PROFESSIONAL TRAINING

murach's
beginning
visual basic
.NET

Anne Prince

D. LEEDS
216-932-3243

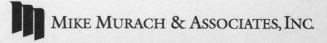

MIKE MURACH & ASSOCIATES, INC.

2560 West Shaw Lane, Suite 101 • Fresno, CA 93711-2765

Author:	Anne Prince
Writer:	Doug Lowe
Researcher:	Matt Stuemky
Editor:	Judy Taylor
Cover Design:	Zylka Design
Production:	Tom Murach

Books in the Murach series

Murach's Beginning Visual Basic .NET

Murach's Visual Basic 6

Murach's Beginning Java 2

Murach's Structured COBOL

Murach's OS/390 and z/OS JCL

Murach's CICS for the COBOL Programmer

10 9 8 7 6 5 4 3 2 1
ISBN: 1-890774-15-4

Contents

Expanded contents

Chapter 3   Visual Basic language essentials (part 1)

Chapter 4   Visual Basic language essentials (part 2)

Section 3 More language essentials

Section 4   Database programming essentials

Chapter 16   An introduction to database programming

Chapter 17   How to develop a database application with ADO.NET

Chapter 18 **How to work with bound controls and parameterized queries**

Section 5 Web programming essentials

Introduction

If you're new to Visual Basic .NET, this book gets you started right. By chapter 3, you'll be developing simple but complete applications. By chapter 5, you'll be doing some serious programming. And by chapter 7, you'll be able to code, test, and debug object-oriented programs with Visual Basic .NET.

But that's just the start. By the time you finish this book, you'll know how to develop multi-form applications; how to develop database applications; and how to develop web applications. You'll also have an entry-level set of professional programming skills that you can use for developing real-world business applications.

Of course, there's a lot more to Visual Basic .NET than one beginning book can cover. But this book gets you started with all of the important features and capabilities of Visual Basic .NET and prepares you for learning more about them on your own. That's why we say that *no other book or course will get you started faster or better than this book.*

5 ways the content gives you a professional start

- If you're a beginner, you'll learn how to code, test, and debug object-oriented Visual Basic programs in the first seven chapters. That's section 1 of this book, and no other book gets you started that fast with such a wide range of skills.

- In section 2, you'll learn how to develop graphical user interfaces at a professional level. This includes the use of common controls, multi-document interfaces, and GUI enhancements like menus, toolbars, and help information.

- In section 3, you'll learn how to use the .NET classes to work with dates, strings, arrays, collections, structures, files, and XML. You'll also learn the additional skills you need for object-oriented programming. These are the programming skills that every professional should have.

- In section 4, you'll learn how to use ADO.NET and the disconnected data architecture of the .NET platform to develop database applications with bound controls, queries, and parameterized queries. Although there's a lot more to database programming than that, this will get you off to a terrific start.

- In section 5, you'll learn how to develop web applications and create and use web services. Here again, there's a lot more to web programming than that, but this will get you started right.

4 ways the instructional approach insures your success

- To help you learn how to develop applications at a professional level, this book presents 18 business applications as examples. That way, you can see the relationships between the Visual Basic code, objects, properties, methods, and events that an application requires, which is essential to your understanding. In contrast, most competing books present trivial applications that have little resemblance to applications in the real world, and that limits your learning potential.

- To solidify your skills, the exercises at the end of each chapter guide you through the development of some of the book's applications. They also encourage you to experiment and challenge you to apply what you've learned in new ways. To give you a maximum amount of practice in a minimum amount of time, you start many of these exercises from partial applications that you download from our web site.

- To help you learn more by reading less, all of the information in this book is presented in "paired pages" with the essential syntax, guidelines, and examples on the righthand page and the perspective and extra explanation on the left. Programmers tell us how much they like this approach because it lets them quickly find what they're looking for. This is particularly useful for a language like Visual Basic because you simply can't remember the hundreds of details that are required for effective programming.

- After you read the first section of this book plus chapter 8, you can read the chapters in section 2, 3, 4, or 5. In other words, you don't have to read all 20 chapters in sequence. We refer to this as "modular organization," and it lets you get the training you need when you need it. Yes, there are some contingencies between some of the chapters, but we let you know about them whenever they're critical.

Who this book is for

This book is for anyone who wants to learn how to use Visual Basic .NET for developing business applications. It works if you have no programming experience at all. It works if you have programming experience with another language like COBOL or Java. It works if you already know Visual Basic 6. And it works if you've already read three or four other Visual Basic .NET books and still don't know how to develop a real-world business application.

If you're completely new to programming, the prerequisites are minimal. First, you need to be familiar with the Windows interface. This means that you have used Windows applications like Word or Excel so you're comfortable with tasks like opening, saving, printing, and closing files. Second, you should know how to use the Windows Explorer to copy folders and files from one location to another.

What software you need for developing Visual Basic .NET applications

To develop Visual Basic .NET applications, you need to be running Windows 2000 or Windows XP on your PC. You also need to install either Visual Studio .NET or Visual Basic .NET on your PC. Although Visual Studio .NET includes other languages and features, you can do almost everything that this book requires with the Standard Edition of Visual Basic .NET, which sells for around $110. The one exception is that you can't create class libraries as shown in chapter 15, but that's insignificant. In contrast, the Professional Edition of Visual Studio .NET sells for about $1,080 and the Upgrade version sells for about $550.

If you want to run the database and web applications on your PC (as opposed to using a database or web server on a network), you also need to install MSDE and IIS on your PC. MSDE is the desktop database engine that comes with Visual Studio or Visual Basic, and IIS is the web server that comes with Windows. To learn how to install these products as well as Visual Studio or Visual Basic, please refer to appendix A in this book. *But please do this before you start the installations, because it's likely to save you some time* (if you don't install the products in the right order, you'll have to re-install some of them).

The downloadable files for this book

If you go to our web site at www.murach.com, you can download the files for this book. These files include:

- The source code and data for all of the applications presented in this book

- The starting source code for many of the exercises in this book

- The data for all of the exercises in this book

- Project descriptions and data for new projects that you can develop on your own

These files, of course, are designed to help you learn faster and better. First, the source code and data for the book applications let you test and review these applications to see exactly how they work. Second, the starting source code for many of the exercises lets you get more practice in less time because you don't have to start every application from scratch. Third, the data for the exercises provides the files and database that the exercises require so you don't have to create test data yourself. And fourth, the project descriptions give you ideas for new projects that you can develop from scratch to test your skill levels.

So before you start the exercises, you should download the files for this book and install them in the proper directories on your PC. To make sure you do that right, please refer to figure A-1 in appendix A.

Support materials for trainers and instructors

If you're a trainer or instructor who would like to use this book for a course, we offer an Instructor's Guide on CD that gives you a complete set of instructional materials. These materials include: the solutions to the exercises in the book; the solutions to the downloadable projects; tests for comprehension; and a complete set of PowerPoint slides that you can use to review and reinforce the content of the book. Taken together, this book, its exercises, its downloadable files, and the instructional materials on CD make a powerful teaching package.

To download a sample of the Instructor's Guide and to find out how to get the complete Guide, please go to our web site at www.murach.com and click on the Instructors link. Or, if you prefer, you can call Karen at 1-800-221-5528 or e-mail karen@murach.com.

Please let us know how this book works for you

When we started this book, our goals were (1) to teach you Visual Basic as quickly and easily as possible; (2) to teach you a set of professional Visual Basic skills that you can use for developing real-world business applications; and (3) to introduce you to all of the major features of Visual Basic .NET so you're prepared to learn more on your own. Now, we sincerely hope that we've succeeded.

So if you have any comments about this book, we would appreciate hearing from you. In particular, we would like to know whether this book has lived up to your expectations. To reply, you can e-mail us at murachbooks@murach.com or send your comments to our street address.

Thanks for buying this book. Thanks for reading it. And good luck with your Visual Basic programming.

Anne Prince
Author

Mike Murach
Publisher

Section 1

The essence of Visual Basic .NET programming

The best way to learn how to develop Visual Basic .NET applications is to start developing them, and that's the approach the chapters in this section take. So in chapter 1, you learn the basic techniques for working in the Visual Basic development environment. Then, in chapter 2, you learn how to use this environment as you develop your first Visual Basic application.

Next, chapters 3, 4, and 5 present the essentials of the Visual Basic language that you will use as you develop your applications. Then chapter 6 shows you how to create and use your own classes as you develop applications. And chapter 7 presents the features that help you test and debug more complex applications.

When you complete the seven chapters in this section, you'll have the essential skills that you need for designing, coding, and testing Visual Basic applications. You'll also have a clear view of what Visual Basic application development is and what you have to do to become proficient at it. That's why we call this section "The essence of Visual Basic .NET programming."

How to get started with Visual Basic .NET

Before you can learn how to develop applications with Visual Basic .NET, you need to become familiar with the .NET Framework, Visual Studio .NET, and the Microsoft Development Environment. So that's what you'll be introduced to in this chapter. Along the way, you'll learn some basic concepts and some basic skills for working with the Development Environment.

Introduction to the .NET Framework and Visual Studio .NET

The *.NET Framework* (pronounced "dot net framework") defines the environment that you use to execute Visual Basic .NET applications and the services you can use within those applications. One of the main goals of this framework is to make it easier to develop applications that run over the Internet. However, this framework can also be used to develop traditional business applications that run on the Windows desktop.

To develop a Visual Basic .NET application, you use a product called *Visual Studio .NET* (pronounced "Visual Studio dot net"). This is actually a suite of products that includes the three programming languages described in figure 1-1. In this book, of course, you'll learn how to use *Visual Basic .NET*, which is designed for rapid application development.

Visual Studio also includes several other components that make it an outstanding development product. One of these is the *Microsoft Development Environment*, which you'll be introduced to in a moment. Another is the *Microsoft SQL Server 2000 Desktop Engine* (or *MSDE*). MSDE is a database engine that runs on your own PC so you can use Visual Studio for developing database applications that are compatible with Microsoft SQL Server. SQL Server in turn is a database management system that can be used to provide the data for large networks of users or for Internet applications.

The two other languages that come with Visual Studio .NET are C# and C++. C# .NET (pronounced "C sharp dot net") is a new language that has been developed by Microsoft especially for the .NET Framework. Visual C++ .NET is Microsoft's version of the C++ language that is used on many platforms besides Windows PCs.

In this figure, you can see that Visual Studio .NET can be used on any PC that runs Windows 2000 or later. You can also see that the applications that are developed with Visual Studio .NET can be run on any PC that runs Windows 98 or later, depending on which .NET components are used by the application. From a practical point of view, though, you can assume that the applications that you develop with Visual Basic .NET will be run on PCs that are using Windows 2000 or later.

This figure also shows that Visual Basic .NET comes in an inexpensive Standard Edition that includes only the Visual Basic language, not C# or C++. All but one of the Visual Basic features presented in this book work with the Standard Edition as well as the full Visual Studio .NET. The one exception is in chapter 15 (class libraries), and I'll be sure to point it out.

Although the three languages shown in this figure are the only three programming languages you can use within Visual Studio .NET, other vendors are free to develop languages for the .NET Framework. For example, Fujitsu has already developed a version of COBOL for the .NET Framework.

Programming languages supported by Visual Studio .NET

Language	Description
Visual Basic .NET	Designed for rapid application development
Visual C# .NET	A new language that combines the features of Java and C++ and is suitable for rapid application development
Visual C++ .NET	Microsoft's version of C++ that can be used for developing high-performance applications

Two other components of Visual Studio .NET

Component	Description
Microsoft Development Environment	The Integrated Development Environment (IDE) that you use for developing applications in any of the three languages
Microsoft SQL Server 2000 Desktop Engine	A database engine that runs on your own PC so you can use Visual Studio for developing database applications that are compatible with Microsoft SQL Server

Platforms that can run Visual Studio .NET

- Windows 2000 and later releases of Windows

Platforms that can run Visual Studio .NET applications

- Windows 98 and later releases of Windows, depending on which .NET components the application uses

Visual Basic .NET Standard Edition

- An inexpensive alternative to the complete Visual Studio .NET package that supports a limited version of Visual Basic .NET as its only programming language

Description

- The *.NET Framework* defines the environment that you use for executing Visual Basic .NET applications.
- *Visual Studio .NET* is a suite of products that includes all three of the programming languages listed above. These languages run within the .NET Framework.
- You can develop business applications using either *Visual Basic .NET* or Visual C# .NET. Both are integrated with the design environment, so the development techniques are similar although the language details vary.
- Besides the programming languages listed above, third-party vendors can develop languages for the .NET Framework. However, programs written in these languages can't be developed from within Visual Studio .NET.

Figure 1-1   Visual Studio .NET and the .NET Framework

Windows Forms and Web Forms applications

You can use Visual Basic .NET for developing the two types of applications shown in figure 1-2. A *Windows Forms application* is a typical Windows application that runs on the user's PC. Each *Windows form* (or just *form*) in the application provides a user interface that lets the user interact with the application. In the example in this figure, the application consists of a single form that lets the user perform either of two calculations: a future value or a monthly investment calculation. Many applications, though, require more than one form.

As part of the user interface, a Windows Forms application uses *Windows Forms controls*. For instance, the form in this figure uses radio buttons, labels, text boxes, and buttons. In the next chapter, you'll start learning how to develop Windows Forms applications.

The other type of application that you can develop with Visual Basic .NET is a *Web Forms application*. Like a Windows Forms application, a Web Forms application consists of one or more *web forms* that can contain controls. Unlike Windows forms, though, web forms are accessed by and displayed in a *web browser*. For instance, the web form in this figure is displayed in the Microsoft web browser, which is called Internet Explorer.

As part of the user interface, a web form uses *Web Forms controls*. These controls are similar to the Windows Forms controls, but they work only with web forms.

In contrast to a Windows Forms application, which runs on the user's PC, the code for a Web Forms application runs on a web server. As this code is executed, it passes the visual portion of the application to the browser running on the client in the form of HTML (Hypertext Markup Language). The browser then interprets the HTML and displays the form. In chapters 19 and 20, you'll learn how to develop Web Forms applications with Visual Basic .NET.

A Windows Forms application running on the Windows desktop

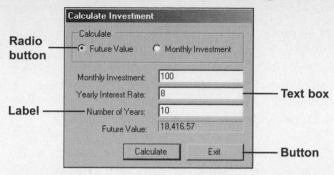

Radio button

Label

Text box

Button

A Web Forms application running in a Web browser

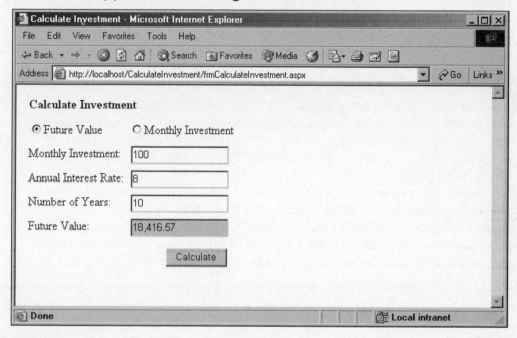

Description

- A *Windows Forms application* runs on the Windows Desktop and can consist of one or more *Windows forms*. These forms provide the graphical user interface (GUI) for the application.

- Each Windows form can contain *Windows Forms controls* like labels, text boxes, buttons, and radio buttons. These controls let the user interact with the application.

- A *Web Forms application* runs on a web server, but its user interface is displayed in a *web browser* on the client machine.

- A Web Forms application consists of one or more *web forms* that provide the user interface for the application. Each form can contain *Web Forms controls* like labels, text boxes, buttons, and radio buttons.

Figure 1-2   Windows Forms and Web Forms applications

The components of the .NET Framework

To give you a more detailed view of the .NET Framework, figure 1-3 presents the main components of this framework. As you can see, the .NET Framework provides a common set of services that application programs written in a .NET language such as Visual Basic .NET can use to run on various operating systems and hardware platforms. The .NET Framework is divided into two main components: the .NET Framework Class Library and the Common Language Runtime.

The *.NET Framework Class Library* consists of segments of pre-written code called *classes* that provide many of the functions that you need for developing .NET applications. For instance, the *Windows Forms classes* are used for developing Windows Forms applications. The *ASP.NET classes* are used for developing Web Forms applications. And other classes let you work with databases, manage security, access files, and perform many other functions.

Although it's not apparent in this figure, the classes in the .NET Framework Class Library are organized in a hierarchical structure. Within this structure, related classes are organized into groups called *namespaces*. Each namespace contains the classes used to support a particular function. For example, the System.Windows.Forms namespace contains the classes used to create forms and the System.Data namespace contains the classes you use to access data.

The *Common Language Runtime*, or *CLR*, provides the services that are needed for executing any application that's developed with one of the .NET languages. This is possible because all of the .NET languages compile to a common intermediate language, which you'll learn more about in the next figure. The CLR also provides the *Common Type System* that defines the data types that are used by all the .NET languages. That way, you can use more than one of the .NET languages as you develop a single application without worrying about incompatible data types.

If you're new to programming, the diagram in this figure probably doesn't mean too much to you right now. For now, then, just try to remember the general structure of the .NET Framework and the terms that I've presented. As you progress through this book, you will become more familiar with each of the terms.

The .NET Framework

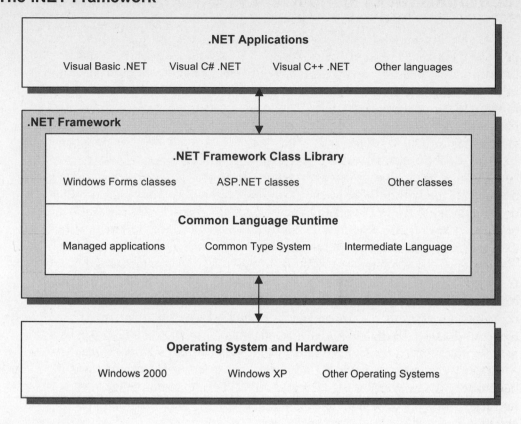

Description

- .NET applications do not access the operating system or computer hardware directly. Instead, they use services of the .NET Framework, which in turn access the operating system and hardware.

- The .NET Framework consists of two main components: the .NET Framework Class Library and the Common Language Runtime.

- The *.NET Framework Class Library* provides pre-written code in the form of *classes* that are available to all of the .NET programming languages. This class library consists of hundreds of classes, but you can create simple .NET applications once you learn how to use just a few of them.

- The *Common Language Runtime*, or *CLR*, is the foundation of the .NET Framework. It manages the execution of .NET programs by coordinating essential functions such as memory management, code execution, security, and other services. Because .NET applications are managed by the CLR, they are called *managed applications*.

- The *Common Type System* is a component of the CLR that ensures that all .NET applications use the same basic data types regardless of what programming languages were used to develop the applications.

Figure 1-3   The components of the .NET Framework

How a Visual Basic application is compiled and run

Figure 1-4 shows how an application is compiled and run when using Visual Basic .NET. To start, you use Visual Studio .NET to create a *project,* which is made of one or more *source files* that contain Visual Basic statements. Most simple projects consist of just one source file, but more complicated projects can have more than one source file. A project may also contain other types of files, such as sound files, image files, or simple text files. As the figure shows, a *solution* is a container for projects, which you'll learn more about in a moment.

You use the Visual Basic *compiler,* which is built into Visual Studio, to compile your Visual Basic source code into *Microsoft Intermediate Language* (or *MSIL*). For short, this can be referred to as *Intermediate Language* (or *IL*).

At this point, the Intermediate Language is stored on disk in a file that's called an *assembly*. In addition to the IL, the assembly includes references to the classes that the application requires. The assembly can then be run on any PC that has the Common Language Runtime installed on it. When the assembly is run, the CLR converts the Intermediate Language to native code that can be run by the Windows operating system.

Although the CLR is only available for Windows systems right now, it is possible that the CLR will eventually be available for other operating systems as well. In other words, the Common Language Runtime makes *platform independence* possible. If, for example, a CLR is developed for the Unix and Linux operating systems, Visual Basic applications will be able to run on those operating systems as well as Windows operating systems. Whether this will happen and how well it will work remains to be seen.

How Visual Basic .NET differs from Visual Basic 6

If you are an experienced Visual Basic 6 programmer, you'll notice that Microsoft has made many changes to Visual Basic for .NET. In fact, the changes are so significant that it's probably best to think of Visual Basic .NET as a new language with a familiar syntax.

Although there are a few changes to the Visual Basic language itself, the most significant change in VB.NET is its reliance on the .NET Framework classes. These classes affect almost every aspect of VB.NET programming, including creating and working with forms and controls, using databases, and even working with basic language features such as arrays and strings.

Although Visual Basic .NET provides an upgrade wizard that lets you convert VB6 applications to VB.NET, it leaves much of the conversion work up to the programmer. As a result, most companies will probably not upgrade their existing VB6 applications to VB.NET. Instead, they'll support their existing VB6 applications and use VB.NET to develop new applications.

How a Visual Basic application is compiled and run

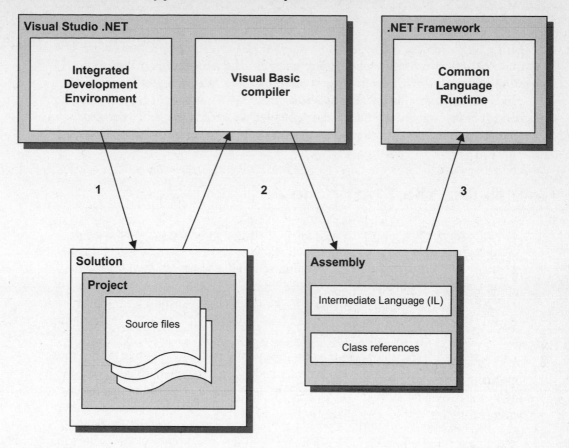

Description

1. The programmer uses Visual Studio's Integrated Development Environment to create a *project*, which includes one or more Visual Basic *source files.* In some cases, a project may contain other types of files, such as graphic image files or sound files.

    A *solution* is a container that holds projects. Although a solution can contain more than one project, the solution for most simple applications contains just one project. So you can think of the solution and the project as essentially the same thing.

2. The Visual Basic *compiler* translates or *builds* the source code into *Microsoft Intermediate Language (MSIL)*, or just *Intermediate Language (IL)*. This language is stored on disk in an *assembly* that also contains references to the classes that the application requires. An assembly is simply an executable file that has an *.exe* or *.dll* extension.

3. The assembly is then run by the .NET Framework's Common Language Runtime. The CLR manages all aspects of how the assembly is run, including converting the Intermediate Language to native code that can be run by the operating system, managing memory for the assembly, enforcing security, and so on.

Figure 1-4   How a Visual Basic application is compiled and run

A tour of the Microsoft Development Environment

With that as background, you're ready to take a tour of the Microsoft Development Environment. This is the *Integrated Development Environment*, or *IDE*, that you use for developing Visual Basic applications. Along the tour, you'll learn some of the basic techniques for working in this environment. You'll also see how some of the terms that you just learned are applied within the IDE.

How to use the Start page

The Start page, shown in figure 1-5, is displayed when you start Visual Studio. From this page, you can open existing projects or create new projects, change your Visual Studio configuration settings, and access various online Visual Studio resources.

Note that the first time you start Visual Studio after installing it, the My Profile link rather than the Get Started link is displayed. You'll find information about the My Profile link in the next figure.

The Start page is actually the home page of a web browser that's built into Visual Studio. The built-in web browser is displayed whenever you access the Start page or when you're accessing Help information. You can return to the Start page at any time by using the Help → Show Start Page command.

In case you aren't familiar with the notation I just used, Help → Show Start Page means to pull down the Help menu from the menu bar and then select the Show Start Page command. We'll use this notation throughout this book because it makes it easier to find the command that you need. Usually, you only need to pull down one menu and select a command. But sometimes, you need to go from a menu to one or more submenus and then to the command. In the second bulleted item in this figure, for example, you go from the Programs menu to the Visual Studio .NET submenu and then to the command.

If you've worked with a web browser such as Internet Explorer before, you'll have no trouble navigating among pages in the Visual Studio browser. A special Web toolbar includes the buttons you can use to go to the previous or next page, stop a download, refresh a page, or return to the home page. This toolbar appears only when you are working in the web browser. When you're working with other Visual Studio tools, such as the Forms Designer or Code Editor, the Web toolbar is replaced by other toolbars.

The nine links located on the left side of the Start page let you access other Visual Studio resources, including a variety of online resources such as online communities and download libraries. If you are an experienced Visual Basic 6 programmer, you may want to explore these links now. But if you're new to Visual Basic, I suggest you wait until you're more experienced with Visual Basic before exploring the online resources.

The Start page

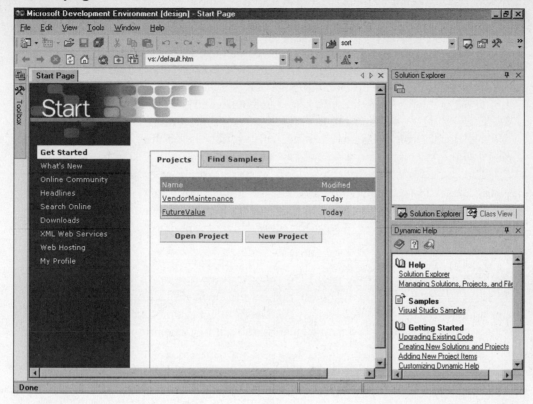

Description

- When you develop applications with Visual Studio, you use its *Integrated Development Environment* (*IDE*). The IDE contains all of the tools you need to develop .NET programs using Visual Basic, C#, or C++.

- To start the Visual Studio IDE, click the Start button in the Windows taskbar, then choose Programs → Microsoft Visual Studio .NET → Microsoft Visual Studio .NET.

- The Start page of the IDE has nine links on the left side that lead to a variety of resources.

- The first time you run Visual Studio after installing it, My Profile is selected rather than Get Started as shown here. After that, Get Started is selected when you start Visual Studio unless you configure Visual Studio to display a different page at startup. The My Profile page is described in figure 1-6.

- As you work with Visual Studio, the Start page will be obscured by other information. But you can return to the Start page at any time by clicking the Start Page tab that's located in the upper left portion of the window, just below the toolbars, or by choosing the Help → Show Start Page command.

Figure 1-5   How to use the Start page

How to customize Visual Studio for use with Visual Basic

The My Profile page, shown in figure 1-6, lets you customize the IDE so it works the way you want it to. You can return to this page at any time to change your settings by calling up the Start page and clicking the My Profile link.

The My Profile page lets you select one of several profiles that configures the Visual Studio environment. For Visual Basic programming, you'll want to use the Visual Basic Developer profile. This profile sets up the keyboard shortcuts and the Visual Studio windows layout to work best with Visual Basic.

You can also use the My Profile link to customize the way the IDE's Help feature works. I recommend you set the Help Filter option to Visual Basic and Related so that when you access Help, you won't have to wade through pages of information on C# or C++. As for the Show Help option, leave it set to Internal Help.

Finally, you can customize Visual Studio to display something other than the Start page as its opening page. The other settings for the At Startup option open the last project you worked on, display the Open Project dialog box so you can open an existing project, display the New Project dialog box so you can create a new project, or just start Visual Studio without opening any page or dialog box.

Note that there are many ways to customize Visual Studio besides the settings available on the My Profile page. The Tools → Customize command lets you customize Visual Studio's toolbars, menus, and keyboard shortcuts in the same way you can for Microsoft Office. And the Tools → Options command has literally hundreds of options you can set to customize Visual Studio. As you become more proficient with Visual Studio, you may want to explore some of these customization options. But while you're just getting started, I recommend you leave them alone.

The My Profile page

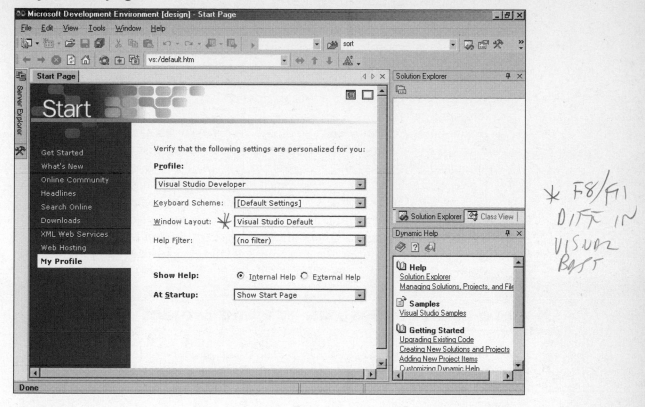

Description

- The My Profile page lets you configure Visual Studio to work the way you want. This page appears the first time you use Visual Studio, but you can return to it at any time by clicking the My Profile link on the Start Page.

- To customize Visual Studio for use with Visual Basic, select Visual Basic Developer for the Profile setting. The Keyboard Scheme and Window Layout settings automatically change to Visual Basic 6, and the Toolbox is displayed on the left side of the window. You'll see the effects of these changes in later figures.

- If you want to filter the help information so that only information related to Visual Basic is displayed, select the Visual Basic or Visual Basic and Related option for the Help Filter setting. You can also change the filter as you use the Help feature.

- By default, help information is displayed as part of the Visual Studio IDE. To display it separately from the IDE, select the External Help option for the Show Help setting.

- To display something other than the Start page when you start Visual Studio, select a different option for the At Startup setting. The other options let you load and display the last solution you worked on, display the dialog box for opening an existing project or for starting a new project, or display an empty environment.

Figure 1-6   How to customize Visual Studio for use with Visual Basic

Solutions and projects

Before you work with Visual Basic projects, you need to understand the distinction between a solution and a project. As figure 1-7 explains, a project is a container that holds Visual Basic source files and other files needed to create an assembly that can be run by the .NET CLR. A project can contain several source files, but all of the source files in a project are compiled together to create a single assembly.

A solution is a container than holds one or more projects. A solution often contains just a single project. In that case, there's not much distinction between a solution and a project.

However, a solution can contain more than one project. Multi-project solutions are most useful for large applications developed by teams of programmers. With a multi-project solution, programmers can work independently on the projects that make up the solution. In fact, the projects don't even have to be written in the same language. For example, a solution can contain two projects, one written in Visual Basic, the other in C#.

How to open or close an existing project

To open a project, click the Open Project button on the Get Started page or use the File→ Open→ Project command. Either way, the Open Project dialog box shown in figure 1-7 is displayed. From this dialog box, you can locate and open your Visual Basic projects.

You can also open a project you've recently worked on directly from the Get Started page, which was shown back in figure 1-5. And you can open recently used projects by choosing the project you want to open from the Recent Projects submenu of the File menu.

At this point, you might be confused about whether you should open projects or solutions. Both are shown in the Open Project dialog box. In figure 1-7, FinancialCalculations.sln is a solution and FinancialCalculations.vbproj is a Visual Basic project.

In most cases, it doesn't matter whether you open the solution or the project. Each way, both the solution and the project files will be opened. If you open the project, Visual Studio automatically opens the solution that contains it. And if you open the solution, Visual Studio automatically opens all of the solution's projects.

In contrast, you can't close a project. Instead, you have to close the solution that contains it. To do that, you use the Close Solution command in the File menu.

The Open Project dialog box

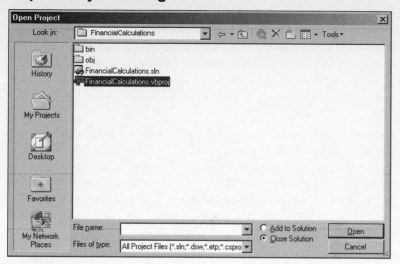

Project and solution concepts

- Every project has a *project file* that keeps track of the files that make up the project and records various settings for the project. Visual Basic project files have the extension *.vbproj*. In this figure, the highlighted file (FinancialCalculations.vbproj) is a project file.

- Likewise, every solution has a *solution file* that keeps track of the projects that make up the solution. The solution file's extension is *.sln*. In this figure, you can see a solution file named FinancialCalculations.sln just above the highlighted project file.

- When you open a project, Visual Studio automatically opens the solution that contains the project. And when you open a solution, Visual Studio automatically opens the projects contained in the solution. So in most cases, it doesn't matter whether you open the project or the solution. Either way, both are opened.

How to open a project

- To open an existing project, use the Open Project dialog box. To access the Open Project dialog box, click the Get Started link in the Visual Studio Start page, then click the Open Project button. Or, use the File → Open → Project command.

- Use the controls in the Open Project dialog box to locate and select the project or solution you want to open.

- After you've worked on one or more projects, the names of those projects will be listed in the Start page and in the File → Recent Projects submenu. Then, you can click a project name to open the project.

How to close a project

- Use the File → Close Solution command.

Figure 1-7   How to open and close an existing project

How to work with the IDE

When you open an existing Visual Basic project, you'll see a screen like the one in figure 1-8. Here, one or more *tabbed windows* are displayed in the main part of the IDE. In this example, the first tab is for the Start page, and the second tab is for a form named frmInvestment.vb, which is displayed in the *Form Designer window* (or just *Form Designer*). You use this window to develop the user interface for a form.

Although it isn't shown in this example, you can also display the code for a form in the *Code Editor window* (or just *Code Editor*). The Code Editor lets you develop the Visual Basic code for an application. In the next figure, you can see what this window looks like.

This figure also illustrates some of the other windows that you use as you develop Visual Basic applications. To add controls to a form, for example, you use the *Toolbox*. And to set the properties of a form or control, you use the *Properties window*. You'll learn more about using these windows in the next chapter. In addition, you can use the *Solution Explorer window* (or just *Solution Explorer)* to manage the files that make up a solution.

This figure also points out two of the toolbars that are available in the IDE. Like other Windows programs, you can use these toolbars to perform a variety of operations, and the toolbars change depending on what you're doing. Of course, you can also perform any operation by using the menus at the top of the IDE. And you can perform some operations using the context-sensitive shortcut menu that's displayed when you right-click anywhere in the IDE.

The Visual Studio IDE with a Form Designer window displayed

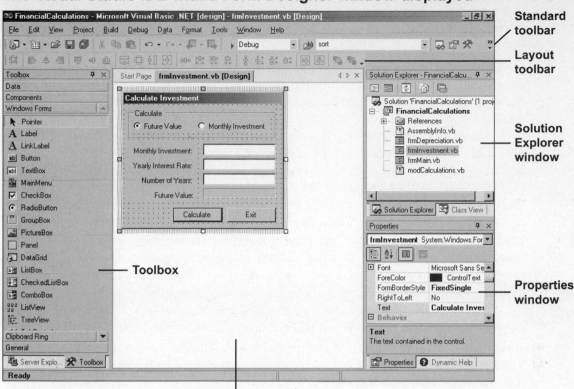

Form Designer window

Description

- The main part of the Visual Studio IDE contains one or more *tabbed windows*. To develop a form, you use the *Form Designer window*. And to develop code, you use the *Code Editor window*. The Code Editor isn't visible in this figure, but is described in figure 1-9.

- To add controls and other items to a form, you use the *Toolbox*. The Toolbox contains a variety of items organized into categories such as Data, Components, Windows Forms, and so on. The items you'll use most are the controls in the Windows Forms category.

- To change the way a form or control looks or operates, you use the *Properties window*. This window displays the properties of the item that's selected in the Form Designer window.

- You use the *Solution Explorer window* to manage project files. You'll learn more about the Solution Explorer in figure 1-10.

- At the top of the Visual Studio window are several toolbars. The Standard toolbar includes standard Windows toolbar buttons such as Open, Save, Cut, Copy, and Paste. On the right side of the Standard toolbar, you'll find several buttons that summon other windows in the IDE. As you work with Visual Studio, you'll find that additional toolbars are occasionally displayed, depending on the function you're performing.

Figure 1-8   How to work with the IDE

How to use the Code Editor

The Code Editor window, shown in figure 1-9, lets you create and edit Visual Basic source code. After you have designed the user interface for your project by placing controls on the form, you'll turn to the Code Editor to develop the Visual Basic statements that make the controls functional. The easiest way to call up the Code Editor is to double-click a control. Then, you can begin typing the Visual Basic statements that will be executed when the user performs the most common action on that control. If you double-click on a button, for example, you can enter the statements that will be executed when the user clicks on that button.

The Code Editor works much like other text editors you've worked with. However, the Code Editor has a number of special features that simplify the task of editing Visual Basic code. For example, color is used to distinguish Visual Basic keywords from variables, comments, and other language elements. And many types of coding errors are automatically highlighted as you type so you can correct them. You'll learn more about working with the Code Editor in the next chapter.

Note that the Code Editor and the Form Designer provide two different ways to work with the same Visual Basic source file. The Code Editor lets you work directly with the Visual Basic statements that make up your application. The Form Designer presents a visual representation of the forms and controls that are implemented by that code.

A project with a Code Editor window displayed

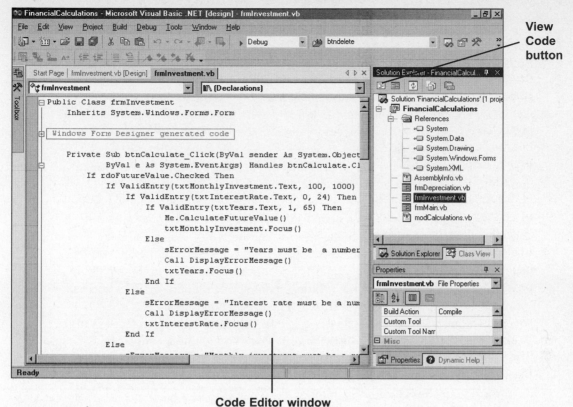

Code Editor window

Description

- The Code Editor window is where you create and edit the Visual Basic code that your application requires. The Code Editor works much like any other text editor you have used, so you shouldn't have much trouble learning how to use it.

- You can display the Code Editor by double-clicking the form or one of the controls in the Form Designer window. Or, you can click the View Code button in the Solution Explorer.

- Once you've opened the Code Editor, you can return to the Form Designer by clicking the (Design) tab at the top of the Code Editor or the View Designer button in the Solution Explorer (to the right of the View Code button). You can also move among these windows by pressing Ctrl+Tab or Shift+Ctrl+Tab.

- It's important to realize that the Form Designer and the Code Editor do not represent two different files. Instead, they provide you with two views of the same Visual Basic source file. The Form Designer gives you a visual representation of the form that is implemented by your Visual Basic code. The Code Editor lets you edit the code for the form.

Figure 1-9   How to use the Code Editor

How to use the Solution Explorer

Figure 1-10 shows the Solution Explorer, which you use to manage the projects that make up a solution and the files that make up each project. As you can see, the files in the Solution Explorer are displayed in a tree view with the files that make up a project subordinate to the project container and the project container subordinate to the solution container. If a container has a plus sign next to it, you can click on the plus sign to display its contents. Conversely, you can hide the contents of a container by clicking on the minus sign next to it.

You can also use the buttons at the top of the Solution Explorer to work with the files in a project. To display the code for a form, for example, you can highlight the form file and then click on the View Code button. And to display the user interface for a form, you can highlight the form file and then click on the View Designer button. For a code file, only the View Code button is available since a code file doesn't contain a user interface.

To identify the files that make up a project, you can look at the icon that's displayed to the left of the file name. The icon for a form file, for example, is a form, and the icon for a code file is a document and the letters VB. As you can see, this project consists of three form files and two code files.

Note, however, that all of the files have the file extension *vb* regardless of their contents. Because of that, I recommend that you give your files names that identify their contents. For example, we add the prefix *frm* to the names of our form files. That way, it's easy to identify the form files when you work with them outside of the Solution Explorer.

The last four files shown in this figure are custom files that we developed for this project. In contrast, the first file (AssmblyInfo) was added automatically when this project was created. This file receives information whenever the project is compiled into an assembly.

This project also includes a folder named References. This folder contains references to the assemblies that contain the namespaces that are available to the project. Remember that the namespaces contain the classes that the application requires. In this case, all of the assemblies were added to the project automatically when this project was created.

This should give you some idea of how complicated the file structure for a single project can be. For this relatively simple application, three form files and one code file were created by the developer. And five namespaces and an assembly file were added to the project automatically.

Although you can't see it here, each Visual Basic program you develop also has access to the Microsoft.VisualBasic namespace. Among other things, this namespace includes the classes that provide the Visual Basic functions you can use in your applications. You'll learn about many of these functions throughout this book.

The Solution Explorer

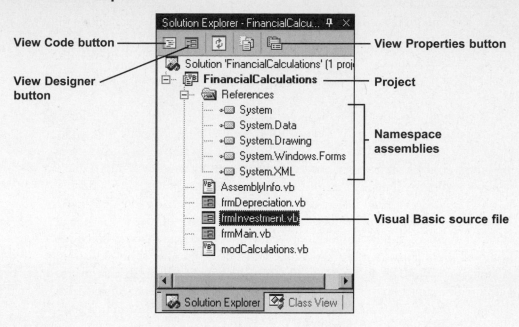

View Code button — View Properties button

View Designer button — View Properties button

Solution 'FinancialCalculations' (1 proj
FinancialCalculations — **Project**
References
System
System.Data
System.Drawing — **Namespace assemblies**
System.Windows.Forms
System.XML
AssemblyInfo.vb
frmDepreciation.vb
frmInvestment.vb — **Visual Basic source file**
frmMain.vb
modCalculations.vb

Solution Explorer   Class View

Description

- You use the Solution Explorer to manage and display the files and projects in a solution. The Solution Explorer lists all of the projects for the current solution, as well as all of the files that make up each project.

- Plus (+) and minus (-) signs in the Solution Explorer indicate groups of files. You can click on these signs to expand and collapse the groups.

- You can perform most of the functions you need using the buttons at the top of the Solution Explorer window. The buttons you'll use most are the View Code and View Designer buttons, which open the Code Editor and Form Designer windows, and the View Properties button, which opens the Properties window.

Project files

- Visual Basic source files are stored with the file extension *.vb*. Each form you create for a project will have its own *form file*. You can also create *code files* that contain Visual Basic code but do not define a form. The Solution Explorer uses different icons to distinguish between form files and code files.

- The AssemblyInfo.vb file is created automatically when the project is created. It contains information about the assembly that's created when you compile the project.

- The References folder contains references to the assemblies for the namespaces that the application can use. These namespaces contain the classes that the project requires. In most cases, all the assemblies that you need are included when the project is created.

- In addition to the assemblies in the References folder, every Visual Basic application you develop has access to the Microsoft.VisualBasic assembly.

Figure 1-10   How to use the Solution Explorer

How to work with the windows in the IDE

In figure 1-11, the Toolbox isn't visible. Instead, it's hidden at the left side of the window. Then, when you need the Toolbox, you can move the mouse pointer over its button to display it. This is just one of the ways that you can adjust the windows in the IDE so it's easier to use. This figure also presents many of the other techniques that you can use.

By default, the Toolbox is displayed as a *docked window* at the left side of the application window. To hide it as shown in this figure, you can click on its Auto Hide button. The Auto Hide button looks like a pushpin, as illustrated by the button near the upper right corner of the Properties window. When a docked window is hidden, it appears as a tab at the edge of the application window.

You can also undock a docked window so it floats in the middle of the IDE. To do that, you drag it by its title bar away from the edge of the IDE or double-click on its title bar. In this figure, for example, you can see that the Solution Explorer window that was docked at the right side of the IDE is now floating in the middle of the IDE. In addition, the Class View window, which was grouped with the Solution Explorer window as a tabbed window, has been separated from the Solution Explorer window. Although we don't recommend this arrangement of windows, it should give you a good idea of the many ways you can arrange them.

As you review the information in this figure, notice that you can't hide, separate, or undock the windows in the main area of the IDE. For the most part, you'll just move between these windows by clicking on their tabs or by using one of the other techniques.

If you experiment with these techniques for a few minutes, you'll see that they're easy to master. Then, as you get more comfortable with Visual Basic, you can adjust the windows so they work best for you.

The IDE with two floating windows and a hidden window

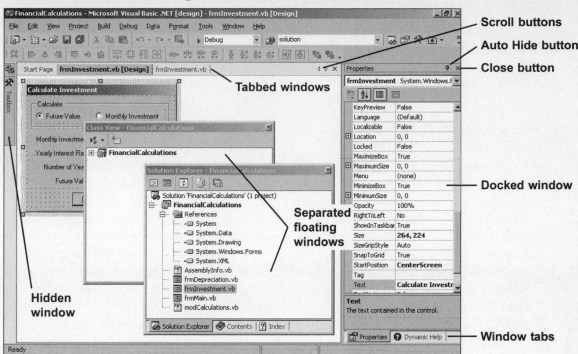

How to rearrange windows

- To close a window, click on its Close button. To redisplay it, click on its button in the Standard toolbar (if one is available) or select it from the View menu.

- To undock a *docked window* so it floats on the screen, drag it by its title bar away from the edge of the application window or double-click on its title bar. To dock a floating window, drag it by its title bar to the edge of the application window or double-click on its title bar to return it to its default location.

- To hide a docked window, click on its Auto Hide button. Then, the window is displayed as a tab at the edge of the screen, and you can display it by placing the mouse pointer over the tab. To change it back, display it and then click on the Auto Hide button again.

- To size a window, place the mouse pointer over an edge or a corner of the window, and then drag it.

- If two or more windows are grouped into tabbed windows, you can display any window in the group by clicking on its tab. If you dock, undock, hide, or unhide a tabbed window, all the windows in the group are docked, undocked, hidden, or unhidden.

- To reset the windows to their default arrangement, you can use the Environment/General settings of the Tools→ Options command. This command is described in chapter 2.

Warning

- Don't fool around with the window layout too much until you have some experience working with Visual Studio. When you're just starting, it's easy to lose track of your windows and to move or close a window and not know how to get it back.

Figure 1-11   How to work with the windows in the IDE

How to test a project

When you develop a project, you design the forms using the Forms Designer and you write the Visual Basic code for the project using the Code Editor. Then, when you're ready to test the project to see whether it works, you need to build and run the project.

How to build a project

Figure 1-12 shows how to *build* a project. One way to do that is to pull down the Build menu and select the Build command that includes the project name. If the project doesn't contain any coding errors, the Visual Basic code is compiled into the Intermediate Language for the project and it is saved on disk in an assembly. This assembly can then be run by the Common Language Runtime.

Usually, though, you don't need to build a project this way. Instead, you can simply run the project, as described in the next topic. Then, if the project hasn't been built before, or if it's been changed since the last time it was built, the IDE builds it before running it.

How to run a project

The easiest way to *run* a project is to click on the Start button that's identified in figure 1-12. Then, the project is built if necessary, the Intermediate Language is executed by the Common Language Runtime, and the first (or only) form of the project is displayed. In this figure, for example, you can see the first form that's displayed when the Financial Calculations project is run. This form contains controls that let you display the other forms of the project.

To test the project, you try everything that the application is intended to do. When data entries are required, you try ranges of data that test the limits of the application. When you're satisfied that the application works under all conditions, you can exit from it by clicking on the Close button in the upper right corner of the form or on a button control that has been designed for that purpose. If the application doesn't work, of course, you need to fix it, but you'll learn more about that in the next chapter.

The form that's displayed when the Financial Calculations project is run

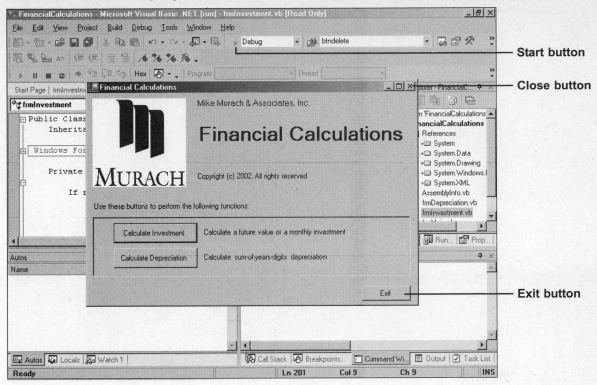

How to build a project apart from running it

- Use the Build → Build *project name* command. Or, right-click on the project in the Solution Explorer and select the Build command from the shortcut menu.
- This *builds* the Intermediate Language for the project and saves it in an assembly.

How to run a project

- The easiest way to run a project from the IDE is to click on the Start button in the Standard toolbar. Then, the program's startup form is displayed on top of the Visual Studio window.
- If the project hasn't already been built, the project is first built and then run when you click on the Start button. As a result, it isn't necessary to use the Build command before you click the Start button.

Two ways to exit from a project that is running

- Click on the Close button in the upper right corner of the startup form.
- Click on the button control that's designed for exiting from the application. This is typically a button that is labeled Exit or Close.

Figure 1-12   How to build and run a project

Perspective

Now that you've read this chapter, you should have a general idea of what the .NET Framework, Visual Studio .NET, and Visual Basic .NET are and how they are related. You should also know how to use Visual Studio's Integrated Development Environment to work with the files in projects and solutions. Now, to get more comfortable with the IDE, you can step through the exercise that follows.

When you're done with this exercise, you should be ready for the next chapter. There, you'll learn more about using the IDE as you develop your first Visual Basic .NET application.

Summary

- *Visual Studio .NET* provides three programming languages: *Visual Basic*, Visual C#, and Visual C++. It also provides the *Microsoft Development Environment* and the *Microsoft SQL Server 2000 Desktop Engine (MSDE)*.

- You can develop two types of programs using Visual Basic .NET. *Windows Forms applications* consist of *Windows forms* that contain *Windows Forms controls*. *Web Forms applications* consist of *web forms* that contain *Web Forms controls*.

- The primary components of the *.NET Framework* are the .NET Framework Class Library and the Common Language Runtime. The *.NET Framework Class Library* provides pre-written code that makes it easier to develop applications, and the *Common Language Runtime* (*CLR*) supports the execution of any application written in a .NET language.

- The Class Library is organized into *namespaces* that contain the classes you need for developing applications.

- When you develop a Visual Basic application, the *source code* is *compiled* into *Intermediate Language* (*IL*) that's saved in an *assembly*. Then, the assembly can be run by the Common Language Runtime.

- You develop Visual Basic .NET applications from within Visual Studio .NET using the *Integrated Development Environment* (IDE). You use the *Form Designer* to design the user interface for a form, and you use the *Code Editor* to enter the Visual Basic code for the form.

- A *solution* consists of one or more projects, and a *project* consists of one or more files. To work with the files in a project, you use the *Solution Explorer*.

- To *build* a project, you use the Build command in the Build menu. To *run* a project, you click on the Start button in the Standard toolbar. And to end a project that's running, you can click on the built-in Close button or on a button control that's provided by the application.

Terms

.NET Framework
Visual Studio .NET
Visual Basic .NET
Microsoft Development Environment
Microsoft SQL Server 2000 Desktop
   Engine (MSDE)
Windows Forms application
Windows form
form
Windows Forms control
Web Forms application
web form
web browser
Web Forms control
.NET Framework Class Library
class
Windows Forms classes
ASP.NET classes
Common Language Runtime (CLR)
Common Type System
managed applications
namespace
project
source file

solution
compiler
Microsoft Intermediate Language (MSIL)
Intermediate Language (IL)
assembly
platform independence
Integrated Development Environment
   (IDE)
project file
solution file
tabbed window
Form Designer window
Form Designer
Code Editor window
Code Editor
Toolbox
Properties window
Solution Explorer window
Solution Explorer
form file
code file
docked window
build a project
run a project

Objectives

- List the three languages that are supported by Visual Studio .NET.

- Describe the main difference between a Windows Forms application and a Web Forms application.

- Describe the two main components of the .NET Framework.

- Describe the use of Microsoft Intermediate Language and the Common Language Runtime.

- Describe the use of each of these windows in the Visual Studio IDE: Form Designer, Code Designer, and Solution Explorer.

- Customize the Visual Studio environment for use with Visual Basic.

- Use the Integrated Development Environment to do any of these operations: (1) Open an existing Visual Basic project or solution; (2) Display the forms in a project; (3) Display the code for each of the forms in a project; (4) Open, hide, and adjust the windows for a project; (5) Build the project; (6) Run the project; or (7) Close the project.

Before you do the exercises in this book

Before you do any of the exercises in this book, you need to download the folders and files for this book from our web site and install them on your C drive starting with C:\VB.NET. For complete instructions, please refer to appendix A.

Exercise 1-1 Tour the Visual Studio IDE

This exercise guides you through the process of customizing Visual Studio for use with Visual Basic, opening an existing Visual Basic project, working with the windows in the IDE, and building and running a project. When you're done, you should have a better feel for the some of the techniques that you will use as you develop Visual Basic applications.

Start Visual Studio and customize it for use with Visual Basic

1. Start Visual Studio and click on the My Profile link on the Start page if it isn't already displayed.

2. Select the Visual Basic Developer option from the combo box at the top of the page. For now, leave the other options the way they are. If you want to, you can come back and change them later.

Open an existing project

3. Click on the Get Started link to display a screen like the one in figure 1-5. Then, click on the Open Project button to display the Open Project dialog box, shown in figure 1-7.

4. Use the drop-down list at the top of the dialog box to locate the project file named FinancialCalculations.vbproj in the C:\VB.NET\Chapter 01\ FinancialCalculations folder. Then, double-click on the file to open the project.

Experiment with the Visual Basic IDE

5. If the Form Designer window for the Calculate Investment form isn't displayed as shown in figure 1-8, highlight the file that contains this form in the Solution Explorer and click on the View Designer button at the top of this window.

6. Highlight the file for the Calculate Investment form in the Solution Explorer and click on the View Code button. A Code Editor window like the one shown in figure 1-9 should be displayed.

7. Click on the tab for the Form Designer window to display it. Then, press Ctrl+Tab to move back to the Code Editor window.

8. Locate the pushpin near the upper right corner of the Toolbox and click on it. The Toolbox should now be displayed as a tab along the left side of the window. Place the mouse pointer over the tab to display the Toolbox, and then move the pointer outside the Toolbox to see that it's hidden again.

9. Undock the Solution Explorer window by dragging its title bar to the center of the screen. Notice that the Properties window expands to fill the space that was occupied by the docked Solution Explorer window. Double-click the title bar of the Solution Explorer window to return the window to its docked position.

10. Click on the plus sign next to the References folder in the Solution Explorer window to see the namespaces that are included in the project. When you're done, click on the minus sign next to the References folder to close it.

Close and reopen the solution

11. Select the File → Close Solution command to close the solution that contains the project. If a dialog box is displayed that asks whether you want to save changes, click on the No button.

12. Reopen the solution by selecting the File → Open Solution command and then locating and selecting the solution file from the dialog box that's displayed.

Build and run the application

13. Build the project by pulling down the Build menu and selecting the Build project name command. This assembles the project into Intermediate Language. It also opens another window, but you don't need to be concerned with that until the next chapter.

14. Run the application by clicking on the Start button in the Standard toolbar. When the first form is displayed, click on the Calculate Investment button to go to the next form. Then, experiment with this form until you understand what it does. When you're through experimenting, click on this form's Exit button to return to the first form.

15. Click on the Calculate Depreciation button to go to another form. Then, experiment with that form to see what it does. When you exit from it, you will return to the first form.

16. Exit from the first form by clicking on either the Close button or the Exit button.

Close the project and exit from Visual Studio

17. Close the project the way you did in step 11.

18. Exit from Visual Studio by clicking on the Close button in the Visual Studio window.

2

How to develop a Windows Forms application

In the last chapter, you learned the basic skills for working with the Visual Basic IDE, you toured a Windows Forms application, and you tested an application with three Windows forms. Now, in this chapter, you'll learn the basic skills for designing, coding, and testing a Windows Forms application. When you're done, you'll be able to develop simple applications of your own.

How to create a new project

When you create a new Visual Basic project, you use the New Project dialog box to set the basic options for the project, such as the project's name and the location at which the project is saved. In addition, you can use the Options dialog box to set some options that affect how Visual Studio handles projects and solutions. You'll learn about these dialog boxes in the topics that follow.

How to use the New Project dialog box to start a new project

To create a new project and set the basic options for that project, you use the New Project dialog box shown in figure 2-1. This dialog box lets you select the type of project you want to create by choosing one of several *templates*. To create a Windows Forms application, for example, you select the Windows Application template. Among other things, this template includes references to all of the assemblies that contain the namespaces you're most likely to use as you develop a Windows application.

The New Project dialog box also lets you specify the name for the project, and it lets you identify the folder in which it will be stored. By default, projects are stored in the Visual Studio Projects folder under the My Documents folder. However, as you'll soon learn, you can change this default. You can also click on the Browse button to select a different location; you can display the drop-down list to select a location you've used recently; or you can type a path directly. If you specify a path that doesn't exist, Visual Studio will create the necessary folders for you.

When you click on the OK button, Visual Studio automatically creates a new folder for the project, using the project name you specify. In the dialog box in this figure, for example, Invoice Total is the project name and C:\VB.NET\Chapter 02 is the location. As a result, Visual Studio will create a folder named Invoice Total in the Chapter 02 folder. You can see the complete path for the new project near the bottom of the New Project dialog box.

When you create a new project, Visual Studio also creates a new solution to hold the project. By default, the solution is given the same name as the project and is stored in the same folder. If that's not what you want, you can click on the More button in the New Project dialog box. This displays additional options that let you create a solution folder above the project folder and provide a separate name for the solution.

Incidentally, the terms *folder* and *directory* are used as synonyms throughout this book. With the introduction of Windows 95, Microsoft started referring to *directories* as *folders*. But most of the Visual Studio documentation still uses the term *directory*. That's why this book uses whichever term seems more appropriate at the time.

The New Project dialog box

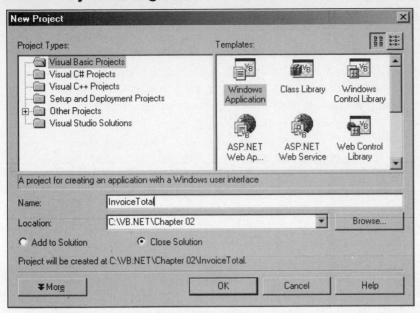

How to create a new project

1. Click on the New Project button on the Start page. Or use the File → Open → Project command. Either way, the New Project dialog box is displayed.

2. Highlight the Visual Basic Projects folder in the Project Types list to display the templates that are available for Visual Basic. Then, highlight the template you want to use. For a Windows Forms application, you highlight the Windows Application template.

3. Enter a name for the project and select the location for the project. A folder with the same name as the project is automatically added to the location you specify.

4. Click on the OK button to start the new project.

Description

*   The project *template* that you select determines the initial files, assembly references, code, and property settings that are added to the project.

*   By default, Visual Studio creates a new solution with the same name as the project and stores the solution file in the same folder as the project. If you prefer, you can create a separate folder for the solution file and give the solution file a different name. To do that, click the More button, then select the Create directory for Solution option and enter the solution name. A folder with this name is then added above the project folder.

Figure 2-1   How to use the New Project dialog box

How to use the Options dialog box to set the options for projects and solutions

To make it easier for you to create new projects, you can set default project and solution options by using the Options dialog box shown in figure 2-2. You can display this dialog box by using the Tools → Options command. To get to the Projects and Solutions options, click the Environment folder if it isn't already open, then click Projects and Solutions.

The Visual Studio projects location option establishes the default location for new projects. To set this option, you can type a path directly into the text box, or you can click Browse to display a dialog box that lets you navigate to the folder you want to use. Note that you can always override the default project location by specifying a different location in the New Project dialog box when you create a new project.

The next two options in this category let you determine if the Output and Task List windows are displayed automatically. Then, the last group of options determines whether or not Visual Studio saves changes to the files when you build and run a project.

As you can see in this figure, you can set a variety of options in addition to the ones described here. You'll learn about some of these options later in this book. However, I suggest that you spend a few minutes exploring the Options dialog box now so you know what options are available. You'll have a chance to do that in the first exercise for this chapter.

The Options dialog box for setting the project options

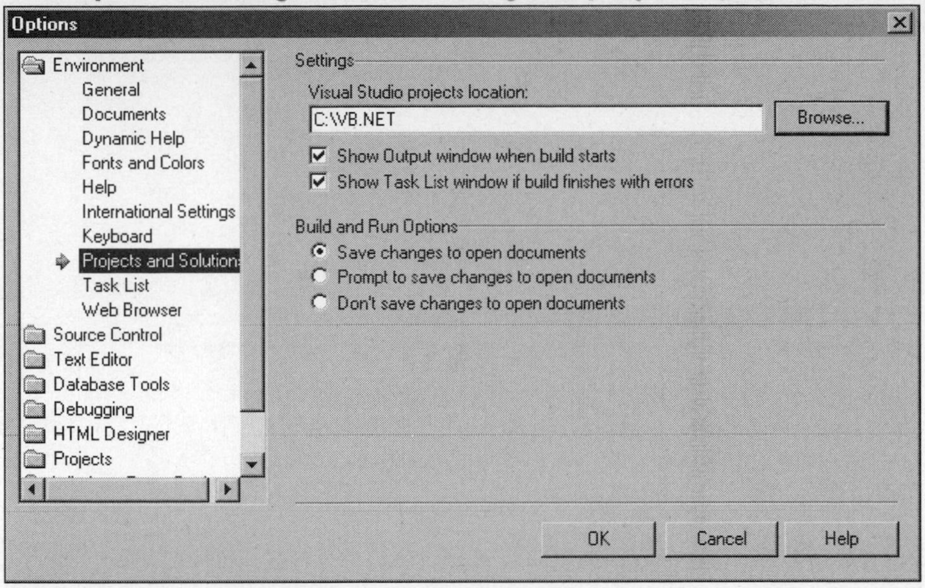

The Projects and Solutions options

Option	Description
Visual Studio projects location	The default location for all projects you start from Visual Studio. You can change this default when you create a new project.
Show Output window when build starts	Indicates whether or not the Output window is displayed automatically when you build a project.
Show Task List window if build finishes with errors	Indicates whether or not the Task List window is displayed if errors are detected during a build operation (see figure 2-16).
Save changes to open documents	Changes made to project files are saved automatically when the project is built and run.
Prompt to save changes to open documents	You are prompted to save changes to project files when the project is built and run.
Don't save changes to open documents	Changes made to project files are not saved when the project is built and run.

How to use the Options dialog box

- To display the Options dialog box, select the Tools → Options command. The Environment folder is open by default, and the General category is displayed.
- To display another category of options, click on that category. To display the categories in another folder, click on that folder to open it.
- Although most of the options should be set the way you want them, you may want to familiarize yourself with the options in each category so you know what's available.

Figure 2-2   How to use the Options dialog box

How to design a form for a Windows application

When you create a new project, the project begins with a single, blank form. You can then add controls to the form and set the properties of the form and controls so they look and work the way you want them to. That's what you'll learn to do in the topics that follow.

The design of the Invoice Total form

Before I show you how to add controls to a form and set the properties of the form and controls, I want to describe the Invoice Total form that I'll use as an example throughout this chapter. This form is presented in figure 2-3. As you can see, the form consists of a eight controls: a text box, five labels, and two buttons.

The Invoice Total form lets the user enter an order total into the text box, and then calculates the discount amount and invoice total for that order when the user clicks on the Calculate button. The discount amount and invoice total are displayed in label controls. For this simple application, the discount amount is always calculated as 20% of the order total. Later in this book, though, you'll see projects in which the discount calculation is more complicated.

After the discount amount and invoice total are calculated for an order, the user can enter a different order total and click on the Calculate button again to display the discount and invoice total for that order amount. This cycle continues until the user clicks on the Close button in the upper right corner of the form or clicks on the Exit button. Then, the form is closed and the application ends.

Note that this application also provides keystroke options for users who prefer using the keyboard to the mouse. In particular, the user can activate the Calculate button by pressing the Enter key and the Exit button by pressing the Esc key. The user can also activate the Calculate button by pressing Alt+C and the Exit button by pressing Alt+X. When the user presses the Alt key, the letters that activate the keys are underlined so the user can tell which ones to press.

The Invoice Total form

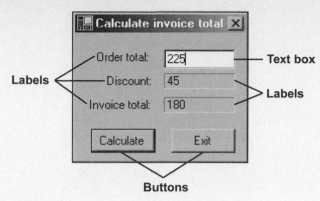

Description

- The Invoice Total form calculates a discount amount and invoice total based on the order total entered by the user.

- The user enters the order total into a text box, and the discount amount and invoice total are displayed in label controls. Label controls are also used to identify the amounts that are displayed on the form.

- After entering an order total, the user can click on the Calculate button to calculate the discount amount and the invoice total. Alternatively, the user can press the Enter key to perform the calculation. For this version of the Invoice Total application, the discount is always calculated as 20% of the order total.

- To calculate another invoice total, the user can enter another order total and then click on the Calculate button or press the Enter key again.

- To close the form and end the application, the user can click on the Close button in the upper right corner of the form or on the Exit button. Alternatively, the user can press the Esc key to exit from the form.

- The user can press Alt+C to perform the calculation or Alt+X to exit from the form. When the user presses the Alt key, the C in the Calculate button will be underlined and the x in the Exit button will be underlined.

Figure 2-3   The design of the Invoice Total form

How to add controls to a form

Figure 2-4 shows how you can use the Toolbox to add controls to a form. The easiest way to do that is to click on the control in the Toolbox, then click the form at the location where you want to add the control. You can then resize the control by dragging one of the control's adjustment handles, and you can move the control by dragging the control to a new location on the form.

If you prefer, you can place and size the control in a single operation by clicking the control in the Toolbox, then clicking and dragging in the form. In this figure, for example, a button is being added to the form.

A third method for adding controls is to simply double-click the control you want to add in the Toolbox. This places the control in the upper left corner of the form. You can then move and resize the control.

A fourth way to add a control is to drag the control from the Toolbox to the form. The control is placed wherever you drop it. You can then resize the control.

Note that if the AutoHide feature is activated for the Toolbox and you move the mouse pointer over the Toolbox tab to display it, the display frequently obscures some or all of the form. This makes it difficult to add controls. As a result, it's a good idea to turn off the AutoHide feature by clicking the pushpin button in the upper right corner of the Toolbox.

After you have added controls to the form, you can work with several controls at once. For example, let's say that you have four text box controls on your form and you want to make them all the same size with the same alignment. To do that, first select all four controls by holding down the Shift key as you click on them or by using the mouse pointer to drag around the controls. Then, use the commands in the Format menu or the buttons in the Layout toolbar to move, size, and align the first three controls relative to the fourth control (the *primary control*). To format the controls relative to a control other than the last one you selected, click on that control to make it the primary control. (The primary control will have different color handles so you can identify it.)

Although these techniques may be hard to visualize as you read about them, you'll find that they're relatively easy to use. All you need is a little practice, which you'll get in the first exercise for this chapter.

A form after some controls have been added to it

Layout toolbar —

Control that's — selected in the Toolbox

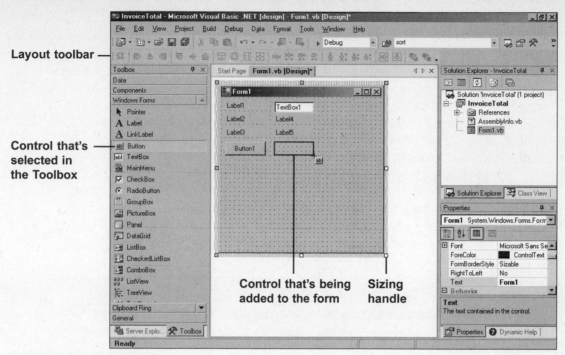

Control that's being added to the form

Sizing handle

How to add a control

- To add a control to a form, select the control in the Toolbox. Then, click in the form where you want to place the control and drag the pointer on the form to size the control.

- You can also add a control by double-clicking it or by dragging and dropping it onto the form. If you double-click on it, the control is placed in the upper left corner of the form. If you drag it, it's placed wherever you drop it. Then, you can move and size the control.

How to select and work with controls

- To select a control on the form, click on it. To move a control, drag it. To size a selected control, drag one of its handles.

- To select more than one control, hold down the Shift or Ctrl key as you click on each control. You can also select a group of controls by clicking on a blank spot in the form and then dragging around the controls.

- To align, size, or space a group of selected controls, click on a control to make it the *primary control*. (By default, the last control you select is the primary control.) Then, use the commands in the Format menu or the buttons on the Layout toolbar to align, size, or space the controls relative to the primary control.

- You can also size all of the controls in a group by sizing the primary control in the group. And you can drag any of the selected controls to move all the controls.

- To change the size of a form to accommodate the controls, click on the form and then drag it by one of its handles.

Figure 2-4   How to add controls to a form

How to set properties

After you have placed controls on a form, you need to set each control's properties so the controls will look and work the way you want them to when the form is displayed. In addition, you need to set some of the properties for the form itself.

To set the properties of a form or control, you work in the Properties window as shown in figure 2-5. To display the properties for a specific control, click on it in the Form Designer window to select the control. To display the properties for the form, click the form's title bar or any blank area of the form.

In the Properties window, you can select a property by clicking it. When you do, a brief description of that property is given at the bottom of the Properties window. To change a property setting, you change the entry to the right of the property name by typing a new value or choosing a new value from a drop-down list.

To display properties alphabetically or by category, you can click the appropriate button at the top of the Properties window. At first, you may want to display the properties by category so you have an idea of what the different properties do. Once you become more familiar with the properties, though, you may be able to find the ones you're looking for faster if you display them alphabetically.

As you work with properties, you'll find that most are set the way you want them by default. In addition, some properties such as Height and Width are set interactively as you size and position the form and its controls in the Form Designer window. As a result, you usually only need to change a few properties for each object.

A form after the properties have been set

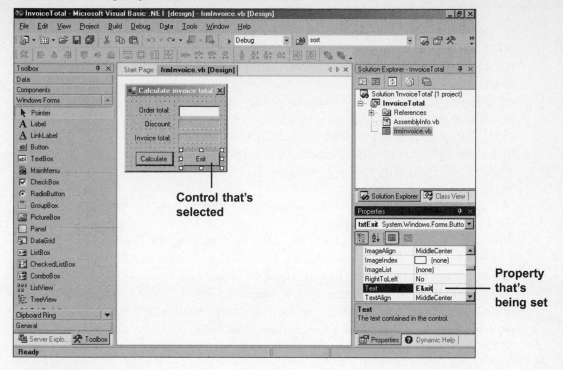

**Control that's
selected**

**Property
that's
being set**

Description

- The Properties window displays the properties for the object that's currently selected in the Form Designer window. To display the properties for another object, click on that object or select the object from the drop-down list at the top of the Properties window.

- To change a property, enter a value into the text box or select a value from its drop-down list if it has one. If a button with an ellipsis (…) appears at the right side of a property's text box, you can click on the ellipsis to display a dialog box that lets you set options for the property.

- To change the properties for two or more controls at the same time, select the controls. Then, the common properties of the controls are displayed in the Properties window.

- When you click on a property in the Properties window, a brief explanation of the property appears in a pane at the bottom of the window. For more information, press F1 to display the help information for the property.

- You can use the first two buttons at the top of the Properties window to sort the properties by category or alphabetically.

- You can use the plus and minus signs displayed to the left of some of the properties and categories in the Properties window to expand and collapse the list of properties.

Note

- If a description isn't displayed when you click on a property in the Properties window, right-click on the window and select Description from the shortcut menu.

Figure 2-5   How to set properties

Common properties for forms and controls

Figure 2-6 shows some common properties for forms and controls. The first two properties apply to both forms and controls. The other properties are presented in two groups: properties that apply to forms and properties that apply to controls. Note that some of the control properties only apply to certain types of controls. That's because different types of controls have different properties.

Since all forms and controls must have a Name property, Visual Studio creates generic names for all forms and controls, such as Form1 or Button1. Often, though, you should change these generic names to something more meaningful, especially if you're going to refer to them in your Visual Basic code.

To make your program's code easier to read and understand, you should begin each name with a two- or three-letter prefix in lowercase letters to identify the control's type. Then, complete the name by describing the function of the control. For instance, you should use a name like *btnExit* for the Exit button and *txtOrderTotal* for the Order Total text box.

For label controls, you can leave the generic names unchanged unless you plan on modifying the properties in your code. For example, the two label controls that will display the calculated discount amount and invoice total should be given meaningful names such as *lblDiscountAmount* and *lblInvoiceTotal*. But there's no reason to change the names for the other three label controls, which display text that won't be changed by the program.

Forms and most controls also have a Text property that is visible when the form is displayed. A form's Text property is displayed in the form's title bar. For a control, the Text property is displayed somewhere within the control. The Text property of a button, for example, is displayed on the button, and the Text property of a text box is displayed in the text box.

As you work with properties, you'll find that you can set some of them by selecting a value from a drop-down list. For example, you can select a True or False value for the TabStop property of a control. For other properties, you have to enter a number or text value. And for some properties, a button with an ellipsis (...) is displayed. Then, when you click this button, a dialog box appears that lets you set the property.

The Name property

- Sets the name you use to identify a form or control in your Visual Basic code.
- Should only be changed if you intend to refer to the form or control in your code. For label controls whose values won't change during your program's execution, you can leave the name set to the default value.
- Use a three-letter prefix to indicate whether the name refers to a form (*frm*), button (*btn*), label (*lbl*), or text box (*txt*).

The Text property

- Sets the text that is displayed on the form or control. The default value is the form or control name, which you'll almost always want to change.
- For a form, the Text value is displayed in the title bar. For controls, the Text value is displayed directly on the control.
- For a text box, the Text value changes when the user types text into the field. As a result, you can use the Text property to access the information entered by the user.
- If you want a text box to be initially blank, be sure to clear its Text property.

Other properties for forms

Property	Description
AcceptButton	Identifies the button that will be activated when the user presses the Enter key.
CancelButton	Identifies the button that will be activated when the user presses the Esc key.
ControlBox	Determines whether a control box will be displayed in the upper left corner of the form.
FormBorderStyle	Sets the border style for the form.
MaximizeBox	Determines whether a Maximize button will be displayed on the form.
MinimizeBox	Determines whether a Minimize button will be displayed on the form.
StartPosition	Sets the position at which the form is displayed. To center the form, set this property to CenterScreen.

Other properties for controls

Property	Description
BorderStyle	Sets the border style for controls.
Enabled	Determines whether the control will be enabled or disabled.
ReadOnly	Determines whether the text in some controls like text boxes can be edited.
TabIndex	Indicates the control's position in the tab order, which determines the order in which the controls will receive the focus when the user presses the Tab key.
TabStop	Determines whether the control will accept the focus when the user presses the Tab key to move from one control to another. Some controls, like labels, don't have the TabStop property because they can't receive the focus.
TextAlign	Sets the alignment for the text displayed on a control.

Figure 2-6   Common properties for forms and controls

How to add a Button control to a form

Now that you know the general techniques for adding controls to a form, the next two figures show you how to add specific controls. To start, figure 2-7 gives a procedure for adding a Button control to a form. You can use a similar procedure to add most other types of controls.

Most forms should have at least two buttons. One button should perform the processing required by the form; the other should close the form without performing any processing. Depending on the requirements of your application, your forms may include other buttons as well.

Because your Visual Basic code will refer to the buttons on your forms, you should always set the Name property for a button to a meaningful name. As mentioned earlier, a common naming recommendation is to use the letters *btn* followed by the value you set for the Text property. If, for example, you set the Text property to *Calculate*, set the Name property to *btnCalculate*.

A form after a Button control has been added to it

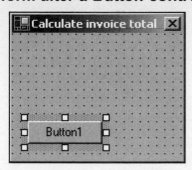

A procedure for adding a Button control to a form

1. Click the Button control in the Toolbox, then click the form where you want the button to appear.

2. If necessary, drag the button to its exact location and resize it.

3. Use the Properties window to change the Name property of the button. Choose a name that describes the action performed by the button, prefixed with the letters *btn*, such as btnCalculate or btnExit.

4. Use the Properties window to change the Text property of the button. Use text that describes the action performed by the button, such as Calculate or Exit.

The Button control after the properties have been set

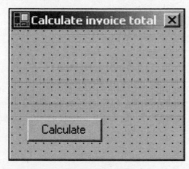

Figure 2-7   How to add a Button control to a form

How to add a Label and a related TextBox control to a form

Label controls are often used alongside TextBox controls to provide captions that tell the user what type of information to enter into each text box. Labels are also used alongside other types of controls, such as ListBox and ComboBox controls, which you'll learn about in chapter 8.

Figure 2-8 gives a procedure that you can follow to add a Label control and a related TextBox control to a form and then set the properties of these controls. For the label, you set the Text property so it identifies the text box. You can also set the TextAlign property of the label to Middle Right so the label text will be next to the text box.

If the label will remain unchanged throughout the program's execution, you can leave its Name property unchanged. However, you should change the Name property of the text box to something meaningful because your code will refer to it. If the label's text is short, you can use the prefix *txt* followed by the label's text value. If, for example, the label reads *Order total*, you can use *txtOrderTotal* for the name of the text box.

A form after a Label and a related TextBox control have been added to it

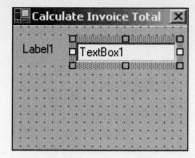

A procedure for adding a Label and a related TextBox control

It is common to use Label and TextBox controls together so the label indicates what information the user should enter into the text box. The procedure that follows shows how to add a label and a related text box to a form.

1. Click the Label control in the Toolbox, then click the form where you want the label to appear. Next, click the TextBox control in the Toolbox and click the form where you want the text box to appear.

2. If necessary, adjust the size of the Label and TextBox controls so the controls are the same height and don't overlap. Then, move the controls so they are positioned next to one another.

3. Use the Properties window to change the Text property of the Label control to the text that you want to appear on the form next to the TextBox control. For example, "Order total:" or "Discount:"

4. Set the Label control's TextAlign property to MiddleRight.

5. Use the Properties window to change the Name property of the TextBox control. Choose a name that describes the contents of the text box, prefixed with the letters *txt*, such as txtOrderTotal.

6. Use the Properties window to clear the Text property of the TextBox control.

The Label and TextBox controls after the properties have been set

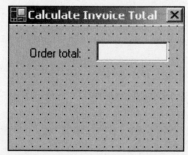

Figure 2-8   How to add a Label and a related TextBox control to a form

How to add navigation features

Windows forms have features that make it easier for users to move around in the forms without using the mouse. These navigation features are described in figure 2-9.

The *tab order* is the order in which the controls on a form receive the *focus* when the user presses the Tab key. The tab order should usually be set so the focus moves left-to-right and top-to-bottom, beginning at the top left of the form and ending at the bottom right. However, in some cases you'll want to deviate from that order. For example, if you have controls arranged in columns, you may want the tab order to move down each column.

The tab order is initially set based on the order in which you add controls to the form. So if you add the controls in the right order, you won't need to alter the tab order. But if you do need to change the tab order, you can do so by adjusting the TabIndex property settings. The TabIndex property is simply a number that represents the control's position in the tab order, beginning with zero. So, the first control in the tab order has a TabIndex of 0, the second control's TabIndex is 1, and so on.

Access keys are shortcut keys that let the user move directly to a control. You set a control's access key by using the Text property. Just precede the letter in the Text property value that you want to use as an access key with an ampersand (&). Then, the user can activate the control by pressing Alt plus the access key.

Note that if you assign an access key to a control that can't receive the focus, such as a label control, pressing the access key causes the focus to move to the next control in the tab order. As a result, you can use an access key with a label control to create a shortcut for a text box control.

Finally, you should usually set the AcceptButton and CancelButton form properties. These properties specify the buttons that are activated when the user presses the Enter and Esc keys. That can make it easier for a user to work with a form. If, for example, the AcceptButton property of the Invoice Total form in figure 2-3 is set to the Calculate button, the user can simply press the Enter key after entering an order total instead of having to use the mouse to click on the Calculate button.

How to adjust the tab order

- *Tab order* refers to the sequence in which the controls receive the *focus* when the user presses the Tab key. You should adjust the tab order so the Tab key moves the focus from one control to the next in a logical sequence.

- Each control has a TabIndex property that indicates the control's position in the tab order. You can change this property to change a control's tab order position.

- If you don't want a control to receive the focus when the user presses the Tab key, change that control's TabStop property to False.

- Label controls don't have a TabStop property so they can't receive the focus.

How to set access keys

- *Access keys* are shortcut keys that the user can use in combination with the Alt key to quickly move to individual controls on the form.

- You use the Text property to set the access key for a control by placing an ampersand immediately before the letter you want to use for the access key. For example, &Invoice sets the access key to *I*, but I&nvoice sets the access key to *n*.

- Since the access keys aren't case sensitive, &N and &n set the same access key.

- A form can use the same access key more than once. Then, pressing the access key once moves to the first control with that access key, pressing it a second time moves to the second control with that access key, and so on. This isn't recommended, though, because there are more efficient ways to provide navigation.

- You can't set the access key for a text box. However, if you set an access key for a label that immediately precedes the text box in the tab order, the access key will take the user to the text box.

How to set the Enter and Esc keys

- The AcceptButton property of the form sets the button that will be activated if the user presses the Enter key.

- The CancelButton property of the form sets the button that will be activated if the user presses the Esc key. This property should usually be set to the Exit button.

- You set the AcceptButton or CancelButton values by choosing the button from a drop-down list that shows all of the buttons on the form. So be sure to create and name the buttons you want to use before you attempt to set these values.

Figure 2-9   How to add navigation features

The property settings for the Invoice Total form

Figure 2-10 shows the property settings for the Invoice Total form. As you can see, you need to change seven properties for the form but only three properties for most of the controls to get the interface to look the way you want it to. In addition, four properties (Name, Text, TextAlign, and TabIndex) account for all but one of the control settings. Depending on the order in which you create the controls, though, you may not need to change the TabIndex settings.

Since the form is designed so it's the right size for the controls it contains, you can set the FormBorderStyle property to FixedSingle. Then, the user won't be able to change the size of the form by dragging the edge of the form. In addition, you can set the MaximizeBox and MinimizeBox properties to False so these boxes aren't displayed on the form and the user can't minimize or maximize the form.

You should also notice the settings for the AcceptButton and CancelButton properties of the form. As described earlier, the AcceptButton property is set to the Calculate button so the user can simply press the Enter key to perform a calculation. To identify this button as the accept button, a dark outline is placed around it. Similarly, the CancelButton property is set to the Exit button so the user can press the Esc key to exit from the application.

Next, notice that the two labels that display the form's calculated results have their BorderStyle property set to Fixed3D. This setting gives the labels a recessed and boxed appearance. In the next figure, you can see how the appearance of the two labels below the text box differs from the appearance of the other three labels.

Incidentally, you could also design this form by using text boxes instead of labels for displaying the Discount and Invoice total values. Then, to prevent the user from entering data into the text boxes, you'd change the ReadOnly properties to True. You'd also change the TabStop properties to False so the focus wouldn't move to these controls. And to change the background color of the text boxes from white to gray, you'd change the BackColor properties. The resulting form would look very much the same.

Finally, please notice the settings for the TabIndex properties of the controls. Here, the settings for the text box and the two buttons are 1, 2, and 3, while the settings for all of the label controls are zero. Since the label controls can't receive the focus, this is just one way these properties could be set. If, for example, the TabIndex properties for the 8 controls were set from 0 through 7, from top to bottom in this summary, the tab order would work the same.

***

On the next page, you'll see an exercise that gives you a chance to practice the techniques that you've learned so far. Because this is a long chapter, this is also a good time to take a break before continuing with the rest of the chapter.

The property settings for the form

Default name	Property	Setting
Form1	FormBorderStyle	FixedSingle
	MaximizeBox	False
	MinimizeBox	False
	StartPosition	CenterScreen
	Text	Calculate invoice total
	AcceptButton	btnCalculate
	CancelButton	btnExit

The property settings for the controls

Default name	Property	Setting
Label1	Text	Order total:
	TextAlign	MiddleRight
	TabIndex	0
Label2	Text	Discount:
	TextAlign	MiddleRight
	TabIndex	0
Label3	Text	Invoice total:
	TextAlign	MiddleRight
	TabIndex	0
TextBox1	Name	txtOrderTotal
	Text	(empty)
	TabIndex	1
Label4	Name	lblDiscountAmount
	Text	(empty)
	TextAlign	MiddleLeft
	TabIndex	0
	BorderStyle	Fixed3D
Label5	Name	lblInvoiceTotal
	Text	(empty)
	TextAlign	MiddleLeft
	TabIndex	0
	BorderStyle	Fixed3D
Button1	Name	btnCalculate
	Text	&Calculate
	TabIndex	2
Button2	Name	btnExit
	Text	E&xit
	TabIndex	3

Note

- Because label controls can't receive the focus, the TabIndex properties for these controls don't matter. What matters is that the text box and the two buttons have TabIndex properties with sequence numbers that move the focus from the text box, to the Calculate button, to the Exit button, and back to the text box.

Figure 2-10   The property settings for the Invoice Total form

Exercise 2-1   Design the Invoice Total form

This exercise will guide you through the process of starting a new project and developing the user interface for the Invoice Total form shown in this chapter.

Start the project

1. Start Visual Studio. If the Start page isn't displayed, click on the Get Started link to display it.

2. Click on the New Project button to display the New Project dialog box. Note the path that's specified for the new project in the Location box. Then, close this dialog box without starting a new project.

3. Select the Tools → Options command to display the Options dialog box. Highlight the Projects and Solutions category in the Environment folder, and then change the Visual Studio projects location setting to C:\VB.NET.

4. If you're interested, take a few minutes to review the other options that are available in this dialog box. Then, close the box.

5. Open the New Project dialog box again and notice that the new project location has changed to the location you specified in the Options dialog box.

6. If necessary, highlight the Visual Basic Projects folder in the Project Types list and then highlight the Windows Application template. Next, enter InvoiceTotal for the name of the project, and add \Chapter 02 to the end of the location path. Finally, click on the OK button to start the new project.

Add controls to the new form

7. Use the techniques in figure 2-4 to add the controls to the form with approximately the same sizes and locations as in that figure.

8. Group the three labels on the left side of the form. Then, use the buttons in the Layout toolbar or the commands in the Format menu to make sure that they're the same size and that they're aligned on their right sides. Repeat this process for the text box and the two labels on the right side of the form, but align these controls on their left sides. Repeat this process a third time to size and align the button controls. Then, size the form so it looks like this, but without the text on the form and its controls:

9. Use the Properties window to set the properties for the form and its controls so it looks like the one above. These properties are summarized in figure 2-10. Also, check the TabIndex properties to make sure that the ones for the text box and buttons are numbered from 1 through 3.

Test the user interface

10. Click on the Start button in the Standard toolbar or press F5 to build and run the project. Because this project consists of a single form, that form will be displayed like this:

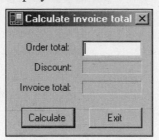

11. Experiment with the form to see what it can do. When you press the Tab key, notice how the focus moves from one control to the other. When you click on a button, notice how it indents and then pops back out just like any other Windows button control. However, nothing happens in response to these button clicks because you haven't yet created the code that implements the button functions.

    Also notice that the Calculate button has a dark outline around it to indicate that its function will be executed if you press the Enter key. (If it doesn't have a dark outline, you haven't set the AcceptButton property of the form to the button.) And when you press the Alt key, an underline should appear under the first *c* in *Calculate* and the *x* in *Exit* to indicate that you can use an access key to activate these buttons. (If underlines don't appear, you haven't set the Text properties of these buttons properly.) As you can see, you've already accomplished a lot without writing a single line of code.

12. If you notice that some of the properties are set incorrectly, click on the Close button in the upper right corner of the form to close the form. Then, make the necessary changes and run the project again. When you're satisfied that the form is working right, close the form to return to the Form Designer window.

Save the project

13. Save the project by highlighting it in the Solution Explorer and then clicking on the Save All button in the Standard toolbar.

14. If you're going to continue on with this chapter, leave the solution open. Otherwise, close it.

How to add code to a form

After you design a form, you write the code that makes the form and its controls work the way you want them to. So that's what you'll learn how to do next. Because you'll learn the essentials of the Visual Basic language in the next three chapters, though, I won't focus on the coding details right now. Instead, I'll focus on the concepts behind the code and the mechanics of adding the code to a form.

Introduction to object-oriented programming

Whether you know it or not, you are using *object-oriented programming* as you design a Windows form with the Visual Studio IDE. That's because each control on a form is an object, and the form itself is an object. These objects are derived from *classes* that are part of the .NET Class Library.

When you start a new project from the Windows Application template, you are actually creating a new *class* that inherits the characteristics of the Form class that's part of the .NET Class Library. Later, when you run the form, you are actually creating an *instance* of your form class, which is known as an *object*.

Similarly, when you add a control to a form, you are actually adding a control object to the form. Each control is an instance of a specific class. For example, a text box control is an object that is an instance of the TextBox class. And a label control is an object that is an instance of the Label class. This process of creating an object from a class can be called *instantiation*.

As you progress through this book, you will learn much more about classes and objects because Visual Basic is an *object-oriented language*. In chapter 6, for example, you'll learn how to use the Visual Basic language to create your own classes. At that point, you'll start to understand what's actually happening as you work with classes and objects. For now, though, you just need to get comfortable with the terms and accept the fact that a lot is going on behind the scenes as you design a form and its controls.

Figure 2-11 summarizes what I've just said about classes and objects. It also introduces you to the properties, methods, and events that are defined by classes and used by objects. As you've already seen, the *properties* of an object define the object's characteristics and data. For instance, the Name property gives a name to a control, and the Text property determines the text that is displayed within the control.

In contrast, the *methods* of an object determine the operations that can be performed by the object. And an object's *events* are signals sent by the object to your application that something has happened that can be responded to. For example, a Button control object generates an event called Click if the user clicks the button. Then, your application can respond by running a Visual Basic procedure that's designed to handle the Click event.

You'll learn more about methods and events in the next three figures. The properties, methods, and events of an object are called the *members* of the object, and are collectively known as the object's *interface*.

A form object and its eight control objects

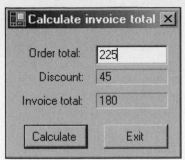

Class and object concepts

- An *object* is a self-contained unit that combines code and data. Two examples of objects you have already worked with are forms and form controls.

- A *class* is the code that defines the characteristics of an object. You can think of a class as a template for an object.

- An object is an *instance* of a class, and the process of creating an object from a class is called *instantiation*.

- More than one object instance can be created from a single class. For example, a form can have several button objects, all instantiated from the same Button class. Each is a separate object, but all share the characteristics of the Button class.

- A class can be based on an existing class. In that case, the existing class is referred to as the *base class*, and the new class inherits the characteristics of the base class.

Property, method, and event concepts

- An object's *interface* consists of a clearly defined set of properties, methods, and events. The properties, methods, and events can be referred to as *members* of the object.

- *Properties* are the data associated with an object.

- *Methods* are the operations that an object can perform.

- *Events* are signals by which an object can notify other objects that something noteworthy has occurred.

- If you instantiate two or more instances of the same class, all of the objects have the same properties, methods, and events. However, the values assigned to the properties can vary from one instance to another.

Objects and forms

- When you use the IDE to design a form, the IDE automatically generates Visual Basic code that creates a new class based on the Form class. Then, when you run the project, a form object is instantiated from the new class.

- When you add a control to a form, the IDE automatically generates Visual Basic code in the Form class that instantiates a control object from the appropriate class and sets the control's properties to the values you have set for the control.

Figure 2-11   Introduction to object-oriented programming

How to refer to properties, methods, and events

As you enter the code for a form in the Code Editor window, you often need to refer to the properties, methods, and events of its objects. To do that, you type the name of the object, a period (also known as a *dot operator*, or *dot*), and the name of the member. This is summarized in figure 2-12.

To make it easier for you to refer to the members of an object, Visual Basic provides the Auto List Members feature shown in this figure. This is part of the Intellisense feature provided by Visual Studio. After you type an object name and a period, this feature displays a list of the members that are available for that object. Then, you can highlight the entry you want by clicking on it, typing the first few letters of its name, or using the arrow keys to scroll through the list. In most cases, you can then complete the entry by pressing the Tab key.

To give you an idea of how properties, methods, and events are used in code, this figure shows examples of each. In the first example for properties, code is used to set the value that's displayed for a text box to 10. In the second example, code is used to set a text box's ReadOnly property to True. Although you can also use the Properties window to set these values, that just sets the properties at the start of the application. By using code, you can change the properties as an application is running.

In the first example for methods, the Focus method of a text box is used to move the focus to that text box. In the second example, the Close method of a form is used to close the active form. Notice in this example that the keyword Me is used instead of the name of the form. In this case, Me refers to the current instance of the active Invoice Total form. As you progress through this book, you'll learn how to use the methods for many types of objects. For now, though, just try to understand the concept.

In the example for an event, the code refers to the Click event of a button named btnExit. The main point here is that the syntax is the same whether you're referring to a property, method, or event of an object. In the next two figures, you'll learn more about events.

A member list that's displayed in the Code Editor window

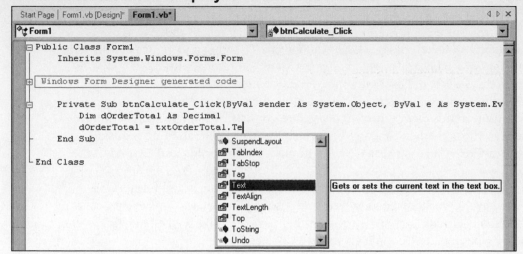

The syntax for referring to a member of an object

```
objectname.membername
```

Statements that refer to properties

txtOrderTotal.Text = 10   Assigns the value 10 to the Text property of the text box named txtOrderTotal.

txtOrderTotal.ReadOnly = True   Assigns the True value to the ReadOnly property of the text box named txtOrderTotal so the user can't change its contents.

Statements that refer to methods

txtMonthlyInvestment.Focus   Uses the Focus method to move the focus to the text box named txtMonthlyInvestment.

Me.Close   Uses the Close method to close the form that contains the method. In this example, Me is a keyword that is used to refer to the current instance of the class.

Code that refers to an event

btnExit.Click   Refers to the click event of a button named btnExit.

How to enter member names when working in the Code Editor window

- To display a list of the available members for an object, type the object name followed by a period (called a *dot operator*, or just *dot*). Then, you can type the first few letters of the member name, and the Code Editor will select the first entry in the list that matches those letters. Or you can scroll down the list to select the member you want. Once it's selected, press the Tab key to insert the member into your code.

- If a member list isn't displayed, select the Tools → Options command to display the Options dialog box. Then, click on the Text Editor item, select Basic, and check the Auto list members and Parameters information boxes.

Figure 2-12   How to refer to properties, methods, and events

How an application responds to events

Visual Basic applications are *event-driven*. That means they work by responding to the events that occur on objects. To respond to an event, you code an *event procedure* (or *event handler*) as shown in figure 2-13.

In this figure, the user clicks on the Exit button on the Invoice Total form. Then, the application responds by executing the event procedure for that object and event. In this case, the event procedure consists of a single statement that uses the Close method to close the form. The Private Sub and End Sub statements are generated by Visual Studio to mark the beginning and the end of the procedure.

This figure also lists some common events for controls and forms. One control event you'll respond to frequently is the Click event. This event occurs when the user clicks on an object with the mouse. Similarly, the DblClick event occurs when the user double-clicks on an object.

Although the Click and DblClick events are started by user actions, that's not always the case. For instance, the GotFocus and LostFocus events can occur when the user moves the focus to or from a control, but they can also occur when the Visual Basic code moves the focus to or from a control. Similarly, the Load event of a form can occur when an application first starts. And the Closed event occurs after the Close method is executed for a form.

In addition to the events shown here, most objects have many more events that the application can respond to. For example, events occur when the user positions the mouse over an object or when the user presses or releases a key. However, you don't typically respond to those events.

Event: The user clicks on the Exit button

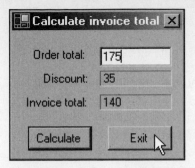

Response: The procedure for the Click event of the Exit button is executed

```
Private Sub btnExit_Click(ByVal sender As System.Object, _
                          ByVal e As System.EventArgs) _
                          Handles btnExit.Click
    Me.Close()
End Sub
```

Common control events

Event	Occurs when...
Click	...the user clicks on the control.
DblClick	...the user double-clicks on the control.
GotFocus	...the focus is moved to the control.
LostFocus	...the focus is moved from the control.

Common form events

Event	Occurs when...
Load	...the form is loaded into memory.
Activated	...the form becomes the active form.
Closing	...the form is closing.
Closed	...the form is closed.

Concepts

- Windows applications work by responding to events that occur on objects.

- To indicate how an application should respond to an event, you code an *event procedure*, which is also known as an *event handler*.

- An event can be an action that's initiated by the user like the Click event, or it can be an action initiated by program code like the Closed event.

Figure 2-13   How an application responds to events

How to create an event procedure

To code event procedures, you work in the Code Editor window as described in figure 2-14. One way to start an event procedure is to select the object and event from the drop-down lists at the top of the window. Then Visual Studio generates the Sub and End Sub statements for you, and you can add the code for the procedure between those two statements.

You can also start an event procedure by double-clicking on an object in the Form Designer window. Then, Visual Studio opens the Code Editor window and generates Sub and End Sub statements for the default event of the object. In this figure, for example, you can see the code that was generated when I double-clicked on the Calculate button on the Invoice Total form.

Whichever method you use to create an event procedure, Visual Studio creates the Sub and End Sub statements for you and places the insertion point on a blank line between them. Then, you can immediately start typing the Visual Basic statements that you want to include in the event procedure.

Note that before you start an event procedure for a control, you should set the Name property of the control as described earlier in this chapter. That way, this name will be reflected in the name of the event procedure as shown in this figure. If you change the control name after starting an event procedure for it, Visual Basic will change the name of the object in the Handles clause, but it won't change the name of the object in the procedure name. And that can be confusing when you're first learning Visual Basic.

Also, I want to warn you not to modify the Sub and End Sub statements that are generated for you when you create an event procedure. Later in this book, you'll learn how to change the Sub statement slightly so that you can use a single event procedure to handle events for several objects. But for now, you should leave the Sub and End Sub statements alone.

A Click event procedure

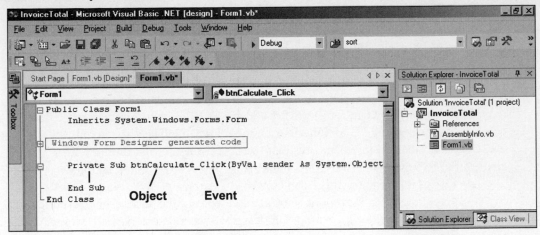

How to create a Click event procedure

1. In the Form Designer, double-click the control for which you want to create an event procedure. This opens the Code Editor and automatically generates the Sub and End Sub statements for the default event.

2. Type the Visual Basic code for the event procedure between the Sub and End Sub statements.

3. When you are finished working on the event procedure, you can return to the Form Designer by clicking the View Designer button in the Solution Explorer window. Or, you can work on other procedures in the Code Editor.

How to start procedures for other events

*   To start a procedure for any event, choose the object and event from the drop-down lists at the top of the Code Editor window. Then, Sub and End Sub statements are generated for the event.

*   To start a procedure for the Load event of a form, double-click the form itself. The Load event is executed when the form is first displayed.

The Sub and End Sub statements

*   The Sub statement that's generated when you create an event procedure includes a Handles clause that names the object and event the procedure handles. The procedure name that's generated consists of the object name, an underscore, and the event name. Thus, btnCalculate_Click is the name of the procedure that handles the Click event of the btnCalculate button.

*   Although you can modify the generated Sub statement, you shouldn't do that unless you want the procedure to handle two or more events. You'll learn how to do that later in this book.

Figure 2-14   How to create an event procedure

The code for the Invoice Total form

Figure 2-15 presents the code for the Invoice Total form. The first thing to notice is that the code starts with a Class statement and ends with an End Class statement. These statements are added automatically when you create a form, and they're your first clue that when you create a form you're actually creating a new class that defines the form. In this case, the class is named Form1, which is the default name for the first form that's added to a Windows application.

Visual Basic also adds an Inherits statement after the Class statement. In this case, the Inherits statement says that the new form is based on the Form class in the System.Windows.Forms namespace of the .NET Class Library.

The rest of the code for this form consists of two event procedures. The first one responds to the Click event of the Calculate button; the second one responds to the Click event of the Exit button. I'll describe this code briefly here so you have a general idea of how it works, but if you're new to programming you may not understand the code completely until after you read the next chapter.

The event procedure for the Click event of the Calculate button calculates the discount amount and the invoice total based on the order total entered by the user and then displays those values in the appropriate label controls. To do that, this procedure starts by defining the variables it will use in its calculations. In this case, three variables are defined, each of which can hold a decimal value.

In the next group of statements, the value in the Text property of the Order Total text box, which is the value entered by the user, is assigned to the variable named dOrderTotal. Because the discount for this version of the program is always 20%, the discount amount is calculated by multiplying the order total by .2, and the resulting value is assigned to the variable named dDiscountAmount. Then, the invoice total is calculated by subtracting the discount amount from the order total, and the result is assigned to the variable named dInvoiceTotal.

The next two statements assign the values of the last two variables to the Text properties of the label controls, which displays the values on the form. Then, the last statement before the End Sub statement executes the Focus method of the Order Total text box, which moves the focus to that control. Otherwise, the focus would remain on the Calculate button that's used to start this event procedure.

The other procedure that's required by this application is for the Click event of the Exit button. It contains just one statement that performs the Close event of the form. So when the user clicks on this button, the form is closed, which ends the application.

Note that all of the shaded code in this figure is generated by Visual Basic when you start the project and start the event procedures. Beyond that, Visual Basic generates other code that is hidden in the Code Editor window under the label "Windows Form Designer generated code" (you can see this label back in figure 2-12). When the application is run, this is the code that implements the form and controls that you designed in the Form Designer. For now, you can just accept the fact that this generated code should work the way you want it to. By the time you finish this book, though, you'll understand what this code does.

The code for the Invoice Total form

```
Public Class Form1
    Inherits System.Windows.Forms.Form

    Private Sub btnCalculate_Click(ByVal sender As System.Object, _
            ByVal e As System.EventArgs) Handles btnCalculate.Click

        Dim dOrderTotal As Decimal
        Dim dDiscountAmount As Decimal
        Dim dInvoiceTotal As Decimal

        dOrderTotal = txtOrderTotal.Text
        dDiscountAmount = dOrderTotal * .2
        dInvoiceTotal = dOrderTotal - dDiscountAmount

        lblDiscountAmount.Text = dDiscountAmount
        lblInvoiceTotal.Text = dInvoiceTotal

        txtOrderTotal.Focus()

    End Sub

    Private Sub btnExit_Click(ByVal sender As System.Object, _
            ByVal e As System.EventArgs) Handles btnExit.Click

        Me.Close()

    End Sub

End Class
```

Description

- The code for the Invoice Total form includes two event procedures. The first one is executed when the user clicks the Calculate button. This procedure calculates the discount amount and invoice total based on the order total entered by the user.

- The second event procedure is executed when the user clicks the Exit button. This procedure closes the form, which ends the application.

- When you use the IDE to create a form, you're actually creating a new class based on the Form class. That's why the code for a Windows form starts with a Class statement and ends with an End Class statement. That's also why the Class statement is followed by an Inherits statement that identifies the Form class. All three of these statements are generated for you, and you don't need to change them. In chapters 6 and 15, you'll learn more about the Class and Inherits statements.

Note

- All of the shaded statements in the code are generated for you.

Figure 2-15   The code for the Invoice Total form

How to detect and correct syntax errors

As you enter the code for a procedure, Visual Basic checks the syntax of each statement. If a *syntax error*, or *build error*, is detected, Visual Basic displays a wavy line under the code in the Code Editor window. In the Code Editor window in figure 2-16, for example, you can see the lines under the reference to two controls named txtDiscountAmount and txtInvoiceTotal.

If you place the mouse pointer over the code in error, a brief description of the error is displayed. In this case, the error message indicates that the name is not declared. If you look back to the property settings in figure 2-10, you'll see the problem is that the prefix for these controls is *lbl*, not *txt*. To correct these errors, you just correct the names in the Code Editor window.

If the *Task List window* is open as shown in this figure, any errors that Visual Basic detects will also be displayed in that window. When you build an application, the Task List window is displayed automatically. But you can also display this window before building an application as described in this figure. Then, you can locate an error by double-clicking on it in the Task List window. This can be useful when you're working with an application that has more code than can be displayed on the screen at one time.

The Code Editor and Task List windows with syntax errors displayed

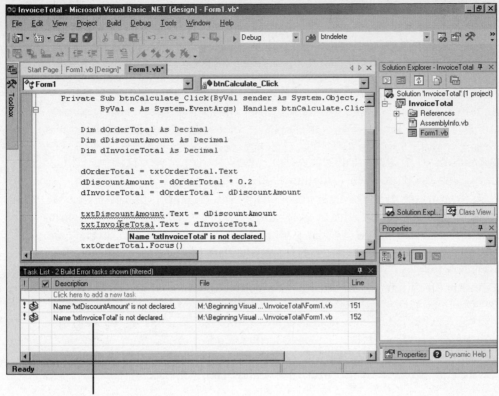

Task List window

Description

- Visual Basic checks the syntax of the code as you enter it. If an error occurs, it's high-lighted with a wavy underline in the Code Editor window, and you can place the mouse pointer over it to display a description of the error.

- If the *Task List window* is open, all of the *syntax errors* (or *build errors*) are listed in that window. Then, you can double-click on any error in the list to take you to its location in the Code Editor window. When you correct the error, it's removed from the *task list*.

- By default, the Task List window is displayed when you build an application that contains a syntax error. To open this window and display the syntax errors before building the application, use the View → Show Tasks → Build Errors command.

Figure 2-16   How to detect and correct syntax errors

How to get help information

As you develop applications in Visual Basic, it's likely that you'll need some additional information about the IDE, the Visual Basic language, an object, property, method, event, or some other aspect of Visual Basic programming. Figure 2-17 shows you several ways you can get that information.

When you're working in the Code Editor window or the Form Designer window, the quickest way to get help information is to press F1 while the insertion point is in a keyword or an object is selected. Then, information about that keyword or object is displayed in a Help Topic window in the main area of the IDE.

Another way to access help information is to select the Contents, Index, or Search command from the Help menu. When you do that, a tabbed window is added to the group that contains the Solution Explorer window. In this figure, for example, you can see the Search window. From this window, you can enter a word or phrase to search for. Then, when you click on the Search button, the results are displayed in the Search Results window. To display information on any of the listed topics, just double-click on the topic.

One final way to get help information is to use the Dynamic Help window. This window is included by default in the group that contains the Properties window. The topics that are displayed in this window are determined by the most recent operations you performed. With all the other ways to get help, though, you probably won't need the Dynamic Help window.

Help information for using the Solution Explorer

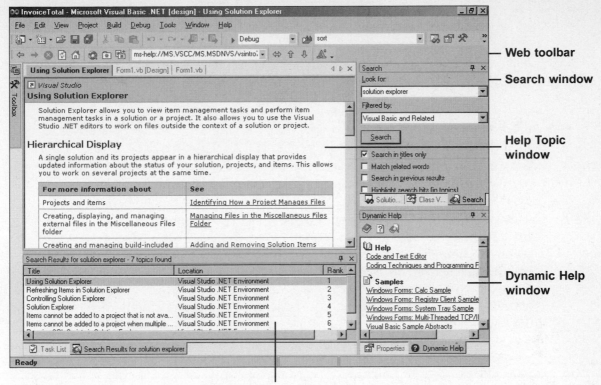

Search Results window

Description

- To display context-sensitive help information, select an object in the Form Designer window or position the insertion point in a keyword in the Code Editor window. Then, press F1. If the Help feature recognizes the object or keyword, information is displayed in the Help Topic window, which replaces the window that contains the Start page.

- You can also get help information by selecting the Contents, Index, or Search command from the Help menu. Then, a tabbed window is combined with the Solution Explorer window, and you can use that window to select the appropriate topic.

- The Contents window lets you select a topic from the table of contents, and the Index window lets you select an entry in the index. When you select a topic or index entry, it's displayed in the Help Topic window.

- The Search window lets you search for information based on keywords you enter. The results of the search are displayed in the Search Results window at the bottom of the screen. Then, you can double-click on an entry to display the related topic.

- The Dynamic Help window provides context-sensitive help depending on the operations you performed most recently. To display one of the listed topics, just click on it.

- When a help topic is displayed, the Web toolbar appears. You can click on the Search button in this toolbar to go to the MSDN online web site. To redisplay the Start page, you can click on the Home button.

Figure 2-17   How to get help information

How to run, test, and debug a project

After you correct any syntax errors that are detected as you enter the code for a project, you'll want to run the project. When the project runs, you'll want to test it to make sure it works the way you want it to and debug it to remove any programming errors you find.

How to run a project

As you learned in chapter 1, before a project can be *run*, it must be *built* into an assembly containing the Intermediate Language that can then be run by the Common Language Runtime. You can build a project without running it as described in figure 2-18, but in most cases you'll want to run the project so you can test and debug it.

To run a project, click the Start button in the Standard toolbar, select the Start command from the Debug menu, or press the F5 key. This builds the project if it hasn't been built already and causes the project's form to be displayed, as shown in this figure. If your project contains two or more forms, you can designate which one of them is displayed when you start your project. You'll learn more about that in chapter 9.

When you close the form for a project, the application ends. Then, you're returned to Visual Studio where you can continue working on your program.

The form displayed when you run the Invoice Total project

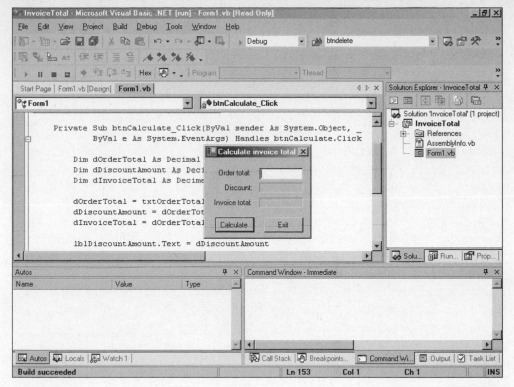

Description

- To *run* a project, click the Start button located in the Standard toolbar, select the Debug → Start menu command, or press the F5 key. This causes Visual Studio to *build* the project and create an assembly. Then, assuming that there are no build errors, the assembly is run so the project's form is displayed over the IDE as shown above.

- If syntax errors are detected when a project is built, they're listed in the Task List window and a dialog box asks whether you want to run the project even though there were build errors. Click No to return to the Code Editor, then correct the build errors and run the project again.

- If you prefer, you can build a project without actually running it by selecting the Build → Build *project name* command. You can then run the project by clicking the Start button or selecting the Debug → Start menu command.

- When you build a project for the first time, all of the components of the project are built. After that, only the components that have changed are rebuilt. To rebuild all components whether or not they've changed, use the Build → Rebuild Solution command.

- If a solution consists of two or more projects, you can build all of the projects at once by using the Build → Build Solution command.

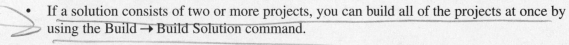

Figure 2-18   How to run a project

How to test a project

Testing refers to the process of running your project to make sure the application works the way it is supposed to. As you test your project, you should try every possible combination of input data and interactions to be certain that the project works correctly in every case. Figure 2-19 provides an overview of the testing process for Visual Basic applications.

To start, you should test the user interface. Make sure that each control is sized and positioned properly, that there are no spelling errors in any of the controls or in the form's title bar, and that the navigation features such as the tab order and access keys work properly.

Next, subject your application to a carefully thought-out sequence of valid test data. Make sure you test every combination of data that the project will handle. If, for example, the project calculates the discount at different values based on the value of the order total, use order totals that fall within each range.

Finally, test the program to make sure that it properly handles invalid data entered by users. For example, type text information into text boxes that expect numeric data. Leave fields blank. Use negative numbers where they shouldn't be allowed. Remember that the goal of testing is to find all of the problems.

As you test your projects, you'll eventually encounter *run-time errors*. These errors, also known as *exceptions*, occur when Visual Basic encounters a problem that prevents a statement from being executed. If, for example, a user enters "ABC" into the txtOrderTotal text box, a run-time error will occur when the program tries to assign that value to a decimal variable.

When a run-time error occurs, a dialog box like the one in this figure is displayed. This dialog box lets you break into the debugger (Break) so you can debug the error or end the application (Continue). When you break into the debugger, you can use the debugging tools that you'll be introduced to in the next figure.

The dialog box that's displayed when a run-time error occurs

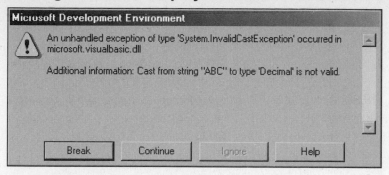

How to test a project

- Begin by testing the user interface. Visually check all the controls to make sure they are displayed properly with the correct text. Use the Tab key to make sure the tab order is set correctly, verify that the access keys work right, and see if both the Esc key and the Exit button properly close the application.

- Continue by testing the application with valid input data. For the Invoice Total application, you should enter a variety of order total amounts to make sure the discount and invoice totals are always calculated properly. For applications with more input controls, you need to test all possible combinations of valid input data.

- Complete your testing by making sure the project properly handles invalid or unexpected data or user actions. For example, leave required fields blank, enter text data into numeric input fields, and use negative numbers where they are not appropriate. Try everything you can think of to make the program fail.

- If a statement in your application can't be executed, a *run-time error*, or *exception*, occurs. Then, if the exception isn't handled by your application, a dialog box like the one above is displayed. At that point, you need to debug the application as explained in the next figure.

Description

- To *test* a project, you run the project to make sure it works properly no matter what combinations of valid or invalid data you enter or what sequence of controls you use.

- Because an application should never end with a run-time error, one of your goals in testing is to force run-time errors.

- In chapter 4, you'll learn how to write applications that test for invalid data so run-time errors won't occur. And in chapter 5, you'll learn how to catch exceptions so they won't cause your application to fail.

Note

- When you press the Enter key to activate the default AcceptButton for a form and an exception occurs, the resulting dialog box may not include a Break button. In that case, you can click on the Continue button to continue the application, and then click on the button that caused the exception. This time, the dialog box will include the Break button.

Figure 2-19   How to test a project

How to debug run-time errors

When a run-time error occurs and you click on the Break button in the dialog box that's displayed, Visual Basic enters *break mode*. In that mode, Visual Basic displays the Code Editor window and highlights the statement that couldn't be executed. It also displays two debugging toolbars. This is illustrated in figure 2-20. Then, you need to find the cause of the exception (the *bug*) by *debugging* the application.

Often, you can figure out what caused the problem just by knowing what statement couldn't be executed. But sometimes, it helps to find out what the current values in some of the variables or properties in the program are. To do that, you place the mouse pointer over a variable or property in the code so a *data tip* is displayed. This tip displays the current value of the variable or property.

In the example in this figure, the current value of the Text property of the txtOrderTotal control is ABC, which isn't numeric data. Since the variable named dOrderTotal requires numeric data, that explains why the highlighted statement can't be executed. If you were to move the mouse pointer over the dOrderTotal variable in this statement, you would see the value 0D, which is its starting value of decimal zero.

Once you find the cause of a bug, you can correct it. But first, you must exit from break mode. To do that, you can click on the Stop Debugging button in the Debug toolbar. Then, you can correct the problem in the Code Editor window and test the application again.

The last of the three debugging techniques that are summarized in this figure lets you stop a program that you can't stop any other way. To do that, you can click on the Break All button in the Debug toolbar. Although you shouldn't need to do that when working with a simple program like the one in this chapter, it can come in handy when you're working with programs that perform loops, which you'll learn about in chapter 4. Then, in chapter 7, you'll learn about the other windows, toolbar buttons, and commands that you can use as you debug more complicated programs.

How a project looks in break mode

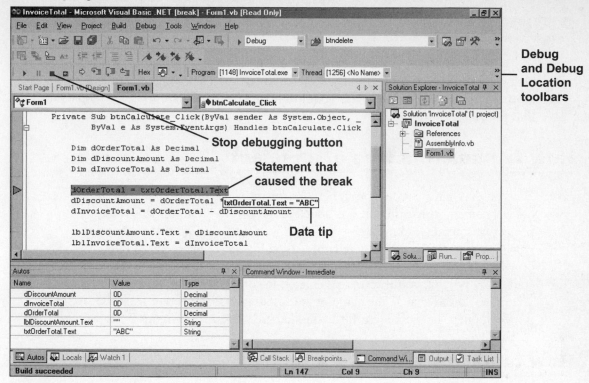

Description

- When an application ends with a run-time error, you need to fix the error. This is commonly referred to as *debugging*, and the error is commonly referred to as a *bug*.

- If you click on the Break button in the dialog box for a run-time error, Visual Basic displays the Code Editor window and highlights the statement that caused the exception.

- When a program enters break mode, the debugging windows and the Debug and Debug Location toolbars are displayed.

Debugging techniques for simple applications

- In *break mode*, you can display the value of a variable or property in a *data tip* by positioning the mouse pointer over it.

- To exit break mode and end the application, click on the Stop Debugging button in the Debug toolbar.

- To enter break mode any time that an application is running, click on the Break All button in the Debug toolbar. This is useful if you need to stop a program that's caught in a loop.

Figure 2-20   How to debug run-time errors

How to name and save the files of a project

When you complete a project or as you're working on it, you may want to change the names of some of the files from their defaults. Then, you'll want to save the files with their new names. You'll learn how to do that in the two topics that follow.

How to name the files of a project

You may have noticed throughout this chapter that I didn't change the default name of the form that was added to the Invoice Total project when the project was created. In most cases, though, you'll want to do that so that the name is more descriptive. You may also want to change the name of the project or solution. For example, if you accepted the default project name when you started the project, you'll want to change it to something more meaningful. Or, you may want to change the name of the solution so it's different from the project name. The techniques for doing that are presented in figure 2-21.

How to save the files of a project

Figure 2-21 also describes how to save the files of a project. Because Visual Basic saves any changes you make to the files in a project when you build the project, you won't usually need to save them explicitly. However, it's easy to do if you need to.

Notice in this figure that two factors determine which files are saved: what's selected in the Solution Explorer and the command you use to perform the save operation. If, for example, a single file is selected, you can use the Save command to save just that file, and you can use the Save All command to save the file along with the project and solution that contain the file. In contrast, if a project is selected in the Solution Explorer, the Save command causes the entire project to be saved, and the Save All command causes the entire solution to be saved.

The Properties window for a form file

How to rename a file, project, or solution

- To rename a file, highlight it in the Solution Explorer window to display its properties and then change the File Name property.

- Be sure not to change or omit the file extension when you rename a file. Remember too that using a three-letter prefix to indicate the contents of the file (like *frm* for a form file) makes it easier to tell what each file represents.

- To change the name of the project, highlight it in the Solution Explorer and then change the Project File property. To change the name of the solution, highlight it in the Solution Explorer and then change the Name property.

- You can also rename a file, project, or solution by right-clicking on it in the Solution Explorer and then selecting the Rename command from the shortcut menu that's displayed. This lets you change the file name directly in the Solution Explorer window.

How to save a file, project, or solution

- You can use the Save and Save All buttons in the Standard toolbar or the Save and Save All commands in the File menu to save a file, a project, or a solution. The files that are saved depend on what's selected in the Solution Explorer window.

- If a single file is selected, the Save command saves just that file and the Save All command saves the file and the project and solution that contain it. If a project is selected, the Save command saves the entire project and the solution that contains it and the Save All command saves the entire solution. And if a solution is selected, both the Save and Save All commands save the entire solution.

- If you try to close a solution that contains modified files, a dialog box is displayed that asks you if you want to save those files.

Figure 2-21   How to name and save the files of a project

Perspective

If you can develop the project that's presented in this chapter, you've already learned a lot. You know how to design an interface that consists of a form and its controls. You know how to enter the code for the event procedures that make the interface work the way you want it to. You know how to build and test a project. And you know some simple debugging techniques.

On the other hand, you've still got a lot to learn. In particular, you need to learn how to code the Visual Basic language. So in the next three chapters, you'll learn the essentials of the Visual Basic language.

Summary

- When you start a new Windows Application project, the project includes a default form. Then, you can add controls to the form by using the Form Designer window, and you can set the properties of the form and controls by using the Properties window.

- A *class* is a template for creating an *object* like a form or control. Each class defines the *members* of the object, which include *properties*, *methods*, and *events*. Collectively, these are known as the object's *interface*.

- To refer to the properties, methods, and events of an object, you type the name of the object followed by a *dot operator* and the member name. The Code Editor window makes this easy for you by listing all of the members that are available for an object.

- Windows applications work by responding to the events that occur on objects. To respond to an event, you code an *event procedure*.

- As you enter code, Visual Basic checks for *syntax errors*. It highlights any errors it finds in the Code Editor window and lists them in the Task List window so you can locate and correct them.

- You can get context-sensitive help for an object in the Form Designer window or for a keyword in the Code Editor window. You can also use the Contents, Index, and Search commands in the Help menu to get information.

- When you *run* a project, Visual Basic first *builds* the project to create an assembly that is then run by the Common Language Runtime.

- You should *test* a project thoroughly to make sure it properly handles all combinations of input, including incorrect or missing data.

- If a statement in the application can't be executed, a *run-time error* (or *exception*) occurs. Then, you must *debug* the application.

- Before you save a project, you should change the name of the default form file so it's more descriptive. If necessary, you can also change the name of the project file or the solution file.

Terms

template	interface	Task List window
primary control	member of an object	task list
tab order	property	build a project
focus	method	run a project
access key	event	test a project
object-oriented programming	dot operator	run-time error
object-oriented language	dot	exception
class	event-driven application	bug
object	event procedure	debug
instance	event handler	break mode
instantiation	syntax error	data tip
base class	build error	

Objectives

- Given the form design, property settings, and code for a simple application, use the skills presented in this chapter to develop and test the application.

- Use any of the help features presented in this chapter to display help information on a given topic.

- Distinguish between a class and an object.

- Give an example of a property, a method, and an event.

- Explain how an application responds to events.

- Distinguish between a syntax error and a run-time error.

- Distinguish between testing and debugging.

- Describe two techniques that you can use for debugging a run-time error.

Exercise 2-2   Code and test the Invoice Total form

In this exercise, you'll add code to the Invoice Total form that you designed in exercise 2-1. Then, you'll build and test the project to be sure it works correctly. You'll also experiment with debugging and review some help information.

Open the project

1. If it's not already open, open the Invoice Total project you started in the last exercise.

Add code to the form and correct syntax errors

2. Double-click on the Calculate button to open the Code Editor window and generate the Sub and End Sub statements for the Click event of this object. Then, enter the code for this procedure as shown in figure 2-15.

3. Select the Exit button (btnExit) from the drop-down list in the upper left corner of the Code Editor window, and select the Click event from the drop-down list in the upper right corner. When you do, the Sub and End Sub statements for the Click event of this object will be generated. Then, enter the statement shown in figure 2-15 for this event procedure.

4. Open the Task List window as described in figure 2-16. If any syntax errors are listed in this window, double-click on the error to move to the error in the Code Editor window. Then, correct the error. Repeat this for any other errors listed in the Task List window.

Test the application

5. Click on the Start button in the Standard toolbar to build and run the project. If you corrected all the syntax errors in step 4, the build should succeed and the Invoice Total form should appear. If not, you'll need to correct the errors and click the Start button again.

6. Enter a valid numeric value in the first text box and click on the Calculate button or press the Enter key to activate this button. Assuming that the calculation works, click on the Exit button or press the Esc key to end the application. If either of these procedures doesn't work right, of course, you need to debug the problems and test the application again.

Enter invalid data and display data tips in break mode

7. Start the application again. This time, enter xx for the order total. Then, click on the Calculate button, which will cause a run-time error and display a dialog box. (Note: If you press the Enter key instead of clicking on the Calculate button, you may get a dialog box that doesn't include the Break button. Then, you can click on the Continue button and try this again.)

8. Click on the Break button to enter break mode, and note the highlighted statement. Then, move the mouse pointer over the variable and property in this statement to display their data tips. This shows that the code for this application needs to be enhanced so it checks for invalid data. You'll learn how to do that in chapter 4. For now, though, click on the Stop Debugging button in Debug toolbar to end the application.

Create syntax errors and see how they affect the IDE

9. When you return to the Code Editor window, close the Task List window by clicking on the Close button in its upper right corner. Next, change the name of one of the labels that are referred to in the code so it's incorrect. Notice that when you move the insertion point out of the name, it's now underlined to indicate an error. Then, place the mouse pointer over the name to display a description of the error.

10. Start the application without correcting the error. A dialog box will be displayed indicating that there are build errors. Click on the No button in this dialog box to end the application and return to the Code Editor window.

11. Notice that the Task List window is displayed again, and it lists the build error that was detected. Double-click on this error and it will be highlighted in the Code Editor window. Correct the error, and it's removed from the Task List window.

Rename the form file and save the project

12. Click on the form file in the Solution Explorer window to display its properties, and notice the value of the File Name property. Instead of changing the setting for this property, though, right-click on the file in the Solution Explorer and select the Rename command from the shortcut menu that's displayed. Then, replace the current file name with the name frmInvoiceTotal.vb. When you press the Enter key, the file will be saved with this name and its File Name property will be updated. Notice, however, that the Class statement in the Code Editor window still refers to the form by its default name (Form1). In chapter 9, you'll learn how and when to change this name.

13. Select the Close Solution command from the File menu. Because the name of the form file was changed but the project wasn't saved, a dialog box will be displayed that asks you if you want to save the changes. Click on the Yes button to save the changes and close the solution.

Experiment with the Help feature

14. Open the project again. Then, to see how context-sensitive help works, place the insertion point in the Focus method in the last statement of the first event procedure and press F1. This should open a Help Topic window that tells you more about this method. Notice that this window replaces the window that contains the Start page.

15. Select the Index command from the Help menu to display the Index window. Type "focus" into the Look for box in this window to see the entries that are listed under this topic. Next, select the Visual Basic and Related item from the Filter by drop-down list to show just the topics related to Visual Basic. Then, click on one or more topics to display them in the Help Topic window.

16. Continue experimenting with the Index feature until you're comfortable with it. Then, experiment with the Contents and Search commands in the Help menu to see how they work. When you're done, click on the Home button in the Web toolbar to see that it redisplays the Start page.

Exit from Visual Studio

17. Click on the Close button for the Visual Studio window to exit from this application. If you did everything and got your application to work right, you've come a long way!

3

Visual Basic language essentials (part 1)

In the last chapter, you learned the basic techniques for adding Visual Basic code to a project. To become a proficient Visual Basic programmer, though, you need to master the Visual Basic language. As a result, this chapter and the two that follow present the language essentials that you'll need for all of the projects you develop. When you finish this chapter, you will be able to write the code for simple applications of your own.

Basic coding skills

To start, the topics that follow present some basic coding skills for Visual Basic. These are the ones that you'll use in all your applications.

How to code with a readable style

When you build an application, Visual Basic makes sure that your code follows all of its rules. If it doesn't, Visual Basic reports syntax errors that you have to correct before you can continue. You saw how that worked in the last chapter.

Besides adhering to the coding rules, though, you should try to write your code so it's easier to read, understand, debug, and maintain. That's important for you, but it's even more important if someone else has to take over the maintenance of your code. You can create more readable code by following coding recommendations like those in figure 3-1.

To illustrate, this figure presents an example of an event procedure. As you can see, this procedure consists of four types of statements: a *procedure declaration*, *variable declarations*, *assignment statements*, and a *conditional statement*. The *end-of-procedure declaration* that ends the procedure is paired with the procedure declaration and is generated along with it.

The first coding recommendation is that you use indentation and extra spaces to align related elements in your code. This is possible because you can use one or more spaces to separate the elements in a Visual Basic statement. In this example, then, the Private Sub and End Sub statements are aligned because they are the first and last statements in the procedure, and all of the other statements are indented. In addition, the statements within the If and Else clauses of the conditional statement are indented and aligned so you can easily identify the parts of this statement.

The second recommendation is to use blank lines before and after groups of related statements to set them off from the rest of the code. This too is illustrated by the procedure in this figure. Here, the code is separated into seven groups of statements. In a short procedure, this isn't too important, but it can make a long procedure much easier to follow.

The third recommendation is to code all the variable declarations at the start of a procedure so they're easy to find. In addition, if the procedure requires many declarations, you can group related declarations and set them off with blank lines.

Throughout this chapter and book, you'll see code that illustrates the use of these recommendations. You will also receive other coding recommendations that will help you write code that is easy to read, debug, and maintain.

As you enter code in the Code Editor window, the Code Editor will automatically assist you in formatting your code. When you press the Enter key at the end of a statement, for example, the Editor will indent the next statement to the same level. Or, if you leave out a space between a variable name and an arithmetic operator, the Code Editor will put the space in for you.

An example of a Visual Basic procedure

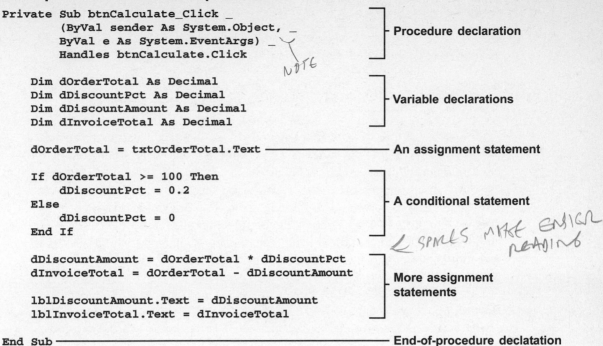

```
Private Sub btnCalculate_Click _
        (ByVal sender As System.Object, _
        ByVal e As System.EventArgs) _
        Handles btnCalculate.Click
```
Procedure declaration   *NOTE*

```
    Dim dOrderTotal As Decimal
    Dim dDiscountPct As Decimal
    Dim dDiscountAmount As Decimal
    Dim dInvoiceTotal As Decimal
```
Variable declarations

```
    dOrderTotal = txtOrderTotal.Text
```
An assignment statement

```
    If dOrderTotal >= 100 Then
        dDiscountPct = 0.2
    Else
        dDiscountPct = 0
    End If
```
A conditional statement

SPACES MAKE EASIER READING

```
    dDiscountAmount = dOrderTotal * dDiscountPct
    dInvoiceTotal = dOrderTotal - dDiscountAmount

    lblDiscountAmount.Text = dDiscountAmount
    lblInvoiceTotal.Text = dInvoiceTotal
```
More assignment statements

```
End Sub
```
End-of-procedure declatation

Types of statements

- *Procedure declarations* identify the *procedures* within an application, and *end-of-procedure declarations* end them.
- *Variable declarations* define *variables*, which are used to store values.
- *Assignment statements* assign values to variables and properties.
- *Conditional statements* determine the order in which statements are performed based on one or more conditions.

Coding rules

- Use spaces to separate the words and operators in each statement.
- Indentation and capitalization have no effect on the operation of a statement.

Coding recommendations

- Use indentation and extra spaces to align statements and clauses within statements.
- Use blank lines before and after groups of related statements.
- Code all variable declarations at the start of the procedure, and group related declarations.

Note

- As you enter code in the Code Editor window, Visual Basic may adjust the capitalization, spacing, and alignment of your code.

Figure 3-1   How to code with a readable style

How to continue a statement from one line to the next

In the first example in figure 3-2, you can see how a long statement is displayed in the Code Editor window. It just continues to the right beyond the boundaries of the window so you can't see it. Although this doesn't affect the way the code is interpreted, it does make editing and printing difficult.

In the second example, you can see how you can use the *continuation character* to continue a statement from one line to the next. Just type a space and the underscore (_) at a logical break point in a statement. Then continue the statement on the next line. This obviously makes your code easier to read.

Another alternative is to use the *word wrap* feature to automatically format long statements as shown in the third example. Two drawbacks to using this feature, though, are (1) that you can't control where the lines break, and (2) you can't control the indentation of the wrapped lines. In general, then, it's better to use continuation characters so you can format the lines so they're as readable as possible.

How a long statement appears in the Code Editor window

```
        Do Until iIndex > iMonths
            dFutureValue = (dFutureValue + txtMonth
            iIndex = iIndex + 1
        Loop
```

How to use continuation characters to format a long statement

```
        Do Until iIndex > iMonths
            dFutureValue = (dFutureValue _
            + txtMonthlyInvestment.Text) _
            * (1 + dInterestRate)
            iIndex = iIndex + 1
        Loop
```

How the word wrap option formats the code

```
        Do Until iIndex > iMonths
            dFutureValue = (dFutureValue +
    txtMonthlyInvestment.Text) * (1 + dInterestRate)
            iIndex = iIndex + 1
        Loop
```

How to continue a statement on the next line

- Type a space followed by an underscore (the *continuation character*) at the end of the line you want to continue. Then, continue the statement on the next line.

Description

- By default, a long statement will continue beyond the right side of the Code Editor window.

- To make a statement more readable, you can divide it at any logical point and continue it on the next line.

- You can use *word wrap* to automatically format long statements to the width of the Code Editor window, but this feature doesn't indent continuation lines.

- To turn the word wrap feature on, use the Edit → Advanced → Word Wrap command.

Figure 3-2   How to continue a statement from one line to the next

How to use comments

Comments can be used to document what a program does, what specific blocks of code do, and what specific lines of code do. Since the Visual Basic compiler ignores comments, you can include them anywhere in a program without affecting how your code works. In figure 3-3, you can see that you code a comment by typing an apostrophe followed by the comment.

This figure also illustrates several ways that you can use comments. At the start of the code, you can see a *block comment*. This type of comment can be used to document information that applies to the entire procedure. Next, you can see an *end-of-line comment* that is coded to the right of a statement. This type of comment can be used to describe what that statement does or what the group of statements does. After that, you can see a *single-line comment* that describes what the block of code that follows is doing.

Comments can also be useful when you're writing and testing code. If, for example, you don't want to delete a line of code but you want to test a procedure without running that line of code, you can type an apostrophe before the line to convert it to a comment. This is sometimes referred to as *commenting out* a line of code. Later, you can restore the line of code just by removing the apostrophe.

Although many programmers sprinkle their code with comments, that shouldn't be necessary if you write your code so it's easy to read and understand. Instead, you should use comments only to clarify portions of code that are hard to understand. The trick, of course, is to provide comments for the portions of code that need explanation without cluttering the code with unnecessary comments. In the example in this figure, of course, none of the comments are needed.

One problem that you run into when using comments is that they may not accurately represent what the code does. This often happens when a programmer changes the code, but doesn't change the comments that go along with it. Then it's even harder to understand the code, because the comments are misleading. So if you change the code that you've written comments for, be sure to change the comments too.

Incidentally, all comments are displayed in the Code Editor window in a different color from the words in the Visual Basic statements. By default, the Visual Basic statements are blue and black (blue for the Visual Basic words and black for the programmer-supplied words), while the comments are green. That makes it easy to identify the comments.

Code that uses comments

```
' ==========================================
' Date:     11/30/01
' Author:   Anne Prince
' Purpose:  Calculate invoice total
' ==========================================

    Dim dOrderTotal As Decimal       'declaration statements
    Dim dDiscountPct As Decimal
    Dim dDiscountAmount As Decimal
    Dim dInvoiceTotal As Decimal

    dOrderTotal = txtOrderTotal.Text

'Calculate the proper discount
    If dOrderTotal >= 100 Then
        dDiscountPct = 0.25
'       dDiscountPct = 0.2
    Else
        dDiscountPct = 0
    End If

    dDiscountAmount = dOrderTotal * dDiscountPct    'calculate discount
    dInvoiceTotal = dOrderTotal - dDiscountAmount   'deduct from total

    lblDiscountAmount.Text = dDiscountAmount        'display results
    lblInvoiceTotal.Text = dInvoiceTotal            'on form
```

- Block comment
- 'declaration statements
- End-of-line comment
- Single-line comment
- A statement that has been commented out

How to code a comment

- Type an apostrophe (') followed by the comment. A comment can be coded to the right of a statement or on a line with no statement. However, a comment can't be coded to the right of a continuation character.

- You can also code a comment by typing the keyword Rem (short for Remark) followed by a space and the comment, but that isn't normally done.

Coding recommendations

- Use comments only for portions of code that are difficult to understand. Then, make sure that the comments are correct and up-to-date.

- If you write your code in a readable style, your code will need few comments.

Description

- *Comments* can be used to document what a procedure does, what specific blocks of code do, and what specific lines of code do. Since comments are ignored by the Visual Basic compiler, they have no effect on the operation of the code.

- During testing, you can *comment out* a line of code by inserting an apostrophe before it. This is useful for testing a new statement without deleting the old statement.

- To comment or uncomment one or more lines of code, you can select the lines and click on the Comment or the Uncomment button in the Text Editor toolbar (see figure 3-5).

Figure 3-3   How to use comments

How to collapse, expand, and print the source code

As you write the code for an application, you may want to *collapse* and *expand* some of the procedures to make it easier to scroll through the code and locate specific procedures. To do that, use the techniques described in figure 3-4. In the Code Editor window in this figure, for example, the event procedure for the Click event of a button named btnCalculate has been collapsed so all you can see is the Sub statement.

To print the code for a form, you use the Print command in the File menu, which is the standard Windows technique for printing. Then, the expanded procedures are printed, but the collapsed procedures aren't. Also, any coding lines that extend beyond the width of the printed page are automatically wrapped.

"PRINT FORM"
-CAN'T PRINT WHOLE PROJ.

The Code Editor window with one of the procedures collapsed

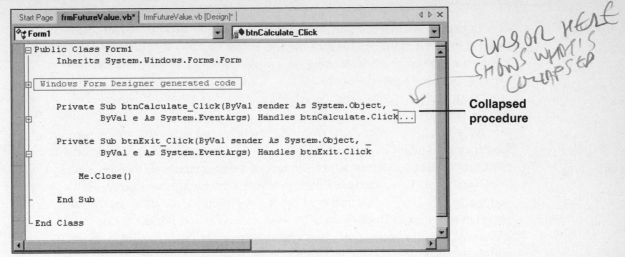

How to collapse and expand the source code

- If a procedure appears in the Code Editor window with a minus sign (-) next to it, you can click on the minus sign to *collapse* the procedure so just the first statement is displayed.

- If a procedure appears in the Code Editor window with a plus sign (+) next to it, you can click on the plus sign to *expand* the procedure so you can see all of it.

- You can also display the code that's generated automatically as you design a form by clicking on the plus sign next to the block of code that's labeled "Windows Form Designer generated code." You don't usually need to change this code, though.

How to print the source code

- To print the source code, select the File → Print command and complete the dialog box that's displayed.

- The code is printed as it appears in the Code Editor window with the statements in the collapsed procedures omitted. Any lines that extend beyond the width of the printed page are automatically wrapped.

Figure 3-4   How to collapse, expand, and print the source code

How to use the Text Editor toolbar

Figure 3-5 shows how you can use the Text Editor toolbar to work with code. If you experiment with this toolbar, you'll find that its buttons provide some useful functions for working with comments and indentation and for moving between procedures.

In particular, you can use the Text Editor toolbar to modify several lines of code at once. For example, you can use this toolbar to add and remove comments from a block of code by selecting the lines and then clicking on the Comment or Uncomment button. Similarly, you can use the Increase Indent and Decrease Indent buttons to adjust the indentation for selected lines of code.

You can also use the Text Editor toolbar to work with *bookmarks*. After you use the Toggle Bookmark button to mark lines of code, you can easily move between the marked lines of code by using the Next and Previous Bookmark buttons. Although you usually don't need bookmarks when you're working with simple applications like the one shown here, bookmarks can be helpful when you're working with applications that contain more than a few pages of code.

If you experiment with the other buttons on the Text Editor toolbar, you'll find that they provide Intellisense features like the ones you learned about in the last chapter for referring to properties, methods, and events. Since most of these features are on by default, though, you'll only need to use these buttons if you turn the associated feature off.

MEMBER LIST = CTRL-SP ON BUTTON

A Code Editor window with the Text Editor toolbar displayed

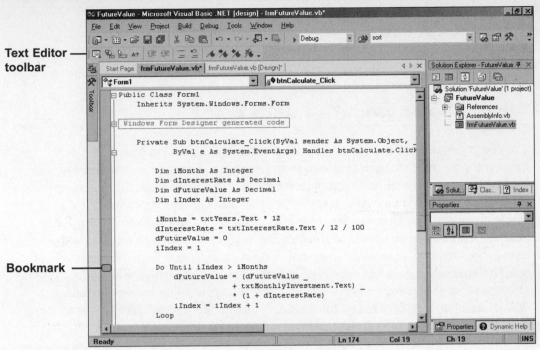

Text Editor toolbar

Bookmark

How to display or hide the Text Editor toolbar

- Right-click in the toolbar area and choose Text Editor from the shortcut menu.

How to use the basic buttons of the Text Editor toolbar

- To comment out or uncomment several lines of code at once, select the lines and click on the Comment or Uncomment button.

- To increase or decrease the indentation of several lines of code at once, select the lines and click on the Increase Indent or Decrease Indent button.

- To move quickly between lines of code, you can use *bookmarks*. To set or remove a single bookmark, move the insertion point into a line of code and click on the Toggle Bookmark button. To move between bookmarks, use the Next Bookmark and Previous Bookmark buttons. To remove all bookmarks, click on the Clear All Bookmarks button.

What the other buttons do

- The first two buttons on the Text Editor toolbar display member and argument information, and the third button displays information about the definition of a property, method, event, variable, or other identifier.

- The fourth button displays a list of keywords that match the characters you type. To use this feature, type one or more characters of a keyword, such as a word in a Visual Basic statement, and then click this button.

Figure 3-5   How to use the Text Editor toolbar

How to work with variables

As you learned earlier in this chapter, *variables* are used to store data that changes as a project runs. In the topics that follow, you'll learn how to declare variables, give them initial values, and change those values as the project runs.

The Visual Basic primitive data types

When you declare a variable, you assign it one of the twelve Visual Basic *primitive data types* that are summarized in figure 3-6. The *data type* defines what kind of information will be stored in the variable. For instance, the String data type is used for any alphanumeric or text characters. The Char data type is used for a single character. The Boolean data type is used for the binary values: True or False. And the Date data type is used to store a value that represents both the date and time.

The next seven data types in this table are *numeric data types*. When you choose one of these, you should make sure that it's appropriate for the size and type of number that the variable must hold. If the number doesn't have digits to the right of the decimal point, for example, you can use one of the *integer data types*: Short, Integer, or Long. They store whole numbers.

To store values with decimal places, you use the Decimal, Single, or Double data type. For business data, you usually use the Decimal type. However, you can also use the Single and Double types, which I'll tell you more about in a moment.

If you declare a variable without specifying a data type, the Object data type is used as the default. This data type can hold a reference to any type of object. In general, though, it's better to specify another data type because it uses fewer system resources and results in code that's easier to understand.

To create variable names that are easy to interpret, you should assign a name that begins with a standard prefix. The suggested prefix for each data type is shown in this figure. By doing this, your code is easier to read and understand, because the data type of each variable is apparent without referring back to the declaration statement.

Now, back to the Single and Double data types, which are used to store data as *floating-point numbers*. This number format provides for very large and very small numbers, but with a limited number of *significant digits*. A *single-precision number* provides for numbers with approximately 7 significant digits, and a *double-precision number* provides for numbers with approximately 14 significant digits. In general, the Double data type is better for business applications because it provides the precision (number of significant digits) that those applications require.

To express the value of a floating-point number, you can use *scientific notation*. This lets you express very large and very small numbers in a sort of shorthand. To use this notation, you type the letter e or E followed by a power of 10. For instance, 3.65e+9 is equal to 3.65 times 10^9, or 3,650,000,000. If you have a mathematical background, of course, you're already familiar with this notation. And if you don't, you probably won't need it for business applications.

[handwritten: NOT NECC, BUT GOOD PRACTICE (TESTED)]

The Visual Basic primitive data types

[handwritten: DANGEROUS IN TRANSLATION!!]

Data type	Prefixes	Description
String	str *or* s	Any number of characters
Char	chr *or* c	A single character *[handwritten: ← NEW]*
Boolean	bln *or* b	A True or False value
Date	dtm	An integer that represents the number of 100-nanosecond units that have elapsed since 12:00 a.m. January 1, 0001
Byte	byt *or* y	A positive integer value from 0 to 255
Short	srt *or* t	An integer from –32,768 to +32,767
Integer	int *or* i	An integer from –2,147,483,648 to +2,147,483,647
Long	lng *or* l	An integer from –9,223,372,036,854,775,808 to 9,223,372,036,854,775,807
Decimal	dec *or* d	A non-integer number with up to 28 significant digits (integer and fraction) that can represent values up to $79,228 \times 10^{24}$
Single	sng *or* f	A single-precision, floating-point number with approximately 7 significant digits
Double	dbl *or* p	A double-precision, floating-point number with approximately 14 significant digits
Object	obj *or* o	An address that refers to an object

[handwritten: —NEW, FASTER THAN SNG, DBL]
[handwritten: → MORE ACC THAN DEC.]

Default values for data types

Data type	Initial value
All numeric types	Zero (0)
Boolean	False
Char	Binary 0
String or Object	Nothing (which means that it has no value)
Date	12:00 a.m. on January 1, 0001

[handwritten: ← NOT EMPTY STRING]
[handwritten: SOME LANG DIFF.]

Description

- A *variable* is used to store data, and each variable is assigned a *data type*. That data type defines what kind of information can be stored by the variable.

- The Visual Basic *primitive data types* are actually aliases for the data types defined by the Common Type System of the .NET Framework.

- When you name a variable, you should start the variable name with the recommended prefix for each data type.

- If you don't declare an initial value for a variable, it receives a default value.

- When a numeric value is converted to a Boolean value, the value 0 becomes False and all other values become True. When a Boolean value is converted to a numeric value, a value of False becomes 0 and a value of True becomes –1.

[handwritten: TRUE = –1 NOT 1]

[handwritten: NO VARIANT (ANY TYPE VAR) IN .NET NOW, USE OBJECT]

Figure 3-6   The Visual Basic primitive data types

How to declare and initialize variables

At the top of figure 3-7, you can see the syntax for declaring a variable. In a summary like this, the *keywords* are in boldface. These are the Visual Basic words that have to be typed exactly as shown. In contrast, the words that aren't in boldface are the ones that you provide replacements for. For instance, you enter a variable name in place of *variablename*, a data type in place of *type*, and an expression in place of *expression*.

Beyond that, you can choose between the items in the syntax summary that are separated by pipes (|) and enclosed in braces ({ }), while the items enclosed in brackets ([ ]) are optional. If you compare the syntax with the coding examples in this figure, you'll soon see how the two are related.

The four keywords at the start of a declaration determine the *scope* of the variable, which determines which part of your code can use it. For now, you can use Dim for all of your declarations, but you'll learn more about scope and the other keywords in chapter 5.

After the keyword for a variable declaration, you code the name of the variable. This is followed by the keyword *As* and the data type for the variable. When you type this keyword followed by a space in the Code Editor window, a list of the available data types is displayed so you can select the one you want.

If you want to assign an initial value to the variable you're declaring, you can follow the data type with an equals sign and the initial value coded as an expression. If you don't assign an initial value, though, the variable is assigned a *default value* depending on its data type, as summarized in the previous figure.

The examples in this figure show various ways of declaring and initializing variables. For instance, the first example shows how to use the Dim keyword to declare a string variable. Because an initial value isn't specified in this statement, the variable will be initialized with a value of Nothing (no value at all).

The second example in this figure shows how to use the Dim statement to define an integer with an initial value of 1. The third example shows how to declare two variables with different data types in a single statement. And the fourth example shows how to declare two variables with the same data type in a single statement. Note that when you declare two or more variables in the same statement, you can't specify initial values for the variables.

The last three examples show how to declare variables using the Private, Public, and Static keywords. Notice in the first of these examples that the value True is assigned to a Boolean variable. True and False are also keywords.

To create variable names that are easy to interpret, you should follow the naming recommendations in this figure. Beyond that, you should be consistent in your use of names. If, for example, the text box that displays the interest rate is named txtInterestRate, you should use dInterestRate as the name of the decimal variable that holds the interest rate.

By the way, the Code Editor automatically adjusts the capitalization of variable names to the way you entered them when you declared them. So do your best to type each variable name properly when you declare it. After that, you can enter the name in all lowercase and the Editor will adjust it for you.

The basic syntax for declaring and initializing a variable

`{Dim|Private|Public|Static} variablename [As type] [= expression]`

Keyword	Meaning
Dim	Declares a variable that can be used within a single procedure or within just a part of that procedure. This is determined by the location of the Dim statement within the procedure.
Private	Declares a variable that can be used by more than one procedure within a class or module.
Public	Declares a variable that can be used by all the classes and modules in a project.
Static	Declares a variable that retains its value from one execution of a procedure to another.

Typical variable declarations

```
Dim sErrorMessage As String          'declares string variable
Dim iIndex As Integer = 1            'declares integer variable
                                     'with initial value of 1

Dim tMonth As Short, dRate As Decimal  'declares 2 variables
Dim iStatus, iRunningValue As Integer  'declares 2 integer variables
Private bAddMode As Boolean = True     'declares Private Boolean variable
                                       'with initial value of True

Public iUserStatus As Integer          'declares Public integer variable
Static iRunningValue As Integer        'declares Static integer variable
```

Naming recommendations

- Start each variable name with its data type prefix in lowercase letters (see the previous figure for a list of prefixes).

- Use uppercase and lowercase letters to make the names easier to read. In particular, capitalize the first letter in all words after the prefix.

- Try to assign meaningful names that are easy to remember as you code, even if that results in longer names.

Description

- You can declare a variable with any of the data types listed in the previous figure. If you omit the As clause, the Object data type is used as the default. However, this usually isn't what you want, so it's a good idea to always specify a data type.

- The Dim, Private, Public, or Static keyword determines the *scope* of a variable. The scope determines which part of your code can use the variable.

- For now, you can use Dim for all the variables that you declare. You'll learn how to use the other scopes in chapter 5.

- The optional equals sign assigns an initial value to the variable. If you don't specify an initial value, the *default value* for the data type is assigned (see figure 3-6).

- You can declare two or more variables in a single statement by separating the variables with commas. If the variables have the same data type, you can code a single As clause for them. Otherwise, you should code an As clause for each variable.

- By default, you must declare a variable before you can use it. Although you can override this default behavior, it isn't recommended.

Figure 3-7   How to declare and initialize variables

How to code assignment statements

After you declare a variable, you can assign it a value by coding an *assignment statement* as summarized in figure 3-8. As the syntax shows, you just code the variable name, an equals sign (known as an *assignment operator*), and an expression for the value. When the statement is executed, the value of the expression is stored in the variable.

The *expression* in an assignment statement can be as simple as a *numeric literal* like 1 or 22.5. It can be the name of another variable. Or it can be an *arithmetic expression*.

To code an *arithmetic expression*, you use *arithmetic operators* to indicate what operations are to be performed on the *operands* in the expression, which can be either literals or variables. For business applications, most arithmetic expressions are relatively simple, so you shouldn't have much trouble understanding them. But you can learn more about coding them in the next figure.

If you look at the examples in this figure, you can see the expressions in some typical assignment statements. Please note in the second example that you can code the same variable name on both sides of the equals sign. In this case, 1 is added to the original value of iMonth and the result is stored in iMonth. In other words, if iMonth has a starting value of 5, this statement assigns a value of 6 to it.

Besides the equals sign, Visual Basic provides for the other assignment operators in this figure. Here again, if you study the examples, you shouldn't have any trouble using them. Although these operators don't provide any new functionality, you can use them to write shorter code. This can be useful when you're working with variables that have long names.

Please note that Microsoft treats a property as a type of variable. As a result, you can use assignment statements to assign values to properties in the same way that you use these statements to assign values to variables.

The syntax of an assignment statement

```
variablename = expression
```

Typical assignment statements

```
iMonth = 1
iMonth = iMonth + 1
dDiscountAmount = dOrderTotal * .2
dInvoiceTotal = dOrderTotal + dDiscountAmount
dChangePercent = (dThisYTDSales – dLastYTDSales) / dLastYTDSales * 100
dArea = (dRadius ^ 2) * 3.1416
```

Arithmetic operators

Operator	Name	Description
+	Addition	Adds the two operands.
-	Subtraction	Subtracts the right operand from the left operand.
*	Multiplication	Multiplies the two operands.
/	Division	Divides the right operand into the left operand.
\	Integer division	Divides the right operand into the left operand and returns an integer quotient.
Mod	Modulo	Divides the right operand into the left operand and returns the remainder.
^	Exponentiation	Raises the left operand to the power of the right operand.
-	Negative sign	Changes the sign of the operand.

\ = INTEGER
MOD = REM.

Other assignment operators (assume i = 13)

Operator	Example	Description	Result
+=	i += 5	i = i + 5	i = 18
-=	i -= 6	i = i - 6	i = 7
*=	i *= 2	i = i * 2	i = 26
/=	i /= 2	i = i / 2	i = 6
\=	i \= 3	i = i \ 3	i = 4
^=	i ^= 2	i = i ^ 2	i = 169

NOTE!
i += 5 → i = i + 5

Description

- An *assignment statement* consists of a variable, an equals sign (the *assignment operator*), and an *expression*. When the assignment statement is executed, the value of the expression to the right of the equals sign is stored in the variable to the left of the sign.

- An *arithmetic expression* consists of one or more *operands* and *arithmetic operators*. All of the operators except the negative sign are *binary operators* because they operate on two operands. The negative sign is a *unary operator* because it operates on just one.

- Since a property is a type of variable, you can use assignment statements to assign values to properties as well as declared variables.

- Besides the equals sign, Visual Basic provides for the other assignment operators shown above. These operators provide a shorthand for coding common operations.

Figure 3-8   How to code assignment statements

How to code arithmetic expressions

Figure 3-9 presents the *order of precedence* of the arithmetic operations. This means that all of the exponentiation operations in an expression are done first, followed by the negative sign operations, followed by multiplication, division, and modulo operations, followed by addition and subtraction operations. If there is more than one operation at each order of precedence, the operations are done from left to right.

Since most arithmetic expressions are relatively short, it's usually not difficult to understand how an expression will be evaluated. However, if there's any chance for confusion, you should use parentheses to override the order of precedence. Then, the expression within the innermost pair of parentheses is evaluated first, followed by each pair of parentheses further out. Within each pair of parentheses, the normal order of precedence applies.

If you study the first group of examples in this figure, you should get a better idea of how the arithmetic operators work. Since addition, subtraction, and multiplication are easy to understand, the first four examples illustrate the division, *integer division*, and *modulo* operators. The first two use Integer data types and the next two use Decimal data types. The last two examples in this group illustrate the use of the negative sign.

In the second group of examples, you can see how parentheses affect the result of an expression. In the second and fourth examples, the parentheses override the order of precedence, so the results with and without parentheses differ dramatically.

Then, in the last group of examples, you can see how the value of an expression is automatically converted to the data type of the variable that it's assigned to in a process called *casting*. In this process, Visual Basic automatically converts less precise data types to more precise types. If, for example, an integer value is assigned to a decimal variable, it is automatically converted to the Decimal data type. Visual Basic also casts the result of an arithmetic expression to the data type of the most precise operand.

Keep in mind, however, that some conversions aren't valid. For example, you can't convert a string that contains nonnumeric data to a numeric data type, and you can't convert an integer with a value of more than 32,767 to a Short variable. If you try to do a conversion like that, a run-time error will occur when the application is run.

The order of precedence for arithmetic operations

1. Exponentiation $\wedge$
2. Negative sign   —
3. Multiplication, division, integer division, and modulo $*, /, \backslash, mod$
4. Addition and subtraction $+, -$

The use of parentheses

- Unless parentheses are used, the operations in an expression take place from left to right in the *order of precedence*.

- To clarify or override the sequence of operations, you can use parentheses. Then, the operations in the innermost sets of parentheses are done first, followed by the operations in the next sets, and so on.

Examples of arithmetic expressions

```
iVarX = 14          'assume for all examples
iVarY = 8           'assume for all examples
dVarA = 8.5         'assume for all examples
dVarB = 3.4         'assume for all examples

iResult = iVarX \ iVarY          'result = 1
iResult = iVarX mod iVarY        'result = 6
dResult = dVarA / dVarB          'result = 2.5
dResult = dVarA mod dVarB        'result = 1.7
iResult = -iVarY                 'result = -8
iResult = -iVarY + iVarX         'result = 6
```

How parentheses can affect the result of an expression

```
iVarX = 10
iVarY = 5

iResultA = iVarX + iVarY * 5       'iResultA is 35
iResultB = (iVarX + iVarY) * 5     'iResultB is 75
dResultA = iVarX - iVarY * 5       'dResultA is -15
dResultB = (iVarX - iVarY) * 5     'dResultB is 25
```

How casting affects the value assigned to a variable

```
dVarA = 5.0
iVarB = 7
iVarC = 9

dResult = (dVarA + iVarB + iVarC) / 4   'dResult is 5.25
dVarA = iVarC                            'dVarA is 9.0
```

Description

- If the value of an expression isn't the same data type as the result variable, the value is automatically converted to the data type of the result. This is called *casting*.

- If the system can't cast the value into the data type of the result variable, a run-time error will occur.

Figure 3-9   How to code arithmetic expressions

How to work with string and date variables

Figure 3-10 summarizes the techniques that you need for working with string and date variables. To start, you should know that a *string* can consist of any letters, numbers, or special characters. To code a literal value for a string, which can be referred to as a *string literal*, you just enclose the characters within quotation marks. This is illustrated by the first example of an assignment statement.

Similarly, you can code a literal value for a date, which can be referred to as a *date literal*, by enclosing the date value within quotation marks or pound signs (#). This is illustrated by the next three examples of assignment statements. Note that the year value must be four digits to avoid possible misinterpretation. And keep in mind that the date is actually stored as an integer value that represents the number of days that have passed since January 1, 0001.

If you want to join, or *concatenate*, two or more strings into one, you use the *concatenation character* (&) to connect them. This is illustrated by the last statement in the second group of examples. Here, two string variables and a literal value that consists of one space are concatenated so the name Bob Smith is assigned to the variable named sFullName.

In the third group of statements, you can see how you can *append* a string to the value in a string variable by using an assignment statement. In the last statement in this group, sName starts with a value of Bob followed by a space. Then, the last name is appended to it so it contains Bob Smith after the statement is executed.

Finally, in the fourth group of statements, you can see how you can accomplish the same thing by using the &= operator. This is just a shorter way to append a string to the string that a variable already contains. Since appending strings is a common practice, though, it's often worth using this operator.

For now, this introduction to strings and dates should be all that you need as you work through the remaining chapters in this section. Keep in mind, though, that many applications require that extensive operations be done on string and date data. So in chapter 11, you can learn how to use all of the Visual Basic features for working with strings and dates.

THERE IS A RANGING FUNCTION IN .NET

INT'L = DD/MM/YYYY
USA = MM/DD/YYYY

The syntax of an assignment statement

```
variablename = expression
```

Simple assignment statements

```
sMessage = "Invalid data entry."      'assigns a string literal
dtmStartDate = #June 1, 2001#         'one way to assign a date literal
dtmStartDate = "June 1, 2001"         'a second way to assign a date literal
dtmStartDate = #6/1/2001#             'a third way to assign a date literal
```

How to concatenate character strings

```
sFirstName = "Bob"                        'sFirstName is Bob
sLastName = "Smith"                       'sLastName is Smith
sFullName = sFirstName & " " & sLastName  'sFullName is Bob Smith
```

How to append one string to another string

```
sFirstName = "Bob"                    'sFirstName is Bob
sLastName = "Smith"                   'sLastName is Smith
sName = sFirstName & " "              'sName is Bob followed by a space
sName = sName & sLastName             'sName is Bob Smith
```

How to append one string to another with the &= operator

```
sFirstName = "Bob"                    'sFirstName is Bob
sLastName = "Smith"                   'sLastName is Smith
sName = sFirstName & " "              'sName is Bob followed by a space
sName &= sLastName                    'sName is Bob Smith
```

Description

- To code a *string literal*, code the value within quotes.
- To code a *date literal*, enclose the date in pound signs (#) or quotes.
- To *concatenate* string variables and string literals, use the *concatenation character* (&). Although you can also use the plus sign to concatenate two strings, this can cause confusion since the plus sign is also used for arithmetic operations.
- When you *append* one string to another, you add one string to the end of another. To do that, you can use assignment statements.
- The &= operator is a shortcut for appending a string expression to a string variable.

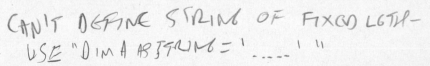

Figure 3-10   How to work with string and date variables

How to code conditional statements

As you write Visual Basic code, you often need to determine when certain operations should be done. For instance, you'll want to execute one or more statements if a certain condition is true and other statements if the condition is false. To get you started, this topic will first show you how to code condition expressions. Then, it will show you how to code two kinds of conditional statements that use those expressions.

How to code conditional expressions

A *conditional expression* is an expression that evaluates to either a True or a False value when it's used in certain statements. You can use conditional expressions in assignment statements to assign a value to Boolean variables or properties. But you also use these expressions in conditional statements like If and Select Case statements.

Figure 3-11 shows how to code conditional expressions. As you code these expressions, you can use *relational operators* like =, <, and >. You can also use *logical operators* like And and Or to create *compound conditions* that consist of two or more conditions.

To evaluate a conditional expression, Visual Basic performs the operations from left to right based on the order of precedence. If you review this order, you can see that arithmetic operations are done first, followed by relational operations and logical operations. Although you can use six logical operators with Visual Basic, the ones you'll use the most are Not, And, and Or.

The first example in this figure tests a variable named sSwitch to see if it contains a value other than Yes. If it does, the expression is True; otherwise the expression is False. Similarly, if the Boolean variable in the second example has a value of True, the conditional expression is True; otherwise, it's False. The third conditional expression is just another way to code the second example because Visual Basic assumes the equals True condition when the condition is coded as just a Boolean variable (or a Boolean property).

In the second to last example, you can see that two or more And operators can be coded in an expression with little chance for confusion. But when you mix two or more logical operators, you usually need to use parentheses to clarify how the expression should be evaluated. This is illustrated by the last example. (If you remove the parentheses, can you tell how the condition will be evaluated?)

After the examples of conditional expressions, you can see two assignment statements that assign True/False values to Boolean variables. In the first statement, if the value in dOrderTotal is greater than or equal to 200, a value of True is assigned to bDiscountRate1; otherwise, a value of False is assigned to it. In the second statement, if the value in dThisYTD is greater than the value in dLastYTD, a value of True is assigned to bSalesIncrease; otherwise, a value of False is assigned. This is one way that you can use conditional expressions. The other way is in conditional statements like the If statement.

Conditional expressions

```
sSwitch <> "Yes"
bNewCustomer = True
bNewCustomer                    'This is the same as bNewCustomer = True
dThisYTD > dLastYTD
iValue = 1
iValue Not > 99
dMonthlyInvestment > 0 And fInterestRate > 0 And iMonths > 0
(dThisYTD > dLastYTD) Or (dLastYTD <= 0 And dThisYTD >= 1000)
```

Assignment statements that assign True/False values to Boolean variables

```
bDiscountRate1 = dOrderTotal >= 200
bSalesIncrease = dThisYTD > dLastYTD
```

Relational and logical operators

Relational operators

=	Equal	<	Less than	>	Greater than
<>	Not equal	<=	Less than or equal to	>=	Greater than or equal to

Common logical operators

Not   Reverses the value of the expression.

And   Connects two or more expressions. If both expressions are true, the entire expression is true.

Or   Connects two or more expressions. If either expression is true, the entire expression is true.

Order of precedence for conditional expressions

1. All arithmetic operations in the usual order of precedence
2. Relational operations
3. Logical operations in this order: Not, And, Or

[handwritten: AND = LOGICAL MULT. OR = LOGICAL ADD. A OR B AND C]

Description

- *Conditional expressions* compare operands and return a Boolean (True/False) value.

- You can use a conditional expression to assign a value to a Boolean variable. If the expression is true, the variable receives a value of True. If the expression is false, the variable receives a value of False.

- You can also use conditional expressions in If statements and Select Case statements as shown in the next two figures.

- You can use the *logical operators* And and Or to create *compound conditions* that consist of two or more conditions, and you can use the Not logical operator to check for the opposite of a condition. Visual Basic also provides three other logical operators that are rarely used: AndAlso, OrElse, and Xor. You can learn more about these in the online help.

- Use parentheses whenever there's any doubt about the sequence in which the operations will be evaluated. Then, the operation within the innermost set of parentheses is evaluated first, followed by each pair of parentheses further out.

Figure 3-11   How to code conditional expressions

*[handwritten: * WON'T EVAL 2ND HALF IF 1ST FALSE]*

How to code If statements

Figure 3-12 presents the syntax of the *block If statement* and the *one-line If statement*. For most coding situations, you'll use the block If statement, because it provides more options and is easier to read. For a series of short If statements that don't require ElseIf clauses, though, you may want to use one-line If statements. A one-line If statement can actually be coded on multiple lines, but only if you use continuation characters. Otherwise, Visual Basic assumes it's a block If statement and checks its syntax accordingly.

This figure also provides four examples that illustrate the many ways that you can code the block If statement. In the syntax, the brackets show that the ElseIf and Else clauses are optional so you don't have to code them. And the ellipsis (...) shows that you can code more than one ElseIf clause if they're needed. Note, however, that every block If statement must end with the words End If.

The first example in this figure shows how you can use an If statement without an Else or ElseIf clause. In this case, if the value in the text box is less than or equal to zero, the Boolean variable bValidData is set to False. Since there isn't an Else clause, the value of bValidData remains unchanged if the condition isn't true.

The second example shows how to use an Else clause. Here, if the value of dOrderTotal is greater than or equal to 100, a value of .2 is assigned to the variable named dDiscountPct. Otherwise, the variable is set to zero.

The third example shows how to use both ElseIf and Else clauses. Here, the value in a variable named iQuantity is tested and an appropriate value is assigned to a variable named dDiscount. If none of the conditions in the ElseIf clauses are true, though, the final Else clause is executed.

The last example in this figure shows how one If statement can be nested within the Then or Else portion of another If statement. This is referred to as *nested If statements*, and you can nest If statements many levels deep. In this example, one If statement is nested within the Then portion of another If statement, but an If statement can also be nested in the Else portion. As you progress through this book, you'll see many variations of nested If statements.

When you code nested If statements, you must make sure that you end the inner statement with the words End If before you continue the coding of the outer statement. Otherwise, Visual Basic will display an error message as you code. This automatic checking helps you code error-free If statements.

In the last example in this figure, you may have noticed that I included a comment after the word Else that describes the condition under which the Else statement will be executed. This is useful in a complex If statement where it's difficult to tell what condition or conditions the Else represents. As with all comments, though, if you change your code by altering the other conditions, you must change the comment to prevent confusion.

The syntax of the block If statement

```
If condition Then
    statements
[ElseIf condition-n Then
    statements] ...
[Else
    statements]
End If
```

MORE THAN 1!

The syntax of the one-line If statement ← *NOT REC'D*

```
If condition Then statements [Else statements]
```

An If...Then statement without an Else clause

```
If txtMonthlyInvestment.Text <= 0 Then
    bValidData = False
End If
```

A simple If...Then...Else statement ← *PREF'D*

```
If dOrderTotal >= 100 Then
    dDiscountPct = 0.2
Else
    dDiscountPct = 0
End If
```

An If statement with ElseIf clauses ← *NEGATIVE LOGIC! NOT REC'D*

```
If iQuantity = 1 Or iQuantity = 2 Then
    dDiscount = 0
ElseIf iQuantity >= 3 And iQuantity <= 9 Then
    dDiscount = 0.1
ElseIf iQuantity >= 10 And iQuantity <=24 Then
    dDiscount = 0.2
ElseIf iQuantity >= 25 Then
    dDiscount = 0.3
Else
    dDiscount = 0
End If
```

Nested If statements — *S/B NO MORE THAN 2 LEVELS (SAME KIND)!*

```
If sType = "Retail" Then
    If iQuantity <= 9 Then
        dDiscount = 0
    ElseIf iQuantity <= 19 Then
        dDiscount = .1
    ElseIf iQuantity >= 20 Then
        dDiscount = .2
    End If        ← MUST CLOSE INNER!
Else '(sType <> "Retail")
    dDiscount = .4
End If
```

Description

- If you type the If keyword and the condition and then press the Enter key, Visual Basic adds the Then and End If keywords automatically.

- You can code a comment after the word Else to note the conditions that it represents.

Figure 3-12   How to code If statements

How to code Select Case statements

Figure 3-13 shows the syntax for the Select Case statement and two of the ways this statement can be used. This statement can be used in place of an If statement with many ElseIf clauses. In the first example, the test expression is just the integer variable iTerms, which can range from 0 through 2. Based on the value in this variable, the value in a variable named dInvoiceTotal is added to one of three variables. Since there isn't a Case Else clause, though, no statement will be executed if the value of the iTerms variable isn't 0, 1, or 2.

In the second example in this figure, the test expression is an integer variable named iQuantity. Then, if iQuantity has a value of 1 or 2, dDiscount is set to zero. If the quantity is from 3 to 9, the discount is .1. If the quantity is from 10 to 24, the discount is .2. If the quantity is greater than or equal to 25, the discount is .3. And if none of these conditions is true (Else), the discount is zero. Note the variety of ways that these values can be specified in a Select Case statement using the To and Is keywords. This example also illustrates the use of a comment to describe the condition under which the Else clause is executed.

The benefit of using the Select Case statement is that your code is usually easier to read and understand than it is when you use multiple ElseIf clauses in an If statement. To appreciate this benefit, compare the second example in this figure to the third example in the previous figure. The results are identical, but which is easier to understand?

The syntax of the Select Case statement

```
Select Case testexpression
    [Case expressionlist
        statements] ...
    [Case Else
        statements]
End Select
```

[handwritten: → EVEN IF 2 SIMILAR COND. EXIST,]
[handwritten: — FIRST COND, THAT SATISFIES WILL WORK!]

A Select Case statement that adds invoice totals to three variables

```
Select Case iTerms
    Case 0
        d30DayTotal += dInvoiceTotal
    Case 1
        d60DayTotal += dInvoiceTotal
    Case 2
        d90DayTotal += dInvoiceTotal
End Select
```

[handwritten: — SHOULD HAVE CASE ELSE - USUALLY FOR SOMETHING WRONG (USE W/EXCEPTION]

A Select Case statement that sets discount percentages

```
Select Case iQuantity
    Case 1, 2
        dDiscount = 0
    Case 3 To 9
        dDiscount = 0.1
    Case 10 To 24
        dDiscount = 0.2
    Case Is >= 25
        dDiscount = 0.3
    Case Else '(< 1)
        dDiscount = 0
End Select
```

How to code the expression list

Keyword	Meaning
To	Specifies a range of values.
Is	Precedes a conditional expression.

Description

- If you type the Select Case keywords and the test expression and then press the Enter key, Visual Basic adds the End Select keywords automatically.

- To make a complex Select Case statement easier to read, you can code a comment after the Case Else keywords that describes the conditions under which the clause will be executed.

Figure 3-13   How to code Select Case statements

The Invoice Total application

Now that you've learned some of the basic statements for writing Visual Basic code, I'll present an application that uses these statements. This application is an enhanced version of the Invoice Total application that you developed in the last chapter.

The user interface and control names

Figure 3-14 presents the user interface for this application, which is the same as it was in the last chapter. This figure also summarizes the names of the three controls that the code refers to so you can see how the code relates to those controls.

The Visual Basic code

Figure 3-14 also presents the code for this version of the Invoice Total application. By now, you should understand all of this code, except for the statements that are generated as you develop the application. So if you have any trouble understanding what any of these statements do, please refer back to the related pages for any clarification that you need.

If you study the code, you should see that the If statement assigns a discount percent of .2 if the order total is greater than or equal to 100. Otherwise, the Else clause assigns a value of zero to the discount percent. This percent is then used to calculate the discount for the order.

You should realize, though, that this application has a few shortcomings. First, if you don't enter a valid order total, the application will end prematurely with a run-time error. Second, the numbers that are displayed for the discount and invoice total values aren't formatted properly for all order total values. In the next chapter, you'll learn how to fix both of these problems.

The Invoice Total form

The names of the controls that are referred to in the Visual Basic code

Object type	Name	Descriptions
TextBox	txtOrderTotal	The only text box on the form
Label	lblDiscountAmount	The first label below the text box
Label	lblInvoiceTotal	The second label below the text box

The code for the modified Invoice Total application

```
Public Class Form1
    Inherits System.Windows.Forms.Form

    Private Sub btnCalculate_Click(ByVal sender As System.Object, _
            ByVal e As System.EventArgs) Handles btnCalculate.Click

        Dim dOrderTotal As Decimal
        Dim dDiscountPct As Decimal
        Dim dDiscountAmount As Decimal
        Dim dInvoiceTotal As Decimal

        dOrderTotal = txtOrderTotal.Text
        If dOrderTotal >= 100 Then
            dDiscountPct = .2
        Else
            dDiscountPct = 0
        End If
        dDiscountAmount = dOrderTotal * dDiscountPct
        dInvoiceTotal = dOrderTotal - dDiscountAmount

        lblDiscountAmount.Text = dDiscountAmount
        lblInvoiceTotal.Text = dInvoiceTotal
        txtOrderTotal.Focus

    End Sub

    Private Sub btnExit_Click(ByVal sender As System.Object, _
            ByVal e As System.EventArgs) Handles btnExit.Click
        Me.Close()
    End Sub

End Class
```

Figure 3-14   The code for the Invoice Total application

Perspective

In this chapter, you learned how to use some of the common Visual Basic statements. These statements let you declare and work with variables and perform conditional processing. With just these statements, you can perform many of the operations that are required by Visual Basic applications. But there's a lot more to learn.

So in the next chapter, you'll learn how to write an application that checks the user entries so it doesn't try to process invalid data. You'll learn how to format the data that is displayed by the user interface. And you'll learn how to code repetitive arithmetic operations. When you finish that chapter, your applications will start to take on a more professional look.

Summary

- Besides following the coding rules of Visual Basic, you should format your code so it's easy to read, understand, debug, and maintain.

- To make long statements easy to read, you should use indentation and the *continuation character*.

- You can use *comments* to document your code, but you should only use them when your code is difficult to understand.

- Visual Basic provides twelve *primitive data types* to store string, Boolean, date, integer, decimal, and floating-point values.

- *Variables* store the values that change as an application runs. Before you can refer to variables in your code, you must *declare* them. Then, you can use *assignment statements* to assign values to the variables.

- You can use numeric variables, *numeric literals*, and *arithmetic operators* to form *arithmetic expressions* that calculate values that can be assigned to numeric variables. If necessary, Visual Basic *casts* a less precise data type to a more precise type during the assignment process.

- You can use string variables, *string literals*, and *concatenation characters* to form string expressions that can be assigned to string variables.

- You can use a few different date formats to assign a *date literal* to a date variable, but the date variable actually receives an integer value that represents the date as the number of 100-nanosecond units since January 1, 0001.

- You can use *relational operators* and *logical operators* to form *conditional expressions* that are evaluated as either True or False.

- You can code If statements and Select Case statements to control the logic of your code based on the True or False values of conditional expressions. You can also code *nested If statements* by coding one If statement within another.

Terms

procedure declaration	primitive data type	unary operator
procedure	numeric data type	order of precedence
variable declaration	integer data type	integer division
assignment statement	floating-point number	modulo
conditional statement	significant digit	casting
end-of-procedure declaration	single-precision number	string
continuation character	double-precision number	string literal
Word Wrap	scientific notation	date literal
comment	keyword	concatenate
block comment	scope	concatenation character
end-of-line comment	default value	append
single-line comment	assignment operator	conditional expression
comment out a statement	expression	relational operator
collapse a procedure	numeric literal	logical operator
expand a procedure	arithmetic expression	compound condition
bookmark	arithmetic operator	block If statement
variable	operand	one-line If statement
data type	binary operator	nested If statements

Objectives

- Given the Visual Basic code for a form that uses any of the language elements presented in this chapter, explain what each statement does.

- Given the form design and specifications for an application that requires only the language elements presented in this chapter, write the code for the application.

- List three coding recommendations that will help make your code easier to read, debug, and maintain.

- Explain how the use of continuation characters can help make your code easier to read.

- Describe the proper use of comments.

- Describe any of the 12 primitive data types.

- Describe the differences between integer, decimal, and floating-point numbers.

- Describe what is stored in Boolean, string, and date variables.

- Describe the differences between arithmetic expressions and conditional expressions.

Exercise 3-1   Enhance the Invoice Total application

In this exercise, you'll enhance the Invoice Total application that you developed in chapter 2.

Copy and open the Invoice Total application

1. Use the Windows Explorer to copy the C:\VB.NET\Chapter 02\InvoiceTotal folder to C:\VB.NET\Chapter 03. Then, open the project ("InvoiceTotal.vbproj") in the Chapter 03\InvoiceTotal folder.

2. If the Code Editor window isn't open, open it. Then, click on the minus sign to the left of the btnCalculate_Click procedure to collapse its code, and click on its plus sign to expand it again.

3. Click on the plus sign before the "Windows Form Designer generated code" so you can review all of the code that's generated for this simple form. This is the code that actually displays the form. Then, click on its minus sign to collapse all of this code again.

Modify and test the code for the Invoice Total application

4. Modify the code for the btnCalculate_Click procedure so it matches the code in figure 3-14.

5. Build and run the application by pressing the F5 key or clicking on the Start button in the Standard toolbar. Then, enter a range of valid order totals to verify that the correct discount is being taken.

6. Enter 233.33 as the order total, and click on the Calculate button. Then, note that the discount and invoice total are displayed with more than two decimal places. In the next chapter, you'll learn how to round and format numbers so only two decimal places are displayed.

7. Enter "10K" as the order total and click on the Calculate button. This time, the application should crash with a run-time error and a dialog box should be displayed. Then, click the Break button to enter break mode.

8. Note the highlighted statement. This shows that the assignment statement can't convert string data to the Decimal data type. In the next chapter, you'll learn how to code the application so it checks for invalid data and asks the user to re-enter it.

9. Click on the Stop Debugging button in the Debug toolbar to end the application.

Exercise 3-2   Enhance the If statement

In this exercise, you'll modify the discount calculation that's used in the Invoice Total application by coding an enhanced If statement.

C12e 205

1. If they're not already open, open the Invoice Total application that you enhanced in exercise 3-1 and open the Code Editor window.

2. Modify the discount calculation so the discount is 20% if the order total is greater than or equal to $500; 15% if the order total is greater than or equal to $250 but less than $500; 10% if the order total is greater than or equal to $100 but less than $250; and zero if the order total is less than $100.

3. Build and run the application. Then, enter a range of valid order totals to verify that the correct discount is being taken. If the application doesn't calculate the correct discounts, exit from the application, correct the code, and test the application again.

Exercise 3-3   Code a Select Case statement

In this exercise, you'll replace the If statement in the Invoice Total application with a Select Case statement.

1. If they're not already open, open the Invoice Total application that you enhanced in exercise 3-2 and open the Code Editor window.

2. Comment out all the lines in the If statement. To do that, you can code an apostrophe at the start of each line. Or, you can select all of the lines and click on the Comment button in the Text Editor toolbar. (If the Text Editor toolbar isn't displayed, you can right-click in the toolbar area to display a shortcut menu, and select Text Editor to display that toolbar.)

3. After the commented out If statement, code a Select Case statement that works the same way the If statement works. Then, test the application to make sure that the correct discounts are being taken. If they aren't, exit from the application, correct the code, and test the application again.

Project 3-1   Calculate area and perimeter

Now that you know how to design a form and write the code for its procedures, you should be able to apply your skills to new projects like this one. In fact, that's how you prove you've mastered the skills that have been presented. That's why the download for this book includes a Word document named Projects that gives you a range of projects for the chapters in this book. The project that follows is one example. It requires just the skills that you've learned so far, although some of the enhancements give you a preview of what you'll learn in the chapters to come.

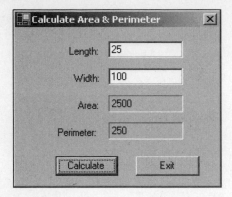

Operation

- The user enters values for the length and width of a rectangle and clicks on the Calculate button or presses the Enter key to activate the Calculate button.

- The application then displays the area and perimeter of the rectangle in the two labels.

Specifications

- The formula for calculating the area: width * length.

- The formula for calculating the perimeter: 2 * width + 2 * length.

- The application should accept fractional decimal values like 10.5 and 20.65 for the user entries.

- Assume that the user will enter valid numeric data for the length and width.

Enhancements

- Add a Clear button to the form that will clear all of the values when you click on it.

- Add numeric formatting and data validation after you read chapter 4.

- Add exception handling after you read chapter 5.

4

Visual Basic language essentials (part 2)

In the last chapter, you learned how to write the code for simple applications. Now, you'll learn some other language essentials. In particular, you'll learn how to write applications that check user entries for validity and that format the data that's displayed. You'll also learn how to write applications that use loops for repetitive processing. When you finish this chapter, your applications will start to take on a more professional look and feel.

How to work with constants and enumerations

In the last chapter, you learned how to use variables. Now, you'll learn how to use constants and enumerations, which are similar.

How to declare and work with constants

A *constant* is like a variable, but its value can't be changed. As the syntax in figure 4-1 shows, you declare a constant and assign it a value in the same statement. You can also use the Private and Public keywords to define the scope of the constant, but you'll learn more about scope in the next chapter. For now, you can omit these keywords from your constant declarations.

Besides the constants you define, you can use any of the constants defined in the classes of the .NET framework. For instance, this figure presents some of the constants in the ControlChars class, which are used to add linefeed, carriage return, and tab characters to a string that will be displayed or printed. When you use constants like these, your code becomes easier to read because you use meaningful names for values that are hard to remember.

In the third example in this figure, you can see how the CrLf constant of the ControlChars class is used. Here, two parts of a string message are separated by this constant. This means that after the first part of the message is displayed or printed, the message will be dropped down one line (a linefeed) and the second part of the message will start at the leftmost position of that line (a carriage return). In other words, when the message is displayed, it will look like this:

```
An error has occurred.
The program will be canceled.
```

The syntax for declaring a constant

```
[Private|Public] Const constantname As type = expression
```

Typical declarations for constants

```
Const iMonths As Integer = 60
Public Const fInterestRate As Single = .125 / 12
```

The syntax for referring to a constant in a class

```
classname.constantname
```

Some of the constants in the ControlChars class

Constant	Description
ControlChars.Cr	Carriage return character
ControlChars.Lf	Linefeed character
ControlChars.CrLf	Carriage return and linefeed combination
ControlChars.Tab	Tab character

Statements that use constants

```
If iIndex = iMonths Then ...
fInterest = fInvestment * fInterestRate
sMessage = "An error has occurred." & ControlChars.CrLf _
          & "The program will be canceled."
```

Description

- A *constant* is similar to a variable, except the value of a constant can't change.
- You can use constants to provide meaningful names for constant values.
- You can use the constants defined in the ControlChars class to format string values that will be displayed or printed. To refer to a constant in a class, you type the class name, a dot, and the constant name.
- To display a list of the constants available in a class in the Code Editor window, type the class name followed by a dot operator.

Figure 4-1   How to declare and work with constants   CURSOR = WINDOWS, FORMS, CURSORS, WAIT CURSOR (ETC)

How to declare and work with enumerations

An *enumeration* is a set of related constants. The enumerations provided by Visual Basic are generally used to set object properties and to specify the values that are passed to functions (you'll learn about functions later in this chapter). For example, the FormBorderStyle enumeration includes a group of constants that you can use to specify settings for the FormBorderStyle property of a form. Some of the constants in that enumeration are shown in figure 4-2.

Besides the enumerations provided by Visual Basic, you can define and use your own enumerations. To do that, you use the Enum keyword, followed by the name of the enumeration as shown by the syntax in this figure. Then, within this statement, you code the names of each of the constants contained in the enumeration. To end the enumeration, you code the End Enum statement.

In most cases, that's all you need to code. Then, each constant within the enumeration is defined as an integer, and each is given a sequential integer value beginning with zero. In the Terms enumeration in this figure, for example, the constant named Net30Days will have a value of zero, the constant named Net60Days will have a value of one, and the constant named Net90Days will have a value of two.

To refer to a constant in an enumeration, you code the name of the enumeration followed by the name of the constant. The first statement in this figure, for example, shows how you can use a constant in the Terms enumeration. And the second statement shows how you can use a constant in the FormBorderStyle enumeration.

The syntax for declaring an enumeration

```
[Private|Public] Enum enumname [As type]
    constantname1
    constantname2
    .
    .
End Enum
```

An enumeration that defines invoice terms

```
Enum Terms
    Net30Days
    Net60Days
    Net90Days
End Enum
```

Some of the constants in the FormBorderStyle enumeration

Constant	Description
FormBorderStyle.FixedDialog	A fixed, thick border typically used for dialog boxes.
FormBorderStyle.FixedSingle	A fixed, single-line border used for most windows.
FormBorderStyle.Sizable	A resizable border.

Statements that use enumeration constants

```
If iIndex = Terms.Net60Days Then ...
frmMessageDialog.FormBorderStyle = FormBorderStyle.FixedDialog
```

Description

* An *enumeration* represents a set of related constants.
* The enumerations defined by Visual Basic are typically used to set object properties and to specify the values that are passed to Visual Basic functions.
* If you code the As clause on an Enum statement, the type you specify must be one of the integer data types (Byte, Short, Integer, or Long). If you omit the As clause, Integer is the default type.
* By default, the first constant in an enumeration is given the value zero, the second constant the value 1, and so on.
* To display a list of the enumerated constants in the Code Editor window, type the name of the enumeration followed by a dot operator.

How to look up predefined enumerations

* Use the Help feature to get information for a function or property. This information usually includes links to related enumerations.
* Use the Contents tab of the Help feature in this sequence: Visual Studio .NET → Visual Basic and C# → Reference → Visual Basic Language → Visual Basic Language and Run-time Reference → Constants and Enumerations.

Figure 4-2   How to declare and work with enumerations

How to use shared members

In most cases, you work with class members like properties and methods through an instance of the class, which is an object. However, you can also work with some members directly from the class that defines them. This type of member is called a *shared member*, and several of the .NET classes provide them.

An introduction to .NET shared members

Figure 4-3 presents some of the shared members you can use in your applications. For example, you can use the shared methods of the Cursor class to hide and display the cursor, and you can use the shared properties of the Cursors class to control what the cursor looks like.

To use a shared member, you type the classname, a dot, and the member name. The examples in this figure show how this works. The first statement uses the Hide method of the Cursor class to hide the cursor. And the second statement uses the WaitCursor property of the Cursors class to change the cursor to an hourglass.

Although this figure presents shared members from just four .NET classes, there are many other .NET classes that have shared members that you might find useful from time to time. Unfortunately, finding the classes that have useful shared members can be a challenge. One way to do that is to search the Help index for keywords related to the operations that you want to perform. Another way is to view the help for the entire .NET Framework Class Library, but that library is huge and its documentation can be overwhelming. A third way is to let this book guide you to the shared members that apply to each of the chapters.

VB6 HAD OWN RUNTIME FUNCTIONS.

The syntax for referring to a member in a class

```
classname.membername
```

Statements that use shared members

```
Cursor.Hide()                              'A shared method that hides the cursor
Cursor.Current = Cursors.WaitCursor        'A shared property that changes the
                                           'cursor to an hourglass
```

Shared methods of the Cursor class

Method	Description
Hide	Hides the cursor.
Show	Displays the cursor.

Shared properties of the Cursors class

Property	Description
AppStarting	Gets the cursor that appears as an application is starting.
Arrow	Gets the arrow cursor.
Cross	Gets the crosshair cursor.
Default	Gets the default cursor.
Hand	Gets the hand cursor.
WaitCursor	Gets the wait cursor, which is typically an hourglass.

Shared methods of the Math class

Method	Description
Max	Returns the larger of two numbers.
Min	Returns the smaller of two numbers.
Round	Rounds a number to the specified precision.
Sqrt	Returns the square root of a number.

MATH.MAX

Shared method of the MessageBox class

Method	Description
Show	Displays a message box.

Description

- A *shared member* is one that can be accessed directly from the class that defines it rather than from an instance of that class.
- To refer to a shared member, you type the class name, a dot, and the member name. The member can be either a property or a method.
- You can identify the shared members in a class by the large yellow S that's displayed in front of the member in the help topic that lists the members for that class.

Figure 4-3   An introduction to .NET shared members

How to use some of the methods of the Math class

To give you an idea of how to use some of the other shared members, figure 4-4 presents four of the shared methods that are available in the Math class in more detail. You can use these methods to perform a variety of mathematical operations.

When you use shared methods, you often have to code one or more *arguments* in the parentheses after the method name. For instance, the Round method requires at least one argument that represents the value to be rounded, plus an optional second argument. The Sqrt method requires just one argument. And the Min and Max methods require two arguments. In contrast, the Hide method of the Cursor class shown in the previous figure doesn't require any arguments.

You use the Round method to round a decimal or double value to a specified number of decimal digits, called the *precision*. For instance, the first statement in this figure rounds the value in the dblShipWeight variable to a whole number, because that's the default. In a case like this, the result can be assigned to an integer variable. In contrast, the second statement specifies two decimal places so the result can't be assigned to an integer variable.

This figure also presents three other shared methods of the Math class: Sqrt, Min, and Max. The Sqrt method calculates the square root of a number. The Min and Max methods return the minimum or maximum of two numeric values that you specify. In contrast to the Round method, these three methods can be used with any of the numeric data types. However, when you use the Min or Max method, the two values you specify must be of the same type.

Four shared methods of the Math class

The syntax of the Round method

```
Math.Round({decimal|double}[, precision])
```

The syntax of the Sqrt method

```
Math.Sqrt(number)
```

The syntax of the Min and Max methods

```
Math.{Min|Max}(number1, number2)
```

Statements that use shared methods of the Math class

```
iShipWeight = Math.Round(dblShipWeight)          'rounds to a whole number
dOrderTotal = Math.Round(dOrderTotal, 2)         'rounds to 2 decimal places
dSqrtValue = Math.Sqrt(dValue)
dMaxSales = Math.Max(dLastYearSales, dThisYearSales)
iMinQty = Math.Min(iLastYearQty, iThisYearQty)
```

Results from shared methods of the Math class

Statement	Result
Math.Round(23.75)	24
Math.Round(23.754, 2)	23.75
Math.Round(23.755, 2)	23.76
Math.Sqrt(20.25)	4.5
Math.Max(23.75, 20.25)	23.75
Math.Min(23.75, 20.25)	20.25

Description

- To use one of the methods of the Math class, you code the class name, a dot, the method name, and one or more *arguments* in parentheses. The arguments provide the values that are used by the method.

- The Round method rounds a decimal or double argument to the specified *precision*, which is the number of significant decimal digits. If the precision is omitted, the number is rounded to the nearest whole number.

- The Sqrt method returns the square root of the specified argument, which can have any numeric data type.

- The Min and Max methods return the minimum and maximum of two numeric arguments. The two arguments must have the same data type.

Visual Basic 6 note

- Visual Basic 6 provided functions instead of shared methods for performing math operations, and those functions aren't available in Visual Basic .NET.

Figure 4-4   How to use some of the methods of the Math class

How to use the Show method of the MessageBox class

Figure 4-5 shows how to use the Show method of the MessageBox class to display a message box to which the user can respond. Since you'll use this method frequently in your Visual Basic programs, you'll want to thoroughly understand it.

The syntax at the top of the figure shows that this method can use five arguments. The first argument is the text message that you wish to display. Although the first argument is the only one that's required, you will typically code the second argument too, which displays a caption in the title bar of the message box.

You can use the third argument to control the buttons that are displayed in the message box. You can use the fourth argument to control the icon that's displayed in the message box. And you can use the fifth argument to control the button that's activated when the user presses the Enter key (the default button). To specify any of the last three arguments, you use the constants in the enumerations that are summarized in this figure.

The first coding example in this figure shows how to display a simple message box with a message and an OK button. From this example, you can see that if you don't specify which buttons to display, only the OK button is displayed. And since this is the only button that's displayed, it's also the default button. In addition, no caption or icon is displayed.

The second example shows how to display a more complex message box. In this example, all of the arguments except the last one are specified. Due to this, the dialog box has a caption, Yes and No buttons are displayed instead of the OK button, and a question mark icon is displayed. Because the default button argument is omitted, the first button is the default.

This example also shows how you can use the value that's returned by the Show method to determine which button the user clicked in the message box. To do that, you code the Show method within a conditional expression and compare the value returned by the method with the constants in the DialogResult enumeration, which correspond to the buttons that can be displayed in the message box. In this example, the value is compared with the DialogResult.Yes constant, which means that the user clicked on the Yes button.

NOTE - SHOWDIALOG IS DIFFERENT

EX. DIM A AS MSGBOXRESULT
RESULT = MSGBOX ("OUR MESS AGE", MSGBOX.OKCANCEL OR
BUTTON
STYLE

Two message boxes displayed by the MessageBox.Show method

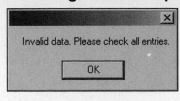
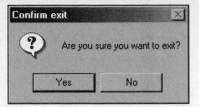

The syntax of the Show method of the MessageBox class

```
MessageBox.Show(text[, caption][, buttons][, icon][, defaultbutton])
```

Examples of the Show method

A statement that displays the first dialog box shown above

```
MessageBox.Show("Invalid data. Please check all entries.")
```

Code that displays the second dialog box shown above

```
If MessageBox.Show("Are you sure you want to exit?", "Confirm exit", _
        MessageBoxButtons.YesNo, MessageBoxIcon.Question) _
        = DialogResult.Yes Then
    Me.Close
Else
    txtOrderTotal.Focus
End If
```

The constants you can use for the Show method arguments

Enumeration	Constants
MessageBoxButtons	OK, OKCancel, YesNo, YesNoCancel, RetryCancel, AbortRetryIgnore
MessageBoxIcon	Information, Error, Warning, Exclamation, Question, Asterisk, Hand, Stop, None
MessageBoxDefaultButton	Button1, Button2, Button3

The constants in the DialogResult enumeration

OK, Cancel, Yes, No, Abort, Retry, Ignore, None

Description

- The Show method of the MessageBox class lets you display a message to the user and accept a response from the user.

- You use the enumerations listed above to specify the buttons and icon that will appear in the message box and the button that's treated as the default.

- If you omit the buttons argument, the OK button is displayed by default. You can display a maximum of three buttons in a message box.

- The second example uses the Show method within an If statement, which tests to determine whether the user clicked the Yes button. The DialogResult enumeration has constants that correspond to the buttons that can be displayed.

Figure 4-5   How to use the Show method of the MessageBox class

How to use Visual Basic functions

A *function* is a type of procedure that returns a value, and Visual Basic provides many functions that provide useful operations. As you will see, functions are similar to shared methods, although the coding details vary slightly. To get the most from Visual Basic, you need to be aware of both the functions and the shared methods that can help you code more easily.

A summary of the Visual Basic functions

In figure 4-6, you can see some of the types of functions that Visual Basic provides. In this chapter, you'll learn how to use the IsNumeric function and three of the formatting functions. You'll learn how to use some of the other types of functions in later chapters of this book.

As the syntax and examples in this figure show, you normally code one or more arguments that are *passed* to the function. Then, the function uses the arguments as it performs its operation and returns a result. The only difference between using a function and using a shared method is that the function name replaces the classname, dot, and method name of a shared method.

To find functions that may be of use to you and to find out how they need to be coded, you can use online help. To get help on the use of a function when you know its name, you can use the online help index. To find specific types of functions like the financial and type conversion functions, you can use the online help index to search by function type. And to examine an alphabetical list of the Visual Basic functions, you can use the help contents. To find this list of functions, open the folders in this sequence: Visual Studio .NET → Visual Basic and C# → Reference → Visual Basic Language → Visual Basic Language and Run-Time Reference → Functions. Then, you can open the group folders within this folder to display the functions that start with specific letters of the alphabet.

Keep in mind, though, that the .NET Framework provides shared members that you may be able to use in place of functions. As a result, some of the functions you find in the online help will refer to an equivalent shared method that you should use in its place. For example, you already learned about the methods of the Math class, which have replaced the Math functions that were available in Visual Basic 6.

The syntax for using a function

```
functionname(arguments)
```

Statements that use a function

```
Len(sLastName)                              'Returns the length of a string
DateDiff(dtmPurchaseDate, dtmReceiptDate)   'Returns a time interval
```

Some of the type conversion functions

Function	Description
CDec	Returns a value of Decimal data type.
CInt	Returns a value of Integer data type.
CStr	Returns a value of String data type.

[handwritten: CONVERT, TO STRING BETTER, CBool]

Some of the string functions

Function	Description
Left	Returns a specific number of characters from the start of a string.
Len	Returns the length of a string.
LTrim	Removes spaces from the start of a string.

Some of the date functions *[handwritten: — LOTS]*

Function	Description
DateDiff	Returns a long value that contains the time interval between two dates.
WeekDay	Returns an integer value representing the day of the week.
WeekDayName	Returns a string value that contains the name of the specified day of the week.

Some of the finance functions

Function	Description
FV	Calculates the future value of a periodic payment amount.
Pmt	Calculates the periodic payment needed to attain a fixed future value.

Some of the formatting functions

Function	Description
FormatNumber	Returns a string that contains the specified expression in a number format.
FormatCurrency	Returns a string that contains the specified expression in a currency format.
FormatPercent	Returns a string that contains the specified expression in a percentage format.
FormatDateTime	Returns a string that contains the specified expression in a date or time format.

Some miscellaneous functions

Function	Description
InputBox	Displays a message in a dialog box, waits for the user to enter text or click a button, and returns a string that contains what the user entered.
IsNumeric	Returns a True value if the specified expression contains numeric data. Otherwise, returns a False value.

Figure 4-6   A summary of the Visual Basic functions

How to use the IsNumeric function for data validation

Figure 4-7 presents the syntax and use of the IsNumeric function. This function returns a Boolean (True or False) value after evaluating the expression that you pass as an argument. If the argument can be cast as a numeric data type without error, the function returns a True value. Otherwise, it returns a False value.

As the example in this figure shows, you typically use the IsNumeric function in an If statement. Then, if the function returns a True value, it's okay for the program to process the data. Otherwise, the program should display an error message so the user can correct the entry. That way, the program won't cause a run-time error by trying to perform arithmetic operations on data that isn't numeric.

Coding like this is called *data validation*, or *validity checking*. However, numeric checking is just one type of data validation. Other common types are *range checking* and *format checking*. In a range check, an entry is tested to make sure that it's within a valid range of values. In format checking, an entry is tested to make sure that it has the required format, like the format for a social security number or telephone number.

Incidentally, the condition in the example in this figure could also be coded as

```
IsNumeric(txtOrderTotal.Text) = True
```

If = True is omitted, though, Visual Basic assumes it for a Boolean expression. In practice, then, a Boolean expression is normally coded without the = True portion of the condition. So that's the way you'll see this type of condition coded throughout this book.

The syntax of the IsNumeric function

```
IsNumeric(expression)
```

An If statement that uses the IsNumeric function

```
If IsNumeric(txtOrderTotal.Text) Then
    dOrderTotal = txtOrderTotal.Text
Else
    MessageBox.Show("You must enter a numeric value.", "Entry error")
End If
```

Results of the IsNumeric function

Expression	IsNumeric(Expression)
24	True
+45	True
-281	True
2+2	False
1E10	True
49y101	False
seven	False

Description

- The IsNumeric function tests whether the value of an expression can be cast as a numeric data type. This function returns a Boolean value, which you can test in a conditional expression. If the Boolean value is True, the value of the expression is numeric.

- *Data validation*, or *validity checking*, is the process of verifying that input from the user is valid. One goal of this verification is to prevent run-time errors during the execution of your program.

- One type of data validation tests that the input is of the expected data type. The IsNumeric function is typically used for this type of validation.

- Two other common types of data validation are (1) *range checking* and (2) *format checking*. In a range test, you test to see whether an entry falls within a valid range of values. In a format test, you test to see whether an entry has a valid format like the format for a telephone number or social security number.

Figure 4-7   How to use the IsNumeric function for data validation

How to use three of the formatting functions

Figure 4-8 shows how to use three of the formatting functions. The FormatNumber function formats a numeric value without a dollar sign. The FormatCurrency function formats a value with a dollar sign. And the FormatPercent function formats a value with a percent sign. All three functions also let you control the number of decimal positions in the result.

Although you can code up to five arguments for each of these functions, you usually code only one or two. The only argument that's required is the first one, which is an expression for the number to be formatted. Then, the second argument indicates the number of decimal digits to be used. The default is determined by your computer's regional setting, which is typically 2, so you can often omit this argument.

If you want to code one or more of the last three arguments, you use the constants in the TriState enumeration shown in this figure. Here again, the defaults for these arguments are determined by your computer's regional settings, and these settings are normally set the way you want them.

The syntax of three of the formatting functions

```
{FormatNumber|FormatCurrency|FormatPercent}(expression
    [, NumDigitsAfterDecimal][, IncludeLeadingDigit]
    [, UseParensForNegativeNumbers][, GroupDigits])
```

The constants in the TriState enumeration

Constant	Description
True	A True value
False	A False value
UseDefault	Use the computer's regional settings

[handwritten: TRISTATE, TRUE FALSE USE THE...]

Statements that use the formatting functions

```
lblDiscountAmount.Text = FormatNumber(dDiscountAmount, 2)
lblInvoiceTotal.Text = FormatNumber(dInvoiceTotal)
lblInvoiceTotal.Text = FormatCurrency(dInvoiceTotal)
lblDiscountPct.Text = FormatPercent(dDiscountPct)
```

Results of the three formatting functions

Expression	Result
FormatNumber(-.888)	-0.89
FormatNumber(-.888, 2)	-0.89
FormatNumber(-.888, 1)	-0.9
FormatNumber(-.888, , TriState.False)	-.89
FormatNumber(-.888, , , TriState.True)	(0.89)
FormatNumber(3000)	3,000.00
FormatNumber(3000, , , , TriState.False)	3000.00
FormatCurrency(3000)	$3,000.00
FormatPercent(-.888)	-88.80%
FormatPercent(-.888, 1)	-88.8%

[handwritten: DEF FOR WINDOWS]

Description

- These three formatting functions are used to format a number for display or printing in number, currency, or percent format. If necessary, these functions round the values to the specified number of decimal places.

- Although you can code up to five arguments for these functions, you usually just code two arguments: the expression to be formatted, which can be as simple as a variable name, and the number of decimal digits to be displayed.

- If you omit the number of decimal digits, your computer's default regional setting is used.

- You can code the last three arguments for a function by using the constants in the TriState enumeration. If a constant isn't specified, TriState.UseDefault is used.

- The IncludeLeadingDigit argument specifies whether a leading zero is to be displayed for fractional numbers. The UseParensForNegativeNumbers argument specifies whether negative numbers are to be displayed within parentheses. And the GroupDigits argument specifies whether digits are to be grouped using the computer's regional settings.

Figure 4-8   How to use three of the formatting functions

The Invoice Total application with data validation and formatting

Now that you have seen all of the skills that you need for adding data validation and formatting to an application, figure 4-9 shows how you can use them to enhance the Invoice Total application of the last chapter. To make this code easier to review, the new code is shaded. As you can see, all of the enhancements are made in the btnCalculate_Click procedure.

The code for data validation

For data validation, the code uses nested If statements. In the outer If statement, the IsNumeric function tests whether the user entry is numeric. If it is, processing passes to the inner If statement. Otherwise, processing passes to the outer Else clause, which displays a message box that tells the user to enter a numeric value. That ends the procedure.

In the inner If statement, the numeric entry is tested to see whether it is greater than a constant named dMinOrderTotal and less than a constant named dMaxOrderTotal. Since these constants are defined at the start of the procedure with values of 10 and 10000, this tests whether the order total is within an acceptable range of values. If it is, processing continues with the statements that follow. But otherwise, processing passes to the inner Else clause, which displays a message box that tells the user what the valid range is. To do that, the code uses the constants a second time.

The benefit of using constants instead of numeric literals is that the constants make the code easy to change if that becomes necessary. Instead of finding and changing the statements that use numeric literals, you just change the two constants at the start of the procedure. This also eliminates the chance that you'll change the literals in one portion of the code but forget to change them in another portion, which would be a programming error.

The code for formatting

Formatting is done in two ways in this program. First, the Round method of the Math class has been used to round the user entry to two decimal places in case the user enters more decimal places than that. Second, the FormatNumber function is used to format the calculated values.

Although the Math.Round method and the FormatNumber function perform similar functions, please note that they work differently. In particular, the Round method returns a number, not a string. In this program, it is used to assign a new rounded number to the original variable. If, for example, the user enters 150.555, the Round method converts it to 150.56. In contrast, the FormatNumber function returns a string, not a number. It is used to display a number, not to change the number itself.

The modified code for the Invoice Total application

```
Private Sub btnCalculate_Click(ByVal sender As System.Object, _
        ByVal e As System.EventArgs) Handles btnCalculate.Click

    Const dMinOrderTotal As Decimal = 10
    Const dMaxOrderTotal As Decimal = 10000

    Dim dOrderTotal As Decimal
    Dim dDiscountPct As Decimal
    Dim dDiscountAmount As Decimal
    Dim dInvoiceTotal As Decimal

    If IsNumeric(txtOrderTotal.Text) Then            'Check for valid data type
        If txtOrderTotal.Text > dMinOrderTotal And _
           txtOrderTotal.Text < dMaxOrderTotal Then  'Check for valid range

            dOrderTotal = txtOrderTotal.Text
            dOrderTotal = Math.Round(dOrderTotal, 2)

            If dOrderTotal >= 500 Then
                dDiscountPct = 0.2
            ElseIf dOrderTotal >= 250 Then
                dDiscountPct = 0.15
            ElseIf dOrderTotal >= 100 Then
                dDiscountPct = 0.1
            Else ' < 100
                dDiscountPct = 0
            End If

            dDiscountAmount = dOrderTotal * dDiscountPct
            dInvoiceTotal = dOrderTotal - dDiscountAmount
            lblDiscountAmount.Text = FormatNumber(dDiscountAmount)
            lblInvoiceTotal.Text = FormatNumber(dInvoiceTotal)
        Else ' Out of range
            MessageBox.Show("Order total must be between " & _
                            dMinOrderTotal & " and " & _
                            dMaxOrderTotal & ".", "Entry error")
        End If
    Else ' Not IsNumeric
        MessageBox.Show("You must enter a numeric value.", "Entry error")
    End If
    txtOrderTotal.Focus()

End Sub
```

Description

- This enhancement to the Invoice Total application uses nested If statements to check the user entry for two types of validity.

- The outer If statement uses the IsNumeric function to test whether the user entry is numeric. The inner If statement tests whether the user entry is within a valid range.

- Two constants are used to provide the minimum and maximum values for the valid range. These constants are then referred to by two sets of statements within the nested Ifs. Later, if you need to change the range values, you can change just the constants; you won't have to change the statements in the nested Ifs.

Figure 4-9   The Invoice Total application with data validation

How to code loops

A *loop* is a sequence of statements that's performed repetitively. To code loops in Visual Basic, you can use the For...Next or the Do...Loop statement. Because the For...Next statement usually leads to more readable code, I'll present that statement first.

How to code For...Next loops

Figure 4-10 presents the syntax of the For...Next statement, which is used to implement a *For...Next loop*. This statement lets you repeat a series of statements for each value of a variable. By default, the value of the variable is incremented by one each time the loop is completed. But if you want to increment the variable by a value other than one, you can include the Step clause in this statement.

The first example in this figure shows a For...Next loop that displays the numbers from zero through four in a message box. To start, this statement initializes a variable named iIndex to zero. Then, the value is increased by one each time Next is reached. This continues until the value is increased beyond the specified end value, at which point the processing exits the loop and continues with the statement that follows the loop.

The second and third examples show how the Step clause can be used. In the second example, a positive step value causes the counter to be increased by 2 each time through the loop. In the third example, a negative step value causes the counter to be decreased by 10 each time through the loop.

The last example in this figure shows how you can use a For...Next statement to calculate the future value of a monthly investment. As you can see, this example uses five variables. The iIndex variable counts the number of loops, and the iMonths variable sets the total number of loops. Then, the dMonthlyInterestRate variable holds the monthly interest rate, the dMonthlyInvestment variable holds the monthly amount being invested, and the dFutureValue variable stores the future value amount for the calculation. For each iteration of the loop, the monthly investment amount is added to the future value variable, which is then multiplied by one plus the monthly interest rate.

In case the math within this loop isn't clear to you, suppose the monthly investment is $100 and the interest rate is one percent a month (.01). Then, the calculation the first time through the loop is this:

```
(0 + 100) * (1 + .01) or (100 * 1.01) which equals 101
```

After this result is assigned to dFutureValue, which had a starting value of zero, the calculation the second time through the loop is this:

```
(101 + 100) * (1 + .01) or (201 * 1.01) which equals 203.01
```

And after this result is assigned to dFutureValue, the loop continues in this way until the calculation has been done once for each month indicated by the iMonths variable.

The syntax of the For…Next statement

```
For counter = start To end [Step step]
    statements
Next [counter]
```

A For…Next loop that displays the numbers 0 through 4

```
Dim iIndex As Integer
For iIndex = 0 To 4
    MessageBox.Show(iIndex)
Next iIndex
```

[handwritten: FASTER, KNOWS WHERE INDEX IS]

[handwritten: iINDEX]

A For…Next loop that adds the numbers 2, 4, 6, 8, 10, and 12 to iSum

```
Dim iSum As Integer            'The default starting value is zero
Dim iIndex As Integer
For iIndex = 2 To 12 Step 2
    iSum += iIndex
Next iIndex
```

A For…Next loop that adds the squares of 25, 15, 5, -5, and -15 to iSumofSquares

```
Dim iSquared As Integer
Dim iSumofSquares As Integer
Dim iIndex As Integer
For iIndex = 25 To -15 Step -10
    iSquared = iIndex ^ 2
    iSumofSquares += iSquared
Next iIndex
```

[handwritten: DON'T CHANGE VAL OF INDEX INSIDE OF LOOP?]

A For…Next loop that calculates a future value

```
Dim dMonthlyInvestment As Decimal
Dim dMonthlyInterestRate As Decimal
Dim iMonths As Integer
Dim dFutureValue As Decimal
Dim iIndex As Integer
For iIndex = 1 To iMonths
    dFutureValue = (dFutureValue + dMonthlyInvestment) _
               * (1 + dMonthlyInterestRate)
Next iIndex
```

[handwritten: EXIT FOR TO GET OUT - ESP. W/ FOR EACH (FULL BUFFER, ETC]

Description

- The For…Next statement is used to implement a *For…Next loop*.
- You typically use a For…Next loop to repeat a series of statements for each value of an index.
- For…Next statements are often used with arrays, which you'll learn about in chapter 12.

*[handwritten: FOR EACH A IN AARRAY (or COLLECTION) **]*

[handwritten: NEXT]

Figure 4-10   How to code For…Next loops

*[handwritten: * UNKNOWN # OF ELEM. (FOR NEXT FASTER)]*

*[handwritten: ** SLOWER]*

How to code Do loops

Figure 4-11 shows how you can use Do…Loop statements to create *Do loops* that perform the same types of repetitive processing as For…Next loops. If you compare the Do loops shown in this figure with the For…Next loops shown in the last figure, though, you'll see that For…Next loops generally lead to simpler code that's easier to understand. As a result, you'll probably use For…Next loops more than Do loops. Nevertheless, it's worth taking a moment to see how Do loops work.

As you can see, this figure shows two versions of the Do…Loop statement. In the first version, the condition is tested *before* the series of statements is executed. In the second version, the condition is tested *after* the series of statements is executed. Testing last means that the loop will always be executed at least one time.

In the examples, you can see how you can use both versions of this statement to calculate a future value like the one in the previous figure. Before the loop begins, you must assign a value of 1 to the iIndex variable because the Do statement itself doesn't provide for that. Otherwise, a default value of 0 will be used and an extra loop will be counted. Similarly, once the loop begins, you must also include a statement like this

```
iIndex += 1
```

to manually increment the iIndex variable because the Do statement itself doesn't provide for that. Here, a value of 1 is added to the current value of the variable each time through the loop. When the value of this variable becomes greater than the value of the iMonths variable, the Do loop ends.

The syntax of the Do statement with the test first

```
Do [{While|Until} condition]
    statements
Loop
```

A Do loop with the test first that calculates future value

```
Dim dMonthlyInvestment As Decimal
Dim dMonthlyInterestRate As Decimal
Dim iMonths As Integer
Dim dFutureValue As Decimal
Dim iIndex As Integer = 1
Do Until iIndex > iMonths
    dFutureValue = (dFutureValue + dMonthlyInvestment) _
                * (1 + dMonthlyInterestRate)
    iIndex += 1
Loop
```

The syntax of the Do statement with the test last   ← *ALWAYS RUNS ONCE*

```
Do
    statements
Loop [{While|Until} condition]
```

A Do loop with the test last that calculates future value

```
Dim dMonthlyInvestment As Decimal
Dim dMonthlyInterestRate As Decimal
Dim iMonths As Integer
Dim dFutureValue As Decimal
Dim iIndex As Integer = 1
Do
    dFutureValue = (dFutureValue + dMonthlyInvestment) _
                * (1 + dMonthlyInterestRate)
    iIndex += 1
Loop While iIndex <= iMonths
```

Description

- The Do statement and Loop statement are used to implement *Do loops*. A Do loop lets you repeat a series of statements as long as a condition is true (While) or until a condition becomes true (Until). You can test the condition either before or after the statements are performed.

- You can use Do loops to perform the same types of repetitive processing as you do with For...Next loops. However, For...Next loops typically lead to simpler code.

- You can also code a While...End While statement to do this type of processing. This statement isn't presented in this book, though, because the Do While statement is easier to use.

Figure 4-11   How to code Do loops

Debugging techniques for programs with loops

When you code programs that use loops, debugging often becomes more difficult because it's hard to tell how the loop is operating. As a result, you may want to use the debugging techniques that are summarized in figure 4-12. These techniques let you stop the execution of a program and enter break mode when a loop starts. Then, you can observe the operation of the loop, one statement at a time.

To stop the execution of a program and enter break mode, you set a *breakpoint*. To do that, you click once in the *margin indicator bar* at the left-hand side of the Code Editor window. The breakpoint is then marked by a red dot. Later, when the application is run, execution will stop just prior to the statement at the breakpoint.

Once in break mode, a yellow arrowhead marks the next statement that will be executed, which is called the *execution point*. In addition, several windows are automatically opened, one of which is the *Autos window*. This window displays the current values of the variables used by the current statement and three statements before and after the current statement. Then, you can see how those variables change each time through the loop.

While in break mode, you can also *step through* the statements in the loop, one statement at a time. To do that, you repeatedly press the F11 key. This lets you observe exactly how and when the variable values change as the loop executes. Once you understand how the loop works, you can remove the breakpoint and press the F5 key to continue normal execution.

Of course, these techniques are also useful for debugging problems that don't involve loops. If, for example, you can't figure out what's wrong with one of the procedures in your application, you can set a breakpoint in that procedure. Then, when the program enters break mode, you can step through the statements in that procedure and observe the changes in the variables as you to try to figure out what's wrong.

How to set a breakpoint in your code

Breakpoint indicator

Margin indicator bar

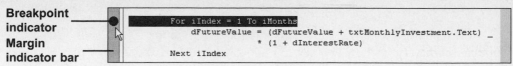

The variables displayed in the Autos window

Execution point

Autos window

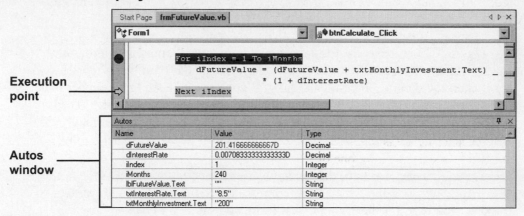

How to set and clear breakpoints

- To set a breakpoint, click in the *margin indicator bar* to the left of a statement. Or, press the F9 key to set a breakpoint at the cursor insertion point.

- To remove a breakpoint, use either technique for setting a breakpoint. To remove all breakpoints at once, use the Clear All Breakpoints command in the Debug menu.

How to work in break mode

- In break mode, a yellow arrowhead marks the current *execution point*, which points to the next statement that will be executed.

- To step through your code one statement at a time, press the F11 key.

- To continue normal processing until the next breakpoint is reached, press the F5 key.

Description

- When you set a *breakpoint* at a specific statement, the program stops before executing that statement and enters break mode. Then, you can step through the execution of the program, one statement at a time.

- In break mode, the *Autos window* displays the current values of the variables in the current statement and three statements before and after the current statement.

- By setting breakpoints, stepping through the code that follows, and observing the changes in the variables, you can learn how a loop works. This is also a useful technique for debugging other portions of code.

Figure 4-12   Debugging techniques for programs with loops

The Future Value application

Now that you've learned the statements for coding loops, I'll present a new application that shows how you can use a loop to calculate and display the future value of a monthly investment.

The form design and properties

Figure 4-13 presents the form design and property settings for a program that calculates the future value of a monthly investment. To do that, the user must enter the monthly investment, the yearly interest rate, and the number of years the investment will be made into the three text boxes on the form. Then, when the user clicks on the Calculate button or presses the Enter key, the application calculates the future value and displays it in the last label on the form.

To make it easy for you to develop this form, this figure also lists the property settings for the form and its controls. Since these settings are similar to the ones you used for the Invoice Total form, you shouldn't have any trouble figuring out what they do.

The form for the Future Value application

The property settings for the form

Default name	Property	Setting
Form1	AcceptButton	btnCalculate
	CancelButton	btnExit
	FormBorderStyle	FixedSingle
	MaximizeBox	False
	MinimizeBox	False
	StartPosition	CenterScreen
	Text	Calculate future value

The property settings for the controls

Default name	Property	Setting
Label1	Text	Monthly Investment:
Label2	Text	Yearly Interest Rate:
Label3	Text	Number of Years:
Label4	Text	Future Value:
Label 5	BorderStyle	Fixed3D
	Name	lblFutureValue
Text1	Name	txtMonthlyInvestment
Text2	Name	txtInterestRate
Text3	Name	txtYears
Button1	Name	btnCalculate
	Text	&Calculate
Button2	Name	btnExit
	Text	E&xit

Additional property settings

- The TextAlign property of each of the four left labels is set to MiddleRight.
- The Text property of each text box and the fifth label is cleared so it's empty.
- The TabIndex properties of the controls are set so the focus moves from top to bottom and left to right.

Figure 4-13   The form design and properties for the Future Value application

The code for the Future Value application

Figure 4-14 presents the code for the Future Value form. Like the code for the Invoice Total form, the code for this form consists of two event procedures: one for the Click event of the Calculate button and one for the Click event of the Exit button. Here again, the main processing occurs in the Click event procedure of the Calculate button.

The first four statements in this procedure declare the variables that will be used by the future value calculation. That includes an index variable that will be used to control the processing of the For...Next loop.

The next two statements assign values to two of these variables so all of the variables used in the future value calculation will be in terms of months. The first assignment statement converts the number of years for the investment to months by multiplying the years by 12. The second assignment statement divides the yearly interest rate by 12 to get a monthly interest rate and then divides that result by 100. That way, the user can enter a value like 7.5 rather than .075.

Once these variables are set, a For...Next loop calculates a new future value for each month of the investment. Since I explained this calculation when I described the fourth example in figure 4-10, I won't do it again here. When this loop ends, the future value is formatted as currency and assigned to the text property of the future value label so it's displayed properly on the form. Then, the focus is moved to the text box for the monthly investment amount so the user can enter the data for another future value calculation.

To keep this program simple, it doesn't provide for data validation. As a result, this program will end with a run-time error if the user enters nonnumeric data in one of the text boxes. In the next figure, though, you can see two ways to add data validation to this program.

The Visual Basic code for the Future Value application

```
Public Class Form1
    Inherits System.Windows.Forms.Form

    Private Sub btnCalculate_Click(ByVal sender As System.Object, _
            ByVal e As System.EventArgs) Handles btnCalculate.Click

        Dim iMonths As Integer
        Dim dInterestRate As Decimal
        Dim dFutureValue As Decimal
        Dim iIndex As Integer

        iMonths = txtYears.Text * 12
        dInterestRate = txtInterestRate.Text / 12 / 100

        For iIndex = 1 To iMonths
            dFutureValue = (dFutureValue + txtMonthlyInvestment.Text) _
                        * (1 + dInterestRate)
        Next iIndex

        lblFutureValue.Text = FormatCurrency(dFutureValue)
        txtMonthlyInvestment.Focus()

    End Sub

    Private Sub btnExit_Click(ByVal sender As System.Object, _
            ByVal e As System.EventArgs) Handles btnExit.Click

        Me.Close()

    End Sub

End Class
```

Description

- This application makes use of a For...Next loop to calculate the future value of a monthly investment amount. If the calculation is to work right, all of the variables that it uses must be converted to the same time period, which in this case is months.

- Since this application doesn't provide data validation, the user will be able to enter invalid data, which will cause run-time errors.

Figure 4-14   The code for the Future Value application

Two ways to provide data validation

As the number of user entries in an application increases, the code that's used for data validation increases in both size and complexity. To illustrate, figure 4-15 shows two ways that data validation can be added to the Future Value program in the previous figure.

In the first example, a compound condition is used to make sure that all three user entries are numeric. If they are, the procedure continues by calculating and displaying the future value. If one user entry isn't numeric, though, a general message is displayed that tells the user to check the entries for validity. When you use a compound condition, you can't tell which of the entries is invalid so you can't provide a specific error message.

In the second example, nested If statements are used to make sure that each user entry is numeric. Then, if one of the entries isn't numeric, the related Else clause displays a specific error message and moves the focus to the text box that contains that entry. When you use this technique, the If statements should check the text boxes from the first to the last, so the user can correct the entry errors in that sequence.

Please note that neither of these techniques provides for range checking, which should normally be done in an application like this. But when you add that code, you have to use more compound conditions or nested If statements so the data validation code becomes even more cumbersome. That's why data validation accounts for a large portion of the code in professional applications.

NESTED IFS, CAN TELL WHICH ONE

Numeric data validation with a compound condition

```
If IsNumeric(txtYears.Text) _
        And IsNumeric(txtInterestRate.Text) _
        And IsNumeric(txtMonthlyInvestment.Text) Then
    iMonths = txtYears.Text * 12
    dInterestRate = txtInterestRate.Text / 12 / 100
    For iIndex = 1 To iMonths
        dFutureValue = (dFutureValue + txtMonthlyInvestment.Text) _
                    * (1 + dInterestRate)
    Next iIndex
    lblFutureValue.Text = FormatCurrency(dFutureValue)
    txtMonthlyInvestment.Focus()
Else
    MessageBox.Show("Invalid data. Please check all entries.", _
                "Entry error")
    txtMonthlyInvestment.Focus()
End If
```

Numeric data validation with nested If statements

```
If IsNumeric(txtMonthlyInvestment.Text) Then
    If IsNumeric(txtInterestRate.Text) Then
        If IsNumeric(txtYears.Text) Then
            iMonths = txtYears.Text * 12
            dInterestRate = txtInterestRate.Text / 12 / 100
            For iIndex = 1 To iMonths
                dFutureValue = (dFutureValue + txtMonthlyInvestment.Text) _
                            * (1 + dInterestRate)
            Next iIndex
            lblFutureValue.Text = FormatCurrency(dFutureValue)
            txtMonthlyInvestment.Focus()
        Else
            MessageBox.Show("Number of years must be numeric.", _
                "Entry error")
            txtYears.Focus()
        End If
    Else
        MessageBox.Show("Yearly interest rate must be numeric.", _
            "Entry error")
        txtInterestRate.Focus()
    End If
Else
    MessageBox.Show("Monthly investment must be numeric.", _
        "Entry error")
    txtMonthlyInvestment.Focus()
End If
```

Description

- When you use a compound condition for data validation, you can't tell which entry is invalid so you can only provide a general error message and move the focus to the first text box.

- When you use nested Ifs for data validation, you can tell which entry is invalid so you can provide a specific error message and move the focus to the text box with the invalid entry.

Figure 4-15   Two ways to provide data validation in the Future Value application

Perspective

If this chapter has succeeded, you now know how to provide data validation and data formatting in your applications. You also know how to use loops in your applications. Those skills start you on your way toward the development of programs at a professional level.

At this point, you should also start to appreciate the many different ways that you can get operations done when you're using Visual Basic. Besides the statements of the language itself, like assignment and If statements, you can use object properties and methods, shared properties and methods, the constants in classes, enumerations, and functions.

In fact, one of your major problems when learning Visual Basic is figuring out what's available to you and which of several alternatives is the best way to do an operation. But that, of course, is what this book is designed to help you do.

Summary

- A *constant* provides a value that doesn't change, and an *enumeration* is a set of related constants. As you write Visual Basic code, you can define your own constants and enumerations, but you can also use the ones provided by Visual Basic.

- *Shared members* are the properties and methods that you can access directly from a class, and Visual Basic provides shared methods for many of the common operations that your programs need to do. To use a shared method, you often need to pass it one or more *arguments*.

- *Functions* are procedures that return a value, and Visual Basic provides functions for many of the common operations that your programs need to do. To use a function, you usually need to pass it one or more arguments.

- *Data validation*, also known as *validity checking*, is the process of checking the user's entries for validity. One goal of data validation is to prevent run-time errors.

- *Loops* are sequences of statements that are executed repeatedly. You can code loops using For…Next statements or Do…Loop statements, although *For…Next loops* are usually easier to use than *Do loops*.

- To debug a program that contains a loop, you can set a *breakpoint* and *step through* the statements in the loop. As you do that, you can use the *Autos window* to observe the changes in the variables that are used.

Terms

constant	data validation	Do loop
enumeration	validity checking	breakpoint
shared member	range checking	margin indicator bar
argument	format checking	execution point
precision	loop	Autos window
function	For...Next loop	step through the code
passing an argument		

Objectives

- Given the Visual Basic code for a form that uses any of the language elements presented in this chapter, explain what each statement does.

- Given the form design and specifications for an application that requires any of the language elements presented in this chapter, write the code for the application.

- Distinguish between a variable and a constant.

- Distinguish between a constant and an enumeration.

- Describe the syntax differences between using a shared method and a function.

- Describe the process of data validation and describe three specific types of data validation.

- Explain how you can use breakpoints, the Autos window, and the stepping through technique to debug errors within loops.

Exercise 4-1   Enhance the Invoice Total application

In this exercise, you'll add data validation and data formatting to the Invoice Total application you developed for the last chapter.

1. Use the Windows Explorer to copy the C:\VB.NET\Chapter 03\InvoiceTotal folder to C:\VB.NET\Chapter 04. Then, open the Invoice Total project for chapter 4.

2. Add data validation and data formatting to the btnCalculate_Click procedure as shown in figure 4-9. Don't just copy the code, though. Try to write the code on your own so you only refer to figure 4-9 when you're stuck.

3. Test the application to make sure that the data is formatted correctly and that the data validation works. Then, enter a value like 10K to make sure the numeric check is working correctly and enter a value like 12000 to make sure that the range check is working correctly.

4. When you're satisfied that the application works correctly, close it.

Exercise 4-2   Develop the Future Value application

In this exercise, you'll develop and test the Future Value application that was presented in this chapter. That will give you a chance to develop another form.

Develop the form and write the code for the application

1. Open the New Project dialog box by selecting the File → New → Project command, and select the Windows Application template from the Visual Basic Projects folder. Next, enter "FutureValue" for the name of the project, and add "\Chapter 04" to the end of the path shown in the Location box. Then, click the OK button to start the new project.

2. Add the controls to the starting form as shown in figure 4-13. Then, set the properties of the form and its controls.

3. Double-click on the Calculate button to open the Code Editor window and generate the btnCalculate_Click event procedure. Then, write the code for this procedure, but don't include data validation. If necessary, you can refer to the code in figure 4-14, but try to write the code without referring to this figure.

4. Add the code for the btnExit_Click procedure, which you should be able to do without referring to figure 4-14.

Test the application

5. Build and run the application, and test it by entering valid data in each of the three text boxes. To start, enter simple values like $100 for the monthly investment, 12% for the yearly interest rate (which is 1% per month), and 1 for the number of years. Then, check to make sure that the calculation and the formatting are correct. If necessary, exit from the application, make the corrections, and test again.

6. After you're sure that the application works for valid data, test it with nonnumeric entries. When you do, the application will fail with run-time errors known as casting exceptions.

7. Test the application one more time with large values like 100 for the interest rate and 1000 for the number of years. This time the application will end with a run-time error known as an overflow exception. This means that the future value got so large that it couldn't be stored in the decimal variable. This points out the need for range checking the entries.

Exercise 4-3   Step through the Future Value application

This exercise guides you through the process of stepping through the code in the loop within the Future Value program.

Set breakpoints and step through the loop

1. In the Code Editor window, set a breakpoint at the For statement by clicking in the Margin Indicator Bar to the left of the statement as shown in figure 4-12. A red dot will indicate that you have successfully set the breakpoint.

2. Run the application, and enter 10 as the monthly investment, 12 as the yearly interest rate, and 1 as the number of years. Then, click on the Calculate button. This will cause the program to enter break mode at the breakpoint with the Autos window displayed. Here, you can see the values of the iMonths and dInterestRate variables, which have already been assigned. In contrast, iIndex and dFutureValue haven't been assigned values yet, so they are set to the default value of zero.

3. Press the F11 key to step into the next statement, which will execute the For statement. Here, you can see that the value of iIndex has been set and its font color has been changed to red. This is done automatically to highlight the variable that has been most recently changed.

4. Press the F11 key again to execute the assignment statement within the For…Next loop, and notice that the value of dFutureValue has been changed. Then, press the F11 key once more to execute the Next statement, and notice that the iIndex variable has been increased by one and the execution point returns to the assignment statement.

5. Continue by pressing the F11 key until iIndex is 12, and notice that the Next statement increases iIndex to 13 and that the execution point steps out of the loop because iIndex is now larger than iMonths.

6. Press the F11 key again, and note the result of the assignment statement. Then, press F11 two more times. After the End Sub statement is executed, the Future Value form is displayed again.

7. Click on the Calculate button again, with the same values entered. This time, when you enter break mode, press the F5 key, which causes execution to continue until another breakpoint is reached. Because the For statement is only executed once in this procedure, the loop runs to completion.

8. Click on the Exit button to exit from the application.

Change the location of the breakpoint

9. Remove the breakpoint from the For statement and try to set one on a Dim statement. Notice that you can't do that because a Dim statement is a declaration, which isn't executed when the application is run.

10. Set a breakpoint at the Next statement and run the application again. Then, enter valid numeric values and click the Calculate button. When you enter break mode, notice that all four variables have already been set.

11. Press the F5 key to continue execution until the next breakpoint. Notice that the breakpoint at the Next statement causes a break for each iteration of the loop. This is because the Next statement is executed each time through the loop.

12. While in break mode, remove the breakpoint that you set at the Next statement. Then, press the F5 key so the application returns to the form and you can click on the Exit button to end the test.

Exercise 4-4   Add data validation to the Future Value application

In this exercise, you will add data validation to the Future Value application.

1. With the Future Value application still open, use nested If statements to add data validation to the btnCalculate_Click procedure, and provide a specific error message for each entry. Try to do this without referring to the code in figure 4-15.

2. Test the data validation routines to make sure they work correctly. In particular, enter nonnumeric entries to make sure they won't cause run-time errors. Then, make sure that the right error message is displayed for each entry and that the focus is moved to the text box that has invalid data.

3. Test the routines with large values like 100 for the interest rate and 1000 for the number of years. When a run-time error occurs, you can see that numeric checking isn't enough. You also need to provide range checking.

4. Add range checks to the program so the monthly investment amount is from 100 to 1000, the yearly interest rate is from 0 to 24%, and the number of years is from 1 to 65. One way to do that is to add three more levels of nested If statements. Then, test the program again to make sure the range tests work correctly.

5. When you're satisfied that the application works correctly under all conditions without failing, close the project.

5

Visual Basic language essentials (part 3)

In this chapter, you'll learn several new skills for coding Visual Basic programs. In particular, you'll learn new ways to organize your code and prevent run-time errors. When you complete this chapter, you'll know all of the essential language elements for developing Visual Basic programs.

How to code and call Sub procedures and functions

So far, all of the procedures you have written have been event procedures, which contain the code that is run when an event occurs for an object. But now, you will learn how to code two types of *general procedures*: Sub procedures and Function procedures. These are procedures that are run when they are called by other procedures, instead of being initiated by an event. As you will see, the use of general procedures lets you organize your code so it's easier to work with.

How to code and call a Sub procedure

Figure 5-1 shows the syntax for coding and calling a *Sub procedure*. The syntax for the Sub statement shows that you code the procedure name after the keyword Sub. After that, you code an argument list in parentheses if the procedure requires that one or more arguments be passed to it. Then, you code the statements of the procedure between the Sub and End Sub statements. If a procedure doesn't require any arguments, it's a good practice to code the parentheses anyway, even though they are optional.

You can code a Sub statement with either the Private or Public keyword. You use Private if you only need to call the procedure from within the same class or module. If you need to call the procedure from another class or module, however, you use the Public keyword. You'll learn more about modules in a moment.

To *call* (execute) a Sub procedure, you use the Call statement. This statement includes a list of any arguments required by the called procedure within parentheses. Even if the called procedure doesn't require arguments, though, you should include the parentheses. If you don't, Visual Basic will add them for you.

As you can see in the syntax for the Call statement, the Call keyword is optional. This means that you can code just the name of a procedure to call it, as shown in the first two examples. As a standard coding practice, I recommend that you omit this keyword whenever you call a procedure that's in the same class or module. Otherwise, you should include it. Also, when you call a procedure in the same class or module, I recommend that you include the Me keyword as illustrated by the first two examples. These recommendations make it easier for you to locate the called procedure.

When you code a Call statement, you must be sure to code the arguments in the same sequence that's used by the argument list in the called procedure. What's more, the data types of the passed arguments must be compatible with the data types of the corresponding arguments in the called procedure. In fact, it's a good coding practice to pass arguments that have the *same* data types as the arguments in the called procedure. Note, however, that the argument names that are passed don't have to be the same as those in the called procedure.

[handwritten: GGN'L PROC vs. FUNC PROC = RET.VAR. ASSOC W/NAME OF PROC.]

The basic syntax of the Sub statement

[handwritten arrow →]

```
[Private|Public] Sub subname[(argumentlist)]
    statements
End Sub
```

A Sub statement that requires no arguments

```
Private Sub ValidateUserEntries()
```

A Sub statement that requires four arguments

```
Private Sub CalculateFutureValue(ByVal Months As Integer, _
        ByVal InterestRate As Decimal, _
        ByVal MonthlyInvestment As Decimal, _
        ByRef FutureValue As Decimal)
```

The syntax of the Call statement

[handwritten: OLD →]

```
[Call] subname[(argumentlist)]
```
[handwritten: → NEW   SUBNAME (...) OR SUBNAME...]

A Call statement that calls a procedure in the same class or module with no arguments

```
Me.ValidateUserEntries()
```

A Call statement that passes four arguments

```
Me.CalculateFutureValue(iMonths, dInterestRate, _
    dMonthlyInvestment, dFutureValue)
```

A Call statement that calls a procedure in another module

```
Call CalculateFutureValue(iMonths, dInterestRate, _
    dMonthlyInvestment, dFutureValue)
```

Description

- A *Sub procedure* is one kind of *general procedure*, which is a procedure that is called from an event procedure or from another general procedure. To define a Sub procedure, you use the Sub statement.

- A Sub procedure can define a list of arguments in parentheses that must be passed to it. To code two or more arguments in this list, separate them with commas.

- To *call* a Sub procedure, you can omit the optional Call keyword and code just the name of the procedure.

- When you call a procedure, the arguments must be in the sequence of the argument list in the Sub procedure with compatible data types. However, the names of the passed arguments don't have to be the same as those in the argument list of the called procedure.

Coding recommendations for Call statements

[handwritten: SUB IN SAME CLASS/MOD, USE "ME." INST OF "CALL"]

- When the Sub procedure is in the same class or module as the Call statement, omit the Call keyword and code Me, dot, and the procedure name to indicate that.

- When the Sub procedure is in another class or module, code the Call keyword followed by the procedure name.

Naming recommendation for Sub procedures

- Start the name of each Sub procedure with a verb and indicate what the procedure does.

Figure 5-1   How to code and call a Sub procedure

When and how to pass arguments by reference and value

When you define the arguments for a procedure, you must specify whether each argument is passed *by value* or *by reference*. To do that, you use the syntax shown in figure 5-2.

By default, an argument is passed by value, which means that the value of the variable is passed to the Sub procedure. Then, the Sub procedure can change the value of the variable that receives the argument without changing the value of the variable in the calling procedure. In fact, the Sub procedure can't change the value of the variable in the calling procedure.

If you want to change the variable in the calling procedure, though, you can pass an argument by reference. Then, the address of the variable is passed to the Sub procedure rather than the value of the variable. In that case, the Sub procedure changes the variable in the calling procedure whenever it changes the value of the variable that receives the argument.

If you look at the Sub procedure in this figure, you can see that the first three arguments are passed by value, but the fourth is passed by reference. As a result, when the Sub procedure changes the fourth argument (FutureValue), the variable in the calling procedure (dFutureValue) is also changed.

[Handwritten annotations:]

VAL BY DEFAULT

COPY SENT

IF CALLING PROC PARA IN (),
LIKE MYSUB B,(A) → WILL ALWAYS
GET BYVAL

SET OF PARAMETERS (W/TYPE) = SIGNATURE

PRIU OVERLOADS SUB MYSUB (A INT, B INT) → CALL X.MYSUB B, C SUB.NET
                          " (A INT')   X.MYSUB B   KNOWS
  - IF SIG NOT SAME = ERROR (A STRING VS A INT)   B4 SUB.

VB6 → OPTIONAL BY REF Y AS INT → IF IS MISSING Y

* OVERLOADS SHOW IN INTELLISENSE (1 OF 2). RT CLICK + GOTO DEF
                                           TAKES YOU TO ORIG.
                                           EXAMPLE IS MSGBOX.

The syntax of the arguments in an argument list

```
[ByVal|ByRef] variablename As type
```

A Sub procedure named CalculateFutureValue that requires four arguments

```
Private Sub CalculateFutureValue(ByVal Months As Integer, _
        ByVal InterestRate As Decimal, _
        ByVal MonthlyInvestment As Decimal, _
        ByRef FutureValue As Decimal)
    Dim iIndex As Integer
    For iIndex = 1 to Months
        FutureValue = (FutureValue + MonthlyInvestment) * (1 + InterestRate)
    Next iIndex
End Sub
```

A Call statement that calls the CalculateFutureValue procedure

```
Me.CalculateFutureValue(iMonths, dInterestRate, _
    dMonthlyInvestment, dFutureValue)
lblFutureValue.Text = dFutureValue
```

Description

- Each argument can be passed to a Sub procedure *by value* or *by reference*.
- If you pass an argument by value, the value of the variable in the calling procedure can't be changed by the called procedure. That's because the value of the variable is passed, not the variable itself.
- If you pass an argument by reference and the called procedure changes the value of the argument, the value of the variable in the calling procedure is changed. That's because the passed argument provides a reference that points to the variable in the calling procedure.
- If you omit the ByVal and ByRef keywords, ByVal is the default.

*[handwritten: IN OO PROG, PROC NOTHING MORE THAN METHOD → ME.SUB1 *]*

[handwritten: PUB VARS SHOULD HAVE PLACEHOLDER (MYCLASS 2.Y) OR ME.2Y — SHOULD LOOK LIKE PROP OF OBJ — PRIVATE NOT]

Figure 5-2   When and how to pass arguments by reference and by value

*[handwritten: * M.S. WANTS US TO GIVE UP PROC & FUNCT.]*

How to code and call a function

Figure 5-3 presents the syntax for coding and calling a *Function procedure*, or just *function*. The main difference between a Sub procedure and a function is that a function always returns a value to the calling procedure. To specify the type of data to be returned, you include the As clause in the Function statement.

The function shown in this figure requires three arguments and returns the future value of an investment. As you can see, the code that calls the function is within an assignment statement, so the value returned by the function is assigned to the text property of the FutureValue label.

Although it's not obvious in this figure, you actually use the Call statement to call a function, just as you do to call a Sub procedure. However, the only time you include the Call keyword to call a function is when you don't want to use the value that the function returns…a rare situation. As a result, you routinely call a function by coding it in an assignment statement, as shown in this figure.

If you compare this function with the Sub procedure in figure 5-2, you can see how similar the coding is. In fact, both the function and the procedure accomplish the same purpose. In general, though, you should use a function when you need a value returned, and you should use a Sub procedure when you don't.

One way to return the value of the function is to code the function name, an equals sign, and an expression, as shown by the function in this figure. When you code the function name, though, be sure to code it without parentheses. That way, it refers to the function's return value and not the function itself.

The other way to return a value from a function is to use the Return statement followed by an expression. In the function in this figure, for example, you could code a statement like this

```
Return dFutureValue
```

in place of the last assignment statement

```
FutureValue = dFutureValue
```

The benefit of coding the Return statement is that it ends the function when it is executed. As a result, it can be coded anywhere in the procedure.

When you call a function, the argument names that you pass don't have to be the same as those used in the function. However, you do have to code the arguments in the same sequence that's used by the argument list in the function, and you have to check that the data types match up. As with a Sub procedure, the passed arguments must have data types that are compatible with the data types of the corresponding arguments in the function. In addition, the variable that the returned value is assigned to must have a data type that's compatible with the data type of the function. In this example, lblFutureValue.Text has the String data type, so it can handle the decimal value that's returned by the FutureValue function. You'll learn more about compatibility between data types later in this chapter.

The basic syntax of the Function statement

```
[Private|Public] Function functionname[(argumentlist)] [As type]
    statements
    {functionname = expression} | {Return expression}
End Function
```

[handwritten: OPT., BUT SHOULDN'T BE]

A function named FutureValue that requires three arguments

```
Private Function FutureValue(ByVal Months As Integer, _
                ByVal InterestRate As Decimal, _
                ByVal MonthlyInvestment As Decimal) _
                As Decimal
    Dim iIndex As Integer
    Dim dFutureValue As Decimal
    For iIndex = 1 To Months
        dFutureValue = (dFutureValue + MonthlyInvestment) _
                * (1 + InterestRate)
    Next iIndex
    FutureValue = dFutureValue
End Function
```

The syntax for calling a function

```
variable = functionname[(argumentlist)]
```

An assignment statement that contains the call to the FutureValue function

```
lblFutureValue.Text = FutureValue(iMonths, _
    dInterestRate, dMonthlyInvestment)
```

Description

- A *Function procedure*, or just *function*, is a general procedure that is similar to a Sub procedure, except that it returns a value.

- To code a function, you use the Function statement. The As keyword in this statement specifies the data type of the value that's returned by the function.

- To return a value to the calling procedure from a function, you can assign a value to the function name or you can code the Return keyword followed by an expression.

- To call a function, you usually code the name of the function as part of an expression in an assignment statement. Then, the function returns its value to the variable you name in the assignment statement.

- Like a general procedure, you can pass arguments to a function either by value or by reference. The default is by value.

Naming recommendation for functions

- The name of each function should indicate the value that it returns to the calling procedure.

[handwritten: — DESCRIPTIVE NAME]

Figure 5-3   How to code and call a function

The Future Value application with a Sub procedure and a function

To illustrate the use of Sub procedures and functions, figure 5-4 shows the Future Value application of the last chapter with a Sub procedure for data validation and a function for calculating future value. By using these called procedures, the code in the Click event procedure for the Calculate button is simplified because it's divided into three procedures. This type of division often makes the code easier to work with.

If you study the code for the Sub procedure named ValidateNumericEntries, you can see that the ValidEntries argument is a Boolean type that is passed by reference. So when this procedure finishes, either a True or False value is returned to the variable named bValidNumericEntries in the calling procedure. Because the default value for a Boolean variable is False, this procedure only has to change it to True if the numeric entries are valid. In practice, a procedure like this is usually coded as a function because it returns a value, but I treated it here as a Sub procedure for illustrative purposes.

If you study the code for the FutureValue function, you can see that a Return statement is used to return the value in the variable named dFutureValue to the calling procedure. In the calling procedure, you can see that the FutureValue call is coded within a FormatCurrency function. As a result, the returned value is formatted before it is assigned to the Text property of the Future Value label.

The Future Value application with a Sub procedure and function

```vb
Public Class Form1
    Inherits System.Windows.Forms.Form

    Private Sub btnCalculate_Click(ByVal sender As System.Object, _
            ByVal e As System.EventArgs) Handles btnCalculate.Click
        Dim iMonths As Integer
        Dim dInterestRate, dMonthlyInvestment As Decimal
        Dim bValidNumericEntries As Boolean

        Me.ValidateNumericEntries(txtMonthlyInvestment.Text, _
            txtYears.Text, txtInterestRate.Text, bValidNumericEntries)
        If bValidNumericEntries Then
            iMonths = txtYears.Text * 12
            dInterestRate = txtInterestRate.Text / 12 / 100
            dMonthlyInvestment = txtMonthlyInvestment.Text
            lblFutureValue.Text = FormatCurrency(FutureValue(iMonths, _
                dInterestRate, dMonthlyInvestment))
            txtMonthlyInvestment.Focus()
        Else
            MessageBox.Show("Invalid data. Please check all entries.", _
                            "Entry error")
            txtMonthlyInvestment.Focus()
        End If
    End Sub

    Private Sub ValidateNumericEntries(ByVal Value1 As String, _
            ByVal Value2 As String, ByVal Value3 As String, _
            ByRef ValidEntries As Boolean)
        If IsNumeric(Value1) And IsNumeric(Value2) And IsNumeric(Value3) Then
            If Value1 > 0 And Value2 > 0 And Value3 > 0 Then
                ValidEntries = True
            End If
        End If
    End Sub

    Private Function FutureValue(ByVal Months As Integer, _
            ByVal InterestRate As Decimal, _
            ByVal MonthlyInvestment As Decimal) As Decimal
        Dim iIndex As Integer, dFutureValue As Decimal
        For iIndex = 1 To Months
            dFutureValue = (dFutureValue + MonthlyInvestment) _
                        * (1 + InterestRate)
        Next iIndex
        Return dFutureValue
    End Function

    Private Sub btnExit_Click(ByVal sender As System.Object, _
            ByVal e As System.EventArgs) Handles btnExit.Click
        Me.Close()
    End Sub

End Class
```

Figure 5-4   The Future Value application when it uses a Sub procedure and a function

How to work with modules and scopes

The procedures that you have written so far have all been associated with a single form class. Within these procedures, all of the variables have had procedure scope. When a procedure or variable can be used by more than one form, however, it sometimes makes sense to code it in a standard module. Then, the procedure or variable can have a broader scope.

How to create and code a module

Besides the form classes that you create for a project, you can create one or more *standard modules*, or just *modules*. A module typically contains procedures and variables that are used by more than one form. In addition, a module can contain a special *Main procedure* that's executed when the application starts.

To create a module, you use the Add New Item dialog box that's shown in figure 5-5. When you complete it, Visual Basic adds the module to the project and generates the Module and End Module statements. Then, you can code variables and procedures between these statements.

As you can see, the module in this figure declares one variable and one Sub procedure. Because the variable is declared with the Public keyword, it can be used by any procedure in any form of the project. Similarly, because the procedure is declared with the Public keyword, it can be called by any procedure in the project. In other words, this variable and procedure have project *scope*.

You can also code variables and procedures within a module using the Private keyword. In that case, they have module scope, which means that they can only be accessed from within the module. Variables can also have other scopes, which you'll learn about next.

The Add New Item dialog box

A module with a public variable and procedure

```
Module modCalculations

    Public n_sErrorTitle As String = "Entry Error"

    Public Sub ValidateNumericEntries(ByVal Value1 As String, _
            ByVal Value2 As String, ByVal Value3 As String, _
            ByRef ValidEntries As Boolean)
        If IsNumeric(Value1) And IsNumeric(Value2) And IsNumeric(Value3) Then
            If Value1 > 0 And Value2 > 0 And Value3 > 0 Then
                ValidEntries = True
            End If
        End If
    End Sub

End Module
```

Description

- A *standard module*, or just *module*, is used to define Sub procedures, functions, and variables that are needed by more than one form in a project. For the forms to access these procedures and variables, they must be defined as Public. A module can also include Private variables and procedures that are only accessible from that module.

- A module is also commonly used to code the start-up procedure that's executed when an application is run, called a *Main procedure*. You'll learn how to code a Main procedure in chapter 10.

- To create a module, select the Project → Add New Item command, and select the Module template from within the Local Project Items folder. Then, enter a name for the module and click Open.

- You declare a module by using the Module statement, which also specifies the name of the module. The declaration ends with the End Module statement. These statements are automatically generated when you create the module.

Figure 5-5   How to create and code a module

How to work with scopes and lifetimes

When you declare a variable, you specify its scope. The scope of a variable determines what code in the application has access to that variable. If a variable is referred to by a statement that is outside of its scope, a syntax error occurs. Figure 5-6 summarizes the four different scopes that a variable can have.

So far, you have only worked with *procedure-level variables*, or *local variables*. These variables are typically coded at the beginning of a procedure and are only available to that procedure.

In contrast, a *block variable* is declared within a block of code, such as a For…Next statement or an If…Then…Else statement. In that case, the variable is available only within the block where it's declared.

If you declare a variable outside of all procedures, it's called a *module-level variable*. These variables are typically coded at the beginning of a class or a module and are available to all of the procedures in that class or module.

The fourth type of scope is namespace scope. When you declare a *namespace variable*, it's available not only to the class or module where it's declared, but to all other procedures in the namespace. Because each project usually has its own namespace, you can think of a namespace variable as a *project variable*.

In addition to scope, each variable has a *lifetime* that determines when the variable exists. In most cases, the expected lifetime of a variable is intuitive because it is so similar to its scope. For example, a procedure-level variable exists while the procedure is executing and a module-level variable exists while the application is executing or the class instance exists. However, there are two types of variables that have lifetimes that are not intuitive.

First, the lifetime of a block variable is the same as for a procedure-level variable, although its scope is only within the block in which it is defined. This means that a block variable exists when the procedure is executing, even though it cannot be referred to except when the block is executing.

Second, the lifetime of a *static* variable is the same as for a module-level variable, although its scope is only within the procedure in which it is defined. This means that a static variable will exist when the application is executing, even though it cannot be referred to except when the procedure is executing. Note that the value of a static variable is retained from one execution of the procedure to another. In contrast, the value of a normal procedure-level variable is reinitialized each time the procedure executes, as you've seen in all the examples in this book so far.

This figure also presents variable declarations within a module that illustrate the coding for various scopes and lifetimes. Although this code isn't functional, it does demonstrate how the declaration keyword and the location of the declaration affect scope and lifetime.

Variable scopes and recommended prefixes for variable names

Scope	Description	Prefix
Procedure	A *procedure-level variable*, or *local variable*, is available only within the procedure where it's declared.	None
Block	A *block variable* is available only within the block of code where it's declared. A block of code is a For…Next, If…End If, or Do…Loop statement.	None
Module	A *module-level variable* is available to all the procedures in the module or class where it's declared. These variables are declared outside of any procedures, usually at the beginning of a module or a class.	m_
Namespace	A *namespace variable* is available to all the procedures in all the classes in the namespace. Since each project is in its own namespace by default, you can usually think of namespace scope as project scope.	n_

How to declare variables of each scope

Scope	Declaration keyword	Location of declaration	Lifetime
Procedure	Dim	Within a procedure but outside a block of code.	While procedure is executing.
Procedure	Static	Within a procedure but outside a block of code.	While application is executing.
Block	Dim	Within a block of code.	While procedure is executing.
Module	Dim or Private	Outside all of the procedures in a module.	While application is executing.
Module	Dim or Private	Outside all of the procedures in a class.	While class is instantiated.
Namespace	Public	Outside all of the procedures in a module or a class.	While application is executing.

Statements that declare variables of each scope

```
Module Module1
    Public n_iNamespace As Integer      'Namespace scope/application lifetime
    Private m_iModule1 As Integer       'Module scope/application lifetime
    Private Sub TestLoop()
        Dim iProcedure As Integer       'Procedure scope/procedure lifetime
        Static iStatic As Integer       'Procedure scope/application lifetime
        For iProcedure = 1 To 10
            Dim iBlock As Integer       'Block scope/procedure lifetime
        Next
    End Sub
End Module
```

Description

- The *scope* of a variable determines what code has access to it. If you try to refer to a variable outside of its scope, you will generate a syntax error.
- The *lifetime* of a variable is the period of time that it's available for use.
- You specify the scope and lifetime of each variable in your application by how and where you declare it.

Figure 5-6   How to work with scopes and lifetimes

The Future Value application with a module

Figure 5-7 presents another version of the code for the Future Value application. This is like the code in figure 5-4, but this time the Sub procedure and function are coded in a module along with a Public variable that has namespace (or project) scope. Although this code isn't completely realistic, it does illustrate the way a module and Public variable can be used.

Because the code is so much like the code in figure 5-4, you can just focus on the highlighted code. As coding standards, the word Call is used to call the procedure in the module and the namespace variable is declared with n_ as its prefix. Also, the Sub procedure and function are declared with the Public keyword so they're available to any class or module in the project.

The benefit of using a module is that its Public variables, procedures, and functions can be used by any of the forms in the project. In addition, the module can be copied into another project so the Public variables and procedures can be used in that project too. This is one way to make variables and procedures available to multiple forms or projects, but you'll learn how to use classes for the same purpose in chapter 6.

- COMPONENTS S/B IN SEP. MODULE,
  EVERYTHING CAN BE IN SAME

- MODULES MAY BE REUSED IN OTHER
  PROJECTS

The code for the Form class

```
Public Class Form1
    Inherits System.Windows.Forms.Form

    Private Sub btnCalculate_Click(ByVal sender As System.Object, _
            ByVal e As System.EventArgs) Handles btnCalculate.Click
        Dim iMonths As Integer
        Dim dInterestRate, dMonthlyInvestment As Decimal
        Dim bValidNumericEntries As Boolean
        Call ValidateNumericEntries(txtMonthlyInvestment.Text, _
            txtYears.Text, txtInterestRate.Text, bValidNumericEntries)
        If bValidNumericEntries Then
            iMonths = txtYears.Text * 12
            dInterestRate = txtInterestRate.Text / 12 / 100
            dMonthlyInvestment = txtMonthlyInvestment.Text
            lblFutureValue.Text = FormatCurrency(FutureValue(iMonths, _
                                    dInterestRate, dMonthlyInvestment))
            txtMonthlyInvestment.Focus()
        Else
            MessageBox.Show("Invalid data. Please check all entries.", _
                        n_sErrorTitle)
            txtMonthlyInvestment.Focus()
        End If
    End Sub

    Private Sub btnExit_Click(ByVal sender As System.Object, _
            ByVal e As System.EventArgs) Handles btnExit.Click
        Me.Close()
    End Sub

End Class
```

The code for the module

```
Module modFutureValue

    Public n_sErrorTitle As String = "Entry error"

    Public Sub ValidateNumericEntries(ByVal Value1 As String, _
            ByVal Value2 As String, ByVal Value3 As String, _
            ByRef ValidEntries As Boolean)
        If IsNumeric(Value1) And IsNumeric(Value2) And IsNumeric(Value3) Then
            If Value1 > 0 And Value2 > 0 And Value3 > 0 Then
                ValidEntries = True
            End If
        End If
    End Sub

    Public Function FutureValue(ByVal Months As Integer, _
            ByVal InterestRate As Decimal, _
            ByVal MonthlyInvestment As Decimal) As Decimal
        Dim iIndex As Integer, dFutureValue As Decimal
        For iIndex = 1 To Months
            dFutureValue = (dFutureValue + MonthlyInvestment) * (1 + InterestRate)
        Next iIndex
        Return dFutureValue
    End Function

End Module
```

Figure 5-7   The Future Value application with a module

How to use structured exception handling

In chapter 4, you learned how to prevent run-time errors caused by invalid data. However, other types of run-time errors can occur. To handle them, you can use Try...Catch...Finally statements, which you'll learn about next. This is referred to as *structured exception handling*.

How to code Try...Catch...Finally statements

When a run-time error occurs during the execution of a program, Visual Basic *throws* an *exception*. Then, if this exception isn't handled by your program, the system displays a dialog box and stops the execution of your code. Since that's not the way a production program should end, your programs need to handle any exceptions that are thrown by its statements.

To implement structured exception handling, you use the Try...Catch... Finally statement that's presented in figure 5-8. This statement lets you *try* a block of code to see if it causes an exception, then *catch* and handle the exceptions.

The example in this figure shows how this statement works. Here, two statements are coded within the Try portion of the statement. One calls the CalculateFutureValue procedure and the other is an assignment statement. Then, if an exception occurs during the execution of the called procedure or the assignment statement, the Catch clause catches and handles it.

In the Catch clause, a variable named eSystem is declared as type Exception. Here, eSystem is a name created by the programmer, and the Exception type is a generic exception class that you can use to get information about any exception. In the next figure, you'll learn about other exception classes.

When an exception is thrown, an Exception object is created from the .NET Exception class. Then, the code in a Catch block can use properties of this object to display information about the error. In this example, the Source and Message properties are used to display the message box shown in this figure.

The Finally clause of this statement contains the code that is executed after the processing in the Try block and any Catch blocks is finished. This means that the code in the Finally block always executes. In the example, the one statement in this block moves the focus to the text box for the monthly investment, which you want to do whether or not an exception is caught.

When you use structured exception handling, you can code more than one Try...Catch...Finally statement. You can also nest these statements. The goal is to catch all exceptions so your applications won't end prematurely.

The basic syntax of the Try...Catch...Finally statement

```
Try
    trystatements
Catch [exception [As exceptionclass]]
    catchstatements...
[Finally
    finallystatements]
End Try
```

A Try...Catch...Finally statement

```
Try
    Me.CalculateFutureValue()
    lblFutureValue.Text = FormatCurrency(dFutureValue)
Catch eSystem As Exception
    MessageBox.Show("An exception has occurred." _
        & ControlChars.CrLf & "Source: " & eSystem.Source _
        & ControlChars.CrLf & "Description: " _
        & eSystem.Message, "Calculate future value")
Finally
    txtMonthlyInvestment.Focus()
End Try
```

The message box displayed by the Catch block in the statement

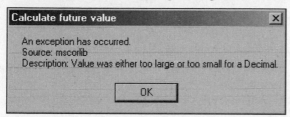

Description

- An *exception* is an error that occurs during the execution of an application. When this happens, your code is said to *throw* an exception. If an exception isn't *caught*, the application stops with a run-time error.

- The Try...Catch...Finally statement lets you catch and handle exceptions. This is known as *structured exception handling*. NO GOTO NOW.

- The Try block contains the code that is to be tested for exceptions, and the Catch blocks contain the code that handles the exceptions. The Finally block contains the code that is executed whether or not an exception occurs.

- If a Try block contains calls to other procedures, the Catch blocks can catch any exceptions that aren't handled by the called procedures.

- When an exception is thrown, an Exception object is created from the .NET Exception class. Then, you can use the properties of the Exception object to get information about the exception. Two of the most useful properties are Source, which gives the source of the exception, and Message, which gives an error message.

WORKS W/CALLS

Figure 5-8   How to code Try...Catch...Finally statements

MSG BOX (EXP. SOURCE. TOPSTRING + CTRCHARS VBCRLF
EXP. TOPSTRING) WILL PRINT REASON + LOC

How to catch specific exception classes

The example in the last figure shows how you can use a single Catch clause to handle any exception that might occur. However, you can also catch specific types of exceptions as shown in figure 5-9.

In the procedure in this figure, you can see a Try…Catch…Finally statement that includes two Catch clauses. The first one catches and handles an overflow exception. This type of exception occurs if the result of an arithmetic operation, like the future value calculation, is too large for the data type it's assigned to. To catch this type of exception, you use the OverflowException class.

The second Catch clause is like the one you saw in the previous figure. Unlike the Catch clause in that figure, the Catch clause in this example won't catch an overflow exception because it's caught by the first Catch clause. However, it will catch any other type of exception that occurs.

This figure also lists some of the other specific exception classes that are available for catching exceptions. Note, however, that you can avoid some of these exceptions by coding your programs carefully. To avoid an InvalidCastException, you can test user entries to make sure they're numeric. And to avoid an OverflowException, you can restrict the range of values the user can enter. Often, though, it's hard to tell when an error will occur so you need to provide structured exception handling for the unexpected exceptions.

An exception-handling routine that checks for a specific exception class

```
If ValidNumericData() Then
    Try
        Me.CalculateFutureValue()
    Catch eOverFlow As OverflowException      'Catch a specific exception
        MessageBox.Show("An overflow exception has occurred.", _
            "Calculate future value")
    Catch eSystem As Exception                'Catch any other exception
        MessageBox.Show("An exception has occurred." _
            & ControlChars.CrLf & "Source: " & eSystem.Source _
            & ControlChars.CrLf & "Description: " _
            & eSystem.Message, "Calculate future value")
    Finally
        txtMonthlyInvestment.Focus()
    End Try
End If
```

Common exception classes in the System namespace

Class	Exception occurs when...
ArgumentException	One of the arguments of a method isn't valid.
DivideByZeroException	A program tries to divide an integer or decimal value by zero.
OverflowException	The result of an arithmetic operation or a conversion is too large for the receiving variable.
FieldAccessException	A program tries to access a private or protected field within a class.
InvalidCastException	A program tries to perform an invalid conversion.
InvalidOperationException	A program tries to a call a method that is invalid.
MemberAccessException	An attempt to access a member of a class fails.
MethodAccessException	A program tries to access a private or protected method within a class.
NullReferenceException	A program tries to remove a reference for a null object.
TypeUnloadException	A program tries to access a class that has not been loaded.

Description

- To catch a specific class of exception, you can name the exception class in the As clause of the Catch clause. Then, the statements in the Catch clause are executed only if that class of exception occurs.

- When you check for specific exceptions, you can include a final Catch clause coded for the Exception class. This will catch any exceptions that aren't specifically handled by the preceding clauses. Otherwise, an exception can occur that isn't handled, which will cause a run-time error.

Figure 5-9   How to catch specific exception classes

How to use the Throw statement ✳

The Throw statement can be used to throw a specific exception from one of the exception classes, which can then be used for testing Try...Catch statements. The Throw statement can also be used to throw new exceptions for error conditions that your procedures detect. These uses are illustrated by the examples in figure 5-10.

In the first example, a Throw statement is used to throw an overflow exception from a FutureValue function. In this case, the name of the exception class is coded as the exception and the message is omitted. This type of statement is useful when you want to test to see whether a Catch block works correctly. The alternative is to try to generate an overflow exception by entering large values for the variables involved in the calculation, which can be time consuming. After you test the Catch block, you remove the Throw statement.

If you omit the message in the parentheses of the Throw statement as in this first example, the default Message property of the exception object is used. If you include a message, though, it replaces the default message. That way, you can display your own message for a specific exception class.

In the second example, two Throw statements are used to throw new exceptions. In both statements, the general Exception class is coded as the exception followed by a specific error message. Then, when the application is run and the exception is thrown, the message in the statement is stored in the Message property of the exception object so it can be displayed by any Catch block that catches it.

Like an exception that's generated by an invalid statement, an exception that's generated by a Throw statement can be handled by the procedure that contains it or by the procedure that calls that procedure. In the examples in this figure, the exceptions need to be handled by the calling procedures since they aren't handled by the procedures that throw them.

ERROR MSG VS THROW — THROW MORE PROFESSIONAL

✳ IF CREATING OWN COMPONENTS, CAN THROW EXCEP. TO BEHAVE LIKE REST OF SYSTEM

The syntax of the Throw statement

```
Throw New exception([message])
```

A procedure that uses a Throw statement to test for an overflow exception

```
Private Function FutureValue(ByVal Months As Integer, _
        ByVal InterestRate As Decimal, _
        ByVal MonthlyInvestment As Decimal) As Decimal
    Dim iIndex As Integer, dFutureValue As Decimal
    For iIndex = 1 To Months
        dFutureValue = (dFutureValue + MonthlyInvestment) _
                    * (1 + InterestRate)
        Throw New OverflowException()
    Next iIndex
    Return dFutureValue
End Function
```

A procedure that uses Throw statements to generate new exceptions

```
Public Sub ValidateNumericEntries(ByVal Value1 As String, _
        ByVal Value2 As String, ByVal Value3 As String, _
        ByRef ValidEntries As Boolean)
    If Not IsNumeric(Value1) Or Not IsNumeric(Value2) _
            Or Not IsNumeric(Value3) Then
        Throw New Exception("All entries must be numeric.")
    Else
        If Value1 <= 0 Or Value2 <= 0 Or Value3 <= 0 Then
            Throw New Exception("All entries must be greater than zero.")
            ValidEntries = True
        End If
    End If
End Sub
```

Description

- The Throw statement throws an exception. You can use the Throw statement to test the structured exception handling code in your application or to generate new types of exceptions.

- To throw a specific exception, you create a new object for that exception class. To throw a general exception, you create a new Exception object.

- If you code a message in the Throw statement, it's substituted for the Message property of the exception object. Otherwise, the Message property is set to the default for the exception class.

- The Source property of the exception object is set to the name of the project.

- An exception can be handled by the procedure that throws it or by the procedure that calls it.

Figure 5-10   How to use the Throw statement

The Future Value application with structured exception handling

To give you a better idea of how structured exception handling works, figure 5-11 presents another version of the code for the Future Value application. This time, a Try...Catch...Finally statement is used to catch all types of errors including invalid user entries. Also, to test one of the Catch blocks, a Throw statement is used in the FutureValue function to throw an OverflowException.

In the btnCalculate_Click procedure, you can see that four statements are included in the Try block. Then, the first Catch block catches an InvalidCastException, which occurs when the user enters invalid numeric data. The second Catch block catches the OverflowException, which occurs when the user enters large values that cause the future value to become so large that it won't fit in the Decimal type. And the third Catch block catches any other exception class. In the Finally block, the focus is moved to the text box for the monthly investment entry, which should be done whether or not an exception occurs.

Because the FutureValue function includes a Throw statement for an OverflowException, that exception will occur each time the function is called. So after you've tested the Catch block for that exception, you can remove the Throw statement.

In practice, you usually don't use structured exception handling as a replacement for data validation the way this example does. Instead, you use data validation to test for conditions like numeric and range validity. But you use structured exception handling to catch any unexpected errors that aren't prevented by the data validation routines.

The Future Value application with structured exception handling

```vbnet
Public Class Form1
    Inherits System.Windows.Forms.Form

    Private Sub btnCalculate_Click(ByVal sender As System.Object, _
            ByVal e As System.EventArgs) Handles btnCalculate.Click

        Dim iMonths As Integer
        Dim dInterestRate As Decimal
        Dim dMonthlyInvestment As Decimal

        Try
            iMonths = txtYears.Text * 12
            dInterestRate = txtInterestRate.Text / 12 / 100
            dMonthlyInvestment = txtMonthlyInvestment.Text
            lblFutureValue.Text = FormatCurrency(FutureValue(iMonths, _
                dInterestRate, dmonthlyinvestment))
        Catch eCast As InvalidCastException
            MessageBox.Show("Invalid data. Please check all entries.", _
                "Entry error")
        Catch eOverFlow As OverflowException
            MessageBox.Show("An overflow exception has occurred.", _
                "Entry error")
        Catch eSystem As Exception
            MessageBox.Show("An exception has occurred." _
                & ControlChars.CrLf & "Source: " & eSystem.Source _
                & ControlChars.CrLf & "Description: " _
                & eSystem.Message, _
                "General error")
        Finally
            txtMonthlyInvestment.Focus()
        End Try

    End Sub

    Private Function FutureValue(ByVal Months As Integer, _
            ByVal InterestRate As Decimal, _
            ByVal MonthlyInvestment As Decimal) _
            As Decimal
        Dim iIndex As Integer
        Dim dFutureValue As Decimal
        For iIndex = 1 To Months
            dFutureValue = (dFutureValue + MonthlyInvestment) _
                        * (1 + InterestRate)
        Next iIndex
        Throw New OverflowException()
        Return dFutureValue
    End Function

    Private Sub btnExit_Click(ByVal sender As System.Object, _
            ByVal e As System.EventArgs) Handles btnExit.Click
        Me.Close()
    End Sub

End Class
```

Figure 5-11   The Future Value application with structured exception handling

How to use structures and classes to work with data types

To complete your understanding of the many ways that Visual Basic helps you perform operations, this topic introduces you to the structures and classes that you can use for working with data types. As you will see, the Visual Basic data types are something more than what they at first seem to be.

The .NET structures and classes that define data types

Each Visual Basic data type is supported by a *structure* or class in the .NET Framework as summarized in figure 5-12. For instance, the Visual Basic Decimal data type is supported by the .NET Decimal structure. The Visual Basic Short data type is supported by the .NET Int16 structure. And the Visual Basic String data type is supported by the String class.

When you declare a variable as one of the Visual Basic data types that's supported by a structure, that structure is a *value type*. Then, the value type holds the data of the variable. If, for example, you declare a variable as a Decimal data type, that variable actually holds the decimal value.

In contrast, when you declare a variable as one of the Visual Basic data types that's supported by a class, an object is created from the class. Then, the variable contains a reference to the object, not the object itself. Because of that, object data types are called *reference types*.

The two reference types defined by the .NET Framework are Object and String. So when you declare a variable as a String data type, that variable actually holds a reference to a String object, which contains the data for the string. And when you declare a variable as an Object data type, that variable actually holds a reference to a generic object. Since the Object class is the base class for all other objects, that means an Object data type can hold a reference to any Visual Basic object.

Most of the time, you can work with the Visual Basic data types without knowing about the underlying .NET structure or class. However, all of the data structures and data classes provide properties and methods that you can use to work with the data. You'll learn about the some of these in figure 5-14. But first you need to know more about data type conversion.

- ELEMENTS IN STRUCTURE WILL BE PUBLIC
  BY DEF. IF "DIM"-ED.

- STRONG DATATYPES NOT AS FORGIVING AS TYPES
  IN VB6

— REMEMBER, OPTION STRICT!

.NET structures that define data types

Structure name	VB data type	What the value type holds
Byte	Byte	An 8-bit unsigned integer
Int16	Short	A 16-bit signed integer
Int32	Integer	A 32-bit signed integer
Int64	Long	A 64-bit signed integer
Single	Single	A single-precision floating-point number
Double	Double	A double-precision floating-point number
Boolean	Boolean	A True or False value
Char	Char	A single character
Decimal	Decimal	A 96-bit decimal value
DateTime	Date	A 64-bit signed integer that represents the number of *ticks* (100-nanosecond units) that have elapsed since 12:00 AM, January 1, 0001

TYPICALLY DEFINED SIZE

.NET classes that define data types

Class name	VB data type	What the reference type holds
Object	Object	A pointer to any type of object
String	String	A pointer to a string object

OBJECTS (ARRAY, TOO)

Description

- Each Visual Basic data type is supported by a structure or a class within the .NET Framework. When you refer to a Visual Basic data type, you're actually using an alias for the associated structure or class.

- A *structure* defines a *value type*, which holds its own data. A class defines a *reference type*, which holds a pointer to the object that holds the data.

- Like a class, a structure has properties and methods. You can use the public properties and methods of a structure to work with variables. And, you can use the shared properties and methods of a structure to perform operations directly from the structure.

— VAL TYPE CAN BE SENT BY REF OR BY VAL

— BEWARE CONVERSION OF ARRAYS FROM VB 6 TO .NET! (.NET 0 BASED ONLY)

Figure 5-12   The .NET structures and classes that define data types

— IMPORTS VISUAL BASIC 6 - POSS, IN .NET

How data type conversion works

As you learned in chapter 3, when you convert data from one data type to another, it is called *casting*. In many cases, Visual Basic does this casting automatically. If, for example, you assign the value of a numeric variable to the Text property of a text box, Visual Basic casts the value to a string. And if you assign the value of an Integer data type to a Decimal data type, Visual Basic casts the integer value to a decimal value.

Figure 5-13 lists the conversions that Visual Basic always does automatically. These are called *widening conversions* because the receiving variable is always wider than the original variable. Because of that, the receiving variable will always be able to hold the value assigned to it.

In contrast, a conversion that's done in the opposite direction is called a *narrowing conversion*. With this type of conversion, the receiving variable may not be wide enough to hold the value of the original variable. When that happens, an InvalidCastException is thrown. Because of that, you should use a narrowing conversion only when you're sure that the receiving variable can hold the value.

In the examples of narrowing conversions, the first three may throw casting exceptions. The fourth example, however, won't throw an exception. That's because the Round function is used to round a Decimal data type before it's assigned to an Integer data type.

By default, Visual Basic can perform both widening and narrowing conversions *implicitly*. That's because the *permissive type semantics* option is on. This means that casting takes place automatically when you assign a variable of one data type equal to a variable of another data type.

However, if this option is set to *strict type semantics*, you have to perform narrowing conversions *explicitly*. To do that, you can use the .NET methods or Visual Basic functions that you'll learn about next. Note that these methods and functions don't stop exceptions from being thrown when a conversion can't be done. They just specify what type of conversion is to be performed.

To change the semantics option, you change the Option Strict property of the project as explained in this figure. Whether or not this option is on, though, you need to be aware of what's happening when you cast a variable from one data type to another. And whenever a casting exception can occur, you need to provide code that prevents it from ending your program.

Widening conversions

[handwritten: NOT AUTO WITH CONV. FROM VB6!]

From this data type	To these data types
Byte	Short, Integer, Long, Decimal, Single, Double
Short	Integer, Long, Decimal, Single, Double
Integer	Long, Decimal, Single, Double
Long	Decimal, Single, Double
Decimal	Single, Double
Single	Double
Double	None
Char	String
Any	Object, String

[handwritten box: ONLY SENDING SPEC. TYPES WHEN SEND PARA TO METH - ELSE SIG. MISMATCH]

Widening conversions that are done implicitly

```
txtInvoiceTotal.Text = dInvoiceTotal
dLength = iLength
sLength = dLength
```

Narrowing conversions that are done implicitly

```
dOrderTotal = txtOrderTotal.Text     'May throw an exception
iLength = dLength                    'May throw an exception
iLength = sNumber                    'May throw an exception
iLength = Math.Round(dLength)        'Won't throw an exception
```

Description

- *Casting* refers to the process of converting an expression from one data type to another.
- A *widening conversion* is one that casts data from a data type with a narrower range of possible values to a data type with a wider range of possible values.
- A *narrowing conversion* is one that casts data from a wider data type to a narrower data type. Because the new data type may not be able to hold the original data, this may throw a casting exception.
- To cast data *implicitly*, you code assignment statements as shown above. To cast data *explicitly*, you can use methods or functions as shown in the next figure. Whether you do a cast implicitly or explicitly, a casting exception will occur if the cast can't be done.
- By default, a project allows implicit narrowing conversions. This is referred to as *permissive type semantics*. If you change this default to *strict type semantics*, all narrowing conversions must be done explicitly.

How to change from permissive to strict type semantics

- Right-click on your project and select Properties. Then, click on the Build page within the Common Properties folder and set the Option Strict property to On.

Figure 5-13   How data type conversion works

*[handwritten: * EXPLICIT SAFER]*

How to use shared methods and functions to convert data

Figure 5-14 presents three ways you can explicitly convert data from one type to another. First, you can use the ToString and Parse methods with any of the data structures defined by the .NET Framework. Second, you can use the shared methods for specific data structures like the ones shown for the Decimal structure. Third, you can use Visual Basic functions.

You can use the ToString method to convert any data type to a string. If you include a formatting argument in parentheses, you can format the string as the cast takes place. The second statement in the first group of examples shows how this works. Here, the ToString method of a Decimal variable is used to cast the decimal value defined in the first statement to a string value. Because the "n" formatting code is specified, the number is formatted with a comma and two decimal places. Otherwise, the string wouldn't have a comma and it would have as many decimal places as the decimal value had. You'll learn more about the formatting codes you can use with strings in chapter 11.

The Parse method performs the reverse operation. It converts a string value to another data type as illustrated by the third statement in the first group of examples. Here, the Parse method of the Decimal structure is used to cast a string variable to a decimal value. Note, however, that this method only recognizes standard numeric characters. A decimal string, for example, can include only a sign, commas, digits, and a decimal point. If it includes any other characters, like a dollar sign or a percent sign, an exception will be thrown.

As this figure shows, the Decimal structure has shared methods for data conversion in addition to the Parse method. To convert a decimal to an integer, for example, you can use a statement like the fourth one in the first group of examples. Notice that this conversion causes any decimal digits to be dropped.

Although this figure only shows four of the shared methods for the Decimal structure, there is one for converting a Decimal data type to every other numeric data type. There are also shared methods for each of the other structures that let you convert that structure to other data types. Besides that, there are shared methods in the Convert class that let you convert any data type to any other data type. These methods should provide all the capabilities that you need.

Nevertheless, Visual Basic also provides functions for data conversion like the ones in this figure. You can use these functions to convert an expression to any of the Visual Basic data types. Here, you can see some of the functions you're most likely to use, but there is one for every data type if you need it.

The second statement in the second group of examples shows how the CDec function can be used to convert a string that contains a number with currency formatting to a decimal. Unlike the Parse method, the string value can include characters like dollar signs and percent signs, which are removed when the conversions are performed. In the third statement, you can see how the CType function can be used to convert an expression to any data type. In this case, a decimal is converted to an integer. In contrast to the conversion that uses the ToInt32 method of the Decimal class, this conversion gives a rounded result.

Methods for data conversion that are included in all the data structures

Method	Description
ToString([formatString])	A public method that converts the value to its equivalent string representation using the specified format. If the format is omitted, the value isn't formatted.
Parse(string)	A shared method that converts the specified string to an equivalent data value.

Some of the shared methods of the Decimal structure for data conversion

Method	Description
ToDouble(value)	Converts the decimal to the Double data type.
ToInt32(value)	Converts the decimal to the Integer data type.
ToInt64(value)	Converts the decimal to the Long data type.
ToSingle(value)	Converts the decimal to the Single data type.

Conversion statements that use shared methods

Statement	Result
`Dim dSales As Decimal = 2574.98`	2574.98
`Dim sSales As String = dSales.ToString("n")`	2,574.98
`dSales = Decimal.Parse(sSales)`	2574.98
`Dim iSales As Integer = Decimal.ToInt32(dSales)`	2574

Some of the Visual Basic functions for data conversion

Function	Description
CDate(expression)	Converts the expression to the Date data type.
CDbl(expression)	Converts the expression to the Double data type.
CDec(expression)	Converts the expression to the Decimal data type.
CInt(expression)	Converts the expression to the Integer data type.
CLng(expression)	Converts the expression to the Long data type.
CStr(expression)	Converts the expression to the String data type.
CType(expression, typeName)	Converts the expression to the specified type.

Conversion statements that use Visual Basic functions

Statement	Result
`Dim sSales As String = "$2,574.98"`	$2,574.98
`Dim dSales As Decimal = CDec(sSales)`	2574.98
`Dim iSales As Integer = CType(dSales, Integer)`	2575

Description

- The ToString and Parse methods are included in all of the data structures.

- There are shared methods for each of the structures as well as shared methods in a Convert class. These methods provide two different ways to do data conversion.

- The Visual Basic functions for data conversion provide the same basic functionality as the methods of the Convert class. However, the Visual Basic functions are easier to code.

Figure 5-14   How to use shared methods and functions to convert data

Three more coding skills

The last topics in this section present three more coding skills. First, you'll learn how to use another function. Second, you'll learn how to use object variables and the For Each statement to work with the controls on a form. Third, you'll learn how to use the With statement. Yes, this is a random collection of skills, but they round out the essentials of the Visual Basic language.

How to use the FV function

Earlier in this chapter, you learned how to create a function for calculating the future value of an investment. But now, you should know that Visual Basic provides a similar function named FV so you didn't really need to code your own. In figure 5-15, you can see the syntax of this function and examples of how it can be used. Note that it provides for five arguments.

The first three arguments are required. These arguments provide the interest rate (rate), the number of periodic payments (numperiods), and the amount of each payment (payment). When you pass these arguments, you must be sure that all three are based on the same time period, like years or months. If, for example, the payment amount represents monthly payments, the other two arguments have to represent the monthly interest rate and the number of months. Curiously, the amount of the payment must be entered as a negative value if you want this function to return a positive result.

The fourth argument lets you specify the present value of an investment. If, for example, you already have money in the investment account you'll be contributing to, you provide that amount as the present value of the investment. Like the payment amount, this amount must be entered as a negative value.

The last argument lets you specify whether the periodic payments will be made at the beginning of each period or at the end of each period. You indicate the value of this argument by using one of the constants in the DueDate enumeration shown in this figure. If omitted, DueDate.EndOfPeriod is used as the default.

Because you've already learned how to write a future value application of your own, you should have a pretty good idea of how the FV function works. To use this function or any other function, though, you don't need to know how it works. You just need to know what arguments to pass to it, and you can use the help information for the function to find that out.

Unfortunately, the help information for some functions is so confusing that you have to experiment before you get the functions to work right. For instance, this FV function can also be used to calculate the future value of a loan. In that case, you enter the third and fourth arguments as positive values. But how and why it works that way is hard to figure out from the help information.

The syntax of the FV function

```
FV(rate, numperiods, payment[, PV][, Due])
```

The constants in the DueDate enumeration

Constant	Description
EndOfPeriod	The periodic payment is made at the end of each period.
BeginOfPeriod	The periodic payment is made at the beginning of each period.

A statement that calculates the future value of a monthly investment

```
lblFutureValue.Text = _
    FormatNumber(FV(dInterestRate, iMonths, -txtMonthlyInvestment.Text, , _
        DueDate.BegOfPeriod))
```

A statement that calculates the future value of a monthly loan payment

```
lblFutureValue.Text = _
    FormatNumber(FV(dInterestRate, iMonths, txtMonthlyPayment.Text))
```

Description

- You use the FV function to calculate the future value of an annuity based on fixed, periodic payments and a fixed interest rate. An annuity can be a loan or an investment.

- For the calculation to work properly, you must base each of the first three arguments (interest rate, number of periods, and periodic payment) on the same time period (months, years, etc.).

- If the payment is money that you pay out, such as deposits to an investment, you should specify it as a negative number, which will return a positive result. For a loan, you should specify the payment as a positive number.

- The PV argument specifies the present value of the annuity (negative for cash already paid out; positive for cash already received). If you omit this argument, the default is zero.

- The Due argument indicates whether the payments will be made at the beginning or the end of each period. To do this, you use the constants in the DueDate enumeration, which are either DueDate.BegOfPeriod or DueDate.EndOfPeriod. The default is EndOfPeriod.

Figure 5-15   How to use the Visual Basic FV function

How to code With statements

The With statement doesn't provide any new capabilities. Its purpose is to let you write code without repeating the name of a specific object. This can save you some typing, and it can make your code easier to read.

In figure 5-16, you can see the syntax for this statement and two coding examples. The first example shows four statements that set three properties and use a method. In this case, the object name (txtMonthlyInvestment) is repeated in all four lines of code. In contrast, the second example shows how this duplication of the object name can be eliminated by using the With statement.

```
Inst. of MYSTRUCTURE.A, MYSTRUCTURE.B
                    ↓
WITH MYSTRUCTURE
    .A
    .B
END WITH
```

The syntax of the With statement

```
With object
    statements
End With
```

Four lines of code without a With statement

```
txtMonthlyInvestment.ReadOnly = False
txtMonthlyInvestment.TabStop = True
txtMonthlyInvestment.ForeColor = Color.Red
txtMonthlyInvestment.Focus()
```

The same code with a With statement

```
With txtMonthlyInvestment
    .ReadOnly = False
    .TabStop = True
    .ForeColor = Color.Red
    .Focus()
End With
```

Description

* The With statement lets you refer to an object more than once without repeating its name each time.
* After you code the name of the object on the With statement, you can omit the object name from any reference to that object between the With and End With statements.

Figure 5-16   How to use the With statement

How to use object variables and the For Each...Next statement

Earlier in this chapter, you learned that two of the primitive data types, Object and String, are based on .NET classes with the same names. Besides that, you can use *object variables* to work with objects created from any of the other .NET classes. Figure 5-17 shows how.

To declare an object variable, you specify the name of a class rather than a data type on the As clause of the declaration statement. Then, you can assign an object to that variable just as you would assign a value to a variable that holds data. Keep in mind, though, that an object variable can only refer to an object with the declared type or an object that's derived from that type. If, for example, an object variable is declared with the TextBox type, it can refer only to a text box object. But if an object variable is declared with the Control type, it can refer to any type of control because all of the control types are derived from the Control class.

Many of the objects you work with in a project are stored in *collections*. For example, each control that you add to a form is stored in a collection of controls for the form. Then, to work with this type of object collection, you can use the For Each...Next statement presented in this figure. This statement loops through the objects in a collection and executes the specified code for each object.

Visual Basic also provides two conditional expressions specifically for working with object variables. You can use a TypeOf...Is expression to test whether an object variable refers to a specific type of object. And you can use the Is expression to test if two object variables refer to the same object.

The two examples in this figure show how these expressions and the For Each...Next statement work. In the first example, a For Each...Next statement is used to loop through the controls on a form. To do that, it declares an object variable with the generic Control type. Then, it uses that variable in the For Each...Next statement to refer to each control in the collection of controls for the form. To refer to that collection, it uses the Controls property of the form. Within the For Each...Next loop, it uses a TypeOf...Is expression to check if the current control is a text box. If it is, a With...End With block is declared using that control. Within this block, three properties are modified. If the control is not a text box, however, the loop continues with the next control.

The second example illustrates the use of the Is expression. It starts by declaring two object variables. Later on (as indicated by the two dots), an If statement tests whether the two object variables refer to the same text box and displays an appropriate message depending on the result of that comparison. Although this example is unrealistic, it should help you understand how you can use the Is expression to work with object variables.

As you study these examples, remember that an object variable is a reference type variable. That means that it points to an object. So in the first example, ctlControl points to each of the objects in the controls collection as the loop is executed. And in the second example, either of the TextBox variables could be assigned a reference to a different object during the execution of the program.

The syntax for declaring an object variable ← PLACEHOLDER FOR OBJ, NOT INSTANT.

```
{Dim|Private|Public|Static} variablename As classname
```

The syntax of the For Each...Next statement for working with the objects in a collection

```
For Each object In collection
    statements
Next [object]
```

Conditional expressions for working with object variables

Expression	Description
TypeOf...Is	Determines whether an object variable refers to an object of a specified type.
Is	Determines whether two object variables refer to the same object.

A loop that changes all of the text boxes on a form

```
Dim ctlControl As Control
For Each ctlControl In Me.Controls
    If TypeOf ctlControl Is TextBox Then
        With ctlControl
            .ReadOnly = False
            .TabStop = True
            .ForeColor = Color.Red
        End With
    End If
Next
```

Code that checks if two variables refer to the same text box

```
Dim txtEntry1 As TextBox = txtMonthlyInvestment
Dim txtEntry2 As TextBox = txtInterestRate
    .
    .
    .
If txtEntry1 Is txtEntry2 Then
    MessageBox.Show("Variables refer to the same control")
Else
    MessageBox.Show("Variables refer to different controls")
End If
```

Description

- An *object variable* is a reference type that points to an object. You can define an object variable for any .NET class that lets you create objects from it.

- You can use a For Each...Next loop to repeat a series of statements for each object in a *collection* of objects.

- The Controls property of a form refers to the controls collection of the form. Each control that you add to a form is automatically included in this collection.

- You can use the TypeOf and Is keywords within conditional expressions that evaluate object variables. For example, you can use the TypeOf keyword to determine if a control is a specific type, such as a text box. And you can use the Is keyword to determine if two text box variables refer to the same control.

Figure 5-17   How to use object variables and the For Each...Next statement

One more version of the Future Value application

To show how the last three skills can be used, figure 5-18 presents yet another version of the code for the Future Value application. This time, the code makes use of a function named ValidNumericData and a Sub procedure named CalculateFutureValue. By now, you should be getting comfortable with Visual Basic code so you should be able to read and understand code like this with little or no help. Nevertheless, some highlights follow.

To start, the btnCalculate_Click procedure calls the ValidNumericData function from an If statement. Then, if the function returns a True value, the Click procedure calls the CalculateFutureValue procedure and moves the focus to the text box for the monthly investment entry. Otherwise, it displays an error message. That's all there is to this Click procedure.

If you look at the Call statements for the function and Sub procedure, though, you can see that no arguments are passed. Instead, the function and Sub procedure work directly with the text box controls. This is possible because all of the controls on a form are available to all of the procedures for a form. Scope isn't an issue the way it is with variables.

In the ValidNumericData function, you can see how the For Each statement is used with the collection of controls on the form. For each control that is a text box, the Text property is tested to see if it's numeric. If it is, the value of the property is rounded to two decimal places, and the foreground color (the text itself) is set to black by using the Black constant in the Color enumeration. Note that the CDec function is coded to convert the Text property from a string value to a decimal value. That's because the Round method can be used only with a decimal or double value. If the value isn't numeric, the foreground color is set to red to highlight the entry error. Then, the focus is moved to the text box, and the return value of the function is set to False. The With statement in this function just shortens the code in the If statement that it contains.

In the CalculateFutureValue procedure, you can see that the FV function is used for the calculation instead of a For...Next loop. In the arguments for the FV function, the periodic payment is specified as a negative value so the future value will be positive. Also, the DueDate.BegOfPeriod constant is used to specify that the payments will be made at the beginning of each period. Note that the FV function is coded within the FormatCurrency function, which is assigned to the Future Value label on the form.

You have now seen four different versions of the code for the Future Value application in this chapter and one in the last chapter. The point is not only to illustrate the essential coding skills that a Visual Basic programmer must have, but also to show the many different ways that Visual Basic provides for getting the same results.

The code for the Form class

```
Public Class Form1
    Inherits System.Windows.Forms.Form

    Private Sub btnCalculate_Click(ByVal sender As System.Object, _
            ByVal e As System.EventArgs) Handles btnCalculate.Click
        If ValidNumericData() Then
            Me.CalculateFutureValue()
            txtMonthlyInvestment.Focus()
        Else
            MessageBox.Show("Invalid data. Please check red entries.", _
                            "Entry error")
        End If
    End Sub

    Public Function ValidNumericData() As Boolean
        Dim ctlControl As Control
        ValidNumericData = True
        For Each ctlControl In Me.Controls
            If TypeOf ctlControl Is TextBox Then
                With ctlControl
                    If IsNumeric(.Text) Then
                        .Text = Math.Round(CDec(.Text), 2)
                        .ForeColor = Color.Black
                    Else
                        .ForeColor = Color.Red
                        .Focus()
                        ValidNumericData = False
                    End If
                End With
            End If
        Next
    End Function

    Public Sub CalculateFutureValue()
        lblFutureValue.Text = _
            FormatCurrency(FV(txtInterestRate.Text / 12 / 100, _
            txtYears.Text * 12, -txtMonthlyInvestment.Text, , _
            DueDate.BegOfPeriod))
    End Sub

    Private Sub btnExit_Click(ByVal sender As Object, _
            ByVal e As System.EventArgs) Handles btnExit.Click
        Me.Close()
    End Sub

End Class
```

Figure 5-18   One more version of the Future Value application

Perspective

At this point, you have been introduced to the essential concepts and skills of the Visual Basic language. That means you should know how to code variable and constant declarations as well as statements like assignment, If, For...Next, For Each, and With statements. That also means that you should know how to use .NET classes, objects, properties, methods, shared members, functions, enumerations, and even structures.

After just three language chapters, that's a lot. But Visual Basic offers a lot, and therefore asks a lot. At this point, you can't be expected to remember the coding details for all of the Visual Basic features, but you should understand how the features work and how they work together. In other words, you should have the big picture. You should also be able to write the code that an application requires by referring to the figures and examples in these chapters.

Summary

- *Sub procedures* and *functions* are *general procedures* that can be called from event procedures or from other general procedures. A function returns a value, but a Sub procedure does not.

- When variables are passed to a general procedure *by value*, they can't be changed by the called procedure. When they're passed *by reference*, they can be changed.

- *Modules* can be used for the variables, Sub procedures, and functions that should be available to all of the procedures in a project.

- A variable's *scope* determines which portions of code can access it, and its *lifetime* determines when it is available. You specify the scope of each variable by where you declare it and the keyword you use to declare it.

- You can use *structured exception handling* to handle the *exceptions* that are *thrown* while your program executes.

- The Visual Basic data types are based on the *structures* and *classes* of the .NET Framework. A structure defines a *value type*, which stores its own data, while a class defines a *reference type*, which stores a reference that points to an object.

- *Casting* is the process of converting a value from one data type to another. *Widening conversions* can always be done, but *narrowing conversions* cause exceptions when the conversion can't be done.

- Casting is done *implicitly* when an expression of one data type is assigned to another data type. Casting can also be done *explicitly* by using shared methods and functions.

- *With* statements simplify the coding of repeated references to the same object.

PLACEHOLDERS, NOT INSTANT.

- *Object variables* are reference types that point to specific objects. You can use the TypeOf and Is keywords with object variables in conditional expressions. And you can use For Each...Next statements to repeat a series of statements for each object in a *collection* of objects.

Terms

general procedure	local variable	structure
Sub procedure	block variable	value type
call	module-level variable	reference type
by value	namespace variable	casting
by reference	project variable	widening conversion
Function procedure	lifetime	narrowing conversion
function	static variable	implicit conversion
standard module	exception	explicit conversion
module	structured exception	permissive type semantics
Main procedure	handling	strict type semantics
scope	throw an exception	object variable
procedure-level variable	catch an exception	collection

Objectives

- Given the Visual Basic code for a form that uses any of the language elements presented in this chapter, explain what each statement does.

- Given the form design and specifications for an application that requires any of the language elements presented in this chapter, write the code for the application.

- Distinguish between event procedures and general procedures and between Sub procedures and functions.

- Distinguish between arguments that are passed by reference and by value.

- Describe the purpose of a standard module.

- Describe each of these scopes: procedure, block, module, and namespace.

- Describe the operation of a Try...Catch...Finally statement.

- Describe the way .NET structures and classes support the Visual Basic data types, and distinguish between value types and reference types.

- Explain how casting is done implicitly or explicitly, and explain the difference between a widening conversion and a narrowing conversion.

- Describe the way object variables and For Each...Next statements can be used to work with a collection of controls.

Exercise 5-1 Add two functions to the Invoice Total application

In this exercise, you'll add a data validation function and a discount calculation function to the Invoice Total application.

1. Open the Invoice Total application that's in the C:\VB.NET\Chapter 05\ InvoiceTotal folder ("InvoiceTotal.vbproj"). This is our version of this project after data validation has been added to it.

2. Test the program to make sure it works no matter what value you enter as the order total.

3. Code a function named DiscountAmount that returns the discount amount when the order total amount is passed to it as an argument. This function should include the If statement that determines the discount percent and the variable that holds the discount percent.

4. Replace the code that used to calculate the discount amount with an assignment statement that receives the discount amount that's returned by the function. Then, test the program to make sure it works the same as it did in step 2.

5. Create a function named ValidEntry that does the numeric and range testing that's currently being done by the program. This function should require the order total entry as an argument, and it should return an Integer value that's 0 if the entry is valid, 1 if the entry isn't numeric, and 2 if the entry isn't in a valid range. Then, the calling procedure should process the data or display error messages based on the value returned by the function. To make this work, you need to move the range checking variables to the module level so they're available to both the function and the calling procedure.

6. Replace the original data validation code with code that uses the ValidEntry function for data validation. Then, test the program to make sure it works the same as it did in step 2 with the same error messages.

7. When you've got this application working right, close the application.

Exercise 5-2 Add a module to the Invoice Total application

In this exercise, you'll move the functions of exercise 5-1 into a module.

1. Open the Invoice Total application that you modified in exercise 5-1. Then, add a module named modInvoiceTotal to this application.

2. Move the functions and constants of the form class to the module. Then, modify the functions and constants so they can be called by statements in the form class.

3. Test the application to make sure it works the way it did before.

Exercise 5-3   Add structured exception handling to the Invoice Total application

In this exercise, you'll add exception handling to the Invoice Total application.

1. Open the Invoice Total application that you developed in exercise 5-2.

2. Without changing any of the existing code, add structured exception handling to the btnCalculate_Click procedure so any exceptions that are thrown by this procedure or by any procedures that it calls will be caught by the Exception class. In the Catch block, the code should display a message box that displays the Message property of the exception as in figure 5-8.

3. To test this procedure, code a Throw statement in the DiscountAmount function to throw an OverflowException with this Message property: "This is a test of the code for handling an overflow exception."

4. Test the application to make sure that it catches the overflow exception. Then, remove the Throw statement and test the application again to make sure it works as it did before you added structured exception handling.

Exercise 5-4   Modify the Future Value application

In this exercise, you'll add structured exception handling to the Future Value application. You'll also use the FV function instead of your own function.

1. Open the Future Value application in the C:\VB.NET\Chapter 05\FutureValue folder ("FutureValue.vbproj"). This is our version of the code after the Sub procedure and function have been added to it, as shown in figure 5-4.

2. Add structured exception handling to the btnCalculate_Click procedure so it catches overflow exceptions in one Catch block and any other exceptions in a second Catch block. Display a different error message for each type.

3. Test the application by entering 100 as the monthly investment, 12 as the yearly interest rate, and 1 as the number of years. Then, write down the future value that's calculated.

4. Test the application by entering 1000, 100, and 1000 for the three entries to force an overflow exception. Then, make sure that the message for this exception is correct, and end the application.

5. Comment out the statement that calls the FutureValue function and modify the code so it uses the FV function instead. Code this function so it assumes that the payment is made at the beginning of each period. Then, test the application by entering the same values as in step 3, and compare the result with the step 3 result. They should be the same.

6. Modify the function call so it specifies payments at the end of each period and test it with the step 3 entries. Could you modify your FutureValue function so it works this way?

7. Test the application by entering 1000, 100, and 1000 for the three entries to force an overflow exception. This time, the exception isn't thrown, and the Future Value in the label is "NaN." Can you explain that? (The answer is that the FV function uses a Double type for the result instead of the Decimal type. As a result, it can hold extremely large values. However, the FormatCurrency function can't format extremely large values so it returns "NaN" for them.)

8. When you're through experimenting, close the application.

Project 5-1   Accumulate test score data

Here's another one of the projects that are available in the Word document named Projects that is included with the downloads for this book. These projects test your ability to apply what you've learned to new applications.

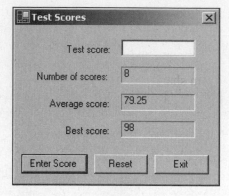

Operation

• The user enters a test score ranging from 0 to 100 and then clicks the Enter Score button or presses the Enter key to activate that button.

• For each score, the application adds one to the number of scores, calculates the average score, and determines what the best score is so far. Then, it displays the results.

• To clear the results so the user can enter another set of scores, the user clicks on the Reset button.

Specifications

• The average score is the sum of all scores divided by the number of scores.

• To make this work, you need to declare module-level variables for the number of scores, the sum of the scores, and the best score.

• Include data validation and/or exception handling so the program won't fail under any circumstances.

6

How to develop object-oriented applications

In the first five chapters of this book, you've learned how to use the classes and objects of the .NET Framework. For instance, you've learned how to use the properties, methods, and events of the form and control objects that are defined by the .NET classes. That's one part of object-oriented programming.

In this chapter, though, you'll learn how to create your own classes and how to use the properties and methods of the objects that are defined by those classes. That's the other part of object-oriented programming. You'll also learn how to create and use classes that contain shared properties and methods.

When you complete this chapter, you'll start to see how the use of business classes can help simplify the development of an application. You'll also have a better understanding of how the .NET classes work.

An Invoice application that uses Invoice objects

To introduce you to object-oriented programming, this chapter presents a simple Invoice application that's implemented by two user-defined classes. One class is an Invoice class that is used to create Invoice objects. The other is the form class that implements the user interface. As you learn how to develop this application, you'll also review some of the concepts and terms that apply to object-oriented programming.

The design of the Invoice class

When you develop an object-oriented application, you start by identifying the *business objects* that the application requires. For a payroll application, for example, two of the business objects are the employees and the payroll checks. For a billing application, some of the business objects are customers, inventory items, and invoices.

Once you've identified all of the objects that the application requires, you design the *class* for each *object* by identifying the *properties* (data) and *methods* (operations) that any project in the application may require. For instance, figure 6-1 lists four properties and two methods for a simple Invoice class. In practice, of course, other properties like invoice date and invoice number would be included for each invoice, and other methods would be included too.

Notice that all of the properties for the Invoice class except CustomerName are read-only. That means that the form class can retrieve the value of these properties, but it can't change them directly. Instead, the Invoice class automatically calculates these values whenever the AddItem method is invoked. In contrast, the WriteInvoice method writes the data for each Invoice object to a file or database after all of the items for an invoice have been processed. You'll understand how this works as you go through the next three figures.

After you design a class for a business object like the Invoice object, you code and test the class, which can be called a *business class*. To do that, you write code that creates *instances* of the class, which are called objects, and you write code that uses the properties and methods of each object. When you create (or *instantiate*) two or more objects from the same class, remember that all the objects have the same properties and methods, but the property values may vary from one object to the next.

Once you've tested the business classes for an application, all of the projects in the application can use them. Often, in fact, two or more projects in the same application will use the same business objects. That's one of the benefits of object-oriented programming, that the code in the classes can be reused.

As you develop these projects, you create *user interface classes* for handling the user interface and *database classes* for saving and retrieving the data for the business objects. This separates the code for the business logic from the code for the user interface and from the code for database operations. That can

The members of an Invoice class

Property	Description
CustomerName As String	Read-write. The customer's name.
OrderTotal As Decimal	Read-only. The total price of the items ordered.
DiscountAmount As Decimal	Read-only. A discount that's based on the order total.
InvoiceTotal As Decimal	Read-only. The OrderTotal minus the DiscountAmount.

Method	Description
AddItem(UnitPrice as Decimal, Quantity As Integer)	Adds an item to the invoice and recalculates the OrderTotal, DiscountAmount, and InvoiceTotal properties.
WriteInvoice( )	Writes the data for the current Invoice object to a file or database.

[handwritten: PUBLIC]
[handwritten: PRIVATE - DISCOUNT (OGAMIN, ARG YS) ORD TOTAL)]
[handwritten: SELECT CASE 500+.3 00±2 00±.1 ELSE,0]
[handwritten: SUB, NO RETURN]

Two Invoice objects that have been instantiated from the Invoice class

Invoice1

CustomerName = Mark Adams
OrderTotal = 139.65
DiscountAmount = 13.96
InvoiceTotal = 125.69

Invoice2

CustomerName = Bill Jones
OrderTotal = 100.00
DiscountAmount = 10.00
InvoiceTotal = 90.00

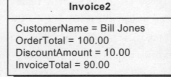

[handwritten diagram: CUSS ↔ DISCOUNT, ORD, INV, DISC, ADD]

Review of class and object concepts

- An *object* is a self-contained unit that has *properties* (data) and *methods* (operations).

- A *class* is the code that defines the properties and methods of an object.

- An object is an *instance* of a class, and the process of creating an object from a class is called *instantiation*.

- If you instantiate two or more instances of the same class, all of the objects have the same properties and methods. However, the properties can have different values.

- A class can be based on an existing class. In that case, the existing class is called a *base class*, and the new class inherits the properties and methods of the base class. *[handwritten: (DERIVED)]*

How to develop the business classes for an application

- Identify the *business objects* that the application requires like customers, invoices, and products.

- Design the classes for the business objects by identifying all the properties and methods that any project in the application will require. These classes can be referred to as *business classes*.

- Code and test the business classes so they're ready for use by any projects in the application.

The two other types of classes that an application requires

- Besides business classes, an application usually requires *user interface classes* and *database classes*. The user interface classes do all of the processing related to the forms. The database classes save and retrieve the data for the business objects.

Figure 6-1   The design of an Invoice class   *[handwritten: METHOD CAN BE IMP AS SUB OR FUNC]*

[handwritten: QUERY INSTANCE IN BGP. OBJ.]

simplify the development of an application, and it makes the application easier to maintain and enhance later on. That is another benefit of object-oriented programming.

As you read the rest of this chapter, please keep in mind that its purpose isn't to teach you how to design the business classes of an application. That unfortunately is a complex subject that is the sole subject of many other books. Instead, the purpose of this chapter is to show you how to code and use business classes. What you've read so far has just been an introduction to object-oriented design.

The specifications for an Invoice application

Figure 6-2 presents the specifications for an Invoice application that uses the Invoice class that's summarized in figure 6-1. Because all of the business processing is going to be done by the methods of the Invoice object, these specifications are primarily for the user interface. This interface consists of the form and the message box shown in this figure.

To create an invoice, the user enters the customer name and the unit price and quantity for the first item ordered, and clicks on the Add Item button. In other words, the unit price and quantity represent the data for one item that the customer has ordered. Normally, this data would include a description of the item, but remember that this application has been simplified for illustrative purposes.

Then, to add additional items to the order, the user enters the unit price and quantity for the next item and clicks the Add Item button again. When there are no more items for an invoice, the user clicks the New Invoice button to start a new invoice. At that time, the message box is displayed.

As this figure explains, this application is implemented by two classes. The user interface class is the form class that you develop by using the Visual Basic IDE. The business class is the Invoice class that you learned about in the previous figure. In the next two figures, you'll see the code for these classes.

Note, however, that the WriteInvoice method isn't used by this application because you won't learn how to work with files or databases until later in this book. As a result, the WriteInvoice method isn't coded in the Invoice class and isn't used by the form class. This also means that this application doesn't use a database class.

WRITE ONLY = SET

READ ONLY = GET (SHOW)

The form and message box for the Invoice application

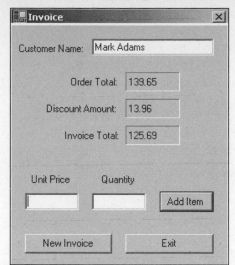
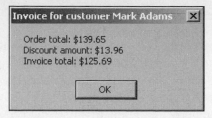

How the application works

- To begin an invoice, the user enters a customer name and the unit price and quantity for the first item and clicks the Add Item button. Then, the invoice application multiplies the unit price and quantity to determine the item total, and it adds that total to the order total, calculates the discount, and determines the invoice total.

- To add another item to the invoice, the user enters a new unit price and quantity and clicks Add Item again.

- To end one invoice and start another, the user clicks the New Invoice button. Then, a message box with the invoice totals is displayed, and the form is cleared.

How the application is implemented

- This application is implemented by a form class and the Invoice class described in the previous figure.

- The form class is a user interface class that defines the form and its controls, accepts the user entries, and responds to any user actions.

- The Invoice class is a business class that defines the properties and methods of each Invoice object and does all the processing for each object.

- Because you haven't learned how to work with files or databases yet, this application doesn't use the WriteInvoice method of the Invoice class at this point (in fact, the method isn't implemented in the Invoice class in this chapter). As a result, the data for each object isn't saved.

Figure 6-2   The specifications for an Invoice application

The code for the form class

If you know what properties and methods a business class offers, you can use them without knowing how they work, just as you use the properties and methods of the .NET classes without knowing how they work. To illustrate, figure 6-3 shows the code for the form class that uses the properties and methods of the Invoice class that are summarized in figure 6-1. Here, the shaded code is the code that refers to the Invoice class, and you should understand all but the second and last lines.

The first shaded line declares an object variable of type Invoice. This means that this variable will be used to refer to the data for the Invoice objects that are created as the application is executed. This variable will be used by the three procedures that follow.

The first procedure is Form1_Load, which means that it is executed when the form is loaded into storage at the start of the application. Within this procedure, a new instance of the Invoice class (an Invoice object) is assigned to the Invoice variable. Then, the focus is moved to the text box for the customer name, and the New Invoice button is disabled so the user can't activate it before any data is entered for the first invoice.

The second procedure provides the code for the Click event of the Add Item button. Here, the first statement calls the AddItem method of the Invoice object with the unit price and quantity values that have been entered by the user as arguments. This method does the processing that's required by each invoice item. Then, the next three statements get the three read-only properties of the Invoice object and update the corresponding labels on the form. The last four statements clear the Unit Price and Quantity text boxes, move the focus back to the Unit Price text box, and enable the New Invoice button.

The third procedure provides the code for the Click event of the New Invoice button. Here, the first statement assigns the customer name entry to the CustomerName property of the Invoice object, and the second statement displays a message box that shows all four properties of the Invoice object.

At this point, a more realistic application would invoke the WriteInvoice method of the Invoice object to save the data for the current invoice in a file or database. But to keep things simple, the Invoice application creates a new Invoice object and assigns it to the Invoice variable. This means that the data for the previous Invoice object is lost. Then, the remaining lines in this procedure clear the labels and text boxes on the form, set the focus to the Customer Name text box, and disable the New Invoice button so the form is ready for the next invoice.

I hope you can now see that you use the properties and methods of business classes just as you use the properties and methods of .NET classes. You don't have to know how these properties and methods are coded. Often, in fact, the senior programmers develop the business classes for an application, and the other programmers use them without knowing how they're coded. In the next figure, though, you can see the code that's behind the properties and methods of the Invoice class.

INVTO J -IT ORDTGR-OJ
DISCAMT -DA

The code for the form class

S/B
PRIVATE
FOR MOD.
LEVEL VAR.

```
Public Class Form1
    Inherits System.Windows.Forms.Form
    Dim Invoice As Invoice          ← CONFUSING.

    Private Sub Form1_Load(ByVal sender As System.Object, _
            ByVal e As System.EventArgs) Handles MyBase.Load
        Invoice = New Invoice()
        txtCustomerName.Focus()
        btnNewInvoice.Enabled = False
    End Sub

    Private Sub btnAddItem_Click(ByVal sender As System.Object, _
            ByVal e As System.EventArgs) Handles btnAddItem.Click
        Invoice.AddItem(txtUnitPrice.Text, txtQuantity.Text)
        lblOrderTotal.Text = FormatNumber(Invoice.OrderTotal)
        lblDiscountAmount.Text = FormatNumber(Invoice.DiscountAmount)
        lblInvoiceTotal.Text = FormatNumber(Invoice.InvoiceTotal)
        txtUnitPrice.Text = ""
        txtQuantity.Text = ""
        txtUnitPrice.Focus()
        btnNewInvoice.Enabled = True
    End Sub

    Private Sub btnNewInvoice_Click(ByVal sender As System.Object, _
            ByVal e As System.EventArgs) Handles btnNewInvoice.Click
        Invoice.CustomerName = txtCustomerName.Text
        MessageBox.Show( _
            "Order total: " & _
                FormatCurrency(Invoice.OrderTotal) & _
                ControlChars.CrLf & _
            "Discount amount: " & _
                FormatCurrency(Invoice.DiscountAmount) & _
                ControlChars.CrLf & _
            "Invoice total: " & _
                FormatCurrency(Invoice.InvoiceTotal), _
            "Invoice for customer " & Invoice.CustomerName)
        Invoice = New Invoice()
        lblOrderTotal.Text = ""
        lblDiscountAmount.Text = ""
        lblInvoiceTotal.Text = ""
        txtCustomerName.Text = ""
        txtUnitPrice.Text = ""
        txtQuantity.Text = ""
        txtCustomerName.Focus()
        btnNewInvoice.Enabled = False
    End Sub

    Private Sub btnExit_Click(ByVal sender As System.Object, _
            ByVal e As System.EventArgs) Handles btnExit.Click
        Me.Close()
    End Sub

End Class
```

Form Load procedure

Add Item button procedure

New Invoice button procedure

Exit button procedure

Figure 6-3   The code for the form class of the Invoice application

*SHOULDN'T NAME SAME AS CLASS → PRIVATE MYOBJINVOICE AS INVOICE — BETTER

The code for the Invoice class

Figure 6-4 presents the code for the Invoice class. As you can see, it begins with a Public Class statement and ends with an End Class statement, with the statements for the class coded in between. In the next four figures, you'll learn how to write all the code for this class. But, here's a preview of it.

The first four statements in this class are declarations for four private variables. These variables are referred to as *instance variables* because they are created when an object is instantiated from a class. They are used to store the data for the properties of each object. Because these variables are defined as private, they cannot be referred to from outside the class.

Below the instance variables are four *property procedures*. These procedures provide access to the four instance variables. Within each of these procedures is a block of code called a *get procedure* that is responsible for retrieving the value of the property from its corresponding instance variable. The CustomerName property also has a *set procedure* that is responsible for setting the value of that property.

Next is a Public Sub procedure that implements the AddItem method, which accepts two arguments, UnitPrice and Quantity. First, this procedure multiplies the values of the two arguments and adds the result to the order total. Then, it calls a Private Function procedure named Discount to return a discount amount, and it subtracts the discount amount from the order total to get the invoice total.

Notice that you always use the Public keyword to identify the properties and methods that can be accessed from other classes. In contrast, you use the Private keyword to declare instance variables so they can't be accessed from other classes. You can also use the Private keyword on Function and Sub procedures that you don't want accessed from other classes.

This illustrates the concept of *encapsulation*, which is one of the key concepts of object-oriented programming. This means that the programmer can hide, or encapsulate, some data and operations of a class while exposing others. For instance, Private variables and Private procedures are completely hidden from other classes, while Public property procedures and Public Function and Sub procedures provide the exposed interface to the data and operations of the class.

In short, encapsulation lets the user of a class think of it as a black box that provides useful properties and methods. This also means that you can change the code within a class without affecting the other classes that use that class. For instance, you can change the discount calculation in the Invoice class without making any change to the form class. This makes it easier to enhance or change an application because you only need to change the classes that need changing.

The code for the Invoice class

```
Public Class Invoice
    Private sCustomerName As String
    Private dOrderTotal As Decimal
    Private dDiscountAmount As Decimal
    Private dInvoiceTotal As Decimal

    Public Property CustomerName() As String
        Get
            Return sCustomerName
        End Get
        Set(ByVal Value As String)
            sCustomerName = Value
        End Set
    End Property

    Public ReadOnly Property OrderTotal() As Decimal
        Get
            Return dOrderTotal
        End Get
    End Property

    Public ReadOnly Property DiscountAmount() As Decimal
        Get
            Return dDiscountAmount
        End Get
    End Property

    Public ReadOnly Property InvoiceTotal() As Decimal
        Get
            Return dInvoiceTotal
        End Get
    End Property

    Public Sub AddItem(ByVal UnitPrice As Decimal, _
            ByVal Quantity As Integer)
        dOrderTotal += UnitPrice * Quantity
        dDiscountAmount = Discount(dOrderTotal)
        dInvoiceTotal = dOrderTotal - dDiscountAmount
    End Sub

    Private Function Discount(ByVal OrderTotal As Decimal) As Decimal
        Dim dDiscountPct As Decimal
        Select Case dOrderTotal
            Case Is >= 500
                dDiscountPct = 0.3
            Case Is >= 200
                dDiscountPct = 0.2
            Case Is >= 100
                dDiscountPct = 0.1
            Case Else
                dDiscountPct = 0
        End Select
        Return Math.Round(OrderTotal * dDiscountPct, 2)
    End Function

End Class
```

Private instance variables

CustomerName property procedure

OrderTotal property procedure

DiscountAmount property procedure

InvoiceTotal property procedure

AddItem method

Private Procedure

Handwritten annotations: "OR STRCustomerName" ; "OR MSTRCustomerName= STRCustomerName" ; "NOT NEEDED" ; "NOT NEEDED"

Figure 6-4   The code for the Invoice class of the Invoice application

Basic skills for creating and using classes

Now that you've seen how a form class and a business class work together, you're ready to learn the basic skills you need to know for creating and using your own classes. The topics that follow present these skills.

How to add a class file to a project

To create a user-defined class, you start by adding a *class file* to your project. To do that, you use the dialog box shown in figure 6-5. When you complete the dialog box, the class will appear in the Solution Explorer with the extension *vb*.

When you add a class to a project, Visual Basic automatically generates the Class and End Class statements so you can enter the code for the class between them. In most cases, you'll start with the declarations for the private instance variables. Then, you'll code a procedure for each property and method that the class provides. You'll learn how to do that in the next two figures.

The dialog box for adding a class and the starting code for the new class

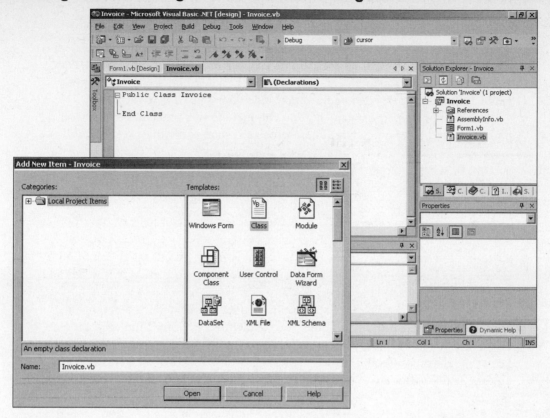

Description

- To add a new class to a project, use the Project → Add Class command to display the Add New Item dialog box. Then, enter the name you want to use for the new class and click Open.

- When you complete the Add New Item dialog box, a *class file* is added to the project. It will appear in the Solution Explorer window with *vb* as the extension.

- The Class and End Class statements are automatically added to the class. Then, you can enter the code for the class between those statements.

Figure 6-5   How to add a class file to a project

How to define properties

You use the Property statement to code a property procedure for each property your class defines. The syntax for this statement is shown in figure 6-6. Here, the As clause indicates the data type of the property. In most cases, each property has a corresponding private instance variable that holds the property's value, and the property should have the same data type as that variable.

Within the Property statement, you can include two procedures: a get procedure and a set procedure. These procedures are sometimes referred to as *accessors* because they provide access to the property values. The get procedure is invoked when a request to retrieve the property value is made, and the set procedure is invoked when a request to set the property value is made.

The three examples in this figure show how you can create *read/write*, *read-only*, or *write-only properties*. As you can see, read/write properties have both a get and a set procedure, read-only properties have only a get procedure, and write-only properties have only a set procedure. A get procedure is identified by the Get and End Get statements, and a set procedure is identified by the Set and End Set statements.

When you start a Property statement, the Get and End Get statements are generated automatically if you enter the ReadOnly keyword. Similarly, the Set and End Set statements are generated automatically if you enter the WriteOnly keyword. If you omit both keywords, both Get and Set pairs are generated automatically. After a Get or Set pair is generated, you just add the code for the procedure.

Because a get procedure returns a value, it is similar to a function. In fact, you use the same techniques for returning a property value that you use for returning the result of a function. The first technique, shown in the read/write property example, is to use a Return statement that includes the value you want to return for the property. The second technique, shown in the read-only example, is to use an assignment statement to assign a value to the property name.

When a Set statement is generated by the IDE, it includes an argument named Value. Then, when another class uses this set procedure, it passes the argument that it wants the value of the property set to. Although you can change the argument name in the set procedure from Value to something else, there's little point in doing so.

You should now be able to understand the property procedures in figure 6-4. The get procedures for all four properties including the three read-only properties just return the values of the corresponding instance variables. In contrast, the set procedure for the read-write property receives a string value as an argument and assigns it to an instance variable.

The Property statement

```
Public [ReadOnly|WriteOnly] Property name As type
    [Get
        [statements]
        {name = propertyvalue} | {Return propertyvalue}
    End Get]
    [Set(ByVal varname [As datatype])
        [statements]
        propertyvalue = newvalue
    End Set]
End Property
```

A property procedure that defines a read/write property

```
Public Property CustomerName() As String
    Get
        Return sCustomerName
    End Get
    Set(ByVal Value As String)
        sCustomerName = Value
    End Set
End Property
```

A property procedure that defines a read-only property

```
Public ReadOnly Property OrderTotal() As Decimal
    Get
        OrderTotal = dOrderTotal
    End Get
End Property
```

A property procedure that defines a write-only property

```
Public WriteOnly Property InterestRate() As Decimal
    Set(ByVal Value As Decimal)
        dInterestRate = Value
    End Set
End Property
```

Description

- You use the Property statement to code a *property procedure* for each property your class defines. The actual property value is usually stored in a private variable with a name that corresponds to the property name.

- A *get procedure* is used by another class to get the value of a property. Often, a get procedure simply returns the value of the instance variable that holds the property value.

- A *set procedure* is used by another class to set the value of a property. Often, a set procedure simply assigns the value passed to the property procedure to the instance variable that holds the property value.

- A *read-only property* has only a get procedure; a *write-only property* has only a set procedure; and a *read/write property* has both a get and a set procedure.

- Visual Basic generates the starting code for a get or set procedure based on whether the ReadOnly or WriteOnly keyword is used. If you omit both, Visual Basic generates the starting code for both get and set procedures.

Figure 6-6   How to define properties

How to define methods

Figure 6-7 shows you how to define the methods for a class. Because methods are nothing more than Public Sub procedures and functions, you should already know how to code them. If you want the method to return a value, you implement the method as a function. If the method doesn't need to return a value, you implement the method as a Sub procedure. And if the method requires that one or more values be passed to it, you code an argument list in parentheses.

The first example in this figure shows a method that accepts two arguments and performs calculations but doesn't return a value. The second example shows a method that requires two arguments and returns a value. The only difference between these methods and Sub and Function procedures is that the methods are coded with the Public keyword.

A method that doesn't return a value

```
Public Sub AddItem(ByVal UnitPrice As Decimal, _
        ByVal Quantity As Integer)
    dOrderTotal += UnitPrice * Quantity
    dDiscountAmount = Discount(dOrderTotal)
    dInvoiceTotal = dOrderTotal - dDiscountAmount
End Sub
```

A method that returns a value

```
Public Function InvoiceTotal(ByVal UnitPrice As Decimal, _
        ByVal Quantity As Integer) As Decimal
    dOrderTotal += UnitPrice * Quantity
    dDiscountAmount = Discount(dOrderTotal)
    dInvoiceTotal = dOrderTotal - dDiscountAmount
    Return dInvoiceTotal
End Sub
```

Description

- You define a method by coding a public Sub or Function procedure.

- If the method doesn't return a value, use a Sub procedure. If the method does return a value, use a Function procedure (or function).

- You define the arguments for a method just as you do for a private Sub or Function procedure.

Figure 6-7   How to define methods

How to create and use an object

Once you have created a user-defined class, you can use the class by following the techniques presented in figure 6-8. To start, you have to create an instance of the class and assign it to an object variable. Then, you can work with the properties and methods defined by the class through the object variable.

To declare an object variable and create an instance of the class with a single statement, you use a Dim statement like the one in the first example in this figure. Here, the New keyword creates an instance of the Invoice class and assigns the newly created object to the Invoice variable.

To declare an object variable without creating an instance of the class, you code a Dim statement without the New keyword as in the second example in this figure. Then, the object variable is assigned a value of Nothing. After that, you can code an assignment statement that uses the New keyword to create an instance of the class and assign it to the object variable.

You've probably noticed that in all of the examples in this chapter, the object variable that holds a reference to an instance of a class is given the same name as the class itself. That makes it easy to identify the class that defines the object. If your application creates two or more instances of a class at the same time, though, you need to define an object variable to hold each instance. In that case, you can still use the class name for one of the object variables if you want, but the others will have to have different names.

After you create an object, you can use the object variable to refer to its properties and methods. To do that, you code the name of the object variable, followed by a dot operator, followed by the name of the property or method and any arguments it requires. If the Auto List Members feature is on, you'll see a list of the properties and methods that are available for the object when you enter the variable name and the dot operator in the Code Editor window. You'll also see the definitions of any arguments that are required by the property or method when you enter its name followed by an opening parenthesis. In other words, this works the same way for a business object that it does for a .NET object.

What should you do when you're finished with an object? Usually, nothing. That's because when a program ends, the Common Language Runtime automatically disposes of any objects used by the program in a process called *garbage collection*. If you want to dispose of an object before the program ends, however, you can *dereference* it by setting its object variable to Nothing as illustrated in this figure. Then, garbage collection can dispose of the object before the program ends.

The Dim statement for an object variable

```
{Dim|Private|Public} variablename As [New] classname
```

How to define an object variable and instantiate an object in one statement

```
Dim Invoice As New Invoice()
```

How to define an object variable and instantiate an object in two statements

```
Dim Invoice As Invoice
Invoice = New Invoice()
```

The syntax for referring to the properties and methods of an object variable

```
variablename.member[(argumentlist)]
```

How to refer to object properties and methods

```
Invoice.CustomerName = txtCustomerName.Text
lblOrderTotal.Text = Invoice.OrderTotal
Invoice.AddItem(dUnitPrice, iQuantity)
```

The syntax for dereferencing an object

```
variablename = Nothing
```

How to dereference an object

```
Invoice = Nothing
```

Description

- Before you can instantiate a class, you must create an object variable to hold the object. The Dim statement that defines the object variable names the class that will be used to create the object.

- To define an object variable and instantiate an object from a class in a single statement, use the New keyword in a Dim statement. To define an object variable and instantiate an object in separate statements, use the New keyword in an assignment statement.

- You can refer to the properties and methods of a user-defined class using the same techniques you use to refer to the properties and methods of any class. Just code the object name followed by the dot operator and the name of the property or method.

- When you enter a property or method for a business object in the Code Editor window, the IDE works just as it does when you enter a property or method for a .NET object. After you type the object name and dot, a list of the members for the object is displayed. After you type the left parenthesis for an argument list, the definitions of the arguments are displayed.

- You can *dereference* an object by setting its object variable to Nothing. When the Common Language Runtime determines that there are no more references to the object, the object is deleted in a process called *garbage collection*.

Figure 6-8   How to create and use an object from a user-defined class

Basic skills for creating and using your own shared members

In chapters 4 and 5, you learned how to use some of the shared properties and methods of some of the .NET Framework classes. Now, you'll learn how to create and use your own shared properties and methods.

How to create and use shared properties and methods

Figure 6-9 shows how to create and use *shared properties* and *shared methods*. To define a shared property, you simply include the Shared keyword on the Property statement. At the top of this figure, for example, you can see the definition of a shared property named CompanyName that gets the value of a private variable. Notice that the variable is also defined with the Shared keyword, which makes it a *shared variable*.

In fact, a shared property procedure can only refer to shared variables or private variables that are defined within the procedure. That makes sense if you remember that the shared property is independent of any instance of the class. As a result, it can't use any variables that belong to an instance.

The statement that follows the property definition in this figure shows how you can use a shared property. In this case, the statement refers to the CompanyName property through the Invoice class. Just by looking at this statement, you can't tell if Invoice is the name of a class or an object variable, but that's okay because it doesn't matter. Although a shared property is a member of a class, you can refer to it either through the class or an instance of the class.

You define and use shared methods in a similar manner. The shared method in this figure is a function that validates the Text property of a control (such as a TextBox control) to make sure the user has entered a valid number. If the Text property is a valid number, the method returns a value of True. If not, the method displays a message box, sets the focus to the control, and returns a value of False.

The last example in the figure shows how you can use this shared method. Here, a pair of If statements are used to validate the entries in the Unit Price and Quantity text boxes before invoking the AddItem method of the Invoice class.

The definition of a shared property in the Invoice class

```
Private Shared sCompanyName As String

Public Shared ReadOnly Property CompanyName() As String
    Get
        Return sCompanyName
    End Get
End Property
```

A statement that uses the shared property

```
lblCompanyName.Text = Invoice.CompanyName
```

The definition of a shared method in a class named ValidData

```
Public Shared Function Numeric(ByVal Control As Control) As Boolean
    Dim bValid As Boolean
    If IsNumeric(Control.Text) Then
        bValid = True
    Else
        MessageBox.Show("Must be numeric.")
        Control.Focus()
        bValid = False
    End If
    Return bValid
End Function
```

A statement that uses the shared method

```
If ValidData.Numeric(txtUnitPrice) Then
    If ValidData.Numeric(txtQuantity) Then
        Invoice.AddItem(txtUnitPrice.Text, txtQuantity.Text)
    End If
End If
```

Description

- A *shared member* is a *shared property* or *shared method* that belongs to the class rather than to the objects created from the class.
- To define a shared member, you use the Shared keyword. Then, you can access that member through the class without creating an instance of the class.
- If you create instances of a class that contains shared members, the shared members are shared across all instances. Then, you can refer to the shared members through the class or though an instance of the class.
- A *shared variable* is a variable declared with the Shared keyword.
- Shared properties and methods can refer only to shared variables or variables declared within the property or method. A shared property or method cannot access a private instance variable.
- A constant that's declared with the Public keyword is implicitly shared. You can't code the Shared keyword on a constant declaration.

Figure 6-9   How to define and use shared properties and methods

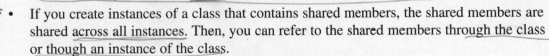

How a shared method can be used in the Invoice application

Perhaps you noticed that the Invoice application in figures 6-3 and 6-4 didn't provide data validation. That was one of several ways that this application was simplified for illustrative purposes. As a result, the application will fail if the user enters invalid data.

In figure 6-10, you can see how a shared method can be used to provide data validation for this application. Here, a new class named ValidData consists of a single shared method named PositiveNumber. This method accepts two arguments: a control and a string that identifies the name of the control. Then, the method checks to make sure the Text property of the control is both numeric and positive (> 0). If it is, the method returns True. If is isn't, the method displays a message box that tells the user what the problem is, sets the focus to the control, and returns False.

To use this method, the only procedure in the form class that needs to be changed is the procedure for the Click event of the Add Item button. This procedure is shown in this figure, and the changes to it are shaded. Here, the PositiveNumber method is used to validate both the unit price and quantity entries before the AddItem method of the Invoice object is invoked. A key point to note is that the form class doesn't have to create an object variable for the ValidData class or instantiate that class before it uses the shared method.

When to use shared properties and methods

Now that you know how to code shared properties and methods, you may wonder when to use them and when to use regular properties and methods. In general, there are two cases when you should use shared properties and methods. The first is when you want to create a property or method that will affect all instances of a class. For example, the CompanyName property in figure 6-9 lets you set a single company name that will be used for all invoices.

The second case is when you want to create a method that isn't tied to the data for a specific object. The PositiveNumber method is an example of this. In fact, to make the ValidData class more useful, you could add a complete set of data validation methods to it that could be used to validate any type of user entry.

The code for the ValidData class

```
Public Class ValidData

    Public Shared Function PositiveNumber(ByVal Control As Control, _
            ByVal FieldName As String) As Boolean
        Dim bValid As Boolean
        If IsNumeric(Control.Text) Then
            If Control.Text > 0 Then
                bValid = True
            Else
                MessageBox.Show(FieldName & " must be positive.")
                Control.Focus()
                bValid = False
            End If
        Else
            MessageBox.Show(FieldName & " must be numeric.")
            Control.Focus()
            bValid = False
        End If
        Return bValid
    End Function

End Class
```

The Click event procedure for the Add Item button

```
Private Sub btnAddItem_Click(ByVal sender As System.Object, _
        ByVal e As System.EventArgs) Handles btnAddItem.Click
    If ValidData.PositiveNumber(txtUnitPrice, "Unit Price") Then
        If ValidData.PositiveNumber(txtQuantity, "Quantity") Then
            Invoice.AddItem(txtUnitPrice.Text, txtQuantity.Text)
            lblOrderTotal.Text = FormatNumber(Invoice.OrderTotal)
            lblDiscountAmount.Text = FormatNumber(Invoice.DiscountAmount)
            lblInvoiceTotal.Text = FormatNumber(Invoice.InvoiceTotal)
            txtUnitPrice.Text = ""
            txtQuantity.Text = ""
            txtUnitPrice.Focus()
        End If
    End If
End Sub
```

Description

- PositiveNumber is a shared method of the ValidData class that accepts two arguments: a control and a string that contains the name of the control. This method checks whether the Text property of the control is both numeric and positive.

- If the Text property of the control contains valid data, the PositiveNumber method returns a value of True. If the data isn't valid, the method displays the name of the field and a description of the problem in a message box, moves the focus to the control, and returns False.

- The Click event procedure for the Add Item button uses the PositiveNumber method to validate the UnitPrice and Quantity fields before invoking the AddItem method of the Invoice class.

Figure 6-10   The use of a shared method in the Invoice application

How to explore classes

At this point, you know how to use the .NET classes as well as any business classes that you or someone else has created. But how do you know what classes are available and what their properties and methods are? Finding that out, in fact, is one of the time-consuming aspects of working with Visual Basic.

To help you do that, Visual Studio provides two tools that let you explore the classes in a solution as well as the thousands of classes that make up the Class Library of the .NET Framework. The Class View window lets you browse the classes that make up the current solution, and the Object Browser lets you browse those classes plus the .NET Framework classes for the solution. After you learn how to use these tools, we'll explore the code that Visual Basic generates for a form class because that's going to be more meaningful to you now.

How to use the Class View window

The Class View window is a tabbed window that's displayed by default in the group with the Solution Explorer window. As figure 6-11 shows, this window contains a hierarchical view of the classes and other programming elements in your solution. The list of classes gives you an overall view of the classes that make up your solution.

The solution shown here is the Invoice application with the data validation that was presented in figure 6-10. Here, I've expanded the class list to show the individual objects that make up the form class named Form1. The list of objects for this class includes event procedures such as btnAddItem_Click and Form1_Load, the individual controls that make up the form, such as btnAddItem and lblDiscountAmount, and a number of other elements that were automatically generated by Visual Basic. If you were to scroll down the Class View window, you would see the two user-defined classes that this solution includes (Invoice and ValidData) along with their properties and methods.

To display the code for an item in the Code Editor window, you can double-click that item in the Class View window. In this figure, for example, you can see the code that was displayed when I double-clicked on the btnAddItem_Click procedure in the Class View window.

The Class View window

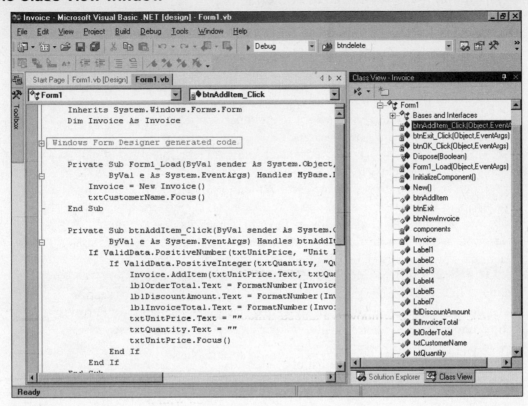

Description

- The *Class View window* lets you browse the current solution's classes.

- The Class View window displays each class and its properties, methods, events, private variables, Sub and Function procedures, and other code elements in a hierarchical tree view. You can expand or collapse the tree by clicking the plus and minus signs.

- The Class View window also displays modules and other solution items.

- To display the Class View window, click the Class View tab that's grouped with the Solution Explorer window or use the View → Class View command.

- You can double-click an item in the Class View window to call up the code that defines that item in the Code Editor.

Figure 6-11   How to use the Class View window

How to use the Object Browser

The Object Browser, shown in figure 6-12, is similar to the Class View window. However, the Object Browser isn't limited to the classes of a specific solution. Instead, the Object Browser is designed to let you explore .NET classes as well. That way, you can determine which of the .NET classes and members are most useful for your application.

When you open the Object Browser, it appears as a tab in the same window as the Code Editor and Form Designer. Then, the Objects pane, located on the left side of the Object Browser window, displays a hierarchical list of classes. When you select a class in the Objects pane, a description of that class is displayed in the Description pane at the bottom of the window. In addition, the members of that class are displayed in the Members pane at the right side of the window, and you can click on any member to display its description in the Description pane. To display additional information about a selected class or member, you can press F1 to display the online Help documentation.

The Object Browser displays classes from the current solution plus classes in the .NET *namespaces* that are listed in the solution's References section. These namespaces are collections of related classes. For a Windows Forms application, the References section includes these five namespaces:

- System, which includes general-purpose system classes.

- System.Data, which includes the database classes you'll learn about in section 4.

- System.Drawing, which includes classes for creating drawings, working with fonts, and printing.

- System.Windows.Forms, which includes classes for creating Windows forms and controls. You learned about several of these classes in chapter 2 and will learn about more of them in chapters 8 through 10.

- System.Xml, which includes classes for working with XML data. You'll learn how to use some of these classes in chapter 14.

The Object Browser also displays two namespaces that are available to every Visual Basic application: Microsoft Visual Basic .NET Runtime and mscorlib. These namespaces include classes that provide the basic features of Visual Basic, such as functions and primitive data types (Integer, Boolean, etc.).

Because the .NET class library is huge, your first experiences with the Object Browser are likely to be overwhelming. But don't get discouraged. As you get more experience with the Object Browser, you'll become familiar with the way the .NET class library is organized. Then, you'll find that browsing classes with the Object Browser is an excellent way to learn about the .NET Framework.

The Object Browser

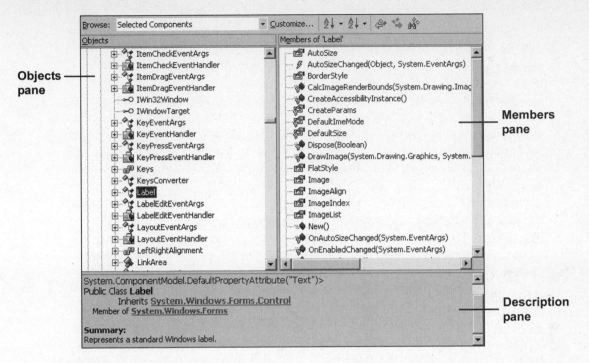

Description

- The *Object Browser* lets you display objects and members that are available to your solution. This includes classes defined in the solution as well as the .NET Framework classes that are listed in the References section of the Solution Explorer.

- To display the Object Browser, press F2 or use the View → Other Windows → Object Browser command.

- The Objects pane displays a hierarchical list of objects, and the Members pane displays the members of the object that is currently selected.

- The Description pane shows information about the selected object or member. This description often includes links you can click to display other objects.

- You can press F1 at any time to call up help on the currently selected object or member.

- You can use the buttons at the top of the Object Browser window to sort or group the items in the Objects list, sort the items in the Members list, navigate forward and backward to previously selected items, and search for objects, definitions, and references.

F2 = OBJ, BROWSER

Figure 6-12   How to use the Object Browser

The generated code for a form class

Although you may not think of the forms you develop as classes, that's what they are. In fact, if you look at the code that Visual Basic generates when you add a form to a project, you'll see that it begins with a Class statement that names the class and ends with an End Class statement.

In the code for the form shown in figure 6-13, for example, the form class is named Form1. This is the default name that's given to the form that's automatically added to a new Windows project. Although you can change the name of the form class by changing the name of the Class statement, you won't usually do that unless the project contains two or more forms. You'll learn more about that in chapter 9.

After the Class statement, Visual Basic generates an Inherits statement that names the Form class in the System.Windows.Forms namespace of the .NET Framework. This statement causes the new form to *inherit* the properties, methods, and events defined by the Form class. The Close method you use to close a form, for example, is inherited from the Form class, and all of the properties you see in the Properties window for a form are inherited from this class. You'll learn more about inheritance in chapter 15.

After the Inherits statement is a #Region directive that groups code so it can be expanded and collapsed within the Code Editor window. That's how Visual Basic hides most of the generated form class code from you. In the Code Editor window, you can click the plus sign next to the #Region directive to reveal the generated form code. If you do expand this code, though, you should avoid modifying it.

In figure 6-13, you can see selected portions of the generated code that's shown when you expand the region directive for the Form1 class of the Invoice application. In particular, this figure shows the code that's related to the Exit button control. However, there is similar code for each control on the form.

To start, there's an object declaration for each control. All of them use the Friend keyword so any other class in the project can access them. They also use the WithEvents keyword so the events of the controls are available to the program. After the As keyword for each variable, you can see the .NET class that the control is based on.

After the object declarations is a Sub procedure named InitializeComponent that is responsible for creating instances of each control and setting each control's initial properties. For example, you can see the statement that creates an instance of the System.Windows.Forms.Button class and assigns it to the object variable named btnExit. Then, you can see a set of six assignment statements that set the Exit button's initial properties.

If you look at all of the generated code for a form class, much of it will still be a puzzle to you. But you'll learn more about that code in chapter 15. Even now, though, this quick look at the code should demonstrate that a form and its controls are implemented by Visual Basic code that is stored in a form class. There is no magic to it.

Some of the code that's generated for the Future Value form

```
Public Class Form1
    Inherits System.Windows.Forms.Form

#Region " Windows Form Designer generated code "
    .
    .
    Friend WithEvents btnExit As System.Windows.Forms.Button ————— Object variable declaration
    .
    .
    Private Sub InitializeComponent()
        .
        .
        Me.btnExit = New System.Windows.Forms.Button() ————————— Instantiation
        .
        .
        Me.btnExit.DialogResult = System.Windows.Forms.DialogResult.Cancel
        Me.btnExit.Location = New System.Drawing.Point(168, 112)
        Me.btnExit.Name = "btnExit"                                         Property assignments
        Me.btnExit.Size = New System.Drawing.Size(80, 23)
        Me.btnExit.TabIndex = 9
        Me.btnExit.Text = "E&xit"
        .
        .
    End Sub

#End Region
    .
    .
End Class
```

Description

- When you add a form to a project, Visual Basic generates the Class and End Class statements for the form. In addition, it generates an Inherits statement that causes the form to be based on the Form class defined by the .NET Framework. Then, you can customize the class by adding controls and code to it.

- Visual Basic also generates code for the controls you add to a form, which are based on classes in the .NET Framework. To display this code, click on the plus sign to the left of the *Windows Form Designer generated code* heading in the Code Editor window.

- For each control used on a form, Visual Basic declares a variable with the appropriate class type. The Friend keyword included in this declaration indicates that the variable is accessible from anywhere in the program, and the WithEvents keyword makes the events defined by the class available to the program.

- Visual Basic also creates an instance of each control and assigns it to the object variable for the control. Then, it assigns the values of any properties you set in the Properties window to the object.

- In addition to the code shown above, Visual Basic generates code for creating and disposing of the form itself.

Figure 6-13   The generated code for a form class

Perspective

Now that you've completed this chapter, you should be able to create simple business classes. You should also be able to use the properties and methods of those classes from another class. These are the basic skills of object-oriented programming. Beyond that, you should be able to create and use classes that contain shared properties and methods.

Although developing your own classes may at first seem like more work than straight coding, you must remember that the benefits of using classes are twofold. First, the code in a class can be used by more than one application. Second, when you develop business classes, you separate the business code from the user interface and database code, which can simplify the development of an application and make it easier to maintain and enhance later on.

Although you have learned some of the basic skills of object-oriented programming in this chapter, you should realize that this has only been a start. So in chapter 15, you'll learn some of the more advanced skills. In particular, you'll learn how to use constructors and inheritance.

Summary

- A *class* defines the *properties* and *methods* of an *object* that is created from the class. An object is an *instance* of a class, and the process of creating an object is known as *instantiation*.

- The *business classes* of an application define the *business objects*. By dividing an application into business classes, *user interface classes*, and *database classes*, you separate the business, interface, and database code. This can make it easier to develop, maintain, and enhance an application.

- Each user-defined class is saved in a separate file known as a *class file*.

- *Instance variables* are private variables that are created when an object is created from the class. The instance variables are used to store the values of an object's properties.

- For each property in a class, you create a *property procedure* to make the property accessible to other classes. Within a property procedure, a *get procedure* retrieves the value of the property and a *set procedure* sets the property's value.

- For each method in a class, you create a Public Function or Sub procedure. You use a Function procedure if the method returns a value and a Sub procedure if it doesn't.

- You can declare an object variable and instantiate a class in a single statement by using the New keyword on the Dim statement. Or you can declare the object variable and create the class instance in separate statements by using the New keyword in an assignment statement.

- To refer to a business object's properties or methods, you code the object name, a dot, and the member name, just as you do when you refer to the members of a .NET object.

- To *dereference* an object, you set its object variable to Nothing.

- A *shared property* or *shared method* is a property or method that you can use without first declaring an object variable or instantiating an object from the class. You use the Shared keyword on the property and method declarations to create shared properties and methods.

- The Class View window and Object Browser let you explore the classes, properties, and methods of a solution. The Object Browser is more expansive because it lets you explore all of the .NET classes that are listed in the References section of the Solution Explorer.

- The code that's generated for a form class defines instance variables for the control objects of a form and assigns values to their properties.

Terms

object	database class	write-only property
property	instance variable	garbage collection
method	property procedure	dereference
class	get procedure	shared member
instance	set procedure	shared property
instantiation	encapsulation	shared method
base class	class file	shared variable
business object	accessor	Class View window
business class	read/write property	Object Browser
user interface class	read-only property	inherit

Objectives

- Given the design of a business class with properties and methods like the ones in this chapter, create a class file that implements the class.

- Given the specifications for a form class that requires the use of a business class, write the code for the form class.

- Given the specifications for a class that contains one or more shared properties or methods, create a class file that implements the class.

- Distinguish among read-only, write-only, and read/write properties.

- Distinguish between a method implemented as a function and a method implemented as a Sub procedure.

- Distinguish between ordinary class properties and methods and shared class properties and methods.

Exercise 6-1   Create the Invoice class

In this exercise, you'll add a class to an Invoice application. Then, you'll use the members and objects of that class from the form class. To give you more practice in less time, you'll start from an application that doesn't use an Invoice class.

Start the Invoice application and review it

1. Open the Invoice application that's in the C:\VB.NET\Chapter 06 folder ("Invoice.vbproj"). This is a version of the Invoice application that's presented in figure 6-3, but it doesn't use an Invoice class so it consists of just a form class.

2. Review the code for the form class. Note that four private variables are declared at the start of the form class. Later, these variables are used by the Click procedures for the Add Item and New Invoice buttons. Note too that this class doesn't provide for data validation. Then, run the application to see how it works.

Add the Invoice class to the project

3. Use the Project → Add Class command to add a class named Invoice to the project.

4. Add the code for the four properties in figure 6-1 to the Invoice class. That includes both the instance variables and the property procedures. If necessary, refer to figure 6-6, but don't just copy the code from figure 6-4.

5. Add the code for the AddItem method that's described in figure 6-1 to the Invoice class. To do that, cut and paste the related code from the form class to the Invoice class. Then, modify the code so it becomes a public method.

Modify and test the code in the form class

6. Modify the code in the form class so it uses the properties and methods of the Invoice class. To do that, you need to: (1) delete the private variable declarations at the start of the class; (2) add a Dim statement for the Invoice object variable; (3) modify the Form1_Load procedure so it instantiates an Invoice object; (4) modify the Click event procedure for the Add Item button so it uses the properties and methods of the Invoice object; and (5) modify the Click event procedure for the New Invoice button so it uses the properties of the Invoice object and instantiates a new Invoice object. If necessary, you can refer to the code in figure 6-3 . When you're done, the application should work the same way it did when you started this exercise.

7. Test the application by entering several orders with valid data for the Unit Price and Quantity fields. If it doesn't work right, fix the errors.

8. After you're sure that the application works for valid data, test it with non-numeric entries. When you do, the application will fail due to casting exceptions because the application doesn't provide data validation.

9. When you're through experimenting, close the solution.

Exercise 6-2   Enhance the Invoice class

In this exercise, you will change the discount calculation and add an additional property to the Invoice class. The new property will be named ItemCount and it will indicate how many items were added to each Invoice object.

Change the discount calculation method

1. Open the Invoice application that you developed in exercise 6-1, and open the Code Editor window for the Invoice class file. Then, comment out the Select Case statement in the Discount function and modify the Return statement so each order gets a 10% discount.

2. Test the application to make sure that every order now receives a 10% discount. Note that you don't have to change the form class to make this work.

Add an ItemCount property

3. Return to the Code Editor window for the Invoice class. Add a new instance variable named iItemCount. The type for this variable should be Integer and its initial value should be zero.

4. Add a new read-only property procedure variable named ItemCount. This property should simply return the value of the iItemCount instance variable.

5. Add a line to the AddItem method that adds one to the iItemCount variable each time the method is run.

6. Go to the event procedure for the New Invoice button in the form class, and adjust the statement that displays the message box so the ItemCount property is displayed in the first line like this: Item count: 3.

7. Test the application to make sure the ItemCount property is displayed properly for each invoice. Note in this case that both the Invoice class and the form class had to be changed.

Add a WriteInvoice method

8. Add a WriteInvoice method to the Invoice class. Because you haven't yet learned how to write the data for an invoice to a file or database, this method should just display a message box that says: Invoice has been written to the database. It shouldn't require any arguments.

9. In the Click procedure for the New Invoice button, invoke the WriteInvoice method before a new Invoice object is created. Then, test the application. This shows how you can simulate a method in a business object before you actually code the working version of the method.

10. When you're through experimenting, close the solution.

Exercise 6-3   Create a ValidData class

In this exercise, you will create and use a class named ValidData with two shared methods named PositiveNumber and PositiveInteger.

Create the ValidData class and add a PositiveNumber method

1. Open the Invoice application. Then, use the Project → Add Class command to add a class named ValidData to the project.

2. Create a shared method named PositiveNumber in the ValidData class that accepts just a control as an argument. This method should return a Boolean value of True if the Text property of the control is a positive number or False if it isn't. This is similar to but different than the PositiveNumber method in figure 6-10.

3. Open the Click event procedure for the Add Item button and add If statements that use the PositiveNumber method to make sure the user enters positive numbers in the Unit Price and Quantity text boxes before invoking the AddItem method. If either text box doesn't contain a valid entry, this procedure should display an appropriate error message and move the focus to that text box.

4. Test the Invoice application to make sure the data validation works. Try leaving the unit price and quantity fields blank, entering negative numbers, and entering non-numeric data. The application should work in all cases.

Add a PositiveInteger method

5. Create a shared member named PositiveInteger in the ValidData class. This method should be like the PositiveNumber method, but it should check to make sure that the Text property of the control contains a whole number. For efficiency, you may want to copy and paste the PositiveNumber method, and then edit it to create the PositiveInteger method.

   Hint: To check to see if the value is an integer, you can use the CInt() function you learned about in chapter 5 to convert the Text property to an integer after you've checked to make sure it's a positive number. Then, you can compare the unconverted Text property to the resulting Integer value. If they are the same, which means that the CInt function didn't drop any decimal positions, the number is an integer.

6. Modify the Click event procedure for the Add Item button so the unit price is validated by the PositiveNumber method and the quantity is validated by the PositiveInteger method. Then, adjust the error message for the quantity entry to reflect this change.

7. Test the application to make sure that the Quantity text box now accepts only whole numbers. Try entering values such as 1.5 and -9.9 for the quantity. Each of these values should be treated as errors.

8. When you're done experimenting, close the solution.

7

How to test and debug an application

In chapters 2 and 4, you learned how to enter break mode when a run-time error occurs, how to use data tips to find out what value a variable or property contains, how to use breakpoints to enter break mode before a specific statement is executed, and how to step through the statements in a program from a breakpoint. These are the basic debugging skills that you need for debugging simple applications.

As your applications get more complicated, though, debugging gets more complicated. In fact, if you've done much programming, you know that testing and debugging are often the most difficult and time-consuming phases of programming. The good news is that Visual Studio offers many other tools for testing and debugging. In this chapter, you'll learn how to use the most useful ones, and you'll also review the tools you've already been introduced to.

Basic debugging techniques

Before you begin debugging, you can set the options that control how Visual Basic handles exceptions. Then, you can use the basic debugging skills that you learned in previous chapters to find and fix most types of exceptions. In the first four figures in this chapter, you'll learn how to set the debugging options; you'll review the techniques for working in break mode; you'll learn more about working with breakpoints; and you'll learn more ways to control the execution of a program.

How to set the options for debugging

Figure 7-1 presents the dialog box you can use to set the options for debugging. Although you can set these options for individual exception classes or for the exception classes in individual namespaces, you're most likely to set them for all the exception classes in the Common Language Runtime. To do that, you highlight the Common Language Runtime Exceptions entry before you set the options.

The first set of options in this dialog box determines what happens when an exception first occurs. By default, the Continue option is selected, so the program will continue instead of breaking into the debugger. In most cases, that's what you want. If you set this option to Break into the debugger, however, you can use the debugging features described in this chapter to set breakpoints and check program variables *before* any exception-handling code is executed.

The second set of options determines what happens if an exception is thrown but isn't handled by the program. In most cases, you'll want to break into the debugger so you can determine the cause of the exception, and that's the default. If you set this option to Continue, though, the program will actually end because it can't continue after an unhandled exception. (This option is provided for programs written in native C++, in which case you can attempt to fix the exception and continue execution.)

By the way, the "Use parent setting" options are enabled when you select one of the categories or exceptions below the Common Language Runtime Exceptions entry. Then, if you specify that option, the settings for the next higher level are applied to the selected category or exception.

The Exceptions dialog box

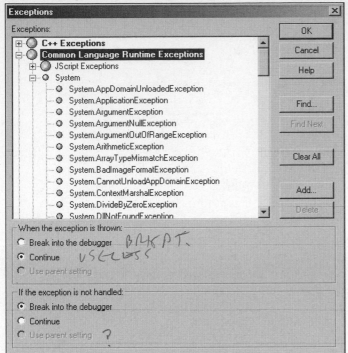

DEBUG → EXCEPTIONS

(handwritten annotations: "BRKPT." next to "Break into the debugger", "USELESS" next to "Continue", "?" next to "Use parent setting")

The options for handling run-time errors

Group	Option	Description
When the exception is thrown	Break into the debugger	Causes the program to enter break mode when an exception occurs, even if exception-handling code is available.
	Continue	Causes the program to continue. If exception-handling code is available, it is executed.
	Use parent setting	The setting of the parent exception is used.
If the exception is not handled	Break into the debugger	Causes the program to enter break mode when exception-handling code isn't available or when the code doesn't correct the problem.
	Continue	Causes the program to end.
	Use parent setting	The setting of the parent exception is used.

Description

- To display the Exceptions dialog box, use the Debug → Exceptions command.
- To set the options for all exceptions in the CLR, select the Common Language Runtime Exceptions entry. To set the options for a category of exceptions or a specific exception, select that category or exception.

Figure 7-1   How to set the options for debugging

How to work in break mode

If the debugging options are set so a program can break into the debugger, the dialog box that's displayed when an exception is thrown includes a Break button that lets you enter *break mode* as shown in figure 7-2. You can also enter break mode by using one of the other techniques listed in this figure.

When you enter break mode after an exception occurs, the statement that was executing is highlighted. Then, you can use the debugging information that's available to try to determine the cause of the exception. For example, you can place the mouse pointer over a variable, property, or expression to display its current value in a *data tip*. You can also look in the Autos window to see the values of the variables that have been changed by statements near the one that was executing when the break occurred. You'll learn more about the Autos window in a moment.

If you want to change the value of a variable or property in break mode before the program continues, you can use one of the techniques you'll learn about later in this chapter. However, you can't change the code for the program like you could in Visual Basic 6. If you need to change the code, you first have to end the program by clicking on the Stop Debugging button in the Debug toolbar. Then, you can make the necessary changes and run the program again.

- CAN SET TO BREAK AT
  CERTAIN CONDITION
- HIT COUNT = # OF
  TIMES BREAKPOINT
  HIT

The Future Value application in break mode

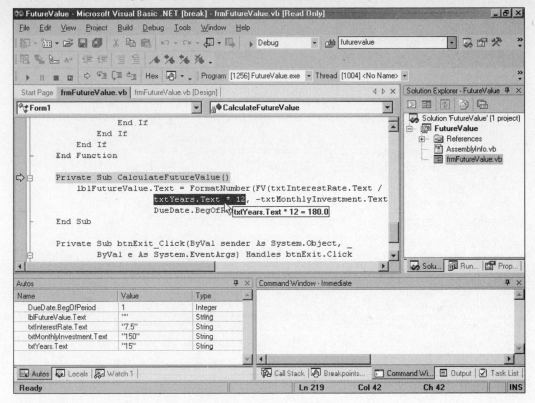

Three ways to enter break mode

- Click on the Break button in the dialog box that's displayed when an exception occurs.
- Choose the Debug → Break All command while the program is executing.
- Set a breakpoint on a statement to enter break mode before that statement is executed.

Description

- When you enter *break mode*, Visual Basic displays the Code Editor window and highlights the next statement to be executed or the statement that was executing when the exception occurred.
- You can use the debugging windows and the Debug and Debug Location toolbars that are displayed in break mode to control the execution of the program and determine the cause of an exception.
- To display the value of a variable or property in a *data tip*, position the mouse pointer over it in the Code Editor window. To display a data tip for an expression, select the expression and then point to it. The expression must not contain a function call.
- To exit break mode and end the program, click on the Stop Debugging button in the Debug toolbar. To continue program execution, press F5 or click on the Continue button in the Standard or Debug toolbar.

Figure 7-2   How to work in break mode

How to use breakpoints

Although you can enter break mode when you encounter an exception, you can also set a *breakpoint* to enter break mode at the statement of your choice. Breakpoints are particularly useful for determining the cause of *logical errors*, which cause a program to produce inaccurate results. Because these types of errors don't cause exceptions to occur, they can be the most difficult to locate.

Figure 7-3 reviews the techniques for setting and clearing breakpoints that you learned in chapter 4. When you run an application after setting a breakpoint, it will enter break mode when it reaches the breakpoint but before the statement at the breakpoint is executed. At that point, you can use the debugging tools described in this chapter to check the state of the application. When you're ready to continue, you can press F5 or click on the Continue button, or you can use the Step commands described in the next figure.

For some applications, you may want to set more than one breakpoint. You can do that either before you begin the execution of the application or while the application is in break mode. Then, when the application is run, it will stop at the first breakpoint. And when you continue execution, the application will execute up to the next breakpoint.

Once you set a breakpoint, it remains active until you remove it. In fact, it remains active even after you close the project. If you want to remove a breakpoint, you can use one of the techniques presented in this figure.

You can also work with breakpoints from the Breakpoints window. To disable a breakpoint, for example, you can remove the check mark in front of the breakpoint. Then, the breakpoint isn't taken until you enable it again. You can also move to a breakpoint in the Code Editor window by selecting the breakpoint in the Breakpoints window and then clicking on the Go To Source Code button at the top of this window. In most cases, though, you'll work with breakpoints in the Code Editor window.

The Future Value application after a breakpoint is taken

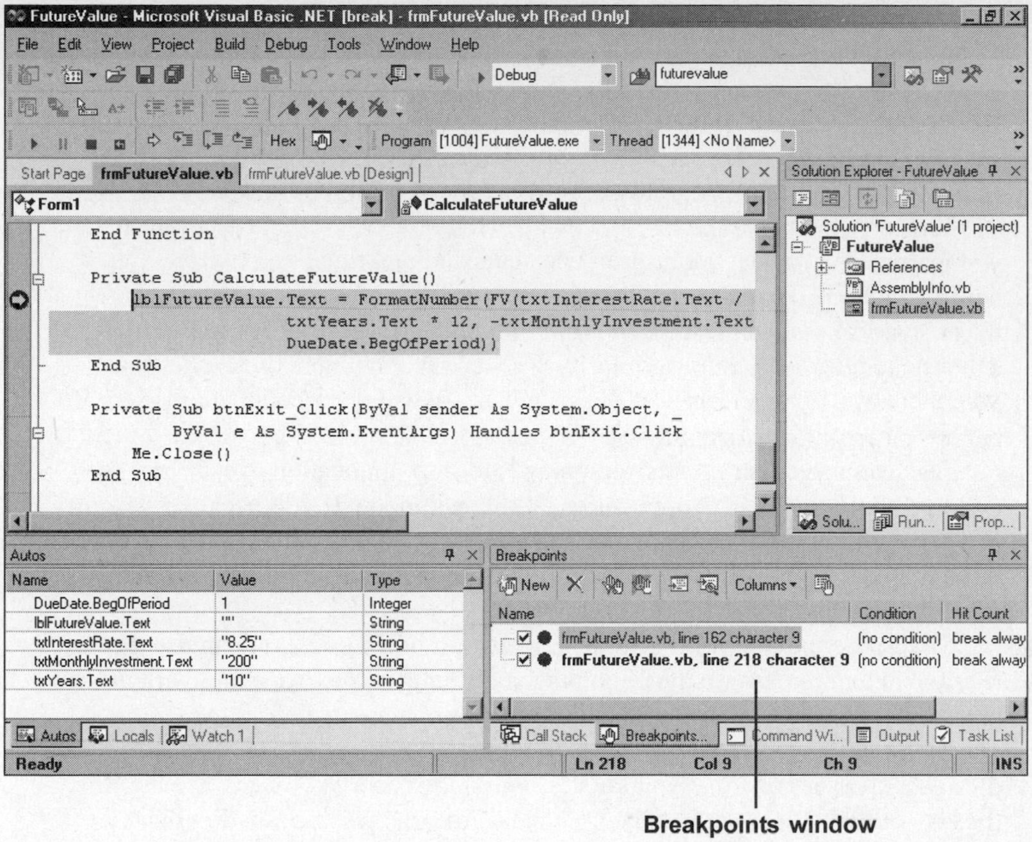

Breakpoints window

How to set and clear breakpoints

- To set a *breakpoint*, click in the margin indicator bar to the left of a statement. Or, press the F9 key to set a breakpoint at the cursor insertion point. You can set a breakpoint before you run an application or while the application is in break mode.

- To remove a breakpoint, use either technique for setting a breakpoint. To remove all breakpoints at once, use the Debug → Clear All Breakpoints command.

Description

- You can set a breakpoint only on a line that contains an executable statement. You cannot set breakpoints on blank lines, comments, or declarative statements.

- When Visual Basic encounters a breakpoint, it enters break mode before it executes the statement that contains the breakpoint.

- The current breakpoints are displayed in the Breakpoints window. This window is most useful for enabling and disabling existing breakpoints, but you can also use it to add, modify, and delete breakpoints and to move to a breakpoint in the Code Editor window.

Figure 7-3   How to use breakpoints

How to control the execution of an application

Once you're in break mode, you can use a variety of commands to control the execution of the program. These commands are summarized in figure 7-4. As you can see, most of these commands are available from the Debug menu or the Debug toolbar, but a couple of them are available only from the shortcut menu for the Code Editor window. You can also use shortcut keys to start a few of these commands.

To *step through* an application one statement at a time, you use the Step Into command. Then, the application enters break mode before each statement is executed so you can test the values of properties and variables and perform other debugging functions. Similarly, the Step Over command executes one statement at a time, except that the statements in called procedures are executed without interruption (they are "stepped over").

You can use either of these commands to start application execution or to restart execution when an application is in break mode. If you use them to start the execution of a typical form class, though, you first step through some of the code that has been generated for the form. For efficiency, then, you normally use these commands after a breakpoint has been reached.

If you use the Step Into command to enter a procedure, you can use the Step Out command to execute the remaining statements in the procedure without interruption. After that, the application enters break mode before the next statement in the calling procedure is executed.

To skip over code that you know is working properly, you can use the Run To Cursor or Set Next Statement command. You can also use the Set Next Statement command to rerun lines of code that were executed before an exception occurred. And if you've been working in the Code Editor window and have forgotten where the next statement to be executed is, you can use the Show Next Statement command to move to it.

One final way to enter break mode is to use the Break All command. This command lets you enter break mode any time during the execution of a program. It's particularly useful for stopping a program that's caught in a processing loop. The shortcut key for this is Ctrl+Break.

Commands in the Debug menu and toolbar

Command	Toolbar	Keyboard	Function
Start/Continue	▶	F5	Start or continue execution of the application.
Break All	❚❚	Ctrl+Break	Suspend execution of the application.
Stop Debugging	■		Stop debugging and end execution of the application.
Restart	⊡		Restart the entire application.
Step Into	⊑≡	F11	Execute one statement at a time. *NO F8 **
Step Over	⊑≡	F10	Execute one statement at a time except for called procedures.
Step Out	⊑≡		Execute the remaining lines in the current procedure.
Show Next Statement	⇨		Display the next statement to be executed. Also available from the shortcut menu for the Code Editor window.

RUN TO CURSOR, ALSO

Commands in the Code Editor window's shortcut menu

Command	Function
Run to Cursor	Execute the application until it reaches the statement that contains the insertion point.
Set Next Statement	Set the statement that contains the insertion point as the next statement to be executed.

Description

- If you use the Step Into or Step Over command to start the execution of an application, Visual Basic will enter break mode before it executes the first statement in the application. If you use the Run to Cursor command, Visual Basic will enter break mode when it reaches the statement that contains the insertion point. In either case, Visual Basic will highlight the current statement in the Code Editor window.

- Once the application enters break mode, you can use the Step Into, Step Over, Step Out, and Run To Cursor commands to execute one or more statements and return to break mode.

- To alter the normal execution sequence of the application, you can use the Set Next Statement command. Just place the insertion point in the statement you want to execute next, issue this command, and click on the Continue button to continue application execution.

- Another way to enter break mode during the execution of an application is to use the Break All command. This is useful when you need to stop the execution of an application that's caught in a loop. To issue the Break All command, you can press Ctrl+Break, or you can switch to the Visual Basic window and click on the Break All button.

NOTE: TIMING CHANGE WHILE IN BREAK POINT — MAY NOT WORK WHEN IN RELEASE MODE!

Figure 7-4   How to control the execution of an application   *IN VS DEFAULT VS. VB*

* F8 —F11 DIFFERENCE

How to use the debugging windows

Now that you know how to work with break mode, you're ready to learn how to use the primary debugging windows. That includes the Autos window, the Locals window, the Watch windows, the Command window, and the Call Stack window. Although Visual Basic also provides a Quick Watch feature you can use to display the values of expressions, you can do that more easily by using data tips. As a result, the Quick Watch feature is described but not illustrated.

How to use the Autos and Locals windows to monitor variables

If you need to see the values of several variables or properties used in the same area of a program, you can do that using the Autos or the Locals window. By default, these windows are displayed in the group of windows in the lower left corner of the IDE when an application enters break mode. If they're not displayed, you can display them by selecting Autos or Locals from the Debug → Windows submenu.

The content of the Autos and Locals windows is illustrated in figure 7-5. The difference between the two is in the amount of information they display and the scope of that information.

The *Locals window* displays information about the variables and controls within the scope of the current procedure. Since that includes information about all of the controls on the form if the code in a form is currently executing, that information can be extensive.

In contrast, the *Autos window* displays information about the variables, properties, and constants used in the current statement, the three statements before that statement, and the three statements after that statement. As a result, the information in this window is usually more limited than it is in the Locals window.

Besides displaying the values of variables and properties, you can use the Autos and Locals windows to change these values. To do that, you simply double-click on the value you want to change and enter a new value. Then, you can continue debugging or continue the execution of the application.

The Autos window

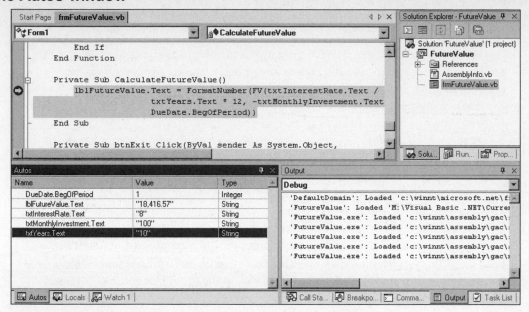

The Locals window

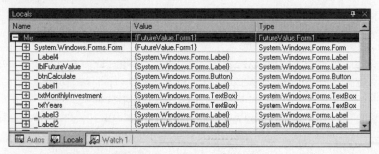

Description

- The *Autos window* displays information about variables, properties, and constants in the current statement and the three statements before and after the current statement. To display the Autos window, click on the Autos window tab or use the Debug → Windows → Autos command.

- The *Locals window* displays information about the variables and controls within the scope of the current procedure. To display the Locals window, click on the Locals tab or use the Debug → Windows → Locals command.

- If you click on the plus sign to the left of the Me keyword at the top of the Locals window for a form object, the properties and variables of the form are displayed. For a module, only variables are displayed.

- To change the value of a property or variable from either window, double-click on the value in the Value column, then type a new value and press the Enter key.

Figure 7-5   How to use the Autos and Locals windows to monitor variables

How to use Watch windows to monitor expressions

By default, the *Watch windows* are also located in the group of windows in the lower left corner of the IDE when an application enters break mode, as shown in figure 7-6. You can use these windows to view the values of *watch expressions* that you enter into these windows. These expressions are automatically updated as the application is executed.

If the Watch 1 window isn't available when an application enters break mode, you can display it by selecting Watch 1 from the Windows/Watch submenu of the Debug menu. You can also display any of the other three watch windows by selecting the appropriate item from this submenu. These windows provide the same features as the Watch 1 window. You can use them if you want to separate the watch expressions into groups.

To add a watch expression, you click in the Name column of an empty row and enter the expression. A watch expression can be any valid Visual Basic expression, and it doesn't have to exist in the application. For instance, the last expression in the Watch window in this figure checks to see if the Future Value variable is greater than 100000 and returns a True or False value. If an expression does exist in the application, though, you can highlight it in the Code Editor window and drag it to the Watch window.

If the expression you add to the Watch window is the name of an object, the Watch window will display a plus sign to the left of the name. Then, you can click on the plus sign to display the properties of the object. A plus sign is also added to an expression if it's the name of an array or a collection (see chapter 12). Then, you can click on the plus sign to display the items in the array.

You can also change the value of a watch expression by clicking on the value in the Value column and entering the new value. And you can delete a watch expression by right-clicking on the expression and selecting the Delete Watch command from the shortcut menu that's displayed. To delete all of the watch expressions in a Watch window, right-click anywhere in the window and select the Select All command. Then, use the Delete Watch command to delete all the expressions. The watch expressions remain in effect until they're deleted.

When and how to use the Quick Watch feature

You can use the Quick Watch feature to display the value of an expression that exists in your application code. To do that, you just highlight the expression and choose Quick Watch from the Debug menu. Remember, though, that you can also display the value of an expression by displaying a data tip, so you really don't need this feature. Its one benefit is that it lets you add its expression to a Watch window by clicking on the Add button in its dialog box.

A Watch window

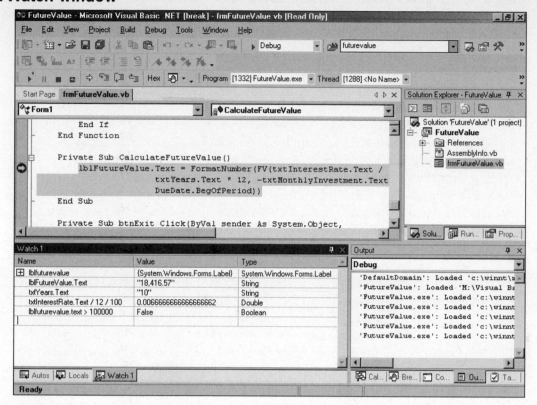

Description

- The *Watch windows* let you view the values of *watch expressions* while an application is in break mode. To display a Watch window, click on its Watch tab. Or, pull down the Debug → Windows/Watch submenu, and choose Watch 1, Watch 2, Watch 3, or Watch 4.

- To add an expression to a Watch window, click on an empty row in the Name column, then type the expression and press the Enter key. You can also highlight an expression in the Code Editor window and then drag it or copy and paste it into a Watch window.

- If an expression is out of scope, the Watch window will display a message instead of a value.

- If you enter the name of an object, an array, or a collection in the Watch window, a tree control will appear next to its name. You can use this control to expand or collapse the entry to show its subentries.

- To change the value of a watch expression, double-click on its value in the Value column, enter the new value, and press the Enter key.

- Any expressions you add to the Watch window remain in effect until they're deleted.

- To delete a watch expression, right-click on the expression in the Watch window and select the Delete Watch command from the shortcut menu. To delete all of the expressions in a Watch window, select the Select All command in the shortcut menu to select the expressions, then use the Delete Watch command.

Figure 7-6 How to use Watch windows to monitor expressions

How to use the Command window to work with values and to execute procedures

Another window that you can use for debugging is the *Command window* that's shown in figure 7-7. By default, this window is located in the group of windows in the lower right corner of the IDE. For debugging, you display this window in Immediate mode as shown in this figure.

You can use the Command window when the variable or property you want to display doesn't appear in the Code Editor window. You can also use the Command window to execute code. For example, you can enter an assignment statement to change the value of a variable or property. Similarly, you can use this window to execute a Sub procedure or function or to display the value returned by the execution of a function. This can be useful for testing the result of a procedure with different arguments. When you do this, you can execute built-in functions as well as user-defined functions.

When you enter commands in the Command window, they're executed in the same context (or scope) as the application that's running. That means that you can't display the value of a variable that's out of scope and you can't execute a private procedure that's in a module that isn't currently executing. If you try to do that, Visual Basic displays a blank line or an error message.

You should also know that the commands that you enter into the Command window remain there until you exit from Visual Studio or explicitly delete them using the Clear All command in the shortcut menu for the window. That way, you can use standard Windows techniques to edit and re-use the same commands from one execution of an application to another without having to re-enter them. Unlike expressions in the Watch window, though, the command results aren't updated as the application executes.

To execute a command that you've already entered in the Command window, just place the insertion point in the command and press the Enter key. This copies the command to the bottom of the window. Then, you can change it if necessary and press Enter to execute it.

Although you use Immediate mode for debugging Visual Basic applications, you can also display the Command window in Command mode. In that mode, you can enter Visual Studio commands. For more information, see the Command Mode, Command Window topic in online help.

The Command window in Immediate mode

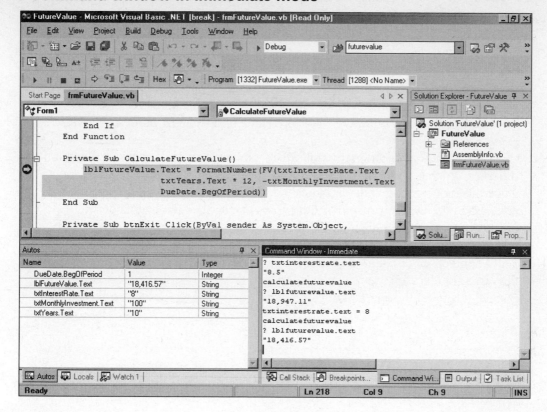

Description

- You can use Immediate mode of the *Command window* to display and assign values from a program during execution. To display this window, click on the Command Window tab or use the Debug → Windows → Immediate command.

- To display a value in the Command window, enter a question mark followed by the expression whose value you want to display. Then, press the Enter key.

- To assign a different value to a variable, property, or object, enter an assignment statement in the Command window. Then, press the Enter key.

- To execute a function or Sub procedure from the Command window, enter its name and any arguments it requires. Then, press the Enter key. If you want to display the result of a function, precede the function call with a question mark.

- To reissue a command, use the Up and Down arrow keys to scroll through the commands until you find the one you want. Then, place the insertion point in the command and press the Enter key to add the command to the bottom of the Command window. Modify the command if necessary, then press the Enter key to execute it.

- To remove all commands and output from the Command window, use the Clear All command in the shortcut menu for the window.

Figure 7-7   How to use the Command window to work with values

How to use the Call Stack window to monitor called procedures

Figure 7-8 shows how to use the *Call Stack window* to monitor the execution of called procedures. This window is located in the group in the lower right corner of the IDE along with the Command and Breakpoints windows. When you display the Call Stack window, it lists all of the procedures that are currently active. In other words, it displays a stack of called procedures, or a *call stack*.

The procedures listed in the Call Stack window appear in reverse order from the order in which they were called. So in this example, the procedure for the Click event of the Calculate button called the CalculateFutureValue procedure. Notice that this window also lists the procedures defined by the Windows objects used by the application. However, these procedures are dimmed so you can easily distinguish them from the procedures that are defined by your application.

The Call Stack window

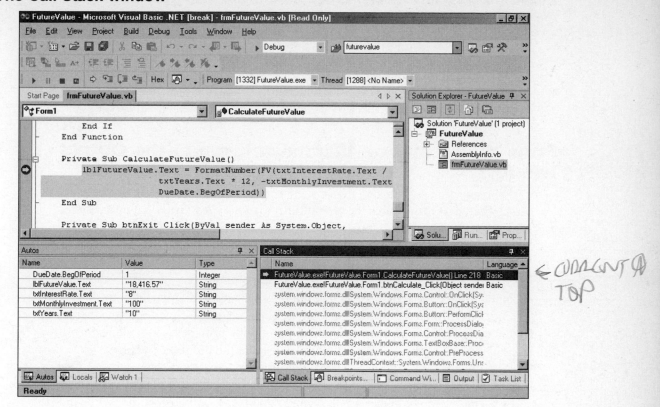

Description

- The *Call Stack window* lists all of the procedures that are active when an application enters break mode. To display this window, click on the Call Stack tab or use the Debug → Windows → Call Stack command.

- In the Call Stack window, the current procedure is listed at the top of the window, followed by the procedure that called it (if any), and so on. This list of procedure names is referred to as a *call stack*.

- You can use the commands in the shortcut menu for the Call Stack window to control what's displayed in this window, including module names and information about parameters.

Figure 7-8   How to use the Call Stack window to monitor called procedures

How to use the Output window

In addition to the debugging windows you've learned about so far, you should know about one more window: the *Output window*. This window is displayed in the lower right group in the IDE. Visual Studio uses this window to display information as you test and debug your applications. You can also use this window to display the information you specify as a program executes.

Project information that's displayed in the Output window

Figure 7-9 illustrates the type of information that's displayed in the Output window. In the first example, you can see the output from a build operation. This output indicates the progress and result of the build. In this case, a single project was built and the build was successful.

The second example in this figure shows output from the execution of an application. Notice that the first seven lines of output identify the files that were required and loaded for the application. Then, the eighth line indicates that an unhandled exception occurred, and the ninth line provides additional information about that error. The last line indicates that the program ended.

In most cases, you won't need the information that's displayed in the Output window. If a build error occurs, for example, the error is displayed in the Task List window and you can use that window to locate and correct the error. And if an unhandled exception occurs, you can use the information in the dialog box that's displayed to identify the cause of the exception. Of course, once you close this dialog box, the error information is only available in the Output window. So if you forget the cause of the error, you can look in this window to refresh your memory.

An Output window that shows the result of a build operation

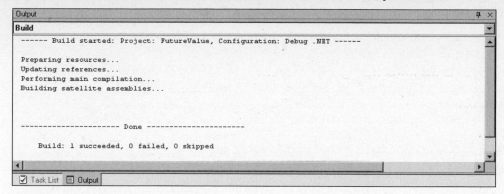

An Output window that shows an unhandled exception

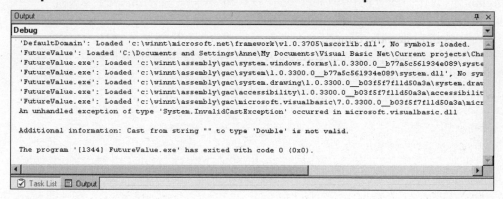

Description

- When you build a project or solution, the progress and results of the build are displayed in the *Output window*. This output includes an indication of how many projects were built successfully, how many builds failed, and how many projects weren't built.

- When you execute a project, the Output window lists the files that were loaded and used by the project. Those files include the .NET Framework runtime library, the executable file for the project, and any namespaces required by the project.

- If an exception occurs during program execution and it's not handled by the application, a description of the exception is included in the Output window. That description may include a *stack trace* that indicates the processing that led up to the error.

- When a project completes execution, the completion code is listed in the Output window.

- You can use the combo box at the top of the Output window to select whether build or debug output is displayed.

Figure 7-9   Project information that's displayed in the Output window

How to use the Debug object to display values in the Output window

In addition to the information Visual Studio displays in the Output window, you can display information that you specify. This can be useful for tracing the execution of a program or for documenting the changing value of a property or variable.

To display information in the Output window, you use the methods of the Debug object shown in figure 7-10. The first two methods, Write and WriteLine, simply write the information you specify to the Output window. In this figure, for example, the WriteLine method is used in the CalculateFutureValue procedure to display the future value each time it's calculated. Unlike the Write method, the WriteLine method adds a line break to the end of the line. That way, the next time one of these methods is executed, the information is displayed on the next line.

The WriteIf and WriteLineIf methods are similar, but they display information only if the specified condition is true. For instance, the example in this figure will display the future value only if it's greater than 20000.

WRITEIF &
WRITELINEIF =
LIKE WRITES
WRITELINE, BUT
ONLY DISPLAY IF
COND. = TRUE

The result of the WriteLine method in the Output window

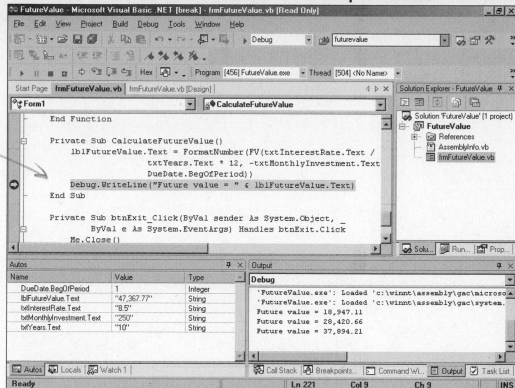

Debug object methods for displaying information

Method	Description
Write(string)	Displays the value of the specified string.
WriteLine(string)	Displays the value of the specified string, followed by a line break.
WriteIf(condition, string)	Displays the value of the specified string if the specified condition is true.
WriteLineIf(condition, string)	Displays the value of the specified string, followed by a line break, if the specified condition is true.

A statement that displays information based on a condition

```
Debug.WriteLineIf(dFutureValue > 20000, _
    "Future value = " & lblFutureValue.Text)
```

Description

- You can use the Write methods of the Debug object to display information in the Output window. This can be useful for tracing program execution or for documenting changes in the values of variables.

Figure 7-10   How to use the Debug object to display values in the Output window

Perspective

As you can now appreciate, Visual Studio provides a powerful set of debugging tools. By using them, you can set breakpoints at the start of critical portions of code. Then, you can step through the statements that follow each breakpoint, and you can review the values of the related variables and properties after each step. If necessary, you can also change values and alter the execution sequence of the statements. With tools like these, a difficult debugging job becomes more manageable.

Summary

- You can set the debugging options to determine whether the debugger is available when an exception is thrown and when the exception isn't handled.

- In *break mode*, you can work with the values of variables, properties, and expressions. You can also set *breakpoints*, control the execution of an application, and monitor called procedures.

- You can work with breakpoints in either the Code Editor window or the Breakpoints window. You can use the Breakpoints window to enable and disable breakpoints and to move to a breakpoint in the Code Editor window.

- You can use the commands in the Debug menu and the shortcut menu for the Code Editor window to control the execution of an application. The most useful commands are the Step commands, which let you execute one or more statements before returning to break mode.

- You can use the *Autos window* and *Locals window* to display and modify the values of properties and variables during program execution.

- You can use the *Watch window* to display the current values of *watch expressions* each time the program enters break mode.

- You can use Immediate mode of the *Command window* to display and modify program values during program execution and to execute Sub procedures and functions.

- You can use the *Call Stack window* to monitor the procedures that are active when an application enters break mode.

- When you build or execute a project, information about that operation is displayed in the *Output window*.

- You can use the methods of the Debug object to display custom information in the Output window as a program executes.

Terms

break mode	Locals window	Call Stack window
data tip	Autos window	call stack
breakpoint	Watch window	Output window
logical error	watch expression	stack trace
step through an application	Command window	

Objectives

- Use the debugging techniques presented in this chapter to determine the cause of run-time or logical errors in any of the applications you develop.

- Describe the differences between the three Step commands that you can use to control the execution of an application.

- Describe the primary difference between the Autos window and the Locals window.

- Describe the differences between the Watch window and the Immediate mode of the Command window.

- Describe the call stack that's displayed in the Call Stack window.

- Explain how you can use the Debug object to display information in the Output window.

Exercise 7-1   Step through an application

In this exercise, you'll step through the code for the Invoice application of chapter 6 that uses an Invoice class. In the process, you'll set breakpoints, use the Autos and Locals windows, and use the buttons in the Debug toolbar for controlling program execution.

Open the project

1. Open the Invoice project in the C:\VB.NET\Chapter 07\Invoice folder. This is our version of the Invoice application that was presented in chapter 6. To start, you may want to review the code in the Invoice class and in the Form1 class.

Set a breakpoint, start the application, and display program values

2. Set a breakpoint on the first statement in the Click event procedure for the Add Item button on the Invoice form. Then, start the program, enter values for the customer name, unit price, and quantity, and click on the Add Item button. The program will then enter break mode.

3. Notice the values that are displayed in the Autos window. In particular, notice that the DiscountAmount, InvoiceTotal, and OrderTotal properties defined by the Invoice class are included in this window because they're used in the three statements that follow the current statement. However, the CustomerName property isn't included in this window because it isn't used until later in the program.

4. Click on the Locals tab to display the Locals window, and then click on the plus sign to the left of the Me keyword. Scroll down in this window until you see the Invoice object. Then, click on the plus sign to the left of this object to display its instance variables and properties. In this window, you can see the CustomerName property because it's within the scope of the current procedure.

5. Press the F11 key to execute the current statement. Since this statement executes the AddItem method in the Invoice class, that method will be displayed in the Code Editor window and the Sub statement will be highlighted. Notice that the values of the arguments defined by this procedure are displayed in the Locals window.

6. Highlight the "UnitPrice * Quantity" expression in the first statement in this procedure. Then, place the mouse pointer over the expression to display its value. Try this again with the "Discount(dOrderTotal)" expression in the next statement. Is a value displayed? Why or why not?

7. Press the F11 key two more times to execute the Sub statement and the statement that calculates the order total. Then, expand the Me keyword in the Locals window to see the value of the OrderTotal property and the dOrderTotal variable.

Use the Step Out and Step Over commands to control program execution

8. Press F11 one more time to execute the statement that calculates the discount. Because this statement calls the Discount function, the execution point moves to the Function statement for that procedure.

9. Click on the Step Out button in the Debug toolbar to execute the statements in the function without entering break mode. The execution point will return to the statement that called this function.

10. Press F11 three more times to return to the calling statement in the Click event procedure. Then, press F11 one more time to complete this statement.

11. Click the Step Over button in the Debug toolbar. That will execute the OrderTotal property in the Invoice class without stopping.

Use the Locals window to change the value of a property

12. Before you continue program execution, set a breakpoint on the last statement in the Click event procedure for the New Invoice button. Then, click on the Continue button in the Debug toolbar. When the Invoice form is displayed, click on the New Invoice button. The invoice confirmation message will be displayed and the program will enter break mode again after you click the OK button.

13. Locate the Quantity text box in the Locals window, expand it to display its properties, and locate the Text property. Double-click in the Value column for this property, then enter 10 and press the Enter key to change its value.

14. Continue program execution, and notice that the value you entered for the Text property of the Quantity text box is displayed on the form. Enter a customer name and unit price and click on the Add Item button. The program will enter break mode when it reaches the breakpoint in the Click event procedure for this button.

Use the Breakpoints window to disable a breakpoint

15. Display the Breakpoints window and remove the check mark from the second breakpoint to disable it. Continue program execution and click on the New Invoice button and then the OK button. This time, the program won't stop at the breakpoint in the Click event procedure.

16. Enter a customer name, unit price, and quantity one more time, and then click on the Add Item button to enter break mode. Click on the Clear All Breakpoints button at the top of the Breakpoints window to remove the two breakpoints. Then, continue program execution.

End the application

17. Click on the Exit button in the Invoice form to end the program. If you're going to continue with the next exercise, leave the project open. Otherwise, close the project.

Exercise 7-2   Use the Command, Watch, and Output windows

In the last exercise, you used the Autos, Locals, and Breakpoints windows. Now, in this exercise, you'll get a chance to experiment with the Command, Watch, and Output windows.

Open the project

1. If it's not already open, open the Invoice project you used in the last exercise.

Use the Command window to work with a variable and function

2. Display the Invoice class in the Code Editor window, and set a breakpoint on the last statement in the AddItem procedure.

3. Start the application, enter values for the unit price and quantity, and click on the Add Item button. In break mode, display the Command window and then display the value of the dOrderTotal variable in this window.

4. Execute the Discount function and display its return value by typing this code into the Command window:

```
? discount(dordertotal)
```

5. Assign a value of 100 to the dOrderTotal variable by entering an assignment statement in the Command window. Then, execute the Discount function again and display its return value.

Use a Watch window to monitor expressions

6. Display the Watch 1 window. Then, highlight the dOrderTotal variable and drag it to that window.

7. Click in the Name column of the first blank row in the Watch window and enter this expression:

```
dordertotal > 1000
```

Notice that the current value of this expression is False. Then, continue program execution.

8. Add additional items to the invoice and check the values in the Watch window each time the program enters break mode. Continue adding items until the value of the second expression is True. Then, click on the Stop Debugging button in the Debug toolbar to end the application.

Use the Output window to display program information

9. Remove the current breakpoint, and add a new breakpoint on the statement in the Click event procedure of the New Invoice button in the form class that creates a new invoice object. Then, add this statement before the breakpoint:

```
Debug.WriteLine("Invoice total: " & lblInvoiceTotal.Text)
```

10. Run the application. Enter the items for an invoice and then click on the New Invoice button and the OK button. When the application enters break mode, display the Output window and notice that the invoice total is displayed in this window.

11. Enter additional invoices if you'd like to see how they're displayed in the Output window. When you're done, end the application, close the project, and close Visual Studio.

Section 2

How to work with Windows forms and controls

This section consists of three chapters that show you how to improve the graphical user interfaces of your applications. Chapter 8 shows you how to work with controls like combo box, list box, radio button, and tab controls. Chapter 9 shows you how to develop applications that consist of two or more Windows forms. And chapter 10 shows you how to enhance a user interface with splash forms, context menus, toolbars, status bars, and help information. Since each of these chapters builds on the previous chapter, you should read these chapters in sequence.

Note, however, that you don't have to read all three chapters before you go on to other sections. Once you finish chapter 8, you'll know how to use the controls and events that are used in the later sections, so you don't have to read chapters 9 and 10 before skipping ahead. If, for example, you want to learn more of the Visual Basic language essentials, you can skip to section 3 after you finish chapter 8. Or, you can skip to section 4 to learn how to work with the data in a database.

How to work with Windows controls

In this chapter, you'll learn how to use the common controls for Windows forms. Then, you'll learn some new skills for working with controls. When you're done, you'll be able to develop forms that use any of the controls presented in this chapter. You'll also have the background you need for learning how to use other controls on your own.

How to work with specific controls

In section 1 of this book, you learned how to use label, text box, and button controls. Although you use these controls on almost every form you develop, their functionality is limited. Because of that, you need to know how to use some of the other controls provided by the .NET Framework.

Common controls for Windows applications

Figure 8-1 summarizes the controls you're most likely to use as you develop Windows applications. All of these controls are available from the Windows Forms tab of the Toolbox. This tab is displayed by default when you're developing a Windows application.

You'll learn how to use a few of these controls in the topics that follow, and you'll learn how to use others in later chapters of this book. However, you won't learn about the LinkLabel and CheckedListBox controls, so I'll describe them briefly here. If you want to learn more about these controls or any of the controls that aren't listed here, you can get the information you need from the online help documentation.

If you want to include a hyperlink like the ones you see in help documents or on web pages, you can use the LinkLabel control. The Text property of this control determines the text that's displayed, and the LinkArea property determines what part of that text is displayed as a hyperlink (the default is all of the text). Then, you can use the LinkClicked event of the control to determine what happens when the hyperlink is clicked. In most cases, this event procedure will display another form in the application, or it will display a web page.

The CheckedListBox control is like the ListBox control you'll learn about later in this chapter, but the items in the list are displayed with a check box next to them. Then, if you select an item, a check mark appears in the check box. And if you select a checked item, the check mark is cleared. You might want to use a list like this to let the user select one or more options that affect the operation of the program. Although you can also create a list box that lets you select more than one item, I think the checked list box is more appropriate for those situations.

COMPONENTS = SOME OLD CONTROLS, SOME JUST SEP. FILES

OUTSIDE FRAMEWORK

Control	Name	Suggested prefix	Description
A	Label	lbl	Displays descriptive information.
A	LinkLabel	lnk	A label that contains hypertext that links to an object or web page when clicked.
ab	Button	btn	Performs an operation when clicked.
abl	TextBox	txt	Lets the user enter or modify a value.
	MainMenu	mnu *INVIS.*	Displays a menu from which the user can select operations.
☑	CheckBox	chk	Turns an option on or off.
◉	RadioButton	rdo	Turns an option on or off. If two or more radio buttons are in a group box or panel, turning one on turns the others off.
	GroupBox	grp	Groups controls. *CONTAINER CONTROL*
	PictureBox	pic	Displays a graphic image. *TAKES MORE MEMORY*
	Panel	pnl	Defines areas of a form. *CAN CHANGE VIS*
	DataGrid *+++*	grd	Displays data in a row and column format, and lets the user add, modify, and delete rows.
	ListBox	lst ✻	Displays a list that the user can select from.
	CheckedListBox	clst ✻	Displays a list that the user can select from. A check mark can be displayed next to items that have been selected.
	ComboBox	cbo ✻✻	Lets the user enter a value or select an item from a list.
	TabControl	tab	Provides tabbed areas that overlay one another. *BETTER THAN MULT WINDOWS*
	ProgressBar	prg	Indicates the progress of an operation.
	ImageList	img	Contains one or more images for use with other controls. *CAN USE W/TOOLBAR (COLLECTION)*
F1	HelpProvider	hlp	Exposes control properties for providing help information.
	ToolTip	ttp	Exposes control properties for displaying ToolTips. *– CAN USE TO SHOW COVERED INFO*
	ContextMenu	cmnu *RT.CLICK*	Displays a context menu for a form or control.
	ToolBar	tlb	Displays a toolbar on the form. *SET OF BUTTONS.*
	StatusBar	sb	Displays a status bar on the form.
!	ErrorProvider	err	Displays an error icon and a ToolTip with the error message.

see 60, 562, 563

* PREFERABLE TO LETTING ENTER

** PREF TO LIST BOX

+++ BUG IN .NET → USING OLD COM CONTROLS → DLL PATCH A M.S. TO BE ABLE TO SEE

Figure 8-1   Common controls for Windows applications

INTRINSIC CONTROLS — IMP. IN RUNTIME CONTROL
– VS –
ACTIVEX CONTROLS — IMP. IN SEP. FILE

How to work with label, text box, and button controls

Since the Invoice Total and Future Value programs that were presented in previous chapters used label, text box, and button controls, you should already be familiar with the basic operations of these controls. However, you may want to know about some of the other properties that affect how they function. The properties you're most likely to use are presented in figure 8-2.

As you know, the main purpose of a label control is to display information. So you almost always set its Text property to the text you want to display when you design the form. If the text will change as the program executes, though, you can set this property in the code for the form.

As you learned in chapter 2, you can include an ampersand (&) in the Text property to indicate the character that can be used to access the control using the keyboard. Note, however, that since a label can't receive the focus, the focus moves to the next control in the tab order that can receive the focus. In the form shown at the top of this figure, for example, the access key for the Invoice number label is the letter I. So if the user holds down the Alt key and presses the letter I, the focus will move to the text box to the right of the label, which is what you want.

In some cases, you may want to include an ampersand in the text that's displayed in the label. To do that, you have to set the UseMnemonic property of the label to False. Then, an ampersand you include in the Text property is treated as a text character.

Several of the text box properties in this figure are used to create multi-line text boxes like the one shown in the form at the top of this figure. To create a text box like this, you set the Multiline property to True. Then, you can set the AcceptsReturn, AcceptsTab, Scrollbars, and WordWrap properties so the control works the way you want it to. These properties, as well as the other text box properties shown in this figure, should be self-explanatory, so I won't describe them in more detail. If you need more information about any of these properties, though, you can refer to the online help documentation.

The last property shown in this figure is the Text property of the button control. Like the label control, you can include one ampersand in this property to define an access key for it. Unlike the label control, if you want to include an ampersand in the text, you can type two ampersands in a row. If, for example, you want to create a Save & Exit button, you can type "Save && Exit" as the Text property.

A form with access keys and a multi-line text box

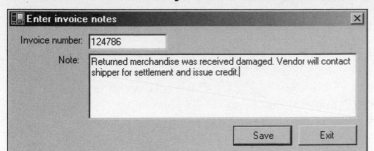

Label control properties

Property	Example	Description
Text	&Invoice number:	The text for the label. If an ampersand (&) is included, the next letter is treated as an access key. Then, the user can press Alt plus this letter to move the focus to the control that follows the label in the tab order. (The label itself can't receive the focus.)
UseMnemonic	True	Determines whether an ampersand (&) in the Text property of the control identifies an access key (True) or a text character (False).

Text box control properties

Property	Example	Description
AcceptsReturn	False	Determines whether return characters can be entered into a text box whose Multiline property is set to True.
AcceptsTab	False	Determines whether tab characters can be entered into a text box whose Multiline property is set to True.
CharacterCasing	Normal	Determines whether characters entered into the text box should be left as entered or converted to upper or lowercase.
HideSelection	False	Determines if the text in the text box is hidden when the control loses focus.
MaxLength	10	The maximum number of characters that can be entered into the text box. The default is 32767.
Multiline	False	Determines whether the text in the text box can occupy more than one line.
PasswordChar	*	The character that's displayed in place of each character entered into the text box. Used to provide security for entering passwords.
ReadOnly	False	Determines whether the user can change the text in the text box.
Scrollbars	None	Determines what scrollbars are displayed in a multi-line text box.
WordWrap	True	Determines whether the lines in a multi-line text box are wrapped automatically when the end of each line is reached.

Button control property

Property	Example	Description
Text	E&xit	The text that will appear on the control. If an ampersand is included, the letter that follows can be used as an access key.

Figure 8-2   How to work with label, text box, and button controls

How to work with combo box and list box controls

Figure 8-3 shows you how to work with *combo boxes* and *list boxes*. In the form at the top of this figure, a combo box lets the user select a number that represents the life of an asset and a list box displays the depreciation amount for each year of the asset's life. To use this form, the user enters the initial cost of the asset and the final value of the asset (which is often zero) in the text boxes. Then, the user selects the life of the asset from the drop-down list of the combo box or enters the number of years into that box. Last, the user clicks on the Calculate button to display the year and depreciation amounts in the list box.

This figure also lists some of the properties and methods you're likely to use as you work with combo boxes and list boxes. To get the *index* value of the item that the user selects, for example, you can use the SelectedIndex property. And to get the value of the selected item, you can use the SelectedItem property. You'll see coding examples that use these properties in the next figure.

One property that applies only to a combo box is the DropDownStyle property. This property determines how the combo box functions. The default is DropDown, which means that the user can either click on the drop-down arrow at the right side of the combo box to display the drop-down list and select an item, or he can enter a value directly into the text box portion of the combo box. Note that the value the user enters doesn't necessarily have to be a value that appears in the list.

If you want to restrict user entries to just the values in the list, you can set the DropDownStyle property to DropDownList. Then, the user can only select a value from the list or enter a value that appears in the list.

The third option for the DropDownStyle property is Simple. Like the DropDown setting, this setting lets the user enter any value into the text box portion of the control. However, instead of having to click on an arrow to display the list, the list is always visible.

When you work with the items in a list box or combo box, you should realize that you're actually working with the items in a collection. To refer to this collection, you use the Items property of the control. Then, you can use the properties and methods that the .NET Framework provides for working with collection objects to work with the items in the collection. The most common properties and methods are summarized in this figure.

The most common event for working with combo boxes and list boxes is the SelectedIndexChanged event. This event occurs when the value of the SelectedIndex property changes, which is when the user selects a different item from the list. For a combo box, you can also use the TextChanged event to detect when the user enters a value into the text box portion of the control. Keep in mind, though, that this event will occur each time a single character is added, changed, or deleted.

** TO ADD ITEMS 3-RUNTIME → LST LIST, ITEMS. ADD "VALUE1"
—USE LOOP FOR MANY...*

A form that contains a combo box and a list box

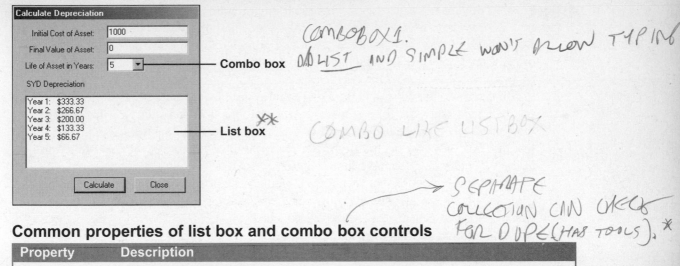

*COMBOBOX1.
DAD LIST AND SIMPLE WON'T ALLOW TYPING*

Combo box

COMBO LIKE LISTBOX

List box

*SEPARATE
COLLECTION CAN CHECK
FOR DUPE (HAS TOOLS). **

Common properties of list box and combo box controls

Property	Description
SelectedIndex	The index value of the selected item. Items are numbered from 0. If no item is selected, this property has a value of –1.
SelectedItem	The contents of the selected item.
Text	The contents of the text box portion of a combo box control.
Sorted	If set to True, the items in the list are sorted alphabetically.
Items	Provides access to the collection of items in a list box or combo box list.
DropDownStyle	Determines whether the text box portion of a combo box control is editable and whether the list portion is always displayed or is displayed when the drop-down arrow is clicked.

ALLOW DROP T/F

Common properties and methods of the Items collection

Property	Description
Count	The number of items in the list.

Method	Description
Add	Adds an item to a list box or combo box list.
Insert	Inserts an item into a list box or combo box list at the specified location.
Remove	Removes an item from a list box or combo box list.
Clear	Removes all items from a list box or combo box list.

Description

- To work with the items in a *list box* or *combo box* list, you use the Items collection of the control that you access through the Items property of the control. To refer to any item in the collection, you use an *index* value.

- If a list box contains more items than can be displayed at one time, a vertical scroll bar is automatically added.

- When the user selects a different item from a list, the SelectedIndexChanged event occurs. When the user enters a value into the text box portion of a combo box, the TextChanged event occurs.

Figure 8-3   How to work with combo box and list box controls

* ENTRY SHOULDN'T SHOW — CHECK FOR ERRORS, DUPES FIRST.

Figure 8-4 presents some code examples for working with combo boxes and list boxes. The first example uses a For…Next loop to load the numbers 1 through 40 into a combo box list named cboLife. This is the combo box from the Calculate Depreciation form you saw in the previous figure that lets the user specify the life of an asset. Each time through the loop, the Add method is used to add the number to the Items collection of the combo box.

In this case, the code is in the Load event procedure for the Form, so the combo box is loaded when the form is loaded. After that, the user can select a value from the combo box and other procedures can use that value. You can see, for example, that the Text property of cboLife is used as the third argument for the SYD function in the second coding example in this figure.

The second example shows how you can load the list box in figure 8-3 when the Click event of the Calculate button occurs. This example begins by invoking the Clear method to clear all items from the list box. Then, a For…Next loop uses the SYD function to add the lines to the list box.

The SYD function is one of the financial functions that come with Visual Basic. It calculates each year's depreciation using a method know as the Sum of the Years' Digits. If you're not familiar with depreciation, keep in mind that you don't have to understand how it works. Just think of it as a function that requires four arguments and returns a yearly depreciation value that is added to a list box. The point of this code is to illustrate the use of the Add method.

Even then, this code may look confusing, but it's easy to understand if you break it down. For each year in the asset's life (iIndex), the Add method is used to add a string to the Items collection of the list box. This string starts with the year followed by a colon and some spaces

```
lstDepreciation.Items.Add ("Year " & iIndex & ":    " &
```

followed by the value derived from the SYD function

```
SYD(txtInitialCost.Text, txtFinalValue.Text, cboLife.Text, iIndex)
```

after the FormatCurrency function is used to format the result.

When you use the Add method of the Items collection to add an item to a list, the item is added at the end of the list. If you want to add the item in another location, you can use the Insert method as illustrated by the third example in this figure. When you use this method, you indicate the index where you want the item inserted along with the value of the item to be inserted. Keep in mind if you use this method that the index values of a collection are zero-based. So the index of the first item is 0, the index of the second item is 1, and so on.

The fourth example in this figure shows how to use the Remove method to remove an item from a list by specifying its index value. The fifth example shows how to use the SelectedItem property to get the value of the selected item. And the last example shows how you can initialize a combo box so that no value is selected. To do that, you set the SelectedIndex property of the control to –1, which is not a valid index value.

Code that loads the combo box in figure 8-3

```
Private Sub Form1_Load(ByVal sender As System.Object, _
        ByVal e As System.EventArgs) Handles MyBase.Load
    Dim iIndex As Integer
    For iIndex = 1 To 40
        cboLife.Items.Add(iIndex)
    Next iIndex
End Sub
```

Code that clears and loads the list box in figure 8-3

```
Private Sub btnCalculate_Click(ByVal sender As System.Object, _
        ByVal e As System.EventArgs) Handles btnCalculate.Click
    Dim iIndex As Integer
    lstDepreciation.Items.Clear()
    For iIndex = 1 To cboLife.Text
        lstDepreciation.Items.Add("Year " & iIndex & ":    " _
            & FormatCurrency(SYD(txtInitialCost.Text, _
                txtFinalValue.Text, cboLife.Text, iIndex)))
    Next iIndex
End Sub
```

A statement that inserts an item into a combo box list

```
cboNames.Items.Insert(iIndex, txtName.Text)
```

A statement that removes an item from a list

```
cboNames.Items.Remove(iIndex)
```

A statement that refers to the selected item in a combo box

```
sSelectedName = cboNames.SelectedItem
```

A statement that initializes a combo box so that no item is selected

```
cboNames.SelectedIndex = -1
```

About the depreciation functions

- The SYD function that's used in the second example is one of the financial functions that comes with Visual Basic. It calculates the yearly depreciation for an item by using the Sum of the Years' Digits method of depreciation.

- The four arguments that the SYD function requires are the initial cost of the item, the final value of the item, the lifetime of the item in years, and the year that the item value should be calculated for. This function returns the depreciation for one year.

- Another function that can be used to calculate depreciation is the SLN function. It calculates straight line depreciation using just the first three arguments that are used for the SYD function (initial cost, final value, and lifetime of the item).

- To find out more about the depreciation functions or other financial functions, use the Index tab of the help feature and type in "financial calculations."

Figure 8-4   Code for working with combo box and list box controls

How to work with check box and radio button controls

Figure 8-5 shows you how to work with *check boxes* and *radio buttons*. The main difference between these two types of controls is that radio buttons in a group are mutually exclusive and check boxes operate independently. In other words, if the user selects a radio button in a group, all of the other buttons are automatically turned off. In contrast, when the user selects a check box, it has no effect on the other check boxes on the form, even if they appear as a group.

To group radio buttons, you can place them in either a group box control or a panel control. You'll learn about these controls in a minute. For now, just realize that if radio buttons aren't placed within one of these controls, all of the radio buttons on the form function as a group.

The property you're most likely to use when working with radio buttons and check boxes is the Checked property. This property can have a value of either True or False to indicate if the control is checked. You can see how this property is used in the two examples in this figure.

In the first example, the Checked property of the Future Value radio button is tested in an If statement. If the value of this property is True, a procedure named CalculateFutureValue is executed. But if the value of this property is False, it indicates that the Monthly Investment radio button is selected. In that case, a procedure named CalculateMonthlyInvestment is executed.

The second example is similar. In this case, though, the Checked property of a check box is tested. If the value of this property is True, the FV function is executed using the DueDate.EndOfPeriod constant for the fifth argument. Otherwise, the DueDate.BegOfPeriod constant is used.

The event you're most likely to work with when you use radio buttons or check boxes is the CheckedChanged event. This event occurs when you check or uncheck one of these controls. You'll see how you can use this event in one of the applications presented later in this chapter.

How to work with group box and panel controls

Figure 8-5 also illustrates how to use GroupBox and Panel controls. Here, you can see that the two radio buttons have been placed inside a *group box* so it's clear that they function as a group. The name of the group, which is displayed in the upper left corner of the group box, is specified by setting the Text property of the control. In contrast, the *panel* control doesn't have a Text property. Because of that, it's more common to use this control to form visual rather than functional groups.

Regardless of which control you use, you should know that if you move one of these controls in the Form Designer window, all of the controls it contains are moved with it. In fact, it's common to use a panel control just to group controls that can be moved together. Then, if you don't want the panel to appear when the form is displayed, you can set its BorderStyle property to None.

DEPRECIATION 0305

A form with two radio buttons, a group box, a panel, and a check box

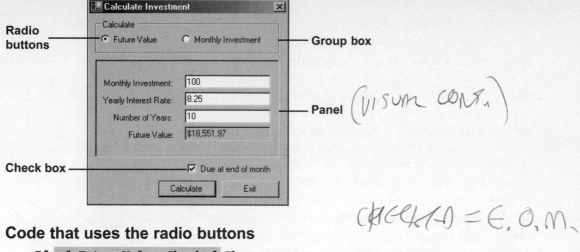

Radio buttons

Group box

Panel (VISUAL CONT.)

Check box

CHECKED = E.O.M.

Code that uses the radio buttons

```
If rdoFutureValue.Checked Then
    CalculateFutureValue()
Else
    CalculateMonthlyInvestment()
End If
```

Code that uses the check box

```
If chkDueAtEnd.Checked Then
    txtFutureValue.Text = _
        FormatNumber(FV(txtInterestRate.Text / 12 / 100, _
            txtYears.Text * 12, -txtMonthlyInvestment.Text, , _
            DueDate.EndOfPeriod))
Else
    txtFutureValue.Text = _
        FormatNumber(FV(txtInterestRate.Text / 12 / 100, _
            txtYears.Text * 12, -txtMonthlyInvestment.Text, , _
            DueDate.BegOfPeriod))
End If
```

Description

- To determine whether a *radio button* or *check box* is checked, you test its Checked property. This property can be set to either True or False.

- When you check or uncheck a radio button or check box, the CheckedChanged event occurs.

- You can use either a *group box* or a *panel* control to group controls. The main difference between the two is that a group box includes a Text property that contains the caption for the control, but a panel control does not.

- Group boxes are typically used to group controls like radio buttons that function as a group. Panel controls are typically used to visually group controls on a form.

- If you move a group box or a panel control, all of the controls it contains move with it.

Figure 8-5   How to work with radio button, check box, group box, and panel controls

How to work with tab controls

The last control I'll present in this chapter is the tab control. This control lets you group other controls on the form into *pages*. Figure 8-6 presents the basic skills for working with tab controls.

As you can see, the form in this figure contains a tab control with two pages, also called *tabs*. The first tab provides controls that let you calculate an investment, and the second tab provides controls that let you calculate depreciation. Notice that these two tabs provide functionality similar to the forms in figures 8-3 and 8-5. The tab control makes it easy to combine related forms like this into a single form.

The event you'll use most often with a tab control is the SelectedIndex-Changed event. This event occurs when the SelectedIndex property of the control changes, which typically happens as a result of a user clicking on another tab. The event procedure shown in this figure, for example, moves the focus to the appropriate control on a tab when that tab becomes the current tab. Notice that this procedure uses the SelectedIndex property to determine which tab is current.

A form that uses a tab control with two tabs

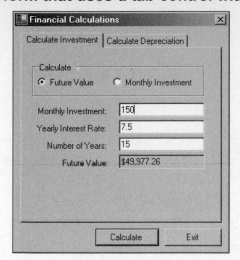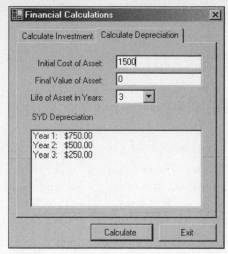

Code that uses the SelectedIndexChanged event of the tab control

```
Private Sub tabCalculations_SelectedIndexChanged _
        (ByVal sender As System.Object, ByVal e As System.EventArgs) _
        Handles tabCalculations.SelectedIndexChanged
    If tabCalculations.SelectedIndex = 0 Then
        If rdoFutureValue.Checked = True Then
            txtMonthlyInvestment.Focus()
        Else
            txtInterestRate.Focus()
        End If
    Else
        txtInitialCost.Focus()
    End If
End Sub
```

Description

- After you add a tab control to a form, you can add *tabs* to it by clicking on the Add Tab link at the bottom of the Properties window or by selecting the Add Tab command from the shortcut menu for the control.

- By default, the tabs are displayed along the top of the tab control. To display them along the left, right, or bottom of the control, change the Alignment property accordingly.

- By default, the tabs you add are displayed in a single row. To create multiple rows of tabs, set the Multiline property to True.

- To remove a tab, select it and then click on the Remove Tab link in the Properties window or select the Remove Tab command from the shortcut menu for the control.

- Each tab in a tab control contains a *page* where you add the controls for the tab. You use the Text property of a page to set the text that's displayed in its associated tab.

- The SelectedIndexChanged event occurs when you move to another tab. You can use the SelectedIndex property of the tab control to determine which tab was selected.

Figure 8-6   How to work with tab controls

Other skills for working with controls

Now that you're familiar with some of the most common Windows controls, you'll want to know about some skills for working with controls in general. These skills will help you work with controls more efficiently.

How to use Tab Order view to set the tab order of controls

In chapter 2, you learned how to use the TabIndex property to change the tab order of the controls on a form. An easier way to change the tab order, though, is to use Tab Order view. This view is illustrated in figure 8-7.

When you display a form in Tab Order view, an index value is displayed at the left of each control that indicates the control's position in the tab order. In the first form in this figure, for example, the Monthly Investment label is the first control in the tab order, followed by the Monthly Investment text box, the Yearly Interest Rate label, and so on. Notice that the index values of the two radio button controls indicate their position in the tab order relative to the group box that contains them, which is what you want.

To change the tab order, you simply click on each control in the appropriate sequence. As you click on each control, the numbers are displayed as shown in the second form in this figure. Here, I clicked on the four text boxes in order, followed by the two buttons and then the group box. That way, when the form is first displayed, the focus will be on the first text box. Then, when the user presses the Tab key, the focus will move through the controls in sequence.

Notice that when I selected the group box control, the main indexes of the radio buttons within this control changed too so that they're the same as the group box. However, the sub index of each radio button didn't change. In other words, the indexes of the radio buttons relative to each other remained the same. If you wanted to change these indexes, though, you could do that by clicking on them just like any other control.

Also notice in the second form that I didn't select any of the label controls. In most cases, it's not necessary to change the tab order of controls that can't receive the focus.

One case where you will want to include a label control explicitly in the tab order is if it defines an access key. In that case, you'll want to position it in the tab order just before the control it identifies. Then, if the user presses the access key for that control, the focus will move to the control it identifies since it's next in the tab order.

A form in Tab Order view before and after the tab order is changed

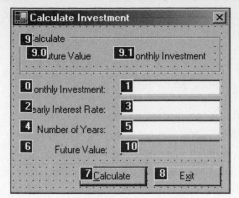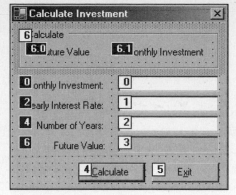

How to use Tab Order view to change the tab order

- To display a form in Tab Order view, select the form and then select the View → Tab Order command. This displays the tab index for each control as in the first form above.

- To change the tab indexes of the controls, click on the controls in the sequence you want to use. As you click, the new tab indexes appear as in the second form above.

- If a control contains other controls, the contained controls are displayed with sub indexes as illustrated by the radio buttons above. Then, you can click on the containing control to change its index and the main indexes of the controls it contains. To change the sub indexes of the contained controls, click on them individually.

Description

- The *tab order* determines the order in which controls receive the focus when the Tab key is pressed. The TabIndex property of the controls determines this order.

- By default, the value of a control's TabIndex property is determined by the sequence in which it's added to the form. The TabIndex property is set to 0 for the first control, to 1 for the second control, and so on.

- One way to change the TabIndex properties of controls is to use the Properties window for each control. If you change this property to an index value that's assigned to another control, the second control that's assigned the index value will come after the first control in the tab order.

- The other way to change the TabIndex properties of controls is to use Tab Order view.

- You won't normally set the tab index for controls like labels that can't receive the focus, unless the control defines an access key. In that case, the TabIndex property of that control should be one less than the control that receives the focus when the access key is pressed.

- You can also skip controls whose TabStop, Enabled, or Visible properties have been set to false unless these properties will change as the form runs.

Figure 8-7   How to use Tab Order view to set the tab order of the controls

How to use the KeyPress event to restrict user entries

The KeyPress event occurs on the control that has the focus each time a key is pressed on the keyboard. It's used most frequently to restrict the characters that the user can enter into a control, which is another way to make sure the user enters valid data.

To restrict user entries, you use code like that shown in figure 8-8. This code responds to the KeyPress event of the Monthly Investment text box on the Future Value form. It lets the user enter only numeric characters. In addition, it lets the user press the backspace key to erase one or more characters that have already been entered. You can use a similar procedure to limit the characters that are entered for a phone number to the ten digits, the left and right parentheses, the hyphen, and the backspace key.

This procedure uses a Select Case statement to perform processing based on which key the user pressed. To determine which key was pressed, it uses the KeyChar property of the e argument that's passed to the procedure, which contains the ASCII character associated with the key. To make it easier to work with keys for non-displayable characters such as the backspace, this ASCII character is converted to an integer value using the Visual Basic Asc function. You can find a list of all the ASCII codes in the Visual Basic documentation, but this figure lists the codes for the most common entry characters.

The key to using the KeyPress event is setting the Handled property of the e argument properly. This property indicates whether the event procedure handled the event. If it didn't (False), the default Windows processing is performed. That's what you want if the user presses a valid key. If the user presses any of the numeric keys listed in the first Case clause in this figure, for example, the default processing will cause the character to be added to the text box. And if the user presses the backspace key, the default processing will cause the last character that was entered to be erased. However, if the user presses any other key, the Handled property is set to True so no processing takes place. In other words, the key is ignored.

If you want to use a KeyPress event procedure for more than one control, you can do that by adding events to the Handles clause in the Sub statement. To illustrate, the Handles clause in the second example in this figure lists the KeyPress event for controls named txtValue1, txtValue2, and txtValue3. If you add events to this clause, though, you should also change the name of the procedure to indicate what it now represents. In this example, the name has been changed to NumericControl_KeyPress to indicate that the procedure is used for the KeyPress event of controls that should receive numeric entries.

Note that it is the Handles clause that determines what events trigger a procedure, not the name of the procedure. As a result, you can use this technique whenever you want to write one procedure that handles more than one event.

A procedure that uses the KeyPress event to restrict entries in a text box

```
Private Sub txtMonthlyInvestment_KeyPress(ByVal sender As Object, _
        ByVal e As System.Windows.Forms.KeyPressEventArgs) _
        Handles txtMonthlyInvestment.KeyPress
    Select Case Asc(e.KeyChar)
        Case 8, 36, 44, 46, 48 To 57 'Backspace key and all numeric keys
            e.Handled = False
        Case Else
            e.Handled = True
    End Select
End Sub
```

ASCII codes for common entry characters

Character	Code	Character	Code
$	36	(	40
,	44	)	41
.	46	-	45
0 to 9	48 to 57	Space	32
		Backspace	8

The Sub statement for a procedure that handles two or more controls

```
Private Sub NumericControl_KeyPress(ByVal sender As Object, _
        ByVal e As System.Windows.Forms.KeyPressEventArgs) _
        Handles txtValue1.KeyPress, txtValue2.KeyPress, txtValue3.KeyPress
```

Description

- The KeyPress event is fired each time a key is pressed. This event is typically used to restrict the characters that the user can enter into a control such as a text box.

- The KeyChar property of the e argument that's passed to the KeyPress event identifies the ASCII character associated with the key that was pressed. You can use the Visual Basic Asc function to convert this key to an integer so it's easy to work with in code. You'll find charts of the ASCII codes in the "ASCII Character Codes" topic in online help.

- You can use the Handled property of the e argument that's passed to the KeyPress event to determine how a key is processed. This property indicates whether or not the event was handled by the procedure.

- For a valid key, set the Handled property to False. Then, the default Windows processing takes place. For a text box, that usually means that the character associated with the key that was pressed is entered into the text box.

- For an invalid key, set the Handled property to True. Then, only the processing you specify (if any) takes place.

- If you allow the use of the Backspace key, the user can use it to erase the characters that have been entered in a control.

- If you want to use the same procedure for the KeyPress event of two or more controls, you can add the extra controls to the Handles clause in the Sub statement as shown above. In that case, it's a good idea to change the name of the procedure so it indicates what the procedure does.

Figure 8-8   How to use the KeyPress event to restrict user entries

How to customize the Toolbox

The .NET Framework provides a variety of controls that you can use in your Visual Basic applications. Many of these controls are available from the Toolbox by default. If you need to use a control that's not in the Toolbox, however, you can customize the Toolbox to include that control. To do that, you use the Customize Toolbox dialog box shown in figure 8-9.

As you can see, you can use this dialog box to add two different types of controls: COM components and .NET Framework components. COM components include ActiveX controls that were used in previous versions of Visual Basic. Because many of these controls have been replaced by components in the .NET Framework, you're not likely to need them.

To add a component to the Toolbox, you simply select the check box for that component. Then, the control is added to the tab that's currently displayed in the Toolbox. If that's not what you want, you can drag the component to another tab. Or, you can add a new tab as described in the figure and then add or drag the component to that tab.

The Customize Toolbox dialog box

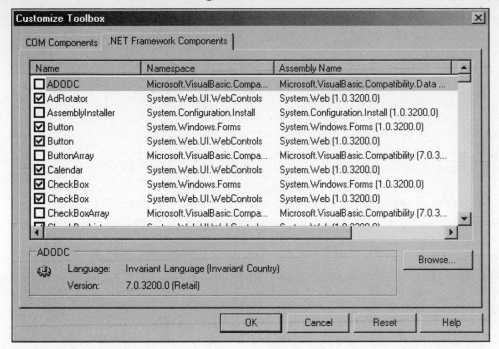

Description

- To display the Customize Toolbox dialog box, select the Tools → Customize Toolbox command. This dialog box lets you add COM components (ActiveX controls) and .NET Framework components. The components that are already in the Toolbox are checked.

- To add one or more components to the Toolbox, check the ones you want to add. To remove components from the Toolbox, uncheck them.

- When you add components to the Toolbox, they're added to the tab that's currently displayed. To create a custom tab for the new components, right-click on the Toolbox and select the Add Tab command from the shortcut menu that's displayed. Then, enter a name for the tab in the text box that's displayed and press the Enter key.

- You can move a component from one tab of the Toolbox to another by dragging it. The tabs that are displayed depend on the type of project you're working on and the window that's currently displayed.

Figure 8-9   How to customize the Toolbox

The Calculate Depreciation form

This chapter closes by presenting the design, property settings, and code for two forms that use many of the controls you learned about in this chapter. The first one is the Calculate Depreciation form you first saw back in figure 8-3. It uses both a combo box and a list box. By studying the code for this form, you will get a much better idea of how you can use combo and list box controls in a real application.

The design and property settings for the form

Figure 8-10 presents the design and property settings for the Calculate Depreciation form. This form calculates the depreciation for each year in the life of an asset using sum-of-years-digits depreciation. Notice here that when the depreciation years extend beyond the end of the list box, a scroll bar is automatically added to the control. That makes it easy for the user to scroll through all the values.

The property settings for the form should be self-explanatory. Like the other forms you've seen in this book, the FormBorderStyle property is set so the user can't change the size of the form, and the StartPosition property is set so the form is displayed in the middle of the screen. In addition, the AcceptButton property is set so the Calculate button is activated when the user presses the Enter key, and the CancelButton property is set so the Exit button is activated when the user presses the Esc key.

You shouldn't have any trouble understanding the property settings for the controls either. You should notice, however, that the DropDownStyle property for the Life combo box is set to DropDownList. That way, the user can only select an item from the list that this combo box provides. In addition, the TabStop property of the list box has been set to False so the focus doesn't move to it when the user presses the Tab key.

The form for the Calculate Depreciation application

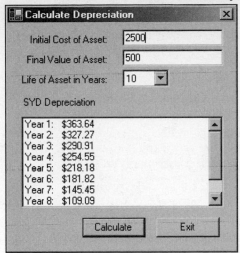

The property settings for the form

Default name	Property	Setting
Form1	Name	frmDepreciation
	FormBorderStyle	FixedSingle
	Text	Calculate Depreciation
	StartPosition	CenterScreen
	AcceptButton	btnCalculate
	CancelButton	btnExit

The property settings for the controls on the form

Default name	Property	Setting
Label1	Text	Initial Cost of Asset:
	TextAlign	MiddleRight
Label2	Text	Final Value of Asset:
	TextAlign	MiddleRight
Label3	Text	Life of Asset in Years:
	TextAlign	MiddleRight
Label4	Text	SYD Depreciation
TextBox1	Name	txtInitialCost
TextBox2	Name	txtFinalValue
ComboBox1	Name	cboLife
	DropDownStyle	DropDownList
ListBox1	Name	lstDepreciation
	TabStop	False

Figure 8-10   The design and property settings for the Calculate Depreciation form

The code for the form

Figure 8-11 presents the code for the Calculate Depreciation form. When this form is first loaded, the Load event procedure loads the values 1 through 40 into the Life combo box. You can refer back to figure 8-4 if you need to refresh your memory about how this code works.

The main procedure for this form is the Click event procedure for the Calculate button. This procedure starts by calling a function named ValidEntry to be sure that the user entries for the initial cost and final value are valid. As you can see, this function accepts three arguments. The first argument is the value to be tested, which is declared as a string. The second and third arguments are the minimum and maximum values that are allowed for the entry. Both of these arguments are declared as decimals.

The first statement in the ValidEntry function uses the IsNumeric function to determine if the entry is numeric. If it is, it then uses the minimum and maximum values that were passed to it as arguments to determine if the entry falls within an acceptable range. If it does, the return value of the function is set to True.

Now, take a closer look at the two If statements in the Click event procedure that call this function. The first one passes the Text property of the Initial Cost text box for the first argument, and it passes numeric literals for the second and third arguments. The second one also passes the Text property of a control for the first argument and a numeric literal for the second argument. However, the third argument uses the CDec function to convert the value in the Initial Cost text box to a decimal. That makes sense because the final value can't be greater than the initial cost, and the maximum value must be passed to the ValidEntry function as a decimal value.

The third If statement in the Click event procedure checks that the SelectedIndex property of the Life combo box isn't equal to –1. If it is, that means that an item wasn't selected.

If any of the user entries are invalid, an error message is displayed and the focus is moved to the control that contains the error. Otherwise, the Click event procedure continues by calculating the depreciation for each year and formatting each year's depreciation for display in the Depreciation list box. You saw this code in figure 8-4 too, so I won't explain it again here. Finally, the procedure moves the focus back to the Initial Cost text box so the user can enter values for another asset.

The Visual Basic code for the Calculate Depreciation form

```
Public Class Form1
    Inherits System.Windows.Forms.Form

    Private Sub frmDepreciation_Load(ByVal sender As System.Object, _
            ByVal e As System.EventArgs) Handles MyBase.Load
        Dim iIndex As Integer
        For iIndex = 1 To 40
            cboLife.Items.Add(iIndex)
        Next iIndex
    End Sub

    Private Sub btnCalculate_Click(ByVal sender As System.Object, _
            ByVal e As System.EventArgs) Handles btnCalculate.Click
        If ValidEntry(txtInitialCost.Text, 500, 1000000) Then
            If ValidEntry(txtFinalValue.Text, 0, CDec(txtInitialCost.Text)) Then
                If cboLife.SelectedIndex <> -1 Then
                    Dim iIndex As Integer
                    lstDepreciation.Items.Clear()
                    For iIndex = 1 To cboLife.Text
                        lstDepreciation.Items.Add("Year " & iIndex & ":    " _
                            & FormatCurrency(SYD(txtInitialCost.Text, _
                                txtFinalValue.Text, cboLife.Text, iIndex)))
                    Next iIndex
                    txtInitialCost.Focus()
                Else
                    MessageBox.Show("You must select a value for the " _
                        & "asset life.", "Entry error")
                    cboLife.Focus()
                End If
            Else
                MessageBox.Show("Final value must be a number " _
                    & "between 0 and the initial cost value.", "Entry error")
                txtFinalValue.Focus()
            End If
        Else
            MessageBox.Show("Initial cost must be a number " _
                & "between 500 and 1,000,000.", "Entry error")
            txtInitialCost.Focus()
        End If
    End Sub

    Private Function ValidEntry(ByVal Entry As String, _
            ByVal MinValue As Decimal, ByVal MaxValue As Decimal) As Boolean
        If IsNumeric(Entry) Then
            If Entry >= MinValue And Entry <= MaxValue Then
                ValidEntry = True
            End If
        End If
    End Function

    Private Sub btnExit_Click(ByVal sender As System.Object, _
            ByVal e As System.EventArgs) Handles btnExit.Click
        Me.Close()
    End Sub

End Class
```

Figure 8-11   The code for the Calculate Depreciation form

The Calculate Investment form

The Calculate Investment form is similar to the Future Value form you saw in earlier chapters. However, it has been enhanced so that it can calculate either a future value or the monthly investment needed to attain a specified future value. Here again, by studying the code for this form, you'll get a much better idea of how you can use radio buttons and a group box in a real application.

The design and property settings for the form

Figure 8-12 presents the design and property settings for the Calculate Investment form. As you can see, two radio buttons have been added to the form within a group box. By default, the Future Value button is selected. Then, the user can calculate a future value by entering a monthly investment, interest rate, and number of years and then clicking on the Calculate button. This is illustrated by the first form shown in this figure.

Although you can't tell by looking at this form, the calculated future value is displayed in a text box rather than in a label. That's necessary because to calculate a monthly investment, the user will need to be able to enter a future value. And, of course, a label can't be used for data entry.

To format this text box so it appears as shown here, the BackColor property of the Control is set to Control, which is a standard system color. In addition, the ReadOnly property of this control has been set to True so the user can't enter a value into it, and the TabStop property has been set to False so the focus doesn't move to this control when the user presses the Tab key. In a moment, you'll see how these properties change as the program executes.

To calculate a monthly investment, the user can click on the Monthly Investment radio button. Then, the form changes to look like the second one in this figure. Notice here that the Future Value text box has been changed so the user can enter a value into it, and the Monthly Investment text box has been changed so a value can't be entered into it.

Two versions of the Calculate Investment form

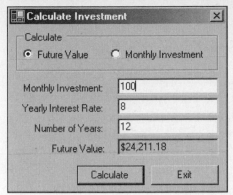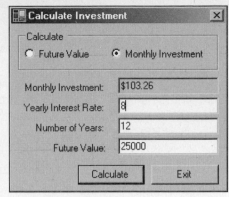

The property settings for the new controls

Default name	Property	Setting
GroupBox1	Text	Calculate
RadioButton1	Name	rdoFutureValue
	Text	Future Value
	Checked	True
RadioButton2	Name	rdoMonthlyInvestment
	Text	Monthly Investment
	Checked	False
TextBox1	Name	txtFutureValue
	ReadOnly	True
	TabStop	False
	BackColor	Control
	Text	(empty)

Description

- The Calculate Investment form can calculate either the future value of a monthly investment or the monthly investment needed to attain a specific future value. The user can choose the operation to perform by clicking on the appropriate radio button.

- Instead of using a label for the future value, this form uses a text box. That way, the user can enter a future value for a monthly investment calculation.

- To limit which controls the user can enter data into and to alter the appearance of those controls, the ReadOnly, TabStop, and BackColor properties of the Future Value and Monthly Investment text boxes are changed as appropriate when the user selects one of the radio buttons in the Calculate group.

Note

- In addition to the properties shown above, you'll want to change the tab order of the controls so they work the way you want them to.

Figure 8-12   The Calculate Investment form and its property settings

The code for the form

Figure 8-13 presents the code for the Calculate Investment form in three parts. Most of the processing for this form is controlled by the Click event procedure of the Calculate button, which starts by checking if the Future Value radio button is selected. If so, it calls a function named ValidEntry to determine if the data in each of the controls is valid. This function works just like the one in the Calculate Depreciation form. Then, if all of the user entries are valid, the Click event procedure calls the CalculateFutureValue procedure to calculate the future value and moves the focus back to the Monthly Investment text box. Otherwise, it displays an appropriate error message.

If the Monthly Investment radio button is selected instead of the Future Value button, similar processing takes place. Instead of calling the CalculateFutureValue procedure, though, this procedure calls the CalculateMonthlyInvestment procedure. And instead of moving the focus to the Monthly Investment text box, it moves it to the Interest Rate text box.

On page 2 of this listing, you can see the code for the two called procedures. Since the CalculateFutureValue procedure is like the one you saw in chapter 5, you should be able to follow it without much trouble. You should also be able to follow the CalculateMonthlyInvestment procedure because it's similar. Instead of using the FV function, though, it uses the Pmt function to calculate the monthly payment. This is another one of the financial functions that come with Visual Basic, and it uses arguments that are similar to those for the FV function.

If the user clicks on the Future Value radio button when the Monthly Investment radio button is selected, the CheckedChanged event of that control is fired. Then, the event procedure for this event changes three properties of the Future Value and Monthly Investment text boxes. Specifically, it changes the ReadOnly property of the Future Value text box to True so the user can't enter a value into this control. It changes the TabStop property of this control to False so the focus doesn't move to this control. And it changes the BackColor property to SystemColors.Control so the control looks disabled.

Next, this procedure changes the ReadOnly, TabStop, and BackColor properties of the Monthly Investment text box so the user can enter a value into this control. Then, this procedure calls a general procedure named ClearControls on page 3 of this listing, which moves a zero-length string to each text box. Last, the CheckedChanged procedure moves the focus to the Monthly Investment text box.

The event procedure for the CheckedChanged event of the Monthly Investment radio button is similar to the one for the Future Value button. However, it reverses the property settings of the Future Value and Monthly Investment text boxes. Then, it clears all the text boxes and moves the focus to the Interest Rate text box.

This should give you some idea of what the code for a professional user interface requires. First, you need to provide complete data validation. Second, you need to adjust the properties of some controls as the application executes so the user can't make a mistake that will cause the program to fail.

The Visual Basic code for the Calculate Investment form   Page 1

```vb
Public Class Form1
    Inherits System.Windows.Forms.Form

    Private Sub btnCalculate_Click(ByVal sender As System.Object, _
            ByVal e As System.EventArgs) Handles btnCalculate.Click
        If rdoFutureValue.Checked Then
            If ValidEntry(txtMonthlyInvestment.Text, 100, 1000) Then
                If ValidEntry(txtInterestRate.Text, 0, 24) Then
                    If ValidEntry(txtYears.Text, 1, 65) Then
                        Me.CalculateFutureValue()
                        txtMonthlyInvestment.Focus()
                    Else
                        MessageBox.Show("Years must be  a number " _
                            & "between 1 and 65.", "Entry error")
                        txtYears.Focus()
                    End If
                Else
                    MessageBox.Show("Interest rate must be a number " _
                        & "between 0 and 24.", "Entry error")
                    txtInterestRate.Focus()
                End If
            Else
                MessageBox.Show("Monthly investment must be a number " _
                    & "between 100 and 1,000.", "Entry error")
                txtMonthlyInvestment.Focus()
            End If
        Else
            If ValidEntry(txtInterestRate.Text, 0, 24) Then
                If ValidEntry(txtYears.Text, 1, 65) Then
                    If ValidEntry(txtFutureValue.Text, 1000, 1000000) Then
                        Me.CalculateMonthlyInvestment()
                        txtInterestRate.Focus()
                    Else
                        MessageBox.Show("Future value must be a number " _
                            & "between 1,000 and 1,000,000.", "Entry error")
                        txtFutureValue.Focus()
                    End If
                Else
                    MessageBox.Show("Years must be a number " _
                        & "between 1 and 65.", "Entry error")
                    txtYears.Focus()
                End If
            Else
                MessageBox.Show("Interest rate must be a number " _
                    & "between 0 and 24.", "Entry error")
                txtInterestRate.Focus()
            End If
        End If
    End Sub
```

Figure 8-13   The code for the Calculate Investment form (part 1 of 3)

The Visual Basic code for the Calculate Investment form   Page 2

```vb
Private Function ValidEntry(ByVal Entry As String, _
        ByVal MinValue As Decimal, ByVal MaxValue As Decimal) As Boolean
    If IsNumeric(Entry) Then
        If Entry >= MinValue And Entry <= MaxValue Then
            ValidEntry = True
        End If
    End If
End Function

Private Sub CalculateFutureValue()
    txtFutureValue.Text = _
        FormatCurrency(FV(txtInterestRate.Text / 12 / 100, _
            txtYears.Text * 12, -txtMonthlyInvestment.Text, 0, _
                DueDate.BegOfPeriod))
End Sub

Private Sub CalculateMonthlyInvestment()
    txtMonthlyInvestment.Text = _
        FormatCurrency(Pmt(txtInterestRate.Text / 12 / 100, _
            txtYears.Text * 12, 0, -txtFutureValue.Text, _
                DueDate.BegOfPeriod))
End Sub

Private Sub rdoFutureValue_CheckedChanged _
        (ByVal sender As System.Object, ByVal e As System.EventArgs) _
        Handles rdoFutureValue.CheckedChanged
    txtFutureValue.ReadOnly = True
    txtFutureValue.TabStop = False
    txtFutureValue.BackColor = SystemColors.Control
    txtMonthlyInvestment.ReadOnly = False
    txtMonthlyInvestment.TabStop = True
    txtMonthlyInvestment.BackColor = SystemColors.Window
    Me.ClearControls()
    txtMonthlyInvestment.Focus()
End Sub

Private Sub rdoMonthlyInvestment_CheckedChanged _
        (ByVal sender As System.Object, ByVal e As System.EventArgs) _
        Handles rdoMonthlyInvestment.CheckedChanged
    txtFutureValue.ReadOnly = False
    txtFutureValue.TabStop = True
    txtFutureValue.BackColor = SystemColors.Window
    txtMonthlyInvestment.ReadOnly = True
    txtMonthlyInvestment.TabStop = False
    txtMonthlyInvestment.BackColor = SystemColors.Control
    Me.ClearControls()
    txtInterestRate.Focus()
End Sub
```

Note

- The Pmt function used in the CalculateMonthlyInvestment procedure is another one of the financial functions that come with Visual Basic. It calculates the monthly payment when the interest rate, number of periods, and future value are supplied as arguments.

Figure 8-13   The code for the Calculate Investment form (part 2 of 3)

The Visual Basic code for the Calculate Investment form   Page 3

```
Private Sub ClearControls()
    txtMonthlyInvestment.Text = ""
    txtInterestRate.Text = ""
    txtYears.Text = ""
    txtFutureValue.Text = ""
End Sub

Private Sub btnExit_Click(ByVal sender As System.Object, _
        ByVal e As System.EventArgs) Handles btnExit.Click
    Me.Close()
End Sub

End Class
```

Figure 8-13   The code for the Calculate Investment form (part 3 of 3)

Perspective

In this chapter, you learned how to use ten of the controls for building Windows applications that are available from the standard Toolbox. These controls, along with the ones you'll learn about in the next two chapters, are the ones you'll use most often. If you need to use any of the controls that weren't presented here, though, you should be able to figure out how to do that on your own. In most cases, it's just a matter of becoming familiar with the properties and events that are available, and you can usually do that by reviewing the documentation for the control and the class it's based on.

Summary

- You can use several properties of a text box control to provide for a multi-line text box, which lets the user enter one or more lines of text.

- The *combo box* and *list box* controls display a list of items that the user can select from. To work with these list items in your program, you use the properties and methods of the Items collection. And to refer to a specific item in a list, you use an *index*.

- The *radio button* and *check box* controls let the user select one or more options. All of the radio buttons in a group are mutually exclusive, but each check box is independent of the others.

- To group radio buttons or other controls, you place them in a *group box* or *panel* control. Then, you can move all of the controls in the group in the Form Designer by moving the group box or panel.

- The tab control lets you group controls into two or more *tabs* rather than creating separate forms for each group. Each of these tabs is a *page* of the tab control.

- You can use Tab Order view of a form to change the tab order of the controls on a form rather than changing the TabIndex properties of the controls directly.

- You can use the KeyPress event of a control to restrict the characters the user can enter into a control.

- You can customize the Toolbox by adding COM and .NET Framework components to it.

Terms

combo box	radio button	page
list box	group box	tab order
index	panel	
check box	tab	

Objectives

- Given the specifications for a form that uses any of the controls presented in this chapter, design and code the form.

- Given a form with two or more controls, set the tab order of the controls using the Tab Order view of the form.

- Given the specifications for a form that uses the KeyPress event to restrict the characters that the user can enter into one or more controls, design and code the form.

- Describe how you work with the items in a combo box list or a list box.

- Distinguish between radio button and check box controls.

- Distinguish between group box and panel controls.

Exercise 8-1   Create the Calculate Investment form

This exercise will guide you through the process of creating the Calculate Investment form of figures 8-12 and 8-13 from the Future Value form presented in earlier chapters.

Open the project and modify the form design

1. Open the Calculate Investment project that's in the C:\VB.NET\Chapter 08\CalculateInvestment folder. This project contains our version of the Future Value form that uses range checking and the FV function.

2. Change the text that's displayed in the title bar of the form to "Calculate Investment," and then add a group box to the top of the form with the text "Calculate." Next, add two radio buttons to this group box and label them "Future Value" and "Monthly Investment." Set the properties of these buttons so the first one is selected by default.

3. Replace the label that displays the future value with a text box, and set its properties so it appears as shown in the first form in figure 8-12.

4. Use the View → Tab Order command to display the form in Tab Order view and set the tab order appropriately.

Modify the code for the form

5. Code a procedure named CalculateMonthlyInvestment that uses the Pmt function to calculate a payment based on the values in the Interest Rate, Years, and Future Value text boxes. Set the last argument to indicate that the payment will be received at the beginning of each period.

6. Add two procedures that respond to the CheckedChanged events of the two radio buttons. These procedures should modify the ReadOnly, TabStop, and BackColor properties so the appropriate control is available for entry. They should also call a procedure named ClearControls that moves an empty string to each text box, and they should move the focus to the first available text box on the form. When you're done, enter the code for the ClearControls procedure.

7. Modify the code for the Click event procedure of the Calculate button so it uses the ValidEntry function to validate the appropriate controls depending on which radio button is selected. Use 1,000 and 1,000,000 as the minimum and maximum values for the future value. If all of the entries are valid, this procedure should call the CalculateFutureValue function or the CalculateMonthlyInvestment function and then move the focus to the first available text box on the form.

8. Test the program to be sure that it works for both a future value and monthly investment calculation. When you're sure it does, close the project.

Exercise 8-2   Create the Calculate Depreciation form

This exercise will guide you through the process of creating the Calculate Depreciation form presented in figures 8-10 and 8-11.

1. Start a new Windows application named CalculateDepreciation and save it in the C:\VB.NET\Chapter 08\CalculateDepreciation folder.

2. Add controls to the default form so it looks like the one in figure 8-10. Then set the properties of the form and the controls as shown in that figure.

3. Double-click on the form to start a procedure for the Load event. Then, enter code in that procedure for loading the combo box with the values 1 to 40.

4. Code a procedure for the Click event of the Calculate button that clears the list box, calculates the depreciation based on the initial cost, final value, and life entered by the user, displays the depreciation for each year in the list box as shown in figure 8-10, and then moves the focus to the Initial Cost text box. You should use the SYD function to calculate the sum-of-years-digits depreciation. Refer to figure 8-11 if you need help.

5. Code a procedure for the Click event of the Exit button so it closes the form. Then, run the program and test it to see if it works with valid data. If not, make the necessary corrections and test it again.

6. Create a function named ValidEntry that works like the one in the Calc⟍
Investment form. Then, add code to the Click event procedure of the C⟍
button that uses this function to validate the data in the Initial Cost an⟍
Value text boxes before calculating the depreciation. The initial cost⟍
a value between 500 and 1,000,000, and the final value should be between ∪⟍
and the initial cost. If a value is invalid, display an appropriate error message
and move the focus to the control in error.

7. Add code to the Click event procedure to test that the user selected an item
from the Life combo box. If an item wasn't selected, display an error message
and move the focus to this combo box.

8. Run the program and test it to make sure that it works with any entries. When
you're sure that it does, end the program but leave the solution open if you're
going to continue.

Exercise 8-3   Use the KeyPress event

In this exercise, you'll enhance the Calculate Depreciation form to restrict the
entries in the Initial Cost and Final Value text boxes to numeric characters.

*TRY
THIS*

1. If it's not already open, open the Calculate Depreciation application that you
created in exercise 8-2.

2. Start a procedure for the KeyPress event of the Initial Cost text box. Then, code
a Select Case statement that tests the value of the KeyChar property of the e
argument that's passed to the procedure. Use the Asc function to convert this
property to an ASCII code.

3. Code two Case clauses within the Select Case statement. The first one should
test for the backspace (8), comma (44), and decimal point (46) and the numbers
0 through 9 (48 through 57). If one of these keys is pressed, the procedure
should set the Handled property of the e argument to False so the default
Windows processing is performed. The second Case clause should test for all
other conditions and set the Handled property to True.

4. Modify the Handles clause of the KeyPress event procedure so it will fire for
both the Initial Cost and Final Value text boxes. Then, change the name of this
event procedure to reflect its function.

5. Run the program. Then, try to enter an alphabetic character into the Initial
Value text box. Does the character appear in that control? Next, try to enter a
value that contains a comma and decimal point in this text box. If this works,
enter a final value, select a life, and calculate the depreciation. Continue testing
until you're sure this works correctly. Then, close the program and close the
project.

Exercise 8-4   Use a tab control

In this exercise, you'll create a form that uses a tab control like the one in figure 8-6. To make that easier to do, you'll use the Calculate Investment and Calculate Depreciation forms you created in exercises 8-1 and 8-2.

1. Start a new Windows application named FinancialCalculations, and save it in the C:\VB.NET\Chapter 08\FinancialCalculations folder.

2. Add a tab control to the default form, name it tabCalculations, and set its TabStop property to False. Add a tab to this control, and then click on the page for the tab and set its Text property to "Calculate Investment."

3. Add Calculate and Exit buttons to the form and set the properties of these controls and the form so it looks like the first one in figure 8-6. Then, change the name of the form class to frmFinancialCalculations so it doesn't conflict with the existing forms you're going to add to the project next.

4. Use the Add→ Add Existing Item command in the shortcut menu for the project to add the Calculate Investment form you created in exercise 8-1 to the project. This creates a copy of the form in the new project folder.

5. Copy all the controls on the Calculate Investment form except for the buttons to the first tab of the tab control on the Financial Calculations form. Then, copy all of the procedures in the Calculate Investment form to the Financial Calculations form. When you're done, close any open windows for the Calculate Investment form and delete this form from the project.

6. Add another tab to the tab control, and set the Text property of the page for this tab to "Calculate Depreciation." Then, add the Calculate Depreciation form you created in exercise 8-2 to the project. Copy and paste all of the controls except the buttons from this form to the new tab, and copy the code for the Load procedure to the Financial Calculations form.

7. Add an If…Else statement to the Click event procedure of the Calculate button that tests the SelectedIndex property of the tab. If it's zero, this procedure should execute the code for calculating an investment. Otherwise, it should execute the code for calculating depreciation. Copy the code for calculating the depreciation from the Calculate Depreciation form. Then, close any open windows for this form and delete it from the project.

8. Double-click on the tab control to start a procedure for the SelectedIndex-Changed event of this control. Then, add code to this procedure that moves the focus to the appropriate control when the user selects the other tab.

9. Run the program to see how it works. Switch back and forth between the two tabs and test them to be sure that they work properly. When you're done, close the program and then close the solution.

9

How to develop a multi-form application

In the last chapter, you saw forms for calculating an investment and for calculating depreciation. Each of these forms was stored in a separate project and operated independently of one another. Another way to implement related forms like these, though, is to include them both in the same project. To do that, you need to learn the skills presented in this chapter.

Basic skills and concepts for developing multi-form applications

Few applications consist of a single form like the ones you've seen so far in this book. Because of that, you need to know how to work with two or more forms in the same project. You'll learn the basic skills and concepts for doing that in the topics that follow.

How to add a form to a project

When you start a new project, it consists of a single blank form. Then, to add another form to the project, you use the Add New Item dialog box shown in figure 9-1. From this dialog box, you select the Windows Form template and then enter the name of the new form. When you click on the Open button, the new form is created with the name you specify. If you look at the code that's generated for this form, you'll see that the class is also given this name (without the file extension, of course).

You can also add an existing form to a project using the Add Existing Item dialog box. This can be useful if you want to use the same form in two different projects or if you want to create a form that's similar to an existing form. Note that when you add an existing form from another project, that form is copied into the new project. That way, you don't have to worry about changing the original form inadvertently. If you did the exercises for the last chapter, you already saw how this works.

— AT LEAST STARTUP + ABOUT FORMS

The Add New Item dialog box

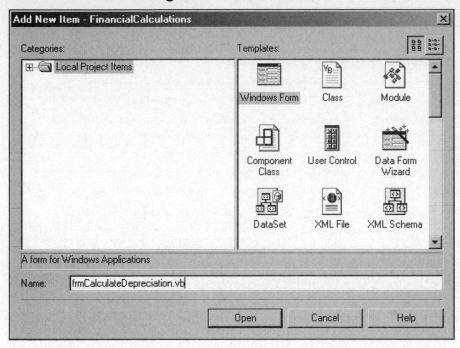

How to add a new form

- Display the Add New Item dialog box by selecting the Project → Add Windows Form command. Or, select the Add → Add Windows Form command from the shortcut menu that's displayed when you right-click on the project in the Solution Explorer.
- To add a new form, select the Windows Form template from the Add New Item dialog box, enter a name for the form, and click on the Open button.

How to add an existing form

- Display the Add Existing Item dialog box by selecting the Project → Add Existing Item command. Or, select the Add → Add Existing Item command from the shortcut menu for the project.
- To add an existing form, select the vb file for the form from the Add Existing Item dialog box and then click on the Open button.

Note

- The Class statement that's generated for the new form will reflect the name you specify in the Add New Item dialog box. Because of that, you may want to change the class statement for the default form to an appropriate name for consistency.

Figure 9-1   How to add a form to a project

How to work with form objects

To work with a form using Visual Basic code, you use the techniques shown in figure 9-2. To start, you declare an object variable for the form. Then, you create an instance of the form class and assign a reference to that instance to the object variable. As with other object variables and classes, you can do that using a single declaration statement with the New keyword as shown in the first statement in this figure. Alternatively, you can declare the variable without the New keyword and then use this keyword in an assignment statement to create an instance of the class and assign it to the object variable.

After you create an instance of a form, you can load and display that form using the Show method as illustrated in the second statement in this figure. This method is a member of the Form class that's defined by the .NET Framework. As you learned in chapter 6, any form you create in Visual Basic inherits the members of the Form class. So you can use any of these members to work with your forms. Some of the other methods you're likely to use are listed in this figure.

Handwritten annotations:

TO SHOW FORM FROM OTHER FORM: **

DIM SECOND FORM AS NEW FORM2 ()

OR

DIM SECOND FORM AS FORM
SECONDFORM = NEW FORM2()*

OR

DIM SECONDFORM AS FORM = NEW FORM2()

SAME

* LATE BINDING   **ELSE, ONLY SHARED METH AVAIL ON ?

VB6 = ALWAYS STARTED W/ SUBMAIN
.NET = ALL HAVE CONSTRUCTOR, BUT
IN BIG PROJ, SUBMAIN STILL BEST.

The syntax for declaring a form variable

```
{Dim|Private|Public|Static} variablename As [New] formname
```

A statement that declares a form variable and creates an instance of the form

```
Dim frmCalculateInvestment As New frmCalculateInvestment()
```

A statement that displays a form

```
frmCalculateInvestment.Show()
```

Typical methods for working with form objects

Method	Description
Show	Loads the form if it isn't already loaded, and then displays the form by setting its Visible property to True.
Hide	Hides the form by setting its Visible property to False.
BringToFront	Displays the form on top of any other forms that are currently displayed.
SendToBack	Displays the form behind any other forms that are currently displayed.

Description

- When an application starts by displaying a form, Visual Basic automatically creates an instance of that form. To display another form from that form or from a class or module, you have to first declare an object variable and create an instance of the form.

- You declare an object variable that will hold a reference to a form just as you do any other object variable. If you include the New keyword on the declaration, an instance of the form class you name is created and assigned to the form variable. Otherwise, you can code an assignment statement with the New keyword to do that.

- After you declare an object variable and assign a form object to it, you can use that variable to work with the properties and methods of the form.

(handwritten notes) (OR VAR) UNLESS REF IN TO SIMPLE CONTROL, ACCESSING 2ND FORM. CONTROL MAY GIVE R/T ERROR. DOESN'T USUALLY WORK W/ACTIVEX CONT. BETTER TO MAKE REPRES. OF PROP RATHER THAN CALL

(handwritten notes) DISPOSE UNLOADS FORM; RELEASE ASSETS.

(handwritten notes) VB6 = LOAD, SHOW, HIDE(LOADED BUT NOT VIS), (CLOSE), DISPOSE .NET =

Figure 9-2   How to work with form objects

(handwritten notes) NOTE! FORM C/B LOADED BUT HIDDEN!

How to change the startup object for a project

By default, the form that's created when you start a project is the form that will be displayed when you run the application. If that's not what you want, you can change the Startup object property of the project as shown in figure 9-3. To change the startup object to another form, for example, you just select the form name from the drop-down list. And to change the startup object to the Main procedure in a module, you select the Sub Main option. You'll learn more about coding a Main procedure in the next chapter.

MODAL = CAN'T DO ANYTHING ELSE TILL
FORM CLOSED. (SHOWDIALOG)

LOAD WON'T WORK ANY MORE

The Property Pages dialog box

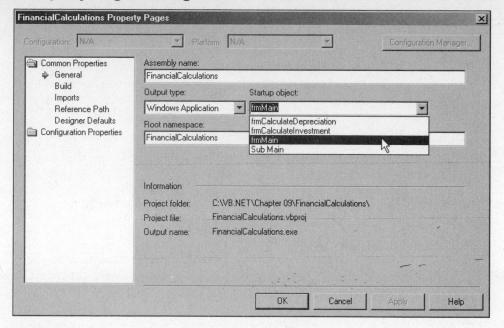

Operation

- To display the Property Pages dialog box for a project, select the Project → Properties command, or select the Properties command from the shortcut menu for the project.

- To change the form that's displayed when the project starts, select the General group in the Common Properties folder. Then, select the form that you want from the Startup object combo box.

- To run the Main procedure in a module when the project starts, select the Sub Main option from the Startup object combo box. See chapter 10 for details on coding a Main procedure.

Figure 9-3   How to change the startup object for a project

Single-document and multiple-document interfaces

Figure 9-4 shows two versions of the Financial Calculations application I'll use as examples in this chapter. These applications let the user calculate an investment or depreciation using forms like the ones you saw in the last chapter. In addition, each application includes a third form that provides a way for the user to access the other forms.

The first version of this application uses a *single-document interface*, or *SDI*. In an SDI application, each form runs in its own application window, and this window is usually shown in the Windows taskbar. Then, you can click on the buttons in the taskbar to switch between the open forms. When you use this interface, each form can have its own menus and toolbars. In addition, a main form called a *startup form* typically provides access to the other forms of the application. In this figure, for example, the startup form includes buttons that the user can click on to display the other forms.

The second version of this application uses a *multiple-document interface*, or *MDI*. In an MDI application, a container form called a *parent form* contains one or more *child forms*. Then, the menus and toolbars on the parent form contain the commands that let you open and view forms, and you can use its Window menu to switch between the open forms. When you close the parent form of an MDI application, all of the child forms are closed and the application ends.

The main advantage of a multiple-document interface is that the parent form manages multiple instances of child forms for you. In contrast, if you create multiple instances of a form in an SDI application, you have to manage them yourself. As you can imagine, that can get unwieldy.

The parent form in the MDI application in this figure also includes a status bar. A bar like this can be set up to display a number of information items. Although you can add a status bar to any form in either an SDI or MDI application, it makes the most sense to use one on the parent form in an MDI application. You'll learn how to create and use a status bar in the next chapter.

Incidentally, you can also develop an *explorer-style interface* with Visual Basic .NET. In this type of interface, a single window is split into two panes just as it is in the Windows Explorer. Then, you can use the left pane to navigate between different parts of the application, and you can use the right pane to work with the application. This type of interface, however, isn't presented in this book.

Single-document interface (SDI) —INDEPENDENT

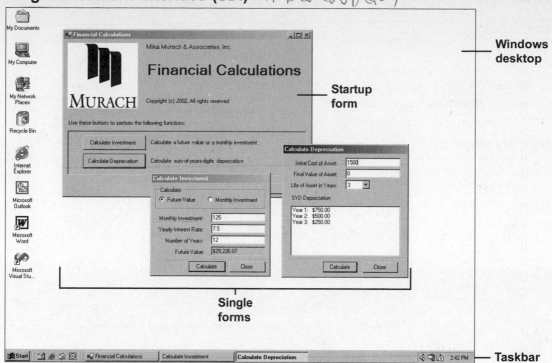

Multiple-document interface (MDI) CONTAINER-LIKE WORD

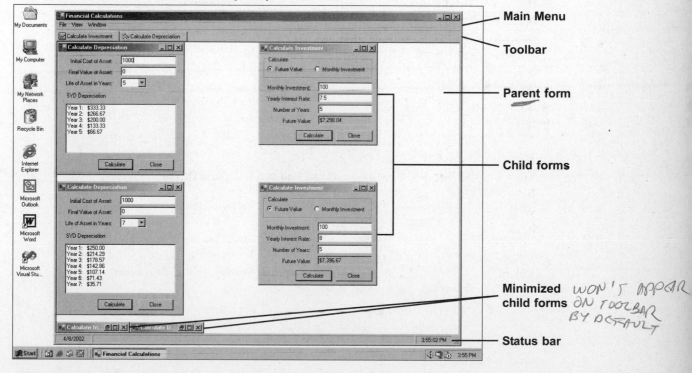

Figure 9-4 Single-document and multiple-document interfaces

How to develop a single-document interface

To develop a single-document interface, you design and code the forms that provide the basic operations of the application. Then, you design and code the startup form that provides access to the other forms.

How to use a startup form

Figure 9-5 presents the startup form for the Financial Calculations application. As you can see, this form gives the user access to the two other forms of this application: the Calculate Investment form and the Calculate Depreciation form. At the beginning of the code for the startup form, you can see the two Dim statements that declare object variables for these forms. Because these statements include the New keyword, an instance of each form will be created when the statements are executed.

The three procedures for the startup form respond to the Click events of the three buttons on the form. When the user clicks on the Calculate Investment button, the Show method of the Calculate Investment form is executed to load and display the form. This method loads the form only the first time the user clicks on the button, though, After that, it simply changes the Visible property of the form to True so it's visible on the screen. That's assuming that the form has been hidden rather than closed between executions of this method. If it's been closed, you can't use the Show method to redisplay the form. That's because when you close a form, the form object is destroyed and you can no longer refer to it. You'll see how to provide for hiding a form rather than closing it a little later in this chapter.

The first time the Show method is executed for a form, that form is displayed on top of the other forms and it receives the focus. If you move the focus to another form, however, that form is displayed on top of the other forms. If you display the Calculate Investment form, for example, and then click on the startup form, the startup form is displayed on top of the Calculate Investment form. Although the Calculate Investment form is technically still visible, it may be hidden behind the startup form so you can't see it. In that case, you have to move the startup form so you can see part of the Calculate Investment form and then click on it to move the focus to it. A better solution, though, is to use the BringToFront method of the form to display it on top of the startup form each time you click on the Calculate Investment button. You can see this method following the Show method of the form.

The event procedure for the Click event of the Calculate Depreciation button contains similar code. And the Click event of the Exit button simply closes the form. Note, however, that if any other forms are open when you click on this button, they are closed as well. That's because the object variables for those forms are declared within the startup form. So when the startup form is closed, those variables go out of scope.

A startup form for the Financial Calculations application

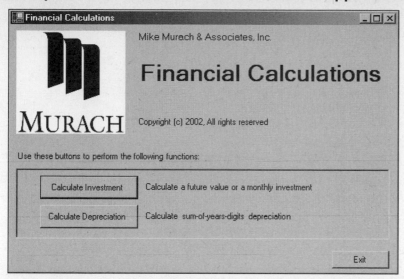

The code for the startup form

```
Public Class frmMain
    Inherits System.Windows.Forms.Form

    Dim frmCalculateInvestment As New frmCalculateInvestment()
    Dim frmCalculateDepreciation As New frmCalculateDepreciation()

    Private Sub btnCalcInvestment_Click(ByVal sender As System.Object, _
            ByVal e As System.EventArgs) Handles btnCalcInvestment.Click
        frmCalculateInvestment.Show()
        frmCalculateInvestment.BringToFront()
    End Sub

    Private Sub btnCalcDepreciation_Click(ByVal sender As System.Object, _
            ByVal e As System.EventArgs) Handles btnCalcDepreciation.Click
        frmCalculateDepreciation.Show()
        frmCalculateDepreciation.BringToFront()
    End Sub

    Private Sub btnExit_Click(ByVal sender As System.Object, _
            ByVal e As System.EventArgs) Handles btnExit.Click
        Me.Close()
    End Sub

End Class
```

Description

- SDI applications that consist of more than one form typically include a *startup form* that directs the user to the other forms of the application.

- A startup form can also load the other forms of the application as it starts so they appear more quickly as the program executes. See chapter 10 for details.

Figure 9-5   How to use a startup form

You should notice here that the Calculate Investment and Calculate Depreciation forms aren't loaded and displayed until the user requests them. In some cases, though, you may want to load all of the forms used by an application when the application starts. Although this takes the application longer to start up, the forms appear quickly once the startup procedure has been completed. You'll see an example of this in chapter 10.

The property settings for the startup form

Figure 9-6 presents the property settings for the startup form in figure 9-5. Besides letting the user display the two calculation forms, this startup form also includes information about the application.

You shouldn't have any trouble understanding the property settings for the form itself. Notice, however, that unlike the other forms you've seen so far in this book, the MinimizeBox and MaximizeBox properties are left at their default values of True so the minimize and maximize buttons are displayed at the right side of the title bar. That way, the user can minimize this form when working with one of the other forms.

Many of the controls on this form are labels that contain text with various font characteristics. For example, the label that displays the text "Financial Calculations" has a font size of 24 points and is displayed in boldface. And the label that displays the text "Mike Murach & Associates, Inc." has a font size of 10 points. (Notice that the UseMnemonic property of this control is set to False so the ampersand (&) will be treated as a character rather than identifying an access key.) The text in all of the other labels is displayed in the default font.

This form also contains a picture box and a panel. Notice that the BorderStyle property of the panel is set to Fixed3D so it appears three-dimensional on the form. Also notice that the Image property of the picture box is set to a bitmap image named Murach logo.bmp. Once you select the image to be displayed, though, Visual Basic displays the type of image you selected in the Image property instead of the name of the image file. For a bitmap image, for example, the property will be set to System.Drawing.Bitmap.

Finally, notice that the SizeMode property of the picture box is set to StretchImage. That causes the image to stretch or shrink to fit the picture box. Other possible settings for this property are AutoSize, which causes the picture box to be sized to the image; CenterImage, which causes the image to be centered in the picture box; and Normal, which causes the image to be placed in the upper left corner of the picture box.

The property settings for the startup form

Property	Setting
Name	frmMain
CancelButton	btnExit
FormBorderStyle	FixedSingle
MaximizeBox	True
MinimizeBox	True
StartPosition	CenterScreen
Text	Financial Calculations

The property settings for the controls on the form

Default name	Property	Setting
PictureBox1	Image	Murach logo.bmp
	SizeMode	StretchImage
Label1	Text	Mike Murach & Associates, Inc.
	Font.Size	10
	UseMnemonic	False
Label2	Text	Financial Calculations
	Font.Size	24
	Font.Bold	True
Label3	Text	Copyright (c) 2002, All rights reserved
Label4	Text	Use these buttons to perform the following functions:
Label5	Text	Calculate a future value or a monthly investment
Label6	Text	Calculate sum-of-years-digits depreciation
Panel1	BorderStyle	Fixed3D
Button1	Name	btnCalcInvestment
	Text	Calculate &Investment
Button2	Name	btnCalcDepreciation
	Text	Calculate &Depreciation
Button3	Name	btnExit
	Text	E&xit

Notes

- The Font property of a control contains a reference to a Font object. To change the font, you change the properties of this object, such as Size and Bold.

- If you click on the Font property and then click on the ellipsis button that appears, a Font dialog box is displayed that lets you change the basic font properties. You can also change individual font properties by expanding the Font group in the Properties window.

- If you select the Image property for a picture box and then click on the ellipsis button that appears, an Open dialog box is displayed that lets you select the image you want to display in the control. After you select the image, the Image property reflects the type of image you selected, such as System.Drawing.Bitmap.

Figure 9-6   The property settings for the startup form

How to design and code forms displayed by a startup form

When you use a startup form to display the other forms of an application, you should follow some basic design and coding guidelines for those forms. Those guidelines are described and illustrated in figure 9-7.

At the top of this figure, you can see the Calculate Investment and Calculate Depreciation forms displayed by the startup form in figure 9-5. Note, however, that there are a couple of differences between these forms and the ones you saw in chapter 8. First, each form contains a Close button instead of an Exit button. That's because an Exit button is typically used for exiting from an application. The users can't exit from the application from these forms, though. They can only close the form.

Second, the title bar of each form contains only a title. The control box and close button have been omitted. That way, the user can only close the form by clicking on the Close button that's provided. That's important, because if the user closed the form using the Close command in the control box or the built-in close button, the form would be unloaded. Then, a new instance of the form would have to be created and loaded the next time the user clicked on its button in the startup form.

You also don't want the form to be unloaded when the user clicks on the Close button. So instead of executing the Close method in the Click event procedure for this button, you execute the Hide method as shown in the code in this figure. Then, the form is simply hidden from view and is displayed again when the Show method is executed. Notice that the procedure in this figure also clears the controls on the form before it's hidden. That way, it will appear to the user as if the form had been closed and reopened.

The Calculate Investment and Calculate Depreciation forms

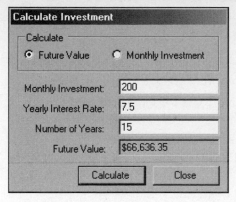 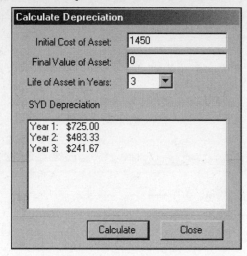

Code that clears and hides the Calculate Depreciation form

```
Private Sub btnClose_Click(ByVal sender As System.Object, _
        ByVal e As System.EventArgs) Handles btnClose.Click
    txtInitialCost.Text = ""
    txtFinalValue.Text = ""
    cboLife.SelectedIndex = -1
    lstDepreciation.Items.Clear()
    Me.Hide()
End Sub
```

Description

- A form that's displayed from a startup form should contain a Close button rather than an Exit button to indicate that the button will close the form and not exit from the application.

- For efficiency, a form that's displayed by a startup form should be loaded only the first time the Show method is issued for that form. To accomplish that, the procedure for the Click event of the Close button on that form should hide the form rather than closing it.

- To prevent the user from using the control box to close (and unload) a form, the ControlBox property of the form should be set to False. This also causes the Close, Minimize, and Maximize buttons to be removed from the form.

- If a form contains data, that data is usually cleared when the form is hidden.

Figure 9-7   How to design and code forms displayed by a startup form

How to develop a multiple-document interface

If the application you're developing requires multiple instances of one or more forms, you'll want to develop a multiple-document interface for it. That way, Visual Basic will manage those instances for you. The good news is that MDI applications are easy to develop, as you'll see in the topics that follow.

How to create parent and child forms

In figure 9-8, you can see the design of a parent form for the Financial Calculations application. Instead of using button controls, this form provides access to its child forms through the main menu. You'll learn how to create a main menu later in this chapter.

You create both parent and child forms as standard Windows forms. Then, you set the IsMdiContainer property of the parent form to True to identify it as the parent form, and you set the MdiParent property of the child forms to the name of the parent form. Note, however, that the MdiParent property can be set only as the program executes. You'll see how to do that in the next figure.

In addition to these two properties, you'll also want to set some of the other properties of the parent and child forms so they work the way you want them to. For example, you usually set the WindowState property of the parent form to Maximized so it uses the entire screen. And you usually set its FormBorderStyle property to Sizable and its MinimizeBox and MaximizeBox properties to True so the form can be minimized, maximized, and sized. In contrast, you usually set the FormBorderStyle property of the child forms to FixedSingle so they can't be resized.

An application with one parent form and two child forms

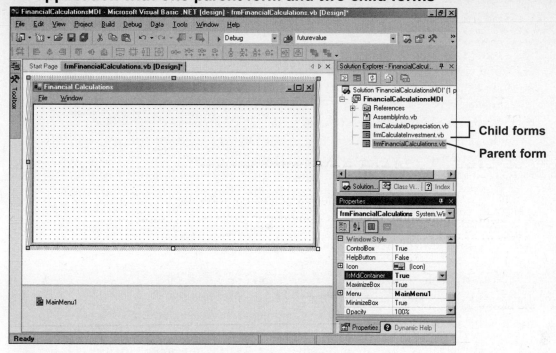

Typical property settings for a parent form

Property	Setting
IsMdiContainer	True to indicate that the form is a parent form.
WindowState	Maximized so the form occupies the entire screen by default.
FormBorderStyle	Sizable so the form can be sized.
MinimizeBox	True so the form can be minimized.
MaximizeBox	True so the form can be maximized.

(handwritten: GT PROP.) *(handwritten: VB6, ONLY ONE PER APP — NOT .NET)*

Typical property settings for a child form

Property	Setting
MdiParent	The name of the parent form. Can only be set at run-time.
FormBorderStyle	FixedSingle so the form can't be resized.
MinimizeBox	True so the form can be minimized.
MaximizeBox	True so the form can be maximized.
StartPosition	WindowsDefaultLocation so the windows are cascaded from the upper left corner of the parent form.

(handwritten: MDI PROP ONLY SET @ RUNTIME IN CHILD)

Note

- An MDI application can also include forms that are used as neither a parent form nor a child form. These forms are usually modal forms, which you'll learn about in the next chapter.

Figure 9-8   How to create parent and child forms

(handwritten: PARENT WILL HAVE DIFF BCKGRND COLOR)

How to write code that works with parent and child forms

Figure 9-9 shows some coding techniques you can use to work with parent and child forms. To start, the first example shows you how to create and display a new instance of a child form. You create a new instance using the New keyword just as you do for any form. Then, you set the MdiParent property of the form to the name of the parent form. Since a child form is usually displayed from the parent form, you can just use the Me keyword to identify the parent form. Finally, you use the Show method to display the form.

Because there may be more than one instance of a child form displayed at the same time, you can't refer to an individual form by name. Instead, you need to use the ActiveMdiChild property of the parent form to refer to the child form that currently has the focus. You can see how this works in the second example in this figure. Here, the If statement checks to be sure that there is an active child form. If there is, that form is closed.

The last coding example in this figure shows how you can use the LayoutMdi method of the parent form to arrange the child forms. To do that, you use the constants in the MdiLayout enumeration. These constants let you tile the windows vertically or horizontally or arrange them in a cascaded layout.

Notice that all of the code in this figure is executed in response to the Click event of a menu item, which occurs when the user selects the item. For example, the code that creates and displays a new instance of a child form is executed in response to the user selecting a menu item named mnuNewInvestment. And the code that closes the active child form is executed in response to the user selecting a menu item named mnuClose. You'll see how to create menu items like these next.

An MDI application with two instances of a child form arranged vertically

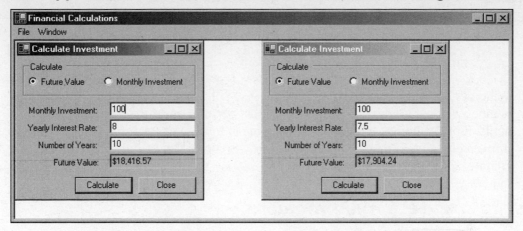

Code that creates and displays a new instance of a child form

```
Private Sub mnuNewInvestment_Click(ByVal sender As System.Object, _
        ByVal e As System.EventArgs) Handles mnuNewInvestment.Click
    Dim frmCalculateInvestment As New frmCalculateInvestment()
    frmCalculateInvestment.MdiParent = Me
    frmCalculateInvestment.Show()
End Sub
```

Code that refers to the active child form

```
Private Sub mnuClose_Click(ByVal sender As System.Object, _
        ByVal e As System.EventArgs) Handles mnuClose.Click
    If (Not Me.ActiveMdiChild Is Nothing) Then
        Me.ActiveMdiChild.Close()
    End If
End Sub
```

Code that arranges the child forms vertically

```
Private Sub mnuTileVertical_Click(ByVal sender As System.Object, _
        ByVal e As System.EventArgs) Handles mnuTileVertical.Click
    Me.LayoutMdi(MdiLayout.TileVertical)
End Sub
```

Description

- Before you display an instance of a child form, you must set its MdiParent property to the name of its parent form. Since a child form is usually displayed by its parent form, you can use the Me keyword to identify the parent form.

- You can use the ActiveMdiChild property of a parent form to refer to the active child form.

- You can use the LayoutMdi method of a parent form to arrange the child forms within the parent form. To specify the type of layout you want, you use the constants in the MdiLayout enumeration.

Figure 9-9   How to write code that works with parent and child forms

How to create and work with a main menu

To provide access to the child forms from a parent form, you can add a main menu to the parent form. That menu can also include items to perform standard Windows operations, such as exiting from the application and switching to another window. And it can include items that perform operations specific to the application. Although you can add a main menu to any type of form, you're most likely to use a menu with a parent form. So that's what I'll illustrate in this chapter.

How to create a main menu

Visual Studio .NET provides an easy-to-use facility for adding a *main menu* to a form, which is the menu that appears at the top of a form. To do that, you start by adding a main menu control to the form as illustrated in figure 9-10. Notice that this control isn't displayed on the form. Instead, it's displayed in the *Component Designer tray* at the bottom of the Form Designer window. This tray is used for components that don't have a visual interface, such as the main menu control. (Although you might think that the main menu control has a visual interface, it actually doesn't. Instead, it just provides the facility that lets you add a main menu to a form.)

When you add a main menu control to a form, the Menu property of the form is automatically set to the name of that control. In addition, the *Menu Designer* is displayed at the top of the form as shown in this figure. Then, you can add menus and menu items by typing the text you want to appear in the Menu Designer anywhere it says "Type Here." When I started typing the text for the first menu in this figure, for example, additional areas opened up below and to the right of that menu. When I entered items below this menu, they appeared as items in that menu as shown in the second screen in this figure. When I completed the first menu, I continued by creating another menu to the right of that menu.

[handwritten notes]
MDI CHILD WILL SHOW MENU
ON PARENT ONLY

USE PROP. "TAG" FOR FORM ID.
SECFORM.TAG =

(IN CHOOSE DEFAULT (BOLD), INVIS. CHECKED, (RADIO CHECK IS ONE ONLY)

The beginning of the main menu for the Financial Calculations application

SEPARATION

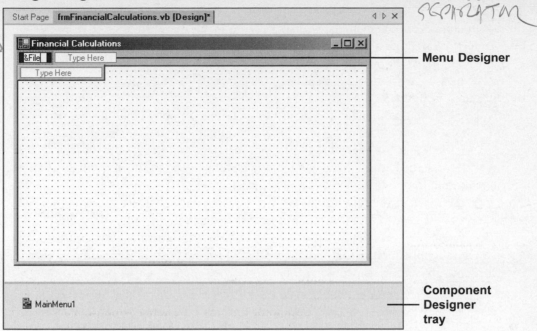

Menu Designer

Component Designer tray

The complete File menu

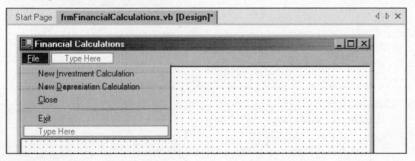

Description

- To create a *main menu*, add a MainMenu control to a form. The control will appear in the *Component Designer tray* at the bottom of the Designer window, and the Menu property of the form will be set to the name of that control.

- To add items to the menu, click wherever it says "Type Here" in the *Menu Designer*, then type the text of the menu item and press the Enter key. Additional entry areas appear below and to the right of the entry.

- When the user selects a menu item, the Click event of that item occurs. Then, you can code a procedure for that event to respond to the selection as shown in figure 9-9.

Figure 9-10   How to create a main menu

How to edit and enhance menus

In addition to the techniques for creating a menu that were presented in the previous figure, you should know about some of the properties that affect how a menu item looks or operates. And you should know about some additional techniques for working with menus. These properties and techniques are presented in figure 9-11.

Each menu and menu item you create is a separate object that has its own properties. When you enter the text for a menu item into the Menu Designer, for example, that text is assigned to the Text property of that item. Like the Text property of some controls, you can include an ampersand in the Text property of a menu item to define an access key for that item.

You can also use properties to display a check mark next to a menu item when it's selected, to define a shortcut key for a menu item, and to disable or hide a menu item. In addition, if you're creating a main menu for a parent form in an MDI application, you can display a list of the open child forms in one of the menus by setting its MdiList property to True. Then, you can switch from one child form to another by selecting it from this menu.

You can also use the commands in the shortcut menu that's displayed when you right-click on a menu item to work with that item. Some of these commands are also presented in this figure. For example, you can use the Insert New command to insert a new menu item above an existing item, and you can use the Edit Names command to display the names of the menu items in the Menu Designer as shown in this figure. Then, you can change the names in the Menu Designer rather than in the Properties window.

If a menu includes two or more groups of commands, you can include a separator bar between the groups. To do that, you can use the Insert Separator command in the shortcut menu for the first menu item in a group. Alternatively, you can create a separator bar by typing a dash for the text of the menu item.

You can also cut, copy, paste, and delete menu items by using the commands in the shortcut menu. These commands are particularly useful for creating shortcut menus, also called *context menus*, since they typically duplicate commands in the main menu. You'll learn more about creating context menus in the next chapter.

A main menu with the menu item names displayed

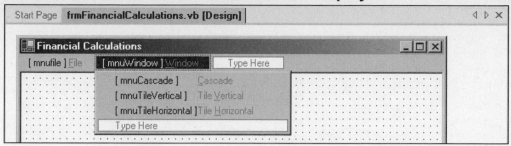

Common menu item properties

Property	Description
Text	The text that will appear in the menu for the item. To provide an access key for a menu item, include an ampersand (&) in this property.
Name	The name that's used to refer to the menu item in code.
Checked	Determines if a check mark appears to the left of the menu item when it's selected.
RadioChecked	Determines if a radio button appears to the left of the menu item when it's selected.
Shortcut	Specifies the shortcut key associated with the menu item.
ShowShortcut	Determines if the shortcut key is displayed to the right of the menu item.
Enabled	Determines if the menu item is available or grayed out.
Visible	Determines if the menu item is displayed or hidden.
MdiList	Determines if a list of the open MDI child windows is included in the menu.

Shortcut menu commands for working with menu items

Command	Description
Insert New	Inserts a new menu item above the selected item.
Insert Separator	Inserts a separator bar above the selected item.
Edit Names	Displays the names of the menu items as shown above so you can change them from the Menu Designer.

Notes

- You can also add a separator bar to a menu by typing a dash (-) for a menu item.
- The shortcut menu for a menu item also includes Cut, Copy, Paste, and Delete commands that you can use to work with the item.
- If a menu item is disabled or hidden, all items subordinate to it are disabled or hidden.
- You can include two or more menu controls on a single form. Then, you can display the appropriate menu as the program executes by changing the Menu property of the form. Alternatively, you can use the properties and methods of the menu items to modify them as the program executes.

Figure 9-11   How to edit and enhance menus

Perspective

Now that you've completed this chapter, you have the basic skills for developing applications that require two or more forms. That includes applications that use a single-document interface and applications that use a multiple-document interface. With these skills, you should be able to develop simple multi-form applications. To enhance those applications, though, you'll want to learn the skills in the next chapter.

Summary

- To work with a form object, you declare a form variable and assign an instance of a form class to it. Then, you can use the form variable to work with the properties and methods of the form object.

- If you want to start an application by displaying a form other than the default form, you can change the Startup object property of the project.

- In a *single-document interface* (*SDI*), each form runs in its own application window. An application with this type of interface typically includes a *startup form* that provides access to the other forms of the application.

- A form that's displayed from a startup form should be designed so the form can be hidden, but not unloaded. That way, it can be redisplayed without having to be instantiated and loaded again.

- In a *multiple-document interface* (*MDI*), a *parent form* contains one or more *child forms* and provides a central location for working with those forms. An MDI application makes it easy to display and manage multiple instances of its child forms.

- A form can include a *main menu* that provides access to basic Windows operations as well as operations specific to the application. When used on a parent form, the main menu typically provides access to the other forms.

- To create a main menu, you add a MainMenu control to a form. Then, the Menu Designer lets you enter the menu items at the top of the form.

- You can modify a menu item by changing its properties in the Properties window. You can also work with a main menu by using the commands in its shortcut menu.

Terms

single-document interface	MDI	main menu
SDI	parent form	Component Designer tray
startup form	child form	Menu Designer
multiple-document interface	explorer-style interface	context menu

Objectives

- Given the specifications for an application that uses a single-document interface, design and develop the application.

- Given the specifications for an application that uses a multiple-document interface, design and develop the application.

- Use the Menu Designer to create a main menu for any form.

- Distinguish between a single-document and a multiple-document interface.

- Describe the purpose of a startup form.

- Describe the general guidelines for designing and coding a form that's displayed by a startup form.

- Explain how you identify the parent and child forms within a project.

- Explain the main purpose of the main menu on a parent form. Then, describe other operations you might make available from a main menu.

Exercise 9-1   Create the SDI application

In this exercise, you'll create the SDI version of the Financial Calculations application. To make that easier, you'll use the Calculate Investment and Calculate Depreciation forms from the chapter 8 applications.

Create a new project and add the existing forms

1. Start a new Windows project named FinancialCalculationsSDI and store it in the C:\VB.NET\Chapter 09\FinancialCalculationsSDI folder.

2. Delete the default form for the project. Then, use the Add Existing Item dialog box to add the frmCalculateInvestment.vb file in the C:\VB.NET\Chapter 08\ CalculateInvestment folder to your project, and change the class name for this form to frmCalculateInvestment.

3. Use the same technique to add the frmCalculateDepreciation.vb file in the C:\VB.NET\Chapter 08\CalculateDepreciation folder to the project, and change the class name for this form to frmCalculateDepreciation.

Create the startup form

4. Add a new form to the project and name it frmMain. Then, modify this form so it looks something like the one in figure 9-5. At the least, this form should include a label that identifies the application and three buttons that let the user display the Calculate Investment and Calculate Depreciation forms and exit from the application. If necessary, you can refer to the property settings in figure 9-6 for help.

5. For the picture box control, you can set the Image property to the Murach logo.bmp file that's in the C:\VB.NET\Chapter 09 folder. Or, you can use any other image that's available to you.

6. Add the code shown in figure 9-5 that creates instances of the Calculate Investment and Calculate Depreciation forms and responds to the Click events of the three buttons.

7. Set the startup form as the startup object for the project, and then run the application. When the startup form is displayed, click on the Calculate Investment button to display the Calculate Investment form. Perform a calculation, and then click on the Exit button to close the form.

8. Click on the Calculate Investment button again to see what happens. Because the form was closed rather than hidden, an error message should be displayed indicating that the program can't access a disposed form. Click on the Continue button in this dialog box to end the application.

Modify the Calculate Investment form

9. Change the Exit button on the Calculate Investment form to a Close button, and change the procedure for the Click event of this button so it hides the form rather than closing it. This procedure should also call the ClearControls procedure so the controls will be empty when the form is redisplayed.

10. Change the ControlBox property of the form to False to remove the control box and close button from the title bar. Then, run the application again.

11. Click on the Calculate Investment button, enter a calculation, and then close the form. Click on the Calculate Investment button again to see what happens. This time, the form should be redisplayed without any data. If it's not, you'll need to correct the problem and test the program again.

12. Perform another calculation, and then click on the startup form to move the focus to that form. Notice that the Calculate Investment form is now hidden behind that form (or at least it will be if you set the StartPosition property of the startup form to CenterScreen). Now, click on the Calculate Investment button one more time to bring that form in front of the startup form. Then, close that form, and close the application.

Modify the Calculate Depreciation form

13. Change the Exit button on the Calculate Depreciation form to a Close button, and change the procedure for the Click event of this button so it hides the form rather than closing it. Then, add code to this procedure that clears the controls on the form before it's hidden.

14. Change the ControlBox property of the form to False, then run the application.

15. Click on the Calculate Depreciation button to display the Calculate Depreciation form. Perform a calculation, then close the form. Click on the Calculate Depreciation button again to make sure this works correctly.

16. Drag the Calculate Depreciation form by its title bar so it's not on top of the startup form. Then, click on the startup form to move the focus to it, and click on the Exit button. Notice that both the startup form and the Calculate Depreciation form are closed.

17. If all of this worked correctly, close the solution. Otherwise, make the appropriate changes until the program works the way it should.

Exercise 9-2   Create the MDI application

In this exercise, you'll create the MDI version of the Financial Calculations application using the forms from the applications presented in chapter 8.

Create a new project and add the existing forms

1. Start a new Windows project named FinancialCalculationsMDI and store it in the C:\VB.NET\Chapter 09\FinancialCalculationsMDI folder.

2. Change the name of the default form class to frmFinancialCalculations so it doesn't conflict with the existing forms that you'll copy into the project, and change the name of the file for this form to frmFinancialCalculations.vb.

3. Use the Add Existing Item dialog box to add the frmCalculateInvestment.vb file in the C:\VB.NET\Chapter 08\CalculateInvestment folder to your project. Then, change the class name for this form to frmCalculateInvestment, set the MinimizeBox and MaximizeBox properties of this form to True, and change the StartPosition property so the form will be displayed in the default position.

4. Use the same technique to add the Calculate Depreciation form in the C:\VB.NET\Chapter 08\CalculateDepreciation folder to the project. Then, change the class name to frmCalculateDepreciation, and set the MinimizeBox, MaximizeBox, and StartPosition properties accordingly.

Create the parent form

5. Set the IsMdiProperty of the Financial Calculations form to True to identify it as a parent form. Then, set the other form properties so the text "Financial Calculations" is displayed in the title bar, the form is sizeable and occupies the entire screen when it's first displayed, and minimize and maximize buttons are available.

6. Add a MainMenu control to the form, and notice that it's displayed in the Component Designer tray at the bottom of the Form Designer. Also notice that a box with the words "Type Here" appears at the top of the form where the menu will be displayed.

7. Use the Menu Designer as described in figure 9-10 to add the File menu with three menu items that will display a new Calculate Investment form, display a new Calculate Depreciation form, and exit from the application. Include access keys if you'd like. Then, use the Properties window to name these three menu items mnuNewInvestment, mnuNewDepreciation, and mnuExit.

8. Add code for the Click event of each menu item. The code for the first two procedures should create a new instance of the form, set the MdiParent property of the form to the Financial Calculations form, and display the form. The procedure for the third item should simply close the form.

9. Run the application. (Since you created the parent form from the default form, this form should already be set as the startup object.) When the Financial Calculations form is displayed, pull down the File menu and select the item that displays an instance of the Calculate Investment form. Notice that this form is displayed in the upper left corner of the parent form.

10. Perform a calculation, and then open another Calculate Investment form. Notice that this form is displayed on top of the other form, but its position is offset so you can see both forms.

11. Open one or more Calculate Depreciation forms and perform calculations to see how this works. When you're done, use the Exit item in the File menu to close the application.

Modify the main menu

12. Right-click on the File menu in the Financial Calculations form to display its menu items. Then, right-click on the Exit item, select the Insert New command, and add a Close menu item. Name this menu item mnuClose.

13. Code a procedure for the Click event of this new menu item so it will close the current child form. Then, run the application again, display two or more child forms, and use this menu item to see how it works. When you're done, exit from the application.

14. Right-click on the Exit item in the File menu again, and select the Insert Separator command to create a separator bar.

15. Click to the right of the File menu where it says "Type Here" and add a Window menu. Change the MdiList property of the Window menu to True so it will display a list of the open child windows. Then, add three items to this menu that will let the user arrange the forms in a cascaded, vertical, or horizontal layout.

16. Right-click in the Window menu and select the Edit Names command. The menu should appear with the names displayed as shown in figure 9-11. Click on each menu item in this menu and enter an appropriate name for it.

17. Code a procedure for the Click event of each of the items in the Window menu. Each procedure should use the LayoutMdi method of the form to arrange the child forms using one of the constants in the MdiLayout enumeration.

18. Run the application again, and display two or more instances of each form. Then, use the items in the Window menu to see how the windows are arranged for each. Use the list of windows in this menu to move from one form to another. When you're done experimenting, close the application, and then close the solution and Visual Studio.

10

How to enhance the user interface

Once you have the forms of an application working right, you can enhance the user interface by adding context menus, toolbars, a status bar, and help information. If the application takes a long time to start up, you may also want to add a splash form that indicates the progress of the startup procedure. By making these additions and changes, you improve the appearance of the application at the same time that you make it easier to use.

How to use special types of forms and procedures

Besides the forms that provide the main functionality of an application, you may need to use forms that perform special functions. In the topics that follow, you'll learn about some of these forms. You'll also learn about a special procedure that you can use to start an application.

How to create and use dialog boxes

[handwritten: CAN MOVE = MODELESS]

When you design an application that consists of two or more forms, the user can typically move back and forth between the various forms as necessary. These types of forms are called *modeless forms*. In some cases, though, you'll want to make sure that the user responds to a form appropriately before returning to another form. To do that, you create a *modal form*, called a *dialog box*, as described in figure 10-1.

A dialog box is a special type of form that returns a result. This result is determined by the value of the DialogResult property of the form. The form in this figure, for example, accepts a password from the user and sets the DialogResult property to DialogResult.OK if the password is correct. As soon as that return value is set, the dialog box is hidden and control returns to the class or module that called it.

Another way to set the result of a dialog box is to set the DialogResult property of a button in the dialog box. Then, when the user clicks on that button, the DialogResult property of the form is set to the DialogResult property of the button. If, for example, you set the DialogResult property of the Cancel button to an initial value of Cancel, that value is returned when the user clicks on that button and the dialog box is hidden. In that case, no code is required for the Click event of that button.

You can also set the DialogResult property of a button to Cancel by setting the CancelButton property of the form to the button's name. Then, the Cancel value is returned when the user clicks on that button and the dialog box is hidden. Here again, no code is required for the Click event of the button.

To display a dialog box, you use the ShowDialog method as shown in the If statement in this figure. This statement also checks the result of the dialog box. You'll see how a statement like this is used later in this chapter.

When you issue the ShowDialog method, the dialog box remains displayed until the DialogResult property of the form is set. If, for example, the user clicks on the Accept button in the dialog box shown here and the password is invalid, an error message is displayed and the user can try entering the password again. If the password is valid or the user clicks on the Cancel button, though, the DialogResult property of the form is set. Then, the form is hidden and control returns to the class or module that displayed it.

A dialog box that accepts a password from the user

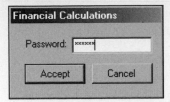

The code for the dialog box

```
Private Sub btnAccept_Click(ByVal sender As System.Object, _
        ByVal e As System.EventArgs) Handles btnAccept.Click
    If txtPassword.Text = "Murach" Then
        Me.DialogResult = DialogResult.OK
    Else
        MessageBox.Show("Invalid password", "Financial Calculations")
        txtPassword.Text = ""
        txtPassword.Focus()
    End If
End Sub
```

An If statement that displays the dialog box and checks the result

```
If frmPassword.ShowDialog = DialogResult.OK Then ...
```

Common property settings for dialog boxes

Property	Setting
FormBorderStyle	FixedDialog
ControlBox	False

Description

- A *dialog box* is a modal form that returns a result. A *modal form* is a form that must be closed or hidden before the application can continue.
- To display a dialog box, you use the ShowDialog method of a form. This method returns a result value that you can test to determine how the user responded.
- You specify the result value of a dialog box by setting its DialogResult property. Or, you can set the DialogResult property of a button in the dialog box. Then, when the user clicks on that button, the DialogResult property of the form is set accordingly.
- To set or test the dialog result value, you use the constants in the DialogResult enumeration. OK and Cancel are the two most common constants.
- If you set the CancelButton property of a form to a button on that form, the DialogResult property of that button is automatically set to Cancel.
- After you set the result value of a dialog box, the dialog box is hidden and control is returned to the class or module that displayed it.

Note

- In contrast to a modal form, you can move the focus from a *modeless form* without closing the form. This is the type of form you've seen so far in this book.

Figure 10-1   How to create and use dialog boxes

How to create and use owned forms   VS PARENT/CHILD

If you want to provide additional information for a form but you don't want to display that information directly on the form, you can create an *owned form*. For instance, the owned form in figure 10-2 gives the titles of the products listed in the combo box in the *owner form*, or *parent form*. That makes it easier to select the right product.

The difference between an owned form and a standard form is that an owned form is closed, minimized, and maximized along with its parent form. In addition, the owned form can't be displayed behind its parent form. However, it can be moved so it doesn't obscure the information on the parent form.

Most owned forms are displayed as modeless forms. That way, after the form is displayed, the user can move the focus back to the parent form. To display an owned form as a modeless form, you use the Show method just as you do for other forms. Before you issue this method, however, you set the Owner property of the form to the parent form as shown in the first coding example in this figure. In this case, the Owner property is set to Me since the owned form is displayed by its parent form. Note that you can't set the owner of a form in design mode. You can only set it as a program executes.

Although it wasn't apparent in figure 10-1, a dialog box is actually an owned form. By default, the parent form of a dialog box is the form that displays it. If you want to name the parent form explicitly, though, you can do that by coding an argument on the ShowDialog method. For instance, the second coding example in this figure names the current form (Me) as the parent form. Although you can also name another form as the parent form, you're not likely to do that.

An parent form and its owned form

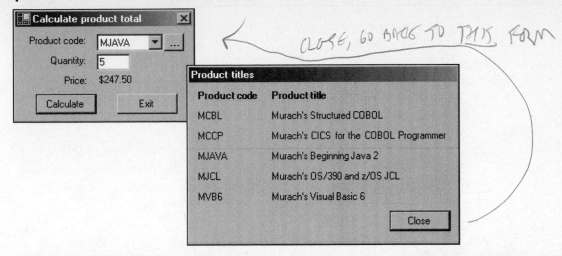

CLOSE, GO BACK TO THIS FORM

Code that establishes the current form as the parent form and displays the owned form as a modeless form

```
frmProductTitles.Owner = Me
frmProductTitles.Show()
```

The ShowDialog method establishes the parent form of a dialog box

```
frmProductTitles.ShowDialog(Me)
```

Description

- An *owned form* is a form that is owned by another form, called an *owner form* or *parent form*. An owned form is closed, minimized, and hidden along with its parent form, and it cannot be displayed behind its parent form.

- If you use the Show method to display an owned form, you can establish the parent form by setting the Owner property of the owned form before you display it.

- A dialog box is an owned form, and the ShowDialog method is used to establish the parent form. If Me is coded as an argument for the method or if no argument is used as in figure 10-1, the current form becomes the parent form.

- When you use a modeless owned form, you can change the focus back and forth between the owned form and its parent form. When you use a dialog box, you can't.

- You can display an owned form in the center of its parent form by setting its StartPosition property to CenterParent.

Figure 10-2   How to create and use owned forms

How to use a splash form

In chapter 9, you learned how to create a startup form that provides access to the other forms of an application. In the example presented in that chapter, the forms of the application were loaded only when the user requested them. In some cases, though, you may want to load all the forms of the application when the application starts. Then, if there's a significant delay before the first screen is displayed by an application, you may want to start the application by displaying a *splash form* (or *splash screen*) like the one at the top of figure 10-3.

This type of screen shows the user that the startup procedure is in progress. Then, to show the user that progress is being made, you can change the text of a label on the splash form as you move through the startup procedure, and you can change the Value property of a progress bar like the one shown in this figure.

The code in this figure shows how you can use the Load event procedure for the startup form to load the primary forms of the application and to show the progress of this startup procedure in a splash form. To start, the procedure declares an object variable for the splash form and creates an instance of this form. Then, it displays the splash form and changes the Text property of the Load Status label to indicate that the Calculate Investment form is being loaded.

Next, the DoEvents method of the Application class is executed. This class is part of the System.Windows.Forms namespace, so it's automatically available to every Windows project you create. Because all of the members of this class are shared, you don't have to create an instance of it to use any of its members.

The DoEvents method passes control to the Windows operating system so it does the events that are already in its queue. Otherwise, Windows decides on the priorities of the events in its queue and executes them based on those priorities. But that may mean that the splash form isn't displayed at the beginning of this procedure, even though the Show method is issued. The DoEvents method is useful whenever you want to make sure that all the commands in the queue are executed before the procedure continues.

The next two statements display and then hide the Calculate Investment form. Then, the value of the progress bar is changed to 50, the Load Status label is changed to indicate that the Calculate Depreciation form is being loaded, and the DoEvents method is executed again so these changes are reflected in the form. Next, the Calculate Depreciation form is displayed and hidden, the progress bar value is changed to 100, and DoEvents is executed one last time. Finally, the splash form is closed. When this procedure ends, the startup form is displayed.

* SEQ. MAY CHANGE HOWEVER, DON'T RELY ON SEQ. IN THIS CASE

A splash form for the Financial Calculations application

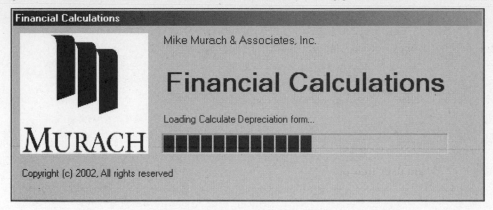

Code that displays the splash form and loads the calculation forms

```
Dim frmCalculateInvestment As New frmCalculateInvestment()
Dim frmCalculateDepreciation As New frmCalculateDepreciation()

Private Sub frmMain_Load(ByVal sender As Object, _
        ByVal e As System.EventArgs) Handles MyBase.Load
    Dim frmSplash As New frmSplash()
    frmSplash.Show()
    frmSplash.lblLoadStatus.Text = "Loading Calculate Investment form..."
    Application.DoEvents()
    frmCalculateInvestment.Show()
    frmCalculateInvestment.Hide()
    frmSplash.prgFormLoad.Value = 50
    frmSplash.lblLoadStatus.Text = "Loading Calculate Depreciation form..."
    Application.DoEvents()
    frmCalculateDepreciation.Show()
    frmCalculateDepreciation.Hide()
    frmSplash.prgFormLoad.Value = 100
    Application.DoEvents()
    frmSplash.Close()
End Sub
```

Description

- A *splash form* can be used to show the progress of a startup procedure and is typically displayed from a startup form.

- You can use a label control on a splash form that changes as the startup procedure executes to tell the user what tasks the application is performing.

- You can use a ProgressBar control on the splash form to show what portion of the startup procedure has been completed.

- The DoEvents method is a shared method of the Application class that ensures that all of the previous commands have been executed before the procedure continues. This method should be issued after the Show method of the splash form to be sure that the splash form is displayed immediately, then again each time the form changes.

Figure 10-3   How to use a splash form

How to use a Main procedure   *CAN START ANY FORM*

In chapter 5, you learned how to use a module to store variables and code used by more than one class. In addition, a module can include a *Main procedure* that's executed when the application starts. This is particularly useful for getting information from the user before displaying the first form of the application or for deciding which form should be displayed first.

Figure 10-4 illustrates how you can use a Main procedure. In the first example in this figure, the Main procedure displays a dialog box like the one you saw in figure 10-1 to get a password. Then, if the password is valid, the procedure starts the application by executing the Run method of the Application class.

To display the first form of the application, you pass an object variable that contains an instance of that form to the Run method. In this procedure, for example, the Run method will display frmMain, the startup form for the Financial Calculations SDI application that you saw in the last chapter. Then, the application will start just as if you had named this form as the startup object for the project.

The second example in this figure also uses the Run method to display the starting form for an application. In this case, the form is the parent form of the Financial Calculations MDI application that you saw in the last chapter. Because the only thing the Main procedure does in this example is display the parent form, you may be wondering why you would want to use this technique. The answer is that when use this technique, you have to declare an object variable for the form. Then, you can use that variable to refer to the form in other procedures in the module. For instance, the module in this example includes two additional procedures that use the object variable for the form to refer to the status bar on that form (which you'll learn more about in a moment). Because of the flexibility this adds to your applications, many developers recommend that you start all of your applications this way.

When you start an application from a Main procedure, you can use that procedure to catch any unhandled exceptions thrown by the application. To do that, you code the Run method within the Try block of a Try…Catch…Finally statement, and you code a Catch clause that will handle any exception, usually by just displaying an error message. Then, after the statements in the Catch block are executed, the program will end. This is a quick and easy way to handle any unexpected errors that occur as an application executes.

A module with a Main procedure that accepts a password before displaying the starting form

```
Module modCalculations
    Private frmPassword As New frmPassword()
    Private frmMain As New frmMain()

    Public Sub Main()
        If frmPassword.ShowDialog = DialogResult.OK Then
            Application.Run(frmMain)
        End If
    End Sub

End Module
```

GOOD FOR LOGIN

NOTE!

A module with a Main procedure that provides for access to the starting form

```
Module modCalculations
    Public sErrorMessage As String
    Private frmFinancialCalculations As New frmFinancialCalculations()

    Public Sub Main()
        Application.Run(frmFinancialCalculations)
    End Sub

    Public Sub DisplayErrorMessage()
        frmFinancialCalculations.sbFinancialCalculations.Text _
            = sErrorMessage
        MessageBox.Show(sErrorMessage, "Financial Calculations")
    End Sub

    Public Sub ClearErrorMessage()
        frmFinancialCalculations.sbFinancialCalculations.Text = ""
    End Sub

End Module
```

Description

- To start an application by executing code rather than by displaying a form, you can use a *Main procedure*. A Main procedure is a procedure named Main that's coded within a module.

- A Main procedure can be used to determine which form to display when an application starts or to perform some processing, such as accepting a password, before the first form is displayed.

- To display the starting form for an application from within a Main procedure, you use the Run method of the Application class. On this method, you specify the name of an object variable that contains a reference to the form object you want to display.

- If you code the Run method within the Try block of a Try…Catch…Finally statement, you can catch any unhandled errors thrown by the application.

- To use a Main procedure as the starting point for an application, you set the Startup object property of the project to Sub Main as described in figure 9-3.

Figure 10-4   How to use a Main procedure

How to create context menus and toolbars

In the last chapter, you learned how to use a main menu to provide access to the functions of an application. Now, you'll learn how to add context menus and toolbars that in many cases duplicate the functions provided by the main menu. However, they can also make these functions more accessible to the user.

How to create a context menu

A *context menu*, also called a *shortcut menu*, is a menu that appears when you right-click on a form or control. The context menu shown in figure 10-5, for example, includes two menu items: one that will clear the entries from the Calculate Investment form and one that will perform the calculation specified by that form. In this case, the context menu is associated with the form, so it's displayed anytime you right-click on the form. However, you can also create context menus for individual controls.

To create a context menu, you add a context menu control to the form as described in this figure. Like the main menu control, this control appears in the Component Designer tray at the bottom of the window. Then, you assign the menu to a form or control by setting the ContextMenu property of that form or control to the name of the menu control. Note that you can assign the same menu control to more than one form control, and you can add as many context menu controls to a form as you need.

When you click on a menu control in the Designer tray, the Menu Designer for that control appears at the top of the form as shown in the second screen in this figure. To create the menu, you simply type the text you want to appear for each menu item where it says "Type Here." In addition, you can use any of the properties and shortcut menu commands you learned about in chapter 9 to work with it. You can refer back to figure 9-11 to review these properties and commands if you need to.

A context menu displayed at run-time

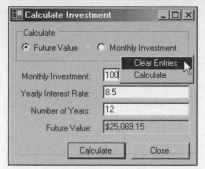

The design of the context menu

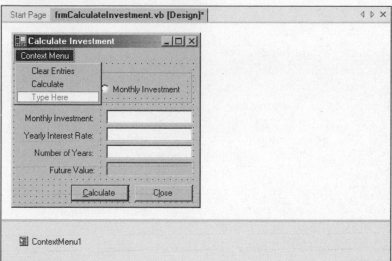

[handwritten notes:]
NEED TO ASSOC. W/ MAIN FORM

CAN SELECT OTHER CONTEXT MNU W/CLICK EVENT

CAN SPEC. WHICH MENU APPEARS BY LOC --- IF E.X > 100 ... (OF FORM!)

Description

- A *context menu* is the menu that's displayed when you right-click on a form or control.

- To create a context menu, add a ContextMenu control to a form. The control will appear in the Component Designer tray at the bottom of the window.

- To add items to the menu, select the menu control so the Menu Designer appears in the upper left corner of the form. Then, click wherever it says "Type Here," type the text of the menu item, and press the Enter key. Additional entry areas appear below and to the right of the entry.

- To assign a menu to a form or control, change the ContextMenu property of the form or control to the name of the menu control. You can assign a context menu to more than one control, and you can create more than one context menu for a form.

- You can set the properties of a context menu item and use the commands in the shortcut menu for a context menu item just as you can for the items in a main menu. See figure 9-11 for details.

Figure 10-5   How to create a context menu

How to create a toolbar

To create a *toolbar*, you add a toolbar control to a form. This control is *docked* at the top of the form below any menus on the form and extends across the full width of the form as shown by the toolbar in figure 10-6. Here, the toolbar includes two buttons that let the user display a Calculate Investment or Calculate Depreciation form. To add buttons like these to a toolbar, you use the ToolBarButton collection editor shown in this figure.

Each button you add to a toolbar can display text, a graphic image, or both. To display text, just set the Text property for that button. To display a graphic image, you first need to create an image list by adding an ImageList control to the form. When you add this control, it's displayed in the Component Designer tray since it doesn't have a visible interface.

After you add an ImageList control to the form, you add the images you want to use on the toolbar buttons to the image list using the Image collection editor that's available through the Images property of the control. Each image you add is assigned an index number that you can then use to refer to the image from the ToolBarButton collection editor. To do that, you set the ImageIndex property of the toolbar button to the index number of the image. But first, you have to set the ImageList property of the toolbar control to the name of the ImageList control that contains the images.

By default, the buttons you add to a toolbar are displayed as standard push buttons. However, you can create other types of buttons by changing the Style property of the button. For example, you can create a button that displays a drop-down list by changing this property to DropDownButton. Then, you use the DropDownMenu property to identify a context menu that you want to display when the user clicks on this button. You can also create a toggle button by changing the Style property to ToggleButton. And you can add a separator between two buttons by changing the Style property to Separator.

Another toolbar button property you should notice is the ToolTipText property. This property lets you specify the text that's displayed when the user places the mouse pointer over the button, called a *ToolTip*. This is particularly useful if the button contains only a graphic image. Then, the ToolTip can contain text that describes the function of the button.

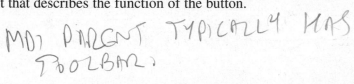

[handwritten: SOLUTION-ADD-NEW ICON]

A toolbar with two toolbar buttons

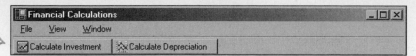

[handwritten: DOCK LETS YOU POSITION IN DIFF. PLACES]

The ToolBarButton Collection Editor dialog box

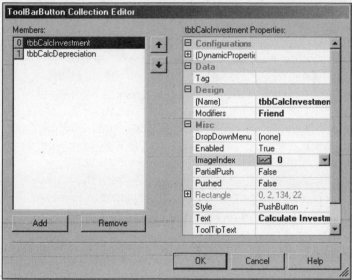

[handwritten: NOTE— DROP DOWN + TOGGLE BUTTON STYLES]

[handwritten: BUTTONS ON PANEL CAN APPEAR W/ APPEAR AP. WILD FORM. "TOOLBAR" DIM X AS NEW A TOOLBARBUTTON X.TEXT = "X42" TOOLBAR. BUTTONS.ADD (X) (ADDS BUTTON)]

Description

- To create a *toolbar*, add a ToolBar control to a form. By default, the toolbar is *docked* at the top of the form below the menus and reaches across the width of the form.

- To add buttons to the toolbar, select the Buttons property in the Properties window and then click on the ellipsis that appears to display the ToolBarButton collection editor. Use the Add button in this dialog box to add a button, then set the button properties.

- To include text on a button, enter the text in the Text property. By default, the text appears below any image that's displayed on the button, but you can display it to the right of the image by changing the TextAlign property of the toolbar to Right.

- To include a graphic image on a button, set the ImageList property of the toolbar to the name of an image list control that includes the image. Then, select the image from the drop-down list for the ImageIndex property of the toolbar button.

- To create an image list, add an ImageList control to the form. Then, select the Images property in the Properties window and click on the ellipsis that appears to display the Image collection editor. Use the Add button in this dialog box to add the images you want to use.

- The ToolTipText property lets you specify the text that's displayed when the user points to the button with the mouse (called a *ToolTip*). You'll want to set this property if the button contains only a graphic image.

[handwritten: ADD IMAGE LIST TO TOOLBAR ↓ USE IMAGE INDEX IN BUTT. COLL. EDITOR TO ASSIGN]

[handwritten: INDEX]

Figure 10-6   How to create a toolbar

[handwritten: TO REMOVE BUTTON, USE "REMOVEAT(1)" -OR- TOOLBAR1.BUTTONS.REMOVE(TOOLBAR1.BUTTONS (1) -OR- FOR EACH X IN XX~~]

How to use code to work with context menus and toolbars

After you create the context menus and toolbars for a form, you need to add the code that makes them work. To do that, you use procedures like the ones shown in figure 10-7. As you can see, you use the Click event of a context menu item to respond to the user clicking on that item just as you do for a main menu item, and you use the ButtonClick event of a toolbar to respond to the user clicking on a button on that toolbar.

The first procedure in this figure is for the Click event of a menu item named mnuClear. This is the first item in the context menu you saw in figure 10-5. The code for this procedure simply calls the ClearControls procedure for the form to clear its controls.

The second procedure in this figure is for the ButtonClick event of the toolbar you saw in the previous figure. This procedure uses the Button property of the e argument that's passed to the procedure to determine which button was clicked. In this case, if the Calculate Investment button was clicked, the procedure executes the Click event procedure for the mnuNewInvestment menu item. To do that, it uses the PerformClick method of that menu item. That way, you don't have to duplicate the code that creates and displays the form. Similarly, if the Calculate Depreciation button is clicked, the Click event procedure of the mnuNewDepreciation menu item is executed.

The third procedure shows how you can show or hide a toolbar using a menu item. In this case, a View menu has been added to the main menu that contains a single item named mnuViewToolbar. This toolbar item is displayed at the top of this figure. As you can see, it uses a check mark to indicate whether or not the toolbar is displayed. Each time you click on a menu item like this, its current status should be changed. A checked item should become unchecked and vice versa, and the toolbar should be hidden or displayed accordingly.

The code for the Click event of this menu item uses the Checked property of the menu item to determine if the toolbar is currently displayed. If it is, this procedure sets this property to False to remove the check mark. It also sets the Visible property of the toolbar to False so it's hidden. Conversely, if the Checked property of the menu item is False, it's set to True so a check mark is displayed, and the Visible property of the toolbar is set to True. Another way to code this procedure is like this:

```
mnuViewToolbar.Checked = Not mnuViewToolbar.Checked
tlbFinancialCalculations.Visible _
    = Not tlbFinancialCalculations.Visible
```

Here, the Not operator is used to reverse the values of the Checked and Visible properties.

A View menu that hides or displays the toolbar

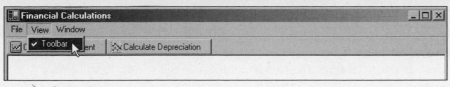

Code for the Click event of a menu item in a context menu

```
Private Sub mnuClear_Click(ByVal sender As Object, _
        ByVal e As System.EventArgs) Handles mnuClear.Click
    Me.ClearControls()
End Sub
```

Code for the ButtonClick event of a toolbar

```
Private Sub tlbFinancialCalculations_ButtonClick _
        (ByVal sender As System.Object, _
        ByVal e As System.Windows.Forms.ToolBarButtonClickEventArgs) _
        Handles tlbFinancialCalculations.ButtonClick
    If e.Button Is tbbCalcInvestment Then
        mnuNewInvestment.PerformClick()
    Else
        mnuNewDepreciation.PerformClick()
    End If
End Sub
```

Code that shows or hides a toolbar depending on a menu selection

```
Private Sub mnuViewToolbar_Click(ByVal sender As System.Object, _
        ByVal e As System.EventArgs) Handles mnuViewToolbar.Click
    If mnuViewToolbar.Checked Then
        mnuViewToolbar.Checked = False
        tlbFinancialCalculations.Visible = False
    Else
        mnuViewToolbar.Checked = True
        tlbFinancialCalculations.Visible = True
    End If
End Sub
```

Description

- You use the Click event of an item in a context menu to respond to the user selecting that item.

- You use the ButtonClick event of a toolbar to respond to the user clicking on one of the buttons in that toolbar. A reference to the button that was clicked is passed to that event in the Button property of the e argument. You can use the Is operator to compare this property with the buttons in the toolbar to determine which one was clicked.

- You can use the PerformClick method of a button or menu item to cause the Click event to occur on that object. This is useful if a toolbar button or menu item duplicates a function that's available from a button or another menu item.

Figure 10-7   How to use code to work with context menus and toolbars

How to create and use a status bar

In addition to menus and toolbars, you can include a status bar on the forms you create. A status bar is typically used to provide general information about an application. Because of that, it's used most often on the parent form of an MDI application.

How to create a simple status bar

Figure 10-8 shows you how to create a *status bar*. In this case, the status bar consists of a single *panel* that displays an error message whenever an error occurs. Although an error message is typically displayed in a message box as well, that message box must be closed before the user can correct the error. Because of that, it can be useful to display information about the error in the status bar to help the user after the message box is closed.

To create a status bar, you use the StatusBar control. By default, this control is docked at the bottom of the form. Then, you can set the Text property of this control as the program executes to display the appropriate text, as illustrated by the code in this figure.

STATUSBAR HAS "SHOW PANELS" PROP

STATUSBAR1.WIDTH = ME.WIDTH → MAKES WIDTH OF FORM

A form with a simple status bar

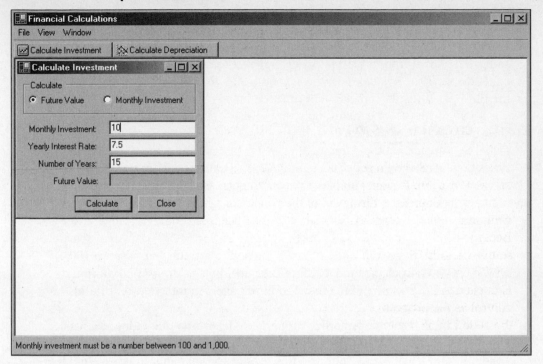

Code that displays an error message in the status bar

```
frmFinancialCalculations.sbFinancialCalculations.Text = _
    "Monthly investment must be a number between 100 and 1,000."
```

Description

- To create a *status bar*, add a StatusBar control to the form. The status bar will be docked at the bottom of the form.

- By default, a status bar consists of a single *panel* that can display text. To display text in that panel, set the Text property of the status bar. This text typically changes as the program executes.

Figure 10-8   How to create a simple status bar

How to add panels to a status bar

By default, a status bar consists of a single panel as shown in the previous figure. However, you can add as many panels to a status bar as you need. The status bar shown in figure 10-9, for example, consists of three panels. The first panel displays the system date, the second panel displays an error message, and the third panel displays the system time.

To add panels to the status bar, you use the StatusBarPanel collection editor shown in this figure. For each panel, you can set a variety of properties. For example, you can set the Alignment property to determine how the information that's displayed within the panel is aligned. You can set the Text property to the starting text that's displayed in the panel. You can set the Icon property to identify an icon that's displayed in the panel. And you can set the ToolTipText property to the text that's displayed when the user places the mouse over the panel.

By default, the width of each panel you add to a status bar is set to 100. However, you can change the width of the panel by setting its Width property. For example, the widths of the first and third panels in the status bar in this figure are set to 80.

You can also use the AutoSize property to determine the width of a panel automatically. If this property is set to Contents, the panel is sized based on its contents. And if it's set to Spring as it is for the second panel in this figure, the panel is sized so it takes up the remaining width of the form. That way, even if the form changes size or other panels in the status bar change size based on their contents, the status bar still occupies the entire width of the form. In either case, you'll want to be sure to set the MinWidth property of the panel to the minimum width you want it to have. The default is 10.

Because the panels of a status bar are stored in a collection, each is assigned a unique index number beginning with 0. In the dialog box shown in this figure, for example, you can see that the three panels displayed in the Members list are given index values of 0, 1, and 2. Then, you can use these index numbers to refer to the panels in the collection from your program. In the procedure in this figure, for example, you can see how the date and time are assigned to the first and third panels (index numbers 0 and 2). In chapter 11, you'll learn more about the properties and methods you can use to work with dates and times.

Notice that this code is executed in response to the Tick event of a timer control. The timer control causes this event to occur at the interval you define in its Interval property. That way, you can update the information in the status bar periodically so it remains current.

A status bar that displays the date, time, and an error message

The StatusBarPanel Collection Editor

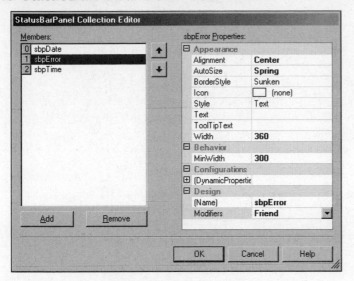

Code that changes the text in two status bar panels at regular intervals

```
Private Sub Timer1_Tick(ByVal sender As System.Object, _
        ByVal e As System.EventArgs) Handles Timer1.Tick
    sbFinancialCalculations.Panels(0).Text = DateTime.Today
    sbFinancialCalculations.Panels(2).Text _
        = FormatDateTime(DateTime.Now, DateFormat.LongTime)
End Sub
```

Description

- To divide a status bar into panels, select the Panels property and then click on the ellipsis that appears to display the StatusBarPanel collection editor. Use the Add button in this dialog box to add a panel, then set the panel properties.

- To specify the exact width of a panel, set the Width property. To size a panel according to its contents, set the AutoSize property to Contents. To size a panel so it takes up the remaining width of the form, set the AutoSize property to Spring.

- After you create panels, you can apply them to the status bar by setting its ShowPanels property to True.

- To display text in a status bar panel, set the Text property of that panel.

How to use a timer control to update information

- To update information in a status bar that changes periodically, use a timer control. To do that, set the Interval property of the control to the number of milliseconds between updates, set the Enabled property to True, and then update the information in the Tick event of the control.

Figure 10-9   How to add panels to a status bar

How to add help information

Because Visual Basic applications use the standard Windows interface, users who are already familiar with other Windows applications should quickly adapt to Visual Basic applications. In addition, you should try to design and develop each application so it is as easy to use as is practical. Nevertheless, almost all applications can benefit from the addition of at least a minimum amount of help information.

One way to add help information to a form is to add a Help menu. Then, you can add items to that menu for various topics. When the user selects one of these items, you can display a dialog box with the appropriate information.

You can also add help information to a form by using ToolTips and context-sensitive help. You'll learn how do that in the two topics that follow.

How to add ToolTips

Earlier in this chapter, you learned how to add ToolTips to toolbar buttons and status bar panels. In addition, you can add ToolTips to each control on a form and to the form itself. Figure 10-10 shows you how.

To add ToolTips, you add a ToolTip control to the form. Then, a ToolTip property becomes available for the form and each of its controls. This property is listed in the Properties window along with the other properties of the form or control. Then, you can set this property to the text you want displayed when the user places the mouse pointer over the form or control. The illustration in this figure, for example, shows the ToolTip for the Initial Cost text box on the Calculate Depreciation form.

- SOME TOOLS ALREADY HAVE TOOLTIPS

A ToolTip that's assigned to a text box

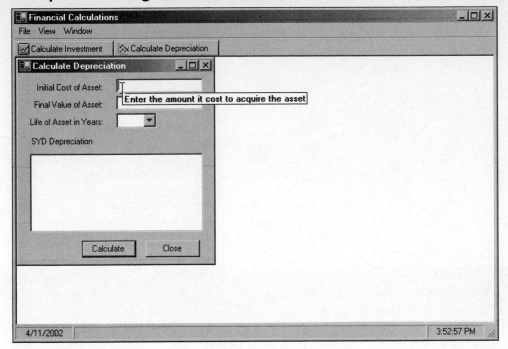

Description

- A *ToolTip* is a brief description of a control that's displayed automatically when you place the mouse pointer over that control.
- To create ToolTips for a form, add a ToolTip control to the form. A control named ToolTip1 will appear in the Component Designer tray at the bottom of the window.
- The ToolTip control makes a property named ToolTip on ToolTip1 available for each control on the form and for the form itself. You can enter the text of the ToolTip for this property in the Properties window.

Note

- If you change the name of the ToolTip control, the name of the ToolTip on ToolTip1 property will change to reflect the name you specify.

Figure 10-10   How to add ToolTips

How to add context-sensitive help

If you want to display help information that's more extensive than what you would normally display in a ToolTip, you can use the HelpProvider control. This control lets you provide *context-sensitive help* for a form or control. Then, the user can display the help for the control that has the focus by pressing the F1 key. If help text isn't provided for that control, the help text for the form is displayed if it's provided.

To specify the help text for a form or control, you use the HelpString property that becomes available when you add a HelpProvider control to the form. The illustration in this figure, for example, shows the help text for the Calculate Depreciation form.

In addition to the HelpString property, the HelpProvider control also provides properties that you can use to build a complete help system that's comparable to one for a commercial application. To do that, you use this control in conjunction with a Help editor like the HTML Help Workshop that comes with Visual Studio .NET. For more information on creating this type of help, see the help documentation for this product.

Context-sensitive help for the Calculate Depreciation form

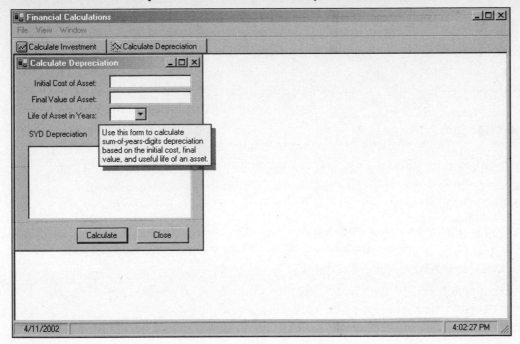

Description

- To provide *context-sensitive help* for a form or control, add a HelpProvider control to the form. A control named HelpProvider1 will appear in the Component Designer tray at the bottom of the window. This control makes several additional properties available for the form and each control it contains.

- To display a text string when the user presses the F1 key for the control that has the focus, enter the text for the HelpString on HelpProvider1 property of the control.

- You can also enter help text for the HelpString property of the form. Then, that text is displayed at the location of the mouse pointer if a help string isn't specified for the control that has the focus.

- You can use the other properties that are exposed by the HelpProvider control to display help that you develop using the HTML Help Workshop that comes with Visual Studio .NET. For more information, see the topic "Providing Help in a Windows Application" in online help.

Notes

- When you enter text for the HelpString on HelpProvider1 property, the ShowHelp on HelpProvider1 property automatically changes from False to True

- If you change the name of the HelpProvider control, the name of the HelpString on HelpProvider1 property will change to reflect the name you specify.

Figure 10-11   How to add context-sensitive help

Perspective

If you take some time to experiment with the features presented in this chapter, you'll see that they're all relatively easy to use. Nevertheless, they can significantly improve the impression that an application makes on its users. More important, they can help the users of an application work more efficiently.

Summary

- You can use a *dialog box* to accept information from the user and return a result value. A dialog box is a *modal form* that must be closed or hidden before the application can continue.

- You can use an *owned form* to display information related to another form. An owned form is closed, minimized, and hidden along with its *parent form*, and it can't be displayed behind its parent form.

- If an application takes more than a few seconds to start up, you can use a *splash form* to display the progress of the startup procedure.

- You can start program execution with a *Main procedure* that simply starts the application and displays the first form or that does some type of processing before displaying the first form.

- You can create a *context menu* that's displayed when the user right-clicks on a form or control. Context menus provide easy access to commonly used functions of an application.

- A *toolbar* can include one or more buttons that provide access to commonly used functions of an application. A toolbar button typically duplicates the function of an item in the main menu.

- You can use a *status bar* to display information to the user as a program executes. A status bar can include one or more *panels* and is typically used on the parent form of an MDI application.

- You can add *ToolTips* to the controls on a form to provide the user with a brief description of what they do. You can also provide *context-sensitive help* for a form or control that's displayed when the user presses F1.

Terms

dialog box	splash form	docked control
modal form	splash screen	ToolTip
modeless form	Main procedure	status bar
owned form	context menu	panel
owner form	shortcut menu	context-sensitive help
parent form	toolbar	

Objectives

- Given the specifications for an application that uses any of the features presented in this chapter, design and develop the application.

- Distinguish between a dialog box and an owned form.

- Describe the use and operation of a splash form.

- Describe the use of a Main procedure in a module, and give two reasons for using one.

- Describe the use and operation of context menus, toolbars, and status bars.

- List two quick ways to provide the user with help information.

Exercise 10-1   Enhance the SDI application

In this exercise, you'll enhance the SDI version of the Financial Calculations application you created in the last chapter so it starts by accepting a password from the user and then displays a splash form as the forms for the application are loaded. You'll also add a Main procedure that starts the application.

Open the project and add a dialog box that accepts a password

1. Use the Windows Explorer to copy the C:\VB.NET\Chapter 09\ FinancialCalculationsSDI folder to C:\VB.NET\Chapter 10. Then, open the chapter 10 SDI project.

2. Add a new form named frmPassword to the project. Then, set the form properties and add controls to the form so it looks something like this:

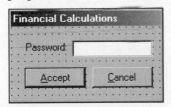

3. Code a procedure for the Click event of the Accept button that tests the value the user enters into the text box. If it's valid, the procedure should set the DialogResult property of the form to DialogResult.OK (you can use your last name as a valid password). Otherwise, it should display an error message, clear the text box, and move the focus back to the text box.

4. Code an event procedure for the Click event of the Cancel button so it sets the DialogResult property of the form to DialogResult.Cancel.

5. Open the Code Editor for the startup form (frmMain). Then, code a procedure for the Load event of the form that declares an object variable for the Password form, creates an instance of the form, and displays the form as a dialog box. This procedure should close the startup form if the return value of the dialog box is equal to DialogResult.Cancel. Otherwise, no special processing should be done.

6. Run the application. When the password dialog box is displayed, enter an invalid password. Then, click on the OK button in the message box that's displayed to return to the password dialog box, and enter a valid password. When the startup form is displayed, exit from the application.

7. Run the application again. This time, click on the Cancel button to see what happens. If the application ends without displaying the startup form, continue with the next step. Otherwise, make the necessary corrections.

8. Delete the procedure for the Click event of the Cancel button. Then, set the CancelButton property of the form to this button. Now, display the properties for the button and notice that the DialogResult property has been set to Cancel. Run the application again and click on the Cancel button to see that this still works.

Add a splash form to the project

9. Add another form to the project named frmSplash. Then, set the properties of the form and add controls to the form so it looks something like the one in figure 10-3. At the least, it should include a label that identifies the application and a label and progress bar that will indicate the progress of the startup procedure.

10. Modify the Load procedure for the startup form so it loads and then hides the Calculate Investment and Calculate Depreciation forms and shows the progress in the splash form. If you need help writing this code, you can refer to figure 10-3.

11. Run the program and enter a valid password. Then, watch carefully or you won't even see the splash form as it's displayed. When the startup form is displayed, end the application.

12. If you want to see the splash form as it's displayed, code this procedure in the startup form:

```
Private Sub SlowDown()
    Dim iIndex, iCount As Integer
    For iIndex = 1 To 100000000
        iCount += 1
    Next iIndex
End Sub
```

Then, call this procedure after each execution of the DoEvents method. When you run the application, you should now be able to see the progress displayed in the splash form. If not, you may have to increase the number of times the loop is performed in the SlowDown procedure.

Create a module with a Main procedure that gets the password and starts the application

13. Add a module to the application. Then, delete the code from the startup form that displays the password dialog box, and move the declarations for the password and splash forms to the module.

14.   Code a Sub procedure named Main in the module that displays the password form as a dialog box and tests the result for a value of DialogResult.OK. If the result is equal to this value, the procedure should use the Run method of the Application class to start the application by displaying the startup form. If you need help, you can refer to the code in figure 10-4.

15.   Change the startup object for the project to Sub Main, and then run the application. If it works, end the application and then close the solution. Otherwise, make the necessary changes to get it to work the way it should.

Exercise 10-2   Add a toolbar to the MDI application

In this exercise, you'll add a toolbar to the parent form of the MDI version of the Financial Calculations application you created in the last chapter. Then, you'll modify the main menu on this form so it lets you hide or display this toolbar.

Open the project and add a toolbar to the parent form

1.   Use the Windows Explorer to copy the C:\VB.NET\Chapter 09\ FinancialCalculationsMDI folder to C:\VB.NET\Chapter 10. Then, open the chapter 10 MDI project.

2.   Add an image list control to the form, and use the Images property of this control to display the Image collection editor. Then, add the two bitmap images in the C:\VB.NET\Chapter 10 folder to this collection.

3.   Add a toolbar named tlbFinancialCalculations to the form, and set the ImageList property of this control to the image list you just created. Then, use the Buttons property of the toolbar to display the ToolBarButton collection editor.

4.   Add two buttons to the toolbar. Name the first one tbbCalcInvestment, set its ImageIndex property to 0, and set its Text property to Calculate Investment. Name the second one tbbCalcDepreciation, set its ImageIndex property to 1, and set its Text property to Calculate Depreciation. When you're done, click on the OK button and notice how the images are displayed above the text in the buttons. If that's not what you want, change the TextAlign property of the toolbar from Underneath to Right.

5.   Double-click on the toolbar to start a procedure for its ButtonClick event. Then, use the Button property of the e argument that's passed to this event to determine which button was clicked. If the Calculate Investment button was clicked, the procedure should execute the Click event of the mnuNewInvestment menu item. Otherwise, it should execute the Click event of the mnuNewDepreciation menu item. If you need help, refer to figure 10-7.

6.   Run the application. When the parent form is displayed, click on the Calculate Investment button to display a Calculate Investment form. Click on this button again to display another form. Then, display one or more Calculate Depreciation forms. When you're done, end the application.

Modify the main menu to hide or display the toolbar

7. Use the Insert New command in the shortcut menu for the Window menu to add a View menu to the main menu of the parent form. Add a Toolbar menu item to this menu, name this menu item mnuViewToolbar, and set its Checked property to True.

8. Double-click on this menu item to start a procedure for its Click event. Then, add code to this procedure to remove its check mark and hide the toolbar if it's checked or add a check mark and display the toolbar if it's not checked.

9. Run the application. When the parent form is displayed, pull down the View menu and notice that the Toolbar item is checked. Click on this item to hide the toolbar. Then, pull down the View menu again to see that the Toolbar item is unchecked. Click on it again to check it and display the toolbar. When you're done, exit from the application, but leave the solution open if you're going to continue.

Exercise 10-3   Add context menus to the MDI application

In this exercise, you'll add a context menu to the Calculate Investment form. In addition, you'll create a context menu for one of the text boxes on this form.

Add a context menu to the Calculate Investment form

1. If it's not already open, open the MDI version of the Financial Calculations application you modified in exercise 10-2.

2. Add a context menu control to the Calculate Investment form, and set the ContextMenu property of the form to this control.

3. Select the context menu control in the Component Designer tray to display the context menu at the top of the form. Then, click on the context menu, add two menu items as shown in figure 10-5, and name them mnuClear and mnuCalculate.

4. Code procedures for the Click events of the menu items. The first one calls the ClearControls procedure of the form, and the second one executes the Click event of the Calculate button.

5. Run the application, display a Calculate Investment form, and perform a calculation. Then, right-click on the form to display the context menu and select the Clear Entries item to clear the controls on the form.

6. Enter the values for another calculation, but don't click on the Calculate button. Instead, display the context menu and select the Calculate item to perform the calculation. Then, exit from the application.

Add a context menu to a control

7. Add another context menu control to the form, and set the ContextMenu property of the Monthly Investment text box to this control. Add two items to this menu. The first one should clear the control, and the second one should increase the value in the control by 10%.

8. Code procedures for the Click events of these two menu items. Then, run the application, display a Calculate Investment form, and perform a calculation.

9. Right-click on the Monthly Investment text box and select the item to clear the control. Then, enter another value in the control, right-click anywhere on the form other than in the Monthly Investment text box, and select the Calculate item from the context menu to perform the calculation.

10. Right-click on the Monthly Investment text box again and select the item to increase the investment by 10% to see how this works. When you're done, close the application, but leave the solution open if you're going to continue.

Exercise 10-4   Add a status bar to the MDI application

In this exercise, you'll add a status bar to the parent form in the MDI version of the Financial Calculations application.

Open the project and add a simple status bar

1. If it's not already open, open the Financial Calculations MDI application and add a status bar control named sbFinancialCalculations to the parent form.

2. Add a module to the project, and add code like that shown in the second example in figure 10-4 that starts the application by using the Run method in a Main procedure to display the parent form. Add the other two procedures in this example to display error messages in a message box and in the status bar and to clear the error message from the status bar.

3. Modify the Calculate Investment and Calculate Depreciation forms so they use the procedures in the module to display error messages and to clear the error message from the status bar when all the user entries are valid or when the form is closing (use the Closing event). Then, run the application, and enter invalid data in each form to see what happens. When you're done, close the application.

Add panels to the status bar

4. Use the Panels property of the status bar to display the StatusBarPanel collection editor. Then, add three panels named sbpDate, sbpError, and sbpTime. For sbpDate and sbpTime, use centered alignment and a width of 80. For sbpError, use centered alignment, but size it so it takes up the remaining width of the form and has a minimum width of 300.

5. Add a timer control to the form, set its Enabled property to True, and set its Interval property to 1000. Then, code a procedure for the Tick event of this control that sets the date and time in the status bar as shown in figure 10-9.

6. Modify the statements in the module that set and clear the error message that's displayed in the status bar so they refer to the second panel. Then, run the application. Are the correct date and time displayed? Does the time change every second? Are errors displayed correctly?

7. When you're done testing the application, close it, but leave the solution open if you're going to continue.

Exercise 10-5   Add ToolTips and help to the MDI application

In this exercise, you'll add ToolTips to the controls on the Calculate Investment form, and you'll add context-sensitive help to the Calculate Depreciation form.

Add ToolTips to the Calculate Investment form

1. Add a ToolTip control to the Calculate Investment form. Then, set the ToolTip on ToolTip1 property for each option button and text box on this form so it contains a brief description of the control.

2. Run the application, display a Calculate Investment form, and place the mouse pointer over each control on the form with a ToolTip to display that ToolTip. When you're done, close the application.

Add context-sensitive help to the Calculate Depreciation form

3. Add a HelpProvider control to the Calculate Depreciation form. Then, set the HelpString property of the form so it contains information about how the form works. In addition, set the HelpString properties for the two text boxes and the combo box so they contain a description of the controls.

4. Run the application and display a Calculate Depreciation form. Press F1 with the focus in each of the first three controls to display the help information for that control. Then, move the focus to the Calculate button and press F1 to display the help information for the form. When you're done, close the application and then close the solution.

Section 3

More language essentials

This section consists of five chapters that show you how to use more of the Visual Basic language essentials. Chapter 11 shows how to work with dates and strings. Chapter 12 shows how to work with arrays and collections. Chapter 13 shows how to work with structures and files. Chapter 14 shows how to use XML for working with files. And chapter 15 presents more of the concepts and skills of object-oriented programming.

You can read the chapters in this section any time after you complete the first eight chapters of this book. We do, however, recommend that you read the five chapters in this section in sequence because each of the later chapters uses features that are presented in earlier chapters. That's not to say you can't skip around if you have a compelling reason to do so, especially if you already have some programming background. The chapters are written as independent units, so you shouldn't have much problem with that. Eventually, though, you're going to want to read all five chapters so you may as well read them in sequence.

How to work with dates and strings

In this chapter, you'll learn how to work with dates and strings. These are two of the primitive data types that are available with Visual Basic, and some special skills are required for working with them. Because dates and strings are used in most programs, the skills in this chapter are ones that every Visual Basic programmer should know how to use.

How to work with dates and times

When you were introduced to data structures in chapter 5, you learned that the Date data type of Visual Basic is supported by the DateTime structure of the .NET Framework. Since a structure is similar to a class, you can use the properties and methods of the DateTime structure to work with dates and times, and that's the preferred way to handle these elements. After you learn how to use the DateTime properties and methods, though, you'll be introduced to some other ways that Visual Basic provides for working with dates and times.

How to get the current date and time

Figure 11-1 presents two DateTime properties that you can use to get the current date and time. If you use the Now property, both the date and time are returned. If you use the Today property, only the date is returned.

Because Now and Today are shared properties, you access them directly through the DateTime structure. For instance, the first example in this figure uses the Today property to get the date, and the second example uses the Now property to get the date and time.

The results of these statements are also shown, but those aren't the actual values that are stored in the variables. Instead, they show what the results are when they're displayed. The date and time are actually stored as the number of *ticks* (100-nanosecond units) that have elapsed since 12:00 AM, January 1, 0001, which makes the dates and times easier to work with numerically.

How to format DateTime values

To control the formatting of dates and times, you can use the four methods of the DateTime structure that are shown in figure 11-1. Although there are other methods for this purpose, these are the ones that are used most frequently. Note, however, that these formats may vary somewhat from the formats that are displayed on your system. The exact formats depend on your computer's regional settings.

VB 6 HAD NOW & ROOM

SOL → PROD → BUILD → OPTION (ETC)

DateTime properties for getting the current date and time

Property	Description
Now	Gets the current date and time.
Today	Gets the current date.

Statements that get the current date and time

Statement	Result
`dtmCurrentDate = DateTime.Today`	12/21/2001
`dtmCurrentDateTime = DateTime.Now`	12/21/2001 4:24:59 AM

DateTime methods for formatting a date or time

Method	Description
ToLongDateString	Converts the DateTime value to a string that includes the day of the week name, the month name, the day of the month, and the year.
ToShortDateString	Converts the DateTime value to a string that includes the numeric month, day, and year.
ToLongTimeString	Converts the DateTime value to a string that includes the hours, minutes, and seconds.
ToShortTimeString	Converts the DateTime value to a string that includes the hours and minutes.

Statements that format dates and times

Statement	Result
`sLongDate = dtmCurrentDateTime.ToLongDateString`	Friday, December 21, 2001
`sShortDate = dtmCurrentDateTime.ToShortDateString`	12/21/2001
`sLongTime = dtmCurrentDateTime.ToLongTimeString`	4:24:59 AM
`sShortTime = dtmCurrentDateTime.ToShortTimeString`	4:24 AM

Description

- The Date data type of Visual Basic is supported by the DateTime structure of the .NET Framework.
- A date is stored as a 64-bit signed integer that represents the number of *ticks* (100-nanosecond units) that have elapsed since 12:00 AM, January 1, 0001.
- The Now and Today properties are shared properties of the DateTime structure, so you can access them directly from that structure.
- The format that's used for a date or time depends on your computer's regional settings.

Figure 11-1   How to get the current date and time and format DateTime values

NOTE! DATETIMEPICKER CONTROL (ALSO MONTH CALENDAR)

How to get information about dates and times

The DateTime structure also provides a variety of properties and methods for getting information about dates and times. These properties and methods are listed in figure 11-2, and the examples in this figure show how they work.

The first statement in this figure uses the Now property to get the current date and time. Then, the second statement uses the Month property to get the month portion of that date, and the third statement uses the Hour property to get the hour portion of the time.

The fourth and fifth statements use the DayOfWeek and DayOfYear properties to get additional information about the current date. The DayOfWeek property returns a number between 0 and 6 that represents the day of the week. And the DayOfYear property returns a number between 1 and 366 that represents the day of the year.

The next two statements show how to use the two methods for getting information about a date. Note that both of these methods are shared, so they're accessed through the DateTime structure. The first method, DaysInMonth, returns the numbers of days in a given month and year. The second method, IsLeapYear, returns a True or False value that indicates if a given year is a leap year.

The last statement uses the Parse method to convert a string that contains a date to a DateTime value. This is the shared method that you use when you need to convert a user entry to a DateTime value. In this example, a literal is used as the string argument, but the argument is usually the Text property of a text box.

For this to work properly, the string that's passed to the Parse method must be in a valid date format. But what constitutes a valid date string? By default, the Parse method accepts any of the standard DateTime patterns, including the following:

```
4/15/2002
4/15/02
4/15/2002 10:25 AM
Apr 15, 2002
April 15, 2002
Monday, April 15, 2002
```

In practice, though, a user is likely to use one of the first three forms to enter just the date or both the date and time. If the user enters just the date, the time portion of the DateTime value is set to 12 AM.

Common DateTime properties

Property	Description
Date	The date portion of a DateTime value.
Month	The month portion of a DateTime value.
Day	The day portion of a DateTime value.
Year	The year portion of a DateTime value.
Hour	The hour portion of a DateTime value.
Minute	The minute portion of a DateTime value.
Second	The second portion of a DateTime value.
TimeOfDay	A TimeSpan value that represents the amount of time that has elapsed since midnight.
DayOfWeek	A constant that represents the day of the week of a DateTime value in the DayOfWeek enumeration. 0 represents Sunday, 1 represents Monday, and so on.
DayOfYear	The numeric day of the year.

Common shared methods of the DateTime structure

Method	Description
DaysInMonth(year, month)	Returns the number of days in a specified month and year.
IsLeapYear(year)	Returns a Boolean value indicating whether a specified year is a leap year.
Parse(string)	Converts the specified string to an equivalent DateTime value or throws an exception if it can't. If the time isn't included in the string, 12 AM is assumed.

Statements that get information about a date or time

Statement	Result
`dtmCurrentDateTime = DateTime.Now`	`12/26/2001 10:26:35 AM`
`iMonth = dtmCurrentDateTime.Month`	`12`
`iHour = dtmCurrentDateTime.Hour`	`10`
`iDayOfWeek = dtmCurrentDateTime.DayOfWeek`	`3`
`iDayOfYear = dtmCurrentDateTime.DayOfYear`	`360`
`iDaysInMonth = DateTime.DaysInMonth(2004, 2)`	`29`
`bLeapYear = DateTime.IsLeapYear(2004)`	`True`
`dtmDateTime = DateTime.Parse("Jan 15, 2003")`	`01/15/2003 12:00:00 AM`

Description

- A TimeSpan value represents an interval of time that's measured in ticks.

- The Parse method can successfully convert any string that takes the form of one of the standard DateTime patterns. This generally works the way you would expect it to. But for more details, you can look up "Date and Time Format Strings" in the help information.

Figure 11-2   How to get information about dates and times

How to perform operations on dates and times

Figure 11-3 presents some of the methods of the DateTime structure that you can use to perform operations on dates and times. Most of these methods let you add a specific number of intervals, like hours, days, or months, to a date or time. However, you can use the Add method to add a TimeSpan value to a date, and you can use the Subtract method to determine the time span between two dates, which is often required in business applications.

The first set of examples in this figure shows how some of the Add methods work. For example, the second statement shows how to add two months to a DateTime value, and the third statement shows how to add 60 days. Similarly, the fourth statement shows how to add 30 minutes, and the fifth statement shows how to add 12 hours.

The second set of examples shows how you can use a TimeSpan variable to determine the number of days between two DateTime values, which is a common business operation. Here, the first statement retrieves the current date, and the second statement assigns a date to another DateTime variable. Next, the third statement uses the Subtract method to subtract the two date values and assign the result to a TimeSpan variable, which represents the number of days, minutes, hours, and seconds between the two dates. Then, the last statement uses the Days property of the TimeSpan structure to extract just the number of days from the TimeSpan value. This is one of several properties of this structure that let you extract the data from a TimeSpan value.

Before I go on, you should know that you can also work with DateTime values within Visual Basic expressions. For instance, the last example in this figure shows how to use two DateTime values in a conditional expression. Here, if the first DateTime value is greater than the second, a Boolean variable is set to True. Otherwise, the variable is set to False. This works because the dates and times are stored as numeric values. You'll use expressions like this frequently when working with dates and times.

DateTime methods for performing operations on dates and times

Method	Description
AddDays(days)	Adds the specified numbers of days to a DateTime value and returns another DateTime value.
AddMonths(months)	Adds the specified number of months to a DateTime value and returns another DateTime value.
AddYears(years)	Adds the specified number of years to a DateTime value and returns another DateTime value.
AddHours(hours)	Adds the specified number of hours to a DateTime value and returns another DateTime value.
AddMinutes(minutes)	Adds the specified number of minutes to a DateTime value and returns another DateTime value.
AddSeconds(seconds)	Adds the specified number of seconds to a DateTime value and returns another DateTime value.
Add(timespan)	Adds the specified TimeSpan value to a DateTime value and returns another DateTime value.
Subtract(datetime) Subtract(timespan)	Subtracts the specified DateTime value from a DateTime value and returns a TimeSpan value. Or, subtracts a TimeSpan value from a DateTime value and returns a DateTime value.

Statements that perform operations on dates and times

Statement	Result
`dtmDateTime = "1/24/2002 13:28"`	1/24/2002 1:28:00 PM
`dtmDueDate = dtmDateTime.AddMonths(2)`	3/24/2002 1:28:00 PM
`dtmDueDate = dtmDateTime.AddDays(60)`	3/25/2002 1:28:00 PM
`dtmRunTime = dtmDateTime.AddMinutes(30)`	1/24/2002 1:58:00 PM
`dtmRunTime = dtmDateTime.AddHours(12)`	1/25/2002 1:28:00 AM

Code that results in a TimeSpan value

Statement	Result
`dtmCurrentDate = DateTime.Today`	12/26/2001
`dtmDueDate = "1/15/2002"`	1/15/2002
`Dim tsDaysTillDue As TimeSpan _` `    = dtmDueDate.Subtract(dtmCurrentDate)`	20.00:00:00
`Dim iDaysTillDue As Integer = tsDaysTillDue.Days`	20

An If statement that uses a DateTime value in a conditional expression

```
If dtmCurrentDate > dtmDueDate Then
    bPastDue = True
Else
    bPastDue = False
End If
```

Description

- The TimeSpan structure has Days, Hours, Minutes, and Seconds properties that let you extract portions of a TimeSpan value.

Figure 11-3   How to perform operations on dates and times

Other ways to work with dates and times

When you use the properties and methods of the DateTime structure to work with dates and times, you write code that is consistent with other .NET code. That's why using the DateTime structure is the preferred way to work with dates and times when you're using Visual Basic .NET.

However, you can also use the Visual Basic properties and functions in figure 11-4 to work with dates and times. These properties and functions are part of the Visual Basic run-time library that's included in the Microsoft.VisualBasic namespace, which is always available to your projects. Because you can get the same results with the properties and methods of the DateTime structure, you don't need to use these properties and functions. Nevertheless, it's worth taking a minute or two to review them in case you encounter them when you're working with someone else's code.

If you scan the properties, you can see that the Today and Now properties get the system date and the system date and time, while the TimeOfDay property gets just the time. In contrast, the DateString and TimeString properties return the date and time as string values.

If you scan the first group of functions, you can see that the Month, Day, and Year functions get the month, day, and year components of a date. The Hour, Minute, and Second functions get the hour, minute, and second components of a time. And the WeekDay function returns a number between 1 and 7 that represents the day of the week. In addition, the MonthName function gets the name of a specified month, and the WeekDayName function gets the name of a specified day of the week.

Finally, if you scan the last group of functions, you can see that the DateAdd function performs the same operations as the Add methods of the DateTime structure. And the DateDiff function subtracts two DateTime values.

To use one of the properties in this figure, you just code the property name without any qualifiers, as in these examples:

```
dtmCurrentDate = Today
sTimeString = TimeString
```

To use one of the functions, you just supply the required arguments as in these examples:

```
iHour = Hour(dtmCurrentDateTime)
iMonth = MonthName(Month(dtmCurrentDateTime))
```

Here, the second statement uses one function within another.

One problem that you run into when you code the Day function is that you have to qualify it with Microsoft.VisualBasic as in this example:

```
iDay = Microsoft.VisualBasic.Day(dtmCurrentDate)
```

That's because Day is a word that's defined in the System.Windows.Forms namespace.

Visual Basic properties for getting the current date and time

Property	Description
Now	Gets the system date and time as a DateTime value.
Today	Gets the system date as a DateTime value.
TimeOfDay	Gets the system time as a DateTime value.
DateString	Gets the system date as a <u>string</u> value with the format mm-dd-yyyy.
TimeString	Gets the system time as a string value with the format hh:mm:ss.

FOR DBMS!

Visual Basic functions for getting information about dates and times

Function	Description
Month(datetime)	Returns the month portion of a DateTime value.
Day(datetime)	Returns the day portion of a DateTime value.
Year(datetime)	Returns the year portion of a DateTime value.
Hour(datetime)	Returns the hour portion of a DateTime value.
Minute(datetime)	Returns the minute portion of a DateTime value.
Second(datetime)	Returns the second portion of a DateTime value.
MonthName(month)	Returns the name of the month specified by an integer between 1 and 12.
WeekDay(datetime)	Returns an integer that represents the day of the week of a DateTime value. 1 represents Sunday, 2 represents Monday, and so on.
WeekDayName(day)	Returns the name of the day specified by an integer between 1 and 7.

Visual Basic functions for performing operations on dates and times

Function	Description
DateAdd(interval, number, datetime)	Adds the specified number of specified intervals to a specified date and returns the resulting DateTime value.
DateDiff(interval, datetime1, datetime2)	Subtracts the value of the first date you specify from the second date and returns the difference as a Long value that contains the number of specified intervals.

Constants in the DateInterval enumeration

Constant	Description	Constant	Description
Day	Day of the month	Quarter	Quarter of the year
DayOfYear	Day of the year	Second	Second
Hour	Hour	Weekday	Day of the week
Minute	Minute	WeekOfYear	Week of the year
Month	Month	Year	Year

Description

- To specify the type of interval for a function, you use the DateInterval enumeration.
- The Day function must be qualified with the Microsoft.VisualBasic namespace since Day is defined as an enumeration in the System.Windows.Forms namespace.

Figure 11-4   The Visual Basic properties and functions for working with dates and times

How to work with strings

Many types of Visual Basic programs require that you work with the characters within strings. If, for example, a user enters the city, state, and zip code of an address as a single entry, your program may need to divide (or *parse*) that single string into city, state, and zip code variables. Or, if a user enters a telephone number that includes parentheses and hyphens, you may need to remove those characters so the number can be stored as a 10-digit integer.

When you create a variable of the String data type, you are actually creating a String object from the String class. Then, you can use the properties and methods of the String class to work with the String object. Another alternative, though, is to create StringBuilder objects from the StringBuilder class so you can use the properties and methods of that class to work with strings. In the topics that follow, you'll learn both ways of working with strings, and you'll also be introduced to the Visual Basic functions for working with strings.

The properties and methods of the String class

Figure 11-5 summaries the properties and methods of the String class that you can use as you work with String objects. As you use these properties and methods, an *index* value is used to refer to a specific character within a string, starting with zero. If, for example, you want to refer to the first character in the string, you use the index value 0. If you want to refer to the second character, you use the index value 1. And so on.

The first property in this figure is the Chars property, which retrieves the character at the position indicated by the index that's used as an argument. In contrast, the Length property returns the number of characters in the string as an integer and doesn't require an argument.

The methods in this figure provide the operations that you'll need as you parse strings and work with them in other ways. In the next figure, you'll see coding examples that will help you see how these methods can be used. But first, take a few minutes to review the operations that these methods provide.

The first two methods in this figure return a Boolean value. The StartsWith method returns a value that indicates whether the string starts with the specified string. And the EndsWith method returns a value that indicates whether the string ends with the specified string.

The next two methods return an integer value that represents an index position. The IndexOf method returns the index of the first occurrence of the specified string. And the LastIndexOf method returns the index of the last occurrence of the specified string. You can also specify the starting position for the search and the number of characters to be searched as arguments.

The next nine methods return a string that has been modified in some way from the original string. The Insert method, for example, lets you insert a string into the original string, and the Remove method lets you remove one or more characters. You'll see how you can use many of these methods in the next figure.

— .NET —

NOTE:
OPTION COMPARE —
- BINARY = ASCII CODE
- TEXT = S/B CASE INSENS.

Properties of the String class

Property	Description
Chars(index)	Gets the character at the specified position.
Length	Gets the number of characters in the string.

Methods of the String class

Method	Description
StartsWith(string)	Returns a Boolean value that indicates whether the string starts with the specified string.
EndsWith(string)	Returns a Boolean value that indicates whether the string ends with the specified string.
IndexOf(string[, startIndex] [, count])	Returns an integer that represents the position of the first occurrence of the specified string starting at the specified position and continuing for the specified number of characters. If the starting position isn't specified, the search starts at the beginning of the string. If the number of characters isn't specified, the string is searched to its end. If the string isn't found, this method returns –1.
LastIndexOf(string[, startIndex] [, count])	Returns an integer that represents the position of the last occurrence of the specified string starting at the specified position and continuing for the specified number of characters. If the starting position isn't specified, the search starts at the end of the string. If the number of characters isn't specified, the string is searched to its beginning. If the string isn't found, this method returns –1.
Insert(startIndex, string)	Returns a string with the specified string inserted beginning at the specified position.
PadLeft(totalWidth [, paddingCharacter])	Returns a string that's right-aligned and padded on the left with the specified character so it's the specified width. If a padding character isn't specified, the string is padded with spaces.
PadRight(totalWidth [, paddingCharacter])	Returns a string that's left-aligned and padded on the right with the specified character so it's the specified width. If a padding character isn't specified, the string is padded with spaces.
Remove(startIndex, count)	Returns a string with the specified number of characters removed starting at the specified position.
Replace(oldString, newString)	Returns a string with all occurrences of the old string replaced with the new string.
Substring(startIndex[, length])	Returns the string that starts at the specified position and has the specified length. If the length isn't specified, all of the characters to the end of the string are returned.
ToLower	Returns a string in lowercase.
ToUpper	Returns a string in uppercase.
Trim	Returns a string with leading and trailing spaces removed.

Handwritten annotations:

FIND: OOP INDEX + 1

Ø BASED!

← EQUIV TO INSTR

CAN'T FIND → -1

{ TRIM END / TRIM START

↳ FASTER THAN STUFF ON 365 ↵

Description

- The characters in a string can be referred to by their *index* positions. The first index position in a string is 0.

Figure 11-5 The properties and methods of the String class

TRIM STRINGS RECEIVED BY DEFAULT!

Typical routines for working with strings

Figure 11-6 presents four string-handling routines that are typical of those required in Visual Basic programs. The first two parse the data in strings. The third one adds characters to a string. And the fourth one replaces some of the characters in a string with other characters. If you can understand the code in these routines, you should be able to write your own routines whenever needed.

The first routine shows how to parse the first name from a string that contains a full name. Here, the full name is assigned to the sFullName variable so you can imagine how the statements that follow work with that name. In practice, though, the name would be entered by a user or read from a file so you wouldn't know what it was.

To start, this routine uses the Trim method to remove any spaces from the beginning and end of the string that a user may have typed accidentally. Next, the IndexOf method is used to get the position of the first space in the string, which should be between the first name and the middle name or last name. If this method doesn't find a space in the string, though, it returns a −1. In that case, the If statement that follows assigns the entire string to the first name variable. Otherwise, the Else portion of this statement use the Substring method to set the first name variable equal to the string that begins at the first character of the string and that has a length that's equal to the position of the first space. In this case, the index of the first space will be 6 so the first 6 characters of the trimmed string will be assigned to the first name variable.

The second routine in this figure shows how to parse a string that contains an address into the components of the address. In this case, a pipe character (|) separates each component of the address. In addition, the string may begin with one or more spaces followed by a pipe character, and it may end with a pipe character followed by one or more spaces.

To remove the spaces from the beginning and end of the string, this routine also uses the Trim method. Then, it uses the StartsWith method to determine whether the first character in the string is a pipe character. If it is, the Remove method removes that character from the string. Similarly, this routine uses the EndsWith method to determine whether the string ends with a pipe character, and the Remove method removes that character if it's there.

The next three statements use the IndexOf method to determine the index values of the first character for each substring other than the first. (The first substring will start at index 0.) To do that, it determines the index of the next pipe character and then adds 1. After that, the next four statements use these index variables as arguments of the Substring method to return the street, city, state, and zip code substrings. The most confusing part of these statements is specifying the length of each substring. If you take a couple of minutes to study these statements, though, I think you'll be able to figure out how they work.

The third and fourth routines show how to add dashes to a phone number and change the dashes in a date to slashes. To add dashes, you simply use the Insert method to insert the dashes at the appropriate locations. And to change dashes to slashes, you use the Replace method.

Code that parses a first name from a name string

```
Dim sFullName As String = " Edward C Koop     "
Dim sFirstName As String
Dim iFirstSpace As Integer
sFullName = sFullName.Trim
iFirstSpace = sFullName.IndexOf(" ")
If iFirstSpace = -1 Then
    sFirstName = sFullName
Else
    sFirstName = sFullName.Substring(0, iFirstSpace)
End If
```

Code that parses a string that contains an address

```
Dim sAddress As String = " |805 Main Street|Dallas|TX|12345| "
Dim iCityIndex, iStateIndex, iZipIndex As Integer
Dim sStreet, sCity, sState, sZipCode As String
sAddress = sAddress.Trim
If sAddress.StartsWith("|") Then
    sAddress = sAddress.Remove(0, 1)
End If
If sAddress.EndsWith("|") Then
    sAddress = sAddress.Remove(sAddress.Length - 1, 1)
End If
iCityIndex = sAddress.IndexOf("|") + 1
iStateIndex = sAddress.IndexOf("|", iCityIndex) + 1
iZipIndex = sAddress.IndexOf("|", iStateIndex) + 1
sStreet = sAddress.Substring(0, iCityIndex - 1)
sCity = sAddress.Substring(iCityIndex, iStateIndex - iCityIndex - 1)
sState = sAddress.Substring(iStateIndex, iZipIndex - iStateIndex - 1)
sZipCode = sAddress.Substring(iZipIndex)
```

Code that adds dashes to a phone number

```
Dim sPhoneNumber As String = "9775551212"
sPhoneNumber = sPhoneNumber.Insert(3, "-")
sPhoneNumber = sPhoneNumber.Insert(7, "-")
```

Code that replaces the hyphens in a date with dashes

```
Dim sDate As String = "12-27-2001"
sDate = sDate.Replace("-", "/")
```

Figure 11-6   Typical routines for working with strings

How to use the StringBuilder class for working with strings

When you use the String class to work with strings, the string is a fixed length, and you can't edit the characters that make up the string. In other words, the String class creates strings that are *immutable*. Then, the only way you can change this type of string is to assign a new string to the String object, which deletes the original string and replaces it with the new string.

Another way to work with strings, though, is to use the StringBuilder class. Then, you create StringBuilder objects that are *mutable* so you can add, delete, or replace characters in the objects. This makes it easier to write some types of string-handling routines.

In figure 11-7, you can see some of the most useful properties and methods for working with the string that's stored in a StringBuilder object. To get the character at a specified position, you can use the Chars property. To get the length of the string, you can use the Length property. And to get or set the capacity of a StringBuilder object, you can use the Capacity property.

Once a StringBuilder object is created, you can use the Append method to add a string at the end of the string that the object already holds. You can also use the Insert, Remove, and Replace methods to insert, remove, and replace characters within the string that the object holds. As you work, the capacity of the object is increased whenever that's necessary. When you're through modifying the object, you can use the ToString method to convert it to a string.

When you use the StringBuilder class, you'll want to include an Imports statement for it as shown in this figure. That way, you can refer to it without qualifying it with the name of the namespace that contains it, System.Text. One curiosity about this namespace is that it's available to the project even though there isn't an assembly for it in the References folder. That's because it's included in the System assembly.

When you create a StringBuilder object, you can code one or two arguments that assign it an initial capacity or an initial value and capacity. The first example in this figure shows how you use a single argument to set the initial capacity. The second example shows how you use two arguments to assign an initial string value of 9775551212 and set the initial capacity to 10 characters.

The next example shows how you can use the Append and Insert methods of the StringBuilder class. Here, the first statement creates a StringBuilder object with an initial capacity of 10 characters, and the second statement uses the Append method to add a string value to the object. Then, the third and fourth statements use the Insert method to insert dashes into the string so it's formatted as a phone number, thus increasing the length of the string. This is something that can't be done with a String object. The last statement uses the ToString method of the StringBuilder object to convert it to a string.

This example shows how the capacity of a StringBuilder object increases automatically when that's necessary. Specifically, the StringBuilder object has a capacity of 10 when it's created, and it remains at 10 when the phone number string is appended because it consists of only 10 characters. However, when the first dash is inserted, the capacity is doubled to 20.

Properties of the StringBuilder class

Property	Description
Chars(index)	Gets the character at the specified position.
Length	Gets the length of the string.
Capacity(characters)	Gets or sets the capacity of the string.

Methods of the StringBuilder class

[handwritten: DON'T DO MANIP W/STRINGBUILDER - STRING FASTER]

Method	Description
Append(string[, count])	Adds the specified string or a string representation of the specified value to the end of the string the specified number of times. If the count is omitted, a single copy of the string is appended.
Append(string, startIndex, count)	Adds a substring of the specified string, starting with the specified position and having the specified length, to the end of the string.
Insert(index, string[, count])	Inserts the specified string or a string representation of the specified value at the specified position in the string the specified number of times. If the count is omitted, a single copy of the string is inserted.
Remove(startIndex, count)	Removes the specified number of characters from the string starting at the specified position.
Replace(oldString, newString [, startIndex][, count])	Replaces all occurrences of the old string with the new string starting at the specified position and continuing for the specified number of characters.
ToString	Converts the StringBuilder object to a string.

A statement that simplifies references to the StringBuilder class

```
Imports System.Text
```

Statements that create and initialize StringBuilder objects

```
Dim sbFullName As New StringBuilder(30)      'Initial capacity is 30
Dim sbPhoneNumber As New StringBuilder("9775551212", 10)
```

Code that creates a phone number and inserts dashes

```
Dim sbPhoneNumber As New StringBuilder(10)    'Capacity is 10
sbPhoneNumber.Append("9775551212")            'Capacity is 10
sbPhoneNumber.Insert(3, "-")                  'Capacity is 20
sbPhoneNumber.Insert(7, "-")                  'Capacity is 20
lblPhoneNumber.Text = sbPhoneNumber.ToString
```

Description

- String objects are *immutable*, which means that they can't be changed. StringBuilder objects are *mutable*, which means that they can be changed.

- To refer to the StringBuilder class, you must either qualify it with System.Text or include an Imports statement for this namespace at the start of the class or module that uses it.

- The capacity of a StringBuilder object is the amount of memory that's allocated to it. That capacity is increased automatically whenever necessary. If you don't set an initial capacity when you create a StringBuilder object, the default is 16 characters.

Figure 11-7   How to use the StringBuilder class for working with strings

Other ways to work with strings

Although the String and StringBuilder classes provide all the properties and methods that you need for working with strings, Visual Basic provides a complete set of functions for working with strings. Here again, these functions duplicate the operations of the .NET classes so you don't need them. Also, using classes and objects is the preferred way to work with strings when you're using Visual Basic .NET. That way, your code is more consistent.

Nevertheless, it's worth taking a minute or two to review the functions that are summarized in figure 11-8. That way, you won't be confused if you come across one of these functions in someone else's code. Curiously, an index value of 1 refers to the first character in a string when you use one of these functions, although it refers to the second character in a string if you use String or StringBuilder properties or methods.

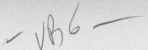

VB6

Visual Basic functions for working with strings   *ALMOST ALL HAVE EQUIV. IN .NET*

Function	Description
Len(string)	Returns the number of characters in the string.
InStr(startIndex, string1, string2)	Returns an integer that represents the position of the first occurrence of the second string in the first string. The search starts at the specified position in the string. If the string isn't found, this function returns 0.
Left(string, length)	Returns the specified number of characters from the beginning of the string.
Mid(string, startIndex[, length])	Returns the specified number of characters from the string starting at the specified position. If the length isn't specified, all of the characters to the end of the string are returned.
Right(string, length)	Returns the specified number of characters from the end of the string.
Replace(string, oldString, newString)	Returns a string with all occurrences of the old string in the string replaced by the new string.
Split(string[, delimiter][, limit])	Parses a string into a one-dimensional array of one or more substrings. If the delimiter isn't specified, space is used. If the limit isn't specified, all substrings are returned.
LCase(value)	Returns a string or character in lowercase.
UCase(value)	Returns a string or character in uppercase.
Trim(string)	Returns a string with leading and trailing spaces removed.
LTrim(string)	Returns a string with leading spaces removed.
RTrim(string)	Returns a string with trailing spaces removed.
Space(number)	Returns a string that contains the specified number of spaces.

SPLIT & JOIN

Description

- When you use Visual Basic functions to work with strings, the first index position is 1.
- The Left and Right functions must be qualified with the Microsoft.VisualBasic namespace because Left and Right are properties in the Windows.Forms.Form namespace.

*NEED VISBASIC NAMESPACE (IMPORTS MICROSOFT.VISUALBASIC)

Figure 11-8   The Visual Basic functions for working with strings

✻ USED TO BE FUNCT. IN V.B.

How to format numbers, dates, and times

Besides the properties and methods for working with strings, the String class provides a Format method that you can use to format numbers, dates, and times. This method can be useful if you ever need to apply special formatting to a number, date, or time. Because this method is complicated, you can first read the pages that follow to get a general understanding of what this method can do. Later, if you ever need to use this method, you can refer back to these pages.

How to format numbers

Figure 11-9 shows how to use the Format method of the String class for formatting numbers. Because this is a shared method, you access it directly from the String class rather than from an instance of this class. The result of this function is a string object that contains the formatted number.

As you can see in the syntax of this function, the first argument is a string. This string contains the format specifications for the value or values to be formatted. I'll have more to say about this in a moment. Following this string, you can specify up to three values that you want to format. In most cases, however, you'll use this method to format a single value.

For each value to be formatted, you code a format specification within the string argument. This specification is divided into three parts. The first part indicates the value to be formatted. Because the values are numbered from zero, you'll usually code a zero to indicate that the first value is to be formatted. The next part indicates the width of the formatted value along with its alignment. In most cases, you'll omit this part of the specification.

The third part of the format specification contains the actual format string. This string can contain from one to three formats. If only one format is specified, it's used for all numbers. If two formats are specified, the first is used for positive numbers and zero values, and the second is used for negative numbers. And if all three formats are specified, the first is used for positive numbers, the second is used for negative numbers, and the third is used for zero values. If you omit the format string altogether, the number is converted to a string without any formatting.

Each format can consist of one of the standard numeric formatting codes listed in this figure. If, for example, you want to format a number as currency, you can code a statement like the first statement in this figure. Here, the format specification indicates that the first value (value 0) should be formatted with the currency format (c). Notice that the format specification is enclosed in braces, and the entire string argument is enclosed in quotes just like any string literal.

If the standard numeric formatting codes don't provide the formatting you want, you can create your own format using the custom codes presented in this figure. For instance, the second statement uses these codes to create a custom currency format. Here, the first format indicates that positive numbers and the

The syntax of the Format method of the String class

```
Format(string, value1[, value2[, value3]])
```

The syntax of a format specification within the string argument

```
{N[, M][:formatString]}
```

Explanation

N	An integer that indicates the value to be formatted.
M	An integer that indicates the width of the formatted value. If M is negative, the value will be left-justified. If it's positive, it will be right-justified.
formatString	A string of formatting codes.

The syntax of a format string

```
positiveformat[;negativeformat[;zeroformat]]
```

Standard numeric formatting codes

C or c	Formats the number as currency with two decimal places.
D or d	Formats an integer with the specified number of digits.
E or e	Formats the number in scientific (exponential) notation with the specified number of decimal places.
F or f	Formats the number as a decimal with the specified number of decimal places.
G or g	Formats the number as a decimal or in scientific notation depending on which is more compact.
N or n	Formats the number with thousands separators and the specified number of decimal places.
P or p	Formats the number as a percent with the specified number of decimal places.

Custom numeric formatting codes

0	Zero placeholder	,	Thousands separator
#	Digit placeholder	%	Percentage placeholder
.	Decimal point	;	Section separator

Statements that format a single number

Statement	Result
`sBalance = String.Format("{0:c}", 1234.56)`	`$1,234.56`
`sBalance = String.Format("{0:$#,##0.00;($#,##0.00)}", -1234.56)`	`($1,234.56)`
`sBalance = String.Format("{0:$#,##0.00;($#,##0.00);Zero}", 0)`	`Zero`
`sQuantity = String.Format("{0:d3}", 43)`	`043`
`sPayment =  String.Format("{0:f2}", 432.8175)`	`432.82`

A statement that formats two numbers

Statement

```
String.Format("Invoice total: {0:c}; Amount due: {1:c}.", 354.75, 20)
```

Result

```
Invoice total: $354.75; Amount due: $20.00.
```

Figure 11-9   How to format numbers

value 0 should be formatted with a decimal and thousands separators (if appropriate). In addition, the first digit to the left of the decimal point and the first two digits to the right of the decimal are always included, even if they're zero. The other digits are included only if they're non-zero.

The format for negative numbers is similar. However, this format includes parentheses, which means that negative numbers will be displayed with parentheses around them as shown in the result for this statement. Notice that the parentheses aren't actually formatting codes. They're simply literal values that are included in the output string. The same is true of the dollar signs.

The third statement is similar to the second one, but it includes an additional format for zero values. In this case, a zero value is displayed as the literal "Zero" as you can see in the result for this statement.

The last two statements show how to use standard formatting codes for integers and decimals. In the first statement, an integer is formatted with three digits since the number 3 is included after the formatting code. In the second statement, a decimal is formatted with two decimal places. As you can see, if the number includes more decimal places than are specified, the number is rounded.

The example at the bottom of this figure shows how you can use the Format method to format two numbers. Notice here that the string argument includes text in addition to the format specifications for each of the two values to be formatted. In this case, the first value is formatted according to the first format specification and is then substituted for the format specification in the resulting string. Similarly, the second value is formatted according to the second format specification and is then substituted for that specification in the resulting string. Notice that when you include two or more format specifications, they must be separated by a semicolon.

How to format dates and times

You can also use the Format method of the String class to format dates and times. This method works the same way that it does for numeric formatting, but you use the standard and custom formatting codes for DateTime values that are presented in figure 11-10. The examples in this figure show how this works. If you understand how to use this method to format numbers, you shouldn't have any trouble using it to format dates and times.

Standard DateTime formatting codes

d	Short date	f	Long date, short time
D	Long date	F	Long date, long time
t	Short time	g	Short date, short time
T	Long time	G	Short date, long time

Custom DateTime formatting codes

d	Day of the month without leading zeros	h	Hour without leading zeros
dd	Day of the month with leading zeros	hh	Hour with leading zeros
ddd	Abbreviated day name	H	Hour on a 24-hour clock without leading zeros
dddd	Full day name	HH	Hour on a 24-hour clock with leading zeros
M	Month without leading zeros	m	Minutes without leading zeros
MM	Month with leading zeros	mm	Minutes with leading zeros
MMM	Abbreviated month name	s	Seconds without leading zeros
MMMM	Full month name	ss	Seconds with leading zeros
y	Two-digit year without leading zero	f	Fractions of seconds (one *f* for each decimal place)
yy	Two-digit year with leading zero	t	First character of AM/PM designator
yyyy	Four-digit year	tt	Full AM/PM designator
/	Date separator	:	Time separator

Statements that format dates and times

Statement	Result
`Dim dtmCurrentDate As Date = DateTime.Now`	12/27/2001 10:37:32 PM
`sShortDate = String.Format("{0:d}", dtmCurrentDate)`	12/27/2001
`sLongDate = String.Format("{0:D}", dtmCurrentDate)`	Thursday, December 27, 2001
`sShortTime = String.Format("{0:t}", dtmCurrentDate)`	10:37 PM
`sLongTime = String.Format("{0:T}", dtmCurrentDate)`	10:37:32 PM
`sCustomDate1 = String.Format("{0:ddd, MMM d, _` `    yyyy}", dtmCurrentDate)`	Thu, Dec 27, 2001
`sCustomDate2 = String.Format("{0:M/d/yy}",_` `    dtmCurrentDate)`	12/27/01
`sCustomTime = String.Format("{0:HH:mm:ss}", _` `    dtmCurrentDate)`	22:37:32

Figure 11-10   How to format dates and times

Perspective

Now that you've completed this chapter, you should be able to use the DateTime structure for working with dates and times and the String and StringBuilder classes for working with strings. These are useful skills that you will use often as you develop Visual Basic programs. You should also be able to use the Format method of the String class to provide custom formatting for numbers, dates, and times, although you probably won't find much need for that.

Summary

- You use the properties and methods of the DateTime structure to work with dates and times.

- DateTime values are stored as the number of *ticks* that have passed since 12:00 AM, January 1, 0001. A tick is 100 nanoseconds.

- You use the properties and methods of the String class to *parse* the substrings within strings and to perform other operations on the characters within strings.

- You use the properties and methods of the StringBuilder class to work with *mutable* strings that are stored in StringBuilder objects.

- You can use the Format method of the String class to format numbers, dates, and times, and you can customize those formats.

- Although you can use Visual Basic properties and functions for working with dates, times, and strings, the preferred way to perform these operations is to use the .NET classes, objects, properties, and methods.

Terms

tick	index	mutable
parse	immutable	

Objectives

- Given the date-handling requirements of an application, write the code that satisfies the requirements.

- Given the string-handling requirements of an application, write the code that satisfies the requirements.

- Given the formatting requirements of an application, use the Format method of the String class to provide the formatting.

- Describe the way a DateTime variable is stored.

- Explain how a String object differs from a StringBuilder object.

Exercise 11-1   Add the date to an Invoice object

Open the Invoice.vbproj application that's in the C:\VB.NET\Chapter 11\
Invoice folder. Then, add an InvoiceDate property to the Invoice class, and set
this property to the current date when the user clicks the New Invoice button.
That property should also be displayed in the first line in the message box for
each Invoice object.

Exercise 11-2   Work with dates and times

In this exercise, you'll use the DateTime and TimeSpan structures. To make
this easier, we'll provide the form so all you have to do is add the code

Open the application and add code to calculate the due days

1. Open the DateHandling.vbproj application that's in the C:\VB.NET\Chapter
    11\DateHandling folder. Within this project, you'll find a form that accepts a
    future date and a birth date from the user and provides buttons for performing
    the due days and age calculations.

2. Add code to calculate the due days when the user enters a future date and
    clicks on the Calculate Due Days button. For simplicity, you can assume valid
    user entries. Then, display the results in a message box like this.

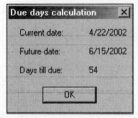

3. Test your code with a variety of date formats to see what formats can be
    successfully parsed. When you're done, close the form.

Add code to calculate the age

4. Add code to calculate the age when the user enters a birth date and clicks on
    the Calculate Age button. Then, display the results in a message box like the
    one that follows. For simplicity, you can assume valid user entries, but be sure
    to take the month and day into account when calculating the age.

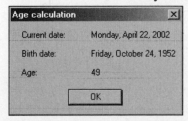

5. Run the application and test your code to make sure it works. Be sure to use
    dates that test whether this works when the month and year of the birth date are
    the same as in the current date. When you're done, close the form.

Exercise 11-3   Work with strings

In this exercise, you'll use methods of the String class to work with strings. To make this easier, we'll provide the form so all you have to do is add is the code.

Open the application and add code to parse a name

1. Open the StringHandling.vbproj application that's in the C:\VB.NET\Chapter 11\StringHandling folder. Within this project, you'll find a form that accepts a name and a phone number from the user and provides buttons for parsing the name and editing the phone number.

2. Add code to parse the name when the user enters a name and clicks on the Parse name button. This code should work whether the user enters a first, middle, and last name or just a first and last name. It should also convert the parsed name so the first letters are uppercase but the other letters are lowercase. The results should be displayed in a message box like this:

3. Test the application to see if it works. Try entering the name in all uppercase letters or all lowercase letters to make sure the parsed name is still displayed with only the first letters capitalized. When you're done, close the form.

Add code to edit a phone number

4. If you've already read chapter 8, add a procedure for the KeyPress event of the phone number text box so the user can only enter the left and right parentheses, hyphens, the digits 0-9, the space, and the backspace.

5. Add code to edit the phone number when the user enters a phone number and clicks on the Edit number button. This code should remove all special characters from the user entry so the number consists of 10 digits, and then format the phone number with hyphens. These results should be displayed in a message box like the one that follows. For simplicity, you don't have to check whether the user enters ten digits.

6. Test the application with a variety of entry formats to make sure it works. When you're done, close the form and then close the solution.

12

How to work with arrays and collections

Arrays and collections are objects that work as containers. As you develop Visual Basic applications, you'll find many uses for arrays and collections. For example, you can use a sales array to hold the sales amounts for each of the 12 months of the year so you can perform calculations on those amounts. Or, you can use a collection to hold all of the Invoice objects that are created during one session of an application. In this chapter, you'll learn the basic concepts and techniques for working with arrays and collections.

How to work with one-dimensional arrays

An *array* is used to store a group of primitive types or objects. Since a *one-dimensional array* is the simplest type of array, you'll start by learning how to declare and use one-dimensional arrays.

How to declare a one-dimensional array

To declare a one-dimensional array, you use the syntax shown in figure 12-1. After you code the array name, which is just like a variable name, you code a number in parentheses that indicates the number of *elements* that the array will be able to hold. This is called the *upper bound* of the array.

Once an array is declared, you can refer to any element in the array by its index value, starting with 0 for the first element in the array. You'll learn more about this in the next figure. Because the indexes start with zero, though, you need to code the upper bound of the array as one less than the number of elements that the array will hold.

To understand how this works, take a look at the first three declaration statements in this figure. Here, the first statement declares an array of integer variables with an upper bound of 11. That means that the index values of the elements in the array will range from 0 to 11, which means that the array will contain 12 elements. Similarly, the second statement declares an array of string variables that will hold 50 elements (index values 0 through 49), and the third statement declares an array of Book objects that will contain 50 elements.

When you declare an array variable and specify the size of the array, an array object is created from the Array class of the .NET Framework. You'll learn more about using the properties and methods of this class later in this chapter. For now, just realize that an array is an object. Because of that, an array variable contains a reference to the array object and not the actual value of the array.

You can also declare an array without indicating its size. To do that, you simply code the declaration without specifying the upper bound. This is illustrated by the fourth statement in this figure, which creates an array of decimal variables. Because the size of the array isn't established, though, an array object isn't created. Instead, the value of the array variable is set to Nothing. Before you can work with the array, then, you must create an array object. To do that, you use the ReDim statement, which you'll learn about later in this chapter.

In most cases, all the elements in an array will contain the same type of data, and you'll declare the array with that data type. If you don't know what type of data an array will contain, however, or you know that it will contain various types of data, you can declare it with the Object data type as shown in the fifth example in this figure. Then, each element can contain data of any type.

Handwritten top margin: OPTION 0, 1, OR UNDER (LB=0) — VB6 → CHECK OPTION BASE IN OLD CODE!

The basic syntax for declaring a one-dimensional array

```
Dim arrayname(upperbound) As type
```

Handwritten: LB, VB DEAD — FROM VB6

Typical statements for declaring one-dimensional arrays

```
Dim iUnitSales(11) as Integer    'Index values are 0 through 11
Dim sBookTitle(49) As String     'Index values are 0 through 49
Dim Book(49) As Book             'An array that holds Book objects
Dim dBookPrice() As Decimal      'An array without a size declaration
Dim oVariableData() As Object    'An array whose elements can contain data
                                 'with different data types
```

Handwritten annotations: PRIV, PUB, FRIEND, ETC. — SAME SCOPE RULES; "2 | 2" next to 11; "OR STRUCTURE (OFTEN)" next to Book objects; "X" next to size declaration

Description

Handwritten: CAN DEFINE W/ KNOWN OR UNKNOWN BOUNDARIES (WHICH CAN DEF. AS RESULT OF CALC.) - AVOID - TAKES TOO MANY RES. → BETTER TO DEF. OVERSIZE

- You can use an *array* to store a group of items instead of using a separate variable for each item. Each item is an *element* of the array, and the length or size of an array is the number of elements it contains.

- A *one-dimensional array* is an array that's based on a single variable factor. To refer to any element in the array, you use an *index* as shown in the next figure.

- To indicate the number of elements an array will contain when you declare the array, you include a number in parentheses after the name of the array. This number indicates the *upper bound* of the array. Because arrays are zero-based, the array will contain one more element than the number you specify.

- You must also specify the type of data that an array will hold when you declare it. This can be any of the primitive data types you learned about in chapter 3 as well as any object data type. If you specify the type as Object, each element can contain a different type of data.

- If you specify the size of an array when you declare it, an array object is created with the specified size, and that object is assigned to the array variable. Then, each element of the array is given a default value depending on its data type.

- If you don't specify the size of an array when you declare it, the value of the array variable is set to Nothing. Then, you must use the ReDim statement to create an array object with the appropriate size as described in figure 12-6.

Note

- Although all of the examples above use the Dim statement, you can use any of the keywords for declaring arrays that you use for declaring variables.

Handwritten at bottom:
- COLL TYP OBJECTS
- ARRAY TYP STRUCTURES

Figure 12-1   How to declare a one-dimensional array

Handwritten: EASIER TO CREATE ARRAY OF STRUCTURES

How to assign values to a one-dimensional array

Figure 12-2 shows how to assign values to the elements of an array. As the syntax at the top of this figure indicates, you refer to an element in an array by coding the array name followed by its *index* in parentheses. The index that you specify must be from 0, which refers to the first element in the array, to the upper bound of the array.

The first two examples in this figure show how you can assign values to the elements of an array by coding one statement per element. Here, the first example creates an array of four decimal values. In this example, the first element holds the value .01, the second holds the value .02, the third holds the value .03, and the fourth holds the value .04. Then, the second example creates an array that holds three string values.

The third example in this figure shows how you can use a loop to assign values to the elements of an array. Here, the statement within the loop uses the index for the loop to access each element of the array. Then, it assigns the value of the index plus 1 to the element. So the first element in the array will have a value of 1, the second element will have a value of 2, and so on.

The syntax and examples at the bottom of this figure show how to declare an array and assign values to the elements in a single statement. Here, you start the array declaration as before, but you omit the upper bound. Then, after the As clause, you code an equals sign followed by the values you want to assign to the elements enclosed in braces. When you use this syntax, Visual Basic creates an array with the number of elements within the braces, and it assigns the values within the braces to each element of the array. For example, the first statement that follows the syntax does the same task as the five statements in the first example of this figure.

(handwritten notes)

| SAFE ARRAY = DIM A (10) AS INT. ← DEFAULT. LOW BOUND 0

! SYSTEM ARRAY = DIM A AS ARRAY = CREATE ARRAY...
      B. CREATE INSTANCE (.... 5TH OVERLOAD LETS YOU
            CHANGE BOUND))

SAFE ARRAYS RUN FASTER
COLLECTIONS RUN SLOWER

WHEN WORKING W/COM COMPONENT = NEED SYSTEM ARRAY, SO CAN USE NON-
!!!!   HAVE TO RECOMPILE COMPONENT!   OBJECT ARRAY IN .NET
            SAFE ARRAY PREDEFINED, CAN'T BE CHANGED.

The syntax for referring to an element of a one-dimensional array

```
arrayname(index)
```

Examples that assign values by accessing each element of an array

Code that assigns values to an array of decimal types

```
Dim dRate(3) As Decimal
dRate(0) = .01
dRate(1) = .02
dRate(2) = .03
dRate(3) = .04
```

Code that assigns values to an array of string objects

```
Dim sBookTitle(2) As String
sBookTitle(0) = "Murach's Beginning Java 2"
sBookTitle(1) = "Murach's Visual Basic 6"
sBookTitle(2) = "Murach's Beginning Visual Basic .NET"
```

Code that uses a loop to assign the values 1-10 to an array

```
Dim iValue(9), iIndex As Integer
For iIndex = 0 to 9
    iValue(iIndex) = iIndex + 1
Next iIndex
```

The syntax for declaring an array and assigning values in one statement

→ WORKS FASTER (IN ONE DIM)

```
Dim arrayname() As type = {value1, value2, value3, ...}
```

Examples that declare an array and assign values in one statement

```
Dim dRate() As Decimal = {.01, .02, .03, .04}
```
← LIST DEFINES SIZE!

```
Dim iUnitSales() As Integer = {125, 203, 157, 194}
```

← NOTE-NO U/B

Description

- To refer to the elements in an array, you use an *index* that ranges from zero to one less than the number of elements in the array. You code this index in parentheses after the name of the array.

- If you initialize an array when you declare it, you don't specify its upper bound. Instead, the size of the array is determined by the number of values you specify.

Figure 12-2   How to assign values to a one-dimensional array

GOOD IDEA: STORE IN COLLECTION, RETRIEVE W/ARRAY

Code examples that work with one-dimensional arrays

Now that you understand how to declare arrays and assign values to the elements, you're ready to review some code examples for working with arrays like the ones in figure 12-3. Here, all three examples work with the array of prices that's declared at the top of this figure. It contains just four decimal values that are indexed by the values 0 through 3.

The first example shows how to use individual elements of an array as you calculate the average value of the elements. Here, the first statement sets the sum variable equal to the sum of the four elements in the array. Then, the second statement computes the average price by dividing the sum by four.

The second example does the same task as the first example, but it uses a For...Next loop to access each element. That way, it will work with 50 or 500 elements as easily as four elements. To change the number of elements that it will work for, you just change the To value on the For statement and the divisor in the expression that calculates the average.

The third example in this figure shows how you can display the elements in the price array, followed by the average price, in a message box. Like the second example, this example uses a For...Next loop to access each element of the array. Within this loop, the value of each element is appended to a string variable. Then, when the loop ends, the average price is calculated and added to the string. The message box that displays the string is shown at the bottom of this figure.

The last example in this figure shows one more way you can calculate the average value of the elements in an array. To do that, this example uses the For Each...Next statement you learned about in chapter 5. Although the example in that chapter showed you how to use this statement with a collection, you can also use it with arrays. In this case, because the array contains decimal values, the For Each statement uses a decimal variable to refer to each element in the array.

This example also uses an integer variable to store the count of the number of elements in the array. This variable is incremented by one each time through the For Each...Next loop. Then, when the loop ends, this variable is used to calculate the average of the elements.

Notice that because you don't have to specify a beginning or ending index on the For Each...Next statement like you do on the For...Next statement, this code will work with an array of any size. So you'll want to consider using this technique whenever you work with an array that may vary in size.

[handwritten annotations:]

TO CREATE SYSTEM ARRAY

→ ARRAY. COPY & ARRAY. CLEAR AVAILABLE (CLEAR FOR SYSTEM. ARRAY)

DIM B AS ARRAY

ARRAY B. CREATE INSTANCE (GETTYPE(STRING), 10)

B. SETVALUE ("ADB", 2)

DIM L AS STRING = B. GETVALUE (2)

* GETTYPE WON'T WORK W/ARRAY OF OBJECTS!

The declaration for an array that contains prices

```
Dim dPrice() As Decimal = {14.95, 12.95, 11.95, 9.95}
```

Code that computes the average of the array

```
Dim dSum As Decimal = dPrice(0) + dPrice(1) + dPrice(2) + dPrice(3)
Dim dAverage As Decimal = dSum / 4
```

Code that uses a For...Next loop to compute the average of the array

```
Dim dSum, dAverage As Decimal
Dim iIndex As Integer
For iIndex = 0 To 3
    dSum += dPrice(iIndex)
Next iIndex
dAverage = dSum / 4
```

Code that displays the array and the average price in a message box

```
Dim dSum, dAverage As Decimal
Dim iIndex As Integer
Dim sMessage As String = "The prices are: " & ControlChars.CrLf
For iIndex = 0 To 3
    sMessage &= dPrice(iIndex) & ControlChars.CrLf
    dSum += dPrice(iIndex)
Next iIndex
dAverage = dSum / 4
sMessage &= ControlChars.CrLf & "The average price is: "
sMessage &= ControlChars.CrLf & dAverage
MessageBox.Show(sMessage, "Price averaging")
```

The message box displayed by the code shown above

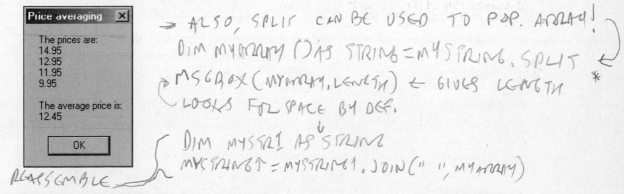

[handwritten notes:]

ALSO, SPLIT CAN BE USED TO POP. ARRAY!
DIM MYARRAY () AS STRING = MYSTRING. SPLIT
MSGBOX (MYARRAY.LENGTH) ← GIVES LENGTH *
LOOKS FOR SPACE BY DEF.

DIM MYSTR1 AS STRING
MYSTRING1 = MYSTRING1. JOIN (" ", MYARRAY)

REASSEMBLE

Code that uses a For Each...Next loop to compute the average price

```
Dim dValue, dSum, dAverage As Decimal
Dim iCount As Integer
For Each dValue In dPrice
    dSum += dValue
    iCount += 1
Next
dAverage = dSum / iCount
```

Figure 12-3   Code examples that work with one-dimensional arrays

[handwritten:] * WORKS, BUT SHOULD HAVE USED "TOSTRING"

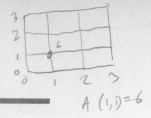

How to work with two-dimensional arrays

If the data in an array varies depending on two factors, you can use a *two-dimensional array* to hold and process the data. Because two-dimensional arrays are commonly used in Visual Basic applications, it's important to learn how to handle them. And once you do, you'll be able to use those same techniques to work with arrays that have more than two dimensions. Although you'll rarely need to work with more than two or three dimensions, Visual Basic actually lets you define arrays with up to 60 dimensions.

How to declare a two-dimensional array

Figure 12-4 shows how to declare a two-dimensional array. You do that by including the upper bound for both dimensions in the declaration, separated by a comma. The first statement in this figure, for example, creates a two-dimensional array of integers. In this case, the first dimension has four elements with index values from 0 to 3, and the second dimension has five elements with index values from 0 to 4.

Like one-dimensional arrays, you can also declare two-dimensional arrays without specifying the upper bound. If you do that, though, you still have to include the comma within the parentheses so Visual Basic knows how many dimensions the array has. This is illustrated by the second statement.

How to assign values to a two-dimensional array

When you work with a two-dimensional array, you can think of it as a *table* that consists of rows and columns. Then, you can use the index for the first dimension to refer to the rows in the table, and you can use the index for the second dimension to refer to the columns in the table. This is illustrated by the table of index values shown in figure 12-4, which consists of four rows and five columns so the index values range from 0,0 to 3,4.

To assign values to the elements of a two-dimensional array, you can code one statement for each element as shown in the first coding example in this figure. This array has three elements in the first dimension and two elements in the second. Then, to refer to an element, you code an index value for each dimension. In other words, you identify both the row and column of the element.

You can also assign values to a two-dimensional array when you declare it as illustrated by the second coding example, which does the same task as the code in the first example. Here, three sets of braces are coded within the outer set of braces. The three inner braces represent the three rows in the array with two columns in each row.

The basic syntax for declaring a two-dimensional array

```
Dim arrayname(upperbound1, upperbound2) As type
```

Typical statements for declaring two-dimensional arrays

```
Dim iItem(3, 4) As Integer    'A two-dimensional array with 4 elements in the
                              'first dimension and 5 elements in the second

Dim dRate(,) As Decimal       'A two-dimensional array without a size
                              'declaration
```
MUST PUT COMMA

The index values for the elements in a two-dimensional array

```
0,0    0,1    0,2    0,3    0,4
1,0    1,1    1,2    1,3    1,4
2,0    2,1    2,2    2,3    2,4
3,0    3,1    3,2    3,3    3,4
```

Code that assigns values to a two-dimensional array of string types

```
Dim sName(2, 1) As String
sName(0, 0) = "Mike"
sName(0, 1) = "Murach"
sName(1, 0) = "Anne"
sName(1, 1) = "Prince"
sName(2, 0) = "Matt"
sName(2, 1) = "Stuemky"
```

Code that creates the array shown above with one statement

```
Dim sName(,) As String = {{"Mike", "Murach"}, {"Anne", "Prince"}, _
                          {"Matt", "Stuemky"}}
```
← HARD SO REMEMBER WHICH DIM IS WHICH

Code that uses nested loops to load a two-dimensional array

```
Dim dRate(4, 1) As Decimal
Dim iIndex1, iIndex2 As Integer
For iIndex1 = 0 To 4
    For iIndex2 = 0 To 1
        dRate(iIndex1, iIndex2) = (iIndex1 + 1) / 100 + (iIndex2 * .005)
    Next iIndex2
Next iIndex1
```

Description

- A *two-dimensional array* varies based on two variable factors and allows data to be stored in a *table* that consists of rows and columns.

- An array can have up to 60 dimensions, but arrays with more than two dimensions are uncommon. The number of dimensions in an array is called its *rank*.

- When you declare a two-dimensional array, you can specify the size of each dimension by coding two numbers separated by commas after the array name. The first number indicates the upper bound of the first dimension, and the second number indicates the upper bound of the second dimension.

- Even if you don't specify the size of the dimensions, you have to code a comma between the parentheses to indicate that the array has two dimensions.

Figure 12-4   How to declare and assign values to a two-dimensional array

The last example in this figure shows how to use nested For…Next loops to assign values to the elements of a two-dimensional array. In this case, the array contains five rows and two columns. To initialize this array, the first For..Next statement cycles through each row, while the second cycles through each column. In this case, the index values not only identify each element that a value is assigned to, but they're also used in the expression that calculates the value for each element. For instance, element 0,0 will be assigned the value of .01; element 0,1 will be assigned .015; element 1,0 will be assigned .02; element 1,1 will be assigned .025; and so on.

Code examples that work with two-dimensional arrays

Figure 12-5 presents some examples that show how to work with two-dimensional arrays. The first example shows how to calculate the sum of the values in a two-dimensional array using nested For…Next loops. Since this code is straightforward, you shouldn't have any trouble understanding it.

The second example is similar, except that it calculates the sum of the values in each row of the array and then displays them in a message box. To do that, it uses nested For…Next loops that cycle through the rows and columns, and it accumulates the values for each row in an element of a one-dimensional array. Then, each time the inner loop ends, the information for the current row is added to a string variable. And when the outer loop ends, that information is displayed in a message box as shown in this figure.

Two-dimensional arrays are also used to perform lookup operations as shown in the last example in this figure. In this case, the array contains sales information for six salespeople, and each of the six rows in this array contains two columns. The first column contains the salesperson's name, and the second one contains the sales total for that salesperson.

The procedure in this example is for the SelectedIndexChanged event of a combo box that contains the same names as the array. Then, when the user selects a name from this combo box, the Do statement in this procedure locates the sales total for that person. To do that, it checks the value in the first column (column 0) of each row until it finds a name that matches the selected name or until it has checked all of the rows in the array. If you take a minute to study the code in this example, you should be able to figure out how it works.

Here again, a procedure like this will work no matter how many rows there are in the array. All you have to do is change the value after the greater-than sign in the Do statement.

Code that calculates the sum of the values in a two-dimensional array

```
Dim iUnitSales(,) As Integer = {{85, 73, 78}, {61, 64, 72}, _
                                {95, 89, 90}, {88, 75, 69}}
Dim iIndex1, iIndex2 As Integer
Dim dTotalUnits As Decimal
For iIndex1 = 0 To 3
    For iIndex2 = 0 To 2
        dTotalUnits += iUnitSales(iIndex1, iIndex2)
    Next iIndex2
Next iIndex1
```

Code that calculates the sum of the values in each row of a two-dimensional array and displays them in a message box

```
Dim iUnitSales(,) As Integer = {{85, 73, 78}, {61, 64, 72}, _
                                {95, 89, 90}, {88, 75, 69}}
Dim iIndex1, iIndex2 As Integer
Dim iTotalUnits(3) As Integer, sMessage As String
For iIndex1 = 0 To 3
    For iIndex2 = 0 To 2
        iTotalUnits(iIndex1) += iUnitSales(iIndex1, iIndex2)
    Next iIndex2
    sMessage &= "Quarter " & iIndex1 + 1 & ": " _
            & iTotalUnits(iIndex1) & ControlChars.CrLf
Next iIndex1
MessageBox.Show(sMessage, "Unit sales by quarter")
```

The message box displayed by the code shown above

Code that looks up a value in a two-dimensional array

```
Dim oSalesData(,) As Object _
    = {{"AdamsA", 3275.68}, {"FinkleP", 4298.55}, {"LewisJ", 5289.57}, _
       {"PotterE", 1933.98}, {"WilliamsL", 4876.32}, {"YangD", 3722.38}}
    .
    .
    .
Private Sub cboEmployees_SelectedIndexChanged(ByVal sender As Object, _
        ByVal e As System.EventArgs) _
        Handles cboEmployees.SelectedIndexChanged
    Dim iIndex As Integer, bMatch As Boolean
    Do Until bMatch Or iIndex > 5
        If oSalesData(iIndex, 0) = cboEmployees.SelectedItem Then
            txtSalesTotal.text = oSalesData(iIndex, 1)
            bMatch = True
        Else
            iIndex += 1
        End If
    Loop
End Sub
```

Figure 12-5   Code examples that work with two-dimensional arrays

More skills for working with arrays

So far in this chapter, you've learned some basic skills for working with arrays. To work with arrays more efficiently, though, you need to learn the skills that are presented in the next three topics.

How to resize an array

Most arrays are declared with a fixed number of elements. For instance, you can declare an array that will hold the sales totals for each month of the year with an upper bound of 11 so it will hold 12 elements. Similarly, you can declare an array with an upper bound of 99 if the actual number of elements in the array will vary from 20 to 100.

Sometimes, though, you don't know how many elements are going to be in an array. Then, you can use the ReDim statement to change the size of the array as the program executes.

Before I present the ReDim statement, you should know that a collection automatically adjusts its capacity to accommodate the elements in the collection. As a result, collections usually work better than arrays for applications that require upper bound changes as a program executes. So you should consider using a collection rather than an array whenever the number of elements is variable. You'll learn about collections starting in figure 12-9.

Nevertheless, figure 12-6 presents the ReDim statement because it represents the traditional way of working with arrays. When you code this statement, you code the array name and the upper bound of each dimension. If the array already contains values, you can also code the Preserve keyword to retain those values. Otherwise, all of the elements in the array will be set to their default values.

The first three statements in this figure illustrate how this works for a one-dimensional array. The first statement declares an array that contains five decimal values. Then, the second statement resizes the array so it contains six elements. Because the Preserve keyword is omitted, the original values are lost. In contrast, the third statement preserves the original values.

You can also use the ReDim statement to create an array object for an array that was declared without an upper bound. This technique can be used when you want to add elements to an array one at a time and you don't know how many elements you will add. In this case, you declare the array variable with no upper bound, then use a ReDim statement before adding each element to increase the capacity of the array by one.

This is illustrated by the coding routine in the middle of this figure. Here, an array that will hold all of the TextBox controls on a form is initially declared with no bounds. Then, a For Each statement cycles through all of the controls on a form. If the control is a TextBox control, a ReDim statement increases the array's capacity and the text box is added to the array.

The basic syntax for resizing an array

```
ReDim [Preserve] arrayname(upperbound1[, upperbound2])
```

Examples that resize a one-dimensional array

The initial array declaration

```
Dim dRate() As Decimal = {.01, .02, .03, .04, .05}
```

A statement that changes the number of elements in the array

```
Redim dRate(5)
```
← NO "AS"

A statement that changes the number of elements and preserves existing values

```
Redim Preserve dRate(5)
```
→ CAN REDIM SMALLER TOO!

Code that resizes an array of text box controls as elements are added to it

```
Dim ctlControl As Control
Dim txtTextBox() As TextBox
Dim iIndex As Integer
For Each ctlControl In Me.Controls
    If TypeOf ctlControl Is TextBox Then
        ReDim Preserve txtTextBox(iIndex)
        txtTextBox(iIndex) = ctlControl
        iIndex += 1
    End If
Next ctlControl
```

Examples that resize a two-dimensional array

The initial array declaration

```
Dim sName(2, 1) As String
```

A statement that changes the number of elements in both dimensions

```
Redim sName(3, 2)
```

A statement that preserves existing values and changes the number of elements in the second dimension

```
Redim Preserve sName (2, 2)
```

Description

- To resize an array, you use the ReDim statement. You can use this statement to increase or decrease the number of elements in the array, but you can't use it to change the number of dimensions.

- By default, the Redim statement clears all of the values from the array. If that's not what you want, you can include the Preserve keyword. Then, existing values are preserved.

- If you include the Preserve keyword, you can only change the size of the last dimension of the array.

- When you resize an array, you're actually creating a new array object that's assigned to the same array variable as the previous array. Because of that, you can't specify a data type when you resize an array. Instead, the new array is created with the same data type as the original array.

Figure 12-6   How to resize an array

The last three statements in this figure show how to resize a two-dimensional array. Here, the first statement declares the array with three rows and two columns, and the second statement resizes both dimensions of the array so that it has four rows and three columns. The third statement shows how you can resize a two-dimensional array when you use the Preserve keyword, but in that case you can only change the size of the second dimension.

How to use the Array class

An array is actually an instance of the .NET Framework's Array class. This class has several properties and methods that are often useful as you work with arrays. Figure 12-7 presents the ones you're most likely to use.

One property you'll use frequently as you work with arrays is the Length property, which returns the number of elements in an array. Because it returns the number of elements in all the dimensions of an array, you're most likely to use this property with one-dimensional arrays. For two-dimensional arrays, you're more likely to use the GetLength method, which returns the length of a single dimension. Another method you'll use frequently is the GetUpperBound method, which returns the upper bound of a given dimension of an array. Note that all three of these methods are based on the number of elements in the dimensions, whether or not these elements contain data.

The first example in this figure shows how you can use both the Length property and the GetUpperBound method. This code calculates the sum and average of the values in an array. To do that, it uses a For…Next loop just like the example you saw in figure 12-3. In this example, however, the GetUpperBound method is used to specify the To value on the For statement, and the Length property is used as the divisor in the expression that calculates the average.

The Sort method of the array class lets you sort the elements in a one-dimensional array. This is illustrated by the second example in this figure. Here, the first statement declares an array that consists of three last names. Then, the Sort method is used to sort the names in that array. Because this method is a shared method, it's accessed through the Array class. After the array is sorted, the code creates a string that contains the data of the elements in sequence and then displays them in a message box like the one in this figure.

The last example in this figure shows how you can use the BinarySearch method to locate a value in a one-dimensional array. This code performs a task that's similar to the one you saw in figure 12-5 for looking up a value in a two-dimensional array. In this case, though, the two columns in the array have been divided into two one-dimensional arrays: one that contains each salesperson's last name and one that contains the sales total for each salesperson. Then, the procedure uses the BinarySearch method to get the index value of the element in the salesperson array that contains the selected salesperson, and this index value is used to get the sales total from the sales amount array.

Common properties and methods of the Array class

Property	Description
Length	Gets the number of elements in all of the dimensions of an array.
Rank	Gets the number of dimensions in an array.

Public method	Description
GetLength(dimension)	Returns the number of elements in the specified dimension of an array.
GetUpperBound(dimension)	Returns the upper bound of the specified dimension of an array.
Initialize	Initializes the elements of an array based on their data type.

Shared method	Description
BinarySearch(array, value)	Searches a one-dimensional sorted array for a specified value and returns the index for that value.
Sort(array)	Sorts the elements in a one-dimensional array into ascending order.

Code that uses the GetUpperBound method and the Length property

```
Dim dPrice() As Decimal = {14.95, 12.95, 11.95, 9.95}
Dim dSum As Decimal, dAverage As Decimal, iIndex As Integer
For iIndex = 0 To dPrice.GetUpperBound(0)
    dSum += dPrice(iIndex)
Next iIndex
dAverage = dSum / dPrice.Length
```

Codes that sorts an array

```
Dim sLastName() As String = {"Prince", "Stuemky", "Murach"}
Dim sMessage As String, iIndex As Integer
Array.Sort(sLastName)        - ASCONDER
For iIndex = 0 To sLastName.GetUpperBound(0)
    sMessage &= sLastName(iIndex) & ControlChars.CrLf
Next
MessageBox.Show(sMessage, "Sorted last names")
```

The message box displayed by the code shown above

Code that uses the BinarySearch method

```
Dim sSalesPerson() As String = {"AdamsA", "FinkleP", "LewisJ", "PotterE"}
Dim dSalesAmt() As Decimal = {3275.68, 4298.55, 5289.57, 1933.98}
...
Private Sub cboEmployees_SelectedIndexChanged(ByVal sender As Object, _
        ByVal e As System.EventArgs)
        Handles cboEmployees.SelectedIndexChanged
    Dim iIndex As Integer
    iIndex = Array.BinarySearch(sSalesPerson, cboEmployees.SelectedItem)
    txtSalesTotal.Text = dSalesAmt(iIndex)
End Sub
```

Figure 12-7   How to use the Array class

For this to work, the table being searched must be in sorted sequence. In addition, the two arrays must be synchronized. In other words, the sales total for the first person in the salesperson array must be in the first element of the sales amount array, the sales total for the second salesperson must be in the second element of the sales amount array, and so on.

How to use arrays with functions and Sub procedures

Figure 12-8 presents the techniques you need for using arrays with functions and Sub procedures. To return an array from a function, you follow the type declaration for the function with parentheses as shown in the first example. Then, you define an array within the code for the function, and you use the Return statement to return that array to the calling procedure. Alternately, you can assign the array to the function name.

To call a function that returns an array, you use the same techniques that you use for calling any other function. For instance, the example in this figure declares an array variable and assigns it the return value of the function. In this case, the function requires an argument that supplies the number of elements that the array should contain.

The second example in this figure shows how to code a procedure that accepts an array as an argument. Here, you can see that you simply follow the name of the argument by parentheses to indicate that it's an array. Then, you can work with the array within the procedure in any way you like.

The code that calls a procedure that accepts an array argument looks just like any other call statement. It simply names the array to be passed within parentheses after the procedure name.

How to return an array from a function

LESS COMMON

The code for a function that returns an array

```vb
Private Function RateArray(ByVal ElementCount As Integer) As Decimal()
    Dim iIndex As Integer
    Dim dRate(ElementCount - 1) As Decimal
    For iIndex = 0 To dRate.GetUpperBound(0)
        dRate(iIndex) = (iIndex + 1) / 100
    Next iIndex
    Return dRate
End Function
```

Code that calls the function

```vb
Dim dRate() As Decimal = Me.RateArray(5)
```

How to code a procedure that accepts an array argument

MORE COMMON

The code for a procedure that sorts an array

WON'T WORK IF

```vb
Private Sub SortArray(ByRef UnsortedArray() As String)
    Array.Sort(UnsortedArray)
End Sub
```

USUALLY GREATER MAX LEN.

Code that declares the array and calls the procedure

```vb
Dim sLastName() As String = {"Prince", "Stuemky", "Murach"}
Me.SortArray(sLastName)
```

Description

- To return an array from a function, you code a set of parentheses after the type declaration of the function to indicate that the return value is an array.

- To pass an array as an argument to a procedure, the argument must be defined as an array in the procedure declaration. To define an argument as an array, you follow the name of the argument with parentheses.

Figure 12-8   How to use arrays with functions and Sub procedures

* STRING BY DEFAULT IS VAL TYPE → BUT WON'T ACCEPT THAT WAY → SEE MSDN REFERENCE

How to work with collections

A *collection* is an object that can hold one or more other objects. In figure 12-6, for example, you saw the use of the Controls collection of a form, which consists of all of the Control objects on the form. Now, in the remaining topics in this chapter, you'll learn how to use five classes of the .NET Framework that let you create and use your own collections.

How to use the Collection class

The Collection class that's presented in figure 12-9 is the basic class for creating collections. It has just four members. The Count property returns the number of items in the collection. The Item property retrieves a specified item from the collection. The Add method adds an item to the collection. And the Remove method deletes a specified item from the collection.

Unlike arrays, collections don't have a fixed size. Instead, the size of a collection is adjusted whenever an item is added or deleted. As a result, you don't have to use the ReDim statement when you're working with collections, which makes them more appropriate for some applications.

Another difference between arrays and collections is that collections aren't data typed. As a result, you can store any type of object in a collection. In fact, you can mix several different types of objects in the same collection, although that usually isn't a good idea.

A third difference between collections and arrays is that the indexes for collections can be either zero- or one-based, depending on the type of collection you are using. For instance, the index of the first item in a collection that's created from the Collection class is 1, not zero.

To illustrate the use of the Collection class, the first example in this figure creates a new Collection object called BookTitles, and then adds three titles to the collection. In this case, all three of the items are string objects.

The second example shows how you can use a For Each loop to access each item in a collection. Here, a message string is built that contains each title in the BookTitles collection. Then, the message string is displayed. Note that this assumes that all the elements in the collection are strings or can be cast to strings. Otherwise, this code won't work.

The third example deletes an item from the BookTitles collection after first displaying a message box to confirm that the user wants to delete the book. In this example, the assumption is that an integer variable named iBookIndex has already been set to the index of the book to be deleted.

One of the limitations of the Collection class is that you can't update an item in the collection. In other words, you can use the Item property to get an item in a collection, but you can't use it to set the item. Often, that's okay because you don't need to update the items in a collection. If you do need to update the items, you can use the ArrayList class shown in the next figure.

Common properties and methods of the Collection class

Property	Description
Count	Gets the number of elements in the collection.
Item(index)	Gets the item at the specified index. The index for the first item in the collection is 1.

← 1 BASED !!

↑

NOTE !!

↑

Method	Description
Add(object)	Adds an element to the collection. → CAN'T ADD DUPLICATE ITEM! ✗
Remove(index)	Removes the item at the specified index.

→ WON'T LIVE IN ()

Code that defines and loads a collection of book titles

```
Dim BookTitles as New Collection
BookTitles.Add("Murach's Beginning Java 2")
BookTitles.Add("Murach's Structured COBOL")
BookTitles.Add("Murach's Visual Basic 6")
```

A For Each loop that accesses each item in a collection

```
Dim sMessage As String
Dim sBookTitle As String
For Each sBookTitle in BookTitles
    sMessage &= sBookTitle & ControlChars.CrLf
Next
MessageBox.Show(sMessage, "BookTitles Collection")
```

✱ LET THROW ERROR, DON'T CATCH, WON'T ADD!

CATCH EXP AS EXCEPTION
IF ERR.NUMBER = 457 THEN
   'DO NOTHING
END IF
KEEPS GOING, WON'T
ADD DUPES!!

The message box displayed by the code shown above

Code that removes an item after first displaying a confirmation message

```
'iBookIndex is the item to be deleted
sMessage = "Are you sure you want to remove "
sMessage &= BookTitles.Item(iBookIndex) & "?"
If MessageBox.Show(sMessage, "Remove Book", _
        MessageBoxButtons.YesNo) = DialogResult.Yes Then
    BookTitles.Remove(iBookIndex)
End If
```

Description

- A *collection* is an object that can hold one or more other objects.
- The Collection class is the basic class for creating and using collections. However, the .NET Framework includes several other classes that provide special features for creating and using collections.

Figure 12-9   How to use the Collection class

→ INDEX STILL USEFUL TO REMOVE ELEM. BY LOOPING THRU.

How to use the ArrayList class

The ArrayList class lets you create a collection that uses an array internally to store its data. However, the size of the array in the ArrayList is automatically adjusted to accommodate new elements, so you never have to use the ReDim statement to resize the collection. In figure 12-10, you can see some of the most useful properties and methods of this class.

To create an array list, you use the New keyword as shown in the first example in this figure. Then, within the parentheses that follow the class name, you can specify the initial capacity of the array. In this example, though, the initial capacity is omitted, so the default capacity of 16 is used.

The second example in this figure shows how you can create, sort, and display a list of names in an array list. Here, the first statement creates the array list with an initial capacity of 3 elements, and the next three statements use the Add method to add three elements to the array. These statements are followed by a statement that uses the Sort method to sort the elements in the array. Then, a For…Next loop is used to construct a string that contains all three of the names. In this loop, the Count property is used to determine the number of elements in the array, and the Item property is used to refer to each item. Finally, a message box is displayed that lists the sorted last names.

Of course, I also could have used a For Each…Next loop to construct the string in this example just as I did in the example in figure 12-9 that uses the Collection class. In that case, I wouldn't need to use the Count or Item property. And I wouldn't need to know that the indexing starts with zero instead of one for a collection that's based on the ArrayList class.

In this example, it's worth noting the difference between the Sort method of the ArrayList class and the Sort method of the Array class shown in figure 12-7. For the Array class, Sort is a shared method that receives the array to be sorted as an argument. For the ArrayList class, Sort isn't a shared method so it's coded for the ArrayList object itself. That's true for the BinarySearch method too.

The last example in this figure illustrates how the capacity of an array list is increased as elements are added to it. In this case, four more names are added to the array list that was created in the previous example. When the first name is added, the capacity is doubled from three to six. Then, the capacity is doubled again when the fourth name, which is the seventh element, is added.

ARRAY LIST → NO KEY, BUT MORE FLEXIBLE → CAN INSERT, REMOVE AT INDEX (SLOWER THAN ARRAY)

Common properties and methods of the ArrayList class

Property	Description
Capacity	Gets or sets the number of elements the array list can hold.
Count	Gets the number of elements in the array list.
Item(index)	Gets or sets the element at the specified index. The index for the first item in the collection is 0.

Method	Description
Add(object)	Adds an element to the end of an array list and returns the element's index.
BinarySearch(object)	Searches an array list for a specified object and returns the index for that object.
Clear	Removes all elements from the array list and sets its Count property to zero.
Contains(object)	Returns a Boolean value that indicates if the array list contains the specified object.
Insert(index, object)	Inserts an element into an array list at the specified index.
RemoveAt(index)	Removes the element at the specified index of an array list.
Sort	Sorts the elements in an array list into ascending order.

A statement that creates an array list with the default capacity

```
Dim BookTitleArray As New ArrayList()     'Initial capacity is 16 elements
```

Code that creates, sorts, and displays an array list of names

```
Dim LastNameArray As New ArrayList(3)     'Initial capacity is 3 elements
Dim sMessage As String, iIndex As Integer
LastNameArray.Add("Prince")
LastNameArray.Add("Stuemky")
LastNameArray.Add("Murach")
LastNameArray.Sort()
For iIndex = 0 To LastNameArray.Count - 1
    sMessage &= LastNameArray.Item(iIndex) & ControlChars.CrLf
Next
MessageBox.Show(sMessage, "Sorted last names")
```

Code that causes the size of the array list of names to be increased

```
LastNameArray.Add("Taylor")               'Capacity is doubled to 6 elements
LastNameArray.Add("Menendez")
LastNameArray.Add("Steelman")
LastNameArray.Add("Schletewitz")          'Capacity is doubled to 12 elements
```

Description

- An ArrayList is a collection that uses an array to store its data, but it automatically adjusts the size of the array to accommodate new elements in the array.

- The default capacity of an array list is 16 elements, but you can specify a different capacity when you create a list and you can set the Capacity property to adjust that capacity. When the number of elements in an array list exceeds its capacity, the capacity is automatically doubled.

- The elements of an array list are automatically defined with the Object data type, so each element can contain any type of data.

- The ArrayList class is part of the System.Collections namespace.

Figure 12-10   How to use the ArrayList class

How to use the SortedList class

You can also implement a collection by using the SortedList class that's described in figure 12-11. A sorted list is useful when you need to look up values in the list based on a key value. If, for example, a sorted list consists of item numbers and unit prices, the keys are the item numbers. Then, the list can be used to look up the unit price for any item number. Each item in a sorted list is actually a DictionaryEntry structure that consists of two properties: Key and Value.

Like an array list, you can set the initial capacity of a sorted list by specifying the number of elements in parentheses when the list is created. Then, if the number of elements in the list exceeds the capacity as the program is executed, the capacity is automatically doubled. Also like an array list, the index for the first item in the collection is zero.

The first example in this figure shows how to create and load a sorted list. When you add an element to a sorted list, you specify the key along with the value associated with that key. In this example, the keys are the names of salespeople, and the values are the sales totals for those salespeople. Although the keys in this list are added in alphabetical order, they wouldn't need to be. The sorted list keeps the keys sorted, no matter what order they're added in.

The second example shows how to look up a value in a sorted list based on a key. Here, the last names of the salespeople are included in a combo box list. Then, when the user selects a name from this list, the procedure for the SelectedIndexChanged event retrieves the sales total for the selected salesperson based on the salesperson's name.

After you review this example, you may want to compare it to the example you saw in figure 12-7 that uses the BinarySearch method to perform the same task. You may remember that since you can only use this method with a one-dimensional array, the names of the salespeople and the sales totals were stored in separate arrays in that example. Then, after the index value of the selected salesperson was retrieved, that index was used to get the sales total for that salesperson. In essence, that's what's happening when you use the SortedList class too. In fact, the keys and the associated values are actually stored in separate arrays. When you use a sorted list, though, you can be sure that the two arrays are synchronized. In addition, you can work directly with key values rather than index values, which makes the code easier to understand.

You may also want to compare the code in this example to the code in figure 12-5 that looks up a value in a two-dimensional table. If you do, you'll see that the code that uses a sorted list is significantly simpler. Because of that, you usually use a sorted list when you need to do this type of lookup.

The third example loads a combo box with keys from a sorted list. To start, you must define a variable of type DictionaryEntry so you can use a For Each loop with it. Then, you can use the Key and Value properties to access each item's key and value elements. In this example, the combo box's Add method is used to add the key value for each item in the sorted list to the combo box.

Common properties and methods of the SortedList class

Property	Description
Capacity	Gets or sets the number of elements the list can hold.
Count	Gets the number of elements in the list.
Item(key)	Gets or sets the value associated with a specified key.

Method	Description
Add(key, value)	Adds an element with the specified key and value to the sorted list.
Clear	Removes all elements from the sorted list.
ContainsKey(key)	Returns a Boolean value that indicates if the sorted list contains the specified key.
ContainsValue(value)	Returns a Boolean value that indicates if the sorted list contains the specified value.
GetByIndex(index)	Gets the value of the element at the specified index. The index for the first item in the collection is 0.
GetKey(index)	Gets the key of the element at the specified index.
Remove(key)	Removes the element with the specified key from the sorted list.
RemoveAt(index)	Removes the element at the specified index from the sorted list.
SetByIndex(index, value)	Sets the element at the specified index to the specified value. The index for the first item in the collection is 0.

(handwritten margin note: INDEX OF 1ST ELEM IS 0)

Properties of the DictionaryEntry structure

Property	Description
Key	The key for the SortedList item.
Value	The value associated with the key.

Code that creates and loads a sorted list

(handwritten note: SYSTEM.COLLECTIONS.)

```
Dim SortedSalesList As New SortedList(6)
SortedSalesList.Add("AdamsA", 3275.68)
SortedSalesList.Add("FinkleP", 4398.55)
SortedSalesList.Add("LewisJ", 5289.75)
SortedSalesList.Add("PotterE", 1933.98)
SortedSalesList.Add("WilliamsL", 4876.32)
SortedSalesList.Add("YangD", 3722.38)
```

Code that looks up a value in the sorted list based on a key

```
Private Sub cboEmployees_SelectedIndexChanged(ByVal sender As Object, _
    ByVal e As System.EventArgs) _
    Handles cboEmployees.SelectedIndexChanged
    txtSalesTotal.Text = SortedSalesList.Item(cboEmployees.SelectedItem)
End Sub
```

Code that loads a combo box from a sorted list

```
Dim EmployeeSalesEntry as DictionaryEntry
For Each EmployeeSalesEntry in SortedSalesList
    cboEmployees.Items.Add(EmployeeSalesEntry.Key)
Next
```

Figure 12-11   How to use the SortedList class

How to use the Queue and Stack classes

Figure 12-12 shows the properties and methods of the Queue and Stack classes. You can use these classes to create *queues* and *stacks*, which are collections with some special features.

Unlike other collections, queues and stacks do not use the Add method to add items or the Item property to retrieve items. Instead, queues use the Enqueue and Dequeue methods to add and retrieve items, and stacks use the Push and Pop methods. These methods highlight the basic differences between queues, stacks, and other types of collections.

You can think of a queue (pronounced *cue*) as a line of items waiting to be processed. When you use the Enqueue method to add an item to the queue, the item is placed at the end of the queue. When you use the Dequeue method to retrieve an item from the queue, the item is taken from the front of the queue. Because items are retrieved from a queue in the same order in which they were added, a queue can be referred to as a first-in, first-out collection.

In contrast, a stack is a first-in, last-out collection. When you use the Push method to place an item on a stack, that item is placed on the top of the stack. If you then push another item onto the stack, the new item is placed on the top of the stack and the item that was previously on the top of the stack moves to second from the top. In contrast, the Pop method retrieves the top item and removes it, so the item that was second from the top moves to the top position.

The two examples in this figure illustrate these differences between queues and stacks. Each example begins by defining a new queue or stack, then adding three names. Next, a Do loop is used to build a string that contains the names in the order that they are retrieved from the queue or stack, and the resulting list is displayed in a message box. If you compare the message boxes for these examples, you can see that the queue names are displayed in the same order that they were added to the queue. But in the stack example, the names are retrieved in the opposite order.

In both examples, the Do loop repeats as long as the Count property is greater than zero. This works because the Dequeue and Pop methods remove the item from the queue or stack, so the Count property is automatically decreased by one each time through the loop. When all of the items have been read from the queue or stack, the Count property reaches zero and the Do loop terminates.

Properties and methods for queues

Property	Description
Count	Gets the number of items in the queue.

Method	Description
Enqueue(object)	Adds the specified object to the end of the queue.
Dequeue	Gets the object at the front of the queue and removes it from the queue.
Clear	Removes all items from the queue.
Peek	Retrieves the next item in the queue without deleting it.

Properties and methods for stacks

Property	Description
Count	Gets the number of items in the stack.

Method	Description
Push(object)	Adds the specified object to the top of the stack.
Pop	Gets the object at the top of the stack and removes it from the stack.
Clear	Removes all items from the stack.
Peek	Retrieves the next item in the stack without deleting it.

Code that uses a queue

```
Dim NameQueue As New Queue
NameQueue.Enqueue("Prince")
NameQueue.Enqueue("Stuemky")
NameQueue.Enqueue("Murach")
Dim sMessage As String
Do While NameQueue.Count > 0
    sMessage &= NameQueue.Dequeue
    sMessage &= ControlChars.CrLf
Loop
MessageBox.Show(sMessage,"Queue")
```

Code that uses a stack

```
Dim NameStack As New Stack
NameStack.Push("Prince")
NameStack.Push("Stuemky")
NameStack.Push("Murach")
Dim sMessage As String
Do While NameStack.Count > 0
    sMessage &= NameStack.Pop
    sMessage &= ControlChars.CrLf
Loop
MessageBox.Show(sMessage,"Stack")
```

Figure 12-12   How to use the Queue and Stack classes

Perspective

In this chapter, you've learned how to use both arrays and collections for working with groups of related data. You've also learned that the .NET Framework provides several different classes that offer special features for working with collections. These include the ArrayList, SortedList, Queue, and Stack classes.

As you develop your own applications, then, you need to decide between the use of an array or collection before you start writing a routine for processing a group of items. Then, if you decide on the use of a collection, you need to choose the most appropriate type of collection. If you make the right decisions, your code will be easier to write, debug, and maintain.

Summary

- An *array* consists of two or more *elements*. The *upper bound* of the array indicates the maximum number of elements that can be stored in the array.

- To refer to an element in an array, you use an *index* value that can range from zero to the upper bound.

- A *one-dimensional array* contains data that varies based on one factor, while a *two-dimensional array* contains data that varies based on two factors. The *rank* of an array indicates the number of dimensions that it has, and Visual Basic provides for up to 60 dimensions.

- To refer to the elements in a two-dimensional array, you use an index that consists of a row value, a comma, and a column value.

- You can use the ReDim statement to resize an array while a program is executing. A better alternative, though, is to use a collection that automatically resizes itself.

- An array is actually an instance of the Array class. As a result, you can use the properties and methods of this class to work with arrays.

- A *collection* is an object that can hold two or more other objects. The Collection class is the generic class that you can use for creating collections.

- The ArrayList and SortedList classes are two more classes for creating collections. The ArrayList class uses an array internally, but automatically adjusts the size of that array whenever needed. The SortedList class lets you look up values in a collection by key value.

- The Queue and Stack classes let you create queues and stacks. A *queue* is a first-in, first-out collection. A *stack* is a last-in, first-out collection.

Terms

array	index	collection
element	two-dimensional array	queue
one-dimensional array	table	stack
upper bound	rank	

Objectives

- Given the specifications for an application that requires the use of a one- or two-dimensional array, code the array handling procedures.

- Given the specifications for an application that requires the use of an ArrayList, SortedList, Queue, or Stack collection, code the collection handling procedures.

- Explain why you shouldn't need to use the ReDim statement.

- Describe the primary benefit of using an ArrayList collection instead of an array.

- Describe the primary benefit of using a SortedList collection.

- Distinguish between a queue and a stack.

Exercise 12-1   Use an array and an array list

This is a simple exercise that will get you started with arrays. It uses the Invoice Total application of chapter 3 so its code should look quite simple to you now.

1. Open the InvoiceTotal.vbproj application that's in the C:\VB.NET\Chapter 12\InvoiceTotal folder. Review the code and run the application to remind yourself how it works.

2. Add code to the form class so the invoice total is added to the next element in an array each time the user clicks on the Calculate button. To do that, you need to declare the array and index variables as module-level variables. For simplicity, the array should provide for just 5 invoice totals.

3. Add code to the exit procedure so all the elements in the array are displayed in a message box when the user clicks on the Exit button, from the first invoice entered to the last. Then, test the program by entering the order totals for from two to five invoices.

4. Modify the exit procedure so the invoice totals in the array are sorted and displayed in a second message box. To sort, use the Sort method of the Array class. Then, test the program again. This time, the first message box should display the invoice totals in their entry sequence and the second one should display them in ascending value sequence.

5. Modify the program so it uses an array list to hold the invoices. When you've got this working right, close the solution.

Exercise 12-2   Use a queue and a stack

This is a simple exercise that will get you started with queues and stacks. It uses the Invoice application of chapter 6, which uses an Invoice class.

1. Open the Invoice.vbproj application that's in the C:\VB.NET\Chapter 12\Invoice folder. Review the code and run the application to remind yourself how it works.

2. Add code to the form class so each Invoice object is added to the next element in a queue each time the user clicks on the New Invoice button. To do that, you need to declare the queue with module-level scope.

3. Add code to the exit procedure so it dequeues the Invoice objects and displays them in a message box like this:

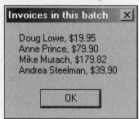

4. Test the program by entering from 2 to 5 invoices. Then, observe that the invoices are displayed in the same sequence that they were entered.

5. Modify the form class so it duplicates the queue processing with a stack. In other words, the program should also add the Invoice objects to a stack, and then display them in a second message box like the one above when the user clicks on the Exit button.

6. Test the program again, and note the sequences in the message boxes. When you've got this working right, close the solution.

Exercise 12-3   Use a two-dimensional array

This exercise will give you a chance to work with a two-dimensional array. Since it requires the use of a combo box, though, you won't be able to do it unless you've already read chapter 8.

1. Open the Attendance.vbproj application that's in the C:\VB.NET\Chapter 12\Attendance folder. This is the start of an application that lets you enter the daily attendance for four weeks. Review the form design and run the program to see what the form looks like. Then, click on the Close button to close the form, which is the only procedure that's already coded.

2. Code a load procedure that adds the numbers 1 through 4 to the combo box and sets the starting value to 1. If necessary, review figures 8-3 and 8-4 to refresh your memory on the use of combo boxes. Then, test the application to make

sure that the combo box has a starting value of 1 and that its list shows the numbers 1 through 4. At this point, the running form should look like this:

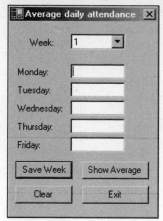

3. Declare a module-level array that provides for five daily attendance values for four weeks. In other words, this is a two-dimensional array with four rows and five columns.

4. Code a procedure for the Click event of the Save Week button that (1) saves the daily attendance entries in the column that corresponds to the week number in the combo box, (2) resets the attendance text boxes, (3) increases the value in the combo box by 1 unless it's already 4, and (4) moves the focus to the text box for Monday. Then, test to see if this appears to work correctly.

5. Code a procedure for the Click event of the Show Average button that calculates and displays the average daily attendance for each of the four weeks as in the message box that follows. Then, test to make sure that everything is working.

6. Code a procedure for the SelectedIndexChanged event of the combo box that occurs when the user selects a week number. This procedure should display the daily attendance values for the week indicated by the combo box. In other words, it should display the array values for that week in the text boxes. Then, test this change.

7. Code a procedure for the Clear button that clears the two-dimensional table, resets the values in the text boxes to zeros, sets the value of the combo box to 1, and moves the focus to the Monday text box. Use nested For loops to clear the table. When you've got this working right, close the solution.

Exercise 12-4   Use a sorted list for a lookup

In this exercise, you'll enhance the Invoice application of chapter 6 so it uses a combo box for item numbers and looks up the related unit prices in a sorted list. Here again, you need to read chapter 8 first so you know how to use the combo box.

1. Open the InvoiceLookup project that's in the C:\VB.NET\Chapter 12\InvoiceLookup folder. Then, review the form in design mode and run the program to see that (1) a combo box has been added for the item number and (2) the Unit Price text box has been changed to read-only. After you modify its code in this exercise, the form will look like this when it's running:

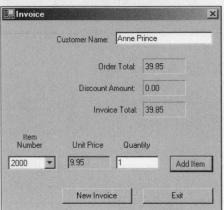

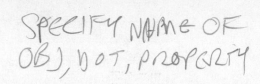

SPECIFY NAME OF OBJ, NOT, PROPERTY

2. Declare a variable for a sorted list that will hold item numbers and unit prices. Then, add code to the Load procedure so these item number and unit price pairs are added to the sorted list and the item numbers are added to the combo box list:

SAVED ITEMS AS STRING, TO WORK W/CBO BOX

    1000 and 19.95
    2000 and 9.95 (as shown above)
    3000 and 29.95
    4000 and 69.95
    5000 and 129.95

3. Code a procedure for the SelectedIndexChanged event of the Item Number combo box. This event should display the related unit price in the Unit Price text box and move the focus to the Quantity text box. Then, test the application to make sure that the correct price is displayed when you select an item from the combo box.

4. Modify the procedure for the Click event of the New Invoice button so no item is selected for a new invoice. Because this will cause the SelectedIndexChanged event of the combo box to fire, you'll also need to modify the procedure for that event so its code isn't executed under this condition. Then, test these modifications.

5. When you're sure everything is working right, close the solution.

* BETTER THAN 2 DIM ARRAY IN THIS CASE

13

How to work with structures and files

To this point in this book, you've learned how to develop applications that get input data from the user, but don't save that data. In practice, though, most business data is saved on disk so it can be retrieved whenever it's needed. In this chapter, then, you'll learn how to write data to disk files and read data from disk files.

How to work with structures

In its simplest form, a *structure* can be thought of as a custom, or user-defined, data type. One of the uses of a structure is to define the data items that are stored in a file. That's why structures are presented in this chapter.

How to declare a structure

Figure 13-1 shows how to declare and use a structure. To start, a structure declaration begins with a Structure statement that names the structure and ends with the End Structure statement. Between these two statements, you declare the variables, or *fields*, that make up the structure.

The structure in this figure, for example, consists of three variables. The first two, named Code and Title, are defined as strings, and the third one, named Price, is defined as a decimal. Note that all three variables are defined with the Dim statement. Because a structure must be defined at the class or module level, the default access for the structure and all of the variables it defines is public. If you want to define a structure and its variables as private, you must use the Private keyword.

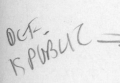

How to use a structure

After you define a structure, you can use it in a declaration just as you would use any other data type. For example, the declaration in this figure declares a variable named Book with the type BookInformation. This variable can hold the data defined by the three fields in the BookInformation structure.

To refer to an individual field within a structure, you follow the variable name with a dot operator and the name of the field as in the next three statements in this figure. Here, each statement refers to one of the fields defined within the structure.

VARNAME. FIELDNAME

The basic syntax for declaring a structure

```
[Public|Private] Structure structurename
    variable declarations
End Structure
```

The declaration for a structure that contains three variables

```
Structure BookInformation
    Dim Code As String
    Dim Title As String
    Dim Price As Decimal
End Structure
```

A statement that declares a variable as a structure type

```
Dim Book As BookInformation
```

Statements that assign values to the fields within a structure variable

```
Book.Code = txtBookCode.Text
Book.Title = txtBookTitle.Text
Book.Price = txtBookPrice.Text
```

Description

- A *structure* can be used to create a custom data type. Then, the structure consists of one or more variable declarations that define the *fields* of the structure.

- Once you define a structure, you can use it in a variable declaration just as you would any other data type. You can also copy a structure from one variable to another, pass a structure to a procedure, and return a structure from a function.

- To refer to a field within a structure, you code the name of the variable that has the structure type, followed by a dot operator and the name of the field.

- One use of a structure is defining the fields in the records that are stored in files.

- A structure must be declared at the class or module level. Because of that, the structure and the variables it declares are public by default.

- Structures can also provide functionality that makes them similar to classes. For more information on the similarity and differences between structures and classes, see the "Structures and Classes" topic in online Help.

Figure 13-1   How to declare and use a structure

An introduction to the System.IO classes

The System.IO namespace provides a variety of classes for processing files and for managing directories, files, and paths. You'll be introduced to those classes in the topics that follow. In addition, you'll learn about the two types of files and streams supported by the System.IO classes and how they're used to perform file I/O.

The classes for managing directories, files, and paths

Figure 13-2 summarizes the classes in the System.IO namespace that you can use to manage directories, files, and paths. As you can see, you can use methods of the Directory class to create or delete a directory or determine if a directory exists. And you can use methods of the File class to copy, delete, or move a file, get or set the attributes of a file, or determine if a file exists. Note that all of the methods in these classes are shared, so you access them directly from the class.

The example in this figure shows how you can use some of these methods. This code starts by declaring a string that holds the path to a directory that contains a file to be processed. Then, the If statement uses the Exists method of the Directory class to determine if this directory exists. If it doesn't, it uses the CreateDirectory method to create it.

If the directory does exist, the code continues by declaring a string that will hold the path to a file named MurachBooks.dat. Then, the If statement that follows uses the Exists method of the File class to determine if this file exists. If it does, it uses the Delete method to delete it.

Before you can include code like this in a program, though, you need to add an Imports statement for the System.IO namespace like the one shown in this figure. If you don't, you can refer to the classes in this namespace only by qualifying each reference with the name of the namespace. For example, you could code the first If statement in this figure like this:

```
If Not System.IO.Directory.Exists(sDir) Then
```

That's a lot of extra typing, though, particularly when you're working with shared methods like the ones shown in this figure. Because of that, I recommend that you always include the Imports statement.

System.IO classes used to work with drives and directories

Class	Description
Directory	Used to create, edit, delete, or get information on directories (folders).
File	Used to create, edit, delete, or get information on files.
Path	Used to get path information from a variety of platforms.

Common methods of the Directory class

Method	Description
CreateDirectory	Creates the directories in a specified path.
Delete	Deletes a directory and its contents.
Exists	Returns a Boolean value indicating whether a directory exists.

Common methods of the File class

Method	Description
Copy	Copies a file from a source path to a destination path.
Delete	Deletes a file.
Exists	Returns a Boolean value indicating whether a file exists.
GetAttributes	Returns a value indicating the attributes of a file.
Move	Moves a file from a source path to a destination path.
SetAttributes	Sets the attributes of a file.

Code that uses some of the Directory and File methods

```
Dim sDir As String = "C:\VB.NET\Files"
If Not Directory.Exists(sDir) Then
    Directory.CreateDirectory(sDir)
Else
    Dim sFile As String = sDir & "\MurachBooks.dat"
    If File.Exists(sFile) Then
        File.Delete(sFile)
    End If
End If
```

A statement that simplifies references to the System.IO classes

```
Imports System.IO
```

Description

- The classes for managing directories, files, and paths are stored in the System.IO namespace.

- To use the classes in the System.IO namespace, you should include an Imports statement. Otherwise, you have to qualify the references to its classes with System.IO.

- All of the methods of the File, Directory, and Path classes are shared, so you don't have to create an instance of the class to use them.

Figure 13-2   The classes for managing directories, files, and paths

How files and streams work

When you use the System.IO classes to do *I/O operations* (or *file I/O*), you can use two different kinds of files: *text files* or *binary files*. To illustrate, figure 13-3 shows the contents of a text file and a binary file as they look when displayed in a text editor. Although both of these files contain the same data and both of them contain the fields defined by the BookInformation structure in figure 13-1, they look quite different.

In a *text file,* all of the data is stored as text characters with one character per byte. Often, the *fields* in this type of file are separated by delimiters like tabs or pipe characters, and the *records* are separated by end of line characters. In the text file in this figure, the fields are separated by pipe characters and the records by end of line characters. Although you can't see the end of line characters, you know they're there because each record starts at the beginning of a new line.

In contrast, the data in a *binary file* can include any of the primitive data types as well as object types. Because of that, the data isn't always displayed properly within a text editor. For example, you can't tell what the value of the Price field is in each of these records because this field is numeric. Also, since the records in a binary file don't end with end of line characters, one record isn't displayed on each line in a text editor.

To handle I/O operations with text and binary files, the .NET Framework uses *streams.* You can think of a stream as the flow of data from one location to another. For instance, an *output stream* can flow from the internal memory of an application to a disk file, and an *input stream* can flow from a disk file to internal memory. When you work with a text file, you use a *text stream.* When you work with a binary file, you use a *binary stream.*

To work with streams and files using the System.IO namespace, you use the classes summarized in this figure. To create a stream, for example, you use the FileStream class. Then, to read data from a text stream, you use the StreamReader class. And to read data from a binary stream, you use the BinaryReader class. You'll learn how to use all of these classes later in this chapter.

Since you can store all of the primitive numeric data types in a binary file, this type of file is more efficient for applications that work with numeric data. In contrast, the numeric data in a text file has to be converted to the primitive types before it can be used in arithmetic operations. That's one reason why binary files are used for most business applications. When an application works primarily with text data, though, text files can be more efficient.

When you save a text or binary file, you can use any extension you want for the file name. In this book, though, *txt* is used as the extension for all text files, and *dat* for all binary files. For instance, the text file in this figure is named MurachBooks.txt, and the binary file is named MurachBooks.dat.

A text file displayed in a text editor

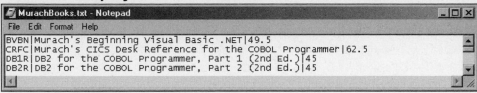

A binary file displayed in a text editor

The two types of files you can process using the System.IO classes

Type	Description
Text	A file that contains text characters. The fields in each record are typically delimited by special characters like tabs or pipe characters, and the records are delimited by a line terminator (usually a carriage return and line feed).
Binary	A file that can contain a variety of data types.

The two types of streams you can use to process files

Stream	Description
Text (Character)	Used to transfer text data to or from a file.
Binary	Used to transfer binary data to or from a file.

System.IO classes used to work with files and streams

Class	Description
FileStream	Provides access to files.
StreamReader	Used to read a stream of characters from a text file.
StreamWriter	Used to write a stream of characters to a text file.
BinaryReader	Used to read a stream of data from a binary file.
BinaryWriter	Used to write a stream of data to a binary file.

Description

- An *input file* is a file that is read by a program; an *output file* is a file that is written by a program. Input and output operations are often referred to as *I/O operations* or *file I/O*.

- A *stream* is the flow of data from one location to another. To write data to a file, you use an *output stream*. To read data from a file, you use an *input stream*. A single stream can also be used for both input and output.

- To read and write text files, you use *text streams*. To read and write binary files, you use *binary streams*.

Figure 13-3   How files and streams work

How to use the FileStream class

To work with input and output streams, you use the FileStream class as shown in figure 13-4. In the syntax at the top of this figure, you can see its arguments. The first two, which specify the path for the file and the mode in which it will be opened, are required. The last two, which specify how the file can be accessed and shared, are optional.

To code the mode, access, and share arguments, you use the FileMode, FileAccess, and FileShare enumerations shown in this figure. If, for example, you want to create a file stream for a file that doesn't exist, you can code FileMode.Create for the mode argument and a new file will be created. Note, however, that this constant causes the file to be overwritten if it already exists. In contrast, if you don't want an existing file to be overwritten, you can code FileMode.CreateNew for this argument. Then, if the file already exists, an exception is thrown as explained in the next figure.

For the access argument, you can code constants that let you read records from the file, write records to the file, or both read and write records. If you omit this argument, the default is to allow both reading and writing of records.

For the share argument, you can code constants that let other users read records, write records, or both read and write records at the same time that the first user is accessing the file. Or, you can code the None constant to prevent sharing of the file. What you're trying to avoid is two users writing to a file at the same time, which could lead to errors. So if you code the access argument as ReadWrite or Write, you normally code the share argument as Read or None. But if you code the access argument as Read, you can use any of the constants as the share argument. That just depends on whether you want to allow other applications to write new data to the file while you're using it.

The coding examples in this figure show two common combinations of arguments used to create a file stream. In the first example, an existing file is opened for reading. Because the share argument is omitted from this example, other programs will be able to read from, but not write to, this file. The second example starts by deleting the file from the first example. Then, it creates a new file stream and assigns it to the same variable that was used by the original file. Because the file no longer exists, the CreateNew constant is used for the mode argument. In addition, the Write constant is used for the access argument so records can only be written to this file.

Once you create a file stream, you don't usually work with it directly. Instead, you work with it using the other System.IO classes you learned about in the previous figure. However, the one method of the FileStream class you may need to use is the Close method.

The Basic syntax for creating a FileStream object

```
New FileStream(path, mode[, access[, share]])
```

Constants in the FileMode enumeration

Constant	Description
Append	Opens the file if it exists and seeks to the end of the file. If the file doesn't exist, it's created. Can only be used with Write file access.
Create	Creates a new file. If the file already exists, it's overwritten.
CreateNew	Creates a new file. If the file already exists, an exception is thrown.
Open	Opens an existing file. If the file doesn't exist, an exception is thrown.
OpenOrCreate	Opens a file if it exists, or creates a new file if it doesn't exist.
Truncate	Opens an existing file and truncates it so its size is zero bytes.

Constants in the FileAccess enumeration

Constant	Description
Read	Data can be read from the file, but not written to it.
ReadWrite	Data can be read from and written to the file. This is the default.
Write	Data can be written to the file but not read from it.

Constants in the FileShare enumeration

Constant	Description
None	The file cannot be opened by other programs.
Read	Allows other programs to open the file for reading only. This is the default.
ReadWrite	Allows other programs to open the file for both reading and writing.
Write	Allows other programs to open the file for writing only.

Common method of the FileStream class

Method	Description
Close	Closes the file stream and releases any resources associated with it.

Code that creates a FileStream object to open a text file for reading

```
Dim sPath As String = "C:\VB.NET\Files\MurachBooks.txt"
Dim BookFileStream As New FileStream(sPath, FileMode.Open, FileAccess.Read)
```

Code that deletes a file and then creates a FileStream object to recreate the file for writing

```
File.Delete(sPath)
BookFileStream = New FileStream(sPath, FileMode.CreateNew, FileAccess.Write)
```

Note

- Operating system level permissions may limit which file access and file share options you can use.

Figure 13-4   How to use the FileStream class

How to use the exception classes for file I/O

In chapter 5, you learned the basic skills for handling exceptions. Now, figure 13-5 summarizes the exceptions that can occur when you perform I/O operations. The three most common exceptions are DirectoryNotFound, FileNotFound, and EndOfStream, but you can code your programs so all three of these exceptions are avoided.

For example, you can avoid a DirectoryNotFound exception by using the Exists method of the Directory class to be sure that the directory exists before you try to use it in the file path for a new file stream. Similarly, you can avoid a FileNotFound exception by using the Exists method of the File class. As you will soon learn, you can also avoid an EndOfStream exception by checking to see whether a file contains more data before trying to read more data.

The coding example in this figure shows how you can use the DirectoryNotFound and FileNotFound exceptions. Here, the Try statement attempts to create a file stream for the file specified in the path variable. Because the mode argument is set to FileMode.Open, a FileNotFound exception is thrown if this file doesn't exist. In that case, the Catch clause for this exception creates the file by passing the FileMode.CreateNew argument to the FileStream. Similarly, if the directory specified by the path argument doesn't exist, the DirectoryNotFound exception occurs. In that case, the Catch clause for this exception creates the directory and creates a new file within that directory when it creates the new file stream. The last Catch clause in this example catches any other I/O exception that might occur.

Often, I/O exceptions are serious problems like hardware problems that a program can't do anything about. In that case, the program should just display an error message and end. If the program consists of a single form, you can end it simply by closing the form as illustrated by the last Catch clause in this figure. Otherwise, you may want to use the technique that was introduced in chapter 10. That is, you can start the application from a Main procedure using the Run method of the Application class coded within a Try statement. Then, a Catch clause can catch and handle the error, after which the program ends.

The exception classes for file I/O

Class	Description
IOException	The base class for exceptions that are thrown during the processing of a stream, file, or directory.
DirectoryNotFoundException	Occurs when part of a directory or file path can't be found.
EndOfStreamException	Occurs when a program attempts to read beyond the end of a stream.
FileLoadException	Occurs when an assembly file can't be loaded.
FileNotFoundException	Occurs when a file can't be found.
PathTooLongException	Occurs when the name of a file or a path is longer than the maximum number of characters allowed by the operating system.

Code that uses exception classes to check for the existence of a file and the directory that contains it

```
Dim sDirectory As String = "C:\VB.NET\Files\"
Dim sFile As String = "MurachBooks.txt"
Dim sPath As String = sDirectory & sFile
Dim BookFileStream As FileStream
Try
    BookFileStream = New FileStream _
                        (sPath, FileMode.Open, FileAccess.ReadWrite)
Catch eFileNotFound As FileNotFoundException
    BookFileStream = New FileStream _
                        (sPath, FileMode.CreateNew, FileAccess.Write)
Catch eDirectoryNotFound As DirectoryNotFoundException
    Directory.CreateDirectory(sDirectory)
    BookFileStream = New FileStream _
                        (sPath, FileMode.CreateNew, FileAccess.Write)
Catch eIO As IOException
    MessageBox.Show("An error has occurred during the opening of file " _
        & sFile & " in directory " & sDirectory & ".")
    Me.Close
End Try
```

Description

- You can use the generic IOException class to catch any I/O error. To catch specific errors, use the exception class for that error.

- To avoid DirectoryNotFound and FileNotFound exceptions, you can use the Exists method of the Directory and File classes to determine if the file and directory exist before referring to them in your program.

- To avoid EndOfStream exceptions, you can determine if the file contains additional data before you read from it. To do that, you use an appropriate method of the class that you use to access the file.

Figure 13-5   How to use the exception classes for file I/O

How to use the System.IO classes for binary files

To process the data in a binary file, you use the BinaryReader and BinaryWriter classes. You'll learn how to use these classes in the figures that follow, and you'll see a complete application that uses these classes.

How to use the BinaryReader class to read from a binary file

Figure 13-6 shows you how to use the BinaryReader class to read data from a binary file. To start, you create a BinaryReader object using the syntax at the top of this figure. As you can see, the only argument is the name of the FileStream object you use to process the file.

As you saw in figure 13-3, there's nothing to indicate where one record ends and another begins in a binary file. Because of that, you can't read an entire record at once. Instead, you have to read one character or one field at a time. To do that, you use the Read methods of the BinaryReader class that are shown in this figure. Note that the methods that read fields indicate the data type of the field to be read. To read a Boolean field, for example, you use the ReadBoolean method. And to read a Decimal field, you use the ReadDecimal method. This figure, though, shows only the most common Read methods. For a complete list of methods, see the online help information for the BinaryReader class.

Before you read the next character or field, you want to be sure that you haven't already read all of the data in the file. To do that, you use the PeekChar method. Then, if there's at least one more character to be read, this method returns that character. Note, however, that this method doesn't advance to the next position in the file. So you can still use one of the Read methods to read the next character or field. If there isn't another character, the PeekChar method returns a value of –1. Then, you can use the Close method to close the binary reader and the associated file stream.

The coding example in this figure shows how you can use some of these methods. Here, a FileStream object is created for an existing file named MurachBooks.dat that will have read-only access, and a new BinaryReader object is created for that file stream. Then, the Do loop that follows is executed until the PeekChar method returns a value of –1, which means the end of the file has been reached.

Within the Do loop, the three fields in each record are read into the BookInformation structure that was defined in figure 13-1. Because the first two fields in each record contain string data, the ReadString method is used to retrieve their contents. And since the third field contains decimal data, the ReadDecimal method is used to retrieve its contents. Then, that structure is added to an array list named Books (see chapter 12 to refresh your memory on array lists). Last, when the Do loop ends, the Close method of the BinaryReader object is used to close both the binary reader and the file stream.

The basic syntax for creating a BinaryReader object

```
New BinaryReader(stream)
```

Common methods of the BinaryReader class

Method	Description
Close	Closes the BinaryReader object and the associated FileStream object.
PeekChar	Returns the next available character without advancing to the next position in the file. If no more characters are available, this method returns -1.
Read	Returns the next available character in the input stream and advances to the next position in the file.
ReadBoolean	Reads a Boolean value from the input stream and advances the current position of the stream by one byte.
ReadByte/ReadBytes	Reads one or more bytes from the input stream and advances the current position of the stream accordingly.
ReadChar/ReadChars	Reads one or more characters from the input stream and advances the current position of the stream accordingly.
ReadDecimal	Reads a decimal value from the input stream and advances the current position of the stream by 16 bytes.
ReadInt32	Reads a 4-byte signed integer from the input stream and advances the current position of the stream by 4 bytes.
ReadString	Reads a string from the input stream and advances the current position of the stream by the number of characters in the string.

Code that reads data from a binary file and stores it in an array list

```
Dim Book As BookInformation
Dim Books As New ArrayList()
Dim sPath As String = "C:\VB.NET\Files\MurachBooks.dat"
Dim BookFileStream As New FileStream(sPath, FileMode.Open, FileAccess.Read)
Dim BookBinaryReader As New BinaryReader(BookFileStream)

Do Until BookBinaryReader.PeekChar = -1
    Book.Code = BookBinaryReader.ReadString
    Book.Title = BookBinaryReader.ReadString
    Book.Price = BookBinaryReader.ReadDecimal
    Books.Add(Book)
Loop
BookBinaryReader.Close()
```

Description

- You use a BinaryReader object to read a single character or an entire field from a binary file. To read a single character, you use the Read method. And to read a field, you use the method that indicates the type of data the field contains.

- You can use the PeekChar method to determine if the input stream is positioned at the end of the stream.

Figure 13-6   How to use the BinaryReader class to read from a binary file

How to use the BinaryWriter class to write to a binary file

Figure 13-7 shows how to use the BinaryWriter class to write data to a binary file. Like the BinaryReader class, the argument that you pass to it is the name of the FileStream object you use to process the file. Unlike the BinaryReader class, though, the BinaryWriter class provides just one method for writing data. This method uses the data types of the variables that it writes to determine what data types to write on the file.

The coding example in this figure illustrates how this works. Here, a file stream is created for a new file that will have write-only access, and a binary writer is created using that file stream. Then, a For...Next loop is used to write the elements in an array list to the file. Because each element in the array list is a structure, each field in the structure is written to the file separately using the Write method. After all of the elements in the array list have been written to the file, the Close method of the BinaryWriter object is used to close both the binary writer and file stream objects.

The basic syntax for creating a BinaryWriter object

```
New BinaryWriter(stream)
```

Common methods of the BinaryWriter class

Method	Description
Close	Closes the BinaryWriter object and the associated FileStream object.
Write	Writes the specified data to the output stream.

Code that writes data from an array list named Books to a binary file

```
Dim sPath As String = "C:\VB.NET\Files\MurachBooks.dat"
Dim BookFileStream As New FileStream(sPath, FileMode.CreateNew, _
    FileAccess.Write)
Dim BookBinaryWriter As New BinaryWriter(BookFileStream)

For Each Book In Books
    BookBinaryWriter.Write(Book.Code)
    BookBinaryWriter.Write(Book.Title)
    BookBinaryWriter.Write(Book.Price)
Next
BookBinaryWriter.Close()
```

Description

- You use a BinaryWriter object to write data to a binary file. In most cases, you'll write one field at a time in a prescribed sequence.

- Unlike the BinaryReader class, which provides several methods for reading fields that contain different types of data, the BinaryWriter class provides a single Write method for writing data to a file. This method determines the type of data being written based on the data types of the variables.

Figure 13-7   How to use the BinaryWriter class to write to a binary file

The design and property settings for the Book Maintenance form

Now that you understand how to use the BinaryReader and BinaryWriter classes, you're ready to see a complete application that uses them. Figure 13-8 presents the design and property settings for this application. Since the property settings are similar to those you've seen throughout this book, I won't say any more about them here.

As you can see, this application consists of a single form that lets the user maintain the records in a file that contains book information. Each record in this file contains the fields in the BookInformation structure you saw earlier, and this application will use an array list that holds this structure to work with the records in this file.

To identify the book to be maintained, the user selects it from the combo box at the top of the form. This combo box contains the titles for all of the books in the file. Then, the data for the selected book is displayed in the text boxes on the form so the user can modify it. If the user changes any of the data in these text boxes, the Update and Cancel buttons become available. Then, the user can click on the Update button to save the changes or on the Cancel button to cancel the changes and redisplay the original data. At this point, though, the changes are only saved within the array defined by the program. To save the changes to the file, the user must click on the Save & Exit button.

The Book Maintenance form

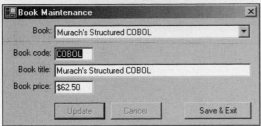

The properties for the form

Property	Value	Property	Value
Text	Book Maintenance	CancelButton	btnCancel
FormBorderStyle	FixedSingle	MaximizeBox	False
StartPosition	CenterScreen	MinimizeBox	False
AcceptButton	btnUpdate		

The properties for the combo box

Default name	Name	DropDownStyle	Sorted
ComboBox1	cboBooks	DropDownList	True

The properties for the text boxes

Default name	Name
TextBox1	txtBookCode
TextBox2	txtBookTitle
TextBox3	txtBookPrice

The properties for the button controls

Default name	Name	Text
Button1	btnUpdate	&Update
Button2	btnCancel	&Cancel
Button3	btnSaveAndExit	&Save && Exit

Description

- The Book Maintenance form lets the user modify existing records in a book file. The user can select the book to be modified from the combo box at the top of the form. Then, the data for that book is displayed in the text boxes on the form.

- If the user changes any of the data for a book, the Update and Cancel buttons become available. Then, the user can save the changes by clicking on the Update button or cancel the changes by clicking on the Cancel button.

- To save the changes back to the file and close the form, the user clicks on the Save & Exit button.

Figure 13-8   The design and property settings for the Book Maintenance form

The code for the Book Maintenance form when it processes a binary file

Figure 13-9 presents the code for the Book Maintenance form. To keep the emphasis on the code for file I/O, this code doesn't include data validation or exception handling. In a production program, though, you would add those routines to a program like this.

To start, you should notice that an Imports statement for the System.IO namespace is included at the beginning of this code so the classes in this namespace can be used without qualification. Then, the BookInformation structure is defined, an array list named Books is declared, and a variable for the BookInformation structure is declared.

Next, a string variable is set to the path for the binary file that's going to be processed by this application, and another variable is declared as a FileStream type. Because the New keyword isn't included on this statement, however, the file stream object isn't instantiated. As you'll see in a minute, this variable is used for both the input stream and the output stream.

Within the Load procedure for the form, a BinaryReader object is declared. Next, the FileStream and BinaryReader objects are instantiated. Then, a Do loop reads the records in the file into the structure and adds the structure to the array list. The last statement in this loop adds the title of each book that is read to the combo box for the form. After all the records have been read and the Do loop ends, both the BinaryReader and FileStream objects are closed. Last, this procedure disables the Update and Cancel buttons so the user can't activate them when the form is first displayed.

When the user selects a book from the combo box on the form, the SelectedIndexChanged procedure is executed. This procedure uses the SelectedIndex property of the combo box to locate the structure for the selected book in the array list of books. Then, it moves the fields in the structure to the text boxes on the form. It also disables the Update and Cancel buttons and moves the focus to the first text box on the form. If the user then makes changes to one of the fields in the text box, the TextChanged procedure on the next page enables the Update and Cancel buttons.

If you look at the Handles clause of the Sub statement for the SelectedIndexChanged procedure, you'll see that it has been modified so it also handles the Click event of the Cancel button. That works because this procedure simply moves the data in the array list to the text boxes on the form. So if the array hasn't been updated with any changes, the changes are lost. Similarly, if the user selects another item from the combo box without updating any changes that have been made, those changes are lost.

✳ SAVED AS BOOKMMN_0402 ✳

The Visual Basic code for processing a binary file   Page 1

```vb
Imports System.IO

Public Class Form1
    Inherits System.Windows.Forms.Form

    Structure BookInformation
        Dim Code As String
        Dim Title As String
        Dim Price As Decimal
    End Structure

    Dim Books As New ArrayList()
    Dim Book As BookInformation
    Dim sPath As String = "C:\VB.NET\Files\MurachBooks.dat"
    Dim BookFileStream As FileStream

    Private Sub Form1_Load(ByVal sender As Object, _
            ByVal e As System.EventArgs) Handles MyBase.Load
        Dim BookBinaryReader As BinaryReader
        BookFileStream = New FileStream(sPath, FileMode.Open, FileAccess.Read)
        BookBinaryReader = New BinaryReader(BookFileStream)
        Do Until BookBinaryReader.PeekChar = -1
            Book.Code = BookBinaryReader.ReadString
            Book.Title = BookBinaryReader.ReadString
            Book.Price = BookBinaryReader.ReadDecimal
            Books.Add(Book)
            cboBooks.Items.Add(Book.Title)
        Loop
        BookBinaryReader.Close()
        btnUpdate.Enabled = False
        btnCancel.Enabled = False
    End Sub

    Private Sub cboBooks_SelectedIndexChanged(ByVal sender As System.Object, _
            ByVal e As System.EventArgs) _
            Handles cboBooks.SelectedIndexChanged, btnCancel.Click
        Book = Books(cboBooks.SelectedIndex)
        txtBookCode.Text = Book.Code
        txtBookTitle.Text = Book.Title
        txtBookPrice.Text = FormatCurrency(Book.Price)
        btnUpdate.Enabled = False
        btnCancel.Enabled = False
        txtBookCode.Focus()
    End Sub
```

Figure 13-9   The code for the form when it processes a binary file (part 1 of 2)

If the user changes the data in any of the text boxes, the TextChanged procedure is executed. This procedure simply enables the Update and Cancel buttons so the user can click on them to update or cancel any changes that have been made. If you look at the Handles clause for this procedure, you can see that it has been modified so it is activated by a change to any one of the text boxes.

If the user clicks on the Update button, the code in that procedure updates the appropriate element in the array list with the data in the text boxes. Then, it disables the Update and Cancel buttons. In addition, if the user changed the title for the book, that title is updated in the combo box list. Finally, the focus is moved to the combo box so the user can select another book.

When the user is done making changes to the records and clicks on the Save & Exit button, the Click event procedure saves the changes to the file. Because there's no way to save modifications to an existing file, this procedure deletes the current file and then recreates it by specifying CreateNew for the mode argument of the file stream.

After the file stream object is created, it's used as the argument for creating a new binary writer object. Then, a For...Next loop cycles through the elements in the array list of books and writes the fields in each element to the new file. Finally, the binary writer, file stream, and form are closed.

The Visual Basic code for processing a binary file   Page 2

```
Private Sub Control_TextChanged(ByVal sender As Object, _
        ByVal e As System.EventArgs) Handles txtBookCode.TextChanged, _
        txtBookTitle.TextChanged, txtBookPrice.TextChanged
    btnUpdate.Enabled = True
    btnCancel.Enabled = True
End Sub

Private Sub btnUpdate_Click(ByVal sender As System.Object, _
        ByVal e As System.EventArgs) Handles btnUpdate.Click
    Book.Code = txtBookCode.Text
    Book.Title = txtBookTitle.Text
    Book.Price = txtBookPrice.Text
    Books(cboBooks.SelectedIndex) = Book
    btnUpdate.Enabled = False
    btnCancel.Enabled = False
    If cboBooks.Items.Item(cboBooks.SelectedIndex) <> Book.Title Then
        cboBooks.Items.Item(cboBooks.SelectedIndex) = Book.Title
    End If
    cboBooks.Focus()
End Sub

Private Sub btnSaveAndExit_Click(ByVal sender As System.Object, _
        ByVal e As System.EventArgs) Handles btnSaveAndExit.Click
    Dim BookBinaryWriter As BinaryWriter
    File.Delete(sPath)
    BookFileStream = New FileStream(sPath, FileMode.CreateNew, _
        FileAccess.Write)
    BookBinaryWriter = New BinaryWriter(BookFileStream)
    For Each Book In Books
        BookBinaryWriter.Write(Book.Code)
        BookBinaryWriter.Write(Book.Title)
        BookBinaryWriter.Write(Book.Price)
    Next
    BookBinaryWriter.Close()
    Me.Close()
End Sub

End Class
```

Handwritten annotations:
- ADDED CONTROLS
- ← STORE BACK IN COLL
- ← IF TITLE CHANGED, CBOBOX ITEM CHANGED
- ← CREATE NEW OBJ. SO WRITE TO FILE
- (COLLECTION)
- WRITE FIELD × FIELD
- *OVERWRITES FILE INST. OF JUST FIELD (DON'T NEED TO DO W/ DBMS)

Figure 13-9   The code for the form when it processes a binary file (part 2 of 2)

How to use the System.IO classes for text files

To process the data in a text file, you use the StreamReader and StreamWriter classes. Unlike the BinaryReader and BinaryWriter classes, these classes let you read and write entire records at one time. Then, if you need to work with the individual fields in a record, you parse the data using the techniques of chapter 11 (if you haven't yet read chapter 11, figures 11-5 and 11-6 provide the information you need). Similarly, before you can write a record, you need to construct it from the individual fields it contains. You'll see how that works in the topics that follow.

How to use the StreamReader class to read from a text file

Figure 13-10 shows how to use the StreamReader class. To create a StreamReader object, you use the name of a FileStream object as the argument. Then, you can use the methods shown in this figure to work with the stream reader object.

The three Read methods let you read a single character, a single line of data (a record), or all of the data from the current position to the end of the file. In most cases, though, you'll use the ReadLine method to read one record at a time. You can also use the Peek method to see if there is additional data in the file before you read from it, and you can use the Close method to close the stream reader and file stream when you're done with them.

The coding example in this figure shows how you can use a stream reader to read the data in a file one record at a time. After the file stream and stream reader are created, a Do loop is used to read the records in the file. The condition on this loop uses the Peek method to check that there is at least one more record. If there is, the ReadLine method is used to read the next record in the file into a string, and that record is parsed into the individual fields that are stored in an array list. When all of the records have been processed, the stream reader and file stream are closed using the Close method of the stream reader.

The basic syntax for creating a StreamReader object

```
New StreamReader(stream)
```

Common methods of the StreamReader class

Method	Description
Close	Closes both the StreamReader object and the associated FileStream object.
Peek	Returns the next available character in the input stream without advancing to the next position in the file. If no more characters are available, this method returns –1.
Read	Reads the next character from the input stream.
ReadLine	Reads the next line of characters from the input stream and returns it as a string.
ReadToEnd	Reads the data from the current position in the input stream to the end of the stream and returns it as a string. Typically used to read the entire contents of a file at once.

Code that reads data from a text file and stores it in an array list

```
Dim Book As BookInformation
Dim Books As New ArrayList()
Dim sPath As String = "C:\VB.NET\Files\MurachBooks.txt"
Dim BookFileStream As New FileStream(sPath, FileMode.Open, FileAccess.Read)
Dim BookStreamReader As New StreamReader(BookFileStream)

Dim sCurrentBook As String
Dim iPosition1, iPosition2 As Integer

Do Until BookStreamReader.Peek = -1
    sCurrentBook = BookStreamReader.ReadLine
    iPosition1 = sCurrentBook.IndexOf("|") + 1
    iPosition2 = sCurrentBook.IndexOf("|", iPosition1) + 1
    Book.Code = sCurrentBook.Substring(0, iPosition1 - 1)
    Book.Title = sCurrentBook.Substring(iPosition1, _
        iPosition2 - iPosition1 - 1)
    Book.Price = sCurrentBook.Substring(iPosition2)
    Books.Add(Book)
Loop
BookStreamReader.Close()
```

Description

- You use a StreamReader object to read data from a text file. Because the records in most text files end with a line terminator (usually a carriage return and a line feed), you'll typically use the ReadLine method to read one record at a time.

- If the fields in a record are delimited by special characters, you need to parse the fields using the techniques of chapter 11.

- You can use the Peek method to determine if the input stream is positioned at the end of the stream.

Figure 13-10   How to use the StreamReader class to read from a text file

How to use the StreamWriter class to write to a text file

Figure 13-11 shows how to use the StreamWriter class to write data to a text file. This class lets you write any data to a text file by using the Write method. In most cases, though, you'll write a single record at a time using the WriteLine method. When you use this method, a line terminator is automatically added to the end of the record. If the fields in the record are separated by special characters, however, you have to add those characters manually.

The coding example in this figure illustrates how this works. This code creates a file stream object for a new file with write-only access and then creates a stream writer object for that file stream. Then, it uses a For...Next loop to write each element in an array list to the file. Because each element consists of three fields, they must be concatenated to form a record. In addition, pipe characters are added between the fields. That way, when a record is read from this file, the pipe characters can be used to parse it into individual fields as you saw in the previous figure. Finally, after all of the records have been written to the file, the stream writer and file stream are closed.

The basic syntax for creating a StreamWriter object

```
New StreamWriter(stream)
```

Common methods of the StreamWriter class

Method	Description
Close	Closes the StreamWriter object and the associated FileStream object.
Write	Writes the specified data to the output stream.
WriteLine	Writes a line of data (a record) to the output stream and appends a line terminator (usually a carriage return and a line feed).

Code that writes data from an array list named Books to a text file

```
Dim sPath As String = "C:\VB.NET\Files\MurachBooks.txt"
Dim BookFileStream As New FileStream(sPath, FileMode.CreateNew, _
    FileAccess.Write)
Dim BookStreamWriter As New StreamWriter(BookFileStream)

For Each Book In Books
    BookStreamWriter.WriteLine(Book.Code & "|" _
                    & Book.Title & "|" _
                    & Book.Price)
Next
BookStreamWriter.Close()
```

Description

- You use a StreamWriter object to write data to a text file. In most cases, you'll use the WriteLine method to write an entire record at once.

- If the fields that make up a record are stored in individual variables, you need to concatenate these variables to construct each record. If the fields in each record are delimited by special characters, you also need to include those characters in the output. However, the line terminator is added automatically.

Figure 13-11   How to use the StreamWriter class to write to a text file

The code for the Book Maintenance form when it processes a text file

Figure 13-12 presents some of the code from the Book Maintenance application that you saw earlier, but this time it uses a text file instead of a binary file. Because this application works just like the one described in figure 13-8, the code for the procedures that aren't shown are the same as those in figure 13-9. If you understand the code in the last two figures, you shouldn't have any trouble understanding the code for the two procedures in this figure.

The Visual Basic code for processing a text file

```
Private Sub Form1_Load(ByVal sender As Object, _
        ByVal e As System.EventArgs) Handles MyBase.Load
    Dim BookStreamReader As StreamReader
    Dim sCurrentBook As String
    Dim iPosition1, iPosition2 As Integer
    BookFileStream = New FileStream(sPath, FileMode.Open, FileAccess.Read)
    BookStreamReader = New StreamReader(BookFileStream)
    Do Until BookStreamReader.Peek = -1
        sCurrentBook = BookStreamReader.ReadLine
        iPosition1 = sCurrentBook.IndexOf("|") + 1
        iPosition2 = sCurrentBook.IndexOf("|", iPosition1) + 1
        Book.Code = sCurrentBook.Substring(0, iPosition1 - 1)
        Book.Title = sCurrentBook.Substring(iPosition1, _
            iPosition2 - iPosition1 - 1)
        Book.Price = sCurrentBook.Substring(iPosition2)
        Books.Add(Book)
        cboBooks.Items.Add(Book.Title)
    Loop
    BookStreamReader.Close()
    btnUpdate.Enabled = False
    btnCancel.Enabled = False
End Sub

Private Sub btnSaveAndExit_Click(ByVal sender As System.Object, _
        ByVal e As System.EventArgs) Handles btnSaveAndExit.Click
    Dim BookStreamWriter As StreamWriter
    File.Delete(sPath)
    BookFileStream = New FileStream(sPath, FileMode.CreateNew, _
        FileAccess.Write)
    BookStreamWriter = New StreamWriter(BookFileStream)
    For Each Book In Books
        BookStreamWriter.WriteLine(Book.Code & "|" _
                        & Book.Title & "|" _
                        & Book.Price)
    Next
    BookStreamWriter.Close()
    Me.Close()
End Sub
```

Figure 13-12 The code for the Book Maintenance form when it processes a text file

Visual Basic functions for file processing

Here again, Visual Basic offers more than one way to do the same operations. This time, Visual Basic offers functions for file processing that duplicate many of the operations that you can do with the System.IO classes. Although it's better to use those classes whenever you can, you should at least be aware of the functions that are available for file processing.

Basic functions

If you've used Visual Basic 6, you may know that it provided a variety of statements for processing files. With Visual Basic .NET, though, those statements are implemented as functions, and additional functions for file processing are also available. These functions are summarized in figure 13-13.

As you can see, these functions let you process binary and text files using techniques similar to the ones you use with the classes in the System.IO namespace. In addition, you can use these functions to process delimited text files (files whose fields are enclosed in quotation marks and separated by commas). Because this format is becoming less common, though, you're not likely to need to do that.

Random access functions

You can also use the Visual Basic functions to process files randomly rather than sequentially. With *random access*, you can read any record in the file by specifying its record number or position. You can also replace existing records without having to rewrite the entire file like you do when you use *sequential access*.

If you need random access in a modern computing environment, though, you usually use a database, not a file. As a result, you're not likely to use the Visual Basic functions for random access.

Visual Basic functions for file operations

Function	Description
Dir	Returns a string representing the name of a file or folder that matches a pattern or file attribute you specify.
EOF	Returns a Boolean value that indicates if the end of a file opened for random access or sequential input has been reached.
FileCopy	Copies a file.
FileClose	Closes a file.
FileDateTime	Returns a Date value that indicates the date and time a file was created or last modified.
FileGet	Returns a record from a random access text file or a binary file.
FileLen	Returns a Long value specifying the size, in bytes, of a file.
FileOpen	Opens a file for input or output.
FilePut	Writes a record to a random access file or a binary file.
FreeFile	Returns an Integer value representing the next available file number for use by the FileOpen function.
GetAttr	Returns a FileAttribute value representing the attributes of a file or directory.
Input	Returns the next field from a delimited text file.
InputString	Retrieves the specified number of characters from a sequential file.
Kill	Deletes one or more files from a disk.
LineInput	Returns the next line of data from a sequential file.
Loc	Returns a Long value indicating the current position within a file.
LOF	Returns a Long value indicating the size, in bytes, of an open file.
Print	Writes the specified output to a sequential file.
PrintLine	Writes the specified output to a sequential file, followed by a carriage return and a line feed.
Seek	Returns a Long value indicating the current read/write position within a file, or sets the position for the next read or write operation.
SetAttr	Sets attribute information for a file.
Write	Writes the specified output to a sequential file, enclosing strings in quotation marks and separating fields with commas.
WriteLine	Writes the specified output to a sequential file, enclosing strings in quotation marks and separating fields with commas, followed by a carriage return and a line feed.

Description

- The Visual Basic 6 statements for file processing have been changed to functions in Visual Basic .NET. You can use these functions along with the other functions for file operations as you work with the data in sequential text files, binary files, and random access files.

Figure 13-13   Visual Basic functions for file operations

Perspective

In this chapter, you learned how to use structures to define custom data types that can be used to identify the individual fields in a record of a file. You also learned a variety of techniques for reading and writing the data in files. With these skills, you should be able to perform the file processing that's required by most of the programs that you're likely to write.

In the next chapter, though, you'll learn how to use XML to work with files. This is a modern method that in some ways makes it easier to work with files. In the future, then, XML files are likely to be used instead of the more traditional text and binary files.

Summary

- A *structure* can be used to create a custom data type that consists of one or more *fields*.

- The Directory, File, and Path classes in the System.IO namespace can be used for managing directories, files, and paths.

- A *text file* contains text characters in fields that are usually delimited by special characters. A *binary file* contains Visual Basic data types.

- I/O exceptions can occur as a program does file operations, and these exceptions can be caught by Try...Catch statements.

- A FileStream object is used to open and close a file. BinaryReader and BinaryWriter objects are used to read and write binary files. And StreamReader and StreamWriter objects are used to read and write text files.

Terms

structure	file I/O	text stream
field	text file	binary stream
record	binary file	random access
input file	stream	sequential access
output file	output stream	
I/O operations	input stream	

Objectives

- Given the specifications for I/O operations that involve text or binary files, write the code for the operations.

- Describe the use of a structure.

- Distinguish between a text file and a binary file.

- Describe the use of a FileStream object.

- Name and describe two common types of I/O exceptions.

- Describe the use of BinaryReader and BinaryWriter objects.

- Describe the use of StreamReader and StreamWriter objects.

Exercise 13-1   Write a binary file

In this exercise, you'll save the Invoice objects that are created by the Invoice application of chapter 6 in a binary file. This will give you a chance to work with the data in business objects instead of the data in structures.

1. Open the Invoice project in the C:\VB.NET\Chapter 13\InvoiceBinary folder. This is a fresh version of the Invoice project of chapter 6. Then, review the code in the form and Invoice classes, and run the application to remind yourself how this application works.

2. Add a method to the Invoice class called WriteInvoice that writes the four properties of each Invoice object to the end of a binary file. The path for the file should be C:\VB.NET\Files\Invoices.dat. The code for this method should open the file, write the properties to it, and close the file. In other words, the file should be opened, written to, and closed each time the method is invoked.

3. Modify the Click procedure for the New Invoice button so it calls the WriteInvoice method before a new invoice is started. Then, test the application by creating from two to five invoices. Note that you can't tell whether it worked or not unless you find the file and open it with a program like NotePad to make sure that it contains data. In exercise 13-2, though, you'll develop a project that reads this file so you can be sure that it has worked correctly.

Exercise 13-2   Read a binary file

In this exercise, you'll read the binary file that you created in exercise 13-1. To save you time, we'll give you the form for the application.

1. Open the InvoiceSummary project in the C:\VB.NET\Chapter 13\ InvoiceSummaryBinary folder. Then, run the application to see that its form looks like this, but without the data:

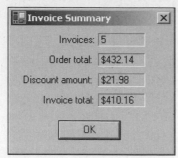

2. Write a load procedure for this form that reads the data from the binary file that you created in exercise 13-1. As it reads each record in the file, this procedure should add one to the invoice count and summarize the three decimal fields. When it finishes reading the records, this procedure should display the invoice count and totals in the labels of the form.

3. Write the code for the OK_Click procedure, which just closes the form. Then, test the application. When you've got it working right, close the project.

Exercise 13-3   Write a text file

This is the same as exercise 13-1, except that you write a text file. This time the starting project is in the C:\VB.NET\Chapter 13\InvoiceText folder. And this time the path for the output file is C:\VB.NET\Files\Invoices.txt. As you write the invoice records, you should separate the fields with pipe characters.

Exercise 13-4   Read a text file

This is the same as exercise 13-2, except that you read the text file you created in exercise 13-3. This time the starting project is in the C:\VB.NET\Chapter 13\InvoiceSummaryText folder.

How to use XML with files

XML is one of the most talked about features of the .NET Framework. Although XML is usually thought of as a way to exchange information in web-based applications, it can also be used to structure data in a text file. In this chapter, you'll learn the basics of creating XML documents. Before you read this chapter, though, you should read chapter 13 so you know how to use traditional text files.

An introduction to XML

The topics that follow introduce you to the basics of XML. Here, you'll learn what XML is and how it is used, the rules you must follow to create a simple XML file, and how to work with XML files in Visual Studio.

What XML is and how it is used

XML, which stands for *Extensible Markup Language*, is a standardized way to structure text information by using *tags* that identify each data element. In some ways, XML is similar to HTML, the markup language that's used to format documents on the World Wide Web. So if you're familiar with HTML, you'll have no trouble learning how to create *XML documents*.

Figure 14-1 shows a simple XML document that contains information about three books. Each book has a code, title, and price. In the next two figures, you'll learn how the tags in this XML document work. But even without knowing those details, you can pick out the code, title, and price for each of the three books represented by this XML document.

XML was designed as a way to structure information that's sent over the World Wide Web. When you use Visual Basic .NET to develop web applications, though, you don't have to deal directly with XML. Instead, the .NET Framework classes handle the XML details for you.

Besides its use for web applications, XML is used internally throughout the .NET Framework to store data and to exchange information between various components of the Framework. In particular, the database features you'll learn about in section 4 rely on XML. When you retrieve information from a database, for example, the .NET Framework converts the database information to XML. But here again, that's done automatically so you don't have to deal with XML directly.

You can also use XML documents as an alternative to the text and binary files that you learned about in chapter 13. In this chapter, for example, you'll learn how to do the same applications with XML documents. This background will also be useful later on when you encounter the XML that's generated for database and web applications.

[handwritten notes:]
- XML HAS NO STD. SET OF ATTRIB.
- ATTRIB VAL ALWAYS STRING
- WHATEVER AFTER = IS ATTRIB.

Data for three books

Code	Title	Price
BVBN	Murach's Beginning Visual Basic .NET	49.50
JAVA	Murach's Beginning Java 2	49.50
ZJCL	Murach's OS/390 and z/OS JCL	62.50

The books.xml document

```xml
<?xml version="1.0" encoding="utf-8" ?>
<!--Book information-->
<Books>
  <Book Code="BVBN">            ⟶ATTRIB
    <Title>Murach's Beginning Visual Basic .NET</Title>  ⟩ ELEM.
    <Price>49.50</Price>
  </Book>
  <Book Code="JAVA">
    <Title>Murach's Beginning Java 2</Title>
    <Price>49.50</Price>
  </Book>
  <Book Code="ZJCL">
    <Title>Murach's OS/390 and z/OS JCL</Title>
    <Price>62.50</Price>
  </Book>
</Books>
```

Description

- *XML*, which stands for *Extensible Markup Language*, is a method of structuring information in a text file using special *tags*. A file that contains XML is known as an *XML document*.

- The XML document in this figure contains information for three books. Each book has an *attribute* called Code and *elements* called Title and Price, which you'll learn more about in the next two figures.

- XML's main use is for exchanging information between different systems, especially via the Internet.

- Many .NET classes, particularly the database and web classes, use XML internally to store or exchange information.

- XML can also be used as an alternative to binary files, delimited text files, or even database systems for storing information.

- When XML is stored in a file, the file name usually has the extension *xml* to indicate that the file contains XML.

- The .NET Framework includes several classes that let you create and read XML data. These classes are in the System.Xml namespace.

Figure 14-1　What XML is and how it is used

XML tags, declarations, and comments

Figure 14-2 shows how XML uses tags to structure the data in an XML document. As you can see, each XML tag begins with the character < and ends with the character >, so the first line in the XML document in this figure contains a complete XML tag. Similarly, the next three lines also contain complete tags. In contrast, the fifth line contains two tags, <Title> and </Title>, with a text value in between. You'll see how this works in a moment.

The first tag in any XML document is an *XML declaration.* This declaration identifies the document as an XML document and indicates which XML version the document conforms to. In this example, the document conforms to XML version 1.0. In addition, the declaration usually identifies the character set that's being used for the document. In this example, the character set is UTF-8, the most common one used for XML documents in English-speaking countries.

An XML document can also contain comments. These are tags that begin with <!-- and end with -->. Between the tags, you can type anything you want. For instance, the second line in this figure is a comment that indicates what type of information is contained in the XML document. It's often a good idea to include similar comments in your own XML documents.

XML elements

Elements are the building blocks of XML. Each element in an XML document represents a single data item and is identified by two tags: a *start tag* and an *end tag*. The start tag marks the beginning of the element and provides the element's name. The end tag marks the end of the element and repeats the name, prefixed by a slash. For example, <Title> is the start tag for an element named Title, and </Title> is the corresponding end tag.

It's important to realize that XML does not provide a pre-defined set of element names the way HTML does. Instead, you create your own element names to describe the contents of each element. Since XML names are case-sensitive, <Book> and <book> are not the same.

A complete element consists of the element's start tag, its end tag, and any *content* between the tags. For example, <Price>49.50</Price> indicates that the content of the Price element is 49.50. And <Title>Murach's Beginning Java 2 </Title> indicates that the content of the Title element is *Murach's Beginning Java 2.*

Besides content, elements can contain other elements, known as *child elements*. This lets you add structure to a *parent element*. For example, a parent book element can have child elements that provide details about each book, such as the book's title and price. In this figure, for example, you can see that the start tag, end tag, and values for the Title and Price elements are contained between the start and end tags for the Book element. As a result, Title and Price are children of the Book element, and the Book element is the parent of both the Title and Price elements.

As the XML document in figure 14-1 shows, an element can occur more than once within an XML document. In this case, the document has three Book

An XML document

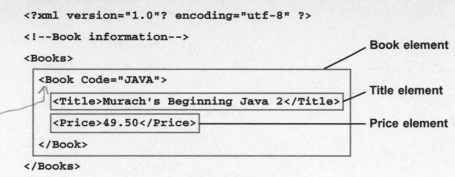

```
<?xml version="1.0"? encoding="utf-8" ?>

<!--Book information-->

<Books>

   <Book Code="JAVA">
      <Title>Murach's Beginning Java 2</Title>
      <Price>49.50</Price>
   </Book>

</Books>
```

Book element

Title element

Price element

Tags, XML declarations, and comments

- Each XML tag begins with < and ends with >.

- The first line in an XML document is an *XML declaration* that indicates which version of the XML standard is being used for the document. In addition, the declaration usually identifies the standard character set that's being used (UTF-8 is the character set that's commonly used for XML documents in English-speaking countries).

- You can include comments to clarify the information in an XML document. Comments begin with the sequence <!-- and end with -->.

Elements

- An *element* is a unit of XML data that begins with a *start tag* and ends with an *end tag*. The start tag provides the name of the element and contains any attributes assigned to the element (see figure 14-3 for details on attributes). The end tag repeats the name, prefixed with a slash (/). You can use any name you want for an XML element.

- The text between an element's start and end tags is called the element's *content*. For example, <Title>Murach's Beginning Java 2</Title> indicates that the content of the Title element is the string *Murach's Beginning Java 2*.

- Elements can contain other elements. An element that's contained within another element is known as a *child element*. The element that contains a child element is known as the child's *parent element*.

- Child elements can repeat within a parent element. For instance, in the example above, the Books element can contain more than one Book element. (Although it isn't likely, each Book element can also contain more than one Title or Price element.)

- The highest-level parent element in an XML document is known as the *root element*. An XML document can have only one root element.

Figure 14-2   XML tags, declarations, comments, and elements

elements, each representing a book. Since each of these Book elements contains Title and Price elements, these elements also appear three times in the document.

Although this example doesn't show it, a given child element can also occur more than once within a parent. For example, suppose you want to provide for books that have more than one author. You could do this by using an Author child element to indicate the author of a book. Then, for a book that has two authors, you simply include two Author child elements within the Book element for that book.

The highest-level parent element in an XML document is known as the *root element*, and an XML document can have only one root element. In the examples in figures 14-1 and 14-2, the root element is Books. For XML documents that contain repeating information, it is common to use a plural name for the root element to indicate that it contains multiple child elements.

XML attributes

As shown in figure 14-3, *attributes* are a concise way to provide data for XML elements. In the books XML document, for example, each Book element has a Code attribute that provides an identifying code for the book. Thus, <Book Code="JAVA"> contains an attribute named Code whose value is JAVA.

Here again, XML doesn't provide a set of pre-defined attributes. Instead, you create attributes as you need them, using names that describe the content of the attributes. If an element has more than one attribute, you can list the attributes in any order you wish. Just separate the attributes from each other with one or more spaces. Note, however, that each attribute can appear only once within an element.

When you plan the layout of an XML document, you will often need to decide whether to use elements or attributes to represent each data item. In many cases, either one will work. In the books document, for example, I could have used a child element named Code rather than an attribute to represent each book's code. Likewise, I could have used an attribute named Title rather than a child element for the book's title.

Because attributes are more concise than child elements, it's often tempting to use attributes rather than child elements. Keep in mind, though, that an element with more than a few attributes soon becomes unwieldy. As a result, most designers limit their use of attributes to certain types of information, such as identifiers like book codes or customer numbers.

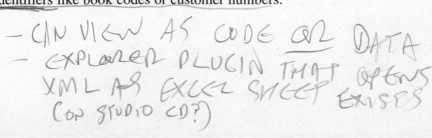

An XML document

```
<?xml version="1.0" encoding="utf-8" ?>

<!--Book information-->

<Books>

  <Book Code="JAVA">———————————————————————— Code attribute

    <Title>Murach's Beginning Java 2</Title>

    <Price>49.50</Price>

  </Book>

</Books>
```

Description

* You can include one or more *attributes* in the start tag for an element. An attribute consists of an attribute name, an equal sign, and a string value in quotes.

* If an element has more than one attribute, the order in which the attributes appear doesn't matter, but the attributes must be separated by one or more spaces.

When to use attributes instead of child elements

* When you design an XML document, you can use either child elements or attributes to represent the data for an element. The choice of whether to implement a data item as an attribute or as a separate child element is often a matter of preference.

* Two advantages of attributes are that they can appear in any order and they are more concise because they do not require end tags.

* Two advantages of child elements are that they are easier for people to read and they are more convenient for long string values.

Figure 14-3   XML attributes

How to work with an XML document in Visual Studio

To create or edit an XML document, you can use the *XML Designer* that comes with Visual Studio as shown in figure 14-4. To create a new XML file and add it to your project, you can use the Project → Add New Item command. To open an existing XML document without adding the file to your project, you can use the File → Open command. Either way, the document is opened in the XML Designer window.

When you use Visual Studio to create a new XML document, the XML declaration is added to the start of the document automatically. As you can see, the declaration in this example includes both the XML version attribute and the encoding attribute that indicates which character set the document uses. Unless you're working in a language other than English, you'll want to leave this attribute set to UTF-8.

When you work in the XML Designer window, the task of editing XML documents is simplified. Tags, content, attributes, values, and comments are color-coded so you can easily tell them apart. When you type a start tag, the XML editor automatically adds the end tag and positions the cursor between the start and end tags. To add a child element, you just press the Enter key, press the Tab key to indent the child element, and type the start tag. And so on. If you work with the XML Designer for a while, you'll quickly see how easy it is to use.

An XML document in the XML Designer window

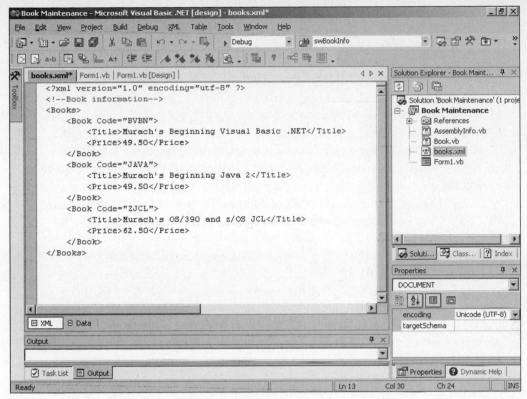

How to add an XML document to a project

- Choose the Project → Add New Item command. In the Add New Item dialog box, select XML document in the Templates box; type a name for the XML document in the Name text box; and click Open. This adds an XML document to your project, opens the document in the XML Designer window, and adds the XML declaration for the document.

How to open an existing XML document

- Use the File → Open command to open an existing XML document without adding the document to your project.

How to edit an XML document in Visual Studio

- When you type a start tag, Visual Studio automatically adds an end tag for the element and positions the insertion point between the start and end tags so you can type the element's content.
- When you type an attribute, Visual Studio automatically adds a pair of quotation marks and positions the insertion point between them so you can type the attribute value.

Figure 14-4   How to work with an XML document in Visual Studio

How to work with an XML document in Data view

Another feature of the XML Designer is its Data view, which is shown in figure 14-5. This view lets you work with XML data in a table that resembles a spreadsheet. To activate Data view, you just click the Data button that's located at the bottom left of the XML Designer window.

When you switch to Data view, the XML Designer examines the XML document's structure to determine the best way to present it in a data table. For simple XML documents such as the ones used in this chapter, the entire table represents the root element. Then, each row in the grid represents one of the root element's children, and the children and attributes of those elements appear as columns.

In this example, then, the table itself represents the Books element. Each row in the table represents one Book element. And the columns represent the Title and Price elements and the Code attribute. In this case, the Title and Price columns appear before the Code attribute because the XML Designer shows child elements before attributes.

Once the document is in Data view, you can change its data by editing the contents of the cells in the data table. For example, to change one of the Book elements, just click the appropriate Title, Price, or Code cell in the table and enter a new value. To delete a Book element, click the box to the left of the row and press the Delete key. And to add a new Book element, just enter the new values for the columns in the last row of the table.

When you switch back to XML view by clicking the XML button at the bottom of the Designer window, you'll see that the XML has been automatically updated to reflect any changes you made to the data. If you deleted a row, that row's Book element is deleted from the XML. And if you added a new row, a new Book element is added to the XML.

The real benefit of the Data view is that it lets you create an XML document by typing a minimum of XML. If, for example, you need to create an XML document that contains 50 Book elements, you start by typing the XML for just one Book element. Then, you switch to Data view and use the data table to enter the data for the rest of the Book elements. It's that easy.

An XML document in Data view

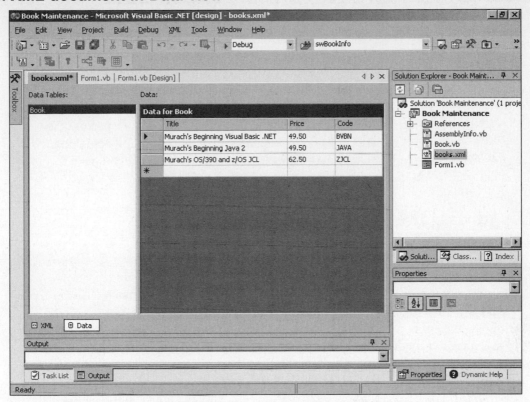

Description

- When you click the Data button at the bottom of an XML Designer window, Visual Studio displays the contents of the XML document as a data table.

- In this example, the entire table represents the Books element. Each Book element is presented as a row. The Title and Price elements and the Code attribute appear as columns.

- To modify any of the elements in the XML document, enter new values in the appropriate columns.

- To add a new row to the XML document, enter values for the columns in the bottom row of the table.

- To delete a row from the XML document, select the row by clicking the box to the left of it, then press the Delete key.

- You can return to the XML source by clicking the XML button at the bottom left of the XML Designer window. When you do, you'll see that the document's XML has been updated to reflect any changes you made.

Figure 14-5   How to work with an XML document in Data view

How to use the XML text classes

In all, the .NET Framework provides nearly 150 different classes for working with XML documents. Fortunately, you don't need to know them all. In this topic, I'll get you started with XML programming by introducing you to two classes. These are the classes that provide the basic services you need to write and read XML documents.

Note that both of these classes reside in the System.Xml namespace. As a result, you should include an Imports System.Xml statement at the beginning of any Visual Basic application that uses either of them. Otherwise, you have to qualify the class names each time you refer to them.

How to use the XmlTextWriter class

If you wanted to, you could use the StreamWriter class that was presented in chapter 13 to create XML files. All you would have to do is build string variables that contain the correct XML tags, and then use the StreamWriter class to write the string variables to a text file.

To make that easier, though, the XmlTextWriter class that's shown in figure 14-6 provides methods that generate the correct XML tags automatically. That way, you don't have to worry about the formatting details. Instead, you can concentrate on the document's structure and content.

When you create a new XmlTextWriter object, you supply two arguments: the filename and the type of encoding to use. Usually, you pass the filename as a string variable that includes the path, and you set the encoding argument to Nothing so the XmlTextWriter uses default encoding (UTF-8). Note that if the file you specify already exists, it's deleted and recreated. So you can't use this technique to add XML to an existing file.

Before you code any statements that write XML, I recommend that you set the XmlTextWriter's Formatting property to Formatting.Indented. That way, the XmlTextWriter will use spaces to indent child elements. This will make your XML files easier to read.

To write XML data, you use one of the Write methods of the XmlTextWriter class. Although this class actually has 27 Write methods, you can create basic XML documents using just the six Write methods in this figure.

To write an XML declaration, you use the WriteStartDocument method. Since this declaration should be the first line in any XML document, you should use this method before you use any of the other Write methods. Similarly, to write a comment to an XML document, you use the WriteComment method. For the argument, you can include any string.

To write a start tag, you use the WriteStartElement method with the name of the element as a string argument. Then, you use the WriteEndElement method without an argument to write the element's end tag.

To write an attribute value, you first use the WriteStartElement method to write the element's start tag. Then, you use the WriteAttributeString method to

The basic syntax for creating a new XmlTextWriter object

```
New XmlTextWriter(filename, encoding)
```

Common properties and methods of the XmlTextWriter class

Property	Description
Formatting	Specifies whether the XmlTextWriter should use indentation to format the XML output. Set to Formatting.Indented if you want indentation.

Method	Description
WriteStartDocument	Writes an XML declaration line at the beginning of a document.
WriteComment(comment)	Writes a comment to the XML document.
WriteStartElement(elementName)	Writes a start tag using the element name you provide.
WriteAttributeString(attributeName, value)	Adds an attribute to the current element.
WriteEndElement	Writes an end tag for the current element.
WriteElementString(elementName, content)	Writes a complete element including a start tag, content, and end tag.
Close	Closes the XmlTextWriter object.

Description

- The XmlTextWriter class lets you write XML data to a text file. If the Formatting property is set to Formatting.Indented, the XmlTextWriter will use indentation to indicate the structure of the information.

- When you create a new instance of the XmlTextWriter class, you specify the name or path of the file where you want to write the XML. If the file already exists, it's deleted and then recreated.

- You also specify the encoding scheme that the document will use when you create an XmlTextWriter object. In most cases, you can specify Nothing for this argument to use UTF-8 encoding.

- To write a single start tag or end tag, use the WriteStartElement or WriteEndElement method. To write a start tag, value, and end tag in a single operation, use the WriteElementString method.

- To write an attribute, first use the WriteStartElement method to write the start tag. Then, use the WriteAttributeString method to write the attribute value.

- The XmlTextWriter class is part of the System.Xml namespace, so your code should include an Imports statement to refer to this namespace.

- If you attempt to create an invalid XML document, an XmlException will be thrown. For example, an XmlException will be thrown if you try to write two XML declarations or if you try to write an end tag before you've written a start tag.

Figure 14-6   How to use the XmlTextWriter class

add an attribute to the start tag. In the WriteAttributeString method, you supply the name of the attribute and the attribute value as arguments.

To create an element that has content but not child elements, you use the WriteElementString method. This method writes a start tag, the content, and an end tag using the name and content values you pass as arguments.

Notice that you don't need to use a WriteStartElement or WriteEndElement method to create a content element that doesn't have children because the WriteElementString method automatically creates the start and end tags. That means you only need to use the WriteStartElement and WriteEndElement methods to create an element that has children. In that case, you use the WriteStartElement method to create the element's start tag; you write the child elements; and you use a WriteEndElement method to write the parent element's end tag.

Code that writes an XML document

Figure 14-7 shows a procedure that creates an XML document like the one that's in figure 14-1. This procedure gets its data from an ArrayList collection of books. The information for each book is stored using a structure called BookInformation. This structure has three members: Code, Title, and Price.

Since the operation of this procedure is straightforward, you shouldn't have any trouble understanding how it works. The heart of the procedure is the For Each loop that writes a Book element for each book in the array list. To write a Book element, the procedure uses the WriteStartElement method to write the start tag for the Book element, and then uses the WriteAttributeString method to add the Code attribute. Next, two WriteElementString methods are used to write the Title and Price elements. Finally, the WriteEndElement method is used to write the end tag for the Book element.

Please notice that the For Each loop is preceded by a WriteStartElement method that writes the start tag for the document's root element. And a WriteEndElement method writes the end tag for the root element after the For Each loop. Then, the Close method is used to close the XmlTextWriter object.

You should also notice how the variable for the path of the XML document is coded:

```
Dim sBookPath As String = "..\books.xml"
```

Here, two dots are used to represent the parent directory of the program that's running. This works when the XML document is part of the project. Of course, you can also code an explicit path for the string variable like this:

```
Dim sBookPath As String = "C:\VB.NET\Files\books.xml"
```

An explicit path works whether or not the XML document is part of the project.

Code that writes the books XML document

```
Structure BookInformation
    Dim Code As String
    Dim Title As String
    Dim Price As Decimal
End Structure

Dim Book As BookInformation
Dim Books As New ArrayList()
Dim sBookPath As String = "..\books.xml"
    .
    .
Private Sub SaveBooks()
    Dim BookWriter As New XmlTextWriter(sBookPath, Nothing)
    BookWriter.Formatting = Formatting.Indented
    BookWriter.WriteStartDocument()
    BookWriter.WriteStartElement("Books")
    For Each Book In Books
        BookWriter.WriteStartElement("Book")
        BookWriter.WriteAttributeString("Code", Book.Code)
        BookWriter.WriteElementString("Title", Book.Title)
        BookWriter.WriteElementString("Price", Book.Price)
        BookWriter.WriteEndElement()
    Next
    BookWriter.WriteEndElement()
    BookWriter.Close()
End Sub
```

Description

- This example saves an array list of Book structures as an XML document. The resulting XML document will be like the one in figure 14-1.

- To set the path for an XML file in the current project, you can use two dots to refer to the parent directory as in:

  `"..\books.xml"`

  This works because the current project is run from the Bin directory, which is the child of the project directory. Of course, you can also use an explicit path.

- After the Dim statement creates the XML document and the Formatting property is set to use indentation, the WriteStartDocument method adds an XML declaration line to the beginning of the document, and a WriteStartElement method is used to write the start tag for the root element, Books.

- The For Each loop writes the XML attribute and elements for each Book in the Books array list.

- After the For Each loop, a WriteEndElement method writes the end tag for Books, the root element. Then, a Close method is used to close the XmlTextWriter object.

Figure 14-7   Code that writes an XML document

How to use the XmlTextReader class

To read an XML document, you can use the XmlTextReader class that's summarized in figure 14-8. In this case, you just supply the name of the XML file as a string when you create a new XmlTextReader object.

Before your code starts reading XML data, you should set the WhitespaceHandling property of the XmlTextReader object to indicate how you want white space handled. *White space* refers to spaces, tabs, and return characters that affect the appearance but not the meaning of an XML document. To simplify the task of processing XML data, you can set this property to WhitespaceHandling.None. This tells the XmlTextReader class to automatically skip over white space in the XML document, so you don't have to write code to deal with it.

Then, to read data from an XML document, you use the various Read methods of the XmlTextReader class. This class treats an XML document as a series of *nodes*, and you can use the basic Read method to read the next node from the file. Because the concept of nodes is so important to reading XML data, the next figure describes them in detail and walks you through the process of reading a simple XML document node-by-node. For now, just realize that every tag in an XML document is treated as a separate node, and each element's content is also treated as a separate node. Attributes, however, are not treated as separate nodes. Instead, an attribute is a part of the node that represents the start tag that contains it.

When you invoke the Read method, the XmlTextReader gets the next node from the XML document and makes that node the *current node*. Then, you can use the XmlTextReader's NodeType, Name, or Value property to retrieve the node's type, name, or value. If you read past the last node in the document, the EOF property is set to True so you can use that to tell when you have reached the end of the file.

In fact, you can process an entire XML document by using just the Read method to read the document's nodes one at a time, by using the NodeType property to determine what type of node has just been read, and by taking appropriate action based on the node type. However, the XmlTextReader has several other methods that simplify the task of dealing with common node types.

The ReadStartElement method starts by confirming that the current node is a start tag. If it is, the method checks to make sure that the name of the start tag matches the name you supply as an argument. If both of these conditions are met, the method then reads the next element. Otherwise, an XmlException is thrown.

The ReadEndElement method is similar, but it checks to make sure the current node is an end tag rather than a start tag, and it doesn't check the element name. If the current node is an end tag, the ReadEndElement method reads the next node. Otherwise, it throws an XmlException.

The ReadElementString method reads content from a simple content element (that is, an element that has content but no child elements). It skips

The basic syntax for creating a new XmlTextReader object

```
New XmlTextReader(filename)
```

Common properties and methods of the XmlTextReader class

Property	Description
WhitespaceHandling	Specifies how the XmlTextReader should handle white space in the XML input. Specify WhitespaceHandling.None to have the XmlTextReader automatically ignore all white space.
NodeType	Gets the type of the current node. Returns a member of the XmlNodeType enumeration.
Name	Gets the name of the current node, if the node has a name.
Value	Gets the value of the current node, if the node has a value.
Item(attributeName)	Gets the value of the specified attribute. Returns an empty string if the current element does not have the attribute.
EOF	True if the XmlTextReader has reached the end of the input.

Method	Description
Close	Closes the XML input file.
Read	Reads the next node.
ReadStartElement(name)	Checks that the current node is a start tag with the specified name, then advances to the next node. An XmlException is thrown if the current node is not a start tag with the specified name.
ReadEndElement	Checks that the current node is an end tag, then advances to the next node. An XmlException is thrown if the current node is not an end tag.
ReadElementString(name)	Reads to the next start tag, checks that the name of the element matches the name specified, then reads the element content and returns it as a string value. An XmlException is thrown if the next element does not match the specified name or if the element does not have simple content.

Description

- The XmlTextReader class lets you read the contents of an XML document one *node* at a time.
- Spaces, tabs, and return characters (known as *white space*) are treated as nodes unless you specify that white space should be ignored by setting the WhitespaceHandling property to WhitespaceHandling.None.
- When you create a new instance of the XmlTextReader class, you can pass the name of the file that contains the XML.
- The various Read methods retrieve input data or verify that the current node is a particular type, then advance the XmlTextReader to the next node.
- You use the Item property to retrieve the value of an attribute. Specify the name of the attribute as a string argument. If the attribute doesn't exist, the Item property returns an empty string.
- The XmlTextReader class is part of the System.Xml namespace, so your code should include an Imports statement to refer to this namespace.

Figure 14-8   How to use the XmlTextReader class

forward over as many nodes as necessary until it reaches a start tag, then confirms that the name of the tag matches the name you supply. If it does, this method reads the element's content node and returns it as a string value. But if the element name doesn't match the name you supply or if the element contains child elements rather than simple content, an XmlException is thrown.

What about attributes? You don't use a separate Read method to retrieve attribute values. Instead, whenever the current node has attributes, you can access those attributes via the Item property. To do that, you supply the name of the attribute as a string argument. To retrieve the Code attribute, for example, use Item("Code").

How the XmlTextReader class reads nodes

To use the XmlTextReader class properly, you need to understand exactly how it reads nodes. To help you with that, figure 14-9 presents a simple XML document and lists all of the nodes contained in that document. Even though this document contains just one Book element with two child elements, there are 12 nodes.

By studying this figure, you can see how the methods of the XmlTextReader class read the nodes. The first node is the XML declaration tag. The second node is the comment. The third node is the start tag for the Books element. And so on.

Notice that when the start tag for the Book element is reached, the Code attribute is available via the Item property. Also notice that the Title and Price child elements each use three nodes: one for the start tag, one for the content, and one for the end tag.

An XML document

XML — NO PREDEF. TAGS

```
<?xml version="1.0">
<!--Book information-->
<Books>
  <Book Code="JAVA">        ← MUST HAVE " "
    <Title>Murach's Beginning Java 2</Title>
    <Price>49.50</Price>
  </Book>
</Books>
```

The XML nodes in the sample document

NodeType	Name	Other properties
XmlDeclaration	xml	
Comment		Value = "Book information"
Element	Books	
Element	Book	Item("Code") = "JAVA"
Element	Title	
Text		Value = "Murach's Beginning Java 2"
EndElement	Title	
Element	Price	
Text		Value = "49.50"
EndElement	Price	
EndElement	Book	
EndElement	Books	

Description

- For the XML declaration and each comment, the XmlTextReader class parses one node.
- For each element without content (usually, a parent element), the XmlTextReader class parses two nodes: an Element node for the start tag and an EndElement node for the end tag.
- For each element with content, the XmlTextReader class parses three nodes: an Element node for the element's start tag, a Text node for the element's text value, and an EndElement node for the element's end tag.
- If an element contains an attribute, the attribute is available via the Item property when the Element node for the element is read.

Notes

- This example assumes that the WhitespaceHandling.None property has been set, so white space is ignored.
- The NodeType, Name, Value, and Item values shown in the table above correspond to the XmlTextReader NodeType, Name, Value, and Item properties.

Figure 14-9   How the XmlTextReader class reads nodes

Code that reads an XML document

Figure 14-10 shows a function that loads the contents of the books document presented back in figure 14-1 into an ArrayList collection of Book objects. I coded this procedure as a function rather than a Sub procedure so it can return True or False to indicate whether the XML document was loaded successfully. Then, the program can proceed accordingly.

The first line of this function creates a new instance of the XmlTextReader class to read the books.xml file, which is in the parent directory. This implies that the file is stored in the project. Then, the second line says that the methods for this object should ignore white space.

After that, a Do Until loop is used to read over any lines in the XML file that occur before the first Book element. When this Do loop finishes, the current node will be the first node in the file whose name is Book. In other words, the current node will be the start tag for the first Book element.

Next, a Do While loop is used to read and process the data for each Book element in the file. This loop begins by using the Item property to retrieve the value of the Code attribute. This works because the Do loop always begins with the XmlTextReader positioned at the start tag for the Book element. After it gets this Code attribute, the loop uses the ReadStartElement method to read the next node, which is the Title element's start tag. Although I could have used a simple Read method here, the ReadStartElement ensures that the XmlTextReader is actually on the Book element before proceeding.

A ReadElementString method then retrieves the content of the Title element, and another ReadElementString method retrieves the content of the Price element. At this point, the reader is positioned at the end tag for the Price element, so a ReadEndElement method reads past that node to the next node. Then, since all the information for the Book element has been read, the procedure adds the book to the Books array list.

If the XML document contains another Book element, the current node will be the start tag for the next Book element, so the Name property will be Book and the loop will repeat. However, if the last Book element has been read, the current node will be the end tag for the Books element, so the loop will end because the Name property will be Books, not Book. In that case, the Close method is called to close the reader object.

If there are errors in the XML document, an XmlException will be thrown by one of the Read methods in the procedure. To catch this type of error, the code that reads the XML document is enclosed in a Try...Catch statement. In this case, the Catch clause catches the XmlException, displays an error message, and returns False to indicate that the function was not able to load the XML document. Otherwise, the statement after the Try...Catch statement sets the return value to True.

Code that reads the books XML document

```
Structure BookInformation
    Dim Code As String
    Dim Title As String
    Dim Price As Decimal
End Structure

Dim Book As BookInformation
Dim Books As New ArrayList()
Dim sBookPath As String = "..\books.xml"
.
.
Private Function BooksLoaded() As Boolean
    Dim BookReader As New XmlTextReader(sBookPath)
    BookReader.WhitespaceHandling = WhitespaceHandling.None
    Try
        Do Until BookReader.Name = "Book"
            BookReader.Read()
        Loop
        Do While BookReader.Name = "Book"
            Book.Code = BookReader.Item("Code")
            BookReader.ReadStartElement("Book")
            Book.Title = BookReader.ReadElementString("Title")
            Book.Price = BookReader.ReadElementString("Price")
            BookReader.ReadEndElement()
            Books.Add(Book)
        Loop
        BookReader.Close()
    Catch exml As XmlException
        MessageBox.Show("There is an error in the XML file.", "XML Error")
        Return False
    End Try
    Return True
End Function
```

(handwritten annotations:) TO PASS COMMENTS, ETC.; NOT MOVING HERE TO NEXT LINE SO...; TO VERIFY END; ADD TO ARR. LIST

Description

- This example loads the XML document in figure 14-1 into an array list of Book structures.

- To set the path for an XML file in the current project, you can use two dots to refer to the parent directory. Or, you can use an explicit path.

- The code that reads the XML document is enclosed in a Try...Catch statement that catches any XmlExceptions that the XmlTextReader might throw. For simplicity, the Catch clause just displays an error message.

- The Do Until loop reads nodes from the XML document until the first Book element is reached. This code skips over the XML declaration, the comment, and the root Books node.

- The Do While loop processes each Book element. For each Book element, the values for the Code attribute and the Title and Price elements are retrieved. Then, the book is added to the Books array list.

Figure 14-10   Code that reads an XML document

(handwritten:) READ ATTRIB.

An XML application

Now that you understand how to use the XmlTextWriter and XmlTextReader classes, you're ready to see a complete application that uses them. This application is an XML version of the Book Maintenance application that was presented in chapter 13, so you should already be familiar it.

The design and property settings for the Book Maintenance form

Figure 14-11 presents the design and property settings for the Book Maintenance application. This application uses a single form that lets the user update the code, title, or price for books stored in an XML document. This document is like the documents you've seen throughout this chapter.

When the user selects a book title from the combo box, the text boxes are filled with the information for that book. Then, if the user changes any of the information, the Update and Cancel buttons are enabled so the user can click Update to record the changes or Cancel to cancel the changes.

When the user clicks the Update button, though, the changes aren't actually saved in the XML document. Instead, they are saved in an array list. Then, when the user clicks the Save & Exit button to end the session, the books in the array list are written to the XML document.

The Book Maintenance form

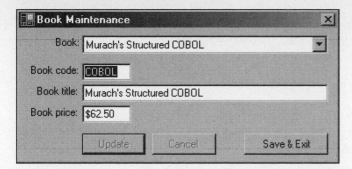

The property settings for the form's controls

Default name	Name	Property	Setting
ComboBox1	cboBooks	DropDownStyle	DropDownList
		Sorted	True
TextBox1	txtBookCode		
TextBox2	txtBookTitle		
TextBox3	txtBookPrice		
Button1	btnUpdate	Text	&Update
Button2	btnCancel	Text	&Cancel
Button3	btnSaveAndExit	Text	&Save && Exit

Description

- This Book Maintenance form lets the user modify existing information in an XML document that contains book information.

- The user can select the book to be modified from the combo box at the top of the form. Then, the data for that book is displayed in the text boxes on the form.

- If the user changes any of the data for a book, the Update and Cancel buttons become enabled. Then, the user can save the changes by clicking the Update button or cancel the changes by clicking the Cancel button. When the user clicks Update or Cancel, the Update and Cancel buttons are disabled.

- To save the changes back to the XML document and close the form, the user clicks the Save & Exit button.

Figure 14-11   The design and property settings for the Book Maintenance form

The code for the Book Maintenance form

Figure 14-12 shows the code for the Book Maintenance application. Because two versions of this application were presented in chapter 13, you shouldn't have much trouble following it. But here's a brief description.

To start, the code for this class defines the BookInformation structure. Then, it declares a Book variable for the structure, a Books variable for an array list, and a string variable for the path of the XML document. This time, the path for the document is coded explicitly.

The Load procedure for the form calls a function named BooksLoaded. This function is identical to the one presented in figure 14-10. It uses the XmlTextReader class to read the XML document and loads an ArrayList object to hold the book information.

The BooksLoaded function returns a Boolean value that indicates whether or not the books in the XML document were successfully loaded into the array list. If this function returns True, the Load procedure loads the combo box (cboBooks) with the title of each book and disables the Update and Cancel buttons. If this function returns False, the Load procedure simply closes the form to end the application.

The Visual Basic code for processing an XML document   Page 1

```
Imports System.Xml
Public Class Form1
    Inherits System.Windows.Forms.Form

    Structure BookInformation
        Dim Code As String
        Dim Title As String
        Dim Price As Decimal
    End Structure

    Dim Book As BookInformation
    Dim Books As New ArrayList()
    Dim sBookPath As String = "C:\VB.NET\Files\books.xml"

    Private Sub Form1_Load(ByVal sender As Object, _
            ByVal e As System.EventArgs) Handles MyBase.Load
        If BooksLoaded() Then
            For Each Book In Books
                cboBooks.Items.Add(Book.Title)
            Next
            btnUpdate.Enabled = False
            btnCancel.Enabled = False
        Else
            Me.Close()
        End If
    End Sub

    Private Function BooksLoaded() As Boolean
        Dim BookReader As New XmlTextReader(sBookPath)
        BookReader.WhitespaceHandling = WhitespaceHandling.None
        Try
            Do Until BookReader.Name = "Book"
                BookReader.Read()
            Loop
            Do While BookReader.Name = "Book"
                Book.Code = BookReader.Item("Code")
                BookReader.ReadStartElement("Book")
                Book.Title = BookReader.ReadElementString("Title")
                Book.Price = BookReader.ReadElementString("Price")
                BookReader.ReadEndElement()
                Books.Add(Book)
            Loop
            BookReader.Close()
        Catch exml As XmlException
            MessageBox.Show("There is an error in the XML file.", "XML Error")
            Return False
        End Try
        Return True
    End Function
```

Figure 14-12   The code for the Book Maintenance form (part 1 of 2)

On page 2, you can see the procedures for handling the user events. In particular, when the user clicks the Save & Exit button, the Click event procedure calls the SaveBooks procedure to rewrite the XML document. Then, it closes the form to end the application.

The SaveBooks procedure is identical to the procedure that was shown in figure 14-7. It uses the XmlTextWriter properties and methods to save an XML file that contains one Book element for each book in the array list. This new file overwrites the existing XML file each time the application is run.

The Visual Basic code for processing an XML document   **Page 2**

```vb
Private Sub cboBooks_SelectedIndexChanged(ByVal sender As System.Object, _
        ByVal e As System.EventArgs) _
        Handles cboBooks.SelectedIndexChanged, btnCancel.Click
    Book = Books.Item(cboBooks.SelectedIndex)
    txtBookCode.Text = Book.Code
    txtBookTitle.Text = Book.Title
    txtBookPrice.Text = FormatCurrency(Book.Price)
    btnUpdate.Enabled = False
    btnCancel.Enabled = False
    cboBooks.Enabled = True
    txtBookCode.Focus()
End Sub

Private Sub Control_TextChanged(ByVal sender As Object, _
        ByVal e As System.EventArgs) Handles txtBookCode.TextChanged, _
        txtBookTitle.TextChanged, txtBookPrice.TextChanged
    btnUpdate.Enabled = True
    btnCancel.Enabled = True
End Sub

Private Sub btnUpdate_Click(ByVal sender As System.Object, _
        ByVal e As System.EventArgs) Handles btnUpdate.Click
    Book.Code = txtBookCode.Text
    Book.Title = txtBookTitle.Text
    Book.Price = txtBookPrice.Text
    Books.Item(cboBooks.SelectedIndex) = Book
    cboBooks.Items.Item(cboBooks.SelectedIndex) = txtBookTitle.Text
    btnUpdate.Enabled = False
    btnCancel.Enabled = False
    cboBooks.Focus()
End Sub

Private Sub btnSaveAndExit_Click(ByVal sender As System.Object, _
        ByVal e As System.EventArgs) Handles btnSaveAndExit.Click
    SaveBooks()
    Me.Close()
End Sub

Private Sub SaveBooks()
    Dim BookWriter As New XmlTextWriter(sBookPath, Nothing)
    BookWriter.Formatting = Formatting.Indented
    BookWriter.WriteStartDocument()
    BookWriter.WriteStartElement("Books")
    For Each Book In Books
        BookWriter.WriteStartElement("Book")
        BookWriter.WriteAttributeString("Code", Book.Code)
        BookWriter.WriteElementString("Title", Book.Title)
        BookWriter.WriteElementString("Price", Book.Price)
        BookWriter.WriteEndElement()
    Next
    BookWriter.WriteEndElement()
    BookWriter.Close()
End Sub
```

Figure 14-12   The code for the Book Maintenance form (part 2 of 2)

Perspective

In this chapter, you've learned the basics of reading and writing XML documents using the XmlTextReader and XmlTextWriter classes. With these skills, you should be able to incorporate simple XML documents into your applications. You'll also have a better appreciation for the way XML is used internally by the database and web applications that you'll learn about in sections 4 and 5.

Please keep in mind, though, that this is just an introduction to XML, and there are many other XML features that I haven't presented here. For example, you can use *XML schemas* to define the layout for an XML file. Then, you can use .NET classes to make sure an XML document conforms to its schema. Another important XML feature is *DOM*, which stands for *Document Object Model*. When you use DOM, an entire XML document is represented as a single XmlDocument object with property collections that represent the XML document's nodes. Before you master XML, then, there's a lot more to learn.

Summary

- *XML* provides a standardized way to structure information in a text file by using *tags* that identify data items.

- An *element* begins with a *start tag* and ends with an *end tag*. An element can contain data in the form of *content* that appears between the tags. It can also contain *child elements*.

- An *attribute* is a name and value that appears within an element's start tag.

- You can use Visual Studio's XML Designer to edit XML data.

- You can use the XmlTextWriter and XmlTextReader classes to write and read XML data. These classes are found in the System.Xml namespace.

Terms

XML (Extensible Markup Language)	child element
tag	parent element
XML document	root element
XML declaration	attribute
element	XML Designer
start tag	white space
end tag	node
content	current node

Objectives

- Use the XmlTextWriter class to write an XML document.

- Use the XmlTextReader class to read an XML document.

- Use the XML Designer to create and edit a new XML document in a project.

- In simple XML documents like the ones in this chapter, identify the following: tags, XML declarations, start tags, end tags, element content, root elements, parent elements, child elements, attributes, and comments.

Exercise 14-1 Write an XML file

In this exercise, you'll save the Invoice objects that are created by the Invoice application of chapter 6 in an XML document.

1. Open the Invoice project in the C:\VB.NET\Chapter 14\Invoice folder. This is a fresh version of the Invoice project of chapter 6. Then, review the code in the form and Invoice classes, and run the application to remind yourself how this application works.

2. Add these methods to the Invoice class:

   a. OpenInvoices, which creates a new XML file named Invoices.xml, writes an XML declaration to the document, and writes a start tag named Invoices for the root element. This should be a shared method that creates an Invoices.xml file in the "C:\VB.NET\Files" folder.

   b. WriteInvoice, which writes an Invoice element for the invoice. The Invoice element should include an attribute named CustomerName and three child elements named OrderTotal, DiscountAmount, and InvoiceTotal.

   c. CloseInvoices, which writes the end tag for the root element (Invoices) and closes the XML file. This should be a shared method.

3. Modify the Load procedure for the form so it calls the OpenInvoices method. Then, modify the Click event procedure for the New Invoice button so it calls the WriteInvoice method before a new invoice is started. Finally, modify the Click event procedure for the Exit button so it calls the CloseInvoices method.

4. Test the application by creating from two to five invoices. To tell whether it worked, use Visual Studio to open the file in the XML Designer window. Then, use both XML and Data view to verify that the XML document is correct.

Exercise 14-2   Read an XML document

In this exercise, you'll read the XML document that you created in exercise 14-1. To save you time, we'll give you the form for the application.

1. Open the InvoiceSummary project in the C:\VB.NET\Chapter 14\InvoiceSummary folder. Then, run the application to see that its form looks like this, but without the data:

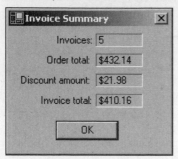

2. Write a Load procedure for this form that reads the data from the XML file that you created in exercise 14-1. As it reads each Invoice element, this procedure should add one to the invoice count and summarize the three decimal fields. When it finishes reading the Invoice elements, this procedure should display the invoice count and totals in the labels of the form.

3. Write the code for the Click event of the OK button, which just closes the form. Then, test the application.

4. Open the XML document in the XML Designer window and edit the document by changing one or more values, adding at least one new invoice, and deleting at least one invoice. Then, run the application again to see the effects of your changes. When you've got it working right, close the project.

15

More skills for object-oriented programming

In chapter 6, you learned some basic skills for working with classes. Now, this chapter will teach you some additional skills for working with classes like using constructors and inheritance. It will also show you how to create and use class libraries to manage the classes you create.

Perhaps even more important, though, this chapter presents an Invoice application and the three business classes that it uses. That will show you how the use of business objects can simplify the development of a large application. And that after all is why you use business objects in the first place.

To get the most out of this chapter, it's a good idea to read chapters 12 and 14 first. That's because they cover collections and XML files, two features that are used in the application in this chapter.

More skills for creating classes

In chapter 6, you learned how to create a class by defining its properties and methods. For simple classes, that's all you need to know. To create more complex classes, though, you'll need the additional skills presented in the topics that follow.

How to define and use constructors

When you use the New keyword to create an instance of a class, Visual Basic automatically assigns default values to all of the instance variables in the new object. If that's not what you want, you can code a special procedure called a *constructor* that's executed when an object is created from a class. Figure 15-1 shows you how to do that.

To create a constructor, you simply create a public Sub procedure named New. Within this procedure, you initialize the instance variables, and you include any additional statements you want to be executed when an object is created from the class.

The first procedure in this figure illustrates a constructor that doesn't accept arguments. This constructor simply assigns a default value of 200 to the instance variable named dCreditLimit. Any other instance variables in this class will be initialized to their default values based on their data types.

The second constructor in this figure accepts two arguments. Then, the constructor assigns the values of those arguments to instance variables. This technique is often used to set property values when an object is created.

This figure also presents two statements that execute the constructors shown here. The first one executes the constructor with no arguments. The second one executes the constructor with two arguments. Although you've seen statements like these before, you should now have a better understanding of how they work. In particular, you should now realize that when you use the New keyword, Visual Basic executes the New method for the class, if one is defined.

A constructor without arguments

```
Public Sub New()
    dCreditLimit = 200
End Sub
```

A constructor with two arguments

```
Public Sub New(ByVal CustomerName As String, CreditLimit As Decimal)
    sCustomerName = CustomerName
    dCreditLimit = CreditLimit
End Sub
```

A statement that calls the constructor without any arguments

```
Invoice = New Invoice()
```

A statement that calls the constructor with two arguments

```
Invoice = New Invoice(txtCustomerName.Text, 500)
```

Description

- You can use a *constructor* to initialize instance variables and perform other initialization operations as an object is created from a class.

- A constructor is simply a public Sub procedure named New. The constructor is executed when you use the New keyword to create an instance of the class, either in the Dim statement that defines the object variable or in an assignment statement that creates an object instance and assigns it to a previously defined object variable.

- If you don't code a constructor, Visual Basic creates a default constructor that initializes all the instance variables to their default values. The default constructor doesn't accept any arguments.

Figure 15-1   How to define and use constructors

NEW TO .NET - LIKE C#, JAVA

How to overload methods

ALLOWS YOU TO USE POLY-MORPHISM. HELPS TO MAKE CODE CLEANER, EASIER TO USE.

When you *overload* a method, you code two or more method procedures with the same name. Each procedure should include the Overloads keyword and must have a unique combination of arguments. The method name combined with the arguments form the method's *signature*.

DIFF # OF ARG, OR DIFF D/T (AT LEAST ONE ARG)

To have a unique combination of arguments, the procedure must have a different number of arguments than the other procedures, or at least one of the arguments must have a different data type. Then, when you refer to an overloaded method, the number of arguments that are passed and the data types of those arguments determine which procedure is executed.

Overloading lets you provide two or more ways to invoke a given method. For example, figure 15-2 shows an overloaded method called AddItem. The first version of the AddItem method accepts two arguments: UnitPrice and Quantity. The second version accepts just one argument, of type LineItem. Later in this chapter, you'll see that the LineItem class has three properties: Description, UnitPrice, and Quantity. So this overloaded method allows a programmer to use the LineItem class to provide the values it needs rather than pass them as separate arguments. Other than this difference, these two methods work the same way.

The coding examples that follow the AddItem methods in this figure illustrate how you would execute each of these methods. The first example passes two arguments to the AddItem method. The second creates a new LineItem object, then passes it to the AddItem method.

As you've worked with the various .NET classes presented in this book, you've probably noticed that when you type the name of a method followed by a left parenthesis, the Intellisense feature displays a list of the method's arguments. You may not have realized, though, that if up and down arrows appear to the left of the argument list, it indicates that the method is overloaded. Then, you can click on the up and down arrows to move from one overloaded method to another. This works with overloaded methods in classes you define as well. For example, the illustration in this figure shows how Intellisense displays the overloaded AddItem methods. In this case, the second of the two methods is currently displayed.

By the way, you can overload any method, including the New method. In fact, one of the most useful applications of overloading is for constructors. Overloading allows you to build a set of constructors that lets you provide various combinations of starting values for an object. For example, figure 15-1 showed two constructors for an Invoice class, one that accepts no arguments and one that accepts two arguments. As a result, you can instantiate an Invoice object from the class using either constructor.

Note, however, that if you overload a constructor, you don't specify Overloads in the Public Sub statement. The Overloads keyword isn't allowed for Sub New procedures.

OVERLOADS MUST HAVE DIFF. SIGS. CAN HAVE EXTRA DUMMY PARAMETER!

An overloaded method that provides for two different argument lists

```
Public Overloads Sub AddItem(ByVal UnitPrice As Decimal, _
        ByVal Quantity As Integer)
    dOrderTotal += UnitPrice * Quantity
    dDiscountAmount = Discount(dOrderTotal)
    dInvoiceTotal = dOrderTotal - dDiscountAmount
End Sub

Public Overloads Sub AddItem(ByVal LineItem As LineItem)
    dOrderTotal += LineItem.UnitPrice * LineItem.Quantity
    dDiscountAmount = Discount(dOrderTotal)
    dInvoiceTotal = dOrderTotal - dDiscountAmount
End Sub
```

A statement that invokes the first AddItem method

```
Invoice.AddItem(txtUnitPrice.Text, txtQuantity.Text)
```

Statements that invoke the second AddItem method

```
Dim LineItem As New LineItem(txtDescription.Text, _
    txtUnitPrice.Text, txtQuantity.Text)
Invoice.AddItem(LineItem)
```

How the Intellisense feature presents overloaded methods

```
Invoice.AddItem(
        ▲2 of 2▼ AddItem (UnitPrice As Decimal, Quantity As Integer)
```
OF VERSONS

Description

- An *overloaded method* is a method that has two or more definitions. Each definition must have a unique *signature*. A method's signature is the name of the method combined with its list of arguments.

- For a method's signature to be unique, it must have a different number of arguments, or one or more of the arguments must be declared with a different data type. Simply using different argument names isn't enough to make the argument list unique.

- When you call an overloaded method, the code that's executed depends on the signature you use to call the method.

- The Overloads keyword is optional, but if you code it on one overloaded method, you must code it on all other overloaded methods that have the same name.

- If you overload constructors, you don't use the Overloads keyword. Instead, you just provide two or more Public Sub New procedures.

- When you type a method name, the Intellisense feature displays the arguments expected by the method. You can click the up or down arrow in this pop-up to display each of the method's overloaded argument lists. In the example above, the second of two signatures is shown.

Figure 15-2   How to overload methods

How to throw argument exceptions

When you create your own user-defined classes, you should make sure that your classes protect themselves from invalid data. In particular, property set procedures should validate the data that is passed to them via the Value argument before they set property values. If the data is invalid, the property shouldn't be changed. Instead, an exception should be thrown to notify the calling procedure that an error has occurred. Methods should also validate arguments passed to them.

Figure 15-3 shows how this validation can be done. Here, the set procedure for a property named Quantity checks to make sure that the value passed to it is greater than zero. If the value is greater than zero, the instance variable named iQuantity is set to the Value argument. But if the value is zero or negative, an exception is thrown instead.

As you learned in chapter 5, the Throw statement takes an exception object as an argument. The .NET Framework defines the three exception classes listed in this figure as standard exceptions you can use when validating arguments. If an argument is out of the range of values acceptable for the property, throw the ArgumentOutOfRangeException. If an attempt is made to set a property to a null value and the property always requires a value, throw the ArgumentNullException. For any other validation errors, throw the ArgumentException.

Notice that all three of these exceptions accept a string argument. You should use this argument to provide a meaningful error message that indicates what is wrong with the data.

If you code a property or method that throws an exception, you might think that you'd code a statement that refers to that property or method within a Try block so that you could catch the exception when it occurs. However, I don't recommend that. Instead, you should validate the data before passing it to the property or method. That way, the exception should never occur. So why include the validation code in the class at all? Because if you design your classes so they're reusable, you can't always count on other programmers validating the data they pass to the class. So including this code makes the class completely self-contained.

A property that validates data in its set procedure

```
Public Property Quantity() As Integer
    Get
        Return iQuantity
    End Get
    Set(ByVal Value As Integer)
        If Value > 0 Then
            iQuantity = Value
        Else
            Throw New ArgumentOutOfRangeException _
                ("Quantity must be greater than zero.")
        End If
    End Set
End Property
```

BETTER TO "DIM" SEPARATELY

Exceptions to throw when validating arguments

Exception	Description
ArgumentOutOfRangeException(message)	Use when the value is outside the acceptable range of values for the property.
ArgumentNullException(message)	Use when the value is null and the property requires a value.
ArgumentException(message)	Use when the value is invalid for any other reason.

An If statement that validates data before setting a property value

```
If iQuantity > 0 Then
    LineItem.Quantity = iQuantity
End If
```

Description

- A class should throw an exception whenever it encounters an error it cannot recover from. The most common type of error a class should check for is an invalid argument passed to a property set procedure or a method.

- If a class detects an invalid argument, it should throw one of the three argument exceptions listed above. The Throw statement should pass a descriptive message as an argument.

- When you refer to a property or method that throws an argument exception, you shouldn't use a Try…Catch block to catch the exception. Instead, you should validate the data before you pass it to the property or method. That way, you can be sure that the exception won't be thrown.

- All of the argument exceptions can be found in the System namespace.

Figure 15-3   How to throw argument exceptions

How to define and use class events

In addition to properties and methods, a class can also define events. Then, when a particular condition occurs, the class can cause the event to be raised. To respond to that event, you can code an event procedure for an object created from the class. Figure 15-4 illustrates how this works.

To define an event, you use an Event statement in the class definition, as shown at the top of this figure. On this statement, you code the name of the event along with any arguments that will be passed to the event procedure when the event is raised. In addition, you'll usually include the Public keyword to indicate that the event is available from outside the class that defines it. This keyword is optional, however, since Public is the default.

To cause an event to be raised, you code a RaiseEvent statement as shown in this figure. On this statement, you name the event you want to raise, and you code values for any arguments defined by the event. Like the arguments you code for procedures, the arguments you code on a RaiseEvent statement must match the arguments defined by the event it raises.

The Event statement shown in this figure declares an event named CreditLimitExceeded that accepts two arguments. The first argument is the customer's credit limit, and the second argument is the invoice total. The AddItem method shown in this figure raises this event if the invoice total for a customer exceeds the customer's credit limit. Notice that the RaiseEvent statement includes an argument list with the two arguments defined by the event.

To use the events defined by a class, the Dim statement for the object variable must include the WithEvents keyword. Then, you can code an event procedure for an event as shown in the last example in this figure. Here, the event procedure for the CreditLimitExceeded event simply displays a message to inform the user that the customer credit limit has been exceeded.

When you include the WithEvents keyword on the Dim statement for an object variable, you should know that the object and its events are included in the drop-down lists at the top of the Code Editor window. That way, you can create an event procedure for the object just as you would for any other object.

- SYNC OR BLOCKING CALL - BLOCKS EXECUTION, UNTIL DONE
  - GUARANTEES EXECUTION OF CODE
- ASYNC - WAITING FOR RETURN, CAN EXEC. OTHER,
  BUT MAY NEVER GET RETURN)
- EVENT-DRIVEN - PROVIDE CODE FOR EVENT HANDLE (HANDLES...)
  OS WATCHES / STARTS PROC.

E = EVENT GENERATED BY CONTROL

The syntax of the Event statement

```
[Public] Event name[(argumentlist)]
```

The syntax of the RaiseEvent statement

```
RaiseEvent name[(argumentlist)]
```

The definition of an event in the Invoice class

```
Public Event CreditLimitExceeded(ByVal CreditLimit As Decimal, _
    ByVal InvoiceTotal As Decimal)
```

A method that raises the event in the Invoice class

```
Public Sub AddItem(LineItem)
    dOrderTotal += UnitPrice * Quantity
    dDiscountAmount = Discount(dOrderTotal)
    dInvoiceTotal = dOrderTotal - dDiscountAmount
    If dInvoiceTotal > dCreditLimit Then
        RaiseEvent CreditLimitExceeded(dCreditLimit, dInvoiceTotal)
    End If
End Sub
```

The code for a form class that uses the event

```
Dim WithEvents Invoice As New Invoice()

Private Sub Invoice_CreditLimitExceeded(ByVal CreditLimit As Decimal, _
        ByVal InvoiceTotal As Decimal) Handles Invoice.CreditLimitExceeded
    Dim sMessage As String
    sMessage = "Credit limit of " & FormatCurrency(CreditLimit)
    sMessage &= " exceeded by " & _
        FormatCurrency(InvoiceTotal - CreditLimit) & "."
    MessageBox.Show(sMessage, "Credit limit exceeded", _
        MessageBoxButtons.OK, MessageBoxIcon.Exclamation)
End Sub
```

Description

- To declare a class event, you code an Event statement at the class level. Then, you can use a RaiseEvent statement in any procedure in the class to cause the event to occur.

- To handle an event from another class, you must declare the class object using the WithEvents keyword. Then, you must create an event procedure for the event using the drop-down lists at the top of the Code Editor window.

- When an event occurs, control is passed to the event procedure for that event. If the event is defined with arguments, the arguments are also passed. When the event procedure completes, control is returned to the statement after the RaiseEvent statement that caused the event to occur.

Figure 15-4   How to define and use class events

How to create a class with a collection property

Most class properties for classes you've seen so far in this book represent a single value, such as a customer's name or an invoice total. However, many applications call for classes that can hold collections of information. For example, an Invoice class might have a collection of line items that record information for each product ordered.

The easiest way to implement a collection property is to simply create a property of type Collection. However, there are several disadvantages to this approach. For starters, the items in a collection aren't typed. As a result, you might inadvertently add the wrong type of data to the collection. In addition, the syntax required to access a Collection property can be cumbersome. For example, to add an item to a collection property named LineItem in a class named Invoice, you would have to code Invoice.LineItem.Add(Item).

A better way to implement a collection in a class is to create the collection as a private instance variable, then create properties and methods that provide access to the collection. Figure 15-5 shows how you can do this. Here, the invoice's line items will be stored in a private collection variable named LineItemCollection. Then, instead of exposing a collection property, the class exposes a LineItem property that lets you access a specific line item, a LineItemCount property that returns the number of line items in the invoice, an AddItem method that adds a line item to the invoice, and a RemoveItem method that removes an item.

Because the only way to add an item to LineItemCollection is through the AddItem method, the class ensures that only LineItem objects are stored in the collection by specifying LineItem as the argument type for the AddItem method. Then, the AddItem method uses the LineItemCollection's Add method to add the line item to the collection.

To provide access to an individual line item, the LineItem property uses an integer argument named Index. A property that uses an argument is known as a *parameterized property*. The value of the argument determines which value the property returns. In this case, the argument is used as an index to retrieve a specific line item from the LineItemCollection variable.

↗HAPPENS OFTEN

The code for an Invoice class that uses a collection property

```
Private LineItemCollection As New Collection()

Public ReadOnly Property LineItem(ByVal Index As Integer) As LineItem
    Get
        Return LineItemCollection.Item(Index)
    End Get
End Property

Public ReadOnly Property LineItemCount() As Integer
    Get
        Return LineItemCollection.Count
    End Get
End Property

Public Sub AddItem(LineItem As LineItem)
    LineItemCollection.Add(LineItem)
End Sub

Public Sub RemoveItem(Index As Integer)
    LineItemCollection.Remove(Index)
End Sub
```

A statement that adds an item to the collection

```
Invoice.AddItem(LineItem)
```

A statement that retrieves the first item in the collection

```
LineItem = Invoice.LineItem(1)
```

Description

- If a property refers to a collection, it's common to create a private collection object to hold the collection. Then, instead of exposing the collection as a property, the class exposes methods to add and remove items from the collection along with a parameterized property that provides access to a single item in the collection.

- A *parameterized property* is a property that accepts an argument. When used with a collection, the argument is an index that's used to retrieve a specific item from the collection.

- Coding a collection property in this way simplifies the syntax you have to use to access the collection and lets you specify what types of objects can be added to the collection.

Figure 15-5   How to create a class with a collection property

COLLECTIONS ARE 1-BASED

An enhanced Invoice application

The topics that follow present the specifications and code for an Invoice application that uses three business classes. This is an enhancement of the Invoice application you saw in chapter 6. Since this is the most complicated example presented in this book, you may have to devote more time to studying it than most of the other examples have required.

Once you understand how this application works, though, you should begin to appreciate how you can use business classes to simplify the development of a large application. Because each business class contains the code for just one type of business object, the use of business classes helps you divide the code for a large application into logical units. Also, because each business object encapsulates the code for its properties and methods, you don't have to concern yourself with that code when you use its properties and methods. The end result is that the coding of the overall project is simplified.

The specifications for the Invoice application

Figure 15-6 presents the specifications for the enhanced Invoice application. The user interface for this application consists of the Invoice form and the three message boxes shown here.

To create an invoice, the user enters the customer name and the description, unit price, and quantity for the first item ordered, then clicks the Add Item button. The application calculates the order total by multiplying the unit price by the quantity, and then calculates a discount based on the order total. The user can then add another item to the order by typing another description, unit price, and quantity and clicking the Add Item button again. When there are no more items for an invoice, the user clicks the New Invoice button to start a new invoice. At that time, the first message box in the figure is displayed to summarize the data for the invoice.

Each time the user clicks on the AddItem button and the invoice total is recalculated, the program checks if the invoice total exceeds the customer's credit limit. If so, the second message box shown in the figure is displayed. To keep things simple, every customer is given a fixed credit limit of $200. In a more realistic example, each customer's credit limit would probably be stored in a file or database along with other customer information.

When the user clicks the Exit button, the invoices that have been entered are written to a file in XML format. Then, the third message box shown in the figure is displayed to indicate how many invoices were written to the file.

The form for the enhanced Invoice application

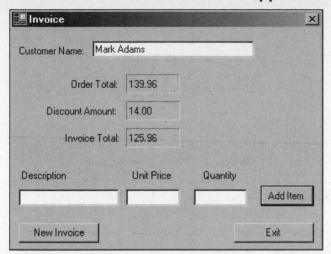

Messages boxes for the enhanced Invoice application

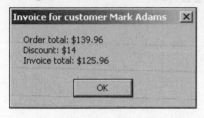 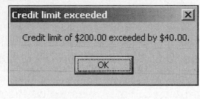 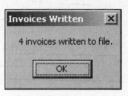

How the application works

- To enter an invoice, the user enters a customer name and the description, unit price, and quantity for the first line item and clicks the Add Item button. To add another item to the invoice, the user enters a new description, unit price, and quantity and clicks Add Item again.

- Each time the user clicks the Add Item button, the program adds the new line item to the invoice and recalculates the invoice totals. If the invoice total exceeds the customer's credit limit, a warning message is displayed.

- To end one invoice and start another, the user clicks the New Invoice button. The program then displays a message confirming the details of the invoice and begins a new invoice.

- When the user clicks the Exit button, the invoices are written to an XML file and a message is displayed to indicate how many invoices were processed.

Figure 15-6   The specifications for an enhanced Invoice application

The design of the classes used by the Invoice application

Figure 15-7 shows the properties, methods, and events for the three classes used by the Invoice application. These three classes work together to enable the application to create and store a batch of invoices, then write the invoices to an XML document.

The InvoiceBatch class represents a collection of invoices that are entered by a user as a batch. This class uses a private Collection variable to store the invoices entered by the user. It provides an Invoice property that retrieves a specified invoice from the collection based on an index value and a Count property that returns the number of invoices in the collection. To add an invoice to the collection, you use the AddInvoice method.

The Invoice class represents a single invoice. Its properties represent the invoice details such as the customer's name, the invoice total, and so on. The Invoice class has a private Collection variable that stores all of the line items for the invoice. The LineItem property retrieves a specified line item and the LineItemCount property returns the number of line items in the collection. To add a line item to the invoice, you use the AddItem method.

The Invoice class also includes a constructor and an event. The constructor simply sets the credit limit for each customer to $200. Then, if an invoice exceeds that limit, the CreditLimitExceeded event is raised. This event passes the credit limit and invoice total as arguments.

The LineItem class has just three properties: Description, UnitPrice, and Quantity. This class represents a single line item for an invoice. It provides a constructor that lets you set all three properties when you create a LineItem object.

Each of these classes has a method that writes data to an XML document. The InvoiceBatch class has a WriteInvoices method that writes all of the invoices in the collection to an XML document. This method calls the WriteInvoice method of the Invoice class to write each invoice to the XML document. And the WriteInvoice method, in turn, calls the WriteLineItem method of the LineItem class to write each line item to the XML document.

So that all of the XML data will be written to the same document, the Invoice.WriteInvoice and LineItem.WriteLineItem classes both accept an XmlTextWriter object as an argument. The InvoiceBatch.WriteInvoices method accepts a Path argument that provides the filename and location for the XML file. This method creates an XmlTextWriter object using the specified path, then passes that object to the Invoice object's WriteInvoice method, which in turn passes it to the LineItem object's WriteLineItem method.

If you haven't yet read chapter 14, you may have trouble understanding all of the details of how these methods work. But even if you don't understand the XML processing these methods do, you should be able to appreciate the way these three classes work together to create a single XML document that represents the entire batch of invoices.

INV BATCH CLASS   INV. CLASS

The InvoiceBatch class

ALL. FOR
STORING
INVOICES
(OBJECTS)

Properties	
Invoice(Index As Integer) As Invoice	Gets the invoice indicated by the index.
Count As Integer	Gets the number of invoices in the batch.
Method	
AddInvoice(Invoice As Invoice)	Adds an invoice to the batch.
WriteInvoices(Path As String)	Writes the invoices to the specified XML file.

The Invoice class

OB. RROC
NAMED ---

ALL. FOR
LINE ITEMS
(OBJECTS)

Constructor ✳	
New()	Creates a new invoice object and sets the credit limit to $200.
Properties	
CustomerName As String	Gets or sets the customer name.
OrderTotal As Decimal	Gets the total of the invoice's line items.
DiscountAmount As Decimal	Gets the discount calculated for the invoice.
InvoiceTotal As Decimal	Gets the invoice total.
LineItem(Index As Integer) As LineItem	Gets the line item indicated by the index.
LineItemCount As Integer	Gets the number of line items for the invoice.
Methods	
AddItem(LineItem As LineItem)	Adds a line item to the invoice.
WriteInvoice(Writer As XmlTextWriter)	Writes the invoice to the specified XML text writer.
Event	
CreditLimitExceeded(CreditLimit As Decimal, InvoiceTotal As Decimal)	Raised if the invoice total exceeds the customer's credit limit.

The LineItem class

HOLDS
DATA
FOR LINE
ITEM,
HAS METH.
TO WRITE
TO XML
FILE

Constructor ✳	
New (Description As String, UnitPrice As Decimal, Quantity As Integer)	Creates a new line item object using the description, unit price, and quantity values specified. 3 ARGS
Properties	
Description As String	Gets or sets the line item description.
UnitPrice As Decimal	Gets or sets the unit price for the line item.
Quantity As Integer	Gets or sets the quantity ordered.
Method	
WriteLineItem(Writer As XmlTextWriter)	Writes the line item to the specified XML text writer.

Figure 15-7   The design of the classes used by the Invoice application

✳ USE TO SEND DATA INITIALLY FOR INSTANCE VARIABLES

The code for the InvoiceBatch class

Figure 15-8 shows the Visual Basic code for the InvoiceBatch class. Here, the private variable InvoiceCollection is a simple Collection object that will hold the invoices for the batch. The Invoice property uses the Index argument to retrieve a specific invoice from the collection. The Count property returns the number of invoices in the collection. And the AddItem method uses the InvoiceCollection object's Add method to add an invoice to the collection.

The WriteInvoices method starts by creating an XmlTextWriter object and writing the start document information and the start tag for the root element (Invoices) to the document. Then, a For Each statement is used to call the WriteInvoice method for each invoice in the collection. The XmlTextWriter object is passed as an argument so the WriteInvoice method of each Invoice object will write its XML information to the same XML document. When all of the invoices have been written, the WriteInvoices method writes an end tag for the root element and closes the XmlTextWriter object.

```
<INVOICES>
  <INVOICE CUSTOMER NAME="JOE">
    <ORDERTOTAL> 23.00
    <DISCOUNT AMOUNT> 10.00
    <INVOICETOTAL> 13.00
```

The Visual Basic code for the InvoiceBatch class

```
Imports System.Xml
Public Class InvoiceBatch

    Private InvoiceCollection As New Collection()

    Public ReadOnly Property Invoice(ByVal Index As Integer)
        Get
            Return InvoiceCollection.Item(Index)
        End Get
    End Property

    Public ReadOnly Property Count() As Integer
        Get
            Return InvoiceCollection.Count
        End Get
    End Property

    Public Sub AddInvoice(ByVal Invoice As Invoice)
        InvoiceCollection.Add(Invoice)
    End Sub

    Public Sub WriteInvoices(Path As String)
        Dim InvoiceWriter As New XmlTextWriter(Path, Nothing)
        InvoiceWriter.Formatting = Formatting.Indented
        InvoiceWriter.WriteStartDocument()
        InvoiceWriter.WriteStartElement("Invoices")
        Dim Invoice As Invoice
        For Each Invoice In InvoiceCollection
            Invoice.WriteInvoice(InvoiceWriter)
        Next
        InvoiceWriter.WriteEndElement()
        InvoiceWriter.Close()
    End Sub

End Class
```

HOW MANY INV IN FILE?

Figure 15-8   The code for the InvoiceBatch class of the Invoice application

The code for the Invoice class

Figure 15-9 shows the code for the Invoice class. Although the listing for this class requires two pages, you shouldn't have any trouble understanding it if you focus on just one part of it at a time.

Like most classes, the Invoice class begins with declarations for several private instance variables. One of them, LineItemCollection, is a Collection object used to hold the line items for the invoice.

After the private instance variable declarations, an Event statement declares the CreditLimitExceeded event that can be raised by the class. Then, the constructor for this class sets the dCreditLimit variable to 200. This variable will be used to determine whether the CreditLimitExceeded event is raised.

The next six procedures are property procedures that provide access to the information that's stored in the private instance variables. Notice that the LineItem property receives an index value as an argument and returns the line item at that index in the line item collection. In contrast, the LineItemCount property simply returns a count of the number of items in this collection.

The AddItem method shown on page 2 of this listing starts by adding a line item to the line item collection. The line item that's added is passed to this method from the calling procedure. Then, this method calculates the invoice totals and checks to see if the invoice total exceeds the customer's credit limit. If so, it raises the CreditLimitExceeded event.

The WriteInvoice method is called by the InvoiceBatch class to write an invoice to the XML document using the XmlTextWriter object that's passed as an argument. After it writes the basic information for the invoice, it uses a For...Next loop to write each line item. To do that, it calls the WriteLineItem method defined by the LineItem class.

The code for the LineItem class

The code for the LineItem class is shown in figure 15-10. The only complication introduced by this class is that it includes data validation to ensure that the UnitPrice value isn't negative and the Quantity value is greater than zero. If it detects invalid data, it throws an ArgumentOutOfRangeException.

Notice that the constructor for this class doesn't set the dUnitPrice and iQuantity instance variables directly. Instead, it uses Me.UnitPrice and Me.Quantity to set these variables via the property set procedures. If the constructor set dUnitPrice and iQuantity directly, the data validation code in the Set procedure would be bypassed.

2 COLLECTIONS, EACH HAS 2 FOR-EACH LOOPS

The Visual Basic code for the Invoice class   Page 1

```vb
Imports System.Xml
Public Class Invoice
    Private sCustomerName As String
    Private dOrderTotal As Decimal
    Private dDiscountAmount As Decimal
    Private dInvoiceTotal As Decimal
    Private dCreditLimit As Decimal
    Private LineItemCollection As New Collection()

    Public Event CreditLimitExceeded(ByVal CreditLimit As Decimal, _
        ByVal InvoiceTotal As Decimal)

    Public Sub New()
        dCreditLimit = 200
    End Sub

    Public Property CustomerName() As String
        Get
            Return sCustomerName
        End Get
        Set(ByVal Value As String)
            sCustomerName = Value
        End Set
    End Property

    Public ReadOnly Property OrderTotal() As Decimal
        Get
            Return dOrderTotal
        End Get
    End Property

    Public ReadOnly Property DiscountAmount() As Decimal
        Get
            Return dDiscountAmount
        End Get
    End Property

    Public ReadOnly Property InvoiceTotal() As Decimal
        Get
            Return dInvoiceTotal
        End Get
    End Property

    Public ReadOnly Property LineItem(ByVal Index As Integer)
        Get
            Return LineItemCollection.Item(Index)
        End Get
    End Property

    Public ReadOnly Property LineItemCount() As Integer
        Get
            Return LineItemCollection.Count
        End Get
    End Property
```

Figure 15-9   The code for the Invoice class of the Invoice application (part 1 of 2)

The Visual Basic code for the Invoice class   **Page 2**

```vb
Public Sub AddItem(ByVal LineItem As LineItem)
    LineItemCollection.Add(LineItem)
    dOrderTotal += LineItem.UnitPrice * LineItem.Quantity
    dDiscountAmount = Discount(dOrderTotal)
    dInvoiceTotal = dOrderTotal - dDiscountAmount
    If dInvoiceTotal > dCreditLimit Then
        RaiseEvent CreditLimitExceeded(dCreditLimit, dInvoiceTotal)
    End If
End Sub

Private Function Discount(ByVal OrderTotal As Decimal) As Decimal
    Dim dDiscountPct As Decimal
    Select Case dOrderTotal
        Case Is >= 500
            dDiscountPct = 0.3
        Case Is >= 200
            dDiscountPct = 0.2
        Case Is >= 100
            dDiscountPct = 0.1
        Case Else '<100
            dDiscountPct = 0
    End Select
    Return Math.Round(OrderTotal * dDiscountPct, 2)
End Function

Public Sub WriteInvoice(ByVal InvoiceWriter As XmlTextWriter)
    InvoiceWriter.WriteStartElement("Invoice")
    InvoiceWriter.WriteAttributeString("CustomerName", sCustomerName)
    InvoiceWriter.WriteElementString("OrderTotal", dOrderTotal)
    InvoiceWriter.WriteElementString("DiscountAmount", dDiscountAmount)
    InvoiceWriter.WriteElementString("InvoiceTotal", dInvoiceTotal)
    Dim LineItem As LineItem
    For Each LineItem In LineItemCollection
        LineItem.WriteLineItem(InvoiceWriter)
    Next
    InvoiceWriter.WriteEndElement()
End Sub

End Class
```

(handwritten annotation: MANY LINE ITEMS)

(handwritten annotation: BACK TO 481)

Figure 15-9   The code for the Invoice class of the Invoice application (part 2 of 2)

The Visual Basic code for the LineItem class

```
Imports System.Xml
Public Class LineItem
    Private sDescription As String
    Private dUnitPrice As Decimal
    Private iQuantity As Integer

    Public Sub New(ByVal Description As String, _
            ByVal UnitPrice As Decimal, ByVal Quantity As Integer)
        sDescription = Description
        Me.UnitPrice = UnitPrice
        Me.Quantity = Quantity
    End Sub

    Public Property Description() As String
        Get
            Return sDescription
        End Get
        Set(ByVal Value As String)
            sDescription = Value
        End Set
    End Property

    Public Property UnitPrice() As Decimal
        Get
            Return dUnitPrice
        End Get
        Set(ByVal Value As Decimal)
            If Value >= 0 Then
                dUnitPrice = Value
            Else
                Throw New ArgumentOutOfRangeException _
                    ("UnitPrice cannot be negative.")
            End If
        End Set
    End Property

    Public Property Quantity() As Integer
        Get
            Return iQuantity
        End Get
        Set(ByVal Value As Integer)
            If Value > 0 Then
                iQuantity = Value
            Else
                Throw New ArgumentOutOfRangeException _
                ("Quantity must be greater than zero.")
            End If
        End Set
    End Property

    Public Sub WriteLineItem(ByVal InvoiceWriter As XmlTextWriter)
        InvoiceWriter.WriteStartElement("LineItem")
        InvoiceWriter.WriteElementString("Description", sDescription)
        InvoiceWriter.WriteElementString("UnitPrice", dUnitPrice)
        InvoiceWriter.WriteElementString("Quantity", iQuantity)
        InvoiceWriter.WriteEndElement()
    End Sub
End Class
```

Figure 15-10   The code for the LineItem class of the Invoice application

The code for the Invoice application's form

Figure 15-11 presents the Visual Basic code for the Invoice application's form. This code is pretty straightforward, so I'll just point out some of the highlights. For starters, the form class creates new InvoiceBatch and Invoice objects. Notice that the declaration for the Invoice object includes the With Events keyword so that the application can respond to the CreditLimitExceeded event.

In the Click event procedure for the AddItem button, the first statement creates a new line item using the information in the Description, Unit Price, and Quantity text boxes. Notice that this data isn't validated before it's used to create a new line item. As a result, an exception will occur if the user enters non-numeric data for the unit price or quantity. If the user enters valid data, though, this procedure continues by adding the new line item to the invoice using the AddItem method of the Invoice object. Then, it updates the order information on the form, clears the text boxes for the next line item, and moves the focus to the Description text box.

The Click event procedure for the New Invoice button starts by setting the CustomerName property of the invoice. Then, it displays a message that confirms the invoice data and adds the invoice to the InvoiceBatch object using the AddInvoice method. Next, it creates a new Invoice object so the user can enter data for another invoice. Finally, it clears the controls on the form and moves the focus to the CustomerName text box.

The Invoice_CreditLimitExceeded procedure handles the Invoice object's CreditLimitExceeded event. This procedure simply displays a message box to let the user know that the customer's credit limit has been exceeded.

The Click event procedure for the Exit button starts by writing the invoices in the InvoiceBatch object to an XML document. To do that, it executes the WriteInvoices method of that object. Then, it displays the number of invoices that were processed and closes the form to end the application.

The Visual Basic code for the form class

```vb
Public Class Form1
    Inherits System.Windows.Forms.Form
    Dim InvoiceBatch As New InvoiceBatch()
    Dim WithEvents Invoice As New Invoice()

    Private Sub btnAddItem_Click(ByVal sender As System.Object, _
            ByVal e As System.EventArgs) Handles btnAddItem.Click
        Dim LineItem As New LineItem(txtDescription.Text, _
            txtUnitPrice.Text, txtQuantity.Text)
        Invoice.AddItem(LineItem)
        lblOrderTotal.Text = FormatNumber(Invoice.OrderTotal)
        lblDiscountAmount.Text = FormatNumber(Invoice.DiscountAmount)
        lblInvoiceTotal.Text = FormatNumber(Invoice.InvoiceTotal)
        txtDescription.Text = ""
        txtUnitPrice.Text = ""
        txtQuantity.Text = ""
        txtDescription.Focus()
    End Sub

    Private Sub btnNewInvoice_Click(ByVal sender As System.Object, _
            ByVal e As System.EventArgs) Handles btnNewInvoice.Click
        Dim sMessage As String
        Invoice.CustomerName = txtCustomerName.Text
        sMessage = "Order total: $" & Invoice.OrderTotal & ControlChars.CrLf
        sMessage &= "Discount: $" & Invoice.DiscountAmount & ControlChars.CrLf
        sMessage &= "Invoice total: $" & Invoice.InvoiceTotal & ControlChars.CrLf
        MessageBox.Show(sMessage, "Invoice for customer " & Invoice.CustomerName)
        InvoiceBatch.AddInvoice(Invoice)
        Invoice = New Invoice()
        lblOrderTotal.Text = ""
        lblDiscountAmount.Text = ""
        lblInvoiceTotal.Text = ""
        txtCustomerName.Text = ""
        txtUnitPrice.Text = ""
        txtQuantity.Text = ""
        txtCustomerName.Focus()
    End Sub

    Private Sub Invoice_CreditLimitExceeded(ByVal CreditLimit As Decimal, _
            ByVal InvoiceTotal As Decimal) Handles Invoice.CreditLimitExceeded
        Dim sMessage As String
        sMessage = "Credit limit of " & FormatCurrency(CreditLimit)
        sMessage &= " exceeded by " & _
            FormatCurrency(InvoiceTotal - CreditLimit) & "."
        MessageBox.Show(sMessage, "Credit limit exceeded") _
    End Sub

    Private Sub btnExit_Click(ByVal sender As System.Object, _
            ByVal e As System.EventArgs) Handles btnExit.Click
        InvoiceBatch.WriteInvoices("C:\VB.NET\Files\InvoiceBatch.xml")
        MessageBox.Show(InvoiceBatch.Count & " invoices written to file.", _
            "Invoices Written")
        Me.Close()
    End Sub

End Class
```

Figure 15-11   The code for the form class of the Invoice application

MARE DISC 4/3

How to use inheritance

Inheritance is one of the key concepts of object-oriented programming. It lets you create a class that inherits members from another class. Inheritance is used throughout the classes in the .NET Framework, and you can use it in the classes you create as well. In the topics that follow, you'll learn how.

An introduction to inheritance

Figure 15-12 introduces you to inheritance. To use inheritance, you create a *derived class* that inherits the properties and methods of a *base class*. Then, the objects that are created from the derived class can use these inherited properties and methods. The derived class can also provide its own properties and methods that extend the base class. In addition, the derived class can *override* properties and methods of the base class by providing replacement definitions for them.

The two tables in this figure illustrate how this works. The first table lists the properties and methods of the Invoice class that was presented earlier in this chapter. The second table lists the properties and methods defined by a TaxableInvoice class that inherits the Invoice class. Because it inherits the Invoice class, the TaxableInvoice class has access to the properties and methods defined by the Invoice class. Notice, however, that the TaxableInvoice class has overridden the AddItem and WriteInvoice methods and provided two new properties of its own: SubTotal and SalesTax. The SubTotal property is used to get the amount that is subject to sales tax, and the SalesTax property provides the sales tax amount.

Incidentally, when you override a method, you're implementing a form of *polymorphism*. With polymorphism, two or more classes can define a property or method with the same name but with different implementations. Then, the procedure that's executed when you refer to a member with that name depends on the class that was used to create the object.

Although you should understand the concept of polymorphism, it has little significance as you develop applications. You just design and code the classes, properties, and methods you need, and polymorphism takes place automatically. I mention it here because polymorphism is a natural result of inheritance.

Note that a derived class doesn't inherit constructors or events from its base class. Because of that, the TaxableInvoice class will have to provide its own constructor and event to duplicate those provided by the Invoice base class.

INHERITS → CAN EXTEND.

OVERRIDABLE → CAN MODIFY QRLL.

MUST OVERRIDE → JUSS EMPTY FRAMEWORK, BUT WANT TO DEFINE AS NECESSARY

Properties and methods for the Invoice base class

Invoice class	
Properties	**Methods**
CustomerName	AddItem
OrderTotal	WriteInvoice
DiscountAmount	
InvoiceTotal	
LineItem	
LineItemCount	

Properties and methods for the derived TaxableInvoice class

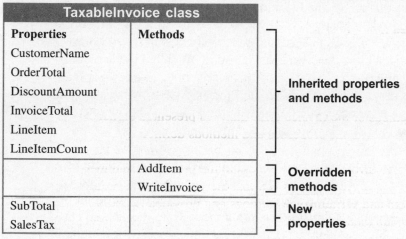

Description

* *Inheritance* lets you create a new class based on an existing class. Then, the new class *inherits* the properties and methods of the existing class. A class that inherits from another class is called a *derived class*. The class it inherits from is called a *base class*.

* A derived class can extend a base class by defining properties, methods, and events that aren't defined in the base class. A derived class can also *override* properties and methods defined in the base class.

* A derived class doesn't inherit constructors or events from its base class.

Figure 15-12   An introduction to inheritance

How to create a base class

Now that you understand how inheritance works, you're ready to learn how to define a base class. This is illustrated in figure 15-13.

To start, you define the properties, methods, and events of the class just as you would for any other class. Then, if you want a class that's derived from this class to be able to override a property or method, you include the Overridable keyword on the Sub, Function, or Property statement that defines the property or method. The code shown in this figure, for example, is for the AddItem method. As you can see, the Sub statement for this method includes the Overridable keyword so that the TaxableInvoice class can override it.

Instance variables that are defined with the Private keyword will be available only to the base class. In many cases, that's what you want. But sometimes, you want to allow derived classes to access instance variables in the base class. For example, any derived class that overrides the AddItem method will need to access the instance variables that are affected by that method. To allow for that, you can define those instance variables with the Protected keyword, as shown in this figure. Any instance variables you define with the Protected keyword are accessible not only to the base class, but also to any other classes that are derived from the base class.

You can also use the Protected keyword for Sub procedures and functions that you want to be accessible from derived classes. If a property or method calls another procedure, for example, you might want to define that procedure as Protected. Then, you could call that procedure directly from the derived class. Otherwise, you could only access it indirectly through the property or method in the base class that uses it.

A method that can be overridden by a class that inherits it

```
Public Overridable Sub AddItem(ByVal LineItem As LineItem)
    LineItemCollection.Add(LineItem)
    dOrderTotal += LineItem.UnitPrice * LineItem.Quantity
    dDiscountAmount = Discount(dOrderTotal)
    dInvoiceTotal = dOrderTotal - dDiscountAmount
    If dInvoiceTotal > dCreditLimit Then
        RaiseEvent CreditLimitExceeded(dCreditLimit, dInvoiceTotal)
    End If
End Sub
```

Protected variables that can be accessed by derived classes

```
Protected dOrderTotal As Decimal
Protected dInvoiceTotal As Decimal
Protected dDiscountAmount As Decimal
Protected dCreditLimit As Decimal
Protected LineItemCollection As New Collection()
```

Description

- You create a base class the same way you create any other class: by defining its properties, methods, and events along with any private code that's required to implement the class.

- If you want a derived class to be able to override a property or method of its base class, you must include the Overridable keyword in the Property, Sub, or Function statement.

- If you don't want a derived class to be able to override a property or method of its base class, you can include the NotOverridable keyword in the Sub, Function, or Property statement. By default, Public properties and methods aren't overridable, so you usually omit this keyword.

[margin note: DEFAULT]

[margin note: →3RD OPTION= MUST OVERRIDE (IMPORTANT) - CREATED EMPTY PLACEHOLDER IN ADVANCE]

- If you want a variable or procedure to be accessible to both the base class and to any class that's derived from that base class, define it as Protected rather than as Private.

Notes

- If you want to prevent a class from being inherited, you can include the NotInheritable keyword in the Class statement. Then, the class cannot be used as a base class.

- If you want to create a class that cannot be instantiated itself but can only be used as a base class, include the MustInherit keyword in the Class statement. This type of class is called an *abstract class*.

[handwritten notes:]
PUBLIC OVERRIDEABLE MY FUN ← MAYBE
" " MUST OVERRIDE ← CLASS NOT VALID UNLESS OVERRIDDEN
PUBLIC MYFUN ← NOT OVERRIDEABLE

Figure 15-13   How to create a base class

[handwritten note at bottom:]
* CONTROL USE OF CODE, AVOID MISUSE, CUST WON'T NEED TO BUY MORE CODE THAN NECC.

How to create a derived class

Figure 15-14 shows how to create a derived class. First, you code an Inherits statement to name the base class. The statement shown at the top of this figure, for example, indicates that the class inherits the Invoice class. That means that any object created from the derived class will have access to the properties and methods of the base class.

After you identify the base class, you can extend its functionality by coding additional properties and methods. In this figure, for example, you can see the declarations for a private constant and two private variables used by the derived class. The constant will be used to calculate the sales tax for an order, and the two variables will be used to hold the subtotal and sales tax for an order. The constant and both variables are used by the AddItem method that overrides the base class method.

This figure shows two ways you can override the AddItem method. In the first example, the method duplicates the processing of the AddItem method in the base class shown in figure 15-13. Then, it includes additional code that calculates the sales tax and the final invoice total. Notice that this method uses four variables (dOrderTotal, dInvoiceTotal, dDiscountAmount, and dCreditLimit) and one procedure (Discount) defined by the base class. Because of that, these variables and procedure must be declared as protected.

Instead of duplicating the code from the base class, the second AddItem method actually executes the AddItem method in the base class. To do that, it uses the MyBase keyword to refer to the base class. Then, the only other code that's included in the method is the code for calculating the sales tax and invoice total.

Notice that both of these methods use the same arguments as the base class method they override. That's a requirement for overriding a property or method. Once you override a property or member, however, you can overload it to provide for a different number of arguments or arguments with different data types.

As I mentioned earlier, a derived class doesn't inherit the constructors of its base class. Because of that, you'll have to code new constructors in the derived class. When you do that, however, you can use the MyBase keyword to refer to a constructor in the base class. For example, you could use MyBase.New() to invoke a constructor in the base class that accepts no arguments.

Derived classes don't inherit events, either. As a result, you'll have to duplicate the Event statement from the base class if the derived class needs to raise the event. If you used the first AddItem method shown in this figure in a derived class, for example, you'd have to code an Event statement for the CreditLimitExceeded event.

WITHIN SOL'N, CAN DRAG-N-DROP FROM PROJ TO PROJ.

MoRE DISC 4/3

An Inherits statement for a class that inherits the Invoice class

```
Inherits Invoice
```

Private variables defined by the derived class

```
Private dSubTotal As Decimal
Private dSalesTax As Decimal
Private Const dTaxRate As Decimal = 0.075
```

The definition of a method that overrides the AddItem method

```
Public Overrides Sub AddItem(ByVal LineItem As LineItem)
    LineItemCollection.Add(LineItem)
    dOrderTotal += LineItem.UnitPrice * LineItem.Quantity
    dDiscountAmount = Discount(dOrderTotal)
    dSubTotal = dOrderTotal - dDiscountAmount
    dSalesTax = dSubTotal * dTaxRate
    dInvoiceTotal = dSubTotal + dSalesTax
    If dInvoiceTotal > dCreditLimit Then
        RaiseEvent CreditLimitExceeded(dCreditLimit, dInvoiceTotal)
    End If
End Sub
```

INHERITS →

COPY & ADD

Another way to implement the AddItem method

```
Public Overrides Sub AddItem(ByVal LineItem As LineItem)
    MyBase.AddItem(LineItem)
    dSubTotal = dInvoiceTotal
    dSalesTax = dSubTotal * dTaxRate
    dInvoiceTotal = dSubTotal + dSalesTax
End Sub
```

CALL & ADD STUFF

(SEE 495)

Description

- To create a derived class, you include an Inherits statement that names the base class. This statement must be coded as the first statement in the class.

- To override a property or method of the base class, you use the same member name and include the Overrides keyword in the Sub, Function, or Property statement. Within that property or method, you can use the MyBase keyword to refer to the property or method you're overriding in the base class.

- You can start an overridden procedure from the Code Editor window by selecting the Overrides item from the first drop-down list and then selecting the procedure you want to override from the second drop-down list.

- An overridden property or method must be defined with the same arguments as the property or method it overrides. Once you override a property or method, though, you can overload it by defining it with different arguments as described in figure 15-2.

- You can also extend the functionality of a base class by coding additional properties and methods in the derived class.

The MyBase keyword

- The MyBase keyword refers to the base class. You can use it to access properties or methods of the base class from a derived class.

Figure 15-14   How to create a derived class

The code for the TaxableInvoice class

Figure 15-15 presents the complete code for the TaxableInvoice class. You've already seen most of the code for this class in the previous figure, but this figure should help you put things together.

Before I describe the code in this figure, I want to point out the modifications that need to be made to the Invoice class that was presented in figure 15-9 in order to allow the TaxableInvoice class to be derived from it:

- The instance variables dOrderTotal, dInvoiceTotal, dDiscountAmount, dCreditLimit, and LineItemCollection must be defined with the Protected keyword rather than the Private keyword.

- The Overridable keyword must be added to the Sub procedures AddItem and WriteInvoice.

The TaxableInvoice class starts with an Inherits statement that names the Invoice class as its base class. Then, it declares two private instance variables and a private constant. The constant provides the tax rate used to calculate the sales tax, and the variables are used to calculate the invoice subtotal and sales tax amount.

Next, two Property procedures define the new read-only properties provided by the TaxableInvoice class. These procedures simply retrieve the contents of the dSubTotal and dSalesTax instance variables.

The AddItem Sub procedure overrides the AddItem method from the base class. This procedure first invokes the base class AddItem method, then calculates the subtotal, sales tax, and invoice total.

The final procedure in the TaxableInvoice class overrides the WriteInvoice method from the base class. This procedure duplicates the code from the base class, but adds statements that write the subtotal and sales tax values to the XML document.

Now that you've seen how inheritance works, you may be wondering whether it makes sense to use it in a case like this. An alternative, for example, would be to define a single class that provides for both taxable and non-taxable orders. Then, the AddItem method could accept a second argument that indicated if the line item should be taxed, or the LineItem class could include a Taxable property. Either way, the solution would be simpler and more flexible than the one shown here.

Keep in mind, however, that I've intentionally kept the examples simple to make it easy for you to understand how inheritance works. As you design more complicated classes, I think you'll begin to see the benefits of using inheritance. In particular, if you can design base classes that are basic enough to be inherited by a number of other classes, you'll see how they can be used as building blocks for a variety of applications.

The Visual Basic code for the TaxableInvoice class

```
Public Class TaxableInvoice
    Inherits Invoice
    Private dSubTotal As Decimal
    Private dSalesTax As Decimal
    Private Const dTaxRate As Decimal = 0.075

    Public ReadOnly Property SalesTax() As Decimal
        Get
            Return dSalesTax
        End Get
    End Property

    Public ReadOnly Property SubTotal() As Decimal
        Get
            Return dSubTotal
        End Get
    End Property

    Public Overrides Sub AddItem(ByVal LineItem As LineItem)
        MyBase.AddItem(LineItem)
        dSubTotal = dInvoiceTotal
        dSalesTax = dSubTotal * dTaxRate
        dInvoiceTotal = dSubTotal - dSalesTax
    End Sub

    Public Overrides Sub WriteInvoice(ByVal InvoiceWriter As _
            System.Xml.XmlTextWriter)
        InvoiceWriter.WriteStartElement("Invoice")
        InvoiceWriter.WriteAttributeString("CustomerName", sCustomerName)
        InvoiceWriter.WriteElementString("OrderTotal", dOrderTotal)
        InvoiceWriter.WriteElementString("DiscountAmount", dDiscountAmount)
        InvoiceWriter.WriteElementString("SubTotal", dSubTotal)
        InvoiceWriter.WriteElementString("SalesTax", dSalesTax)
        InvoiceWriter.WriteElementString("InvoiceTotal", dInvoiceTotal)
        Dim LineItem As LineItem
        For Each LineItem In LineItemCollection
            LineItem.WriteLineItem(InvoiceWriter)
        Next
        InvoiceWriter.WriteEndElement()
    End Sub
End Class
```

(see 493)

Figure 15-15   The code for the TaxableInvoice class

How to create and use class libraries

So far, the classes you've seen have been created as part of a Windows project. If you want to be able to use the classes you create in two or more projects, however, you'll want to store them in class libraries. Simply put, a *class library* consists of a collection of related classes. When you use a class library, you can use any of the classes in the library without copying them into the project.

Before I go on, you should know that if you have the Standard edition of Visual Basic, you won't be able to create class libraries. In that case, you may want to skip the remaining topics of this chapter. However, I recommend that you read them anyway so you understand how class libraries work and what the benefits of using them are.

How class libraries work

Figure 15-16 illustrates the difference between using classes created within a Windows project and classes created within a class library project. As you can see, classes that are created in a Windows project must be included in every project that uses them. In contrast, classes that are created in a class library project exist separately from any project that uses them. Because of that, they are available to any project that has access to the class library.

One of the benefits of using class libraries is that the size of each project that uses them is reduced. That's because each project includes only a reference to the class library rather than the code for each class it needs. And because the classes in a class library are already compiled, Visual Studio doesn't have to compile them every time you build the application. This results in faster compile times.

Another benefit of using class libraries is that they simplify maintenance. If, for example, a class library resides on a network server, you can change that library without changing any of the applications that use the library. When you're done, the modified library is immediately available to the projects that use it.

But probably the main benefit of using class libraries is that they let you create reusable code. If you design your classes carefully and place them in a library, you can reuse them in other projects that require similar functions. In some cases, you can use the classes directly. In other cases, you can use inheritance to create new classes based on the classes in the library.

Two projects that use the same classes

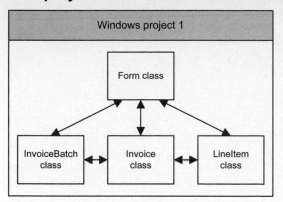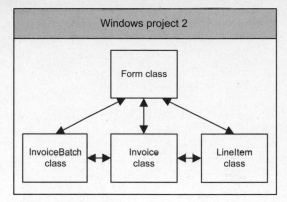

Two projects that use the same class library

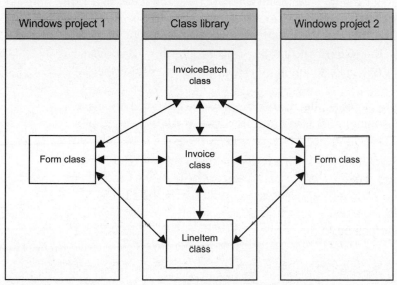

Description

- *Class libraries* provide a central location for storing classes that are used by two or more applications.

- When you store a class in a class library, you don't have to include the class in each application that uses it. Instead, you include a reference to the class library in those applications.

- When you modify a class in a class library, the changes are immediately available to all the applications that use it.

- To create a class library, you develop a class library project. Then, when you build the project, Visual Basic creates a *DLL file* for the class library. It's this *DLL* that you refer to from any application that needs to use the class library.

Figure 15-16   How class libraries work

How to create a class library project

To create a class library project, you use the Class Library template that's available from the New Project dialog box. After you complete this dialog box, Visual Basic creates a class library project that consists of a single class named Class1. Then, you can enter the code for this class and create additional classes using the techniques you've already learned. Or, if the classes you want to place in the library already exist in other projects, you can delete the Class1.vb file, then use the Project → Add Existing Item command to copy the classes into the class library project.

Figure 15-17 shows a class library project named InvoiceLib that includes three classes. These are the same classes used by the Invoice application you saw earlier in this chapter. In this case, though, they're stored in a class library project instead of in the Windows project that uses them.

When you're done designing a class library, you build it to create an assembly. The assembly for a class library is a *DLL file*, or just *DLL*. This is a file with the *dll* extension that contains the executable code for the class library. This file is stored in the Bin folder beneath the project folder for the project. Then, you can include a reference to this file in other projects as described in the next topic.

As you are developing a class library, it is often useful to create the class library as a project in a solution that also has a Windows form project. That way, you can use the Windows form project to test the class library. To add a new class library project to an existing solution, right-click the solution in the Solution Explorer, then choose Add → New Project. You can also add an existing class library project to a solution by choosing Add → Existing Project.

A class library project that includes three classes

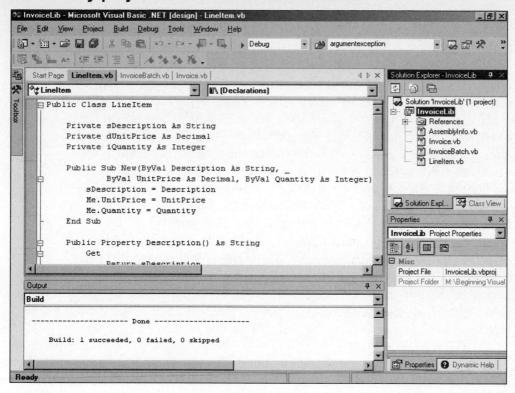

Description

- To create a class library project, display the New Project dialog box. Then, select the Class Library template and enter a name and location for the project.

- By default, a class library project includes a single class named Class1. You can modify this class any way you want or delete it from the project. You can also add additional classes using the Project → Add Existing Item command.

- To compile a class library project, select the Build → Build Solution command. Then, the class library is compiled into a DLL file that's stored in the Bin folder for the project.

Figure 15-17   How to create a class library project

How to add a reference to a class library

Figure 15-18 shows how the Invoice application that was presented earlier in this chapter can be adapted to use a class library. In the Solution Explorer window, you can see that this project includes a form class (Form1.vb) but no other class files. Instead, this version of the Invoice application includes a reference to the InvoiceLib class library that contains the classes it needs.

To add a reference to a class library in a project, you use the Add Reference dialog box shown in this figure. From this dialog box, you can click on the Browse button to locate the DLL file for the class library you want to refer to. Then, when you select that file, it's added to the list of selected components at the bottom of the Add Reference dialog box. When you click on the OK button, a reference to this file is added to the References folder in the Solution Explorer. Then, you can use the classes in the referenced class library.

If you have created a class library as a project in the same solution with a Windows form application, you can add a reference to the class library by selecting the project from the Projects tab of the Add Reference dialog box instead of locating the DLL for the project. Then, when you have the application working the way you want it, you can remove the class library project from the solution and add a reference to the DLL file for this project.

How to use the classes in a class library

Once you have added a reference to a class library to your project, you can use the classes in the class library the same way you use classes in the .NET Framework library. First, you can add an Imports statement at the beginning of the Visual Basic source file that names the class library to make it easier to refer to the classes it contains. In the Code Editor window in this figure, for example, you can see the Imports statement for the InvoiceLib class library.

After you add the Imports statement, you can use the classes in the library as if they were created as a part of the same project. A complication arises, however, if the class you want to refer to in the class library has the same name as a class in another namespace in the project or has the same name as the namespace that contains the project (which is usually the same as the project name). In that case, you have to qualify the name of the class so Visual Basic knows where to look for it. In this figure, for example, you can see that the Dim statement for the Invoice object qualifies the name of the Invoice class with the name of the class library since Invoice is also the name of the project.

A project that includes a reference to the InvoiceLib class library

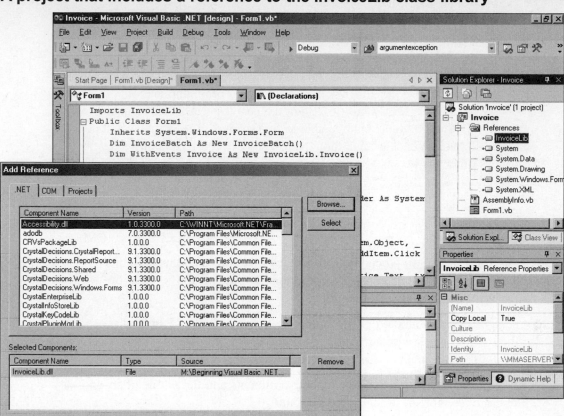

An Imports statement that simplifies access to the InvoiceLib class library

```
Imports InvoiceLib
```

How to use a class library

- Add a reference to the class library to your project by right-clicking the References folder in the Solution Explorer and selecting the Add Reference command from the shortcut menu that's displayed. Then, in the Add Reference dialog box, click the Browse button in the .NET tab, then locate the DLL for the class library and double-click it to add it to the Selected Components list at the bottom of the Add Reference dialog box.

- If the class library project is included in the same solution as the client project, that project will appear in the list at the top of the Projects tab. Then, you can add a reference for the class library by double-clicking on the project name.

- Once you have created a reference to the class library, you can include an Imports statement that names the class library. You can then use the classes in the class library without qualification. (In the example above, the Invoice class is qualified because it's also the name of the project.)

Figure 15-18   How to use a class library

Perspective

In this chapter, you learned a variety of skills for developing your own classes. In particular, you learned how to use features such as overloading and inheritance. You learned how to organize classes into class libraries. And you saw how business classes can be used to simplify the development of an application.

What you didn't learn is how to design the business classes for a business application, although you should be able to find many full-length books about it. With this chapter as background, though, you should start to recognize the need for a business object or two as you develop an application. And you should be able to develop the classes for those objects when you do recognize that need.

Summary

- A *constructor* is a Sub procedure named New that is called when an object is created from a class. You can use constructors to initialize class properties to values other than the standard defaults.

- You can *overload* a method by providing two or more Sub or Function procedures for the method, each with a different combination of arguments. The procedure name and the arguments form the procedure's *signature*.

- A class can validate property and method arguments and throw one of several argument exceptions if it detects invalid data.

- You use the Event statement to define a class event and the Raise Event statement to raise an event that's been defined.

- If a class contains an internal collection, you can provide methods to add or remove items from the collection. In addition, you can use a property with an index argument, also known as a *parameterized property*, to access individual items in the collection.

- *Inheritance* lets you create a new class based on an existing class. The existing class is called the *base class* and the new class is called the *derived class*.

- A derived class inherits the properties and methods of a base class, but you can add additional properties or methods or *override* the properties and methods of the base class.

- *Class libraries* are collections of classes that are stored in a single assembly so they can be used easily in other projects.

Terms

constructor	inherit	abstract class
overloaded method	derived class	class library
signature	base class	DLL
parameterized property	override	
inheritance	polymorphism	

Objectives

- Use the class programming elements presented in this chapter to create and use classes that include constructors, overloaded methods, argument validation, event definition, and collection properties.

- Use the inheritance features presented in this chapter to create a base class and a derived class that inherits the base class.

- Given one or more finished classes, create a class library project containing the classes, then use the class library to access the classes in a project.

- Describe the process of overloading a method or a constructor.

- Describe the effect of inheritance in creating a derived class from a base class.

- List two benefits of using class libraries.

Exercise 15-1   Modify the Invoice application

In this exercise, you'll modify the Invoice application presented in this chapter by adding an overloaded method and an overloaded constructor to the Invoice class and adjusting the form class to use the new method and constructor.

Add an overloaded AddItem method

1. Open the Invoice project in the C:\VB.NET\Chapter 15\Invoice folder. This is a fresh version of the Invoice application presented in figures 15-6 through 15-11.

2. Add an overloaded version of the AddItem method to the Invoice class. The new AddItem method should accept three arguments: a string named Description, a decimal named UnitPrice, and an integer named Quantity. The overloaded AddItem method should create a new LineItem object using these arguments, then duplicate the processing provided by the original AddItem method.

3. Modify the form class so that it calls the new AddItem method to add line items to the invoice. Then, run and test the application to make sure it works properly.

Add a new constructor

4. Add a new constructor to the Invoice class. The new constructor should accept a single argument named CustomerName to provide an initial value for the CustomerName property. The credit limit should still be set to $200 for each customer.

5. Modify the form class so it uses the new constructor. Although accepting a customer name as an argument in a constructor seems like a minor change to the class, it requires substantial changes to the form class:

    a. Instead of creating a new invoice object each time the user clicks on the New Invoice button, you should create the new invoice object only when the user types a new customer name. The best way to do that is to create an event procedure to handle the Leave event of the Customer Name text box. (The Leave event is raised when the focus moves out of the text box.)

    b. Since you can't add line items to an invoice that doesn't exist, you should disable the Add Item button until the user enters a customer name. Then, when the user clicks the New Invoice button, you should disable the Add Item button.

    c. If the user changes the customer name after an invoice object is created, you shouldn't create a new invoice object. Instead, you should just set the invoice's CustomerName property to the new name. The easiest way to check if an invoice object exists is by checking if the Add Item button is enabled.

6. Run the application and test it to make sure everything works properly. To make sure the XML is being written correctly, use the File → Open → File command to open the XML document and view it using the XML Designer. When you're certain the program is working right, close the solution.

TAXABLE INVOICE.

Exercise 15-2   Create a derived class

In this exercise, you'll implement the TaxableInvoice class that was described
in this chapter.

1. Open the Invoice project in the C:\VB.NET\Chapter 15\TaxableInvoice folder.
   This version has a modified form that looks like this:

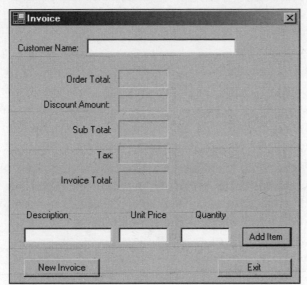

2. Modify the Invoice class so that it can be used as a base class for the
   TaxableInvoice class. You'll need to change the Private keyword for the
   instance variables and the Discount function to Protected and add the
   Overridable keyword to the Sub statements for the AddItem and WriteInvoice
   methods.   *SO CAN ACCESS*

3. Add a new class named TaxableInvoice to the project, then add the code
   necessary to inherit the Invoice class and implement the properties and
   methods indicated in figure 15-12. Be sure to display the subtotal and sales tax
   in the lblSubTotal and lblSalesTax labels and write the subtotal and sales tax
   values to the XML document in the WriteInvoice method. If possible, do this
   without looking at figure 15-15.   *(SEE 485-493)*

4. Modify the code for the form class so that it uses the new TaxableInvoice class
   rather than the Invoice class. Then, test the application to make sure it works
   properly. To tell whether it worked, use the File → Open → File command to
   open the XML document and verify that the XML includes the calculated
   subtotal and sales tax for each invoice.

Exercise 15-3   Create a class library

In this exercise, you'll create a class library for the classes used by the Invoice application of exercise 15-1, and you'll create a modified version of your solution that uses the class library.

1. Create a new Class Library project named InvoiceLib. Delete the empty Class1.vb class file, then use the Project → Add Existing Item command to add the InvoiceBatch, Invoice, and LineItem classes from the project you created for exercise 15-1.

2. Use the Build → Build Solution command to build the class library, then close the solution.

3. Create a new Windows Application project named InvoiceApp. Delete the empty Form1.vb form class, and then use the Project → Add Existing Item command to add the Form1.vb file from the project for exercise 15-1.

4. Add a reference to the InvoiceLib assembly you created in steps 1 and 2 and add an Imports statement to the beginning of the Form1.vb file. Then, run the project and enter several invoices to make sure the application works correctly. When you're done, end the program and close the solution.

TAXABLE INVOICE

Exercise 15-4   Create two new classes

In this exercise, you'll modify the Invoice application so that instead of entering an item description, the user selects an item from a drop-down list. Then, the application looks up the description and price for the selected item. To make this work, you'll create and use two new classes named Product and Inventory.

Open the project and review the form

1. Open the Invoice project in the C:\VB.NET\Chapter 15\InvoiceLookup folder. This version has a modified form that looks like this:

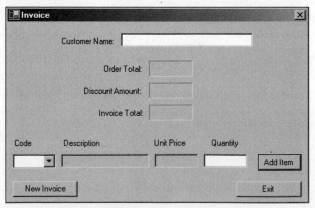

Notice that the txtDescription and txtUnitPrice text boxes have been changed to read-only and a combo box named cboCodes has been added.

Create the Product class

2.   Add a class named Product to the project. The Product class represents an inventory item and should have the following members:

Constructor	
New(Code As String, Description As String, Price As Decimal, QuantityOnHand As Integer)	Creates a new product and sets the code, description, price, and quantity on hand to the specified values.
Properties	
Code As String	Gets the product code.
Description As String	Gets or sets the product description.
Price As Decimal	Gets or sets the product price. This property should check that the value is greater than or equal to zero. If it isn't, it should throw an ArgumentOutOfRange exception.
QuantityOnHand As Integer	Gets or sets the number of product units currently on hand. This property should check that the value is greater than or equal to zero. If it isn't, it should throw an ArgumentOutOfRange exception.
Method	
ReduceQuantity(Amount As Integer)	Reduces the quantity on hand by the specified amount.
Event	
BackOrder(Quantity As Integer)	Raised if the Amount argument that's passed to the ReduceQuantity method is greater than the quantity on hand. If this event is raised, the ReduceQuantity method should set the quantity on hand to zero and pass the backordered quantity to the event.

Create the Inventory class

3.   Add a class named Inventory to the project. This class represents a collection of Product objects. It should use a private SortedList object to store the products and should have the following members:

Constructor				
New()	Creates a new Inventory object and loads the four products shown below into the product collection.			
	Code	**Description**	**Price**	**QuantityOnHand**
	EN1	Ethernet card	39.95	10
	PC6	6-foot patch cable	12.95	10
	PC10	10-foot patch cable	14.95	10
	SW16	16-port switch	99.95	10

Property	
Product (Code As String) As Product	Gets the Product with the specified code.
Method	
Add(Product As Product)	Adds the product to the collection of products.

Modify the form class to use the new classes

4. Add Dim statements to create variables that hold a new Inventory object and a Product object. You'll need to include the WithEvents keyword on the Product object so you can handle the BackOrder event.

5. Add a Form Load procedure that includes a For...Next loop that loads each product's Code property into the combo box (cboCodes).

6. Code a procedure to handle the SelectedIndexChanged event for the combo box. This procedure should retrieve the Product from the Inventory object using the code selected by the user, display the description and price in the Description and Unit Price text boxes, and move the focus to the Quantity text box.

7. In the procedure for the Click event of the Add Item button, call the ReduceQuantity method of the Product object to reduce the quantity on hand by the amount the user enters into the Quantity text box. Also, at the end of this procedure, clear the combo box selection and move the focus to the combo box.

8. Code a procedure to handle the BackOrder event for the Product object. This procedure should display a message box similar to this one:

9. Test the application by creating from two to five invoices. To tell whether it worked, use the File → Open → File command to open the file in the XML Designer window. Then, use both XML and Data view to verify that the XML document shows the correct information for the invoices you entered.

Section 4

Database programming essentials

Chapters 13 and 14 show you how to work with the data in files because files are still commonly used for some purposes. For major applications, though, the data is commonly stored in databases. That's why this section is devoted to the essentials of database programming. When you complete it, you should be able to develop complete database applications that use the latest data access method, which is called ADO.NET.

To start this section, chapter 16 introduces you to the concepts and terms that you need to know when you develop database applications with ADO.NET. Then, chapter 17 shows you how to develop a simple database application with ADO.NET and a data grid control. Last, chapter 18 shows you how to use other techniques for developing database applications with ADO.NET.

As you read these chapters, please remember that they represent little more than an introduction to database processing with ADO.NET, even if they seem quite complicated at times. In fact, there are many other controls and techniques that you can use as you develop more sophisticated applications. And database processing is a complicated subject indeed.

1

35% MSSQL

MOST
POWERFUL → 35% ORACLE

36% ALL OTHER:
ACCESS, DBII, DBIII, ETC.

DECISION BASED ON
PLATFORM, SIZE OF DB

MOSTLY
UNIX

ORACLE

MSSQL

ACCESS, ETC.   WINDOWS

USERS

SIZE

JAVA - MOSTLY ORACLE   { MORE JAVA
                                AVAIL FOR
                                ORACLE
                                THAN VB

VB - MOSTLY MSSQL

IN ACCESS, USER IS ADMIN.

ORACLE/UNIX, ADMIN, TOTALLY SEP. *

MORE TRAINING, MORE $

16

An introduction to database programming

Before you can develop a database application, you need to be familiar with the concepts and terms that apply to database applications. In particular, you need to understand what a relational database is and how you work with it using SQL and ADO.NET. So that's what you'll learn in this chapter.

To illustrate these concepts and terms, this chapter presents examples that use the *Microsoft SQL Server Desktop Engine* (*MSDE*). MSDE, which comes with Visual Basic .NET, is a scaled-back version of Microsoft *SQL Server 2000*. And SQL Server 2000 is the database you're most likely to use as you develop database applications with Visual Basic .NET.

An introduction to multi-user database applications

In case you aren't familiar with multi-user systems, the two topics that follow introduce you to the essential hardware and software components of a multi-user system. Then, the rest of this chapter presents additional information on these components and how you use them in database applications.

The hardware components of a multi-user system

Figure 16-1 presents the three hardware components of a multi-user system: the clients, the network, and the server. The *clients* are usually the PCs that are already available on the desktops throughout a company. And the *network* is the cabling, communication lines, network interface cards, hubs, routers, and other components that connect the clients and the server.

The *server* is a computer that has enough processor speed, internal memory (RAM), and disk storage to serve the clients of the system. This computer is usually a high-powered PC, but it can also be a midrange system like an AS/400 or UNIX system, or even a mainframe system. When a system consists of networks, midrange systems, and mainframe systems, often spread throughout the country or world, it is commonly referred to as an *enterprise system*.

To back up the files of a multi-user system, a server usually has a tape drive or some other form of offline storage. It often has one or more printers or specialized devices that can be shared by the users of the system. And it can provide programs or services like e-mail that can be accessed by all the users of the system.

In a simple multi-user system, the clients and the server are part of a *local area network* (*LAN*). However, two or more LANs that reside at separate geographical locations can be connected as part of a larger network such as a *metropolitan area network* (*MAN*) or a *wide area network* (*WAN*). In addition, individual systems or networks can be connected over the Internet. In chapter 19, you'll learn how to develop Internet applications.

A simple multi-user system

[handwritten: - SERVER MIGHT BE TEMPORARY CONDITION - LIKE USING PRINTER FROM OTHER COMPUTER (OR NAPSTER)]

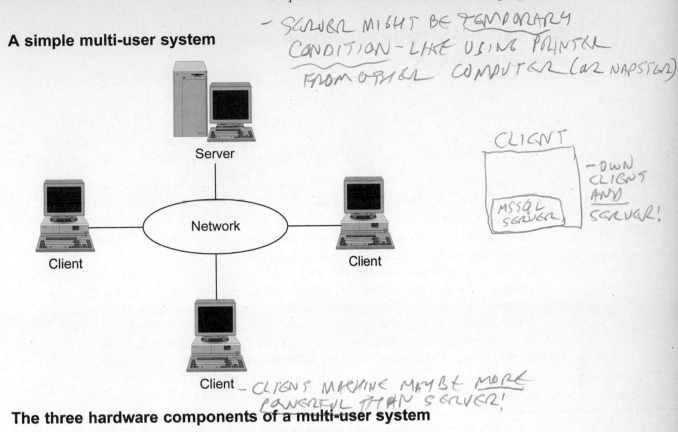

[handwritten: CLIENT - OWN CLIENT AND SERVER! MSSQL SERVER]

[handwritten: Client _ CLIENT MACHINE MAY BE MORE POWERFUL THAN SERVER!]

The three hardware components of a multi-user system

- The *clients* are the PCs, Macintoshes, or workstations of the system.

- The *server* is a computer that stores the files and databases of the system and provides services to the clients.

- The *network* consists of the cabling, communication lines, and other components that connect the clients and the servers of the system.

Multi-user system implementations

- In a simple multi-user system like the one shown above, the server is typically a high-powered PC that communicates with the clients over a *local area network* (*LAN*). ✳

- The server can also be a midrange system, like an AS/400 or a UNIX system, or it can be a mainframe system. Then, special hardware and software components are required to make it possible for the clients to communicate with the midrange and mainframe systems.

- A system can also consist of one or more PC-based systems, one or more midrange systems, and a mainframe system in dispersed geographical locations. This type of system is commonly referred to as an *enterprise system*.

- Individual systems and LANs can be connected and share data over a *metropolitan area network* (*MAN*), a *wide area network* (*WAN*), or the Internet.

Figure 16-1   The hardware components of a multi-user system

[handwritten: ✳ MAINLY, LIMITED ACCESS]

*Handwritten margin note (top): * LOTS OF SECURITY (INTERNET NO)*

The software components of a multi-user database application

*Handwritten margin note (left): NOVELL * MS NETWORKS * INTERNET*

Figure 16-2 presents the software components of a typical multi-user database application. In addition to a *network operating system* that manages the functions of the network, the server requires a *database management system* (*DBMS*) like Oracle or Microsoft SQL Server. This DBMS manages the databases that are stored on the server.

In contrast to a server, each client requires *application software* to perform useful work. This can be a purchased software package like a financial accounting package, or it can be custom software that's developed for a specific application. This book, of course, shows you how to use Visual Basic .NET for developing custom software for database applications.

Although the application software is run on the client, it uses data that's stored on the server. To make this communication between the client and the *data source* possible when a Visual Basic .NET application is being used, the client requires a *.NET data provider*.

The .NET Framework comes with two data providers. The *SQL Server data provider* is designed specifically for use with SQL Server databases (2000 or later) and provides the most efficient access to those databases. The *OLE DB data provider* is less efficient than the SQL Server data provider, but it can be used with a variety of data sources including Oracle and SQL Server.

Once the software for both client and server is installed, the client communicates with the server via *SQL queries* (or just *queries*) that are passed to the DBMS through the .NET data provider. These queries are written in a standard language called *SQL*, which stands for *Structured Query Language*. SQL lets any application communicate with any DBMS. After the client sends a query to the DBMS, the DBMS interprets the query and sends the results back to the client. (In conversation, SQL is pronounced as either *S-Q-L* or *sequel*.)

When the processing for an application is divided between the clients and the server as illustrated in this figure, the system can be referred to as a *client/server system*. In this case, the DBMS is processing the queries so the server is doing part of the work. Theoretically, at least, this balances the workload between the clients and the server so the system works more efficiently. In contrast, in a file-handling system, the clients do all of the work because the server is used only to store the files that are used by the clients.

Handwritten margin note (right): WE WILL CREATE CLIENTS

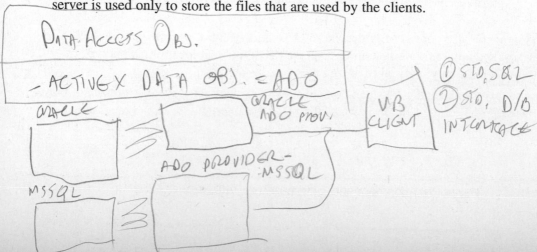

Client software, server software, and the SQL interface

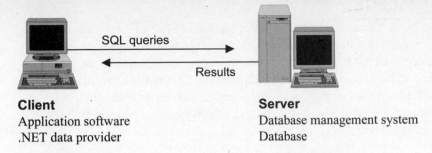

Client
Application software
.NET data provider

Server
Database management system
Database

Server software

- To store the databases of the client/server system, each server requires a *database management system* (*DBMS*) like Microsoft SQL Server.

Client software

- The *application software* does the work that the user wants to do. This type of software can be purchased or developed.

- The *.NET data provider* lets the client application communicate with the *data source*. To work with a SQL Server 2000 or later database, you can use the *SQL Server data provider*. To work with other databases, you use the *OLE DB data provider*.

The SQL interface

- The application software communicates with the DBMS by sending *SQL queries* through the .NET data provider. When the DBMS receives a query, it provides a service like returning the requested data (the *query results*) to the client.

- *SQL* stands for *Structured Query Language*, which is the standard language for working with a relational database.

Client/server versus file-handling systems

- When the processing done by an application is divided between the client and the server, the system can be referred to as a *client/server system*.

- When the clients of a network access the data that's stored in files on a server, none of the processing is done on the server. As a result, a file-handling system isn't a client/server system.

Note

- Since SQL is a standard language, vendors other than Microsoft offer database management systems that are based on it. Two common examples on enterprise systems are Oracle and IBM's DB2.

Figure 16-2   The software components of a multi-user database application

An introduction to relational databases

In 1970, Dr. E. F. Codd developed a model for a new type of database called a *relational database*. This type of database eliminated some of the problems that were associated with standard files and other database designs. By using the relational model, you can reduce data redundancy, which saves disk storage and leads to efficient data retrieval. You can also view and manipulate data in a way that is both intuitive and efficient. Today, relational databases are the de facto standard for database applications.

How a table is organized

The model for a relational database states that data is stored in one or more *tables*. It also states that each table can be viewed as a two-dimensional matrix consisting of *rows* and *columns*. This is illustrated by the relational table in figure 16-3. Each row in this table contains information about a single vendor.

In practice, the rows and columns of a relational database table are often referred to by the more traditional terms, *records* and *fields*. In fact, some software packages use one set of terms, some use the other, and some use a combination. We use these terms interchangeably throughout this book.

If a table contains one or more columns that uniquely identify each row in the table, you can define these columns as the *primary key* of the table. For instance, the primary key of the Vendors table in this figure is the VendorID column. In this example, this column contains a number that is generated automatically by the DBMS, which SQL Server refers to as an *identity column*. Note, however, that a primary key doesn't have to be an identity column.

In addition to primary keys, some database management systems let you define additional keys that uniquely identify each row in a table. If, for example, the VendorName column in the Vendors table contains unique data, it can be defined as a *non-primary key*. In SQL Server, this is called a *unique key*, and it's implemented by defining a *unique key constraint*. The only difference between a unique key and a primary key is that a unique key can contain a null value and a primary key can't.

Indexes provide an efficient way to access the rows in a table based on the values in one or more columns. Because applications typically access the rows in a table by referring to their key values, an index is automatically created for each key you define. However, you can define indexes for other columns as well. If, for example, you frequently need to sort the Vendor records by zip code, you can set up an index for that column. Like a key, an index can include one or more columns.

The Vendors table in the Accounts Payable database

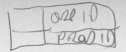

Primary key   **Columns**   **Rows**

VendorID	VendorName	VendorAddress1	VendorAddress2
1	US Postal Service	Attn: Supt. Window Services	PO Box 7005
2	National Information Data Ctr	PO Box 96621	
3	Register of Copyrights	Library Of Congress	
4	Jobtrak	1990 Westwood Blvd Ste 260	
5	Newbrige Book Clubs	3000 Cindel Drive	
6	California Chamber Of Commerce	3255 Ramos Cir	
7	Towne Advertiser's Mailing Svcs	Kevin Minder	3441 W Macarthur Blvd
8	BFI Industries	PO Box 9369	
9	Pacific Gas & Electric	Box 52001	
10	Robbins Mobile Lock And Key	4669 N Fresno	
12	City Of Fresno	PO Box 2069	
13	Golden Eagle Insurance Co	PO Box 85826	
15	ASC Signs	1528 N Sierra Vista	
16	Internal Revenue Service		

Concepts

- A *relational database* uses *tables* to store and manipulate data. Each table consists of one or more *records*, or *rows*, that contain the data for a single entry. Each row contains one or more *fields*, or *columns*, with each column representing a single item of data.

- Most tables contain a *primary key* that uniquely identifies each row in the table. The primary key often consists of a single field, but it can also consist of two or more fields.

- In addition to primary keys, some database management systems let you define one or more *non-primary keys*. In SQL Server, these keys are called *unique keys*, and they're implemented using *unique key constraints*. Like a primary key, a non-primary key uniquely identifies each row in the table.

- A table can also be defined with one or more *indexes*. An index provides an efficient way to access data from a table based on the values in specific columns. An index is automatically created for a table's primary and non-primary keys.

Figure 16-3   How a table is organized

How the tables in a database are related

The tables in a relational database can be related to other tables by values in specific columns. The two tables shown in figure 16-4 illustrate this concept. Here, each row in the Vendors table is related to one or more rows in the Invoices table. This is called a *one-to-many relationship*.

Typically, relationships exist between the primary key in one table and the *foreign key* in another table. The foreign key is simply one or more columns in a table that refer to a primary key in another table. In SQL Server, relationships can also exist between a unique key in one table and a foreign key in another table. For simplicity, though, I'll assume relationships are based on primary keys.

To define a relationship in SQL Server, you create a *foreign key constraint*. A foreign key constraint prevents records from being added to the foreign key table if a related record doesn't exist in the primary key table. In addition, with versions of SQL Server before 2000, a foreign key constraint prevented the primary key of a record in the primary key table from being changed if it had related records in the foreign key table. It also prevented a record in the primary key table from being deleted if it had related records in the foreign key table. With SQL Server 2000, however, changes to a primary key can be applied, or *cascaded*, automatically to a foreign key table. Similarly, if a record is deleted from the primary key table, the related records in the foreign key table can be deleted.

Although one-to-many relationships are the most common, two tables can also have a one-to-one or many-to-many relationship. If a table has a *one-to-one relationship* with another table, the data in the two tables could be stored in a single table. Because of that, one-to-one relationships are used infrequently.

In contrast, a *many-to-many relationship* is usually implemented by using an intermediate table that has a one-to-many relationship with the two tables in the many-to-many relationship. In other words, a many-to-many relationship can usually be broken down into two one-to-many relationships.

The relationship between the Vendors and Invoices tables

Primary key

VendorID	VendorName	VendorAddress1
94	Abbey Office Furnishings	4150 W Shaw Ave
95	Pacific Bell	
96	Wells Fargo Bank	Business Mastercard
97	Compuserve	Dept L-742
98	American Express	Box 0001
99	Bertelsmann Industry Svcs. Inc	28210 N Avenue Stanford
100	Cahners Publishing Company	Citibank Lock Box 4026
101	California Business Machines	Gallery Plz
102	Coffee Break Service	PO Box 1091
103	Dean Witter Reynolds	9 River Pk Pl E 400

InvoiceID	VendorID	InvoiceNumber	InvoiceDate	InvoiceTotal
97	119	120197	1/17/2002	4901.26
98	95	112897	1/17/2002	46.21
99	95	112797	1/18/2002	39.77
100	96	112897	1/18/2002	662
101	103	112697	1/19/2002	1367.5
102	48	112697	1/19/2002	856.92
103	95	112697	1/19/2002	19.67
104	114	112597	1/20/2002	290
105	95	112597	1/20/2002	32.7
106	95	112497	1/21/2002	16.33

Foreign key

Concepts

- The tables in a relational database are related to each other through their key fields. For example, the VendorID field is used to relate the Vendors and Invoices tables above. The VendorID field in the Invoices table is called a *foreign key* because it identifies a related row in the Vendors table.

- To define a foreign key in SQL Server, you create a *foreign key constraint*. Then, you can't add records to the table with the foreign key unless there's a matching primary key in the related table.

- With versions of SQL Server before SQL Server 2000, a foreign key constraint also kept you from changing a primary key value or deleting a primary key record if related records existed in the foreign key table. With SQL Server 2000, however, updates and deletes can be *cascaded* automatically to the foreign key table.

- Three types of relationships can exist between tables. The most common type is *a one-to-many relationship* as illustrated above. A table can also have a *one-to-one relationship* or a *many-to-many relationship* with another table.

Figure 16-4   How the tables in a database are related

How the fields in a table are defined

When you define a field in a table, you assign properties to it as indicated by the design of the Invoices table in figure 16-5. The most critical property for a field is its Datatype property, which determines the type of information that can be stored in the field. With SQL Server 2000, you can choose from *system data types* like the ones in this figure, and you can define your own data types that are based on the system data types. As you define each field in a table, you generally try to assign the data type that will minimize the use of disk storage because that will improve the performance of the queries later.

In addition to a data type, you can use defaults and check constraints to help maintain the validity of the data. A *default* provides a default value for a field when the user or the program doesn't enter anything into the field. Otherwise, if Null values aren't allowed in the field, an error will occur.

In contrast, a *check constraint* defines the acceptable values for a field. For example, you can define a check constraint for the Invoices table in this figure to make sure that the value in the InvoiceDueDate field is always greater than or equal to the value in the InvoiceDate field. Because a constraint is specified at the table level, not the field level, it can refer to two or more fields in the table.

After you define the constraints for a database, they're managed by the DBMS. If, for example, a user tries to add a record with data that violates a constraint, the DBMS sends an appropriate error code back to the application without adding the record to the database. The application can then respond to the error code.

Another alternative is to validate the data that is going to be added to a database before the program tries to add it. That way, the constraints shouldn't be needed and the program should run more efficiently. In practice, though, both data validation and constraints are commonly used. That way, the programs run more efficiently if the data validation routines work, but the constraints are there in case the data validation routines don't work or aren't coded.

The Server Explorer design view window for the Invoices table

Column Name	Data Type	Length	Allow Nulls
InvoiceID	int	4	
VendorID	int	4	
InvoiceNumber	varchar	10	
InvoiceDate	smalldatetime	4	
InvoiceTotal	money	8	
PaymentTotal	money	8	
CreditTotal	money	8	
TermsID	int	4	
InvoiceDueDate	smalldatetime	4	

[handwritten: GIVES FIELDS AND CHARACTERISTICS OF.]

Columns

Default Value	
Precision	10
Scale	0
Identity	Yes
Identity Seed	1
Identity Increment	1
Is RowGuid	No
Formula	

Common SQL Server data types

Type	Description
bit	A value of 1 or 0 that represents a True or False value.
char, varchar, text *[handwritten: No STRING]*	Any combination of letters, symbols, and numbers.
datetime, smalldatetime	Alphanumeric data that represents a date and time. Various formats are acceptable.
decimal, numeric	Numeric data that is accurate to the least significant digit. The data can contain an integer and a fractional portion.
float, real	Floating-point values that contain an approximation of a decimal value.
int, smallint, tinyint	Numeric data that contains only an integer portion.
money, smallmoney	Monetary values that are accurate to four decimal places.
binary, varbinary, image	Binary strings and image data.
timestamp, uniqueidentifier	A value that is always unique within a database.

[handwritten: IDENTITY = YES = UNIQUE IDENTIFIER → [InvID]]

Description

- The *data type* that's assigned to a field determines the type of information that can be stored in the field. Depending on the data type, you can also specify the length, precision, and scale for the field.
- To restrict the values that a field can hold, you can define *check constraints*. These constraints are defined at the table level and can refer to one or more fields in the table.
- If you specify a *default value* for a field, that value is used if another value isn't provided.

Figure 16-5   How the fields in a table are defined

[handwritten: P/K WON'T ALLOW NULL]

How to use SQL to work with the data in a relational database

In this topic, you'll learn about the four SQL statements that you can use to manipulate the data in a database: the Select, Insert, Update, and Delete statements. Because of the way Visual Basic .NET works, you won't need to write any SQL statements for the applications in this book. However, you'll be able to master the material in the next two chapters more easily once you have a general idea of what these statements do and how they're coded. There are also other SQL statements that you can use to define the data in a database, but the programmer usually doesn't use them. As a result, they aren't presented in this book.

Although SQL is a standard language, each DBMS is likely to have its own *SQL dialect*, which includes extensions to the standard language. So when you use SQL, you need to make sure that you're using the dialect that's supported by your DBMS. In this chapter and throughout this book, all of the SQL examples are for Microsoft SQL Server's dialect, which is called *Transact-SQL*.

How to query a single table

Figure 16-6 shows how to use a Select statement to query a single table in a database. In the syntax summary at the top of this figure, you can see that the Select clause names the fields to be retrieved, and the From clause names the table that contains the fields. You can also code a Where clause that gives criteria for the records to be selected. And you can code an Order By clause that names one or more fields that the results should be sorted by and indicates whether each field should be sorted in ascending or descending sequence.

If you study the Select statement below the syntax summary, you can see how this works. Here, the Select statement retrieves fields from a table named Invoices. It selects a record from the Invoices table only if it has a balance due that's greater than zero. And it sorts the returned records by invoice date in ascending sequence (the default).

Please note in this Select statement that the last field in the query, BalanceDue, is calculated by subtracting PaymentTotal and CreditTotal from InvoiceTotal. In other words, a field by the name of BalanceDue doesn't actually exist in the database. This type of field is called a *calculated field*, and it exists only in the results of the query.

This figure also shows the *result table*, or *result set*, that's returned by the Select statement. A result table is a logical table that's created temporarily within the database. When an application requests data from a database, it receives a result table.

If you're a professional programmer who develops database applications, you should eventually learn how to write Select statements. For simple Visual Basic applications, though, you can use the Query Builder to generate the Select statements you need, which is what you'll learn to do in the next chapter.

Simplified syntax of the Select statement

```
Select field-1 [, field-2]...
From table-1
[Where selection-criteria]
[Order By field-1 [Asc|Desc] [, field-2 [Asc|Desc]]...]
```

A Select statement that retrieves and sorts selected fields and records from the Invoices table

```
Select InvoiceNumber, InvoiceDate, InvoiceTotal,
    PaymentTotal, CreditTotal,
    InvoiceTotal - PaymentTotal - CreditTotal As BalanceDue
From Invoices
Where InvoiceTotal - PaymentTotal - CreditTotal > 0
Order By InvoiceDate
```

The result table defined by the Select statement

InvoiceNumber	InvoiceDate	InvoiceTotal	PaymentTotal	CreditTotal	BalanceDue
P-0608	11/24/2001	20551.18	0	0	20551.18
989319-497	11/30/2001	2312.2	0	0	2312.2
989319-487	12/1/2001	1927.54	0	0	1927.54
97/553B	12/9/2001	313.55	0	0	313.55
97/553	12/10/2001	651.29	0	0	651.29
97/522	12/13/2001	1962.13	0	0	1962.13
203339-13	12/15/2001	17.5	0	0	17.5
0-2436	12/20/2001	10976.06	0	0	10976.06
963253272	12/22/2001	61.5	0	0	61.5
963253271	12/22/2001	158	0	0	158
963253269	12/22/2001	26.75	0	0	26.75
963253267	12/22/2001	23.5	0	0	23.5

Concepts

- The result of a Select statement is a *result table*, or *result set*, like the one shown above. A result table is a logical set of records that consists of all of the fields and records requested by the Select statement.

- A result table can include *calculated fields* that are calculated from other fields in the table.

- To select all of the fields in a table, you can code an asterisk (*) in place of the field names. For example, this statement will select all of the fields from the Invoices table:

```
Select * From Invoices
```

Note

- When you use ADO.NET to work with a database as described in the next two chapters, you can use the Query Builder to generate the Select statements that you need so you don't have to master the SQL syntax.

Figure 16-6   How to query a single table

How to join data from two or more tables

Figure 16-7 presents the syntax of the Select statement for retrieving data from two tables. This type of operation is called a *join* because the data from the two tables is joined together into a single result table. For example, the Select statement in this figure joins data from the Invoices and Vendors table into a single result table.

An *inner join* is the most common type of join. When you use an inner join, records from the two tables in the join are included in the result table only if their related fields match. These matching fields are specified in the From clause of the Select statement. In the Select statement in this figure, for example, records from the Invoices and Vendors tables are included only if the value of the VendorID field in the Vendors table matches the value of the VendorID field in one or more records in the Invoices table. If there aren't any invoices for a particular vendor, that vendor won't be included in the result table.

Although this figure shows only how to join data from two tables, you should know that you can extend this syntax to join data from additional tables. If, for example, you want to include line item data from a table named InvoiceLineItems in the results shown in this figure, you can code the From clause of the Select statement like this:

```
From Vendors
    Inner Join Invoices
        On Vendors.VendorID = Invoices.VendorID
    Inner Join InvoiceLineItems
        On Invoices.InvoiceID = InvoiceLineItems.InvoiceID
```

Then, in the field list of the Select statement, you can include any of the fields in the InvoiceLineItems table.

The syntax of the Select statement for joining two tables

```
Select field-list
From table-1
    Inner Join table-2
    On table-1.field-1 {=|<|>|<=|>=|<>} table-2.field-2
[Where selection-criteria]
[Order By field-list]
```

A Select statement that joins data from the Vendors and Invoices tables

```
Select VendorName, InvoiceNumber, InvoiceDate, InvoiceTotal
From Vendors Inner Join Invoices
    On Vendors.VendorID = Invoices.VendorID
Where InvoiceTotal >= 500
Order By VendorName, InvoiceTotal Desc
```

The result table defined by the Select statement

VendorName	InvoiceNumber	InvoiceDate	InvoiceTotal
IBM	Q545443	10/27/2001	1083.58
Ingram	31359783	1/5/2002	1575
Ingram	31361833	1/5/2002	579.42
Malloy Lithographing Inc	0-2058	12/21/2001	37966.19
Malloy Lithographing Inc	P-0259	11/29/2001	26881.4
Malloy Lithographing Inc	0-2060	12/21/2001	23517.58
Malloy Lithographing Inc	P-0608	11/24/2001	20551.18
Malloy Lithographing Inc	0-2436	12/20/2001	10976.06
Pollstar	120197	1/17/2002	1750
Reiter's Scientific & Pro Books	C73-24	11/30/2001	600
United Parcel Service	989319-457	12/7/2001	3813.33

Concepts

- A *join* lets you combine data from two or more tables into a single result table.
- The most common type of join is an *inner join*. This type of join returns records from both tables only if their related fields match.

Figure 16-7   How to join data from two or more tables

How to add, update, and delete data in a table

Figure 16-8 presents the basic syntax of the SQL Insert, Update, and Delete statements. You use the Insert statement to insert one or more records into a table. As you can see, the syntax of this statement is different depending on whether you're adding a single record or selected records.

To add a single record to a table, you specify the name of the table you want to add the record to, the names of the fields you're supplying data for, and the values for those fields. The example in this figure adds a record to a table named Terms, which contains three fields: TermsID, TermsDescription, and TermsDueDays. Because the value of the TermsID field is generated automatically, though, it's not included in the Insert statement. If you're going to supply values for all the fields in a table, you can omit the field names, but then you must be sure to specify the values in the same order as the fields appear in the table.

To add selected records to a table, you include a Select statement within the Insert statement. Then, the Select statement retrieves fields from one or more tables based on the conditions you specify, and the Insert statement adds those records to another table. In the example in this figure, the Select statement selects all the fields from the records in the Invoices table that have been paid in full and inserts them into a table named InvoiceArchive.

To change the values of one or more fields in a table, you use the Update statement. On this statement, you specify the name of the table you want to update, expressions that indicate the fields you want to change and how you want to change them, and a condition that identifies the records you want to change. In the example in this figure, the Update statement changes the TermsID value to 4 for each record in the Invoices table that has a TermsID value of 1.

To delete records from a table, you use the Delete statement. On this statement, you specify the table you want to delete records from and a condition that indicates the records you want to delete. The Delete statement in this figure deletes all the records from the Invoices table that have been paid in full.

Although you may eventually want to learn how to code Insert, Update, and Delete statements, you won't need to know how to code them if you use the development techniques that are presented in the next two chapters. Instead, these statements will be generated automatically based on the Select statement that's used to retrieve the data that's being modified.

How to add a single record

The syntax of the Insert statement for adding a single record

```
Insert Into table-name [(field-list)]
    Values (value-list)
```

A statement that adds a single record to a table

```
Insert Into Terms (TermsDescription, TermsDueDays)
    Values ("Net due 90 days", 90)
```

How to add selected records

The syntax of the Insert statement for adding selected records

```
Insert Into table-name [(field-list)]
    Select-statement
```

A statement that adds selected records from one table to another table

```
Insert Into InvoiceArchive
    Select * From Invoices
    Where InvoiceTotal - PaymentTotal - CreditTotal = 0
```

How to update records

The syntax of the Update statement

```
Update table-name
    Set expression-1 [, expression-2]...
    Where selection-criteria
```

A statement that changes the value of the TermsID field for selected records

```
Update Invoices
    Set TermsID = 4
    Where TermsID = 1
```

How to delete records

The syntax of the Delete statement

```
Delete From table-name
    Where selection-criteria
```

A statement that deletes all paid invoices

```
Delete From Invoices
    Where InvoiceTotal - PaymentTotal - CreditTotal = 0
```

Note

- When you use ADO.NET to work with a database as described in the next two chapters, you don't have to write your own Insert, Update, and Delete statements. Instead, they're generated for you.

Figure 16-8   How to add, update, and delete data in a table

An introduction to ADO.NET

ADO.NET is the primary data access method for the .NET Framework. It provides the classes that you use as you develop database applications with Visual Basic .NET, and it is an improved version of *ADO (ActiveX Data Objects)*, which was the primary access method of Visual Basic 6. In the next three topics, you'll learn the ADO.NET concepts that you need to know as you develop database applications.

How the basic ADO.NET components work

To work with data using ADO.NET, you use a variety of ADO.NET components. Figure 16-9 shows how the primary ones are used for Windows applications.

To start, the data used by an application is stored in a *dataset* that contains one or more *data tables*. To load data into a data table, you use a *data adapter*. The main function of the data adapter is to manage the flow of data between a dataset and a database. To do that, it uses *data commands* that define the SQL statements to be issued. The data command for retrieving data, for example, defines a Select statement. Then, the data command connects to the database using a *data connection* and passes the Select statement to the database. After the Select statement is executed, the result table it produces is sent back to the data adapter, which stores the results in the data table.

To update the data in a database, the data adapter uses a data command that defines an Insert, Update, or Delete statement for a table. Then, the data command uses the data connection to connect to the database and perform the requested operation.

Although it's not apparent in this figure, the connection to the database is closed after the requested operation is performed by the DBMS. Then, the connection is opened again when it's needed. That means that once your application retrieves data, it has no direct connection with the data in the database. Instead, it must work with a copy of the data that's stored in the dataset. The architecture that's used to implement this type of data processing is referred to as a *disconnected data architecture*. Although this is more complicated than a connected architecture, the advantages offset this complexity.

One of the advantages of using a disconnected data architecture is improved system performance due to the use of fewer system resources for maintaining connections. Another advantage is that it makes ADO.NET compatible with ASP.NET web applications, which are inherently disconnected. In chapter 19, you'll learn more about ASP.NET web applications.

When you use the ADO.NET components in your programs, you'll see that they are implemented by .NET classes. For instance, the classes for the SQL Server data provider are in the System.Data.SqlClient namespace, and the classes for the OLE DB data provider are in the System.Data.OleDb namespace. The classes for all of the other components, like the data table and dataset, are in the

CAN HAVE XML VIEW OF TABLES

Basic ADO.NET components in a Windows application

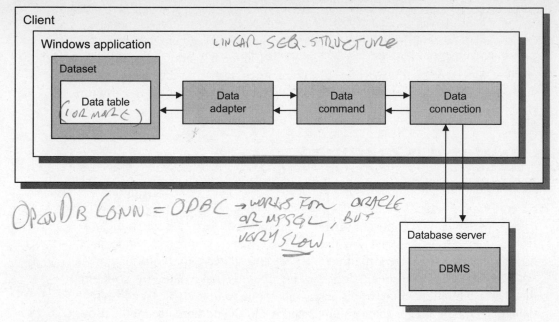

LINEAR SEQ. STRUCTURE

OpenDB Conn = ODBC → WORKS FOR ORACLE OR MSSQL, BUT VERY SLOW.

Description

- The data used by an application is stored in a *data table* within a *dataset*. A data table has a row and column format like a table in a relational database, and a dataset can contain one or more data tables.

- To retrieve data from a database and store it in a data table, a *data adapter* issues a Select statement that's stored in a *data command*. Next, the data command uses a *data connection* to connect to the database and retrieve the data. Then, the data is passed back to the data adapter, which stores the data in the dataset.

- To update the data in a database based on the data in a data table, the data adapter issues an Insert, Update, or Delete statement that's stored in a data command. Then, the data command uses a data connection to connect to the database and update the database.

- After data is retrieved from a database or updated in a database, the connection is closed and the resources used by the connection are released. This is referred to as a *disconnected data architecture.*

- All of the ADO.NET components are implemented by classes in the .NET Framework. However, the specific classes used to implement the data connection, data command, and data adapter depend on the .NET data provider you use.

- ADO.NET uses XML to define the structure of the data in a dataset and to transmit the data to and from a database. In most cases, though, you won't need to work directly with the XML that's generated.

Figure 16-9   How the basic ADO.NET components work

NO COMM. TIL YOU REQ. DATA

System.Data namespace, which makes sense if you realize that these components are independent of the database due to the disconnected data architecture.

You should also know that ADO.NET uses XML to transmit data to and from a database. That's possible because the structure of a dataset in ADO.NET is defined by XML. Usually, this use of XML is done behind the scenes, so you don't have to work with XML directly. In contrast, if you've read chapter 14, you know that you have to work with XML directly if you want to use it with files.

How a dataset is organized

As I mentioned a moment ago, the result table that's returned from the execution of a Select statement is stored in a dataset within the application. Then, the application can work directly with that data as you'll see in the next two chapters. To understand how that works, however, you need to understand how a dataset is organized. Figure 16-10 presents the essential information.

The first thing you should notice in this figure is that a dataset is structured much like a relational database. It can contain one or more tables, and each table can contain one or more columns and rows. In addition, each table can contain one or more constraints that can define a unique key within the table or a foreign key of another table in the dataset. If a dataset contains two or more tables, the dataset also defines the relationships between those tables.

Although it's not apparent in this figure, you should know that each of the groups of objects in the diagram is stored in a collection. All of the columns in a table, for example, are stored in a collection of columns, and all of the rows are stored in a collection of rows. Then, you can use the techniques you learned in chapter 12 to work with the items in these collections. Note, however, that when you develop applications using the techniques presented in the next two chapters, you won't need to work with these collections directly. You'll have a better idea of why that is after you read those chapters.

SERVER EXPLORER = ALLOWS LOOK INSIDE D/B
ADD CONN → REFRESH → SHOW COMP W/ D/B. → CAN FIND
ALL D/B ON SYS, OR NAME SPEC. ONE → TEST CONN. →
"CONN. STRING" SENT TO D/B TO OPEN. THEN, "TREE" EXPLORER
LETS YOU VIEW DATA. CAN ALSO CHANGE DATA IN FIELDS.

The basic dataset object hierarchy

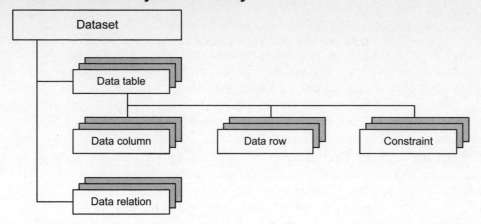

Concepts

- A dataset object consists of a hierarchy of one or more data table and data relation objects.

- A data table object consists of one or more data column objects and one or more data row objects. The data column objects define the data in each column of the table, and the data row objects contain the data for each row in the table.

- A data table can also contain one or more constraint objects that are used to maintain the integrity of the data in the table. A unique key constraint ensures that the values in a column, such as the primary key column, are unique. And a foreign key constraint determines how the records in one table are affected when corresponding records in a related table are updated or deleted.

- The data relation objects define how the tables in the dataset are related. They are used to manage constraints and to simplify the navigation between related tables.

- Because a dataset doesn't inherit relationships from the data source, you have to define them yourself. When you define a data relation object, the appropriate constraint objects are automatically added to the tables involved in the relationship.

- All of the classes used to implement the dataset object hierarchy are available from the System.Data namespace. This namespace is included in all of your Windows applications by default.

- All of the objects in a dataset are stored in collections. For example, the data table objects are stored in a data table collection, and the data column objects are stored in a data column collection. Usually, though, you don't need to refer to the collections directly.

Figure 16-10   How a dataset is organized

Concurrency and the disconnected data architecture

Although the disconnected data architecture has advantages, it also has some disadvantages. One of those is the conflict that can occur when two or more users retrieve and then try to update data in the same row of a table. This is called a *concurrency* problem. This is possible because once a program retrieves data from a database, the connection to that database is dropped. As a result, the database management system can't manage the update process.

To illustrate, consider the situation shown in figure 16-11. Here, two users have retrieved the Vendors table from a database, so a copy of the Vendors table is stored on each user's PC. These users could be using the same program or two different programs. Now, suppose user 1 modifies the address in the row for vendor 123 and updates the Vendors table in the database. And suppose that user 2 modifies the phone number in the row for vendor 123 and then tries to update the Vendors table in the database. What will happen? That will depend on the *concurrency control* that's used by the programs.

When you use ADO.NET, you have two choices for concurrency control. By default, a program uses *optimistic concurrency*, which checks to see whether a row has been changed after it was retrieved. If it has, the update or deletion will be refused and a *concurrency exception* will be thrown. Then, the program should handle the error. For example, it could display an error message that tells the user that the row could not be updated and then retrieve the updated row so the user can make the change again.

In contrast, the *"last in wins"* technique works the way its name implies. Since no checking is done with this technique, the row that's updated by the last user overwrites any changes made to the row by a previous user. For the example above, the row updated by user 2 will overwrite changes made by user 1, which means that the phone number will be right but the address will be wrong. Since errors like this corrupt the data in a database, optimistic concurrency is used by most programs, which means that your programs have to handle the concurrency exceptions that are thrown.

If you know that concurrency will be a problem, you can use a couple of programming techniques to limit concurrency exceptions. One is for a program to update the database frequently so other programs can retrieve the current data. The program should also refresh its dataset frequently so it contains the recent changes made by other programs.

Another way to avoid concurrency exceptions is to work with datasets that contain just one row. That way, it's less likely that two programs will update the same row at the same time. In contrast, if two programs retrieve the same table, they will of course retrieve the same rows. Then, if they both update the same row in the table, even though it may not be at the same time, a concurrency exception will occur when they try to update the database.

Of course, you will understand and appreciate this more as you learn how to develop your own database applications. As you develop them, though, keep in mind that most applications are multi-user applications. That's why you have to be aware of concurrency problems.

Two users who are working with copies of the same data

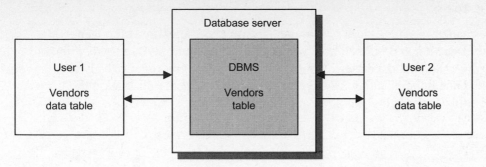

What happens when two users try to update the same row

- When two or more users retrieve the data in the same row of a database table at the same time, it is called *concurrency*. Because ADO.NET uses a disconnected data architecture, the database management system can't prevent this from happening.

- If two users try to update the same row in a database table at the same time, the second user's changes could overwrite the changes made by the first user. Whether or not that happens, though, depends on the *concurrency control* that the programs use.

- By default, ADO.NET uses *optimistic concurrency*. This means that the program checks to see whether the database row that's going to be updated or deleted has been changed since it was retrieved. If it has, a *concurrency exception* occurs and the update or deletion is refused. Then, the program should handle the exception.

- If optimistic concurrency isn't in effect, the program doesn't check to see whether a row has been changed before an update or deletion takes place. Instead, the operation proceeds without throwing an exception. This is referred to as *"last in wins"* because the last update overwrites any previous update. And this leads to errors in the database.

How to avoid concurrency errors

- For many applications, concurrency rarely occurs. As a result, optimistic concurrency is adequate because the users will rarely have to resubmit an update or deletion that is refused.

- If concurrency is likely to be a problem, a program can be designed so it updates the database frequently and so the dataset is refreshed frequently. That way, concurrency is less likely to occur.

- Another way to avoid concurrency is to design a program so it retrieves and updates just one row at a time. That way, there's less chance that two users will retrieve and update the same row at the same time.

Figure 16-11   Concurrency and the disconnected data architecture

Perspective

This chapter has introduced you to the hardware and software components of a multi-user system and described how you use ADO.NET and SQL to work with the data in a relational database. With that as background, you're now ready to develop a database application. In the next two chapters, then, you'll learn the essential skills for building Windows applications that use ADO.NET.

Summary

- A multi-user system typically consists of *clients* and *servers* connected by a *network*.

- The data used by a *client/server system* is typically stored in a *relational database* that's managed by a *database management system* (*DBMS*).

- *Application software* running on the client communicates with the DBMS by sending *SQL queries* through the *.NET data provider*. Then, the DBMS processes the query and returns any *query results*.

- The data in a relational database is stored in *tables* that consist of *rows* (*records*) and *columns* (*fields*). Each table typically has a *primary key* that uniquely identifies each row in the table.

- The tables in a relational database are related to each other through their *primary keys* and *foreign keys*. Most relationships are *one-to-many*.

- To retrieve data from a table, you use a SQL Select statement that stores the rows and columns you request in a *result table*, or *result set*. You can also use a Select statement to *join* the data from two or more tables.

- To add records to a table, you use the SQL Insert statement. To update records in a table, you use the SQL Update statement. And to delete records from a table, you use the SQL Delete statement.

- The data used by an application is stored in a *data table* within a *dataset*. A *data adapter* manages the flow of data between a database and a dataset.

- A data adapter passes SQL statements defined by *data commands* to a database for processing. To connect to the database, a data command uses a *data connection*.

- ADO.NET uses a *disconnected data architecture*. That means that after the requested processing is performed, the connection to the database is closed and must be opened again to perform further processing.

- A *concurrency* problem occurs when two users retrieve the same row in a database table and try to update it. Then, if *optimistic concurrency* is used for *concurrency control*, the second update will be refused and a *concurrency exception* will be thrown. Otherwise, the second update will overwrite the first, which is referred to as "*last in wins.*"

Terms

Microsoft SQL Server Desktop Engine (MSDE)
SQL Server 2000
client
server
network
enterprise system
local area network (LAN)
metropolitan area network (MAN)
wide area network (WAN)
network operating system
database management system (DBMS)
application software
.NET data provider
SQL Server data provider
OLE DB data provider
data source
SQL query
query
SQL (Structured Query Language)
query results
client/server system
relational database
table
record
row
field
column
primary key
identity column
non-primary key
unique key
unique key constraint

index
foreign key
foreign key constraint
cascaded update
cascaded delete
one-to-many relationship
one-to-one relationship
many-to-many relationship
data type
system data type
check constraint
default value
SQL dialect
Transact-SQL
calculated field
result table
result set
join
inner join
ADO.NET
ADO (ActiveX Data Objects)
data table
dataset
data adapter
data command
data connection
disconnected data architecture
concurrency
concurrency control
optimistic concurrency
concurrency exception
"last in wins"

Objectives

- Describe the hardware components of a typical multi-user system.

- Describe the software components of a typical multi-user database application.

- Explain how a table in a relational database is organized.

- Explain how the tables in a relational database are related.

- Describe the use of these SQL statements: Select, Insert, Update, Delete.

- Describe the use of these ADO.NET components: data adapter, data command, data connection, dataset, data table.

- Compare the structure of a dataset with the structure of a relational database.

- Describe concurrency, optimistic concurrency control, and "last in wins."

17

How to develop a database application with ADO.NET

Now that you know the concepts and terms that you need for database programming, this chapter shows you how to develop simple database applications of your own. After you learn how to use the Data Adapter Configuration Wizard to create the data adapter, command, and connection objects, you'll learn how to create and work with a dataset and how to use a data grid control to work with the data in the dataset.

How to use the Data Adapter Configuration Wizard

The easiest way to create the components you need to work with a database is to use the Data Adapter Configuration Wizard. The topics that follow lead you step by step through the process of using this wizard. When you're done, you'll have the data adapter, command, and connection objects you need for developing a database application.

How to start the wizard

To start the Data Adapter Configuration Wizard, display the Toolbox, click on the Data tab to display the data components, and then double-click on the data adapter component you want to use. When you do that, the first dialog box of the wizard is displayed as shown in figure 17-1. This dialog box describes the function of the wizard.

This also adds a data adapter to the Component Designer tray at the bottom of the designer window. Then, as you proceed through the wizard's dialog boxes, the data adapter is configured depending on the information you provide. To proceed with the configuration, you can click on the Next button.

If you want to define the data adapter and the other data components without using the wizard, you can click on the Cancel button from this dialog box. Then, you can use the Properties window to set the properties for the data adapter, and you can use the Data tab of the Toolbox to create the other components you need. Because the wizard quickly and easily creates all the components you need, however, I recommend that you use it whenever possible.

The dialog box that's displayed when you start the Data Adapter Configuration Wizard

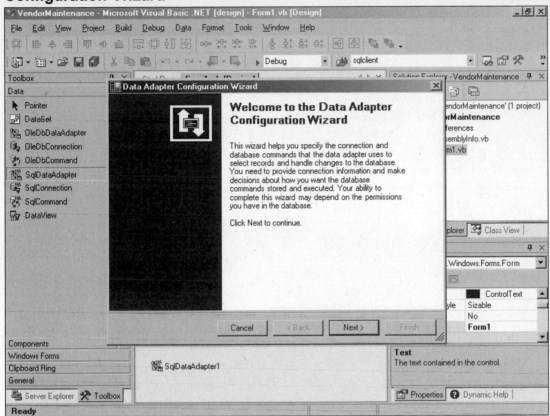

Description

- The Data Adapter Configuration Wizard helps you create the data adapter, connection, and command objects for working with a database.
- To start the wizard, simply double-click on the OleDbDataAdapter or SqlDataAdapter component in the Data tab of the Toolbox. The data adapter is then added to the Component Designer tray at the bottom of the designer window, and the first dialog box of the wizard is displayed.
- The first dialog box displays a welcome message and describes the function of the wizard. To continue with the wizard, click on the Next button.
- If you click on the Cancel button from the wizard's Welcome dialog box, the wizard is canceled. Then, you can set the properties of the data adapter from the Properties window, and you can create the other ADO.NET objects using the components in the Data tab of the Toolbox.

Figure 17-1   How to start the wizard

How to define the connection

The next dialog box helps you define the connection object as illustrated in figure 17-2. From this dialog box, you can select an existing connection (one you've used previously), or you can click on the New Connection button to display the Data Link Properties dialog box shown here. This dialog box helps you identify the database that you want to access and provides the information you need to access it.

When the Data Link Properties dialog box is first displayed, the Connection tab is visible. In this tab, you select the name of the server that contains the database you want to access; enter the information that's required to log on to the server; and select the name of the database you want to access. How you do that, though, varies depending on whether you're using MSDE on your own PC or whether you're using a database on your company's or school's computer.

If you're using MSDE on your own PC and you've installed MSDE and attached the AccountsPayable database to it as described in the appendix, the server name should be the name of your computer followed by \VSdotNet. On my computer, for example, the server name is ANNE\VSdotNet. Next, for the log-on information, you should select the Use Windows NT Integrated security option. Then, MSDE will use the log-in name and password that you use for your computer as the name and password for the database too. As a result, you won't need to provide a separate user name and password in the Connection tab of this dialog box. Last, you select the name of the database that you want to connect to. When you're done, you can click on the Test Connection button to be sure that the connection works.

In contrast, if you're using a database that's on your company's or school's server, you need to get the connection information from the network administrator, the database administrator, or your instructor. That will include the server name, log-on information, and database name. Once you establish a connection to a database, you can use that connection for all of the other applications that use that database.

If you use the SQL Server data provider to access a SQL Server database, the data provider communicates directly with the database. If you use the OLE DB data provider, though, that data provider communicates with the OLE DB provider for the database you're accessing. In that case, you need to use the Provider tab of the Data Link Properties dialog box to select the provider you want to use. This tab lists the available providers, and the default provider is the one for SQL Server.

The dialog boxes for defining a connection

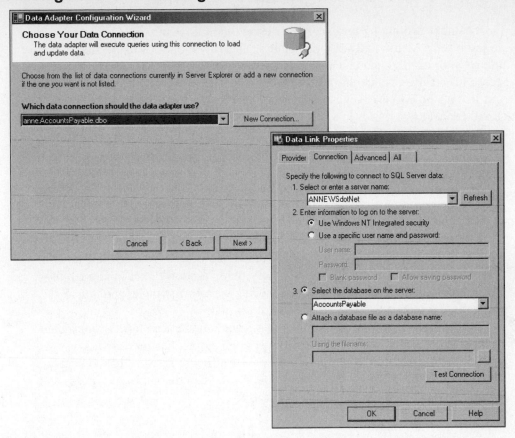

Description

- The Choose Your Data Connection dialog box asks you to identify the data connection you want to use. If you've already defined a data connection, you can select it from the drop-down list. Otherwise, you can click on the New Connection button to create a connection.

- When you click the New Connection button, the Connection tab of the Data Link Properties dialog box is displayed. You use this dialog box to provide the information that's needed to connect to the database.

- If you're creating an OleDbDataAdapter, the default is to use the OLE DB provider for SQL Server. If that's not what you want, you can select a different OLE DB provider from the Provider tab. The information that's required on the Connection tab will vary depending on the provider you choose.

- To be sure that the connection is configured properly, you can click on the Test Connection button. Then, click on the OK button to return to the wizard.

Figure 17-2   How to define the connection

How to define the SQL statements

The next two dialog boxes let you define the SQL statements that your program will use to work with the database. The three options in the first dialog box let you use SQL statements, create new stored procedures, and use existing stored procedures. Since this book doesn't cover the use of stored procedures, you'll learn how to use SQL statements here. If you already know how to use stored procedures, however, you shouldn't have any trouble doing that.

If you select the Use SQL statements option and click on the Next button, the wizard displays the second dialog box in this figure. This dialog box lets you enter the Select statement you want to use to retrieve data. Alternatively, you can click on the Query Builder button to use the Query Builder to build the Select statement as described in the next figure. Because that's the easiest way to create the Select statements that you need, that's what you'll usually do.

The Select statement in this figure selects several fields from a table named Vendors, and it sorts the records by the VendorName field. You saw this table in the last chapter. Notice that the primary key field, VendorID, isn't included in this query. Because the primary key is needed to perform update and delete operations, however, the wizard will add it for you.

Before I go on, you should realize that Select queries can have a significant effect on the performance of a client/server application. The more fields and records that are returned by a query, the more traffic the network has to bear. When you design a query, then, you should try to keep the number of fields and records to the minimum required by a project.

The dialog boxes for defining the SQL statements

(handwritten margin notes: QUERY STAY OUTSIDE OF D/B ; OUT IN D/B ; ALREADY IN D/B)

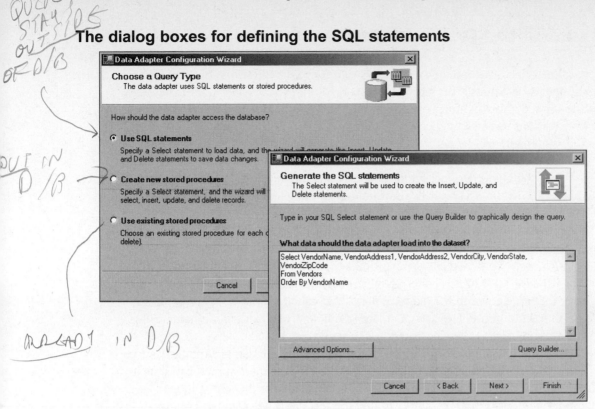

Description

- You use the Choose a Query Type dialog box to select whether the database will be accessed using SQL statements, new stored procedures, or existing stored procedures.

- If you choose to use SQL statements, the Generate the SQL statements dialog box is displayed when you click on the Next button. This dialog box lets you enter the Select statement that will be used to retrieve the data. You can also click on the Query Builder button from this dialog box to build the Select statement interactively (see figure 17-4).

- If you don't include a table's primary key in the Select statement, the wizard adds it for you. Then, it generates Insert, Update, and Delete statements based on the Select statement. If that's not what you want, you can change the advanced options as described in figure 17-5.

- Stored procedures are beyond the scope of this book, but if you're familiar with them, there are two other options you can use. If you choose to create new stored procedures, a dialog box is displayed that lets you enter a Select statement. Then, the wizard generates stored procedures with the appropriate Select, Insert, Update, and Delete statements. If you choose to use existing stored procedures, the wizard displays a dialog box that lets you select the stored procedures to use for select, insert, update, and delete operations.

Figure 17-3   How to define the SQL statements

How to use the Query Builder

Figure 17-4 shows the *Query Builder* window you can use to build a Select statement. You can use this graphical interface to create a Select statement without even knowing the proper syntax for it. Then, when you get the query the way you want it, you can click on the OK button to return to the wizard and the Select statement will be entered for you. This is usually easier and more accurate than entering the code for the statement directly into the wizard dialog box.

When the Query Builder window first opens up, the Add Table dialog box is displayed. This dialog box lists all of the tables in the database you selected. Then, you can use it to add one or more tables to the *diagram pane* of the Query Builder window so you can use them in your query. In this figure, for example, you can see that the Vendors table has been added to the diagram pane.

In the *grid pane*, you can see the fields that are going to be included in the query. To add fields to this pane, you just check the boxes before the field names that are shown in the diagram pane. You can also enter an expression in the Column column to create a calculated field, and you can enter a name in the Alias column to give the calculated field a name.

Once the fields have been added to the grid pane, you can use the Sort Type column to identify any fields that should be used to sort the returned rows and the Sort Order column to give the order of precedence for the sort if more than one field is identified. Here, for example, the rows will be sorted in ascending sequence by the VendorName field. Similarly, you can use the Criteria column to establish the criteria to be used to select the rows that will be retrieved by the query. For example, to retrieve only the rows for California vendors, you can specify CA in the Criteria column for the VendorState field. Since no criteria are specified in this query, all of the rows will be retrieved.

As you create the query, the *SQL pane* shows the current version of the resulting Select statement. You can also run this query at any time to display the selected records in the *results pane*. That way, you can be sure that the query works the way you want it to.

IN ADD TABLE - VIEWS (ALREADY EXEC.)

The Query Builder window

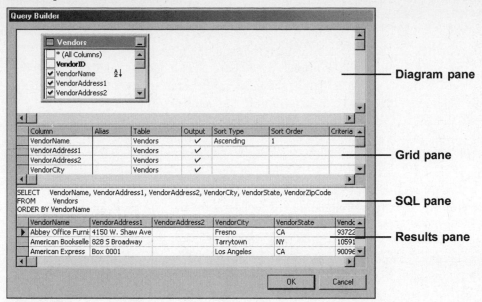

Diagram pane

Grid pane

SQL pane

Results pane

Description

- When you first start the *Query Builder*, the Add Table dialog box is displayed. You can use this dialog box to select the tables you want to include in the query. Then, those tables are displayed in the *diagram pane*.

- To include a column from a table in the query, click on the box to its left. Then, that column is added to the *grid pane*. You can also select all the columns at once by checking the * (All Columns) item.

- To create a calculated field, enter an expression in the Column column and then enter the name you want to use for the column in the Alias column.

- To sort the returned rows by one or more columns, select the Ascending or Descending option from the Sort Type column for those columns in the sequence you want them sorted. You can also use the Sort Order column to set the sort sequence directly.

- To specify selection criteria (like a specific value that the field must contain to be selected), enter the criteria in the Criteria column.

- To use a column for sorting or for specifying criteria without including it in the query results, remove the check mark from the Output column.

- As you select columns and specify sort and selection criteria, the Query Builder builds the Select statement and displays it in the *SQL pane*.

- You can also use the Query Builder shortcut menu to work with a query. To display the results of a query, for example, select the Run command from this menu. The results are displayed in the *results pane*.

Figure 17-4   How to use the Query Builder

How to control the Insert, Update, and Delete statements that are generated

If you click on the Next or Finish button from the Generate the SQL Statements dialog box, the wizard completes the configuration. That includes using the Select statement you specified as the basis for generating Insert, Update, and Delete statements that can be used to modify the database when changes are made to the dataset. If the program you're developing won't allow for data modification, however, you won't need the Insert, Update, and Delete statements. In that case, you should click on the Advanced Options button to display the dialog box shown in figure 17-5. Then, click on the first check box to turn this option off so the extra statements aren't generated.

If you leave the first option checked, which is the default, you can use the second option to provide for optimistic concurrency. And you can use the third option to determine if the dataset will be refreshed after each insert or update operation. These options are also on by default and the simplest solution is to accept the defaults.

As you should remember from the last chapter, *optimistic concurrency* applies to updates and deletions. If this option is on, the wizard adds code to the Update and Delete statements that checks the data in the database rows that are going to be updated or deleted against the original values in these rows. Then, if the data has changed, the update or deletion is refused and a concurrency exception is thrown. That way, one user can't make changes to rows that have been changed by another user and thus write over those changes. For that reason, you almost always use optimistic concurrency for multi-user applications that insert, update, and delete records, but you should turn this option off for read-only applications.

When you choose the Refresh the Dataset option, the wizard generates two additional Select statements. One comes after the Insert statement that's used to add a new record to the database, and it retrieves the new record into the dataset. This is useful if you add records to a table that contains an identity column (a column whose value is generated automatically), columns with default values, or columns whose values are calculated from other columns. That way, the information that's generated for these columns by the database is available from the dataset. Similarly, the wizard adds a Select statement after the Update statement that's used to modify a record so any column values that are calculated by the database will be available from the dataset.

Of course, if the values that are generated by the database aren't used by your application, it isn't necessary to refresh the dataset with this information. In fact, it would be inefficient to do that. In some cases, though, you need to refresh the dataset for your application if you want it to work properly.

The dialog box for setting advanced SQL generation options

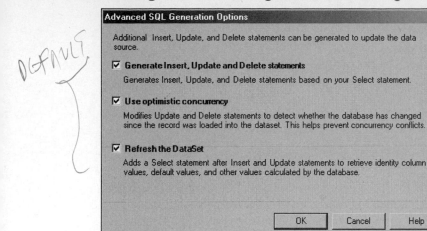

DEFAULT

Description

- If you click on the Advanced Options button from the Generate the SQL statements dialog box, the Advanced SQL Generation Options dialog box is displayed. This dialog box lets you set the options related to the generation of the Insert, Update, and Delete statements that will be used to update the database.

- If your application doesn't need to add, change, or delete records in the database, you should remove the check mark from the Generate option. Then, the other options become unavailable.

- The Use optimistic concurrency option determines whether or not the program checks to be sure that the records that are updated or deleted haven't been changed by another user after they were retrieved. If this option is checked, the wizard adds code to the Update and Delete statements to provide for this checking.

- If you remove the check mark from the Use optimistic concurrency option, records are updated and deleted whether or not they've been changed by another user after they were accessed.

- The Refresh the DataSet option determines whether or not the dataset is refreshed after an insert or update operation. If this option is selected, a Select statement that retrieves the affected row is executed after each Insert and Update statement.

Figure 17-5   How to control the Insert, Update, and Delete statements that are generated

How to complete the configuration

After it generates the SQL statements, the wizard displays the dialog box shown in figure 17-6. This dialog box lists the SQL statements that were generated so you can be sure that you selected the correct options. If not, you can use the Back button to return to the appropriate dialog box and make corrections.

The Results dialog box also indicates that it generated *table mappings*. Table mappings are what the data adapter uses to map the data in the database to a data table in a dataset. For example, the table mappings for the data adapter created in this chapter indicate that the source table identified by the Select statement will be mapped to a data table named Vendors. And the columns within the source table will be mapped to columns in the dataset with the same names. Although you can change the name of the data table or any of the data columns and even the way the columns are mapped, you don't usually need to do that.

The dialog box that displays the configuration results

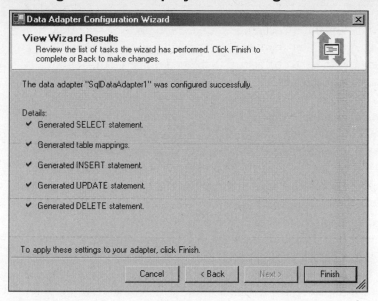

Description

- When you click on the Next button from the Generate the SQL statements dialog box, the wizard completes the configuration and displays the results in the View Wizard Results dialog box. To create the adapter with this configuration, click on the Finish button.
- In addition to Select, Insert, Update, and Delete statements, the wizard generates *table mappings.* The table mappings map the fields in the source table with fields in the data table that's created when you generate a dataset from the data adapter (see figure 17-8).
- Although you can use the TableMappings property of the data adapter to change the table mappings, you shouldn't need to do that.

[handwritten: NOBODY CHANGES THIS]

Figure 17-6   How to complete the configuration

The objects created by the Configuration Wizard

When you click on the Finish button in one of the Configuration Wizard dialog boxes, the wizard creates data adapter and connection objects based on the information you specified. These objects are displayed in the Component Designer tray as you can see in figure 17-7. Then, you can click on either of these objects to display and work with its properties in the Properties window.

When you select the data adapter object, three links appear at the bottom of the Properties windows. You can use the first link, Configure Data Adapter, to redisplay the dialog boxes of the Configuration Wizard so you can change the configuration. You can use the second link to generate a dataset from the data adapter as you'll see in the next figure. And you can use the third link to preview the data that's defined by a data adapter as you'll see later in this chapter.

In addition to the data adapter and connection objects, the wizard also creates one or more command objects. At the least, it creates a command object that defines the Select statement that will be used to retrieve data. In addition, if you indicated that you wanted the wizard to generate Insert, Update, and Delete statements, a command object is created for each of these statements. Although you might think that these objects would be displayed in the Component Designer tray, they usually aren't. My guess is that this is a bug in Visual Basic.

Even if the command objects don't appear in the Component Designer tray, you can still review their properties by selecting them from the list of objects at the top of the Properties window. You can also access these objects through the data adapter object. In the Properties window in this figure, for example, you can see the property of the data adapter that refers to the Select command: SelectCommand. If you scroll down this window, you can see the properties for the Insert, Update, and Delete commands too. You'll learn more about working with these properties later in this chapter. For now, just realize that if you expand the property for one of these commands by clicking on the plus button next to the property, you can work with the properties of the command object it defines.

The objects created by the Data Adapter Configuration Wizard

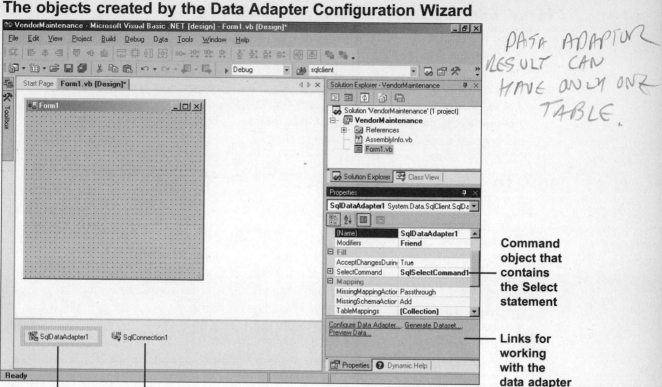

DATA ADAPTER RESULT CAN HAVE ONLY ONE TABLE.

Command object that contains the Select statement

Links for working with the data adapter

COMMAND LOGIN IN ADAPTOR

Data adapter object

Connection object

Description

- When the configuration is complete, the data adapter and connection objects created by the wizard are displayed in the Component Designer tray. To display the properties for either of these objects, just click on it.

- The wizard also creates the command objects that will be used to execute the Select, Insert, Update, and Delete statements against the database. You can access these objects through properties of the data adapter as shown above. Or, you can select the object from the drop-down list at the top of the Properties window.

- You can use the links that are displayed in the Properties window or the commands in the Data menu to work with the data adapter.

Visual Basic bug

- Occasionally, the command objects created by the Configuration Wizard appear in the Component Designer tray, but most of the time they don't.

Figure 17-7   The objects created by the Configuration Wizard

How to work with a dataset

Each data adapter defines a single result table that can be used in an application. Before you can use the result table, though, you have to load the data for it into a dataset. So in the topics that follow, you'll learn how to generate a dataset for an application and load data into it. Then, for applications that make changes to the data in a dataset, you'll learn how to write those changes back to the original database.

How to generate a dataset   *CAN HAVE MANY TABLES*

Figure 17-8 shows you how to generate a dataset. When the Generate Dataset dialog box is first displayed, the New option is selected so you can create a new dataset with the default name or the name you supply. Then, you can choose the tables to be included in the dataset from the list of tables in this dialog box. In this example, only one data adapter was created, so only one table is listed. If you create more than one data adapter for a form, though, there will be one table for each adapter listed in this dialog box. Then, you can include more than one table in the dataset.

When you complete the Generate Dataset dialog box, Visual Basic generates a dataset class that defines the data to be stored in the dataset. In addition, if the Add this dataset to the designer option is selected, Visual Basic creates a dataset object based on the class. If that's not what you want, you can remove the check mark from this option so only the class is generated. If you do that, though, you have to create a dataset object through code. In most cases, then, you'll leave this option checked so the dataset object is created for you.

You can also use this dialog box to modify an existing dataset. To do that, select the dataset you want to modify from the Existing combo box. Then, you can add or remove tables from the dataset by checking or unchecking the appropriate tables. If you do that, though, keep in mind that Visual Basic changes the original dataset class, but not the dataset object that was created from it. Because of that, you'll need to create a new dataset object as well.

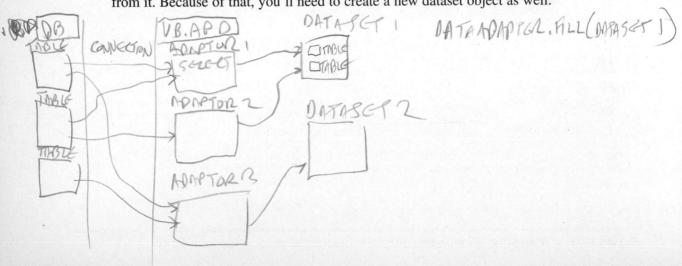

The dialog box for generating a dataset

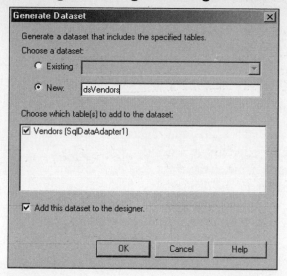

Description

- A dataset allows you work with the data defined by the Select statement in a data adapter. To generate a dataset, select the data adapter or the form it's associated with, and then choose the Data→ Generate Dataset command or click on the Generate Dataset link that's displayed in the Properties window.

- In the Generate Dataset dialog box that's displayed, select the New option and enter the name you want to use for the dataset class that will be created. Then, select the tables you want to include in the dataset from the list that's provided.

- The list of tables that's displayed in this dialog box includes the result tables defined by the data adapters in the project (each data adapter defines a single result table). A dataset can include any or all of the tables in the list.

- The name for each table in the list is taken from the name of the source table in the Select statement for the data adapter. If the Select statement defines a join, the name of the first source table in the statement is used.

- To add an instance of the dataset class that's created to the application, select the Add this dataset to the designer option (this is the default). If you don't select this option, you have to create an instance of the dataset class in the code for the application.

- You can also use the Generate Dataset dialog box to change an existing dataset. If you've already defined one or more datasets, the Existing option will be selected when you display this dialog box and you can select the dataset you want to change from the drop-down list. Then, you can add or delete tables from the dataset.

Figure 17-8   How to generate a dataset

The dataset schema file, class, and object

Figure 17-9 shows the dataset schema file, class, and object that are created when you generate a dataset. The *schema file* defines the structure of the dataset, including the tables it contains, the columns that are included in each table, the data types of each column, and the constraints that are defined for each table. The schema is then used by the dataset class to implement the dataset.

Like the other ADO.NET objects you've seen, dataset objects are displayed in the Component Designer tray since they don't have a visual interface. By default, a dataset object is given the same name as the class it's created from with a number added to the end. For example, the dataset class in this figure is named dsVendors and the dataset object is named DsVendors1. If you created another dataset object from the same class, it would be named DsVendors2. And so on.

A dataset schema file, class, and object

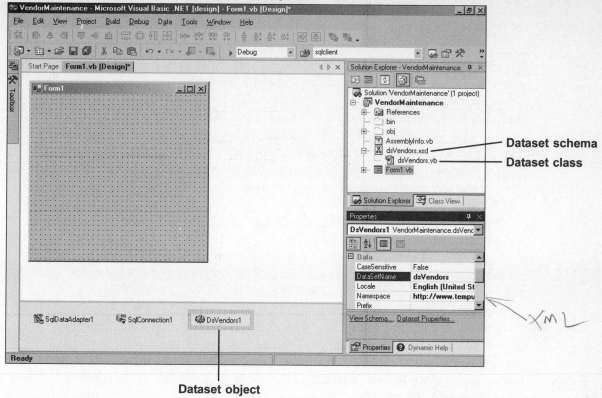

Dataset schema

Dataset class

Dataset object

Description

- When you generate a dataset, Visual Basic creates a dataset *schema file* that defines the structure of the dataset. This file is listed in the Solution Explorer and is given the name you specify in the Generate Dataset dialog box with a file extension of *xsd*.

- The dataset generator also creates a dataset class. By default, this class isn't displayed in the Solution Explorer. To display it, click on the Show All Files button at the top of the Solution Explorer and then expand the schema file for the dataset. The dataset class will appear below the schema file.

- If you selected the option in the Generate Dataset dialog box to add the dataset to the designer, a dataset object is added to the Component Designer tray. This object is given the same name as the dataset class, but with a numeric suffix.

Common dataset properties

Property	Description
Name	The name of the dataset object.
DataSetName	The name of the class that the dataset is derived from.

Figure 17-9   The dataset schema file, class, and object

How to load and unload a dataset

Before you can work with a dataset, you have to load data into it. To do that, you use the Fill method of the data adapter as shown in figure 17-10. The first statement in this figure, for example, loads the data defined by a data adapter named SqlDataAdapter1 into a dataset named DsVendors1. Notice that only the name of the dataset, and not the name of the data table, is used in this method. That's because a data adapter defines a single table even though a dataset can contain more than one data table. So this Fill method stores the data it retrieves in the table identified by the TableMappings property of the data adapter.

If you want to name the table for clarity, though, you can do that as illustrated in the second statement in this figure. This assumes that the dataset name is DsAP1 and the table name is Vendors.

If you want to know how many records were loaded into a dataset, you can retrieve the return value of the Fill method as illustrated in the third statement in this figure. Here, the return value is assigned to an integer variable. Then, you can use this variable any way you like within your program. For example, you might want to use it to keep a count of the number of records in the dataset as the user adds, modifies, and deletes records.

You can also use the Fill method to refresh the contents of a dataset during the execution of a program. To do that, you can use one of two techniques. First, you can use the Clear method of the dataset or a data table within the dataset to remove all the rows from that dataset or data table as illustrated in the last two statements in this figure. Then, you can use the Fill method to load the table with new data. This is the preferred method, and it's usually the most efficient.

Second, you can use the Fill method without clearing the dataset or data table. Then, if the table being refreshed is defined with a primary key, the records in the existing table are updated by the records in the database table. That, however, can be a time-consuming process if the table contains a large number of records. That's why we recommend that you clear the table first. If the table isn't defined with a primary key, the newly retrieved records are appended to the existing records, which isn't usually what you want. In that case, you'll want to be sure to clear the dataset or data table before executing the Fill method.

Another way to refresh a dataset is to refresh each row as it's added or updated. You already learned how to use the Data Adapter Configuration Wizard to provide for that, and you'll learn more about how that works later in this chapter. This technique is usually more efficient than refreshing the entire data table or dataset because only new or modified records are refreshed. On the other hand, if other users will be modifying the same table at the same time, you may want to refresh the entire table periodically so it reflects the changes made by other users.

*(handwritten: RETURNS HOW MANY RECORDS AS INTEGER (IF COPIED) *)*

How to load a data table

The basic syntax of the Fill method for a data adapter

```
dataAdapter.Fill(dataSet[.dataTable])
```
(handwritten: OVERLOADS AVAILABLE)

A statement that loads the data table defined by a data adapter into a dataset

```
SqlDataAdapter1.Fill(DsVendors1)
```

A statement that names the data table to be loaded

```
SqlDataAdapter1.Fill(DsAP1.Vendors)
```

A statement that retrieves the return value from a Fill method

```
iRowCount = SqlDataAdapter1.Fill(DsVendors1)
```

How to unload a dataset or data table

The syntax of the Clear method for a dataset or data table

```
dataset[.datatable].Clear()
```

A statement that clears all the tables in a dataset

```
DsVendors1.Clear()
```

A statement that clears a single data table

```
DsAP1.Vendors.Clear()
```

Description

- The Fill method retrieves rows from the database using the Select statement specified by the SelectCommand property of the data adapter. The rows are stored in a data table within the dataset you specify. *(handwritten: WIZARD CREATED - ACT AS PROPERTIES OF D/A OBJ)*

- In most cases, you don't need to specify the name of the table where you want the results stored. Instead, it's stored in the table identified by the data adapter. However, you may want to code the table name for clarity.

- When the Fill method is executed, the connection object that's associated with the SelectCommand object is opened automatically. After the dataset is loaded, the connection object is closed.

- If you use the Fill method to refresh a table that already contains data, it will merge the rows retrieved from the database with the existing rows in the dataset based on the table's primary key. If the table isn't defined with a primary key, the Fill method appends the rows to the end of the table.

- The Fill method is implemented as a function that returns an integer value with the number of rows that were added or refreshed as shown by the third Fill example above.

- The Clear method removes all the data from the data table or dataset you specify. You can use this method to clear the data from a table that isn't defined with a primary key before you refresh that table. You can also use it to improve the efficiency of a retrieval operation for a table with a primary key.

(handwritten: CLEAR THEN FILL MUCH FASTER)

Figure 17-10   How to load and unload a dataset

(handwritten: DIM RECNUM AS INT / RECNUM = SQLDATAADAPTOR1.FILL(MYDATASET1...) / MSGBOX(RECNUM TOSTRING) GOOD IDEA TO CHECK #! CHANGE W/O APPARENT)

How to update the database with changes made to a dataset

Figure 17-11 shows how to use the Update method of a data adapter to update a database with the changes made to a dataset. Notice in the syntax of this method that, just like the Fill method, you can specify the name of a dataset on this method or a data table within a dataset. In most cases, though, you'll just name the dataset as shown in the first statement in this figure. Then, the table identified by the data adapter is updated.

When you execute the Update method, Visual Basic checks the RowState property of each row in the table to determine if it's a new row, a modified row, or a row that should be deleted. If it's a new row, the Insert statement identified by the InsertCommand property of the data adapter is used to add the row to the table in the database. Similarly, the Update statement identified by the UpdateCommand property is used to update a modified row, and the Delete statement identified by the DeleteCommand property is used to delete a row. After each Insert or Update statement is executed, the RowState property of the affected row is updated to reflect that it has not changed. After a Delete statement is executed, the row is simply deleted from the dataset.

If you want to know how many records were updated, you can retrieve the return value of the Update method as illustrated in the second example in this figure. You might want to use this value to display a message to the user that indicates the number or records that were updated. Or, you might want to use it to determine if the update completed successfully. In the next chapter, though, you'll learn other ways to test for the successful completion of an update operation.

To be sure that changes have been made to a dataset before executing the Update method, you can use the HasChanges method of the dataset. This method returns True if the dataset has been updated and False if it hasn't. You can see how this method is used in the third example in this figure.

The syntax of the Update method for a data adapter *RETURNS DATA TO D/B*

```
dataAdapter.Update(dataSet[.dataTable])
```

A statement that updates a database with the data in a dataset

```
SqlDataAdapter1.Update(DsVendors1)
```

A statement that retrieves the return value from an Update method

```
iUpdateCount = SqlDataAdapter1.Update(DsVendors1)
```

Code that checks for changes to the dataset before updating the database

```
If DsVendors1.HasChanges Then
    SqlDataAdapter1.Update(DsVendors1)
End If
```

Constants in the DataRowState enumeration

Constant	Description
Added	The row has been added to the dataset.
Deleted	The row has been deleted from the dataset.
Modified	The row has been changed.
Unchanged	The row has not changed.

Description

- The Update method saves changes made to the data table identified by the data adapter to the database the data was retrieved from. To do that, it checks the RowState property of each row in the data table to determine if the row has changed. This property contains one of the constants in the DataRowState enumeration shown above.

- If the RowState property of a row indicates that the row has been deleted, the SQL Delete statement for the data adapter is executed for the row. If it indicates that the row has been modified, the SQL Update statement is executed. And if it indicates that the row has been added, the SQL Insert statement is executed.

- Before you execute the Update method, you should check if any changes have been made to the dataset. To do that, you can use the HasChanges method of the dataset. This method checks the RowState property of each row in the dataset to determine if changes have been made and returns a True or False value.

- The Update method is implemented as a function that returns an integer value with the number of rows that were updated. *DELETED, ADDED, MODIFIED.*

Figure 17-11   How to update the database with changes made to a dataset

IF MY DATASET HAS CHANGES THEN
SQLDATASETADAPTOR.UPDATE(MYDATASET)

How to use a data grid control with a dataset

GRID IS RESULT OF QUERY

Now that you've learned how to create and work with a dataset, you're ready to learn how to display the data it contains on a form so the user can work with it. In this chapter, you'll learn how to use a data grid control to display all of the rows and columns in a dataset at once. Then, in the next chapter, you'll learn how to use text boxes and combo boxes to display the data in individual fields of a single row.

A Vendor Maintenance form that uses a bound data grid control

Figure 17-12 presents a Vendor Maintenance form that displays the contents of the Vendors dataset that was created from the Select statement shown in figure 17-3. The *data grid control* on this form lets the user add, modify, and delete records from the dataset. To do that, the control is *bound* to the dataset. You'll learn how to bind a data grid to a dataset in just a moment.

For now, just realize that when a data grid is bound to a dataset, it automatically displays the data in that dataset. Likewise, it automatically updates the dataset when the user adds, modifies, or deletes a record. That means that the only code that's required is the code that loads the dataset and updates the database. Because of that, using a data grid control is the quickest and easiest way to provide access to a dataset.

The design of the Vendor Maintenance form

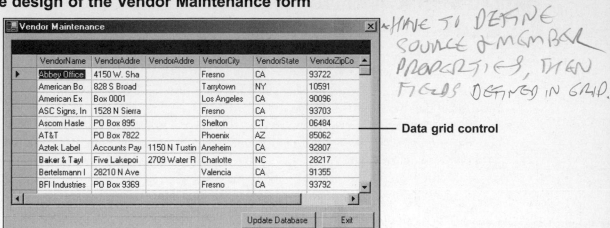

— Data grid control

(handwritten margin note:) HAVE TO DEFINE SOURCE & MEMBER PROPERTIES, THEN FIELDS DEFINED IN GRID.

Description

- The Vendor Maintenance form lets the user view, add, modify, and delete records in the Vendors table. To do that, it uses a *data grid control*, which displays data in a row and column format.

- The data grid control provides built-in functionality for maintaining the data in a data table. Because of that, no code is required to display the data or to implement the add, modify, and delete operations.

- When this form is first loaded, it retrieves data from the database and stores it in the data table used by the data grid.

- When the user clicks on the Update Database button, the database is updated with changes made to the dataset. The user can click on this button after one record or a group of records have been added or changed.

- To use the built-in functionality of a data grid control, you must *bind* it to a data table as described in figure 17-13. Then, you can work with the data as described in figure 17-15.

Figure 17-12   A Vendor Maintenance form that uses a bound data grid control

How to bind a data grid control to a dataset

Figure 17-13 shows the data grid control on the Vendor Maintenance form in design view. Here, you can see the two properties for binding a data grid control to a dataset in the Properties window. The DataSource property identifies the dataset, and the DataMember property identifies the data table within the dataset that the control is bound to.

The technique that's used to bind a data grid control to a dataset is called *complex data binding*. With this type of binding, a control can be bound to more than one element of a data table. When you use complex data binding with a data grid, for example, the grid is bound to the entire table.

Incidentally, when you drop down the list for the DataSource property, you'll see that you can select a dataset or a table within a dataset. If you select a table, you don't need to set the DataMember property. Either way, the result is the same so the technique you use is a matter of preference.

A data grid control that's bound to a Vendors table

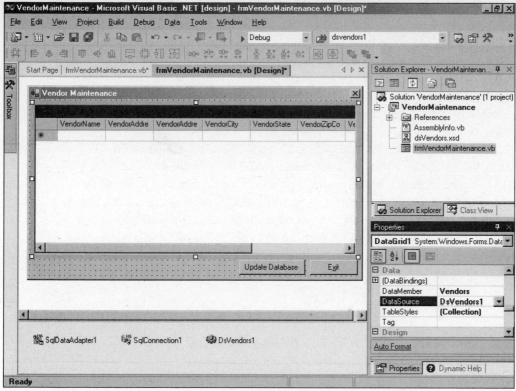

The properties for binding a data grid control to a dataset

Property	Description
DataSource	The name of a data source, such as a dataset.
DataMember	The name of a data table associated with the data source.

Description

- You bind a data grid control to a dataset using a technique called *complex data binding*. This just means that the control is bound to more than one data element. A data grid control, for example, is bound to an entire table.

- To bind a data grid control, you set its DataSource and DataMember properties as indicated above. Then, all of the rows and columns in the table you specify are displayed in the data grid.

Note

- You can also set the DataSource property so it points to a specific data table. In that case, you set the DataMember property to (none).

Figure 17-13   How to bind a data grid control to a dataset

The code for the Vendor Maintenance form

Figure 17-14 presents the code for the Vendor Maintenance form. As you can see, two procedures provide all of the code that's required for working with the dataset. The Fill method in the Load event procedure retrieves the data from the database into the dataset, which loads the data grid. And the Update method in the Click event procedure for the Update Database button updates the database with the changes that have been made to the dataset, but only if any changes have been made.

Of course, we've deliberately kept this application as simple as possible so you can focus on the basic skills for creating and working with ADO.NET objects. In practice, you usually won't use a data grid control to manage the maintenance functions of a dataset. And you usually will have to handle any concurrency exceptions that are thrown by an application. As you will see in the next chapter, then, database programming can get complicated in a hurry.

The Visual Basic code for the Vendor Maintenance form

```
Public Class Form1
    Inherits System.Windows.Forms.Form

    Private Sub Form1_Load(ByVal sender As System.Object, _
            ByVal e As System.EventArgs) Handles MyBase.Load

        SqlDataAdapter1.Fill(DsVendors1)

    End Sub

    Private Sub btnUpdate_Click(ByVal sender As System.Object, _
            ByVal e As System.EventArgs) Handles btnUpdate.Click

        If DsVendors1.HasChanges Then
            SqlDataAdapter1.Update(DsVendors1)
        End If

    End Sub

    Private Sub btnExit_Click(ByVal sender As System.Object, _
            ByVal e As System.EventArgs) Handles btnExit.Click

        Me.Close()

    End Sub

End Class
```

Description

- The dataset that contains the vendor records is loaded in the procedure for the Load event of the form so this data is available when the form is first displayed.

- Because the user can click on the Update Database button without having made any changes to the dataset, the code for the Click event procedure for this button checks for changes before performing the update.

Figure 17-14   The code for the Vendor Maintenance form

How to work with the data in a data grid control

If you haven't used a data grid control before, you may be wondering how to work with the data it displays. So figure 17-15 summarizes the techniques for doing that. In addition, it presents some basic properties you can use to control the appearance and operation of a data grid control. Since these properties are self-explanatory, I'll focus on the operational techniques here.

First, to modify an existing row, you simply click in the column whose value you want to change and enter the change. Then, the change is saved to the dataset when you press the Tab key to move to the next column or the Enter key to move to the next row. The change is also saved if you click anywhere else in the data grid.

To delete a row, you start by clicking on the row header to the left of the row to select it. Then, you press the Delete key to delete it. Note that the row is deleted immediately without any confirmation.

To add a new row, you scroll to the last row in the data grid. This row has an asterisk in the row header and the value (null) in each column. Then, you can enter the appropriate value in each column as shown in the form at the top of the figure. Note that as soon as you begin entering a new record, a pencil appears in the row header and another blank record is added at the bottom of the control.

If you realize that you've made a mistake as you enter a value in a column, you can press the Esc key to cancel the change. Then, the column returns to its original value. You can also return the values in all of the columns in a row to their original values by pressing the Esc key twice. Note, however, that this works only if you don't have the CancelButton property of the form set to a button control. If you do, the Click event of that button is executed the second time you press the Esc key.

The Vendor Maintenance form with a record being added to the data grid

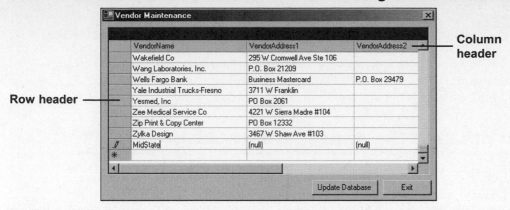

Basic properties for controlling the appearance and operation of a data grid control

Property	Description
AllowSorting	Determines whether the rows in the grid can be sorted by any column. By default, the rows are sorted in the order specified by the Select statement. If no order is specified, the rows are displayed in the same order that they're retrieved from the database.
ReadOnly	Determines whether rows can be added, changed, and deleted. The default is False, which means that the rows can be modified.
PreferredColumnWidth	The default width of each column in the control. This property must be set before the control is bound.

Basic techniques for working with the data in a data grid

- To add a row, scroll to the bottom of the dataset, click in the row that has an asterisk (*) in the row header, and enter the data for each column. By default, the columns in a new row contain null values.

- To change the value of a column, just click in the column and enter the change. A pencil appears in the row header to indicate the row is being changed. When you press the Tab key to move to the next column, the change is saved to the dataset.

- To delete a row, click on the row header to select the row and then press the Delete key.

- To cancel a change to a column, press the Esc key. To cancel all the changes made to a row, press the Esc key twice.

- If the AllowSorting property is set to True (the default), you can click on a column header to sort by that column. The first time you click the header, the rows are sorted in ascending sequence. The second time, they're sorted in descending sequence.

- To change the width of individual columns at run time, drag the line to the right of the column header to the desired width. You can also double-click on this line to change the column width so it accommodates the widest value in the column.

Figure 17-15   How to work with the data in a data grid control

Other skills for working with ADO.NET objects

The last three topics of this chapter present some additional skills for working with ADO.NET objects. These skills will help you understand the ADO.NET objects better and work with them more efficiently.

How to preview the data in a data adapter

Before you create a dataset from a data adapter, you may want to be sure that the data adapter retrieves the correct data. To do that, you can preview the data as shown in figure 17-16. Here, you can see the data that's retrieved and used by the Vendor Maintenance form.

When you first display the Data Adapter Preview dialog box, the Results box will be empty. Then, you can click on the Fill Dataset button to retrieve the data defined by the data adapter in the Data adapters combo box. If more than one data adapter is defined, you can select the one you want to use from this combo box. When you make a selection and click on the Fill Dataset button, the results are displayed in the Results box.

Notice that the value of the Target dataset combo box in this example is Untyped Dataset. That means that no dataset has been generated from the data adapter. Because of that, no structural information about the data is available. If you preview the data in a data adapter after creating a dataset for it, however, you can select the dataset from this combo box. Then, the names of the columns in the dataset are displayed in the Results box even before the data is retrieved. In addition, if the dataset contains two or more tables, those tables are listed in the Data tables list, and you can select the table that holds the data you want to display.

Keep in mind, though, that the main reason for previewing the data in a data adapter is to be sure it's what you want *before* you generate a dataset for it. Because of that, you'll typically work with an *untyped dataset* as shown in this figure.

The dialog box for previewing the data in a data adapter

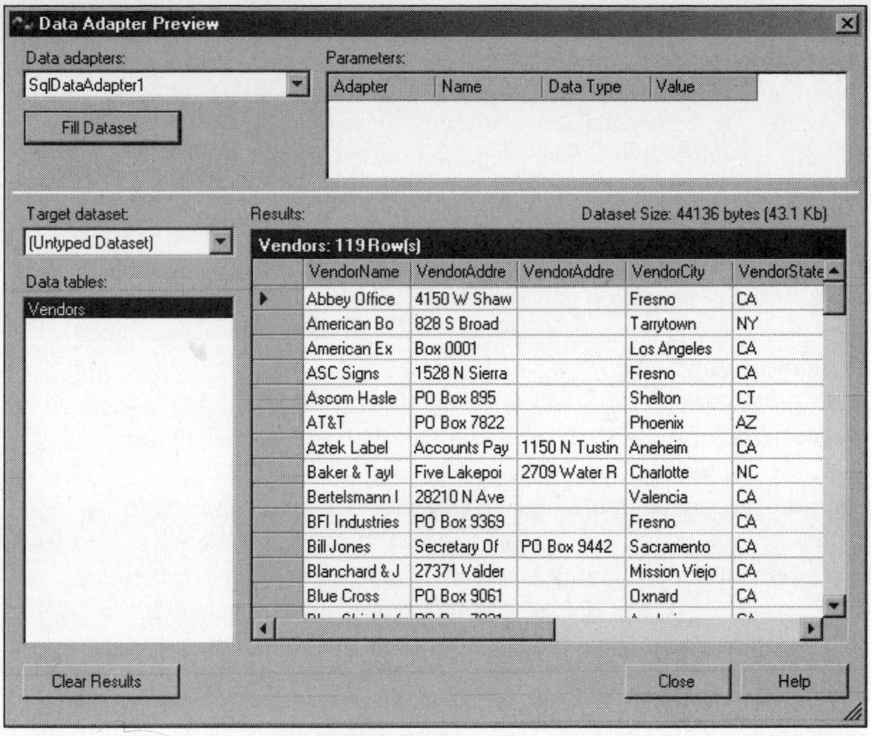

Description

- To preview the data in a data adapter, select the Data → Preview Data command, or click on the Preview Data link that's displayed in the Properties window for the data adapter. This displays the Data Adapter Preview dialog box.

- To display the data specified by a data adapter, select the data adapter from the combo box at the top of the dialog box and then click on the Fill Dataset button. The results are displayed in the Results box.

- You can sort the results by clicking on the header for the column you want to sort by. Click once to sort in ascending sequence. Click again to sort in descending sequence.

- You can change the width of a column by dragging the line to the right of its column header or by double-clicking on this line to change the column width so it accommodates the values in all the rows.

- If you've already created a dataset from a data adapter, you can select the dataset from the Target dataset list. Then, the column headers for the columns in that dataset are displayed in the Results box before the results are retrieved. Otherwise, the results are saved in an *untyped dataset* whose structure is unknown until the data is retrieved.

- If the dataset you select contains two or more tables, you can select the table you want to display by highlighting it in the Data tables list.

Figure 17-16   How to preview the data in a data adapter

How to review the properties for generated ADO.NET objects

To help you understand how the data adapter, command, and connection objects work, figure 17-17 presents some of the properties of these objects and shows you an easy way to review them. To do that, you can use the Properties window for the data adapter as shown at the top of this figure.

As you can see, the data adapter includes properties that refer to the related Select, Insert, Update, and Delete commands. If you expand the property for one of these command objects, you can see the properties of that object. In this figure, for example, you can see the properties of the Update command object used by the Vendor Maintenance form.

The most important property of a command object is the CommandText property. This property contains the SQL statement that's issued when the Update method is executed to update the database. In this case, the CommandText property contains the Update statement that will be used to update the database with changes made to a row in the dataset. I'll have more to say about this statement and the Insert and Delete statements in the next figure. For now, just realize that you can display the full text of the CommandText property in a ToolTip by pointing to the property with the mouse, or you can click on the ellipsis button that appears when you select the property to display the statement in the Query Builder window.

In addition to the CommandText property, each command object has a Connection property. This property refers to the connection object that provides the information for connecting to the database. If you expand the Connection property, you can see the properties of the connection object as shown in this figure. The most important property is the ConnectionString property. This property provides the information that the command object will use to connect to the database. The connection string in this figure, for example, can be used to connect to a database named AccountsPayable in a data source named Anne. Although this string also contains other information, you usually don't need to worry about it since it's generated for you based on the information you supply to the Configuration Wizard.

In addition to the properties I've mentioned so far, each object has a Name property. When the Configuration Wizard creates these objects, it gives them generic names like SqlDataAdapter1, SqlConnection1 and SqlSelectCommand1. In most cases, you won't need to change these names. If the form you're developing uses more than one data adapter, though, you may want to name these objects to reflect their contents and thus make them easier to work with.

If you change the name of one of these objects, the properties in related objects are changed automatically. If you change the name of the connection object, for example, the Connection properties in all of the related command objects are changed. And if you change the name of a command object, the related property in the data adapter object is changed.

The UpdateCommand property for a data adapter

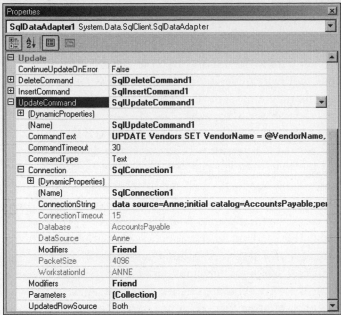

Common data adapter, command, and connection properties

Object	Property	Description
Data adapter	SelectCommand	The name of the command object that contains the SQL Select statement for retrieving records from the database.
	InsertCommand	The name of the command object that contains the SQL Insert statement for adding records to the database.
	UpdateCommand	The name of the command object that contains the SQL Update statement for changing records in the database.
	DeleteCommand	The name of the command object that contains the SQL Delete statement for deleting records from the database.
Command	CommandText	The SQL statement for the operation.
	Connection	The name of the connection object used to connect to the database.
Connection	ConnectionString	The connection information used to connect to the database.

Description

- You can use the Properties window to review the properties that are generated by the Configuration Wizard for the data adapter, command, and connection objects.

- The properties in the Update group for a data adapter include the insert, update, and delete command objects. You can expand these objects to see their properties, and you can expand the connection object within each command object to see its properties.

- To work with the SQL statement in a CommandText property, you can click on the ellipsis button that appears when that property is selected. This displays the statement in the Query Builder window.

Figure 17-17   How to review the properties for generated ADO.NET objects

How to interpret the generated SQL statements

When you execute the Update method of a data adapter to update a database, Visual Basic issues the SQL statements associated with the data adapter's Insert, Update, and Delete statements. To help you understand what these statements do, figure 17-18 presents the statements that were generated for the Vendor Maintenance form. Although these statements may look complicated, the information presented here will give you a good idea of how they work.

To start, notice that the Insert statement in the first example is followed by a Select statement. This statement retrieves the row that was just added to the database table and uses it to update the row in the dataset. That way, the VendorID field in the dataset is set to the value of the VendorID field that's generated by the database. You may remember that this Select statement is added if you select the Refresh the DataSet option when you configure the data adapter.

A Select statement is also added after the Update statement, as shown in the second example. It retrieves the database row that was just updated and uses it to refresh the row in the dataset. In this case, though, this statement isn't necessary because none of the data for a changed row is generated by the database. As a result, you could delete this statement to improve the efficiency of the operation.

Another option that affects the SQL statements that are generated is the Use optimistic concurrency option. If you select this option, code is added to the Where clauses of the Update and Delete statements that checks to be sure that none of the fields have changed since they were retrieved from the database. You can see this code in the second and third examples in this figure. It compares the current value of each field in the database against the original value of the field, which is stored in the dataset. If none of the values have changed, the operation is performed. Otherwise, it's not.

Most of the statements in this figure use one or more *parameters*, which are variables whose names start with an at sign (@). For example, parameters are used in the Values clause of the Insert statement and the Set clause of the Update statement to refer to the current values of the fields in the dataset. They're used in the Where clauses of the Update and Delete statements to refer to the original value of each field in the dataset. And one is used in the Where clause of the Select statement after the Update statement to refer to the current record. In addition, the Where clause of the Select statement after the Insert statement includes a *system function* named @@IDENTITY. While the names of the parameters are based on the data table that's being used, @@IDENTITY is used throughout SQL Server to refer to the most recent value generated for an identity field. The wizard inserts parameters and system functions when it creates the command objects for a data adapter. Then, before each statement is executed, Visual Basic substitutes the appropriate value for each variable.

This should give you more perspective on how the dataset is refreshed and how optimistic concurrency is provided when you use ADO.NET. Because of the disconnected data architecture, these features can't be provided by the database management system or by ADO.NET. Instead, they are provided by the SQL statements that are generated by the Configuration Wizard.

SQL that inserts a vendor row and refreshes the row in the dataset

```
INSERT INTO Vendors (VendorName, VendorAddress1, VendorAddress2,
                     VendorCity, VendorState, VendorZipCode)
VALUES (@VendorName, @VendorAddress1, @VendorAddress2,
        @VendorCity, @VendorState, @VendorZipCode);
SELECT VendorName, VendorAddress1, VendorAddress2,
       VendorCity, VendorState, VendorZipCode, VendorID
FROM Vendors WHERE (VendorID = @@IDENTITY) ORDER BY VendorName
```

SQL that updates a vendor row and refreshes the row in the dataset

```
UPDATE Vendors
SET VendorName = @VendorName, VendorAddress1 = @VendorAddress1,
    VendorAddress2 = @VendorAddress2, VendorCity = @VendorCity,
    VendorState = @VendorState, VendorZipCode = @VendorZipCode
WHERE   (VendorID = @Original_VendorID)
    AND (VendorAddress1 = @Original_VendorAddress1
     OR @Original_VendorAddress1 IS NULL AND VendorAddress1 IS NULL)
    AND (VendorAddress2 = @Original_VendorAddress2
     OR @Original_VendorAddress2 IS NULL AND VendorAddress2 IS NULL)
    AND (VendorCity = @Original_VendorCity)
    AND (VendorName = @Original_VendorName)
    AND (VendorState = @Original_VendorState)
    AND (VendorZipCode = @Original_VendorZipCode);
SELECT VendorName, VendorAddress1, VendorAddress2, VendorCity,
       VendorState, VendorZipCode, VendorID
FROM Vendors WHERE (VendorID = @VendorID) ORDER BY VendorName
```

A SQL Delete statement that deletes a vendor row

```
DELETE FROM Vendors
WHERE   (VendorID = @Original_VendorID)
    AND (VendorAddress1 = @Original_VendorAddress1
     OR @Original_VendorAddress1 IS NULL AND VendorAddress1 IS NULL)
    AND (VendorAddress2 = @Original_VendorAddress2
     OR @Original_VendorAddress2 IS NULL AND VendorAddress2 IS NULL)
    AND (VendorCity = @Original_VendorCity)
    AND (VendorName = @Original_VendorName)
    AND (VendorState = @Original_VendorState)
    AND (VendorZipCode = @Original_VendorZipCode)
```

Description

- If you select the Use optimistic concurrency option when you create a data adapter, the wizard adds code to the Update and Delete statements that checks that the data hasn't changed since it was retrieved.

- If you select the Refresh the DataSet option, the wizard adds a Select statement after the Insert and Update statements that refreshes the new or modified row in the dataset.

- The SQL statements use *parameters* to identify the new values for an insert or update operation. Parameters are also used for the original field values, which are used to check that a row hasn't changed for an update or delete operation. The values for these parameters are stored in and retrieved from the dataset.

- If a table contains an identity field, the *system function* named @@IDENTITY is used to identify the value that's generated for a new row so the row in the dataset can be updated.

Figure 17-18   How to interpret the generated SQL statements

Perspective

In this chapter, you learned the basic skills for creating and working with ADO.NET objects. But there's a lot more to learn about ADO.NET. So in the next chapter, you'll learn how to use ADO.NET with bound controls like text boxes. You'll also learn how to validate the data in a dataset and how to handle ADO.NET errors.

Summary

- You can use the Data Adapter Configuration Wizard to create a data adapter and the connection and command objects it uses to work with a database.

- The Wizard can generate the Insert, Update, and Delete statements that will be used to update the database from the Select statement you specify.

- The *Query Builder* provides a visual interface you can use to generate a Select statement based on the selections you make.

- After you create a data adapter, you can generate a dataset *schema file* that defines the structure of the dataset in which the data adapter will store the data it retrieves. You can also generate and instantiate a dataset class.

- To load data into a data table, you use the Fill method of the data adapter. To remove all the data from a dataset or data table, you use the Clear method of the dataset or data table. And to update the database with changes made to a data table, you use the Update method of the data adapter.

- You can use *complex data binding* to bind a *data grid control* to a data table. Then, the data grid control displays the data in the data table automatically. It also provides for adding, updating, and deleting rows in the table.

Terms

Query Builder	schema file
diagram pane	data grid control
grid pane	bound control
SQL pane	complex data binding
results pane	untyped dataset
optimistic concurrency	parameter
table mappings	

Objectives

- Given the data requirements for a form, use the Data Adapter Configuration Wizard to define a data adapter that provides access to that data.

- Given the specifications for a program that uses a data grid control to work with the data in a dataset, design and code the program.

- Describe the objects that the Data Adapter Configuration Wizard generates and explain how they're related.

- Explain how you use a data adapter and dataset to work with the data in a database.

- Define complex data binding and explain how you use it with a data grid.

Exercise 17-1   Create a data adapter and preview the data

In this exercise, you'll create a data adapter using the Data Adapter Configuration Wizard. Then, you'll preview the data defined by that data adapter.

Before you start these exercises...

If you're going to use MSDE on your own PC to do the database exercises for this book, you need to install MSDE and attach the Accounts Payable database to it. If you haven't already done that, please refer to appendix A. Similarly, if the Accounts Payable database is going to be on the server at your company or school, you need to find out what information you need for establishing a connection to the database.

Start a new project and create the data adapter

1. Start Visual Studio, and then start a new project named VendorMaintenance in the C:\VB.NET\Chapter 17 folder.

2. Open the Toolbox, click on the Data tab, and then double-click on the SqlDataAdapter component to start the Data Adapter Configuration Wizard.

3. Click on the Next button in the Welcome dialog box to display the dialog box for selecting the connection. Then, click on the New Connection button to display the Data Link Properties dialog box.

4. Enter the information for connecting to the Accounts Payable database into the Connection tab of this dialog box. Then, click on the Test button to make sure the connection works. If it doesn't, fix the entries and test it again. Once you have it working, click on the OK button to return to the previous dialog box.

5. Click on the Next button to display the Choose a Query Type dialog box. Make sure the Use SQL statements option is selected, and then click on the Next button to display the Generate the SQL statements dialog box.

6. Click on the Query Builder button to display the Query Builder window. Highlight the Vendors table in the Add Table dialog box that's displayed, and then click on the Open button to add the table to the diagram pane of the Query Builder. Click on the Close button to close the Add Table dialog box.

7. Check the VendorName, VendorAddress1, VendorAddress2, VendorCity, VendorState, and VendorZipCode fields in the Vendors table. Then, select the Ascending option from the Sort Type column of the VendorName field in the grid pane. A Select statement like the one shown in the SQL pane in figure 17-4 should be generated.

8. Right-click in the diagram pane and select the Run command from the shortcut menu that's displayed. The results of the query will be displayed in the results pane. If the results look like those shown in figure 17-4, click on the OK button to return to the Wizard. Otherwise, correct the query.

9. Click on the Next button in the Generate the SQL statements dialog box to display the View Wizard Results dialog box. This dialog box should indicate that Select, Insert, Update, and Delete statements were generated along with table mappings. Click on the Finish button to create the data adapter, command, and connection objects.

Review the properties of the ADO.NET objects and preview the data

10. Click on the data adapter object in the Component Designer tray to display its properties in the Properties window. Then, click on the plus sign to the left of the SelectCommand group to display and review the properties for the command object that contains the Select statement. Next, click on the plus sign to the left of the Connection group to display and review the properties for this object.

11. Expand the InsertCommand group for the data adapter, click on the CommandText property, and then click on the ellipsis button that's displayed. The Insert and Select statements that are executed when a record is added to the database will be displayed in the Query Builder window. Review these statements, and then close this window. Repeat this procedure for the UpdateCommand and DeleteCommand groups.

12. With the data adapter still selected, click on the Preview Data link at the bottom of the Properties window to display the Data Adapter Preview dialog box. Click on the Fill Dataset button to display the results of the Select statement in the Results box.

13. To widen the VendorName column so you can see all the data in each row, double-click on the line to the right of the column header. When the mouse pointer is in the right position, a double-headed arrow will appear. Repeat this procedure for other columns you want to widen. Then, review the results and close the dialog box.

14. Save the project and keep the solution open if you're going to continue with the next exercise. Otherwise, close the solution.

Exercise 17-2 Create the Vendor Maintenance form

In this exercise, you'll create a Vendor Maintenance form like the one shown in figure 17-12 that uses a data grid control to work with the data in a dataset.

Open the project and generate the dataset

1. If it's not already open, open the project you created in exercise 17-1.

2. Select the data adapter object in the Component Designer tray, and then click on the Generate Dataset link at the bottom of the Properties window to display the Generate Dataset dialog box.

3. With the New option selected, enter dsVendors for the name of the dataset. Then, make sure that the Vendors table and the Add this dataset to the designer option are selected, and click on the OK button. A dataset schema file named dsVendors.xsd should appear in the Solution Explorer, and a dataset object named DsVendors1 should appear in the Component Designer tray.

Design and code the form

4. Add two button controls to the default form, name them btnUpdate and btnExit, and change their Text properties so they look like the buttons shown in figure 17-13. Then, change the properties of the form so it looks like the one in this figure.

5. Double-click on the form to open the Code Editor window and start a Load event procedure. Then, enter a statement to fill the dataset.

6. Start a procedure for the Click event of the Update button, and then enter a statement to update the database. This statement should be executed only if changes have been made to the dataset.

7. Start a procedure for the Click event of the Exit button, and then enter a statement to close the form.

8. Return to the Form Designer window and add a data grid control to the form. Size and position the form and its controls so it looks like the one shown in figure 17-13. Then, select the data grid control and set the DataSource and DataMember properties so they refer to the Vendors table in the dataset you created.

Build and test the form

9. Click on the Start button in the Standard toolbar to build and run the project. The form that's displayed should look like the one in figure 17-12.

10. Change the data in any row and column of the data grid. (You can widen the columns first if you want to so you can see all of the data.) Notice the pencil icon that appears in the row header of the changed row to indicate that it's being changed. Now, press the Tab key to move to the next column and update the row in the dataset.

11. Scroll to the bottom of the data in the data grid, and click in the first column of the last row (the one with an asterisk in its row header). The word (null) will appear in each column to indicate that no data has been entered. Then, enter your name and address as the data for the new record, pressing the Tab key to move from one column to the next. (You can skip the VendorAddress2 column since this value isn't required.) Notice that a VendorID column appears to the right of the other columns even though you didn't select this column in your query. Also notice that a value has been generated for this column and you can't change it. When you press the Tab key from this column, the new record is added to the dataset.

12. Click on the Update Database button to apply the changes to the database. Then, click on the column header for the VendorName column to sort the vendors by vendor name. This will move the vendor you just added to the appropriate position in the data grid. Click on the VendorName column header again to see that the vendors are now sorted in descending sequence by vendor name.

13. Locate the record you just added and click on its row header. Then, press the Delete key to delete it from the dataset, and click on the Update Database button to delete it from the database. When you're through experimenting, close the form.

14. If you want to experiment with the AllowSorting, ReadOnly, and PreferredColumnWidth properties of the data grid to see how they work, do that now. When you're through experimenting, close the solution.

18

How to work with bound controls and parameterized queries

In the last chapter, you learned how to use a data grid control that's bound to a dataset to work with the data in that dataset. Now, you'll learn how to work with controls like text boxes and combo boxes that are bound to datasets. You'll also learn how to use parameterized queries that let you retrieve just one row into a dataset. When you're through with this chapter, you'll have a much better idea about what you have to do to create a database application in the real world.

How to use bound controls to display individual data columns

In the topics that follow, you'll learn how use bound text box controls to display the data in individual columns of a data table. When you bind controls to individual data columns, the data in the current row of the table is displayed in those controls. Then, you can navigate through the other rows to display the data they contain.

A Vendor Display form that uses bound controls

To illustrate the basic skills for working with bound controls, I'll use the Vendor Display form shown in figure 18-1. This form lets the user display the data in a table of Vendors. To do that, each text box on this form is bound to an individual column in the Vendors table. Then, the user can click on the navigation buttons that are provided to move from one row in this table to another.

Notice that the number of the current row and the total number of rows in the table are displayed in a label between the navigation buttons. That helps give the users a feel for where they are in the table. Keep in mind, though, that if the table contains a large number of rows, you'll want to provide a way for the user to access a row directly rather than having to scroll through hundreds of rows to get to a specific row. You'll learn two different ways to do that later in this chapter.

Before I go on, you should notice that this form doesn't display the state code from the VendorState field in the State text box. Instead, it uses the StateName field from a States table to display the full state name. Although this may not be realistic (most applications would just display the state code), this will illustrate the use of a join in a data adapter. You'll see the Select statement that includes this join when I present the property settings for this form.

The Vendor Display form

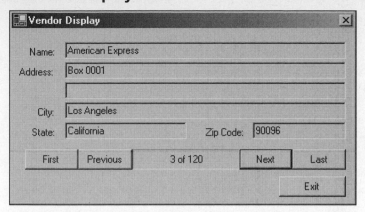

Description

- The Vendor Display form lets you display the data in a single row of the Vendors data table. To do that, each of the text boxes on this form is bound to an individual column in the table.

- When this form is first displayed, it contains the data from the first row in the Vendors table. To navigate to another row, the user can click on the First, Previous, Next, or Last button.

- To give users an idea of where they are in the table, this form includes a label control that indicates the position of the row that's currently displayed and the total number of rows in the table.

- Instead of displaying the VendorState field from the Vendors table in the States text box, this form displays the StateName field from a table named States. That means that the data adapter has to get data from two tables.

- Although the navigation provided by this form is acceptable for a dataset that contains a small number of records, it isn't acceptable for datasets that contain more than a few dozen records.

The data adapter used by this form

- This form uses a data adapter that joins selected columns from the Vendors and States tables in the database. See figure 18-4 for details.

Figure 18-1   A Vendor Display form that uses bound controls

How to bind text box controls

Figure 18-2 shows how to bind a text box control to a data column. To do that, you expand the DataBindings group for the control in the Properties window and then select the appropriate column from the drop-down list for the Text property. In this case, the Name text box is being bound to the VendorName column of the Vendors table. This type of binding is called *simple data binding* because the control is bound to a single data element. In this case, the control is bound to a single column value in the Vendors table.

When you run a form with bound text box controls, the values in the bound columns of the current row are automatically assigned to the Text properties of the controls. That, of course, means that the values are displayed within the text boxes. Then, as you move from one row to another, the data in the controls changes to reflect the data in the current row. In addition, if you change the data in one or more of the bound controls, those changes are saved to the row when you move to another row. (Although the Vendor Display form doesn't provide for modifications, it could easily be changed to do so.) One of the keys to using bound controls, then, is knowing how to navigate through the rows in a data table.

A text box that's bound to a column in the Vendors data table

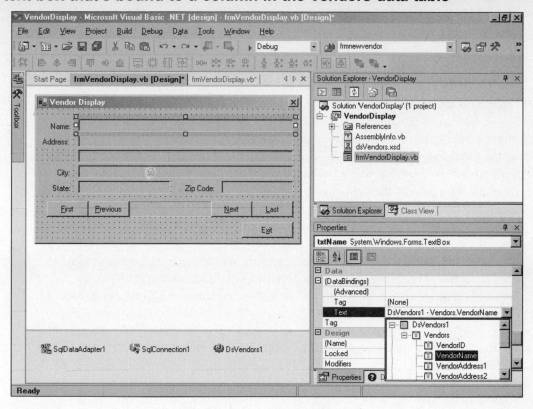

How to bind a text box control to a data column

- To bind a text box control to a data column, set the Text property in the DataBindings group to the name of the data column. This type of binding is called *simple data binding* because the control is bound to a single data element, in this case, a single column value.

- When a text box is bound to a data column, the value of that column in the current record is displayed in the control as the program executes. In addition, if the value of the control changes, that value is saved in the data table.

- The drop-down list that's available for the Text property lists all of the datasets, data tables, and data columns that are available to the project, so you can navigate through this list to locate the column you want.

Figure 18-2   How to bind text box controls

How to navigate through the rows in a data table

By default, when you display a form that contains bound controls, the controls reflect the data in the first row of the table they're bound to. Then, to move to other rows in the table, you use a BindingManagerBase object as described in figure 18-3. This object lets you manage all of the controls on the form that are bound to the same table.

To create a BindingManagerBase object, you use the syntax shown at the top of this figure. As you can see, you use the BindingContext property of the form (Me) to refer to its BindingContext object. This object contains information about the bound controls on the form. When you refer to this object, you specify the name of the dataset and data table that the controls you want to work with are bound to. Then, a BindingManagerBase object is created for those controls, and you can use this object to navigate through the rows in the data table.

The first coding example in this figure shows how you can create a binding manager base for the Vendors table. Here, the first statement declares the variable that will hold the reference to the binding manager base, and the second statement uses the BindingContext property of the form to create the binding manager base. Notice that both the dataset and the data table names are passed to the BindingContext property. That's necessary even if the dataset contains a single table.

The second coding example shows how to use the binding manager base to navigate through the rows in the data table. Notice that the Handles clause of this event procedure has been modified so it handles the Click event of four buttons. These buttons let the user move to the first row, the next row, the previous row and the last row in the data table. To determine which button was clicked, this procedure uses a Select Case statement that checks the Name property of the sender argument that's passed to the procedure. This property contains the name of the button that was clicked. If, for example, the Name property contains the value "btnFirst," you know that the user clicked the First button. Then, the code should move to the first row in the data table so its data is displayed.

To move to a specific row in a data table, you set the Position property of the binding manager base. To move to the first row, for example, you set the Position property to 0 since the collection of rows in a table is zero-based. To move to the next row in a table, you add one to the Position property. To move to the previous row, you subtract 1 from the Position property. And to move to the last row, you set the Position property to the value of the Count property minus one. (Since the Count property indicates the number of rows in the table, you must subtract one to convert this number to the index value of the last row.)

Notice that before you move to the previous row, you have to check that the first row isn't already displayed. If you don't, the Position property will be set to -1, which isn't a valid index value. Similarly, before you move to the next row, you have to check that the last row isn't already displayed. Otherwise, the Position property will be set to an index value that's beyond the bounds of the table.

The syntax for creating a BindingManagerBase object

```
bindingManagerBase = Me.BindingContext(dataSet, tablename)
```

Common BindingManagerBase properties

Property	Description
Position	A zero-based index that indicates the current position in the data table.
Count	The number of rows in the data table.

Code that creates a BindingManagerBase object

```
Dim VendorsBindingManager As BindingManagerBase
VendorsBindingManager = Me.BindingContext(DsVendors1, "Vendors")
```

Code that provides for navigating through the rows in a dataset

```
Private Sub NavigationButtons_Click(ByVal sender As System.Object, _
        ByVal e As System.EventArgs) Handles btnFirst.Click, _
        btnPrevious.Click, btnNext.Click, btnLast.Click
    Select Case sender.Name
        Case "btnFirst"
            VendorsBindingManager.Position = 0
        Case "btnPrevious"
            If VendorsBindingManager.Position > 0 Then
                VendorsBindingManager.Position -= 1
            End If
        Case "btnNext"
            If VendorsBindingManager.Position _
                    < VendorsBindingManager.Count - 1 Then
                VendorsBindingManager.Position += 1
            End If
        Case "btnLast"
            VendorsBindingManager.Position _
                = VendorsBindingManager.Count - 1
    End Select
End Sub
```

Description

- You use the BindingManagerBase object to manage all of the controls on a form that are bound to the same data table.

- To create a BindingManagerBase object, you use the BindingContext property of the form. This property contains a reference to the form's BindingContext object, which is created automatically when controls on the form are bound to the columns in a data table.

- The BindingManagerBase object ensures that all controls that are bound to the same data table are synchronized. That way, when you move to another row, the data-bound controls will display the values in that row.

- If the form provides for updating the rows in a data table, moving from one row to another causes any changes made to the current row to be saved to the data table.

Figure 18-3   How to navigate through the rows in a data table

The property settings for the Vendor Display form

Figure 18-4 presents some of the property settings for the Vendor Display form. Before you look at those, though, look at the Select statement that's used by the Vendors data adapter that's used for the form. This statement uses a join to combine information from the Vendors and States tables into a single data table. In this case, the join is based on the VendorState and StateCode fields in the joined tables, and the StateName field in the States table is included in the result table. That way, the state name can be displayed in the form rather than the state code.

The property settings for the data-bound text boxes should be easy to understand. The Text property of each of these controls is bound to the appropriate data column of the Vendors table in the dataset named DsVendors1. The Name text box, for example, is bound to the VendorName column, and the States text box is bound to the StateName column. Notice that when you join data from two or more tables, the result table is given the name of the first table named on the From clause of the Select statement. In this example, then, the table is named Vendors.

The other property settings shown here are for the label that displays the number of the current row and the total number of rows in the table. It's displayed with a fixed, three-dimensional border, and the text it contains will be centered in the control. In a moment, you'll see how the contents of this control change as the program executes.

Because this form doesn't provide for data modification, the ReadOnly properties of all of the text boxes have been changed to True and the TabStop properties have been set to False. In addition, no Insert, Update, or Delete statements were generated when the data adapter was created. In fact, the wizard couldn't generate these statements from the Select statement. That's because the Select statement joins data from two tables, but only one table can be updated at a time. Since the wizard would have no way of knowing which table you want to update, it's not possible for it to generate the appropriate statements. Because of that, you would have to make some changes to this form before you could use it as a maintenance form. You'll see one way to do that later in this chapter.

The Select statement for the Vendors data adapter

```
Select VendorID, VendorName, VendorAddress1, VendorAddress2,
    VendorCity, VendorZipCode, StateCode, StateName
From Vendors
Inner Join States On VendorState = StateCode
Order By VendorName
```

Property settings for the data-bound text boxes

Name	Text (DataBindings) as shown in the Properties window
txtName	DsVendors1 - Vendors.VendorName
txtAddressLine1	DsVendors1 - Vendors.VendorAddress1
txtAddressLine2	DsVendors1 - Vendors.VendorAddress2
txtCity	DsVendors1 - Vendors.VendorCity
txtState	DsVendors1 - Vendors.StateName
txtZipCode	DsVendors1 - Vendors.VendorZipCode

Property settings for the row position label

Property	Setting
Name	lblPosition
BorderStyle	Fixed3D
TextAlign	MiddleCenter

Description

- The Select statement that's used to retrieve the data that's displayed on the form joins data from the Vendors and States tables. That way, the form can display the StateName field from the States table instead of the state code that's stored in the VendorState field of the Vendors table.

- Because this form doesn't provide for updating data, Insert, Update, and Delete statements aren't generated. In addition, the ReadOnly properties of each of the text boxes is set to True so the data in the controls can't be modified, and the TabStop property of each text box is set to False so the focus doesn't move to those controls when the user presses the Tab key.

- The dataset class is given the name dsVendors, and the dataset object is generated with the name DsVendors1.

Figure 18-4   The property settings for the Vendor Display form

The code for the Vendor Display form

Figure 18-5 presents the Visual Basic code for the Vendor Display form. To start, this code declares a variable that will hold a reference to the binding manager base for the bound controls on the form. Then, the Load event procedure for the form is executed.

In the Load event procedure, the first statement uses the Fill method of the data adapter to load the data into the DsVendors1 dataset. Then, the second statement creates the BindingManagerBase object for the Vendors table of that dataset. And the third statement calls the DisplayPosition procedure to format the label so it indicates the current position in the table.

The DisplayPosition procedure uses both the Position and Count properties of the binding manager base to display the appropriate information. Because the Position property hasn't been set explicitly at this point, it defaults to 0. Because of that, the first record in the table is displayed on the form after the Load procedure has been executed.

When the user clicks on one of the navigation buttons to display another record, the event procedure that's executed sets the Position property so the requested row is displayed on the form. This is the key to this program, and you already saw how this code works. Then, after the new position is established, the DisplayPosition procedure is called to format the position label so it reflects the new position.

If this seems at all complicated, you can do exercise 18-1 right now to help clarify these development procedures. This exercise, which starts on the next page, will guide you through the development process. Otherwise, you can continue with the text and come back to this exercise later.

The Visual Basic code for the Vendor Display form

```
Public Class Form1
    Inherits System.Windows.Forms.Form

    Dim VendorsBindingManager As BindingManagerBase

    Private Sub Form1_Load(ByVal sender As System.Object, _
            ByVal e As System.EventArgs) Handles MyBase.Load
        SqlDataAdapter1.Fill(DsVendors1)
        VendorsBindingManager = Me.BindingContext(DsVendors1, "Vendors")
        Me.DisplayPosition()
    End Sub

    Private Sub DisplayPosition()
        lblPosition.Text = VendorsBindingManager.Position + 1 & " of " _
                        & VendorsBindingManager.Count
    End Sub

    Private Sub NavigationButtons_Click(ByVal sender As System.Object, _
            ByVal e As System.EventArgs) Handles btnFirst.Click, _
            btnPrevious.Click, btnNext.Click, btnLast.Click
        Select Case sender.Name
            Case "btnFirst"
                VendorsBindingManager.Position = 0
            Case "btnPrevious"
                If VendorsBindingManager.Position > 0 Then
                    VendorsBindingManager.Position -= 1
                End If
            Case "btnNext"
                If VendorsBindingManager.Position _
                        < VendorsBindingManager.Count - 1 Then
                    VendorsBindingManager.Position += 1
                End If
            Case "btnLast"
                VendorsBindingManager.Position _
                    = VendorsBindingManager.Count - 1
        End Select
        Me.DisplayPosition()
    End Sub

    Private Sub btnExit_Click(ByVal sender As System.Object, _
            ByVal e As System.EventArgs) Handles btnExit.Click
        Me.Close()
    End Sub

End Class
```

Figure 18-5   The code for the Vendor Display form

Exercise 18-1   Create the Vendor Display form

This exercise guides you through the process of creating the Vendor Display form of figure 18-1. That will give you practice using the BindingManagerBase object to perform navigation functions.

Start the project and create the ADO.NET objects

1. Start Visual Studio, and then start a new Windows Application project named VendorDisplay in the C:\VB.NET\Chapter 18 folder.

2. Double-click on the SqlDataAdapter component in the Data tab of the Toolbox to start the Data Adapter Configuration Wizard.

3. Click on the Next button in the Welcome dialog box to display the Data Connection dialog box. Then, select the data connection you created for the application in chapter 17 from the combo box in this dialog box and click on the Next button.

4. Click on the Next button in the Query Type dialog box to use SQL statements with the data adapter, then use the Query Builder to create the Select statement shown in figure 18-4.

5. When you're done with the Query Builder, close its window and then click on the Advanced Options button to display the Advanced SQL Generation Options dialog box. Remove the check mark from the Generate Insert, Update and Delete statements option since this application won't allow those operations. Then, click on the OK button to return to the Generate the SQL statements dialog box.

6. Click on the Next button and note in the next dialog box that only a Select statement and table mappings were generated. Click on the Finish button to create the data adapter, connection, and command objects.

7. Click on the data adapter in the Component Designer tray, and then click on the Generate Dataset link at the bottom of the properties window. Use the Generate Dataset dialog box that's displayed to create a dataset named dsVendors that contains the Vendors table. Make sure that you select the option to add an instance of this dataset to the designer.

Design the form and bind the controls

8. Add the text box controls shown in figure 18-1 that will display data from the Vendors table. Name these controls as indicated in figure 18-4, and bind the Text property of each control as indicated in that figure. Then, set the ReadOnly property of each of these controls to True and the TabStop property to False.

9. Add the navigation buttons and row position label. Set the properties of the row position label as shown in figure 18-4. Name the navigation buttons btnFirst, btnPrevious, btnNext, and btnLast, and set the Text properties of these controls so they appear as shown in figure 18-2.

10. Add the Exit button and set its Name and Text properties appropriately. Then, set the properties of the form so it appears as shown in figure 18-2.

Add the code and test the application

11. Double-click on the form to start a Load event procedure. Then, code a statement that fills the Vendors dataset with the data specified by the data adapter.

12. Run the application. The data for the first vendor in the Vendors table should be displayed in the text boxes on the Vendor Display form. If it's not, return to the Form Designer and correct the binding properties of the text boxes so the data is displayed properly. When this works the way it should, close the form and return to the Code Editor window.

13. Declare a module-level variable for the binding manager base, and assign the appropriate binding context object to this variable in the Load procedure for the form.

14. Code a procedure named DisplayPosition that displays the number of the current row and the total number of rows in the Vendors table in the label between the navigation buttons. Then, call this procedure from the Load event of the form.

15. Start a procedure for the Click event of the First button. Then, change the name of this procedure to NavigationButtons_Click, and change the Handles clause so it handles all four navigation buttons.

16. Code a Select Case statement in this procedure that moves to the appropriate row in the Vendors table depending on which button the user clicked. Be sure to provide for the user clicking on the First or Last button when the first or last row is already displayed. If you need help, you can refer to figure 18-5.

17. Code a statement that calls the DisplayPosition procedure after the Select Case statement. Then, complete the code for this program by creating a procedure that closes the form when the user clicks on the Exit button.

18. Run the application. Test the navigation buttons to be sure they work properly, and check that the correct information is displayed in the row position label. If you encounter any problems, end the application, fix the problems, and test the application again.

19. When you're sure the application works correctly, close the form and the solution.

How to use bound controls to add, update, and delete data rows

Once you understand how the binding manager base works, you shouldn't have any trouble using it to navigate through the rows in a data table as illustrated in the Vendor Display form. But you can use the binding manager base for more than just navigation. You can also use it to add, update, and delete rows from a table. You'll learn how to do that in the topics that follow.

A Vendor Maintenance form that uses bound controls

Figure 18-6 presents a Vendor Maintenance form that lets the user add, modify, and delete records from a table of vendors. When this application first starts, the data for the first vendor in the table is displayed just as it is on the Vendor Display form. Instead of providing navigation buttons that let the user move to another vendor, though, the Vendor Maintenance form lists all of the existing vendors in a combo box at the top of the form. Then, the user can select a vendor from this combo box to display the data for that vendor, which is clearly more efficient than using the controls shown in figure 18-1.

Once the data for a vendor is displayed, the user can modify the data for that vendor or delete the vendor. Alternatively, the user can click on the Add button to add a new vendor.

In addition to the combo box that lists the vendors, this form uses a combo box that lists the state names from the States table. When the user selects a state from this list, the state code in the current row is updated. You'll see how that's accomplished in a minute. For now, just realize that I included this combo box to illustrate how you can use a combo box to update data as well as to illustrate the use of two data adapters with a single form. In this case, one data adapter is used to retrieve data from the Vendors table, and one is used to retrieve data from the States table.

When the Vendor Maintenance form is first displayed and each time a different vendor is selected, the Update and Cancel buttons on the form are disabled. But the program enables these controls if the user changes any of the data on the form. Then, the user can click on the Update button to save the changes or on the Cancel button to cancel the changes. In contrast, the Add and Delete buttons are enabled when the form is first displayed and each time a different vendor is selected, but they're disabled when the user changes the data in the current row. The program enables these buttons again when the user accepts or cancels the changes.

The Update Database button is also disabled when this form is first displayed. It's enabled after the user clicks on the Update button to save changes to the Vendors table. Then, the user can click on this button to save all the changes made to the Vendors table to the Accounts Payable database.

The Vendor Maintenance form

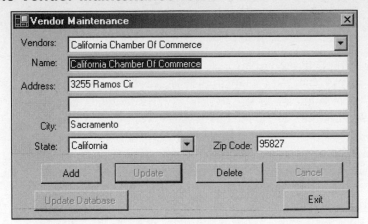

Description

- The Vendors combo box at the top of this form lists the names of all of the vendors in the Vendors table. To modify or delete a vendor, the user selects that vendor from the combo box to display its information on the form.

- To delete the current row from the dataset, the user can click on the Delete button. Before the row is deleted, a confirmation message is displayed.

- To modify the current row, the user can type over the existing data. Then, the Update and Cancel buttons are enabled. To save the changes to the dataset, the user can click on the Update button. To cancel the changes, the user can click on the Cancel button.

- To add a new row, the user can click on the Add button. Then, the controls on the form are cleared so the user can enter the data for the new row. To save the changes to the dataset, the user can click on the Update button. To cancel the changes, the user can click on the Cancel button.

- To update the database with the changes made to the dataset, the user can click on the Update Database button. This button becomes available when a row is added, changed, or deleted.

The two data adapters used by this form

- The first data adapter retrieves data from the Vendors table. This data is used to display the list of vendors in the Vendors combo box and to display the information for a vendor the user selects from the combo box.

- The second data adapter retrieves data from the States table. This data is used to display a list of the state names in the States combo box, associate a state name with a state code in a Vendors row, and check that a zip code is valid for a state.

Figure 18-6   A Vendor Maintenance form that uses bound controls

How to bind combo box and list box controls

Figure 18-7 shows how to bind combo box controls like the ones used on the Vendor Maintenance form. To do that, you can use both complex data binding and simple data binding. The complex data binding provides for displaying all of the values in one column of a table in the list portion of the control. And the simple data binding provides for displaying and updating a single value in a single data column. These techniques also work with list box controls.

To complex-bind a combo box control, you use the DataSource and DisplayMember properties. The DataSource property identifies the table the control is bound to, and the DisplayMember property identifies the column whose values are displayed in the list portion of the control. In this figure, for example, the DataSource property of the States combo box is set to the States table, and the DisplayMember property is set to the StateName column. That way, this combo box will list all of the state names in the States table so the user can select one of them.

The Vendors combo box for this application is also bound with complex binding so all of the vendor names in the Vendors table are displayed in the combo box list. In this case, the DataSource property is set to the Vendors table, and the DisplayMember property is set to the VendorName column.

In contrast, you use the SelectedValue and ValueMember properties to simple-bind a combo box control. You do that when you want to update a field in a row of a data table based on the combo box selection. To do that, you use the SelectedValue property to identify the data table and column that should be updated. For instance, the States combo box in this figure is simple-bound to the VendorState column in the Vendors table, which contains the state code for the vendor. In this case, though, the state code isn't the value that's displayed in the combo box. So for this to work, the ValueMember property must be set to the StateCode column in the States table. Then, when the user selects a state name in the State combo box list, the related StateCode value from the States table is stored in the VendorState column of the current row in the Vendors table.

Although the DisplayMember and ValueMember properties are different in this example, you should realize that they don't have to be. In other words, the values that are displayed in the combo box list can be the same as the values that are stored in the list. If, for example, you display the state codes in the States combo box list instead of the state names, you can set the DisplayMember property to StateCode. Then, when the user selects a state code from the combo box, that value is stored in the VendorState column of the current row in the Vendors table.

Although this may seem complicated at first, you'll soon be able to get the result you want by using the four properties that are summarized in this figure. With complex data binding, you can display the values of one column in a data table in a combo box list or list box. With simple data binding, you can update a column in another data table with a value taken from the first data table.

A combo box that uses simple and complex binding

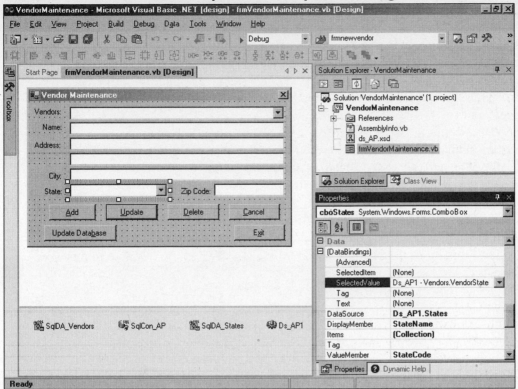

DROPDOWN LIST, SD CBO CAN'T BE KILLED IN BY USER (handwritten annotation)

Combo box and list box properties for binding

Property	Description
DataSource	The name of the data table that contains the data displayed in the list.
DisplayMember	The name of the data column whose data is displayed in the list.
SelectedValue	The name of the data column that the control is bound to.
ValueMember	The name of the data column whose value is stored in the list. This value is used to update the value of the data column specified by the SelectedValue property of the control.

FIRST - FILL DATASET IN FORM LOAD (handwritten annotation)

Description

- To complex-bind a combo box or list box to a data table so all the values in a column of a data table are included in the list, use the DataSource and DisplayMember properties.

- To simple-bind a combo box or list box to a data column so the value of that column changes when the user selects an entry from the list, use the SelectedValue and ValueMember properties. Then, the value of the data column specified by the ValueMember property is used to update the data column specified by the SelectedValue property.

Figure 18-7   How to bind combo box and list box controls

SQLDATAADAPTER1 . FILL (DATASET 1) (handwritten annotation)

How to add, update, and delete data rows

To add, update, and delete rows using the binding manager base, you use the methods shown in figure 18-8. To add a new blank row, for example, you use the AddNew method. Then, after the user enters the data for the row, you use the EndCurrentEdit method to save the row to the data table. Alternatively, you can use the CancelCurrentEdit method to remove the new row from the table.

You also use the EndCurrentEdit and CancelCurrentEdit methods to save and cancel changes made to an existing row. Note that you don't explicitly start the edit of an existing row. Instead, that happens automatically when the user changes the data in a bound control.

Finally, you use the RemoveAt method to delete a specific row. Notice that you identify the row to be deleted by specifying its index value. If you want to delete the current row, for example, you can specify the index value using the Position property of the binding manager base as shown in the example in this figure.

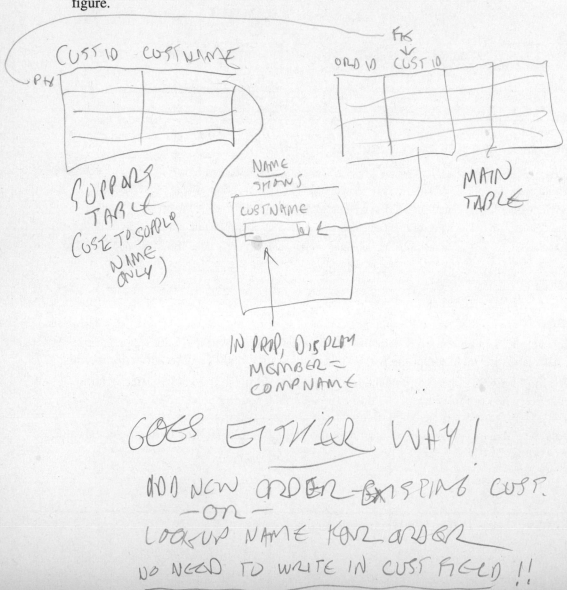

Common BindingManagerBase methods

Method	Description
AddNew	Adds a new blank row to a data table.
RemoveAt(index)	Deletes the row with the specified index from a data table.
EndCurrentEdit	Ends the edit by saving the changes to the current row.
CancelCurrentEdit	Reverses the changes made to the current row.

A statement that adds a new row to a dataset

```
VendorsBindingManager.AddNew()
```

A statement that removes the current row from a dataset

```
VendorsBindingManager.RemoveAt(VendorsBindingManager.Position)
```

A statement that saves the changes to the current row and ends the edit operation

```
VendorsBindingManager.EndCurrentEdit()
```

A statement that cancels the changes to the current row

```
VendorsBindingManager.CancelCurrentEdit()
```

Description

- When you add a new row using the AddNew method, the Position property of the binding manager base is set to one more than the position of the last row in the data table.

- You can use the EndCurrentEdit and CancelCurrentEdit methods to cancel or save the changes to an existing row or a new row that was added using the AddNew method.

[handwritten notes]
ME. MYBINDINGMGR = ME. BINDINGCONTEXT (DATASET II, "ORDERS")
BTN NEXT =
MYBINDINGMGR.POSITION = MYBINDINGMGR. POSITION + 1

Figure 18-8   How to add, update, and delete rows

[handwritten] KU PO-UPDATES

The property settings for the Vendor Maintenance form

Figure 18-9 presents some of the property settings for the Vendor Maintenance form. The first thing you should notice is that this form uses two data adapters: one for the Vendors table and one for the States table. However, both tables are stored in the same dataset, which is named Ds_AP1.

Like the text boxes on the Vendor Display form, the Text property of each text box on the Vendor Maintenance form is bound to a column in the Vendors table. In addition, the SelectedValue property of the States combo box is bound to the VendorState column of the Vendors table. Then, this combo box is complex-bound to the States table so it contains a list of the state names associated with the state codes. That way, the user can select a state from the combo box list rather than having to enter a state code manually.

The Vendors combo box is also complex-bound to the VendorName column of the Vendors table. That way, the user can select a vendor from the list instead of having to navigate through the records to find the one to be modified or deleted. You'll see how this lookup operation is implemented in a minute when I show you the code for this form. For now, notice that because this combo box isn't used to update a column in the Vendors table, its SelectedValue property is left at (none) and its ValueMember property isn't specified.

In addition to the StateCode and StateName columns, the States data adapter retrieves the FirstZipCode and LastZipCode columns. These columns contain the range of zip codes that are valid for the state. As you'll see in a moment, they're used to validate the zip code entered by the user.

Before I go on, you should notice that the MaxLength property of each text box on this form has been changed from the default. When you use the data in a text box to update a column in a table, you'll want to be sure that the user doesn't enter more characters than are allowed by the column definition. In this case, you want to be sure that the user doesn't enter more than 50 characters into the VendorName, VendorAddress1, VendorAddress2, and VendorCity columns or more than 10 characters into the VendorZipCode column. The easiest way to do that is to set the MaxLength property, which specifies the maximum number of characters the user can enter into the control.

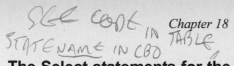

The Select statements for the data adapters

Data adapter	Select statement

SqlDA_Vendors	`Select VendorID, VendorName, VendorAddress1, VendorAddress2,`
	`        VendorCity, VendorState, VendorZipCode`
	`From Vendors`
	`Order By VendorName`

SqlDA_States	`Select StateCode, StateName, FirstZipCode, LastZipCode`
	`From States`
	`Order By StateName`

Property settings for the data-bound text boxes

Name	Text (DataBindings) as shown in the Properties window	MaxLength
txtName	Ds_AP1 - Vendors.VendorName	50
txtAddressLine1	Ds_AP1 - Vendors.VendorAddress1	50
txtAddressLine2	Ds_AP1 - Vendors.VendorAddress2	50
txtCity	Ds_AP1 - Vendors.VendorCity	50
txtZipCode	Ds_AP1 - Vendors.VendorZipCode	10

Property settings for the data-bound combo boxes

Property	Vendors	States
Name	cboVendors	cboStates
DropDownStyle	DropDownList	DropDownList
DataSource	Ds_AP1.Vendors	Ds_AP1.States
DisplayMember	VendorName	StateName
SelectedValue (DataBindings)	(None)	Ds_AP1 - Vendors.VendorState
ValueMember		StateCode

Notes

- Because the data in the States table will not be updated, Insert, Update, and Delete statements aren't generated for it.

- The dataset class is given the name ds_AP, and the dataset object is generated with the name Ds_AP1. This dataset includes the two tables defined by the Vendors and States data adapters.

- The MaxLength properties of the text boxes are set so that the user can't enter more characters than are allowed by the columns they're bound to.

Figure 18-9   The property settings for the Vendor Maintenance form

The code for the Vendor Maintenance form

Figure 18-10 presents the code for the Vendor Maintenance form. It starts by defining three public variables used by the form. The first two will hold Boolean values that will determine when certain processing is done, and the third one will hold a reference to the binding manager base.

When the form is first loaded, both the States and Vendors tables are populated. But first, the bLoading variable is set to True. That way, the code in the Control_DataChanged procedure isn't executed during the loading process. This variable is changed back to False after the tables are loaded.

Notice in this procedure that the Vendors table is loaded after the States table. That's necessary because the States combo box associates the VendorState column in the Vendors table with a column in the States table. But if the States table hasn't been loaded, this association can't be applied for the first Vendor that's displayed.

Next, the Load procedure calls the SetMaintenanceButtons procedure, which sets the Enabled property of the Add, Update, Delete, and Cancel buttons. In this case, a value of True is passed to this procedure, so the Add and Delete buttons are enabled and the Update and Cancel buttons are disabled. Finally, the Load procedure disables the Update Database button to indicate that no changes have been made to the dataset, and it creates the BindingManagerBase object.

When the user selects a vendor from the Vendors combo box, the SelectedIndexChanged event procedure is executed. This procedure starts by setting the Position property of the binding manager base to the SelectedIndex property of the combo box. In other words, it positions the binding manager base to the selected row. This works because the items in the combo box are in the same sequence as the rows in the Vendors table, and both use a zero-based index. Note that if the user makes any changes to the current row before selecting another vendor, those changes are automatically saved when the binding manager base is repositioned.

After the binding manager base is repositioned, the SetMaintenanceButtons procedure is called to enable the Add and Delete buttons and disable the Update and Cancel buttons. Next, the Enabled property of the Update Database button is set to the value of the HasChanges property of the dataset. That way, if any changes have been made to the dataset, the Update Database button is enabled. This code is necessary because when the user changes the data in a row, the Update Database button is disabled so the user can't click on it until the changes are accepted or canceled. So using the HasChanges property is the easiest way to reset the Enabled property of this control.

The next procedure is executed when the user clicks on the Add button. This procedure starts by executing the AddNew method to add a new row to the Vendors table. Then, it calls the SetMaintenanceButtons procedure to disable the Add and Delete buttons and enable the Update and Cancel buttons. To do that, a value of False is passed to the procedure. It also disables the Update Database button so the user can't click on it until the new record is accepted or canceled.

The Visual Basic code for the Vendor Maintenance program   Page 1

```
Public Class Form1
    Inherits System.Windows.Forms.Form

    Dim bLoading As Boolean
    Dim bNewRow As Boolean
    Dim VendorsBindingManager As BindingManagerBase

    Private Sub Form1_Load(ByVal sender As System.Object, _
            ByVal e As System.EventArgs) Handles MyBase.Load
        bLoading = True
        SqlDA_States.Fill(Ds_AP1)
        SqlDA_Vendors.Fill(Ds_AP1)
        bLoading = False
        Me.SetMaintenanceButtons(True)
        btnUpdateDB.Enabled = False
        VendorsBindingManager = Me.BindingContext(Ds_AP1, "Vendors")
    End Sub

    Private Sub SetMaintenanceButtons(ByVal bAddDeleteMode As Boolean)
        btnAdd.Enabled = bAddDeleteMode
        btnUpdate.Enabled = Not bAddDeleteMode
        btnDelete.Enabled = bAddDeleteMode
        btnCancel.Enabled = Not bAddDeleteMode
    End Sub

    Private Sub cboVendors_SelectedIndexChanged(ByVal sender As System.Object, _
            ByVal e As System.EventArgs) Handles cboVendors.SelectedIndexChanged
        VendorsBindingManager.Position = cboVendors.SelectedIndex
        Me.SetMaintenanceButtons(True)
        btnUpdateDB.Enabled = Ds_AP1.HasChanges
        txtName.Focus()
    End Sub

    Private Sub btnAdd_Click(ByVal sender As System.Object, _
            ByVal e As System.EventArgs) Handles btnAdd.Click
        VendorsBindingManager.AddNew()
        Me.SetMaintenanceButtons(False)
        btnUpdateDB.Enabled = False
        cboStates.SelectedIndex = -1
        bNewRow = True
        txtName.Focus()
    End Sub

    Private Sub Control_DataChanged(ByVal sender As System.Object, _
            ByVal e As System.EventArgs) Handles txtName.TextChanged, _
            txtAddressLine1.TextChanged, txtAddressLine2.TextChanged, _
            txtCity.TextChanged, txtZipCode.TextChanged, _
            cboStates.SelectedIndexChanged
        If Not bLoading Then
            Me.SetMaintenanceButtons(False)
            btnUpdateDB.Enabled = False
        End If
    End Sub
```

Figure 18-10   The code for the Vendor Maintenance form (part 1 of 3)

Next, the Add procedure sets the SelectedIndex property of the States combo box to –1 so no value is selected in this combo box. Then, it sets the bNewRow variable to True to indicate that a new record is being added. Finally, it moves the focus to the Name text box so the user can begin entering the data for the new vendor.

The last procedure on the first page of this listing is executed when the user changes the data in the current row. Notice that a single procedure handles the TextChanged event for all the text boxes as well as the SelectedIndexChanged event for the States combo box. Within this procedure, the SetMaintenanceButtons procedure is called to enable the Update and Cancel buttons and to disable the Add and Delete buttons. Then, the Update Database button is disabled so the user can't click on it until the changes are updated or canceled. Notice that this code isn't executed when the form is loaded.

If the user changes the data in a row and then clicks on the Update button, the Update procedure on page 2 of this listing starts by executing a procedure named ValidData. This procedure checks that the user has entered data for the required fields. In this case, it checks the Name, City, and ZipCode text boxes and the States combo box. It also checks to be sure that the zip code is within the valid range identified by the FirstZipCode and LastZipCode columns in the row for the state. To do that, it uses the index of the States combo box to identify the row in the States table that contains the selected state.

If invalid data is detected, an error message is displayed and the return value of the ValidData function is set to False. Otherwise, the return value is set to True so the Update procedure will continue with the update operation.

To save the changes to the current row, the Update procedure issues an EndCurrentEdit method. Then, if the current row is a new row, this procedure sets the SelectedIndex property of the Vendors combo box to the position of the last row in the table, which is the position of the new row. That way, the name of the new vendor is displayed in the combo box. It also sets the bNewRow variable to False so the program is ready for the next operation. The last three statements in this procedure call the SetMaintenanceButtons procedure to disable the Update and Cancel buttons and enable the Add and Delete buttons, enable the Update Database button, and set the focus to the Vendors combo box so the user can select the next vendor to be processed

Similar code is included in the Click event procedure for the Cancel button. Instead of issuing an EndCurrentEdit method, however, this procedure issues a CancelCurrentEdit method to reverse the changes made to the current row. And instead of setting the Enabled property of the Update Database button to True, this procedure sets it to the HasChanges property of the dataset. That way, if this button was enabled before the current row was changed and the changes were canceled, it will be enabled again. Otherwise, it will be disabled. In addition, if the user canceled the addition of a new record, this procedure sets the Position property of the binding manager base to the SelectedIndex property of the Vendors combo box. That causes the data for the vendor that was selected before the user clicked on the Add button to be displayed on the form, since this vendor is still selected in the combo box.

The Visual Basic code for the Vendor Maintenance program   Page 2

```vb
Private Sub btnUpdate_Click(ByVal sender As System.Object, _
        ByVal e As System.EventArgs) Handles btnUpdate.Click
    If ValidData() Then
        VendorsBindingManager.EndCurrentEdit()
        If bNewRow Then
            cboVendors.SelectedIndex = VendorsBindingManager.Count - 1
            bNewRow = False
        End If
        Me.SetMaintenanceButtons(True)
        btnUpdateDB.Enabled = True
        cboVendors.Focus()
    End If
End Sub

Private Function ValidData() As Boolean
    Dim sErrorMessage As String
    If txtName.Text = "" Then
        sErrorMessage = "Name required."
        txtName.Focus()
    ElseIf txtCity.Text = "" Then
        sErrorMessage = "City required."
        txtCity.Focus()
    ElseIf cboStates.SelectedIndex = -1 Then
        sErrorMessage = "State required."
        cboStates.Focus()
    ElseIf txtZipCode.Text = "" Then
        sErrorMessage = "Zip code required."
        txtZipCode.Focus()
    ElseIf txtZipCode.Text < Ds_AP1.States.Rows _
            (cboStates.SelectedIndex).Item("FirstZipCode") _
        Or txtZipCode.Text > Ds_AP1.States.Rows _
            (cboStates.SelectedIndex).Item("LastZipCode") Then
        sErrorMessage = "The zip code is invalid."
        txtZipCode.Focus()
    End If
    If sErrorMessage = "" Then
        ValidData = True
    Else
        ValidData = False
        MessageBox.Show(sErrorMessage, "Data entry error", _
            MessageBoxButtons.OK, MessageBoxIcon.Error)
    End If
End Function

Private Sub btnCancel_Click(ByVal sender As System.Object, _
        ByVal e As System.EventArgs) Handles btnCancel.Click
    VendorsBindingManager.CancelCurrentEdit()
    If bNewRow Then
        VendorsBindingManager.Position = cboVendors.SelectedIndex
        bNewRow = False
    End If
    Me.SetMaintenanceButtons(True)
    btnUpdateDB.Enabled = Ds_AP1.HasChanges
    cboVendors.Focus()
End Sub
```

Figure 18-10   The code for the Vendor Maintenance form (part 2 of 3)

The first procedure on page 3 of this listing is executed when the user clicks on the Delete button. This procedure starts by displaying a message box to confirm that the user wants to delete the record. If the user responds by clicking on the Yes button, a RemoveAt method is executed to remove the current row. Then, the SetMaintenanceButtons procedure is called to reset the Add, Update, Cancel, and Delete buttons, the Enabled property of the Update Database button is set appropriately, and the focus is moved to the Vendors combo box.

The next procedure is the event procedure that's executed when the user clicks on the Update Database button to apply the changes that have been made to the Vendors table to the database. It starts by issuing an Update method to perform this update. Notice that this procedure doesn't check if changes have been made to the dataset before issuing this method. That's because this procedure can be executed only if the Update Database button is enabled, and this button is enabled only if changes have been made to the dataset.

After the database is updated, this procedure issues a Clear method to clear the records from the Vendors table. Then, it issues a Fill method to refresh the table with the current data in the database. Next, it sets the SelectedIndex property of the Vendors combo box to 0 so the first Vendor is selected. This also causes the SelectedIndexChanged procedure for this combo box to be executed. You can look back to the first page of this listing to see what this procedure does.

The last procedure for this form is for the Click event of the Exit button. This procedure starts by checking if any changes have been made to the dataset that haven't been saved to the database. If so, a message box is displayed to ask the user if the form should be closed without saving the changes. If the user responds by clicking on the Yes button, the form is closed. Otherwise, it remains open. If no changes have been made to the dataset, the form is closed without displaying a message box.

* * *

If the coding for this form seems complicated, you should know that this is typical of database programs when insertions, updates, and deletions are made to a dataset and to the related database tables. Remember too that this is a simple application with limited data validation and no exception handling. So a production program is likely to be far more complicated. To get a better feel for this type of programming, you can do the exercise that starts on the next page.

The Visual Basic code for the Vendor Maintenance program   **Page 3**

```
Private Sub btnDelete_Click(ByVal sender As System.Object, _
        ByVal e As System.EventArgs) Handles btnDelete.Click
    Dim iResult As DialogResult _
        = MessageBox.Show("Delete " & cboVendors.Text & "?", _
          "Confirm Delete", MessageBoxButtons.YesNo, _
          MessageBoxIcon.Question)
    If iResult = DialogResult.Yes Then
        VendorsBindingManager.RemoveAt(VendorsBindingManager.Position)
        Me.SetMaintenanceButtons(True)
        btnUpdateDB.Enabled = Ds_AP1.HasChanges
        cboVendors.Focus()
    End If
End Sub

Private Sub btnUpdateDB_Click(ByVal sender As System.Object, _
        ByVal e As System.EventArgs) Handles btnUpdateDB.Click
    SqlDA_Vendors.Update(Ds_AP1.Vendors)
    Ds_AP1.Vendors.Clear()
    SqlDA_Vendors.Fill(Ds_AP1)
    cboVendors.SelectedIndex = 0
    cboVendors.Focus()
End Sub

Private Sub btnExit_Click(ByVal sender As System.Object, _
    ByVal e As System.EventArgs) Handles btnExit.Click
    If Ds_AP1.HasChanges Then
        Dim iResult As DialogResult _
            = MessageBox.Show("You have made changes that have not " _
            & "been saved to the database. " & ControlChars.CrLf _
            & "If you continue, these changes will be lost." _
            & ControlChars.CrLf & "Continue?", "Confirm Exit", _
              MessageBoxButtons.YesNo, MessageBoxIcon.Question)
        If iResult = DialogResult.Yes Then
            Me.Close()
        End If
    Else
        Me.Close()
    End If
End Sub

End Class
```

Figure 18-10   The code for the Vendor Maintenance form (part 3 of 3)

Exercise 18-2   Create the Vendor Maintenance form

This exercise guides you through the process of creating the Vendor Maintenance form of figure 18-6. That will give you practice using the BindingManagerBase to add, update, and delete rows in a data table.

Start the project and create the ADO.NET objects

1. Start a new project named VendorMaintenance in the C:\VB.NET\Chapter 18 folder.

2. Use the wizard to create two data adapters with the Select statements shown in figure 18-9 that use the AccountsPayable connection. Generate Insert, Update, and Delete statements for the Vendors table, but omit these statements for the States table. Name the data adapters as in this figure. When you complete the configuration, notice that a single connection object is used by both of the data adapters.

3. Generate a dataset that includes the tables defined by both data adapters. Name this dataset ds_AP, and be sure to add an instance of this dataset to the designer.

Design the Vendor Maintenance form and bind its controls

4. Use figure 18-7 as a guide to add the text boxes and combo boxes to the Vendor Maintenance form. Then, name and bind these controls as indicated in figure 18-9 and set the MaxLength properties of the text boxes as shown.

5. Add all the button controls to the form, set the Text property of these controls so they appear as shown in figure 18-7, and name the controls appropriately.

6. Set the properties of the form so it appears as shown in figure 18-7. Also set the AcceptButton property to the Update button and the CancelButton property to the Cancel button.

Code the Vendor Maintenance form

7. Switch to the Code Editor window and declare a module-level variable named VendorsBindingManager that will hold an instance of the BindingManagerBase class.

8. Start a procedure for the Load event of the form, and add code to load the Vendors and States tables. Then, code a statement to create the binding manager base object for the Vendors table.

9. Code a procedure for the SelectedIndexChanged event of the Vendors combo box that sets the position of the binding manager base to the selected vendor.

10. Run the application. The first vendor in the Vendors table should be displayed. Drop down the States combo box to see that it lists all the state names. Then, drop down the Vendors combo box list to see that it contains the names of all the Vendors. Select a name to display a different vendor. If this doesn't work, close the form, correct the problem, and run the application again. When you're done, close the form and return to the Code Editor.

11. Enter the remaining code for this form as shown in figure 18-10 and run the application again.

12. Select a vendor from the combo box list and click on the Delete button. When the confirmation message is displayed, click on the No button so the row isn't deleted.

13. Change the data in one of the bound controls. The Update and Cancel buttons should now be enabled, but the Add and Delete buttons should be disabled. Click on the Cancel button to see that the field returns to its original value, the Update and Cancel buttons are disabled again, and the Add and Delete buttons are enabled again.

14. Change the data in a control and click on the Update button to update the dataset. The Update Database button should become available. Click on this button to update the database. Then, select the vendor you just changed from the Vendors combo box to verify that the update was successful.

15. Click on the Add button to display a new blank row. Enter the data for a new vendor and then click on the Update button to save the row to the dataset. The Update Database button should become available. Click on the Delete button to delete the vendor you just added, and click on the Yes button when the confirmation message is displayed. The Update Database button should be disabled once again because the dataset has been returned to its original state.

16. Add another new vendor, but this time update the database. Then, select the vendor you just added, delete it, and update the database.

17. Continue experimenting until you're sure this form works the way it should. Then, close the form and the solution.

How to use a parameterized query to retrieve data

The database applications you've seen so far have retrieved all of the rows from the Vendors table when they start. That works because the Vendors table contains a manageable number of rows. But what if you need to work with a table that contains hundreds or even thousands of rows? In that case, you need to restrict the number of rows that are retrieved at any one time. In addition to making your program more efficient, this helps reduce concurrency errors. That's because the less data you retrieve, the less likely it is that another user will retrieve and change the same data.

To reduce the number of rows a program retrieves, you can use a variety of techniques. One technique is to filter the rows based on one or more columns in the table. To filter a table of customers, for example, you could let the user enter a last name and state. Then, the program could retrieve and display all the customers that meet those criteria, and the user could select from those customers. Another technique is to retrieve a single row based on a unique value entered by the user, like a vendor number or customer number.

To implement either of these techniques, you use a *parameterized query*. With this type of query, you retrieve just the rows you want each time the query is executed. You'll learn more about parameterized queries and how they work in the topics that follow.

A Vendor Maintenance form that uses a parameterized query

Figure 18-11 presents the design of a Vendor Maintenance form that uses a parameterized query. The main difference between this form and the form presented earlier in this chapter is that this form doesn't retrieve all the vendor rows when it starts. Because of that, the user can't select a vendor from a combo box to display the data for that vendor. Instead, the user must enter a Vendor ID and then click on the Get Vendor button to retrieve an existing vendor row. Or, the user can click on the Add button to add a new row. In that case, though, the user does *not* enter a Vendor ID. That's because it's an identity field, so its value is generated by the database when the record is added.

Like the Vendor Maintenance form presented earlier, this form also provides Update, Delete, and Cancel buttons that the user can use to work with the rows in the Vendors table. Notice, however, that this form doesn't include an Update Database button. Instead, each time the user clicks on the Update button to add or modify a row or on the Delete button to delete a row, both the dataset and database are updated. That makes sense because this program is designed to work with only one row at a time. In addition, because the program updates the database immediately, the most current information will always be available to other users.

The Vendor Maintenance form that uses a parameterized query

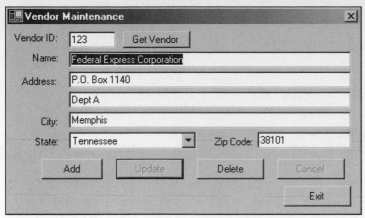

Description

- This Vendor Maintenance form is designed so it retrieves only one vendor record at a time. That's more efficient for working with tables that contain a large number of records. That also makes sense if concurrency is an issue because the program only holds one record at a time and the data it retrieves is always current.

- To retrieve a vendor, the user enters a Vendor ID and clicks on the Get Vendor button. Then, if a row is found with that Vendor ID, the row is retrieved and its data is displayed on the form.

- After a row is retrieved, the user can modify it by entering the changes in the text boxes and then clicking on the Update button that becomes available. This saves the changes to the dataset and updates the row in the database.

- The user can also delete an existing row by clicking on the Delete button. Then, the row is deleted from the dataset and the database.

- To add a new row, the user can click on the Add button and then enter the data for the new vendor. To save the data to the dataset and add the new row to the database, the user can click on the Update button.

Figure 18-11   A Vendor Maintenance form that uses a parameterized query

How to create a parameterized query

A *parameterized query* is a query that contains one or more *parameters*. Usually, the parameters are coded in the Where clause of a Select statement as shown at the top of figure 18-12. Here, the parameter will be used to retrieve the row for a vendor with a specific Vendor ID. This is the parameterized query that's used by the Vendor Maintenance program you saw in the last figure. Before this query is executed, of course, you need to set the value of this parameter to the Vendor ID of the vendor you want to retrieve.

If a Select statement will be processed by the SQL Server data provider, you used *named parameters*, whose names must begin with an at sign (@). The named parameter shown in the query in this figure, for example, is @VendorID. Notice that the name given to this parameter is the same as the name of the column it's associated with. Although that's not required, it makes it easy for you to remember the name when you set its value.

To set the value of a parameter, you use the Parameters collection of the command object that contains the Select statement. To access that object through the data adapter that defines it, you use the SelectCommand property. This is illustrated by the first assignment statement in this figure. Notice here that the parameter is referred to by name. Then, an appropriate value is assigned to the parameter's Value property.

In this example, the value that's assigned to the parameter is the value in the Text property of a VendorID text box. Then, this value is substituted for the parameter in the Select statement. For example, if the Text property contains a value of 94, the Select statement that's issued will look like this:

```
Select VendorID, VendorName, VendorAddress1, VendorAddress2,
    VendorCity, VendorState, VendorZipCode
From Vendors
Where VendorID = 94
```

That way, only the vendor with a VendorID of 94 will be retrieved.

You can also refer to a parameter in the Parameters collection by its index value. This is illustrated by the second assignment statement in this figure, which refers to the parameter with an index value of zero. If the Select statement contains two or more parameters, however, you should use names instead of index values so you can be sure you're referring to the appropriate parameter.

If you use the OLE DB data provider, you can't use named parameters. Instead, you indicate the location of a parameter by coding a question mark as shown in the query in this figure. When you set the parameter value, though, you can still refer to it by name. The name you use is the name of the column it's associated with, as illustrated by the assignment statement in this figure.

To make it easy to create a parameterized query, you can use the Query Builder that you learned about in chapter 17. To do that, you simply enter a named parameter or a question mark in the criteria for the appropriate column. Then, the parameter is generated for you.

How to use a parameterized query with a SQL Server data adapter

A parameterized query for a SQL Server data adapter

```
Select VendorID, VendorName, VendorAddress1, VendorAddress2,
    VendorCity, VendorState, VendorZipCode
From Vendors
Where VendorID = @VendorID
```

A statement that assigns a value to the SQL Server parameter by name

```
SqlDA_Vendors.SelectCommand.Parameters("@VendorID").Value _
    = txtVendorID.Text
```

A statement that assigns a value to the SQL Server parameter by index

```
SqlDA_Vendors.SelectCommand.Parameters(0).Value _
    = txtVendorID.Text
```

How to use a parameterized query with an OLE DB data adapter

A parameterized query for an OLE DB data adapter

```
Select VendorID, VendorName, VendorAddress1, VendorAddress2,
    VendorCity, VendorState, VendorZipCode
From Vendors
Where VendorID = ?
```

A statement that assigns a value to the OLE DB parameter

```
OleDA_Vendors.SelectCommand.Parameters("VendorID").Value _
    = txtVendorID.Text
```

Description

- A *parameterized query* is a query that contains one or more *parameters*. In most cases, you'll use parameters in the Where clause of a Select statement.

- To create a parameterized query for a SQL Server data adapter, you use *named parameters*. The name of a named parameter must begin with an at sign (@).

- To create a parameterized query for an OLE DB data adapter, you code a question mark for each parameter. Then, the parameter is given the name of the column it's associated with.

- Before you can execute a parameterized query, you must set the values of the parameters. To do that, you can work with the Parameters collection of the SelectCommand property of the data adapter, or you can work with the Parameters collection of the command object that contains the Select statement.

- You can identify the parameter you want to work with by its name or by its index value. Like most collections, the Parameters collection is zero-based.

- To create a parameter using the Query Builder, just type the name of the parameter or a question mark into the Criteria column.

- By default, a parameter is defined so it's appropriate for use with the column it's associated with. To view or change the definition of a parameter, expand the SelectCommand property of the data adapter, click on the Parameters property, then click on the ellipsis that's displayed to display the Collection Editor dialog box.

Figure 18-12   How to create a parameterized query

The code for the Vendor Maintenance form

Figure 18-13 presents the code for the Vendor Maintenance form. Before I describe this code, you should know that except for the Select statement for the Vendors data adapter that you saw in the last figure, the properties for this form are the same as for the maintenance form you saw earlier in this chapter. So I won't present them again here. You can refer back to figure 18-9 to review those properties if you need to.

The Load procedure for the form starts by filling the States table. Then, it sets the SelectedIndex property of the States combo box to –1 so no state is selected when the form is first displayed. Next, the Load procedure calls a procedure named SetEntryControls. This procedure enables or disables the five text boxes and the combo box that are used to enter vendor data along with the Delete button depending on the Boolean value that's passed to it. In this case, a value of False is passed to the procedure so the controls are disabled. That way, the user won't be able to enter any data without first retrieving a vendor or clicking on the Add button to add a new vendor. Notice that the Enabled property of the Delete button is set only if a new row isn't being added. That way, this button will be disabled while a new record is being added.

The next statement in the Load procedure calls the SetMaintenanceButtons procedure. Because a value of True is passed to this procedure, it enables the Add and Delete buttons and disables the Update and Cancel buttons just as it did in the previous maintenance program. In addition, it enables the VendorID text box and the GetVendor button so the user can retrieve a vendor.

Finally, the Load procedure creates the binding manager base used by the form. Notice that this procedure doesn't load the Vendors table. Instead, a record is loaded into this table only after the user enters a valid Vendor ID and clicks on the Get Vendor button.

To restrict the characters that the user can enter into the Vendor ID text box, this program includes a procedure for the KeyPress event of that control. This procedure lets the user use only the backspace key and the numbers 0 through 9 in this text box. All other keys are ignored. That way, the Vendor ID will always be an integer.

The Visual Basic code for the Vendor Maintenance form   **Page 1**

```
Public Class Form1
    Inherits System.Windows.Forms.Form

    Dim bLoading As Boolean
    Dim bNewRow As Boolean
    Dim VendorsBindingManager As BindingManagerBase

    Private Sub Form1_Load(ByVal sender As System.Object, _
            ByVal e As System.EventArgs) Handles MyBase.Load
        SqlDA_States.Fill(Ds_AP1)
        cboStates.SelectedIndex = -1
        Me.SetEntryControls(False)
        Me.SetMaintenanceButtons(True)
        VendorsBindingManager = Me.BindingContext(Ds_AP1, "Vendors")
    End Sub

    Private Sub SetEntryControls(ByVal bEditMode As Boolean)
        txtName.Enabled = bEditMode
        txtAddressLine1.Enabled = bEditMode
        txtAddressLine2.Enabled = bEditMode
        txtCity.Enabled = bEditMode
        cboStates.Enabled = bEditMode
        txtZipCode.Enabled = bEditMode
        If Not bNewRow Then
            btnDelete.Enabled = bEditMode
        End If
    End Sub

    Private Sub SetMaintenanceButtons(ByVal bAddDeleteMode As Boolean)
        btnAdd.Enabled = bAddDeleteMode
        btnUpdate.Enabled = Not bAddDeleteMode
        btnDelete.Enabled = bAddDeleteMode
        btnCancel.Enabled = Not bAddDeleteMode
        txtVendorID.Enabled = bAddDeleteMode
        btnGetVendor.Enabled = bAddDeleteMode

    End Sub

    Private Sub txtVendorID_KeyPress(ByVal sender As Object, _
            ByVal e As System.Windows.Forms.KeyPressEventArgs) _
            Handles txtVendorID.KeyPress
        Select Case Asc(e.KeyChar)
            Case 8, 48 To 57
                e.Handled = False
            Case Else
                e.Handled = True
        End Select
    End Sub
```

Figure 18-13   The code for the Vendor Maintenance form (part 1 of 4)

When the user clicks on the Get Vendor button to retrieve a vendor, the Click event procedure for this button is executed. It starts by declaring an integer variable that will be used to hold the number of records that are retrieved. You'll see why that's necessary in a moment. Next, this procedure checks that the user entered a Vendor ID. If not, an error message is displayed and the focus is moved back to the Vendor ID text box. If so, the bLoading variable is set to True so the code in the Control_DataChanged procedure won't be executed when the controls are loaded with the vendor data. Then, the parameter in the Select statement for the Vendors data adapter is set to the value of the Vendor ID text box. Before this statement is executed, though, the Vendors data table is cleared so it no longer contains any record that was retrieved previously.

After the Vendors table is cleared, the Fill method is used to retrieve the row for the selected vendor and load it into this table. Notice that the return value of this method, which contains the number of records that were retrieved, is stored in the iRecords variable. Then, the procedure checks this variable to determine if a record with the specified Vendor ID was found. If the value of this variable is zero, which means that the Vendor ID wasn't found, the SetEntryControls procedure is called to disable the entry controls, an error message is displayed, and the focus is moved back to the Vendor ID text box. Otherwise, the entry controls are enabled and the focus is moved to the Name text box. In either case, the bLoading variable is set to False to indicate that the load operation has completed.

When the user clicks on the Add button, the Click event procedure of this button starts by blanking out the Vendor ID text box and clearing the Vendors table to remove the current row. Then, it adds a new row to the Vendors table, and it sets the bNewRow variable to True to indicate that a row is being added. Finally, it sets the entry controls and maintenance buttons appropriately, it sets the SelectedIndex property of the States combo box to −1, and it moves the focus to the Name text box so the user can begin entering the data for the new vendor.

The procedure that's executed when the user changes the value in any of the data entry controls, Control_DataChanged, is the same as the one in the Vendor Maintenance program you saw earlier in this chapter. It sets the maintenance buttons so the user can update or cancel the changes to the current row.

The Visual Basic code for the Vendor Maintenance form   Page 2

```
Private Sub btnGetVendor_Click(ByVal sender As System.Object, _
        ByVal e As System.EventArgs) Handles btnGetVendor.Click
    Dim iRecords As Integer
    If txtVendorID.Text <> "" Then          IF NOT EMPTY,
        bLoading = True
        SqlDA_Vendors.SelectCommand.Parameters("@VendorID").Value _    ASS. VAR. TO PARA
            = txtVendorID.Text
        Ds_AP1.Vendors.Clear()
        iRecords = SqlDA_Vendors.Fill(Ds_AP1)      FILL DATASET
        If iRecords = 0 Then
            Me.SetEntryControls(False)
            MessageBox.Show("Vendor record not found.", "Entry error")
            txtVendorID.Focus()
        Else
            Me.SetEntryControls(True)
            txtName.Focus()
        End If
        bLoading = False
    Else
        MessageBox.Show("You must enter a Vendor ID.", "Entry error")
        txtVendorID.Focus()
    End If
End Sub

Private Sub btnAdd_Click(ByVal sender As System.Object, _
        ByVal e As System.EventArgs) Handles btnAdd.Click
    txtVendorID.Text = ""
    Ds_AP1.Vendors.Clear()
    VendorsBindingManager.AddNew()
    bNewRow = True
    Me.SetEntryControls(True)
    Me.SetMaintenanceButtons(False)
    cboStates.SelectedIndex = -1
    txtName.Focus()
End Sub

Private Sub Control_DataChanged(ByVal sender As System.Object, _
        ByVal e As System.EventArgs) Handles txtName.TextChanged, _
        txtAddressLine1.TextChanged, txtAddressLine2.TextChanged, _
        txtCity.TextChanged, txtZipCode.TextChanged, _
        cboStates.SelectedIndexChanged
    If Not bLoading Then
        Me.SetMaintenanceButtons(False)
    End If
End Sub
```

IN REFRESH BUTTON:

SQLDATAADAPTOR1 . SELECTCOMMAND. PARAMETERS("@CUSTID").
VALUE = TXTBOX4. TEXT

Figure 18-13   The code for the Vendor Maintenance form (part 2 of 4)

SQLDATAADAPTOR1 . FILL(DATASET1)

The procedure for the Click event of the Update button is similar to the event procedure in the previous maintenance program. The biggest difference is that in addition to updating the dataset, this procedure updates the database. To do that, it calls a procedure named UpdateDatabase that contains the Update statement.

If the update is for a new record, the Update procedure continues by setting the Vendor ID text box to the Vendor ID that was generated by the database. As you may recall from the last chapter, that's possible because an Insert statement that's generated by the Configuration Wizard is followed by a Select statement that refreshes the row in the dataset. That way, any data that's generated by the database is available to the program.

Notice that this procedure doesn't set the position of the binding manager base when a new row is added like the previous maintenance program did. That's because the Vendors table in this program never contains more than one row at a time. Because of that, the binding manager base is always positioned at the first row.

The Visual Basic code for the Vendor Maintenance form   **Page 3**

```vb
Private Sub btnUpdate_Click(ByVal sender As System.Object, _
        ByVal e As System.EventArgs) Handles btnUpdate.Click
    If ValidData() Then
        VendorsBindingManager.EndCurrentEdit()
        Me.UpdateDatabase()
        If bNewRow Then
            txtVendorID.Text = Ds_AP1.Vendors.Rows(0).Item("VendorID")
            bNewRow = False
        End If
        Me.SetMaintenanceButtons(True)
        txtVendorID.Focus()
    End If
End Sub

Private Function ValidData() As Boolean
    Dim sErrorMessage As String
    If txtName.Text = "" Then
        sErrorMessage = "Name required."
        txtName.Focus()
    ElseIf txtCity.Text = "" Then
        sErrorMessage = "City required."
        txtCity.Focus()
    ElseIf cboStates.SelectedIndex = -1 Then
        sErrorMessage = "State required."
        cboStates.Focus()
    ElseIf txtZipCode.Text = "" Then
        sErrorMessage = "Zip code required."
        txtZipCode.Focus()
    ElseIf txtZipCode.Text < Ds_AP1.States.Rows _
            (cboStates.SelectedIndex).Item("FirstZipCode") _
        Or txtZipCode.Text > Ds_AP1.States.Rows _
            (cboStates.SelectedIndex).Item("LastZipCode") Then
        sErrorMessage = "The zip code is invalid."
        txtZipCode.Focus()
    End If
    If sErrorMessage = "" Then
        ValidData = True
    Else
        ValidData = False
        MessageBox.Show(sErrorMessage, "Data entry error", _
            MessageBoxButtons.OK, MessageBoxIcon.Error)
    End If
End Function

Private Sub UpdateDatabase()
    SqlDA_Vendors.Update(Ds_AP1.Vendors)
End Sub
```

Figure 18-13   The code for the Vendor Maintenance form (part 3 of 4)

The procedures for the Click events of the Cancel, Delete, and Exit buttons are also similar to the ones in the previous maintenance program, so you shouldn't have any trouble figuring out how they work. Notice, however, that like the Update procedure, the Delete procedure updates the database as well as the dataset. That way, other users who may be accessing this table won't be able to retrieve the deleted row.

* * *

Here again, this coding is typical of database programs when insertions, updates, and deletions are made to a dataset and to the related database tables. Because of the inherent complexity in this type of program, the coding isn't easy to read, write, test, or debug. And this is a simple application with limited data validation and no exception handling.

The Visual Basic code for the Vendor Maintenance form   **Page 4**

```
    Private Sub btnCancel_Click(ByVal sender As System.Object, _
            ByVal e As System.EventArgs) Handles btnCancel.Click
        VendorsBindingManager.CancelCurrentEdit()
        Me.SetMaintenanceButtons(True)
        If bNewRow Then
            bNewRow = False
            Me.SetEntryControls(False)
        End If
        txtVendorID.Focus()
    End Sub

    Private Sub btnDelete_Click(ByVal sender As System.Object, _
            ByVal e As System.EventArgs) Handles btnDelete.Click
        Dim iResult As DialogResult _
            = MessageBox.Show("Delete " & txtName.Text & "?", _
              "Confirm Delete", MessageBoxButtons.YesNo, _
              MessageBoxIcon.Question)
        If iResult = DialogResult.Yes Then
            VendorsBindingManager.RemoveAt(VendorsBindingManager.Position)
            Me.UpdateDatabase()
            txtVendorID.Text = ""
            cboStates.SelectedIndex = -1
            Me.SetMaintenanceButtons(True)
            Me.SetEntryControls(False)
            txtVendorID.Focus()
        End If
    End Sub

    Private Sub btnExit_Click(ByVal sender As System.Object, _
            ByVal e As System.EventArgs) Handles btnExit.Click
        If btnUpdate.Enabled Then
            Dim iResult As DialogResult _
                = MessageBox.Show("You have made changes that have not " _
                & "been saved to the database. " & ControlChars.CrLf _
                & "If you continue, these changes will be lost." _
                & ControlChars.CrLf & "Continue?", "Confirm Exit", _
                  MessageBoxButtons.YesNo, MessageBoxIcon.Question)
            If iResult = DialogResult.Yes Then
                Me.Close()
            End If
        Else
            Me.Close()
        End If
    End Sub

End Class
```

Figure 18-13   The code for the Vendor Maintenance form (part 4 of 4)

Exercise 18-3   Create and use a parameterized query

To give you practice using a parameterized query, this exercise has you add a parameterized query to the Vendor Maintenance form. To make that easier to do, you'll start from a Vendor Maintenance form that already has the appropriate controls and most of the code that makes it work.

Open the project and create the parameterized query

1. Open the project named VendorMaintenance in the C:\VB.NET\Chapter 18\VendorMaintenanceWithParameter folder. Then, display the form design to see that it includes a text box for entering a Vendor ID and a button for retrieving a vendor.

2. Click on the Vendors data adapter, and then click on the Configure Data Adapter link at the bottom of the Properties window to start the Configuration Wizard. Step through the dialog boxes until the one that shows the Select statement is displayed, and then click on the Query Builder button to display the Query Builder window.

3. Create a parameter named @VendorID for the VendorID column. To do that, type the name of the parameter into the Criteria column. Then, remove the sort specification from the VendorName column. When you're done, click on the OK button and finish the configuration.

Complete the code for the program

4. Double-click on the GetVendor button to start a procedure for its Click event, and add a statement to this procedure that sets the value of the @VendorID parameter in the Select statement to the value in the Vendor ID text box. Next, add code to clear the Vendors table and then fill it with the selected vendor. Also add a statement that calls the SetEntryControls procedure to enable the controls for editing. Then, set the bLoading variable to True at the beginning of this procedure so the code in the Control_DataChanged procedure isn't executed when the vendor row is loaded, and change this variable back to False at the end of the procedure. Finally, move the focus to the Name text box.

5. Run the program. When the form is displayed, enter the value 94 in the Vendor ID text box and then click on the Get Vendor button. Is the vendor row displayed? If not, make the necessary changes to get this to work properly. Then, enter 200 for the Vendor ID to see what happens if the vendor isn't found. Notice that the data entry controls and the Delete button are enabled, which isn't what you want. Finally, delete the Vendor ID and then click on the Get Vendor button to see what happens. If an unhandled exception occurs, click on the Continue button in the dialog box that's displayed to end the program.

6. Add code to the GetVendor procedure that checks if the Vendor ID text box is empty. If it is, the program should display an appropriate error message and move the focus back to the Vendor ID text box.

7. Add code that checks if the requested vendor is found. To do that, you'll need to get the return value of the Fill method. If the vendor isn't found, the program should disable the entry controls, display an appropriate error message, and move the focus back to the Vendor ID text box.

8. Run the program again and retrieve vendor number 94. Then, try to retrieve vendor number 200 again to see what happens. This time, an error message should be displayed and the data entry controls and the Delete button should be disabled. Delete the Vendor ID and then click on the Get Vendor button. If you coded this procedure correctly, an error message should be displayed. If so, click the OK button in the message box and then end the program.

9. Add a statement to the Update procedure that will update the database with a new or modified row after that row is saved to the dataset. Then, add a statement that will display the Vendor ID for a new row in the Vendor ID text box. Finally, add a statement to the Delete procedure that will delete a row from the database after it's deleted from the dataset.

10. Run the program and try adding, modifying, and deleting records. Watch how the controls are enabled and disabled as the program executes. If anything doesn't work correctly, fix the program and then test it again. Otherwise, close the program and close the solution.

How to handle data exceptions

Both ADO.NET and the .NET data providers provide specific classes you can use to catch the data exceptions that may occur as your database applications are running. You'll learn how to work with these classes in the topics that follow. In addition, you'll learn some specific procedures for handling update errors.

How to handle ADO.NET errors

Even if you check bound controls for valid data, ADO.NET errors can occur when you operate on ADO.NET components. Figure 18-14 presents some of the most common of those errors. As you can see, you can catch any ADO.NET error using the DataException class. In addition, you can catch specific errors using the other classes shown here. All of these classes are members of the System.Data namespace.

Like the exception classes you learned about earlier in this book, each ADO.NET exception class has a Message and Source property that you can use to display information about the error. The error-handling code shown in this figure, for example, catches errors caused by the EndCurrentEdit method and then uses a message box to display the Message property of the exception object. Notice that the first Catch clause catches constraint exceptions, the second Catch clause catches null exceptions, and the third Catch clause catches any other data exceptions. As in the other error-handling routines you've seen in this book, the last Catch clause is included to catch any other exceptions that might occur.

One of the data exception classes that isn't illustrated by this example is the DbConcurrencyException class. This is the exception you use to catch concurrency exceptions, which you learned about in chapter 16. This exception can occur when you execute the Update method of a data adapter. Although you might think that this error would be generated by the database rather than ADO.NET, it's not. To understand why, you need to remember that the SQL statements that are executed for an update operation contain code that checks that a row hasn't changed since it was retrieved. But if the row has changed, the row with the specified criteria won't be found and the SQL statement won't be executed. When the data adapter discovers that the row wasn't updated, however, it realizes there was a concurrency error and throws an exception. You'll learn more about how and when to handle this exception later in this chapter.

Common ADO.NET exception classes

Name	Description
DataException	The general exception that's thrown when an ADO.NET error occurs. — *WON'T GET IF BUILT W/WIZARD*
DbConcurrencyException	The exception that's thrown if the number of rows affected by an Insert, Update, or Delete operation is zero. This exception is typically caused by a concurrency violation. *← NOTHING TO WORK ON*
ConstraintException	The exception that's thrown if an operation violates a constraint. *→ TRYING TO VIOLATE INTEG*
NoNullAllowedException	The exception that's thrown when an add or update operation attempts to save a null value in a column that doesn't allow nulls. *LIKE P.K. OR DIVISION OR PROD. DESCRIP, ETC. THAT ARE ABS. VITAL*

 MOST → MP.

Common properties of the ADO.NET exception classes

Property	Description
Message	A message that describes the exception.
Source	The name of the object that caused the exception.

Error-handling code for the EndCurrentEdit method

```
Try
    VendorsBindingManager.EndCurrentEdit()
Catch eConstraint As ConstraintException
    MessageBox.Show(eConstraint.Message, "Constraint error")
Catch eNull As NoNullAllowedException
    MessageBox.Show(eNull.Message, "Null error")
Catch eData As DataException
    MessageBox.Show(eData.Message, "ADO.NET error")
Catch eSystem As Exception
    MessageBox.Show(eSystem.Message, "System error")
End Try
```

Description

- An ADO.NET exception is an exception that occurs on any ADO.NET component. All of these exceptions are members of the System.Data namespace.

- In most cases, you'll include validation code in your programs to make sure that exceptions like ConstraintException and NoNullAllowedException don't occur. Then, you can just use the DataException class to catch any unexpected ADO.NET exception.

- A DbConcurrencyException occurs if the return value of an Insert, Update, or Delete statement that's issued by the Update method of a data adapter indicates that the row wasn't processed. That's typically the result of an operation that tries to modify or delete a row that has been changed by another user. It can also be the result of an operation that tries to add a row with a unique constraint that already exists in the table.

★ EXCEPT FOR BAD DATA OVER NETWORK

Figure 18-14   How to handle ADO.NET errors

EXCEPTION STRUCTURE ALWAYS SAME

How to handle data provider errors

Figure 18-15 describes the two exception classes you can use to catch errors encountered by a data provider. As you can see, there's one class for each of the two data providers supported by the .NET Framework. You use the SqlException class to catch errors encountered by the SQL Server data provider, and you use the OleDbException class to catch errors encountered by the OLE DB data provider.

Unlike the other types of exceptions, the SQL and OLE DB exceptions include a collection of one or more error objects. You can refer to this collection through the Errors property of the exception object. Then, you can loop through this collection to display information about each of the errors.

The code in this figure shows how this works. Here, a Fill method that retrieves data from the Vendors table of a SQL Server database is executed within the Try clause of a Try...Catch statement. The first Catch clause in this statement catches any ADO.NET error that occurs as described in the previous figure. Then, the second Catch clause catches any error that occurs on the SQL Server data provider and assigns the exception object to a variable named eSql.

The code within this Catch clause starts by declaring three variables. The first one is an integer variable named iError that will be used to loop through the errors in the error collection. The second variable, named SqlErrors, is declared as an SqlErrorCollection object. The value that's assigned to this variable is the Errors property of the SqlException object, which contains a reference to the error collection of that object. Finally, the third one is a string variable named sErrorSummary that will be used to format the errors for display.

Next, this code uses a For...Next loop to get information about each of the errors and format it in the error summary variable. Like other collections, the error collection is zero-based. So this loop starts with the error item that has an index value of zero. Then, it continues through the last item in the collection, whose index value is identified by the Count property of the collection minus one. When the loop ends, the error summary is displayed in a message box.

Notice in this code that two properties of each error object are included in the error message: Number and Message. A third property you might want to use is Source, which contains the name of the provider that generated the error. In addition to the properties of the individual error objects, the exception object itself has Number, Message, and Source properties that you can use to get information about the error. In fact, in many cases, these properties will provide all the information you need.

.NET data provider exception classes

Name	Description
SqlException	The exception that is thrown when a warning or error is returned by SQL Server. This class can be found in the System.Data.SqlClient namespace.
OleDbException	The exception that is thrown when a warning or error is returned by an OLE DB data source. This class can be found in the System.Data.OleDb namespace.

Error-handling code for the Fill method of a SQL Server data adapter

```
Try
    SqlDA_Vendors.Fill(Ds_AP1)
Catch eData As DataException
    MessageBox.Show(eData.Message, "ADO.NET error")
Catch eSql As SqlClient.SqlException
    Dim iError As Integer
    Dim SqlErrors As SqlClient.SqlErrorCollection = eSql.Errors
    Dim sErrorSummary As String
    For iError = 0 To SqlErrors.Count - 1
        sErrorSummary = sErrorSummary & SqlErrors(iError).Number & " - " _
                                      & SqlErrors(iError).Message _
                                      & ControlChars.CrLf
    Next iError
    MessageBox.Show(sErrorSummary, "SQL Server error")
Catch eSystem As Exception
    MessageBox.Show(eSystem.Message, "System error")
End Try
```

Common properties of data provider exception and error objects

Property	Description
Number	An error number that identifies the type of error.
Message	Text that describes the error.
Source	The name of the provider that generated the error.

Description

- Whenever the data provider (SQL Server or OLE DB) encounters a situation it can't handle, an Exception object (SqlException or OleDbException) is created.
- The Exception object contains a collection of error objects (SqlErrorCollection or OleDbErrorCollection) that contain information about the error. You can use the Errors property of the exception object to loop through the errors in this collection.
- You can also use the Number, Message, and Source properties of the exception object to determine the cause of an error. The Number and Source properties contain the same information as the first error object, and the Message property contains a concatenation of the messages in all the error objects.

Figure 18-15 How to handle data provider errors

How to handle update errors

The technique you use to handle the errors that can occur when a database is updated depend on whether you're updating multiple rows as in the first Vendor Maintenance program presented in this chapter or a single row as in the second maintenance program. When you update a single row, you can use a procedure like the first one in figure 18-16. Here, the Update statement is coded within a Try...Catch statement that includes three Catch clauses. The first one will catch a concurrency exception, the second one will catch a SQL Server exception, and the third one will catch any other exception. In each case, the program simply displays an error message to the user.

In a production program, you would want to include some additional processing for a concurrency error. For example, you might want to retrieve the updated row so the user can apply the changes again.

When you're updating multiple rows, you'll want to use a different technique. That's because by default, if an error occurs while one of the rows is being updated, the update operation ends and an exception is thrown. So any rows after the row that caused the error aren't processed.

To avoid this situation, you can set the ContinueUpdateOnError property of the data adapter to True. Then if an error occurs during the update, the data adapter doesn't throw an exception. Instead, it flags the row to indicate that it has an error, and it continues the update operation until all of the rows in the data table have been processed.

To flag an error, the data adapter sets the HasErrors property of the row to True, and it sets the RowError property of the row to a description of the error. It also sets the HasErrors property of the table and dataset to True. That way, you can use these properties to check for errors before checking each individual row.

The second example in this figure shows one way you can use this update technique. The first thing you should notice here is that the Update method isn't coded within a Try...Catch statement. That's because no exception will be thrown when an error occurs.

After the Update method is executed, this code checks the HasErrors property of the dataset to determine if any errors were encountered. If so, this code loops through the rows in the Vendors table to locate the ones with errors. To do that, it starts by declaring an object variable as a data row. Then, it uses that variable in a For Each...Next statement that checks the HasErrors property of each row in the table. If it finds an error, it formats a message string so it includes the name of the vendor. After it locates all of the rows in error, this code displays a message box that lists all the vendors that weren't updated. As in the single-row update example, this code could perform some additional processing for each error. Because that processing will vary from one shop to another, however, I haven't included it here.

Code that handles a single-row update

```
Try
    SqlDA_Vendors.Update(Ds_AP1.Vendors)
Catch eConcurrency As DBConcurrencyException
    MessageBox.Show("This row has been changed by another user." _
        & ControlChars.CrLf & "The update has not been processed.", _
        "Concurrency error")
Catch eSql As SqlClient.SqlException
    MessageBox.Show(eSql.Message, "SQL Server error")
Catch eSystem As Exception
    MessageBox.Show(eSystem.Message, "System error")
End Try
```

Code that handles a multi-row update

```
SqlDA_Vendors.Update(Ds_AP1.Vendors)
If Ds_AP1.HasErrors Then
    Dim VendorRow As DataRow
    Dim sMessage As String
    sMessage = "The following rows were not updated:" _
        & ControlChars.CrLf & ControlChars.CrLf
    For Each VendorRow In Ds_AP1.Vendors
        If VendorRow.HasErrors Then
            sMessage &= VendorRow("VendorName") & ControlChars.CrLf
        End If
    Next
    MessageBox.Show(sMessage, "Update errors")
End If
```

Description

- When you perform a single-row update, you can use the DbConcurrencyException class to catch a concurrency error. Then, you can process the error as appropriate.

- When you perform a multi-row update, an exception will be thrown and the update operation will end if a concurrency error (or any other error) occurs on a row. To avoid that, you can set the ContinueUpdateOnError property of the data adapter to True. Then, no exception is thrown and the update operation will process the remaining rows.

- If the ContinueUpdateOnError property is set to True and an error occurs on the update of a row, the HasErrors properties of the row, table, and dataset are set to True. In addition, the RowError property of the row is set to a description of the error. You can use these properties to identify the rows in error and process them appropriately.

Figure 18-16   How to handle update errors

Perspective

One goal of this chapter has been to teach you the skills you need for developing database programs in the real world when using bound controls. The other goal has been to introduce you to the complexity of this type of programming. Keep in mind, though, that the three database chapters in this book are just an introduction to database programming. Before you can master database programming, you need to learn many other skills.

Summary

- You can use *simple data binding* to bind a text box control to a column in a data table. Then, the value of the column in the current row is displayed in the control, and any changes to that value are saved to the data table.

- You can use a form's BindingManagerBase object to manage the bound controls on the form. This object lets you specify the current position within the rows of a data table and makes sure that all controls are synchronized.

- You can complex-bind a combo box or list box control to a column in a data table so all the values in that column are displayed in the control's list. You can also simple-bind a combo box or list box control to a data column so the value in the current row can be displayed and updated using the control.

- You can use the methods of a BindingManagerBase object to add a new row to a data table, delete an existing row from a data table, save changes to the current row in a data table, and cancel changes to the current row.

- You can use a *parameterized query* to modify a Select statement each time it's executed. A parameterized query contains one or more *parameters* whose values can vary from one execution to the next.

- A program can use a parameterized query to retrieve and work with a single row at a time. This can be more efficient than working with all the rows in a table at once, particularly if the table contains a large number of rows.

- You can use the ADO.NET exception classes to catch ADO.NET errors, and you can use the SqlException or OleDbException class to catch data provider errors.

- When you perform a multi-row update, you'll want the data adapter to process all the rows without throwing an error. Then, you can use the properties of the row, table, and dataset to handle any errors that occurred.

Term

simple data binding

parameterized query

parameter

named parameter

Objectives

- Given the specifications for an application that displays data from a data table in bound controls, design and code the application.

- Given the specifications for an application that provides for adding, modifying, and deleting rows in a data table using bound controls, design and code the application. The application may process one or more records at a time.

- Add exception-handling code that catches ADO.NET and data provider errors to any ADO.NET application.

- Describe the function and use of a BindingManagerBase object.

- Describe the differences between the way you might handle concurrency errors for a single-row update and a multi-row update.

Exercise 18-4   Add exception-handling code to the parameterized Vendor Maintenance form

In this exercise, you'll modify the parameterized Vendor Maintenance form you worked on in the last exercise so it handles data exceptions using the ADO.NET and .NET data provider exception classes.

1. Open the Vendor Maintenance application you created in exercise 18-3 that uses a parameterized query.

2. Open the Code Editor window and add a Try statement to the Load procedure that will catch any errors that occur when the States table is loaded. This statement should include Catch clauses that catch ADO.NET errors, data provider errors, and any other errors that might occur. Each Catch clause should display an error message that includes the Message property of the exception object.

3. Add a similar Try statement to the procedure that loads the Vendors table.

4. Add Try statements to the procedures that add a new row to the Vendors table, update a new or modified row in that table, cancel an add or update operation, and delete a row. These statements need to catch ADO.NET or system errors but not data provider errors.

5. Create a procedure named UpdateDatabase that contains a statement that updates the database with changes to the Vendors table. Then, replace the statements in the Update and Delete procedures that update the database with calls to the UpdateDatabase procedure.

6. Add a Try statement to the UpdateDatabase procedure. This statement should include four Catch clauses. The first one should catch a concurrency error, the second one should catch any other data error, the third one should catch any

data provider error, and the fourth one should catch any other error. For all but the data provider error, the program should display an error message that includes the Message property. For a data provider error, the program should display an error message that includes information about each error in the errors collection.

7. Code Throw statements as described in chapter 5 to test that all the Catch clauses work. When you're sure that they do, remove the Throw statements and then close and save the solution.

Exercise 18-5 Add code to the Vendor Maintenance form to handle concurrency errors

In this exercise, you'll add code to the Vendor Maintenance form that will handle any errors that occur during the update operation.

1. Open the Vendor Maintenance application you created in exercise 18-2.

2. Open the Form Designer window, select the Vendors data adapter, and set its ContinueUpdateOnError property to True.

3. Open the Code Editor window and locate the procedure for the Click event of the Update Database button. Add an If statement to this procedure after the statement that updates the database that checks for errors in the Vendors table. If the table has errors, this procedure should check each row for errors. For each row that has an error, the procedure should add the vendor name from that row to a string variable. When all the rows have been checked, the procedure should display a list of the vendors that weren't updated.

4. Build the project, but don't run it.

5. To test that your code works, use the Solution Explorer to locate the executable file for the project (it's in the Bin directory). Double-click on this file to run the project, then double-click on it again. You now have two instances of the form running.

6. Use one instance to modify two rows and then update the database. Switch to the other instance and make changes to the same two rows and at least one other row. Update the database to see what happens. If this works correctly, a message box should be displayed that indicates that the two rows that were already changed couldn't be updated. Any other rows you modified, though, should have been changed. To make sure they were, close the form and then run the project again and display these rows.

7. When you're sure this works correctly, close both forms and then switch to Visual Studio and close the solution.

Section 5

Web programming essentials

The first four sections of this book presented the programming essentials for developing Windows applications. Now, this section will present the essentials for developing web applications. In chapter 19, you'll learn the skills you need to develop web forms. And in chapter 20, you'll learn the skills you need to develop web services.

As will see, you use many of the same skills for developing web applications that you use for developing Windows applications. That's one of the many benefits that you get from using the .NET Framework. So if you understand the material presented so far, you'll soon be developing web applications.

19

How to develop a Web Forms application

Like a Windows Forms application, a Web Forms application consists of one or more forms along with the code used to implement those forms. Because web forms run in a web browser rather than on the Windows desktop, however, they must be processed differently from Windows forms. Once you understand these differences, you shouldn't have any trouble developing web applications.

An introduction to ASP.NET web applications

Before you learn the specific skills for developing web applications, you should have a basic understanding of how they work. In addition, you should know about some special system requirements for developing web applications.

How ASP.NET web applications work

Figure 19-1 illustrates how *ASP.NET* web applications work. As you can see, an *HTTP request* is sent from a browser running on a *client* to a *web server* running *IIS* (*Internet Information Services*). Among other things, an HTTP request includes the *URL* (*Universal Resource Locator*) for the web page to be displayed. Then, the server locates that web page and processes it to produce the *HTML* (*HyperText Markup Language*) that describes the page. Finally, the HTML is sent back to the client in the form of an *HTTP response*, and the page is displayed in the browser.

When a web page is displayed in the browser, the user can interact with it using the *ASP.NET Server controls* on the page. If the user clicks on a button control, for example, the page is *posted* back to the server. That simply means that another HTTP request is sent to the server and the page is processed again. This time, though, the HTTP request indicates that the user clicked on a button. Because of that, additional processing is performed based on the code in the Click event procedure for that button. Then, the HTML that describes the updated page is sent back to the client again to complete the *round trip*.

Keep in mind that each time an HTTP request is sent to the server, the code for the web page is restarted from the beginning. That's because the program ends as soon as the HTML for a page is generated. Otherwise, the program would be idle while it waited for the user to perform another action, which would be a waste of the server's resources. The drawback to this is that the values in the web page aren't maintained between executions. In other words, web applications are *stateless*. As you'll soon see, however, many of the controls that you use on web forms can retain their own data, called a *view state*. That's just one way that Visual Basic makes developing web applications quick and easy.

Although web applications are commonly run over the Internet, they can also be run from a local server. For instance, the applications in one department of a company can be run from a local server that serves a local area network. In this case, you still access the applications from a web browser, but they aren't transmitted over the Internet.

When you develop web applications, you can use a web server with IIS that's available on a local area network. Or, you can install IIS on your own PC. In that case, your PC runs both the web browser to access the applications and the server software that runs the applications.

The operation of an ASP.NET web application

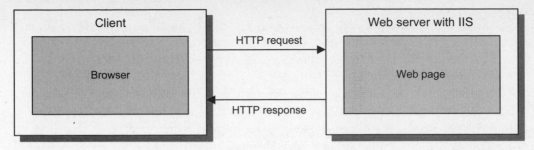

Description

- To start a web application, the user enters the web address, or *URL* (*Universal Resource Locater*), for the application's starting web page in a web browser. This information is sent to the *web server* as part of an *HTTP* (*HyperText Transfer Protocol*) *request*.

- When the server receives the HTTP request, it locates the code for the web page and executes it to create *HTML* (*HyperText Markup Language*). This HTML is then sent back to the *client* as part of an *HTTP response*, and the page is displayed in the browser.

- For this to work, the web server must be configured with *Internet Information Services* (*IIS*). One of the jobs of IIS is to pass requests for *ASP.NET web pages* on to *ASP.NET* for processing. *ASP.NET* is a server-side technology that lets you create web pages at run time.

- A user can interact with an ASP.NET web page by using *ASP.NET Server controls*. These controls are similar to Windows Forms controls, but some of them can be used to send the page back to the server in a process called *posting*. Then, the server processes the web page using application code and sends it back to the client. This entire process is referred to as a *round trip*.

- All web applications are said to be *stateless*. That means that the values that a web page contains are not retained on the server after they're sent back to the client. However, many of the controls you use on web forms can retain the data they contain, called a *view state*.

- The term *web server* can refer to both (1) the computer that stores the software and web pages that are needed for web applications and (2) the server software like IIS that manages HTTP requests and sends and receives web pages.

- Although web applications are commonly accessed over the Internet, they can also be accessed from a local server. For development, IIS can be installed on your own PC so it runs both the web browser and the web server.

Figure 19-1   How ASP.NET web applications work

System requirements for ASP.NET web applications

To develop ASP.NET web applications, you need a client and a server with the software shown in figure 19-2. On both the client and server machines, you need Windows 2000 or later. In addition, you need a browser on the client so you can test your applications.

On the server, you need the .NET Framework, which provides the classes used by ASP.NET along with the Common Language Runtime. You need Internet Information Services, which manages the web pages on the server. And you need a program to manage the files in your web applications.

One program for managing the files in your web applications is *Microsoft FrontPage Server Extensions* (*FPSE*). This program comes with IIS and is installed and configured along with IIS by default. It's typically used with web applications that are deployed to a web server on the Internet. Because FPSE uses reference pointers to access the server, you don't have to have special access privileges for creating files and directories.

However, if you're deploying an application to a local server or your own PC rather than to the Internet, you may want to use *file-share access* instead of FPSE. Unlike FPSE, file-share access lets you use standard Windows-based commands to create the files and directories you need. In this case, you need to have appropriate access privileges, but that usually isn't a problem. Because file-share access is the default when you create a web application in Visual Basic .NET, you need to change that default as described in this figure if you want to use FPSE.

If you want to install IIS on your own PC, you can do that from the Windows Control Panel as summarized in this figure (a complete procedure for installing IIS is presented in the appendix of this book). Note, however, that IIS should be installed before the .NET Framework or Visual Studio .NET. If it's not, you'll need to reinstall Visual Studio .NET after installing IIS, and you'll need to repair the .NET Framework as described in the appendix.

Software requirements for developing ASP.NET web applications

Client

- Windows 2000 or later
- A standard browser such as Internet Explorer or Netscape Navigator

Server

- Windows 2000 or later
- Microsoft .NET Framework
- Internet Information Services 5.0 or later
- Microsoft FrontPage Server Extensions (optional)

How to install IIS on your own PC

- IIS comes with Windows 2000 and later operating systems. IIS should be installed prior to installing the .NET Framework and Visual Studio .NET.

- To install IIS for Windows 2000 or later, display the Windows Control Panel, double-click on Add/Remove Programs, then click on Add/Remove Windows Components. Then, select Internet Information Services (IIS) from the list of components that are displayed, and complete the installation.

- If you install IIS after installing Visual Studio .NET, you will need to reinstall Visual Studio.

- If you install IIS after installing the .NET Framework, you will need to repair the Framework.

- A complete procedure for installing IIS is presented in the appendix of this book.

When to use Microsoft FrontPage Server Extensions

- You can use *Microsoft FrontPage Server Extensions* (*FPSE*) to manage the files in your ASP.NET web applications. By default, FPSE is installed and configured along with IIS.

- FPSE is used most often with web applications that are deployed to a remote server on the Internet. Because FPSE uses reference pointers to access the server, you don't have to worry about having the appropriate access privileges for creating files and directories.

- If you're deploying a web application to a local server, you typically use *file-share access* to manage the files in the application. This is the default for web applications developed in Visual Basic .NET.

- You can change the default file access method from the Web Settings category in the Projects folder of the Options dialog box. You can change the file access method for an existing project from the Web Settings category in the Common Properties folder of the Properties dialog box for the project.

Figure 19-2   Software requirements for ASP.NET web applications

How to design a form for a web application

In general, you use the same techniques to design a web form as you use to design a Windows form. The differences are in the controls that you use and the properties that are available for those controls and the forms that contain them.

The design of the Calculate Investment form

To illustrate how you design a web form, I'll use the Calculate Investment application shown in figure 19-3. You saw a Windows version of this application earlier in this book. It consists of a single form that calculates a future value or monthly investment based on the information supplied by the user.

Each *web form* you create defines a *web page* that can be displayed in a web browser. As you design a web form by adding controls and setting properties, Visual Basic generates the appropriate HTML for the form. This HTML, which includes references to the controls on the form, is stored in a file with the *aspx* extension. This extension tells IIS that the file should be processed by ASP.NET. The user can display the form defined by the aspx file by entering the location of that file in a browser. In this figure, for example, you can see the address of the Calculate Investment form.

You should also notice that this form uses many of the same types of controls that were used for the Windows version of this application. In a moment, though, you'll see that these are special controls that are used only for web applications. As you already know, some of these controls can maintain their own view state. In addition, some of them can cause the page to be posted back to the server. You'll learn more about that later in this chapter.

The Calculate Investment form displayed in a browser

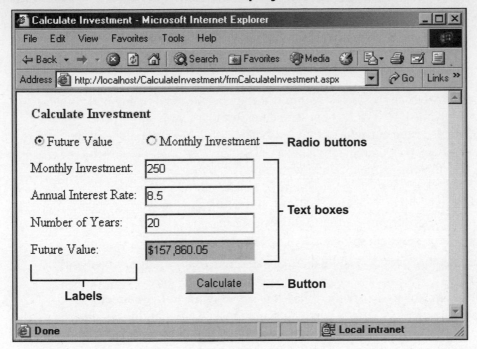

Description

- To design the user interface for a web application, you create *web forms* that define *web pages*. To do that, you use controls and techniques similar to those you use to create Windows forms.

- When you use the Visual Basic IDE to create a web page, the HTML code is generated for you. Because of that, you can create a web application without knowing HTML.

- You can use page and control events to control the processing that's performed for a web page. You can also use the properties of some controls to determine whether the view state of the control is maintained and whether a change to the control causes the page to be posted back to the server.

Figure 19-3   The design of the Calculate Investment form

How to create a web application

Figure 19-4 shows the New Project dialog box for creating a web application. It looks much the same as the dialog box for a Windows application, except that the project location must be on the IIS server. If you're developing a web application that will reside on your own computer, that location is http://localhost as shown in the figure. If the application will reside on another web server, you'll need to find out the address of that server.

To complete the entry for the server location, you enter the name of the directory where you want the project stored. In this example, the directory is named CalculateInvestment. Then, when you finish the application, all of the files for the project except the solution file will be stored in that directory under the appropriate directory for the web server. If, for example, you're running IIS on your own PC, the project files will be stored in

```
C:\Inetpub\wwwroot\CalculateInvestment
```

because Inetpub\wwwroot is the directory structure that's created when you install IIS.

What happens to the solution file? It is stored in the default directory for Visual Studio projects. That's why you should make sure that this default directory is set the way you want it before you create a new web application. Note that this directory isn't identified by the dialog box in this figure.

When you create a web application, a web form named WebForm1 is automatically added to it. Then, you can use the Visual Basic IDE to design the form, as you'll see in the next figure.

The New Project dialog box for a web application

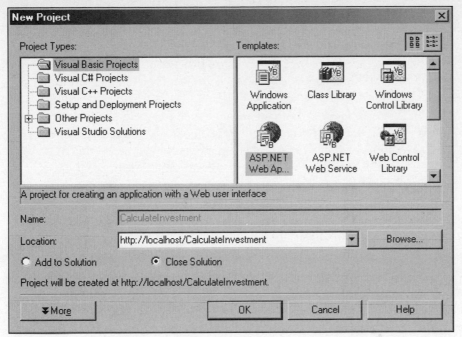

Description

- To create a web application, select the ASP.NET Web Application template from the New Project dialog box. Then, select the IIS server where the project will reside and enter the name of the directory where you want the project stored.

- Visual Basic creates a directory with the name you specify in the \Inetpub\wwwroot directory of the IIS server and stores all the project files in that directory.

- Visual Basic also creates a directory with the name you specify in the default directory for Visual Studio and stores the solution file there. If you want to store the solution in a different directory, change the default directory before you create the project or copy the solution to another directory after you create the project.

- By default, an ASP.NET web application consists of a single web form named WebForm1. This form appears in the Solution Explorer with the *aspx* extension. This extension indicates that the file should be processed by ASP.NET.

Figure 19-4   How to create a web application

How to use the Web Form Designer

Figure 19-5 shows the *Web Form Designer* that you use to design a web form. To add controls to a web form, you can use the Toolbox just as you do for a Windows form. To set the properties for the form or its controls, you use the Properties window. And to manage the files in the project, you use the Solution Explorer.

The ASP.NET Server controls you can use on a web form are available from the Web Forms and HTML tabs of the Toolbox. The controls you're most likely to use as you develop web applications are the *Web Server controls* in the Web Forms tab. These controls are new to .NET and provide functionality that wasn't available with traditional HTML elements. In addition, you can work with them using properties, methods, and events just like other .NET objects.

The controls in the HTML tab provide access to the traditional HTML elements. These controls, called *HTML Server controls*, can be processed on either the client or the server. In contrast, the Web Server controls can only be processed on the server, which means that the page must first be posted back to the server. Because of that, you may want to use the HTML Server controls whenever it's appropriate to perform client-side processing. Remember, though, that these controls don't provide the same functionality as the Web Server controls. In particular, they can't be used to save the view state of the control. Because of that, I'll focus on the Web Server controls in this chapter, since they're the ones you're most likely to use.

In addition to the Web Server controls and HTML Server controls, you can use the *validation controls* in the Web Forms tab of the Toolbox to validate the data on the form. You can use these controls to validate data in either Web Server or HTML Server controls. In this figure, you can see that the Calculate Investment form uses several validation controls. You'll learn more about how to use these controls later in this chapter.

The Calculate Investment form displayed in the Web Form Designer window

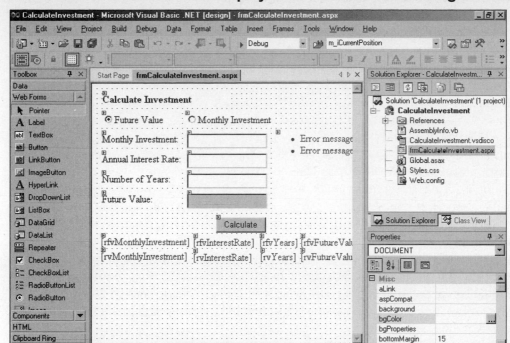

Description

- To design web forms, you use the *Web Form Designer*. This designer lets you add controls and components from the Toolbox. Then, you can set the properties for the page and controls in the Properties window.

- The *HTML Server controls* in the HTML tab of the Toolbox map directly to traditional HTML elements and can be processed on either the client or the server.

- The *Web Server controls* in the Web Forms tab of the Toolbox provide more built-in functionality than the HTML Server controls, but they can only be processed on the server. These controls have properties, methods, and events just like other .NET objects.

- The Web Forms tab of the Toolbox also includes *validation controls* that you can use to perform common validation checks on Web Server or HTML Server controls.

Figure 19-5   How to use the Web Form Designer

Common properties for web pages and controls

Figure 19-6 presents the properties for web pages and Web Server controls that you're most likely to use as you develop web forms. For a web page, for example, you can use the IsPostBack property to determine when a page is being loaded for the first time and when it's being posted back to the server. You can use this property to perform initialization code when the page is first loaded.

The PageLayout property of a web page determines how the form is displayed in the Web Form Designer window. By default, it's displayed in grid layout. This is the layout you saw in the previous figure, and it's the layout you'll typically use to design web forms. With this layout, you can position controls exactly where you want them on the form using *absolute positioning*.

The other layout option is flow layout. With this layout, controls are positioned relative to one another. Because of that, the position of the controls can change when the page is displayed depending on the size of the browser window and the resolution of the display. In most cases, you'll want to use grid layout so the position of the controls doesn't change. The exception is if you want users to be able to access the page from older browsers that don't support absolute positioning.

Most of the properties shown here for Web Server controls provide functionality that's similar to that of Windows controls. For example, you can use the ID property to name a control. And can use the AccessKey property to define an access key for a control. The AutoPostBack and EnableViewState properties, however, are unique to Web Server controls.

The AutoPostBack property lets you determine if the page is posted back to the server when the user changes the value of a control. Note that this property is only available with certain controls, such as the check box, drop-down list, and radio button controls. Also note that this property isn't available with the button controls. That's because these controls are almost always used to post a page back to the server, so that's how they're designed by default.

Earlier in this chapter, I mentioned that a Web Server control can maintain its view state. To do that, the EnableViewState property of the control must be set to True, which is the default. If this property isn't set to True, you'll need to use another technique to maintain data when a page is posted back to the server. For more information, see the online help topic, "Introduction to Web Forms State Management."

The CausesValidation property is also unique in that it determines whether the validation controls on the form are activated when the user clicks on any of the button controls (button, link button, or image button). You'll learn more about this in the next figure.

Common web page properties

Property	Description
IsPostBack	Gets a Boolean value that indicates if the page is being loaded for the first time or is being posted back from the client.
PageLayout	The layout that's displayed in the Web Form Designer window. The possible values are GridLayout and FlowLayout. GridLayout is the default.
Title	The text that's displayed in the title bar of the browser when the web page is displayed.

Common Web Server control properties

Property	Description
AccessKey	Identifies the letter that can be used as a shortcut key.
AutoPostBack	Determines whether the page is posted back to the server when the value of the control changes. Available with controls such as a check box, drop-down list, or text box. The default value is False.
CausesValidation	Determines whether page validation occurs when you click on the button, link button, or image button. The default value is True.
EnableViewState	Determines whether the control maintains its view state across HTTP requests. The default value is True.
Enabled	Determines whether the control is functional. The default value is True.
ID	The name that's used to refer to the control.
TabIndex	The control's position in the tab order.
Text	The text that's displayed in the control.
ToolTip	The text that's displayed in a ToolTip when the mouse pointer is placed over the control.
Visible	Determines whether a control is displayed or hidden.

Notes

- By default, a button control is treated as a *submit button* that posts the page back to the server when the button is clicked. If that's not what you want, you can set the CommandName property of the control to make the control a *command button*. Then, you can code an event procedure for the Command event of the button to respond to the user clicking on that button.

- If the user clicks on a button control whose CausesValidation property is set to True, the data validation that's specified in each of the validation controls on the page is checked and the appropriate error messages are displayed.

- By default, Web Server controls retain their view state across HTTP requests. That means that all of the property values a control contains are maintained when a page is posted to the server and sent back to the client. If that's not what you want, you can set the control's EnableViewState property to False.

Figure 19-6   Common properties for web pages and controls

How to use the validation controls

Figure 19-7 summarizes the *validation controls* you can use with web forms and presents some of the most important properties for these controls. If you want to be sure that the user enters a value into a control, for example, you can use a required field validator control. If you want to compare the value a user enters into a control with a constant value or a property of another control, you can use a compare validator control. And if you want to make sure that the user enters a value within a given range, you can use a range validator control.

You can also use two or more validation controls to validate the data in a single server control. If you look back to figure 19-5, for example, you'll see that two validation controls are included for each text box on the Calculate Investment form. The first one is a required field validator control that checks that the user entered a value. The second one is a range validator control that checks that the value is within a given range.

Each validation control you use is associated with a specific control on the form through its ControlToValidate property. Then, when the user clicks on a button whose CausesValidation property is set to True, all of the controls that have validation controls associated with them are validated. If the data they contain is valid, the page is posted to the server. Otherwise, the appropriate error messages are displayed.

When an error occurs, the Display property of the validation control determines how the message in the ErrorMessage property is displayed. The possible values for the Display property are Static, which lets you allocate space for the error message in the page layout; Dynamic, which causes space to be added for displaying the error message when an error occurs; and None. If you choose None, you can use a validation summary control to display a list of the error messages in a predefined location.

A summary of the validation controls

Name	Description
RequiredFieldValidator	Checks that an entry has been made.
CompareValidator	Compares an entry against a constant value or a property of another control.
RangeValidator	Checks that an entry is within a specified range. If the control is left blank, the range validation is not performed.
RegularExpressionValidator	Checks that an entry matches a pattern, such as a telephone number or an e-mail address, that's defined by a regular expression.
CustomValidator	Checks an entry using validation code that you write yourself.
ValidationSummary	Displays a summary of error messages from the other validation controls.

Common validation control properties

Property	Description
ControlToValidate	The ID of the control to be validated.
Display	Determines how an error message is displayed. Specify Static to allocate space for the message in the page layout, Dynamic to have the space allocated when an error occurs, or None to display the errors in a validation summary control.
ErrorMessage	The message that's displayed when the validation fails.
Text	The text that's displayed for the control in design view. If you leave this property blank, the ID property is displayed.

Additional properties of the CompareValidator control

Property	Description
ControlToCompare	The name of the control whose value you want to use in the comparison.
Operator	An operator that identifies the comparison to be performed.
Type	The data type of the values you want to compare.
ValueToCompare	The value you want to use in the comparison.

Additional properties of the RangeValidator control

Property	Description
MinimumValue	The minimum value that's allowed for the control being validated.
MaximumValue	The maximum value that's allowed for the control being validated.
Type	The data type of the values to be compared.

Description

- You can use *validation controls* to test user input, set an error state, and produce error messages. The validation is performed when the user clicks on a button control whose CausesValidation property is set to True.
- Each validation control is associated with a specific Web Server or HTML Server control. You can associate one or more validation controls with a single server control.
- The validation controls work by running client-side script. Then, if the validation fails, the page isn't posted back to the server.

Figure 19-7   How to use the validation controls

The property settings for the controls on the Calculate Investment form

To help you understand how the Calculate Investment form works, take a look at some of the properties for the controls on this form in figure 19-8. First, notice that the AutoPostBack property of both the radio buttons on this form are set to True. That way, when the user clicks on one of these buttons, the page is posted back to the server so it can be reformatted for the selected calculation.

Also notice that the GroupName property for both of the radio buttons is set to CalculateOption. Unlike radio button controls on a Windows form, you can't group radio buttons on a web form using a group box or panel control. Instead, you have to set the GroupName property of each control in the group to the same name. Then, only one button in the group can be selected at a time.

Finally, notice that the CausesValidation property of the Calculate button is set to True. That way, the user entries will be validated when the user clicks on this button. Remember that this validation occurs before the page is posted back to the server.

The last part of this figure shows the properties for some of the validation controls on this form (not all of the validation controls are shown because of space constraints, but the others are similar). Most of these properties should be self-explanatory. The first required field validator control, for example, makes sure that the user enters a value in the Monthly Investment text box. If not, the message specified in the ErrorMessage property is displayed.

Notice that the Enabled property of the required field validator control for the Future Value text box is set to False. That's because the ReadOnly property of this text box is set to True for a future value calculation, which means that the user can't enter a value into it. Because of that, the validation controls associated with this text box are disabled. If the user clicks on the Monthly Investment radio button to perform a monthly investment calculation, however, the program will set the ReadOnly property of the Future Value text box to False and it will re-enable the controls that validate it.

This figure also shows the property settings for two of the range validator controls on the form. Notice the settings for the Type property of these controls. For the monthly investment text box, this property is set to Currency. This causes the value entered by the user, along with the values specified in the MinimumValue and MaximumValue properties of the validation control, to be converted to the Currency data type before they're compared. Similarly, the value in the Interest Rate text box and the minimum and maximum values for the range validator control for that text box are converted to Double before they're compared.

In addition to the properties shown here, the Display property of each validation control is set to None. That way, any error that occurs as the data is validated will be displayed in the validation summary control on the form. Because it isn't necessary to change any of the properties of this control, it's not listed in this figure.

The property settings for the radio button controls

ID	Text	GroupName	Checked	AutoPostBack
rdoFutureValue	Future Value	CalculateOption	True	True
rdoMonthlyInvestment	Monthly Investment	CalculateOption	False	True

The property settings for the other Web Server controls

Default ID	Property	Value
TextBox1	ID	txtMonthlyInvestment
TextBox2	ID	txtInterestRate
TextBox3	ID	txtYears
TextBox4	ID	txtFutureValue
	ReadOnly	True
	BackColor	Control
Button1	ID	btnCalculate
	Text	Calculate
	AccessKey	C
	CausesValidation	True

The property settings for some of the validation controls

Default ID	Property	Value
RequiredFieldValidator1	ID	rfvMonthlyInvestment
	ControlToValidate	txtMonthlyInvestment
	ErrorMessage	You must enter a monthly investment.
RequiredFieldValidator4	ID	rfvFutureValue
	ControlToValidate	txtFutureValue
	ErrorMessage	You must enter a future value.
	Enabled	False
RangeValidator1	ID	rvMonthlyInvestment
	ControlToValidate	txtMonthlyInvestment
	MinimumValue	100
	MaximumValue	1000
	Type	Currency
	ErrorMessage	Monthly investment must be a decimal value between 100 and 1000.
RangeValidator2	ID	rvInterestRate
	ControlToValidate	txtInterestRate
	MinimumValue	0
	MaximumValue	24
	Type	Double
	ErrorMessage	Interest rate must be a decimal value between 0 and 24.

Note

- The Display property of each of the validation controls is set to None since the errors are displayed in a validation summary control.

Figure 19-8   The property settings for the controls on the Calculate Investment form

How to view the HTML for a web form

Before I go on, you should know that you can display the HTML that's generated for a web form from within the Visual Basic IDE. To do that, you click on the HTML button at the bottom of the Web Form Designer window. Then, the HTML Editor window is displayed as shown in figure 19-9. Although you can edit the HTML code from this window, you shouldn't do that unless you have a thorough understanding of how HTML works.

To help you understand the HTML code that's shown, this figure lists some of the most common *HTML tags* that are used to define a page. In general, one tag is coded at the beginning of a definition and one is coded at the end. For example, the <HTML> and </HTML> tags indicate the beginning and end of a page, and the <body> and </body> tags indicate the beginning and end of the body of the page. The body of a page contains the information that's actually displayed on the page. Within the body, the <form> and </form> tags contain the actual definition of the web form. Notice that this form is defined with the runat="server" attribute. That means that the code for this form will run on the server, which is the case for all ASP.NET web forms.

Within the <form> and </form> tags are special ASP.NET tags for each Web Server control on the form. For example, each label control is enclosed in <asp:label> and </asp:label> tags, and each text box control is enclosed in <asp:textbox> and </asp:textbox> tags. Within these tags are the property settings for each control.

Now, take a look at the tag at the top of this file. In particular, notice the Codebehind attribute. Although you can't see all of this attribute in this figure, it names the file that contains the Visual Basic code for this form. In this case, the file is named frmCalculateInvestment.aspx.vb.

After the Codebehind attribute is an Inherits attribute that names the class for the form. In this case, because the class hasn't been renamed from its default, the name is WebForm1. This attribute, along with the CodeBehind attribute, provides the information ASP.NET needs to process a web page when it's requested.

The Calculate Investment form displayed in the HTML Editor window

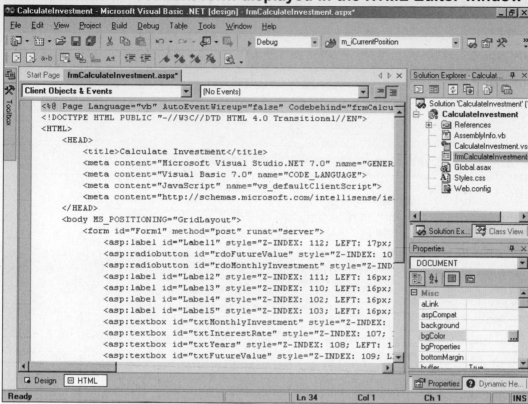

Common HTML tags used to define a web form

Start tag	End tag	Description
\<HTML\>	\</HTML\>	The definition of a page
\<HEAD\>	\</HEAD\>	The definition of a page header
\<title\>	\</title\>	The title that's displayed in the browser's title bar
\<body\>	\</body\>	The part of the page that's displayed in the browser
\<form\>	\</form\>	The definition of a web form
\<asp:...\>	\</asp:...\>	The definition of a Web Server control
\<!	\>	A comment

Description

- As you develop a web form, Visual Studio generates HTML code that defines the form and its controls. You can view and modify this code by clicking on the HTML button at the bottom of the Web Form Designer window.

- For relatively simple web forms, you probably won't need to work directly with HTML.

Figure 19-9   How to view the HTML for a web form

How to code, test, and debug a web application

Although the basic techniques for coding, testing, and debugging web applications are the same as those you use for Windows applications, there are some differences you'll want to know about. You'll learn about those differences in the topics that follow.

How to work in the Code Editor window

Figure 19-10 presents the Code Editor window for the Calculate Investment form. (Actually, this code is from a modified version of the Calculate Investment form that doesn't include validation controls. I omitted those controls so you could see some of the code beyond the initial declarations.) The first thing you should notice here is that the form inherits the Page class in the System.Web.UI namespace of the .NET Framework. This class defines the properties, methods, and events that provide the functionality required by all web pages.

Next, notice that the declaration for each control that was added to the form is included after the Inherits statement rather than in the generated code section as it would be in a Windows form. Also notice that each control is based on a class in the System.Web.UI.WebControls namespace. Because each declaration includes the WithEvents keyword, you can respond to any events defined by those classes from within your application.

If you expand the section in the Code Editor window for the generated code, you'll see that it contains only two procedures. One is for the Init event of the page. You'll learn more about that event in the next figure. The other is for a procedure named InitializeComponent that's called from the Init procedure. This procedure is used to initialize any components used by a web form just as it is for a Windows form. In addition to this code, Visual Basic generates code for the Load procedure of the page. As you can see, this procedure consists of a comment that indicates that you should place your initialization code for the page in that procedure. You'll see one way to use this procedure when you learn how to use ADO.NET with web forms later in this chapter.

In addition to the generated code, of course, you can add code that responds to page and control events. To do that, you can use the same techniques that you use to develop the code for a Windows form. If you double-click on a button control in the Web Form Designer window, for example, Visual Basic starts a procedure for the Click event of that control. You can also use the drop-down lists at the top of the Code Editor window to start an event procedure. And you can code general procedures directly into the window.

As I mentioned earlier, the Visual Basic code for a web form is stored in a file with the *aspx.vb* extension. Although you can display this file by selecting the aspx file in the Solution Explorer and clicking on the View Code button, you can't see it in the Solution Explorer by default. To display it, click on the Show All Files button. Then, it will appear under the aspx file.

The Code Editor window with the code for the Calculate Investment form

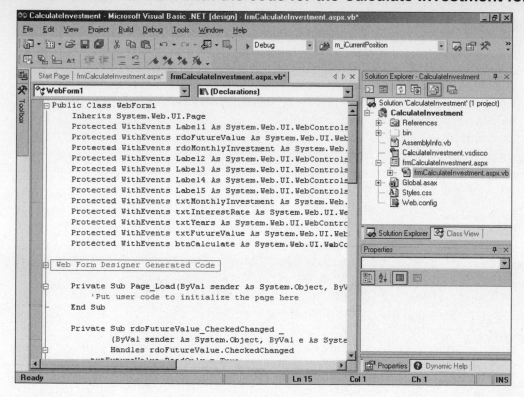

Description

- You develop the code for a web form by coding event procedures and general procedures just as you do for a Windows form.

- The code you add to a form is saved in a file with the aspx.vb extension. To see this file in the Solution Explorer, click on the Show All Files button at the top of the Solution Explorer window.

Notes

- A web form inherits the System.Web.UI.Page class defined by the .NET Framework. This class defines the basic functionality for all web pages.

- The declaration for each control you add to a web form is included near the top of the class definition for the form. The WithEvents keyword is included for each declaration so you can write code for the control's events.

- The hidden code in the generated code section includes an Init event procedure for the page (see figure 19-11) and a general procedure that initializes any components used by the page.

Figure 19-10   How to work in the Code Editor window

How to use ASP.NET page and control events

Figure 19-11 presents some of the common events for working with web pages and controls. The Init and Load events of a page occur whenever a page is requested from the server. The Init event occurs first, and it's used by ASP.NET to restore the view state of the page and its controls. Because of that, you don't usually add your own code to this event. Instead, you'll add it to the Load event procedure. You can use this event to perform operations such as updating control properties and restoring control values. Of course, if the view state is saved with the controls, this may not be necessary. This event can also be used to perform data binding, as you'll see later in this chapter.

The last page event shown here, Unload, occurs just before the page is discarded. From the procedure for this event, you can perform cleanup functions such as closing files and database connections and discarding object references. Although garbage collection will take care of this automatically if you don't, it may not take care of it immediately. That means that resources may be retained unnecessarily, which can be a problem on a busy server. Because of that, we recommend that you do this cleanup work explicitly whenever an application uses resources that might be retained otherwise.

The control events shown here are similar to the ones you use with Windows controls. For example, you use the Click event of a button control to respond to the user clicking on that button, you use the CheckedChanged event to respond to the user clicking on a radio button or checking or unchecking a check box, and you use the SelectedIndexChanged event to respond to the user selecting an item from a list such as a drop-down list.

In this figure, you can see the code for the Click event of the Calculate button on the Calculate Investment form. This procedure simply tests the value of the Checked property of the Future Value radio button. If it's True, it means that the radio button is selected and the CalculateFutureValue procedure is executed. Otherwise, the CalculateMonthlyInvestment procedure is executed.

Common ASP.NET page events

Event	Occurs when...
Init	A page is requested from the server. ASP.NET uses this event to restore the view state of the page and its controls.
Load	A page is requested from the server. This event occurs after the Init event, and you typically use it to perform initialization operations such as data retrieval and binding. You can also use this event to restore values to controls or to change control properties.
Unload	A page is discarded. You typically use this event to close files, close database connections, discard object references, etc.

Common ASP.NET control events

Event	Occurs when...
Click	The user clicks on a button, link button, or image button control.
TextChanged	The user changes the value in a text box.
CheckedChanged	The user selects a radio button in a group of radio buttons or selects or unselects a check box.
SelectedIndexChanged	The user selects an item from a list box, a drop-down list, a check box list, or a radio button list.

Code for the Click event of the Calculate button

```
Private Sub btnCalculate_Click(ByVal sender As System.Object, _
        ByVal e As System.EventArgs) Handles btnCalculate.Click
    If rdoFutureValue.Checked Then
        Me.CalculateFutureValue()
    Else
        Me.CalculateMonthlyInvestment()
    End If
End Sub
```

Description

- All of the events associated with an ASP.NET web page and Web Server controls are executed on the server. Because of that, the page must be posted back to the server to process any event for which you've coded an event procedure.

- The Init and Load events are executed each time a web page is requested from the server. That can happen as a result of the user entering the URL for the page in a browser or as a result of the page being posted back to the server.

- If you want certain code to be processed only the first time a web page is requested, you can check the value of the page's IsPostBack property. If this property is False, the page is being processed for the first time. But if the property is True, the page is being processed as a result of it being posted back to the server.

Figure 19-11   How to use ASP.NET page and control events

The code for the Calculate Investment form

Figure 19-12 presents the complete code for the Calculate Investment form. Because this code is similar to the code for the Windows version of this form that you saw in chapter 8, you shouldn't have any trouble understanding how it works. I'll describe it here briefly, though, and then highlight some of the differences between these two programs.

The event procedure for the CheckedChanged event of the Future Value radio button is executed when the user clicks on this control to select the Future Value option. Note that this option is selected when the form is initially displayed. So this procedure is executed only after the user has selected the Monthly Investment option and then selects the Future Value option again.

This procedure starts by setting the ReadOnly property of the Future Value text box to True so the user can't enter a value into it. This is the value that the program will calculate from the other values on the form. Then, it sets the BackColor property of the control to the system color for a control so it will be obvious to the user that a value can't be entered. It also sets the Enabled properties of the two validation controls associated with this text box to False so the value in the control isn't validated.

The opposite processing is performed on the Monthly Investment text box and its associated validation controls. That way, the user will be able to enter a value into this control and that value will be validated. The last statement in this procedure calls the ClearControls procedure to clear the Text properties of all the text boxes on the form.

The event procedure for the CheckedChanged event of the Monthly Investment radio button includes similar code, but the property settings are reversed. That way, the appropriate text boxes are always available for user entry, and the validation controls are enabled and disabled accordingly.

The Visual Basic code for the Calculate Investment form   Page 1

```
Public Class WebForm1
    Inherits System.Web.UI.Page

    Private Sub rdoFutureValue_CheckedChanged _
            (ByVal sender As System.Object, ByVal e As System.EventArgs) _
            Handles rdoFutureValue.CheckedChanged
        txtFutureValue.ReadOnly = True
        txtFutureValue.BackColor = SystemColors.Control
        rfvFutureValue.Enabled = False
        rvFutureValue.Enabled = False
        txtMonthlyInvestment.ReadOnly = False
        txtMonthlyInvestment.BackColor = SystemColors.Window
        rfvMonthlyInvestment.Enabled = True
        rvMonthlyInvestment.Enabled = True
        Me.ClearControls()
    End Sub

    Private Sub rdoMonthlyInvestment_CheckededChanged _
            (ByVal sender As System.Object, ByVal e As System.EventArgs) _
            Handles rdoMonthlyInvestment.CheckedChanged
        txtFutureValue.ReadOnly = False
        txtFutureValue.BackColor = SystemColors.Window
        rfvFutureValue.Enabled = True
        rvFutureValue.Enabled = True
        txtMonthlyInvestment.ReadOnly = True
        txtMonthlyInvestment.BackColor = SystemColors.Control
        rfvMonthlyInvestment.Enabled = False
        rvMonthlyInvestment.Enabled = False
        Me.ClearControls()
    End Sub

    Private Sub ClearControls()
        txtMonthlyInvestment.Text = ""
        txtInterestRate.Text = ""
        txtYears.Text = ""
        txtFutureValue.Text = ""
    End Sub
```

Figure 19-12   The code for the Calculate Investment form (part 1 of 2)

The code shown in part 2 of this figure is for the Click event of the Calculate button and the two procedures it calls. These two procedures perform the requested calculation, format the result, and then assign it to the Text property of the appropriate text box.

If you compare the code for this form to the code for the Windows version of this form shown in figure 8-13 of chapter 8, you'll notice several differences. First, the Windows form uses nested Ifs and a ValidEntry function to validate the data the user enters. Although you could use code like this in a web form too, it makes more sense to use the validation controls instead. Then, these controls are validated on the client, which means that a round trip to the server isn't necessary.

Second, the code for the Windows form sets the focus to the appropriate text box after a calculation is performed, after a different option is selected, and each time an error occurs. When you process web forms, though, there's no way to set the focus to a specific control. Because of that, the user has to click in a control or tab to it before entering a value.

Finally, the Windows form includes a procedure for the Click event of the Exit button, which is used to close the form. This isn't possible with a web form because a web page doesn't have a Close method. Instead, the form is closed when the user closes the browser or navigates to another page.

The Visual Basic code for the Calculate Investment form   **Page 2**

```
Private Sub btnCalculate_Click(ByVal sender As System.Object, _
        ByVal e As System.EventArgs) Handles btnCalculate.Click
    If rdoFutureValue.Checked Then
        Me.CalculateFutureValue()
    Else
        Me.CalculateMonthlyInvestment()
    End If
End Sub

Private Sub CalculateFutureValue()
    txtFutureValue.Text _
        = FormatCurrency(FV(txtInterestRate.Text / 12 / 100, _
          txtYears.Text * 12, -txtMonthlyInvestment.Text, 0, _
          DueDate.BegOfPeriod))
    Exit Sub
End Sub

Private Sub CalculateMonthlyInvestment()
    txtMonthlyInvestment.Text _
        = FormatCurrency(Pmt(txtInterestRate.Text / 12 / 100, _
          txtYears.Text * 12, 0, -txtFutureValue.Text, _
          DueDate.BegOfPeriod))
End Sub

End Class
```

Figure 19-12   The code for the Calculate Investment form (part 2 of 2)

How to test and debug a web application

Figure 19-13 shows how to test and debug a web application. Before you do that, though, you need to set the starting page for the application. That's because Visual Basic doesn't automatically set the default form as the starting form for a web application like it does for a Windows application. To set the starting page, you simply right-click on the form for that page in the Solution Explorer and select the Set as Start Page command from the shortcut menu that's displayed. Once you've done that, you can use one of the three ways to test the program that are summarized in this figure.

To start, you can test a single form by running it within a Browse window in the Visual Studio IDE. This technique is appropriate for making sure that the page looks the way you want it to and that the basic functions work properly. However, you can't use the debugging tools in this window, and you can't navigate to pages outside your application.

To thoroughly test and debug a web application, you run it in your default browser. The easiest way to do that is to click on the Start button in the Standard toolbar. Then, if an error occurs, error information is displayed in the browser. This information points to the statement that caused the error and identifies the cause of the error. However, you can't switch to break mode when an error message like this is displayed. That's because the application ends execution after it sends a response to a client.

To debug a web application, you have to set a breakpoint before you start program execution. Then, when the program reaches the breakpoint, it will enter break mode. From break mode, you can use all of the debugging tools you learned about in chapter 7.

The Calculate Investment form displayed in a Browse window

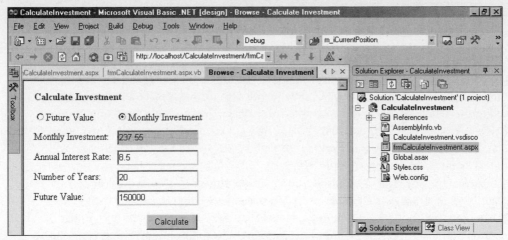

How to select the starting web form for an application

- Before you use one of the techniques that displays forms in your default browser, you must select the starting form for the application. To do that, right-click on the form in the Solution Explorer and select the Set As Start Page command from the shortcut menu.

How to test a single form in the Browse window

- Right-click on the form in the Solution Explorer and select the Build and Browse command from the shortcut menu. The project is compiled and the selected form is displayed in a Browse window within the Visual Studio IDE.

- To stop the browse, close the Browse window.

How to test an application in the default browser without debugging

- Select the Debug → Start Without Debugging command. The project is compiled and the starting page is displayed in your default browser.

- To end the application, close the browser.

How to test and debug an application in the default browser

- Select the Debug → Start command or click on the Start button in the Standard toolbar. Then, the project is compiled and the starting page is displayed in your default browser.

- If an error occurs, error information that includes the statement that caused the error is displayed in the browser. Then, you can close the browser, set a breakpoint at the statement in error, and start the application again. When the program reaches the breakpoint, it will enter break mode. Then, you can use the debugging tools to debug the application.

- To end the application, close the browser, select the Debug → Stop Debugging command, or click on the Stop Debugging button in the Debug toolbar.

Figure 19-13   How to test and debug a web application

How to use ADO.NET with web applications

Like Windows forms, web forms are often used to access data from a database using ADO.NET as presented in Section 4 of this book (if you haven't read that section yet, you need to before you continue with this chapter). For example, when you develop web forms for database applications, you can use the Data Adapter Configuration Wizard that's presented in chapter 17 to generate data adapter, connection, and command objects. You can also generate a dataset using the technique you learned in that chapter.

However, the processing that you can perform when you bind Web Server controls to a dataset is limited when compared to what you can do with Windows controls. Specifically, you can't use Web Server controls to update the data in a dataset. Instead, you have use code to do that, but since that programming technique is beyond the scope of this book, it isn't covered in Section 4. Nevertheless, the remaining topics in this chapter will get you started using ADO.NET in web applications. In particular, you'll learn how to use bound controls to display information in a web page.

A Vendor Display form that uses ADO.NET

To illustrate how you can use ADO.NET in a web form, I'll use the Vendor Display form shown in figure 19-14. This form is similar to the Vendor forms you saw in chapter 18. It allows the user to select a vendor from a drop-down list at the top of the form. This list is bound to a data table that contains the names and IDs of all the vendors in the Vendors table, as indicated by the Select statement for the first data adapter shown in this figure. Then, the ID of the selected vendor is used to retrieve the data for that vendor as defined by the parameterized query in the second Select statement.

The Vendor Display form

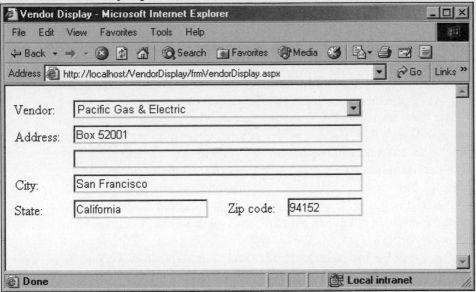

The Select statements for the two data adapters used by the form

Data adapter	Select statement
SqlDA_VendorNames	`Select VendorID, VendorName From Vendors` `Order By VendorName`

SqlDA_Vendors	`Select VendorID, VendorName, VendorAddress1, VendorAddress2,`
	`    VendorCity, VendorState, VendorZipCode, StateName`
	`From Vendors`
	`Inner Join States On VendorState = StateCode`
	`Where VendorID = @VendorID`

Description

- The Vendor Display form displays information for the vendor that's selected from the drop-down list at the top of the form. To do that, it uses two data adapters.
- The first data adapter retrieves the vendor IDs and vendor names that are used by the drop-down list. This data is stored in a dataset named DsVendorNames1, and the drop-down list is bound to this dataset (see figure 19-15).
- The second data adapter retrieves the data for one vendor based on the value in the @VendorID parameter. This data is stored in a dataset named DsVendors1, and each of the text boxes is bound to a field in this one-row dataset (see figure 19-16).

Note

- The bound controls on a web form can be used to retrieve data from a dataset, but not update it.

Figure 19-14   A Vendor Display form that uses ADO.NET

How to bind Web Server controls to multiple rows of a data source

Several of the Web Server controls can be bound to multiple rows of a data source. To do that, you use the control properties shown in figure 19-15. As you can see, the properties you use to bind a data grid, data list, or repeater control are identical to the properties you use to bind a Windows data grid control. Because of that, you shouldn't have any trouble using these controls.

You can also bind a drop-down list like the one in the Vendor Display form to a data source. To do that, you use the five properties shown in this figure. As you can see, these properties are similar to the ones that you use with Windows controls, even though most of their names are different. Although you can use this type of binding with any of the Web Server controls that provide a list, I'll focus on the drop-down list here since it's the control used in the Vendor Display form.

Like the data grid control, the DataSource and DataMember properties of a drop-down list identify the dataset and data table that contain the data to be bound to. Then, the DataTextField property identifies the field to be displayed in the list, and the DataValueField property identifies the field whose value is stored in the list. That makes it possible to display one field and store another. Finally, the DataTextFormatString property lets you specify the format for numeric values displayed in the list. You can use many of the standard numeric formatting codes within the format specification. For more information, see the online help topic on this property.

This figure also presents the property settings for binding the drop-down list of vendors on the Vendor Display form to the table that contains the vendor names and IDs. As you can see, the DataSource property names the DsVendorNames1 dataset, and the DataMember property names the Vendors table. Then, the DataTextField property names the VendorName field, which is the field that's displayed in the drop-down list. Finally, the DataValueField property names the VendorID field so this value is stored in the list. That way, when the user selects a vendor name, the ID for that vendor can be used to retrieve the vendor information.

In contrast to a Windows form, a web form doesn't have a binding manager to manage the bound controls on the form. Because of that, the controls aren't automatically bound to the data source when the program is run. Instead, you have to use the DataBind method of each control to bind it to the data source specified in its binding properties. The statement shown in this figure, for example, binds the drop-down list to its data source. Note that because the data source for this control doesn't change as the program executes, you only need to bind it after the data source is initially loaded. If the data source for a control changes as the program executes, however, you have to rebind it to that data source. That's the case with the text box controls on the Vendor Display form, as you'll see in the next topic.

The properties for binding a data grid, data list, or repeater control to a dataset

Property	Description
DataSource	The name of a data source, such as a dataset.
DataMember	A member associated with the data source, such as a data table. If the data source contains only one bindable member, you don't need to set this property.

The properties for binding a drop-down list, list box, radio button list, or check box list control to a data source

Property	Description
DataSource	The name of a data source, such as a dataset.
DataMember	A member associated with the data source, such as a data table. If the data source contains only one bindable member, you don't need to set this property.
DataTextField	The field in the data member whose value is displayed in the list.
DataValueField	The field in the data member whose value is stored in the list.
DataTextFormatString	The format of the items displayed in the list.

The property settings for binding the drop-down list on the Vendor Display form

Property	Value
DataSource	DsVendorNames1
DataMember	Vendors
DataTextField	VendorName
DataValueField	VendorID

A statement that binds the drop-down list to its data source

```
ddlVendors.DataBind()
```

Description

- The data grid control displays information from a data source in a row and column format, just like the data grid control you use with Windows forms. The data list and repeater controls are similar to the data grid control, but they use different display formats and have less built-in functionality.

- The drop-down list, list box, radio button list, and check box list controls provide functionality similar to the combo box, list box, radio button, and check box controls you use with Windows forms.

- Because web forms don't have a binding manager like Windows forms, you must bind the controls to the data source as the program executes. You must do that any time the data source changes. To bind a control to its data source, you use the DataBind method of the control.

Figure 19-15   How to bind Web Server controls to multiple rows of a data source

How to bind Web Server controls to a single field of a data source

You can also bind some of the Web Server controls, including the text box control, to a single field of a data source. To do that, you create a *data-binding expression* for the control as illustrated in figure 19-16.

To create a binding expression for a control, you display the DataBindings dialog box for the control as described in this figure. In this case, the dialog box for the State text box on the Vendor Display form is displayed. When you first display this dialog box, the Text property is selected in the Bindable Properties list. In most cases, that's what you'll want. If you want to bind to a different property, though, just select that property from the list.

Next, you select the field that you want the control bound to from the list of fields in the available data tables. Notice that the fields are listed under the *default view* for the table. The default view provides a way of filtering the rows in the table so that only the row or rows you specify are available. That can be important when you're working with bound controls on a web form, because they can only be bound to a table or view that contains a single row. In this case, though, a filter isn't required because the program uses a parameter to retrieve a single row into the table.

Like the drop-down list you learned about in the last topic, you have to use the DataBind method of a text box control to bind it to the data source specified by its binding properties as the program executes. In this case, though, because the data source is the default view and because this view changes each time the user selects a vendor from the drop-down list, the text box controls must be rebound each time the view changes. You'll see how that works when you see the code for this form in the next figure.

The DataBindings dialog box for the State text box on the Vendor Display form

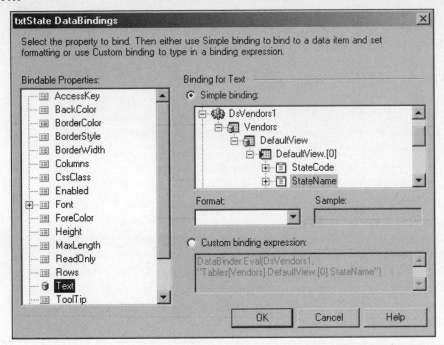

Description

- To bind a text box to a data source, you use the DataBindings dialog box to create a *data-binding expression*. To display the DataBindings dialog box, select the control you want to bind, select the DataBindings property in the Properties window, then click on the ellipsis that appears for the property.

- By default, the Text property is selected in the list of bindable properties. If that's not what you want, you can select any of the other properties in the list.

- To bind the control to a field in a dataset, expand the dataset in the Simple binding list until you can see a list of the fields and then select the field. Notice that the fields are listed under the *default view* for the dataset.

- You can also format the value that's displayed in the text box by selecting an option from the Format combo box.

- After you create a data-binding expression for a property, the property is displayed in the Properties window with a database symbol like the one shown next to the Text property above.

- Because web forms don't have a binding manager, you can't bind a control to the current record. Instead, you have to filter the table that contains the field that a control is bound to so it contains a single row, or you have to fill the table with a single row. Then, you can use the DataBind method of the control to bind it to a field in that row.

- You can use the same technique to bind other Web Server controls to a data source.

Figure 19-16   How to bind Web Server controls to a single field of a data source

The code for the Vendor Display form

Now that you know how to bind Web Server controls to a data source, you're ready to see the code for the Vendor Display form. This code is presented in figure 19-17, and it consists of just two procedures. The first one handles the Load event of the form, and the second one handles the SelectedIndexChanged event of the drop-down list.

The Load procedure fills the DsVendorNames1 dataset and binds the drop-down list control to this dataset. Note, however, that this is only done if the IsPostBack property of the page is False, or the first time the page is loaded. This works because this dataset isn't needed after the page is loaded for the first time. That's because the data it contains is stored in the drop-down list, which maintains its view state from one execution to the next.

Remember that the program ends each time a page is generated, and it is restarted each time a page is posted back to the server. For efficiency, then, you don't want to reload the drop-down list each time the program is restarted. That's why the If logic is needed in the Load procedure.

The SelectedIndexChanged procedure is executed after the Load procedure each time the user selects a vendor from the drop-down list, provided that the page is posted back to the server. For that to happen, though, the AutoPostBack property of the drop-down list must set to True.

The first two statements in the SelectedIndexChanged procedure get the data for the selected vendor. To do that, the first statement sets the parameter of the query to the value of the item selected from the drop-down list. Since the DataValueField property of the drop-down list is set to the VendorID, this means that the vendor ID is used as the parameter. Then, the second statement fills the DsVendors1 dataset with the row for this vendor. After that, the text boxes in the form are bound to the values in this row. When this procedure ends, the program ends, and the page is sent back to the browser so the user can view the data for the selected vendor and then select another vendor.

The Visual Basic code for the Vendor Display form

```
Public Class WebForm1
    Inherits System.Web.UI.Page

    Private Sub Page_Load(ByVal sender As System.Object, _
            ByVal e As System.EventArgs) Handles MyBase.Load
        If Not IsPostBack Then
            SqlDA_VendorNames.Fill(DsVendorNames1)
            ddlVendors.DataBind()
        End If
    End Sub

    Private Sub ddlVendors_SelectedIndexChanged(ByVal sender As System.Object, _
            ByVal e As System.EventArgs) Handles ddlVendors.SelectedIndexChanged
        SqlDA_Vendors.SelectCommand.Parameters("@VendorID").Value _
            = ddlVendors.SelectedItem.Value
        SqlDA_Vendors.Fill(DsVendors1)
        txtAddress1.DataBind()
        txtAddress2.DataBind()
        txtCity.DataBind()
        txtState.DataBind()
        txtZipCode.DataBind()
    End Sub

End Class
```

Figure 19-17   The code for the Vendor Display form

Perspective

Now that you've read this chapter, you should have a basic understanding of how web applications work, and you should have a good feel for what's involved in developing them. With that background, you should now be able to develop simple web applications of your own. As you might guess, there's a lot more to developing web applications than what's presented here. But the goal of this chapter is just to get you started.

Summary

- Web applications work by sending *HTTP requests* for web pages from a browser running on a client to a web server running *IIS*. The web server processes the request and then sends an *HTTP response* back to the client so it can display the page in the browser.

- IIS is used to manage the web pages on a web server. It comes with Windows 2000 and later operating systems and is required for ASP.NET web applications.

- An *ASP.NET web page* is defined using *HTML* and *ASP.NET Server controls*. With ASP.NET, web pages can be created at run time.

- You can *post* a web page back to the server using some of the server controls. Then, the page is processed using application code and is sent back to the client to complete the *round trip*.

- Because web applications are *stateless*, the values that a web page contains are not retained on the server after they're sent back to the client. However, some of the server controls can retain their own data, called a *view state*.

- To define a web page, you create a web form using the Web Form Designer. This designer lets you add controls from the Toolbox and set the properties of the page and its controls in the Properties window.

- *HTML Server controls* map to traditional HTML elements and can be processed on either the client or the server. *Web Server controls* can only be processed on the server, but they provide improved functionality.

- *Validation controls* let you validate user entries on the client before a page is posted back to the server.

- As you develop a web form, the HTML that defines the form is generated for you. You can view this code from the HTML Editor window.

- You use the Code Editor window to develop the code for a web form just as you do for a Windows form. This code can respond to events that occur on the web page or Web Server controls.

- You can test and debug a web application in your default browser using standard techniques. You can also test a single form in the Browse window of the IDE.

- You can use ADO.NET components in a web form to define a data source for controls on the form. Then, you can bind controls to the data source to display the data it contains. However, you can't update this data using bound controls.

- A web form doesn't have a binding manager like a Windows form. Because of that, you have to bind controls as the program executes. In addition, if a control is bound to a single field in a data source, that data source must contain a single row.

Terms

URL (Universal Resource Locater)
HTTP (HyperText Transfer Protocol)
HTTP request
web server
client
HTML (HyperText Markup Language)
HTTP response
IIS (Internet Information Services)
ASP.NET web page
ASP.NET
ASP.NET Server controls
posting a web page
round trip
stateless application
view state

Microsoft FrontPage Server Extensions
  (FPSE)
file-share access
web form
web page
Web Form Designer
HTML Server controls
Web Server controls
validation controls
absolute positioning
HTML tags
submit button
command button
data-binding expression
default view

Objectives

- Given the specifications for a web application that performs a calculation, develop and test the form.

- Given the specifications for a web application that retrieves and displays data using ADO.NET and bound controls, develop and test the form.

- Describe the processing that takes place on the client and on the web server as an ASP.NET web application is executed.

- Explain what it means for a web application to be stateless, and describe one way you can maintain the state of the controls on a form.

- Explain what it means for a web page to be posted to the server, and explain how you provide for posting in a web form.

Exercise 19-1   Create the Calculate Investment form

In this exercise, you'll create the Calculate Investment application presented in this chapter. Then, you'll test the application using the Browse window, and you'll debug it using your default browser.

To do the exercises in this chapter and the next, you'll need a web server with IIS. If you don't have access to a web server with IIS, you can install IIS on your own PC using the information in figure 19-2 and appendix A as a guide.

Start a web application

1. Start Visual Studio. Then, pull down the Tools menu and select the Options command to display the Options dialog box. Highlight the Projects and Solutions category in the Environment folder, and then change the Visual Studio projects location to C:\VB.NET\Chapter 19. This is where the solution for the web application you create in this exercise will be stored.

2. Click on the New Project button in the Start page to display the New Project dialog box. Then, highlight the ASP.NET Web Application template, select the location of the IIS server where you want the project stored, and enter the name CalculateInvestment for the project. Click on the OK button to create the project.

3. Start the Windows Explorer, and then navigate to the Inetpub directory. Expand this directory so you can see the wwwroot directory. Then, expand this directory. You should see a directory named CalculateInvestment. Close the Explorer and return to Visual Studio.

Design the user interface for the form

4. Use the Web Forms tab of the Toolbox to add the label, radio button, text box, and button controls shown in figure 19-5 to the default form.

5. Set the Text properties of the Label controls so they appear as shown in this figure, and set the Title property of the form to "Calculate Investment." Then, set the properties of the radio button, text box, and button controls as shown in figure 19-8.

6. Rename the default form file to frmCalculateInvestment.aspx. Then, click on the HTML button in the lower left corner of the Web Form Designer window to display the HTML Editor window.

7. Review the HTML code to get a feel for the information it contains and how it's organized. In particular, look at the first tag to see that it names the file that contains the code for this form and indicates that the page will inherit the form class. Also look at the code for the Web Server controls to see how the information they contain corresponds to the properties of the controls. When you're done reviewing this code, click on the Design button to return to the Web Designer window.

Add the code for the form

8. Double-click on the Future Value radio button to open the Code Editor window and start the procedure for the CheckedChanged event of this control. Then, add the code shown in figure 19-12 for this event, omitting the code for the validation controls since you haven't added them yet.

9. Use the drop-down lists at the top of the Code Editor window to start the procedure for the CheckedChanged event of the Monthly Investment radio button. Add the code for this event as shown in figure 19-12, once again omitting the code for the validation controls.

10. Enter the rest of the code for this form using standard techniques.

Test and debug the form

11. Right-click on the form in the Solution Explorer and select the Build and Browse command to display the form in a Browse window. Enter appropriate values for a future value calculation, and then press the Enter key or click on the Calculate button to post the page to the server. It should be redisplayed with the calculated future value. Continue testing to make sure the form works with valid values. Then, close the Browse window.

12. Set the Calculate Investment form as the starting form for the application by right-clicking on it in the Solution Explorer and then selecting the Set As Start Page command. Then, click on the Start button in the Standard toolbar to display the page in your default browser. Click in the Visual Studio IDE, pull down the Debug menu, and select the Break All command. A message should be displayed indicating that there's no source code available.

13. Return to the browser. Then, enter "xxx" in the Monthly Investment text box and press the Enter key to see the error message that's displayed. Make a note of the statement that caused the error, and then close the browser.

14. Set a breakpoint at the statement that caused the error and start the program again. Enter the invalid data again and press the Enter key. This time, the program should enter break mode so you can debug it.

15. When you're done debugging the application, click on the Stop Debugging button to end it.

Add the validation controls and test the program again

16. Add the validation controls shown in figure 19-5 to this form, and set the properties of these controls using the settings in figure 19-8 as a guide.

17. Add the code for the validation controls shown in the two CheckedChanged procedures in figure 19-12.

18. Run the program again in either the Browse window or your default browser. Then, enter invalid values in one or more of the text boxes to see what happens. If error messages aren't displayed, you may need to check the settings of your validation controls or debug the program.

19. When you have the program working the way you want, close and save the solution.

Exercise 19-2   Create the Vendor Display form

In this exercise, you'll create the Vendor Display form illustrated in this chapter.

1. Start a new web application with the name VendorDisplay. Then, set the Title property for the default form to "Vendor Display" and change the name of the form file to frmVendorDisplay.aspx.

2. Use the Data Adapter Configuration Wizard that you learned how to use in chapter 17 to create the data adapters with the Select statements shown in figure 19-14. Then, generate datasets for these data adapters and name them dsVendorNames and dsVendors.

3. Use the Web Forms tab of the Toolbox to add the controls shown in figure 19-14 to the form. Set the Text properties of the label controls so they appear as shown in that figure, set the ID property of the drop-down list to ddlVendors, and set the ID properties of the text box controls to txtAddress1, txtAddress2, txtCity, txtState, and txtZipCode. Also, set the AutoPostBack property of the drop-down list to True.

4. Set the data binding properties of the drop-down list as shown in figure 19-15. Then, use the DataBindings dialog box as described in figure 19-16 to bind each text box to the appropriate field in the DsVendors1 dataset.

5. Modify the code for the Load procedure of the form so it loads the DsVendorNames1 dataset and then binds the Vendors drop-down list to this dataset. This code should only be executed the first time the form is loaded.

6. Code a procedure for the SelectedIndexChanged event of the Vendors drop-down list. This procedure should set the value of the parameter in the Select statement for the Vendors data adapter to the Vendor ID of the vendor selected from the drop-down list. Then, it should load the Vendors dataset with the row for this vendor and bind the text box controls to this row.

7. Run the application and test it to be sure it works properly. When you're done, close and save the solution.

20

How to create and use web services

In addition to web applications, you can use Visual Basic .NET to create web services. Web services allow you to store common processing routines on a web server, where they're available to programmers who need to use the routines in their applications. In this chapter, you'll learn the basic concepts and skills you need to create and use web services.

Web services involve the use of XML (the eXtensible Markup Language), which is covered in chapter 14. You don't have to read chapter 14 before reading this chapter because XML works behind the scenes, without any coding considerations on your part. However, chapter 14 will give you a better sense of what's going on as you access web services, so I recommend that you read it soon if you're going to be using web services regularly.

An introduction to web services

Simply put, a *web service* is a class that resides on a web server and can be accessed via the Internet or an intranet. As a result, ASP.NET or other applications can access the web service from any computer that's connected to the Internet or a local intranet.

What web services are used for

Web services are becoming an integral part of web development. One use of web services is to allow applications to interact with one another. For example, an airline might *publish* (make available for general use) a web service that provides flight schedules. Then, a travel agency could build an application that accesses the flight schedule service. Or, a book publisher might publish a web service that processes orders. Then, a bookstore could build an application that automatically sends orders to the publisher. As more companies create web services and publish them on the Internet, applications that use these services will become more popular.

Another use for web services is to aid in the development of *distributed web applications*, where the code and data can be stored on and shared among different computers. For example, web developers can separate the user-interface elements of an application from the business logic that processes user entries by placing the business logic in a web service. That makes it possible to provide two interfaces to the same web service: a web interface provided by a web application that can be run from any computer that has a browser and Internet access, and a Windows interface provided by a Windows application that's installed on the user's computer.

How web services work

Figure 20-1 illustrates how web services work. As you can see, the web service is accessed from a web page running on a web server. In this example, the web service and the application's web pages reside on two different web servers. Although that doesn't have to be the case, this arrangement illustrates how web services can be used to create distributed applications. The server that hosts the web service must have both Microsoft's Internet Information Services (IIS) and the .NET Framework installed.

Notice that the web page and the web service communicate using XML. Actually, web services use a rather complicated collection of protocols that are built on XML. These protocols include *WSDL*, which stands for *Web Services Description Language,* and *SOAP*, which stands for *Simple Object Access Protocol*. Fortunately, all of this is taken care of for you when you create and use a web service. As a result, you don't usually have to deal directly with XML, WSDL, or SOAP.

The operation of a distributed ASP.NET web application

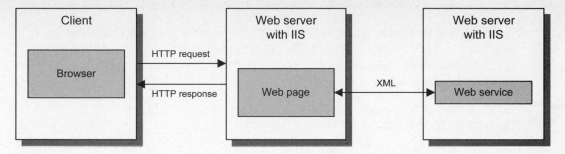

Description

- A *web service* is a class that resides on a web server and can be accessed by web applications or other web services to implement distributed ASP.NET web applications. A web service can also be accessed by Windows applications.

- Web services typically contain business logic that's coded as a collection of public methods.

- Like web applications, web services must reside on a web server with IIS. Although they can reside on the same server as the web applications that use them, they can also reside on a separate server.

- Information is passed between a web page and a web service using XML (the eXtensible Markup Language). XML uses custom tags to define information, rather than standard tags that are universally understood. As a result, the web service must contain a document written in the *Web Services Description Language* (*WSDL*) that describes how the web service works and how clients can interact with it.

- If the web page and web service reside on the same server, the XML is passed as part of an HTTP request or response. If the web service resides on a different web server, the *Simple Object Access Protocol*, or *SOAP*, is used to facilitate the HTTP request and response.

- Because web services aren't tied to a proprietary technology, programs written in any language and running on any operating system can access a web service.

Figure 20-1   How ASP.NET web services work

How to create a web service

To create a web service, you start by creating a web service project. Then, you use the Code Editor window to develop the public and private code. The following topics show you how.

How to start a web service project

Figure 20-2 shows the New Project dialog box for creating a web service. From this dialog box, you identify the location of the web server and the name of the directory where the web service will reside just as you do for a web application. Then, all of the files for the project are stored in that directory on the web server, and the solution file is stored in a directory with the same name within the default Visual Studio directory.

When you first start a web service project, it contains a single web service named Service1. The definition of this service is stored in a file with the extension *asmx*, as you can see in this figure. Like the aspx extension that's used for web pages, the asmx extension tells IIS that the file should be processed by ASP.NET.

As you can see in this figure, the default web service is displayed in a Component Designer window. This window is similar to the Component Designer tray you've seen in earlier chapters. It's used to hold any non-visual components you add to the web service. If the web service will access a database, for example, any ADO.NET components you add to the web service will appear in this window. Because a web service doesn't have a visual interface, however, no design surface is provided.

The New Project dialog box and a new ASP.NET Web Service project

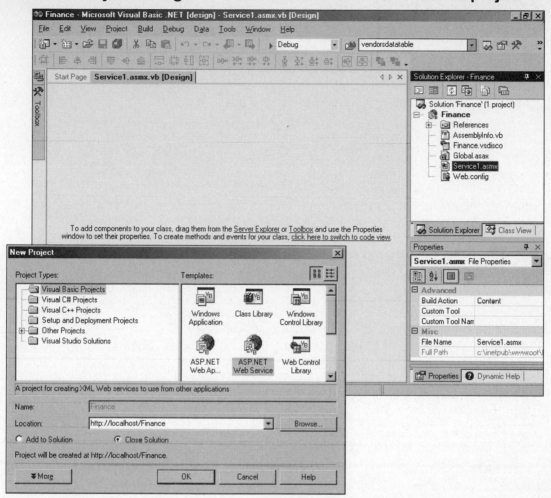

Description

- To start a web service project, display the New Project dialog box and select the ASP.NET Web Service template. Then, select the IIS server and enter the name of the directory where you want the project files stored. Visual Basic creates this directory in the Inetpub\wwwroot directory of the IIS server.

- Visual Basic also creates a directory with the name you specify in the default directory for Visual Studio and stores the solution file there.

- By default, a web service project consists of a single web service named Service1. This web service appears in the Solution Explorer with the *asmx* extension.

- When you start a new web service project, a Component Designer window is displayed for the default web service. You can use this window to add components, like the ADO.NET components presented in section 4, to the web service.

Figure 20-2   How to start a web service project

How to develop the code for a web service

Figure 20-3 presents the starting code for a web service. You'll want to note several things about this code. First, like everything else that's built on the .NET Framework, a web service is implemented as a class. In this case, the class inherits the WebService class, which provides the web service with access to the ASP.NET objects commonly used by web services.

Second, notice the WebService *attribute* that precedes the class definition. An attribute is similar to a keyword (like Public or Private) that provides information to the runtime as to how the code should be used. In this case, the WebService attribute identifies the namespace that will contain the web service. The default is tempuri.org, which is a temporary namespace that you can use during development of a web service. If you publish a web service so it's available to other users, however, you'll want to change this name to something unique. That way, if someone else publishes a web service with the same name, the two can be distinguished by the namespace that contains them.

The WebService attribute can also contain a description of the web service. If you publish a web service, you'll want to include this information to provide potential users of the service with information about what it does. You'll see an example of how you code this information in the next figure.

Finally, notice the WebMethod attribute that's commented out in the web service. You use this attribute to identify a public method as a *web method*, which is a method that's accessible from outside the service. Aside from the WebMethod attribute, you code a web method just as you would any other method. In addition, you can include private variables and procedures that are used by the web method.

One key difference between a web service and a regular Visual Basic class is that a web service cannot have properties. You can define public variables, but those variables aren't accessible to clients that use the web service. As a result, web methods are the only interface a client has to a web service.

You can still implement properties using web methods, though. To retrieve the value of a property, for example, you can use a web method that's coded as a function that returns the value of the variable for the property. And to set the value of a property, you can use a Sub procedure that accepts the value of the property and assigns it to a variable.

In addition to the asmx file that contains the code for the web service, you'll notice that the project includes a file with the extension *vsdisco*. This file is used for *dynamic discovery*, which is a process ASP.NET uses to locate web services. Note, however, that dynamic discovery is used only during application development. If you publish a web service, you'll usually create a *static discovery file* (file extension *disco*) that lets other clients "discover" your web service. However, publishing a web service is beyond the scope of this book, so you'll only see *vsdisco* files in the web service projects you work with in this chapter.

The starting code for a web service

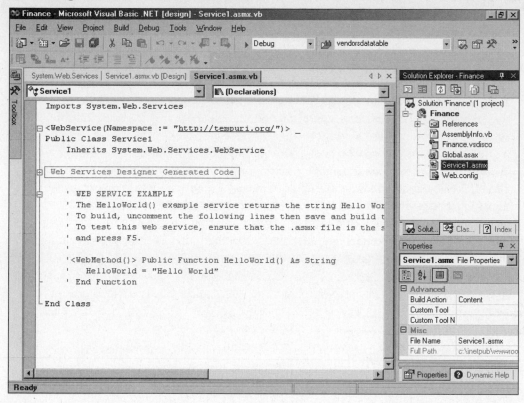

Description

- A web service is implemented as a class that inherits the WebService class of the System.Web.Services namespace. This class provides the basic functionality for all web services.

- You develop the code for a web service by coding *web methods*. A web method is a Public procedure with the WebMethod *attribute* (`<WebMethod()>`). A web service can also include private code that's not available from outside the service.

- Web services don't support property declarations or public variables. Instead, you can use public functions to get the values of private variables, and you can use public Sub procedures to set the values of private variables.

- You can use the WebService attribute (`<WebService()>`) to identify the namespace for the web service. The default namespace is http://tempuri.org. If a web service is made public, it must have a unique namespace to distinguish it from other web services with the same name.

- The WebService attribute can include a description of the web service. This description is displayed on the help and service description pages for the service.

Figure 20-3   How to develop the code for a web service

The code for the Financial Calculations web service

To illustrate how you can use a web service, figure 20-4 presents the code for a Financial Calculations web service. This service contains two web methods that perform future value and monthly investment calculations. As you can see, each method is coded as a function that accepts the values required to perform the calculation and returns the result of the calculation. Since you've seen these calculations many times throughout this book, you shouldn't have any trouble understanding how they work.

Notice that both web methods start with a WebMethod attribute. In this case, the attribute is coded on a separate line that's continued to the line that contains the Function statement. Although that's not required, it can improve the readability of a web service that contains private procedures in addition to web methods. So we recommend that you use this format for all your web services.

Also notice the WebService attribute at the beginning of the web service. This attribute identifies the namespace for the web service as

`http://murach.com/`

This namespace is used to uniquely identify the web service. Although it isn't required, it is common practice to use an Internet domain name to help ensure that the namespace is unique.

The WebService attribute in this example also includes a brief description of the web service. You'll see one way this information is used in the next figure.

The Visual Basic code for the Financial Calculations web service

```vb
Imports System.Web.Services

<WebService(Namespace:="http://murach.com/", _
            Description:="Provides financial calculations")> _
Public Class FinancialCalculations
    Inherits System.Web.Services.WebService

    <WebMethod()> _
    Public Function FutureValue( _
            ByVal Years As Integer, _
            ByVal MonthlyInvestment As Decimal, _
            ByVal InterestRate As Decimal) As Decimal
        FutureValue = FV(InterestRate / 12 / 100, Years * 12, _
                    -MonthlyInvestment, 0, DueDate.BegOfPeriod)
    End Function

    <WebMethod()> _
    Public Function MonthlyInvestment( _
            ByVal Years As Integer, _
            ByVal InterestRate As Decimal, _
            ByVal FutureValue As Decimal) As Decimal
        MonthlyInvestment = Pmt(InterestRate / 12 / 100, Years * 12, _
                        0, -FutureValue, DueDate.BegOfPeriod)
    End Function

End Class
```

Figure 20-4   The code for the Financial Calculations web service

How to test a web service

After you develop a web service, you can test it without having to create a client program that uses it. To do that, you simply build and run the web service in your default browser or in a Browse window just as you would a web application. When you do that, a *Service help page* like the first one shown in figure 20-5 is displayed.

The Service help page identifies the web service and displays the description you specified in the WebService attribute. It also includes a link to the *service description* for the web service. This is the XML document you learned about in figure 20-1 that contains the WSDL that describes the web service. If you're interested in what this document looks like, you can click on this link to display it.

Finally, the Service help page lists the web methods that are available from the web service. If you click on the link for one of these methods, a *Service Method help page* for that method is displayed. The second screen in this figure, for example, is the help page for the MonthlyInvestment method.

If a method requires arguments, the Service Method help page lists them by name and lets you enter values for them. Then, when you click on the Invoke button, the method is executed and the XML that's generated as a result is displayed. In this figure, for example, you can see the XML that's generated when the MonthlyInvestment method is executed using the values shown. If you're familiar with XML, you can see that the actual result of the calculation is contained within <decimal> and </decimal> tags. These tags are generated based on the return type of the MonthlyInvestment method.

Although you can't see it in this figure, the Service Method help page also contains sample SOAP and HTTP requests and responses. If you're interested in what this code looks like, you may want to scroll down so you can see it. In general, though, you don't need to worry about how it works.

In this figure, the help pages and XML output are displayed in windows within the Visual Basic IDE. Because of that, you can't use the debugging tools to test the web service. To do that, you need to run the web service in your browser. Then, you can set breakpoints and debug the web service using standard debugging techniques. Before you do that, though, you need to set the starting page for the project just as you do for a web application.

Help pages for the Financial Calculations web service

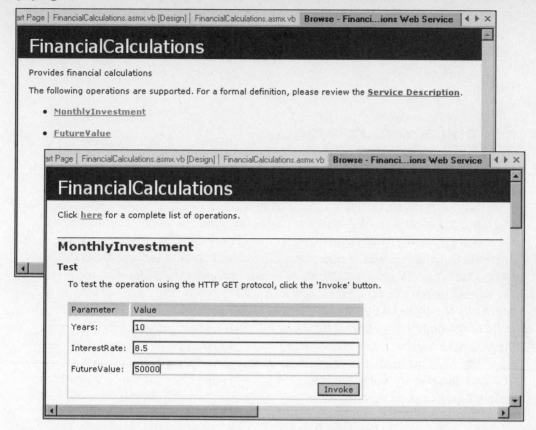

XML output for the MonthlyInvestment web method

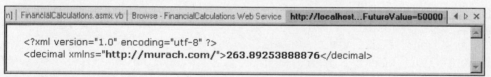

Description

- To test a web service in your default browser, click on the Start button in the Debug toolbar. To test a web service in a Browse window, select the Build and Browse command from the shortcut menu for the web service. In either case, a *Service help page* like the first one shown above is displayed.

- To test any of the web methods defined by the web service, click on the link for that method. Then, enter any required parameters in the *Service Method help page* that's displayed and click on the Invoke button. A page that shows the XML output for the method is displayed.

- When you use your browser to test a web service, you can set breakpoints and debug the web service just as you do for a web application. Before you can test a web service in your browser, though, you have to set the starting page as you do for a web application.

Figure 20-5   How to test a web service

How to consume a web service

After you build and test a web service, you can use it from any project that requires the services it provides. To do that, you first have to add a reference to the web service. Then, you can create an instance of it and use it like any other class.

How to add a web reference

To add a web reference to a project, you use the Add Web Reference dialog box shown in figure 20-6. From this dialog box, you can enter the address of the asmx file for the web service into the Address combo box. If you've added a reference to the web service to a project recently, you can also select it from the list that drops down from the combo box. Alternatively, if the web service has been published, you can use one of the directories that are available from the left pane of this dialog box to locate it, or you can enter the address of the disco file for the web service.

After you identify the web service, its description is displayed in the left pane of the dialog box. This is the same information that's displayed in the Service help page you saw in the last figure. You can use it to test or review the available web methods or to display the service description for the web service. You can also display the service description by clicking on the View Contract link in the right pane. When you're sure you've located the web service you want, you can click on the Add Reference button to add a reference to the service to the project.

The dialog box for adding a web reference

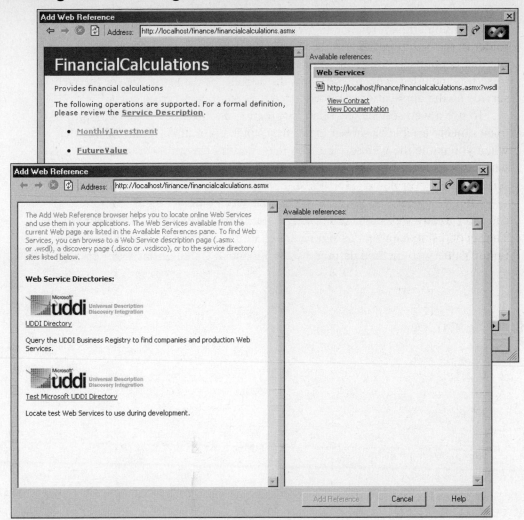

Description

- To add a reference to a web service to a project, right-click on the project file in the Solution Explorer and select the Add Web Reference command from the shortcut menu to display the Add Web Reference dialog box.

- To locate a web service, enter the address of its aspx or disco file in the Address box. You can also use the two Microsoft links to locate web services that have been made public. Then, information about the service is displayed, and you can click on the Add Reference button to add a reference to the web service to your project.

Figure 20-6   How to add a web reference

How to use a web service

After you add a reference to a web service, it appears in the Web References folder in the Solution Explorer as shown in figure 20-7. In addition to the wsdl file that contains the description of the web service, a static discovery file (disco) is included. This file contains the address of the asmx file for the web service so the application can locate and execute it as necessary.

To use a web service, you start by creating an instance of it and assigning it to an object variable as shown in the first statement in this figure. Notice that when you name the web service, you must qualify it with the name of the server where it's located. In this case, because the web service resides on the local service, the server name is localhost.

After you assign an instance of the web service to an object variable, you can refer to any web method defined by the service using standard techniques. The second statement in this figure, for example, shows how you refer to the FutureValue web method defined by the Financial Calculations web service.

The Solution Explorer with a reference to the Financial Calculations web service

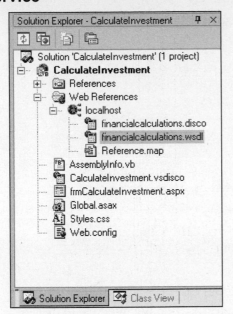

A statement that creates an instance of the Financial Calculations web service

```
Private FinancialCalculations As New localhost.FinancialCalculations()
```

A statement that executes the FutureValue method of this web service

```
txtFutureValue.Text = FormatCurrency( _
    FinancialCalculations.FutureValue(txtYears.Text, _
    txtMonthlyInvestment.Text, txtInterestRate.Text))
```

Description

- After you add a reference to a web service to a project, it's listed under the Web References folder in the Solution Explorer. The disco file contains the address of the asmx file for the web service. The wsdl file contains a description of the web service.

- To use a web service in an application, you can create an instance of it using a declaration statement with the New keyword like the one shown above. The reference to the web service must include the name of the server where it resides.

- After you create an instance of a web service, you can execute its web methods using the same techniques you use to execute a method of any object.

Figure 20-7   How to use a web service

Perspective

Although the web service presented in this chapter is trivial, it demonstrates the techniques you can use to develop more substantial web services. As a result, the basic skills you've learned here are enough to get you started developing your own web services. And, you'll be prepared to learn the more complicated aspects of web service programming when the need arises.

Summary

- An ASP.NET *web service* is a class that resides on a web server with IIS. A web service contains processing code and can be accessed by a web application, another web service, or a Windows application.

- Information is passed to and from a web service using *XML* within an HTTP request or response. If the web service is on a remote server, *SOAP* is used to facilitate the HTTP request or response.

- You develop a web service as part of an ASP.NET web service project. Within a web service, you define one or more *web methods* that provide the interface to the web service.

- You can test a web service independently of a client application using the *help pages* that are displayed when you build and run the web service.

- To use a web service in a client application, you add a web reference. Then, you can create an instance of the web service and execute its methods using standard techniques.

Terms

web service	web method
publish	dynamic discovery
distributed web application	static discovery file
WSDL (Web Services Description Language)	Service help page
SOAP (Simple Object Access Protocol)	service description
attribute	Service Method help page

Objectives

- Given the specifications for a web service, code it, test it, and use it in a web application.

- Explain how XML and SOAP are used with web services.

- Explain the purpose of the WebService and WebMethod attributes.

- Describe the basic technique for implementing a property in a web service.

Exercise 20-1   Create the Financial Calculations web service

In this exercise, you'll create and test the Financial Calculations web service you saw in this chapter.

Start a web service project

1. Start Visual Studio. Then, pull down the Tools menu and select the Options command to display the Options dialog box. Highlight the Projects and Solutions category in the Environment folder, and then change the Visual Studio projects location to C:\VB.NET\Chapter 20.

2. Click on the New Project button in the Start page to display the New Project dialog box. Then, highlight the ASP.NET Web Service template, select the location of the IIS server where you want the project stored, and enter the name Finance for the project directory.

3. When you click on the OK button, the Component Designer window will be displayed. Close this window. Then, rename the Service1.asmx file to FinancialCalculations.asmx.

Code and test the web service

4. Display the Code Editor window for the web service. Then, add a description to the WebService attribute as shown in figure 20-4, but leave the namespace at the default.

5. Add the web methods shown in figure 20-4. Then, right-click on the asmx file and select the Set as Start Page command from the shortcut menu that's displayed.

6. Right-click on the asmx file again and select the Build and Browse command. A Service help page like the first one shown in figure 20-5 will be displayed. Click on the MonthlyInvestment link in this help page to display the Service Method help page. Enter the values shown in figure 20-5 and click on the Invoke button. XML output like that shown in this figure should be displayed. If not, close the Browse window and the window that contains the XML and then correct the code for the web method and test it again.

7. When you have the MonthlyInvestment web method working correctly, return
    to the Service help page by clicking on the *here* link at the top of the Service
    Method help page. Then, click on the FutureValue link and test this method.
    This time, after you're sure the method works correctly, enter invalid data to
    see what happens. Then, close the window that contains the output and return
    to the Service help page one more time.

8. This time, click on the Service Description link to display the wsdl file. Scroll
    through this file to see the type of information it contains. Then, close the
    Browse window and close the project.

Exercise 20-2   Use the Financial Calculations web service

In this exercise, you'll modify the Calculate Investment application that you
created for chapter 19 so it uses the web service you just created.

1. Open the solution for the Calculate Investment project you created in chapter
    19. Then, use the Add Web Reference dialog box as described in figure 20-6 to
    add a reference to the Financial Calculations web service you just developed.

2. Code a declaration statement like the one in figure 20-7 at the beginning of the
    Financial Calculations form class. Now, replace the two statements in the Click
    event procedure of the Calculate button that call the CalculateFutureValue and
    CalculateMonthlyInvestment procedures with statements that call the
    FutureValue and MonthlyInvestment methods of the web service. Use the
    statement shown in figure 20-7 as a guide if needed. Finally, delete the
    CalculateFutureValue and CalculateMonthlyInvestment procedures.

3. Test the application. When you're sure it's working properly, end the
    application. Then, close the solution and exit from Visual Studio.

Appendix A

How to install and use the software and downloadable files for this book

To develop the applications presented in this book, you need to have Visual Studio .NET or the Standard Edition of Visual Basic .NET installed on your system. In addition, if you're going to develop database applications that use databases stored on your own PC rather than on a remote server, you need to install MSDE (Microsoft SQL Server 2000 Desktop Engine). And if you're going to develop web applications that use a web server that's on your own PC, you need to install IIS. This appendix describes how to install these products. It also describes the files for this book that are available for download from our web site and tells you how you can use them.

How to use the downloadable files

Throughout this book, you'll see complete applications that illustrate the material presented in each chapter. To help you understand how they work, you can download the source code and data for these applications from our web site. Then, you can open and run them in Visual Studio.

These files come in a single download that also includes the source code and data you'll need for the exercises at the end of each chapter. In addition, it includes descriptions of other projects you may want to do to practice your skills and the data you'll need to do them. Figure A-1 describes how you download, install, and use these files.

When you download the single install file and execute it, it will install all of the files for this book in the Murach\Beginning VB.NET directory on your C drive. Within this directory, you'll find a directory named Exercise starts that contains a single directory named VB.NET that contains all of the files and directories you'll need for the exercises presented in this book. Before you use these files and directories, though, you'll want to copy (not move) the VB.NET directory that contains them to the root directory of your C drive. That way, it will be easy to locate the files and directories you need as you're working on the exercises. In addition, if you make a mistake and want to restore a file to its original state, you can do that by copying it from the directory where it was originally installed.

You'll also find a directory named Book applications within the C:\Murach\Beginning VB.NET directory. This directory contains the source code for all the Windows applications in this book. Within this directory, you'll find a directory for each chapter that has complete applications. Then, within each chapter directory, you'll find a directory that contains the source files for each application. You can use Visual Studio to open and run these applications.

You may also need to prepare your system for using the databases that come with this book. That's the case if you want to use these databases on your own PC rather than using databases that have been installed on a remote server. Then, you'll need to install MSDE on your system, and you'll need to attach the databases for this book to MSDE. You can learn how to do that in figure A-3.

You may also need to prepare your system for developing and running web applications. That's the case if these applications will be deployed to a web server on your own PC. Then, you need to install IIS on your system as described in figure A-4. In addition, to use the web applications that come with this book, you'll need to copy the project files for these applications to the appropriate directory and then configure the applications for use with IIS. The procedure for doing that is presented in figure A-5.

What the downloadable files for this book contain

- The source code and data for all of the applications presented in the book
- The starting source code and data for all of the exercises included in the book
- Descriptions and data for projects that take you beyond the exercises

How to download and install the files for this book

- Go to www.murach.com, and go to the page for *Murach's Beginning Visual Basic .NET*.
- Click on the link for "FREE download of the book applications." Then, download "All book files." This will download one file named bvbn_allfiles.exe to the root directory of your C drive.
- Use the Windows Explorer to find the install file (C:\ bvbn_allfiles.exe). Then, double-click on this file and respond to the dialog boxes that follow. This installs the files in directories that start with C:\Murach\Beginning VB.NET.

How to prepare your system for doing the exercises

- Some of the exercises have you start from existing projects. The source code for these projects is in the C:\Murach\Beginning VB.NET\Exercise starts\VB.NET directory. Before you use these projects, you'll want to copy (not move) this VB.NET directory and all of its subdirectories to the root directory of the C drive. From that point on, you can find the programs and files that you need in directories like C:\VB.NET\Chapter 01, C:\VB.NET\Chapter 02, C:\VB.NET\Files, C:\VB.NET\Databases, etc.

How to use the source code for the applications presented in this book

- The source code for the Windows applications presented in this book can be found in chapter directories in the C:\Murach\Beginning VB.NET\Book applications directory. You can view this source code by opening the project or solution in the appropriate directory.
- Before you can run the applications for the programs that process a data file, you'll need to prepare your system for doing the exercises as described above. That way, the files used by these programs will be in the correct directories.

How to prepare your system for using the databases

- If you're going to use the databases that come with this book on your own PC, you'll need to install MSDE and then attach the databases to MSDE as described in figure A-3.

How to prepare your system for developing web applications

- If you're going to be developing or running web applications on a web server on your own PC, you'll need to install IIS as described in figure A-4.
- Before you can open the web applications that come with this book, you'll need to copy the project files for these applications to IIS and then configure the applications for use with IIS as described in figure A-5.

Figure A-1   How to use the downloadable files for this book

How to install the .NET Framework and Visual Studio .NET

If you've installed Windows applications before, you shouldn't have any trouble installing Visual Studio .NET. You simply insert the first Visual Studio CD, and the setup program starts automatically. This setup program will lead you through the steps for installing Visual Studio as summarized in figure A-2.

Before I describe this procedure, you should know that if you're going to develop web applications as described in chapters 19 and 20 of this book and you're going to deploy these applications on a web server on your own PC, you'll want to install IIS before running the Visual Studio .NET setup program. You can find out how to do that in figure A-4. This figure also explains what to do if you install IIS after running the Visual Studio setup program.

The first step of the installation procedure for Visual Studio .NET (or the Standard Edition of Visual Basic .NET) is to update the Windows components. During this step, the components of the .NET Framework will be installed on your system. The second step is to install Visual Studio itself. Although you will have a variety of options for what's actually installed, it's safest to just accept the defaults unless you're familiar with the various components and know exactly what you need. The final step is to apply any updates that have become available since the product was released. Note that if you don't do that and updates are available, a link will appear on the Visual Studio Start page that you can use to install the updates.

The Visual Studio .NET setup program

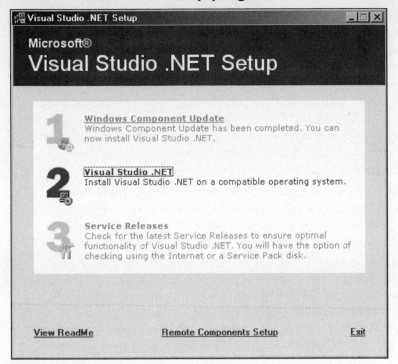

How to install Visual Studio .NET

- To install Visual Studio .NET, insert Disc 1 of the Visual Studio .NET CDs and the setup program will start automatically.

- If the .NET Framework has not been installed on your system, you will need to install it before installing Visual Studio .NET. To do that, click on the Windows Component Update link in the Setup dialog box.

- After the .NET Framework is installed, click on the Visual Studio .NET link and follow the instructions to install Visual Studio .NET. When the Options page is displayed, you can usually just accept the default options unless you have special requirements.

- After you install Visual Studio .NET, click on the Service Releases link to check for and install any updates that are available.

What if you're using Visual Basic .NET

- The setup program for the Standard Edition of Visual Basic .NET is similar to the setup program for Visual Studio .NET, but fewer options are available on the Options page.

Warning

- If you're going to develop the web applications for chapters 19 and 20 and you're going to use a web server that's on your own PC, you need to install IIS before installing the .NET Framework. See figure A-4 for details.

Figure A-2   How to install the .NET Framework and Visual Studio .NET

How to install MSDE and use it with our databases

By default, the files you need to install MSDE are copied to your hard drive when you install Visual Studio. Then, you can simply run the Setup.exe program as described in figure A-3 to install MSDE. Otherwise, you can locate and run this program from the Visual Studio CDs as described in this figure. Note that this setup program doesn't display any dialog boxes or give any options like most setup programs do. In other words, it executes without interruption.

After you install MSDE, you'll notice a server icon near the right side of the windows taskbar. If you double-click on this icon, the SQL Server Service Manager dialog box shown at the top of this figure is displayed. You can use this dialog box to start, continue, pause, or stop the SQL Server engine. By default, SQL Server is started each time you start your PC. If that's not what you want, you can remove the check mark from the Auto-start option in this dialog box. Then, you can start SQL Server whenever you need it using this dialog box.

Although you don't need to know much about how MSDE works to use it, you should know that when you run the setup program, it creates a copy of SQL Server with the same name as your computer appended with VSdotNET. For example, the copy of SQL Server on my system is named ANNE\VSdotNET as you can see in the SQL Server Service Manager dialog box in this figure. After this server is created, you can add databases to it. Then, you can create connections to those databases that you can use in your Visual Basic programs.

If you want to use the databases that are available with the download for this book, you can do that without much trouble. First, you'll need to download and install these files and then copy the VB.NET directory that's created to the root directory of your C drive as described in figure A-1. Then, you can run the batch file named DB_Attach.bat in the C:\VB.NET directory. This batch file runs a SQL Server script named DB_Attach.sql that attaches the databases to the copy of SQL Server running on your computer.

The SQL Server Service Manager

How to install and use MSDE

- Use the Windows Explorer to navigate to this directory: C:\Program Files\Microsoft Visual Studio .NET\Setup\MSDE. Then, double-click on the Setup.exe file to run it and install MSDE. When you're done, restart your PC.

- After you install MSDE, SQL Server will start automatically each time you start your PC. An icon will appear near the right side of the Windows taskbar to indicate that this service is running. To manage this service, double-click on the icon or select the Start → Programs → MSDE → Service Manager command to display the dialog box shown above.

- The setup program creates a copy of SQL Server with your computer name appended with VSdotNET. You can use the Data Adapter Configuration Wizard to define connections to the databases you add to this server as described in chapter 17.

How to attach the databases for this book to MSDE

- If you're going to use the AccountsPayable and MurachBooks databases used by the programs and projects for this book on your own PC, you need to attach them to MSDE. To do that, you can use the batch file and SQL script that are downloaded and installed along with the other files for this book.

- To attach the databases to MSDE, copy the VB.NET directory used by the exercises to the root directory of your C drive as described in figure A-1. Then, use the Windows Explorer to navigate to the C:\VB.NET directory, and double-click on the DB_Attach.bat file to run it.

Note

- If you didn't select the option to install MSDE when you installed Visual Studio .NET, you can install it directly from Disc 3 of the Visual Studio .NET CDs. To do that, insert this CD, navigate to the Program Files\Microsoft Visual Studio .NET\Setup\MSDE directory, and double-click on the Setup.exe file to run it.

Figure A-3   How to install MSDE and use it with our databases

How to install IIS

If you're going to develop web applications and web services as described in chapters 19 and 20, you'll need access to a web server running IIS. If you don't have access to a web server, you can install IIS on your own PC. Figure A-4 shows you how.

To install IIS, you display the Add/Remove Programs dialog box and then click on the Add/Remove Windows Components link as shown in this figure. When you do, the Windows Components Wizard starts and the second dialog box shown in this figure is displayed. This dialog box lists all the available Windows components. The components that are currently installed have a check mark in front of them. To install another component (in this case, IIS), just check it, click on the Next button, and complete the dialog boxes that are displayed.

As I mentioned earlier, if you're going to use IIS, you should install it before you install the .NET Framework or Visual Studio .NET. If you install Visual Studio first, you'll need to reinstall it after installing IIS. And if you install the .NET Framework first, you'll need to repair it after installing IIS. To do that, you can execute the command shown in this figure. This command runs an executable file named dotnetfx.exe that can be found on one of the Visual Studio .NET installation CDs.

The dialog boxes for installing IIS

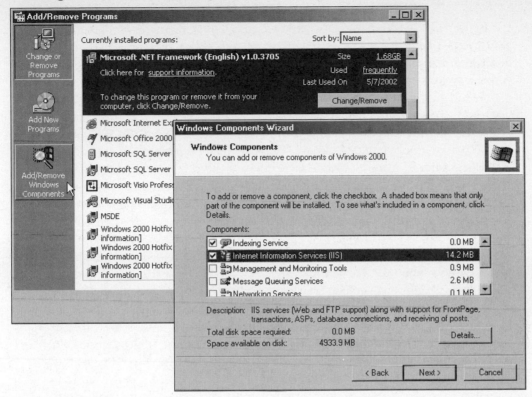

Description

- To install IIS, display the Windows Control Panel, and double-click on the Add/Remove Programs icon to display the Add/Remove Programs dialog box. Then, click on Add/Remove Windows Components to display the Windows Components Wizard, select Internet Information Services (IIS) from the list of components that are displayed, and click on the Next button to complete the installation.

When to install IIS

- IIS should be installed prior to installing the .NET Framework and Visual Studio .NET.
- If you install IIS after installing the .NET Framework, you will need to repair the Framework. To do that, insert the Visual Studio .NET Windows Component Update CD. Then, click on the Start button in the Windows taskbar, choose the Run command, and enter this command:

```
<CD Drive>:\dotNetFramework\dotnetfx.exe /t:c:\temp /c:"msiexec.exe /fvecms
c:\temp\netfx.msi"
```

- If you install IIS after installing Visual Studio .NET, you will need to reinstall Visual Studio. To do that, use the Add/Remove Programs dialog box.

Figure A-4   How to install IIS

How to use the downloaded web applications

Before you can open and run the web applications that you've downloaded for this book, you'll need to copy them to the web server. Then, you'll need to configure them for use with IIS. If IIS is installed on your own system, you can do that by using the procedure in figure A-5.

When you install IIS on your system, it creates a directory named Inetpub on your C drive. Within this directory is a directory named wwwroot. This is where all of your web applications and services must be stored. To start, then, you'll need to copy the folder for each web application to this directory. You'll find these folders in the C:\Murach\Beginning VB.NET\Book applications\IIS files directory that's created when you install the files for this book.

After you copy the files to IIS, you'll need to configure each application for use by IIS. To do that, you use the Internet Services Manager program shown in this figure. When you first start this program, it will list the available web servers in the left side of its window. In most cases, this list will include just the web server on your PC. Then, you can expand the node for this server and then expand the node for the default web site to display the IIS applications.

Next, locate the application you copied to the web server, and notice that it is displayed with a folder icon rather than an IIS icon like most of the other items in the list. In this figure, for example, you can see the folder for the CalculateInvestment application. To configure this application for IIS, display its properties as described in this figure, and then click on the Create button in the Directory tab. When you do, you'll notice that the icon for the application changes from a folder icon to an IIS icon. To complete the configuration, click on the OK button in the Properties dialog box.

The Internet Services Manager and the properties for an IIS application

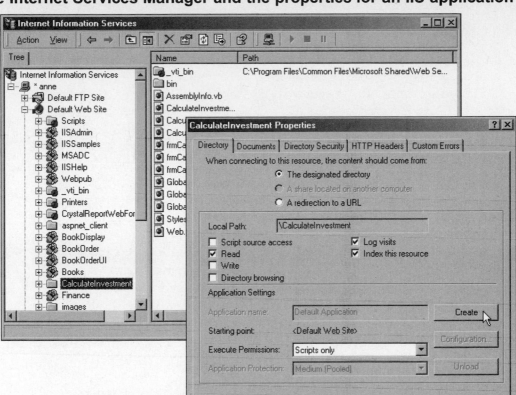

How to use the downloaded web applications

1. Use the Windows Explorer to navigate to the C:\Murach\Beginning VB.NET\Book applications\IIS files directory. Then, copy the folder for the application you want to use to the C:\Inetpub\wwwroot directory.

2. Start the Internet Services Manager program using the Start → Programs → Administrative Tools → Internet Services Manager command.

3. Expand the server node (anne in the window shown above) and the Default Web Site node to display the available applications. Then, right-click on the application folder you just copied and select the Properties command from the menu that's displayed to display the Properties dialog box for that folder.

4. Display the Directory tab and then click on the Create button to configure the application for use with IIS. The icon in the Internet Services Manager window will change from a folder to an IIS application icon like those shown above. Click on the OK button to accept the property changes, and then close the Internet Services Manager program.

Figure A-5   How to use the downloaded web applications for this book

Appendix B

Coding and syntax conventions

Throughout this book, you've learned how to code Visual Basic .NET statements and functions, how to use Visual Basic and .NET methods and properties, and so on. This appendix summarizes the coding rules you have to follow and the syntax conventions that are used in the syntax summaries in the figures. As you work with Visual Studio, many of these coding details are taken care of for you by the Intellisense feature. Still, the coding conventions are summarized here in case you ever have a question about them.

Coding rules and guidelines

General coding rules
1. Use spaces to separate the words and operators in each statement.
2. Indentation and capitalization have no effect on the operation of a statement.

Comments
1. Type an apostrophe followed by the comment.
2. A comment can be coded to the right of a statement or on a line with no statement.
3. A comment can't be coded to the right of a continuation character.

Continuations
To code a statement on more than one line so it's easier to read, type a space followed by an underscore (the continuation character) at the end of the first line. Then, type a return and continue the statement on the next line.

Coding recommendations
1. Use indentation and extra spaces to align statements and clauses within statements.
2. Use blank lines before and after groups of related statements.
3. Code all variable declarations at the start of the procedure, and group related declarations.

Syntax conventions

Boldfaced element	Indicates that the element must be entered exactly as shown.
Regular-font element	Indicates that the element is provided by the programmer.
[option]	Indicates an option that may be coded but isn't required.
[option | option]	Indicates a set of alternative options, one of which may be coded.
{ option | option }	Indicates a set of alternative options, one of which must be coded.
...	Indicates that the preceding option may be repeated multiple times.

Coding examples

Syntax: `{Dim|Private|Public|Static}` name `[As` type`] [=` expression`]`

Examples:
```
Dim sErrorMessage As String

Private bAddMode As Boolean = True

Public iCount As Integer = 1
```

Syntax:
```
Select Case testexpression
    [Case expressionlist
        statements] ...
    [Case Else
        statements]
End Select
```

Example:
```
Select Case iQuantity
    Case 1, 2
        dDiscount = 0
    Case 3 To 9
        dDiscount = 0.1
    Case 10 To 24
        dDiscount = 0.2
    Case Is >= 25
        dDiscount = 0.3
End Select
```

Index

A

X

Y